Golden Rule

AMERICAN POLITICS AND POLITICAL ECONOMY SERIES

Edited by Benjamin I. Page

Thomas Ferguson

Golden Rule

*The Investment Theory of
Party Competition and the Logic of
Money-Driven Political Systems*

THE UNIVERSITY OF CHICAGO PRESS

Chicago and London

THOMAS FERGUSON is professor of political science at
the University of Massachusetts, Boston.

The University of Chicago Press, Chicago 60637
The University of Chicago Press, Ltd., London
© 1995 by The University of Chicago
All rights reserved. Published 1995
Printed in the United States of America

04 03 02 01 00 99 98 97 96 95 5 4 3 2 1

ISBN (cloth): 0–226–24316–8
ISBN (paper): 0–226–24317–6

Library of Congress Cataloging-in-Publication Data

Ferguson, Thomas, 1949–
    Golden rule : the investment theory of party competition and the
logic of money-driven political systems / Thomas Ferguson.
        p.   cm.—(American politics and political economy)
    Includes bibliographical references and index.
    ISBN 0-226-24316-8
    1. Business and politics—United States.   2. Campaign funds—
United States.   3. Political parties—United States.   4. United
States—Economic policy.   I. Title.   II. Series.
JK467.F47   1995   94-40580
324'.4'0973—dc20   CIP

⊗ The paper used in this publication meets the minimum requirements of the American National Standard for Information Sciences—Permanence of Paper for Printed Library Materials, ANSI Z39.48–1984.

Contents

PART ONE

The Investment Theory of
Party Competition

Politics, Social Science, and the Golden Rule:
Reading the Handwriting on the Wall

In the same hour came forth fingers of a man's hand, and wrote
over against the candlestick upon the plaister of the wall of the
king's palace. . . . MENE, MENE, TEKEL, UPHARSIN. This is the
interpretation of the thing: MENE; God hath numbered thy kingdom, and finished it. TEKEL; thou art weighed in the balances,
and art found wanting. PHERES; thy kingdom is divided and given
to the Medes and the Persians.

Book of Daniel

A REVERENT and quite nonsectarian nod to the charitable deduction is
about as close to religious themes as the Public Broadcasting System's
Nightly Business Report ever comes. One memorable evening in late October 1992, however, the talking heads who normally find inspiration
on Wall Street decided suddenly to borrow their evening story line
from the famous tale of Belshazzar's feast in the Book of Daniel.

Just as in the Old Testament original, a ceremonial royal banquet
provided the setting—in this instance, the regular fall meeting of the
Business Council at Hot Springs, Virginia, where a special camera crew
had been dispatched. And, again, as in the older episode, the sumptu-
ous repast was significant less in its own right than as the artistic back-
drop for reflections on a mighty empire's succession crisis—in this case,
the 1992 presidential campaign, about which a select group of Business
Council leaders had agreed to be interviewed on camera.

First on the air that night was Ford Motor Chair Harold Poling. In
contrast to many others in his industry, the auto executive still enjoyed
not only honor but profits. Nevertheless, his view of the campaign of
incumbent President George Bush was not sanguine. To many, indeed,
it sounded like a last judgment on the man whom he had accompanied
only a few months before on an ill-fated trip to Tokyo. Poling was,
according to the introductory voice-over, "pointedly" maintaining
neutrality, pending further clarification of the candidates' views on
trade and other issues. After him came Bethlehem Steel Chair Walter
Williams, who offered the evening's first real revelation: that deep "dis-

3

illusionment" with one of the most ardently free enterprise–oriented regimes in American history was "pushing [many businesses] to [Democratic nominee Bill] Clinton."

John Young, chair of Hewlett-Packard and a longtime Republican, followed. Some days before, Young and Apple Computer Chief Executive Officer John Sculley had led a phalanx of Silicon Valley executives in a mass public endorsement of the Arkansas governor. Now, once again on camera, Young sonorously reaffirmed his new convictions. Next in the parade was another onetime Republican stalwart, Southern California Edison Chair Howard Allen. The utility executive came startlingly to the point:

> It's contrary to my basic instincts as a Republican and the way my father reared me, but there are certain things that government should have oversight on and not just sit back and say that competition will solve everything . . . it hurts me to say that and my father would turn over in his grave if he heard me say it.

It fell to Martin-Marietta CEO Norman Augustine to sum up the evening's discussion. "I think," the defense industry executive observed, "the Democrats are moving more towards business, and business is moving more toward the Democrats."[1]

In the account in the Book of Daniel, King Belshazzar did not initially get the message. But at least he recognized there was one: as soon as he saw the moving hand, he "cried out loud to bring in the astrologers, the Chaldeans, and the soothsayers." When they proved unable to decipher the inscription, he had the good sense to heed his queen. He summoned the prophet Daniel.

No such lucidity attended 1992's high-tech reenactment of the incident. This time, when the handwriting flashed on the electronic walls of some 2 million homes, no one batted an eye (apart from viewers of the program, who dialed up a specially advertised 900 number, seeking more information in disproportionately heavy numbers).

Instead, a few months later, President Clinton—with Apple's Sculley and Federal Reserve Chair Alan Greenspan ensconced in the audience next to Hillary Rodham Clinton—unveiled his long-awaited economic program in a special address to a joint session of Congress. Although his proposed five-year deficit reduction plan strikingly resembled a scheme put forward by Ross Perot that candidate Clinton had attacked all during the campaign, and was shortly to win a public endorsement from many of America's largest businesses, the president's call to raise taxes on the very wealthiest Americans struck a strangely sensitive nerve. Somehow, in a miracle of doublethink, many of the astrologers, Chaldeans, and soothsayers who provide most of what passes for political analysis in America descried ominous signs that the new administration was flirting with the specter of class war.[2]

If war had in fact been declared, it was certainly of a novel kind. Only one side seemed to be mobilizing. As Japan, with an unemployment rate far below that of the United States, prepared to embark on a much larger fiscal stimulus program, the president scaled back his own promised stimulus initiative to a paltry $16 billion—an amount less than the measurement errors in many parts of his new budget. Then, as some of his own Treasury appointees questioned the need for any action, the president dropped the measure altogether after a single rebuff by the Senate. With members of his economic team putting out word that a key indicator of their success would be the state of the bond market, the president also postponed action on two additional campaign promises: to raise the minimum wage, which had stayed fixed for more than a decade, and to require American employers to invest in training workers. He also withdrew (or declined to send forward) the nominations of several prominent liberal activists whose views piqued conservative critics, and handed the hot potato of labor law reform to a special commission not due to report for a year. In the midst of these switches, the president also struggled to find a compromise that he and the top military brass, if not necessarily gay Americans serving their country in the armed forces, could live comfortably with.

By abandoning plans for a fiscal stimulus as economic growth slowed in the rest of the world and cutbacks in military spending and massive exports of American jobs overseas continued, the president was in effect throwing the entire burden of reviving the economy on the bond market and the Federal Reserve. The hope was that a credible deficit reduction program would induce the Fed to lower short-term interest rates, and reduce investors' fears of inflation. With the Fed cooperating, investors would then buy quantities of long-term bonds and push down long-term interest rates. Despite its short-run plausibility, however, this strategy carried with it a self-defeating catch-22 that guaranteed that ordinary Americans would feel increasingly beleaguered for a long time to come, regardless of what happened to the deficit: given their virtual paranoia about inflation, both the Fed and financial markets were certain to demand a return to higher rates at the first signs of a recovery.

But that was a problem for the future. In the meantime, the Cheshire-cat economic upturn—now you see it, now you don't—was fanning widespread anxieties about a "jobless recovery," and the new round of stridently partisan wrangling on the budget could not fail to stir up additional unease. As consumer confidence plunged, and the

White House stumbled from one snafu or scandal to another, the president's popularity went into free fall.

Once again, a mighty empire was in crisis. Amid savage media attacks, a siege mentality enveloped the White House. With the president ordering air strikes against a successor of the Medes and the Persians, more calls went out to the astrologers, Chaldeans, and soothsayers. Their replies were all but unanimous. As though an invisible hand were directing them, the sages brushed off public concerns about the slow pace of economic recovery. Instead, they chorused, the president was in trouble because he had strayed too far to the *left of center*. To have any hopes of salvaging his presidency, the chorus continued, the president must repudiate the liberals who had hijacked his programs and recruit experienced, senior "centrist" advisers who could help him get back on track in the middle of the road.[3]

Bombarded with this advice for many days by newspapers, magazines, television, and many private sources, the White House eventually got the message. On May 29 came a stunning announcement: David Gergen, an intimate of many of the top business figures most opposed to Clinton in 1992 and a premier architect of the Reagan agenda that Clinton was pledged to reverse, was rejoining the White House as a special counselor to the president.

With this much-heralded "return to the middle of the road," the logjam that had held up the president's budget in Congress now began to break up. After further trimming to please conservative critics, the new "government of national unity" (as it would be styled in Italy or Latin America) secured passage of a markedly deflationary budget that even many proponents admitted would weigh heavily on the economy for a long time to come. Then it set about scaling down plans for sweeping reform of the health-care system while cranking up a campaign in favor of a particularly rigid and uncompromising version of the controversial North American Free Trade Agreement (NAFTA).[4] Though many details remained to be ironed out, three points were already evident: First, because from the start the president had ruled out "single-payer" ("Canadian-Style") health care, whatever health plan finally evolved would be comparatively expensive, and likely in the end either to force curtailment of services or hefty rises in taxes of one sort or another. Second, the best hope the administration could hold out to average Americans anxious about the export of their jobs overseas was its highly publicized campaign to *force another country* (Japan) to live better. Third, the pillars of Hercules that marked the outermost limits of respectable political discourse in the United States had just relocated—once again, to the right. The debacle of Clinton's first months in office, all respectable opinion now agreed, proved the bankruptcy of the liberal or "left" alternative.[5]

Now my point in retracing this latest uncanny turn in America's public life is not that the right-wing media reduced to ashes the good intentions of some backwoods naïfs within months after they entered office. Quite the contrary, a major ingredient in the disaster clearly derived from the new administration's elephantine attempts to cover its own retreat from its economic promises by highlighting social issues—first by showcasing Robert Reich and Vernon Jordan as heads of a transition team that recruited the cream of Wall Street and Lloyd Bentsen, the Senate's literal six-million-dollar-man, to run the economy; then by rushing headlong into the gays in the military debacle at the very moment it was completing plans to take over (much of) Perot's deficit program while turning its back on efforts to stimulate the economy, retrain workers, and raise the minimum wage; and finally by striving so ostentatiously to field the perfect politically correct cabinet that a good idea became a painful and embarrassing joke. As discussed in this volume's essay on the 1992 election (chapter 6), such playing to stereotypes has a clear, identifiable function (and by now, a long history) in a Democratic party that is supposed to represent ordinary working Americans but is actually run by investment bankers and their allies. But it is also very dangerous—especially when a country faces literally years of slow growth and high unemployment under an administration whose political base strikingly resembles the Seattle Space Needle.

Nor, certainly, would it be wise to suggest that, with or without Gergen around to play high-tech sandman, the president cannot recover, at least to the extent of possibly squeaking through to reelection in 1996. If for reasons spelled out later in this book, the Clinton presidency is always likely to be a strange combination of Kennedy style and Carter substance, it would be rash to jump to the conclusion that our latest Southern president is shortly fated to be gone with the wind. As a graduate student, I sat in on one of the first courses ever offered by an American university on "political business cycles." That course was team-taught, but one of its leaders was a distinguished economist whom President Clinton appointed to the Council of Economic Advisors. I will, accordingly, be surprised if in 1996, if no other year, the Clinton administration cannot contrive a "national development bank," the promise of yet another "middle-class tax cut" or, at least, a few well-timed cuts in interest rates to quicken both the economy and the pulse of liberals for a few strategic months. With help from the rest of the world (by no means guaranteed) and vast sums of campaign money, such moves might provide the racer's edge, particularly in a three-horse race marked, as it surely will be, by massive public cynicism and low voter turnout.

Instead, my point is less complicated—that it is high time both social scientists and voters learned to read the handwriting on the wall. That Clinton strongly resembles a registered Republican and might well go down in history as the most conservative Democratic president since Grover Cleveland was entirely predictable. Anyone should have seen it who had followed what might be termed the "Golden Rule" of political analysis—to discover who rules, follow the gold (i.e., trace the origins and financing of the campaign, along the lines laid down in the first essay in this book). Indeed, some people did see it—though many of those who bothered to look were active participants in financial markets and thus had no incentive to talk.

By contrast, the armies of people who live by words, who report, observe, and comment in public on American politics had virtually nothing of substance to say before, during, or after the 1992 election. Instead, in the manner of a children's storybook or a morality play, the press and politicians talked incessantly about character, as if the key question facing America were whether it would be better to have a steady navigator, a street bully, a hockey goalie, a cancer survivor, a war hero, or a hillbilly from Oxford as president. When they didn't descant upon character or "toughness," they flapped about the horse race, about "spin," or consultants, or "who was electable." When they spoke of issues, it was usually to debate details of a tax cut that was too small to do anyone any good and that was, in any case, unlikely ever to happen.

But it is a simple fact that virtually all the issues that both elites and ordinary Americans think about outside of or alongside campaigns—work and employment, free trade or protection, health care, the future of U.S. production, the cities, taxes—are critically important not only to voters, but to well-organized investor blocs, businesses, and industries. And it is another simple fact that many such groups invest massively in candidates.

During the campaign, however, we heard at best about fundraising totals. Or a few names, as though that told anyone anything. In a front-page story in early March 1992, for example, *USA Today* informed readers that actress Dixie Carter was backing Clinton, that Ed Asner had contributed to Tom Harkin and rock singer Don Henley had donated to Paul Tsongas. Quoting a study whose authors should have known better, the paper also indicated that "philanthropists" were the group most heavily represented among donors to Pat Buchanan's uniquely acerbic campaign.[6]

In December 1991, when Jerry Brown first attempted to make an issue out of the corrupting effects of campaign finance, he was ridiculed by the Democratic Party's leaders, the other candidates, and the press. The networks, which have surely done more to lower public standards of taste in the past half-century than any group this side of Las Vegas, and party leaders, who virtually without exception double as handsomely remunerated lobbyists, claimed that any mention of Brown's 800 number for small donors during television debates would demean the campaign. (This noble commitment to good taste, however, proved short-lived. Soon one issue about the leading Democratic aspirant dominated the airwaves and the newspapers: Did he or didn't he? The reference was not to a hairdresser.)

The record of the academy over the last twenty years—or indeed, over the last half-century—is scarcely better. For most scholars Rockefeller is a foundation; Lamont, Seth Low, and Widener are libraries, and Brookings is an institute, to which they aspire to be duly grateful. Serious discussion of money, industrial structure, and politics scarcely exists, save among a thin stratum of gifted students of comparative politics. Most detailed studies of politics and money are highly stylized. Among these are the many studies of political action committees (PACs), where serious mismeasurement of the independent variable is virtually guaranteed, since PACs comprise a comparatively small part of politically significant money in most national elections; the older tradition of "phone books" listing large donors, which recall the Comte de Buffon's lucubrations on the animal world, and which, after almost half a century, have yielded little more than the generalization that generalizations are hazardous and the cautionary bromide (which is certainly true) that money doesn't buy everything; and a thin literature on congressional elections, which is sometimes seriously meant and occasionally productive of some insights, but remains blind to the ways (discussed in chapter 1 in this volume and elaborated in the appendix) that money-driven political systems shift the whole political spectrum around and comprehensively influence candidates' electoral appeals.[7]

Early in my life I worked briefly in Washington and on Wall Street. Ever since, I have intermittently returned to each. I have also observed firsthand how several major foreign political systems function. I wrote the original version of the first essay in this book (chapter 1) because I was convinced that modern students of politics resemble adherents of Ptolemy in a Copernican world—and that the now fashionable "rational choice" approaches to analyzing electoral systems produced not rigor but mortis.[8] It was high time, I thought, to spell out precisely what was wrong with the celebrated "median voter" approach to electoral democracy and to put forward a clear alternative, in which—*as long as basic property rights do not emerge as the dominating issue*—competition between blocs of major investors drives the system.

This first essay attracted a considerable amount of attention—rather more, indeed, than a simple citation count would suggest. Among the most interesting responses were several from analysts working in the highly controversial gray area where neoclassical microeconomics now meets political analysis. Though in principle the issues they raised were uncomplicated and of broad concern, their arguments tend to be formulated in rather technical terms.

To avoid putting off readers unfamiliar with microeconomics and the applications of what are somewhat grandiloquently labeled "rational choice" methods to political science and history, my review of the ensuing discussion appears in the appendix to this book instead of directly after chapter 1. Anyone who chooses can thus move directly from the original essay to the more accessible case studies of various elections which follow in chapters 2 through 6.

But I hope very much that any reader who takes this shorter path will eventually be inspired to try the appendix. A royal road to comprehending the complex relations between money and politics will probably never be found. But this appendix presents what I hope is the next-best alternative: a serious inventory and reply to the major objections leveled by the critics of the investment approach.

Because the discussion is really concerned not with technique but with perennial issues in social theory, I have made every effort to make it accessible. It sharpens the considerations advanced in the earlier essay by working through the case of the "median voter" in some detail. By systematically considering how problems of political money affect the logic of the conventional model, it becomes embarrassingly obvious how flimsy that much-touted construct really is. The conventional model breaks down even in very straightforward cases which should display it to best advantage. Simply extending the discussion a bit more also points up fallacies in the cases advanced by other critics of the original essay—both the critique in terms of "rational expectations" put forward by Richard McKelvey and Peter Ordeshook as well as the objections from the "retrospective voting" school, according to which even a completely uninformed electorate is able to control policy by just voting the rascals out.

This appendix will also, I trust, dispose forever of suggestions that the study of political ideas or "rhetoric" is somehow antithetical to serious efforts to come to terms with the realities of money-driven politics. On the contrary, as I emphasize there, investment in ideas is an absolutely fundamental part of the American political system, going well beyond the jejune notions of "agenda setting" that have dominated academic writing (which sees agendas set by, for example, clusters of American states). And, as Lance Bennett has recently emphasized, the investment approach to party competition is basic to understanding why American campaign appeals are the asthenic compounds they are. In the next few years, I expect, we will learn to measure some of these phenomena a bit more precisely.[9]

The other essays in the book put this investment approach to practical use, analyzing real political coalitions in the spirit of the first essay. Chapters 2–4 "From 'Normalcy' to New Deal," "Monetary Policy, Loan Liquidation, and Industrial Conflict" [a coauthored study of the Federal Reserve System in the Depression], and "Industrial Structure and Party Competition in the New Deal") add up to a detailed empirical and theoretical critique of our understanding of one of twentieth-century America's great formative political experiences—the New Deal. Drawing on a large amount of archival evidence—including many letters and documents whose import is still imperfectly assimilated—these essays show how a bloc of capital-intensive, multinationally oriented businesses came to power during the Great Depression by reinventing the Democratic Party.

The third of these essays (chapter 4, "Industrial Structure and Party Competition in the New Deal: A Quantitative Assessment") brings together the results of more than a decade of work in archives to present a detailed quantitative study of the financing of the 1936 presidential campaign. It also contains an extensive discussion of the statistical methods I believe are best suited for analyzing presidential elections, and a long discussion of potential pitfalls.

The remaining two essays in the book, chapters 5 and 6, bring the story down to our own time, by examining the disintegration of the New Deal system since the late seventies. The first of these, on the 1988 election, amounts to a review essay on the main political developments from the pivotal 1973–74 recession to Bush's succession to the presidency. (Though it does not presuppose familiarity with my coauthored *Right Turn*, it does in effect function as a kind of sequel, since the former broke off with the 1984 election.)[10] In contrast to most other academic treatments of this period, the discussion of the party system and the business community is framed throughout in a global context, with considerable attention paid to foreign economic policy developments within the G7. The essay analyzes how these eventually led to the erosion of the Reagan coalition and the revival of business opposition to the GOP inside the Democratic Party.

The last essay in the book discusses the collapse of the Bush presidency and the rise of what became the "Clinton coalition." It also presents a lengthy analysis, drawn from many primary sources, of Ross Perot, whose meteoric career on the national political stage repays close study as the *ne plus ultra* of what the investment approach is pointing to about our political system.

The lamentable state of the social science literature on money and politics tempts anyone who trys to engage the question afresh to plead that if he or she has failed to see farther, it is because one is standing on the shoulders of pygmies (indeed, all too frequently, subsidized pygmies). But the real situation is not as bad as this sounds. It is certainly true that the normally sunny dispositions of many well-known political scientists, and perhaps slightly fewer economists and historians, seem to cloud over when questions of politics, industrial structure, and pecuniary resources come up. It is also regrettably the case that serious work in this field is unlikely to be supported by any foundation or grants agency whatsoever. But withal, scholarship remains a social endeavor. I have certainly benefited from a great deal of help, which I have tried to acknowledge at the beginning of each of the essays in this book.

A few people, however, deserve special mention. At the head of the list is Ben Page, the editor of the University of Chicago Press American Politics and Political Economy series. He first persuaded me that this study was worth undertaking and could actually be published. Even more importantly, however, at several points near the end he played an absolutely decisive role in encouraging me to complete it. Without him, there would be, literally, no book. I owe almost as much to John Tryneski of the University of Chicago Press—not least for the patience and good humor he displayed while waiting for Godot (who, I believe, did not have two young children, and thus perhaps had less of an excuse).

Over the last few years I have profited greatly from virtually constant interchange with a number of gifted analysts of comparative politics and economics, including Bruce Cumings, Robert Johnson, James Kurth, Stephen Magee, and Alain Parguez. It is also a pleasure to acknowledge my considerable debts to Walter Dean Burnham, Gail Russell Chaddock, Erik Devereux, James Galbraith, David Hale, Stanley Kelley, David Noble, Edward Reed, Sherle Schwendiger, Jeri Scofield, and Meredith Woo-Cumings. I was very fortunate to have two very able scholars as coauthors, Gerald Epstein and Joel Rogers. (One of the essays with Epstein is included in this book, in chapter 3. This was very much a joint work and the order of our names was settled by the alphabet when the essay originally appeared in the *Journal of Economic History.* It seemed only right to adhere to the same convention for the version in this book.) Ed Beard and Acting Provost Fuad Safwat of the University of Massachusetts, Boston, also helped my research in significant measure. Goresh Hosangady provided invaluable statistical assistance time and again, while Michael Kagay responded to numerous requests for assistance with polling data. Suggestions and comments that were often very helpful and stimulating came from two anonymous referees for the University of Chicago Press (one of whom, Theodore J. Lowi, promptly declassified his identity) and a member of the press's editorial board.

My wife, Anne McCauley, contributed many suggestions about both the form and the content of this study, while my daughters Louisa and Chloe made sure I was never tempted to rest. To the three of them this book is dedicated.

NOTES

1. The interviews with members of the Business Council appeared as part of a special series of programs on money and elections. I served as a consultant to the series and appeared in several segments. Gregory MacArthur, its producer, kindly made available to me full transcripts of the interviews, which I checked against a video of the final program.

2. The comparison to Perot's plan was initially encouraged by the administration, until the Texan declared against the program. See, e.g., the discussion in chapter 6 in this volume, as well as the news coverage in the major media, which is easily available and, to save space, will not be traced here unless some particular detail is vital. Many business figures weighed in with their various views on the president's plan soon after he introduced it. But a major document witnessing to its support among important parts of big business is the letter released by Illinois Congressman Dan Rostenkowski dated May 25, 1993. This is signed by some fifty of the largest businesses in the United States and flatly endorses the bill reported out by Rostenkowski's committee, which contained virtually all the parts of the proposal that occasioned most of the controversy and were subsequently modified in the Senate. Among the firms which enlisted on the president's side in the alleged class war were AlliedSignal, Ameritech, Anheuser-Busch, Avon, BP America, Colgate-Palmolive, Delta Air Lines, Dow Corning, Electronic Data Systems, Emerson Electric, the GAP, GenCorp, General Electric, General Mills, General Motors, General Signal, Hallmark Cards, Honeywell, Hughes Aircraft, IBM, Jim Walter, Kellogg, Levi Strauss, 3M, Marriott, Mars, Owens-Corning Fiberglas, Philip Morris, Procter & Gamble, Quaker Oats, Ryder, Sara Lee, Southern California Edison, Southland, Tenneco, Time Warner, Walt Disney, and Westinghouse. General Electric's chair attached a brief comment asking for more spending cuts, and a few other firms added other observations. I suppose it is too much to hope that appending this list of firms will save us from a flock of articles and dissertations in the coming years about "Bill Clinton and the dilemmas of the autonomous state."

3. Measuring the tone of press coverage is in its infancy in the social sciences. All one can do is try one's best to carefully summarize main themes. In this and other essays in the book, I have, accordingly, stuck wherever possible to noting truly repetitious

themes that I hope can command general assent. But see the discussion of media coverage following Clinton's speech in Fairness and Accuracy in Reporting's very helpful *Extra,* April/May 1993, p. 8; this reviews many programs and articles such as the *Washington
Post*'s "Is Clinton Pitting Class Against Class?" of February 21, 1993. This article also
quotes David Brinkley's criticism, in a speech to a trucking association after the 1992
election, of the Democrats for practicing "long-standing class warfare." The article also
notes that many of the journalists making such comments are themselves very affluent.

University presses are forced to operate in what one school of French historians is
wont to call *la longue durée.* Thus some parts of chapter 6's analysis of the Clinton administration, and particularly the likely fate of its economic program, that were originally
written as forecasts have become contemporary history. It may, accordingly, be worth
mentioning that chapter 6 was essentially completed within a week or so of the president's budget speech of February 1993. At that time I sent to press a much shorter analysis of the Clinton program, with a very direct prediction of the likelihood of the dollar
difficulties that actually materialized in the summer of 1994. This appeared as "'Organized Capitalism,' Fiscal Policy, and the 1992 Democratic Campaign," in Lawrence Dodd
and Calvin Jillson, eds., *New Perspectives On American Politics* (Washington, D.C.: Congressional Quarterly Press, 1993), pp. 118–39.

4. This book went to press long before the conclusion of the great debate over the
North American Free Trade Agreement, and an extended comment on the final outcome
is obviously out of the question. I daresay, however, that readers of chapter 6 are unlikely to find anything surprising about the president's stance, or those of his allies.

Note, however, in relation to the Gergen appointment and the Clinton administration's efforts to redramatize itself, the discussion in the *Boston Globe,* November 12, 1993.
There Robert Kuttner reports that during the summer of 1993 the administration discussed the possibility of pushing for a version of the NAFTA accord that would have
contained much stronger labor provisions, including one that would have linked reductions in tariffs to rises in Mexican wages. A number of major unions were prepared to
support the treaty in the event the administration opted for this alternative, as were key
House Democratic leaders such as Richard Gephardt.

But urged on by, among others, the Democratic Leadership Council, which wanted
to weaken unions and attract more business support, the Clinton administration rejected
this approach in favor of one built around an appeal to Republican votes and, of course,
massive lobbying by the business community.

I have independently confirmed the gist of Kuttner's account. My sources add that
while some American consumer goods producers did support efforts to raise Mexican
wages, the rest of the business community favored the more sweeping approach the
president eventually adopted. Is it too much to hope that no one will ever ask again
whether the investment banking presence in the Democratic Party matters?

5. See, e.g., a typical comment by William Safire in the *New York Times,* September
20, 1993 (referring to the earlier period). Given the multiplicity of editions that the *Times*
and most other papers now issue, it is impractical and potentially very misleading to
note the pages of particular articles in references. Note that when articles are retrieved
from computer-assisted data banks, there often are no page numbers supplied at all,
even in the original indexes.

6. See *USA Today,* March 6–8, 1992.

7. Thomas Ferguson, "Money and Politics," in vol. 2 of Godfrey Hodgson, ed., *Hand-*

books to the Modern World—The United States (New York: Facts On File, 1992), reviews the main facts and literature that addresses these questions. See also Frank Sorauf, *Money in American Elections* (Glenview, Il.; Scott, Foresman, 1988). There are numerous reviews of the PAC literature. See, e.g., Larry J. Sabato, *PAC Power* (New York: Norton, 1985). Mark S. Mizruchi, *The Structure of Corporate Political Action* (Cambridge: Harvard University Press, 1992) is another particularly thoughtful contribution, although I would disagree with a number of points in his discussion, as well as his reliance on PAC data for much, although not all, of his analysis. A particularly unfortunate feature of the recent PAC literature is a concentration on congressional elections in the early eighties, when much of the business community coalesced in political movements designed to move the U.S. political agenda sharply to the right. The discovery by some researchers that this process—which I and others wrote about at the time—in fact occurred, along with experimental designs that often obscure (weaker, but eventually important) counter-tendencies, nourishes the view that significant political differences within the business community do not in fact exist.

All students of money and politics, incidentally, owe substantial debts to Herbert Alexander, whose publications and data archives are invaluable and quite literally irreplaceable.

The extent to which reality has outstripped the scholarly literature on these questions is hard to convey, but one example may be telling. In many parliamentary democracies it is now quite common for corporations and investors formally to retain members of parliament as advisers for fees. In the United States, on the other hand, it is becoming increasingly common for congressional staffers to strike up various arrangements whereby they are paid (sometimes through one or another legal dodge, such as "consulting fees") by interested parties. The degree of statistical misspecification in ordinary voting models of politics is thus becoming ever more baroque.

8. The text of every previously published essay in this book has been revised and expanded, often considerably, and a substantial amount of material appears here for the first time.

Earlier versions of chapters (or parts of chapters) appeared as follows. Chap. 1: in Paul Zarembka, ed., *Research in Political Economy* 6 (1983); reprinted by permission of JAI Press, Inc. Chap. 2: in *International Organization* 38, no. 1 (Winter 1984); reprinted with the permission of MIT Press. Chap. 3: in *The Journal of Economic History*, vol. 44 (December 1984); reprinted by permission. Chap. 4: in *Sociological Perspectives*, 34, no. 4 (1991); reprinted by permission of JAI Press, Inc. Chap. 5: in *Socialist Review* 19, no. 4 (1989); reprinted by permission of Duke University Press. And in "Unbearable Lightness of Being," in Benjamin Ginsberg and Alan Stone, eds., *Do Elections Matter?* (Armonk, N.Y.: M. E. Sharpe, 1986); reprinted with permission. Chap. 6: in Lawrence C. Dodd and Calvin Jillson, eds., *New Perspectives on American Politics* (Washington, D.C.: Congressional Quarterly, Inc., forthcoming); reprinted with permission. Appendix: in *American Review of Politics* (Winter 1993); reprinted with permission.

9. See Lance Bennett, *The Governing Crisis* (New York: St. Martin's, 1992) and the discussion in the appendix. At a couple of points in his discussion, Bennett asks whether the main effect of money in the political system does not consist in bringing about the disintegration of the system to the exclusion of larger patterns such as those suggested in the various studies in this book (in which investment banks, various multinationals, and other definite business groups play major roles even in the Democratic Party). The

NAFTA debate should now have resolved this question. American politics is not simply disintegrating; new, historically specific, political coalitions and patterns of policies are emerging.

10. Thomas Ferguson and Joel Rogers, *Right Turn: The Decline of the Democrats and the Future of American Politics* (New York: Hill & Wang, 1986).

Party Realignment and American Industrial Structure:
The Investment Theory of Political Parties in Historical Perspective

I. INTRODUCTION

IN MID-SEPTEMBER 1912 a gentleman representing Woodrow Wilson, the Democratic nominee for president of the United States, came calling on Mr. Frank A. Vanderlip. At that time Vanderlip was one of the most prominent businessmen in America. Quoted frequently in the press and recognized as a leading Progressive, he served on the boards of 12 major corporations, including E. H. Harriman's Union Pacific Railroad, the mammoth U.S. Realty and Improvement Co., and four sizable banks. He was also a trustee of New York University and the Stevens Institute, a member of the executive committee of the New York Chamber of Commerce, and active in the National Civic Federation. Most important, however, he was president of the National City Bank of New York, after J. P. Morgan & Co. probably the most important bank in America.

Nothing in the record suggests that the banker felt any embarrassment at receiving the envoy of a party associated in American folklore (and much subsequent academic writing) with straitened Southern and Western farmers. It is easy to understand why: the visitor was Henry Morgenthau Sr., himself a director a dozen corporations (including the big, multinationally oriented Underwood Typewriter Co.) and a major figure in Manhattan real estate.

As was his custom with anything important, Vanderlip later wrote a detailed account of the encounter to James Stillman. Along with William Rockefeller (younger brother of the even more famous and wealthier John D.), Stillman had been prominently associated with the bank for many years. He was probably its largest stockholder. Now retired in France, he superintended the bank by remote control. Almost every other day brought a long letter from Vanderlip, describing his activities and decisions. After reading the letters, Stillman would write back his comments and instructions, dispatching them once in a while by secret courier or sometimes sending them in code. Because the months prior to the 1912 election had been filled with acrimonious controversies that importantly affected National City, especially the discussions of what eventually became the Federal Reserve Act, Vanderlip could be sure of Stillman's attention as he related how

> I had a two-hour session with [Charles D.] Hilles, the chairman of the Republican Campaign Committee, and one of equal length with Morgenthau, who is Chairman of Wilson's finance committee, and who is, with [William G.] McAdoo, practically directing the campaign. Hilles is not hopeful. I think the most [William Howard] Taft really hopes for is to get a larger vote than [Theodore] Roosevelt, although he believes that sentiment is swinging back to him some, and there is some evidence of that. . . . I had a very thorough going over of the administration with Hilles and I must say the result did not improve my views any of its efficiency. There never has been any clear understanding in the White House in regard to the National City Company [National City's newly organized and controversial securities affiliate], and the whole disposition was to avoid trouble and to pass the question along. My conversation with Morgenthau left me more pessimistic about the political outlook than I have been at all. I am afraid not a great deal that is good is likely to come out of a Wilson administration. At least, I am afraid that a good deal that is foolish and ill considered may come out of it. I think Wilson is really pretty well imbued with the "Money Trust" idea, and I fear he lacks the sincerity that I believed at one time he had. Morgenthau told me positively that it would not be his plan to have any extra session of Congress and that he proposed to take up banking legislation before the tariff; that he favors a central bank and one of the arguments he proposed to use is that the people are now under all the evil conditions of an unrestrained central bank, through the operations of the "Money Trust"; that there is a "Money Trust" that is practically a central bank, without any legislative control, and that they might much better replace it with a real central bank that will do them some good and will be controlled. I can see how just such stuff as this would appeal to Wilson's mind, but I am disgusted with his thinking and using such clap trap. He has told Morgenthau that the Aldrich Bill [which many major American banks sponsored] never can be passed, because it bears the Aldrich name. They have got to get up another bill which he supposes will have to be about 60% the Aldrich Bill to start with and probably will be 80% before they got it passed, but it must have another name.
>
> This is about as scientific an attitude toward the banking question as you would expect from Tim Murphy. Morgenthau tells me that [New York attorney Samuel] Untermeyer is preparing for a thoroughgoing

campaign to begin after election—I believe the date is November 20th—and has got a lot of men working on it now. His whole ambition is to, in some way, get a white-wash for his character. He has offered a hundred thousand dollars (all of this is quite confidential, of course) if he can be assured of a foreign mission. Indeed, he would give any amount for an important one, and has even the audacity to think that he might possibly be appointed to England. Wilson will make no promises whatever and they have accepted only $10,000 as yet and probably will accept no more. He would also like to be Attorney General. Morgenthau says that, of course, is quite impossible, although he could imagine that he might be sent to some post of about the grade of Italy.[1]

As a primary source for the study of modern American politics, this letter is uncommonly rich. Even on casual reading it brims with exciting implications for a wide range of issues now extensively debated by social scientists and historians—the impact of financial innovation on American political development, for example; or the relationship between congressional investigations (like that Untermeyer had just directed into banking practices on behalf of the so-called Pujo Committee) and the evolution of the national political agenda; or the role of professionalization in U.S. diplomacy of the period; or the significance of class and, perhaps, ethnic factors in elite politics. With more deliberate attention to the letter's historical context and stylistic idiosyncrasies still more would be revealed. A reading that was sensitive to the political choices other leading businessmen made during the same election, for instance, could certainly throw rare light on several first-order mysteries of the great American organism of that epoch, notably the delicate balance of rivalry and cooperation that characterized the "Money Trust" before World War I, and the precise ways in which the preferences of its members, allies, and opponents translated into party politics and public policy.

But perhaps the most important reflections suggested by this correspondence concern this essay's central theme: the primary and constitutive role large investors play in American politics. For much about this missive's tone and contents—the famous banker's condescension toward the White House (where "the whole disposition was to avoid trouble and to pass the question along," while—as Stillman and Vanderlip were both well aware—securing National City's vital interests); the Olympian assurance which acts as though nothing could be more natural than that top operatives of *both* major parties should drop by for intimate campaign discussions; or the matter-of-fact disdain with which Vanderlip relates to Stillman that the "Archangel Woodrow" (as H. L. Mencken called him) doesn't really believe what he is saying

about what was probably the campaign's prime issue—bank reform—
and that he has no plans to appoint Untermeyer, the archenemy of the
big banks, to high diplomatic post—almost irresistibly raises a series of
subversive doubts about the basic conceptual framework that most recent studies of American politics rely on to understand the workings
of the political system over time and as a whole.

As summed up in the "critical realignment theory" elaborated by
a succession of scholars since the late 1950s, this view understands
political change primarily—though of course not exclusively—in
terms of changing patterns of mass voting behavior.[2] Most American
elections, it considers, are contests within comparatively stable and coherent "party systems." While any number of short-term forces may
momentarily alter the balance of power within a particular party system, and cumulative, long-run secular changes may also be at work,
the identity of individual party systems rests on durable voting coalitions within the electorate. So long as these voting blocs (which in
different party systems may be defined variously along ethnic, class,
religious, racial, sexual, or a plurality of other lines) persist, only marginal changes are likely when administrations turn over. Characteristic
patterns of voter turnout, party competition, political symbols, public
policies, and other institutional expressions of the distribution of
power survive from election to election.

"Normal politics," of course, is not the only kind of politics that
occurs in the United States. The "critical realignments" of critical realignment theory refer to a handful of exceptional elections—those
associated with the New Deal and the Great Depression of the 1930s,
the Populist insurrection of the 1890s, the Civil War, and the Jacksonian era are most frequently mentioned, though other dates have
also been proposed—in which extraordinary political pressures find
expression. Associated with the rise of new political issues, intense social stress, sharp factional infighting within existing parties, and the
rise of strong party movements, these "critical" or "realigning" elections sweep away the old party system. Triggering a burst of new legislation and setting off or facilitating other institutional changes that may
take years to complete, such elections establish the framework of a
new pattern of politics that characterizes the next party system.

With few exceptions, the higher stakes involved in realigning elections do not sway realignment theorists from their emphasis on popular control of public policy.[3] The sweeping changes in the political system that occur are again ascribed to voter sentiment. By raising the
salience of political issues, most analysts suggest, critical elections facilitate a large-scale conversion of new voters from one party to another,

or a mass mobilization of new voters into the political system. Either way, the partisan division of the electorate alters decisively.

An illuminating and sophisticated variation on classic liberal electoral themes, critical realignment theory continues to be widely held by both social scientists and historians. It has also inspired increasing numbers of journalists, consultants, and political activists professionally concerned with interpreting political events. But in recent years skeptical appraisals of the theory have proliferated and many of its claims have come in for heavy criticism (Lichtman, 1976, 1980, 1982; Kousser, 1980; Benson, Silbey, and Field, 1978; Ferguson, 1986).

The pivotal arguments raised against conventional versions of critical realignment theory undermine precisely the aspect of the theory that the Vanderlip-Stillman exchange challenges so vividly: the inspired confidence in what might be termed "voter sovereignty." As several studies have argued in detail, evidence is mounting that the durable voter coalitions which are supposed to underlie party systems never existed, and that so-called critical realignments are not only very difficult to define, but simply have not witnessed major, lasting shifts in voter sentiment.[4] In the words of one sophisticated quantitative study of American voting patterns by three scholars very sympathetic to the realignment perspective (Clubb, Flanigan, and Zingale, 1980, p. 119),

> [E]lectoral change during the historical periods usually identified as realignments was not in every case either as sharp or as pervasive, nor was lasting change as narrowly confined to a few periods, as the literature suggests. Although these periods were marked by both deviating and realigning electoral change, which shifted the balance of partisan strength within the electorate toward one or the other of the parties, these shifts did not involve the massive reshuffling of the electorate that some formulations of the realignment perspective describe. Moreover, indications of substantial continuity of the alignment of electoral forces across virtually the whole sweep of American electoral history can be observed. . . . [E]lectoral patterns do not, by themselves, clearly and unequivocally point to the occurrence of partisan realignment.

To this evidence of massive public policy change without correspondingly sweeping electoral realignment, and other difficulties, adherents of critical realignment theory respond variously. The common denominator in virtually all their replies, however, is a determination to shore up the theory by making it even more complicated, "more multidimensional." The hope is to supplement the already complex electoral analysis with more and more variables—conducting more detailed studies, for example, of the president and the electorate, Congress and the electorate, the president, Congress, and the electorate, etc.[5]

But it is doubtful that such moves will do more than postpone the inevitable. As an earlier paper argued (Ferguson, 1986), adding baroque variations to already complex themes is likely only to generate rococo variations on the same themes—and provide very little additional illumination. Nor are these efforts likely to constitute an effective reply to the direct evidence emerging from both quantitative and case studies indicating that the relationship between public policy change and party platforms, electoral margins, and voting behavior is weak and unstable.[6]

It is time, therefore, to recognize that the chief reason why no social scientists have succeeded in specifying unambiguous *electoral* criteria to identify "partisan realignment" may well be that there are no such criteria to be found. And it is high time, accordingly, to begin developing a different approach—a fresh account of political systems in which business elites, not voters, play the leading part; an account that treats mass party structures and voting behavior as dependent variables, explicable in terms of rules for ballot access, issues, and institutional change, in a context of class conflict and change within the business community.

The present paper represents an attempt to revise conventional accounts of American party systems and critical realignments along precisely these lines. Parties, the paper argues, are not what critical realignment theory (and most American election analyses) treat them as, viz., as Anthony Downs defined them in his celebrated formalization of the liberal (electoral) model of parties and voters, the political analogues of "entrepreneurs in a profit-seeking economy" who "act to maximize votes" (Downs, 1957a, pp. 295 and 300). Instead, the fundamental market for political parties usually is not voters. As a number of recent analysts have documented (Burnham, 1974, 1981; Popkin et al., 1976; Ginsberg, 1982), most of these possess desperately limited resources and—especially in the United States—exiguous information and interest in politics. The real market for political parties is defined by major investors, who generally have good and clear reasons for investing to control the state. In a two-party system like that of the United States, accordingly, incidents like those recounted in Vanderlip's letter to Stillman are far more typical of U.S. parties than the usual median voter fantasy. Blocs of major investors define the core of political parties and are responsible for most of the signals the party sends to the electorate.

During realignments, I shall argue, basic changes take place in the core investment blocs which constitute parties. More specifically, realignments occur when cumulative long-run changes in industrial structures (commonly interacting with a variety of short-run factors, notably steep economic downturns) polarize the business community, thus bringing together a new and powerful bloc of investors with durable interests. As this process begins, party competition heats up and at least some differences between the parties emerge more clearly.

Since the business community typically polarizes only during a general crisis, it is scarcely surprising that in such cases voters also begin to shake, rattle, and roll. Only if the electorate's degree of effective organization significantly increases, however, does it receive more than crumbs. Otherwise all that occurs is a change of personnel and policy that, because it may reflect nothing more than a vote of no confidence in the current regime, bears no necessary relation to *any* set of voting patterns or consistent electoral interests. Assuming that the system crisis eventually eases (possibly, but *not necessarily,* because of any public policy innovation), the fresh "hegemonic bloc" that has come to power enjoys excellent prospects as long as it can hold itself together. Benefiting from incumbency advantage and the chance to implement its program, the new bloc's major problem is to manage the tensions among its various parts, while of course making certain that large groups of voters do not become highly mobilized against it—either by making positive appeals to some (which need not be the same from election to election) or by minimizing voter turnout, or both.

The discussion comprises the following major sections.

Section 2 outlines the basic notions of the investment theory of parties and applies them to the problem of critical realignment. This effort involves two separate tasks: first, to explain clearly why voters can only rarely define public policy through elections; second, to indicate how businesses (and, in some party systems, labor or middle-class organizations) importantly influence or control political parties and elections. Now the first problem, the paper argues, has already been completely solved by recent contributions to the so-called economic theory of democracy developed by Downs and other theorists. Also, the paper proposes that by pursuing the logic of the arguments developed in one of these recent essays, "What Have You Done for Me Lately? Toward an Investment Theory of Voting" (Popkin et al., 1976), an easy solution materializes to the second—the question of how elections and policies are in fact controlled. Building on these arguments, the present paper contrasts the "investment theory of political parties" point by point with conventional voter-centered models of elections. As part of this exercise, the paper reconsiders aspects of Mancur Olson's famous analysis of *The Logic Of Collective Action* to gain a

clearer view of the unique advantages major investors enjoy in providing themselves with what look to all other actors in the system
like "public goods" (Olson, 1971).

How to test the theory is considered next. Section 3 begins with a
brief discussion of criteria for recognizing "large" investors and similar
definitional issues. To demonstrate the existence and stability of the
investor coalitions that the theory posits, the paper develops a method
for the graphical analysis of industrial (and, where necessary, agricultural) structures. By analyzing how blocs of investors whose interests
center in different parts of the economy map into multidimensional
issue space, this technique produces spatial models of the distribution
of major investors within the political system—models that can be estimated with actual data to reveal whether a coalition really exists.
When analyzed developmentally, such models can also indicate
whether these coalitions are becoming more or less coherent.

Section 4,the longest part of the paper, presents a series of sketches
of the major investor blocs that have dominated the various party systems in American history. Necessarily stylized and subject to further
revision, these accounts largely bring together research gathered for
longer studies which have appeared or will appear separately.

Finally, section 5 ties up loose ends and considers the possibilities
for enhancing the power of ordinary voters in advanced industrial societies in light of the investment theory of parties.

II. FROM ELECTORAL TO INVESTMENT THEORIES OF POLITICAL PARTIES

Ironically, it was Anthony Downs's classic formalization of the liberal
theory of elections and public policy which took the first and perhaps
most important step down the path toward an alternative account. For
by the middle of *An Economic Theory of Democracy,* Downs (1957a, p.
258) concluded:

> The expense of political awareness is so great that no citizen can af-
> ford to bear it in every policy area, even if by doing so he could dis-
> cover places where his intervention would reap large profits.

This and similar observations led Downs into a pathbreaking analysis
of the costs and benefits of becoming informed about public affairs and
choosing between alternative courses of action. At several points
Downs recognized that the logic of an information cost model potentially undermined democratic control of public policy, for if voters cannot bear these costs they have no hope of successfully supervising the
government.[7] But Downs did not finally give much empirical weight

to this possibility, and his work became famous as a demonstration of how voters controlled government policy in countries similar to the United States.[8]

More recent analysis has demonstrated, however, that serious application of Downs's ideas about information costs to actual political systems leads to many striking conclusions, which stand both traditional voting analyses and Downs's preferred models of democratic control on their heads.

The most important of these contributions is that of Samuel Popkin and his associates. A pioneering attempt to incorporate the cost of obtaining and processing information into the analysis of voter behavior, their paper presents a detailed critique of the conventional "socialization" approach to partisan identification and mass political choices. In this view, which work done during the 1950s on *The American Voter* (Campbell, et al., 1960) appeared to support, an individual's attachments to political parties are shaped by non- or a-rational group and family socialization experiences involving a minimum of cognitive orientation.[9] By reanalyzing data presented in several earlier studies along Downsian lines, however, Popkin et al. demonstrate that the orientation of most voters toward politics is and has been primarily cognitive rather than affective.

Following a path Downs himself briefly explored,[10] Popkin et al. suggest that voters are only acting rationally when they cut information costs by using shortcuts like partisan identification or demographic facts to evaluate complex vectors of political variables. But—and here lies one major part of their paper's interest for this essay—Popkin et al. (1976, p. 787) also provide a clear argument and a series of vivid examples illustrating how, in a political system like that of the United States, where even highly motivated voters face comparatively enormous costs when they attempt to acquire, evaluate, and act upon political information, effective electoral control of the governmental process by voters becomes most unlikely:

[T]he understanding that information is costly leads to expectations about the voter which differ from those of the SRC or citizen-voter [i.e., "socialization"] model. Whereas citizen-voters are expected to have well developed opinions about a wide range of issues, a focus on information costs leads to the expectation that only some voters— those who must gather the information in the course of their daily lives or who have a particularly direct stake in the issue—will develop a detailed understanding of any issues. Most voters will only learn enough to form a very generalized notion of the position of a particular candidate or party on some issues, and many voters will be ignorant about most issues.

As a consequence it is not necessary to assume or argue that the voting population is stupid or malevolent to explain why it often will not stir at even gross affronts to its own interests and values. Mere political awareness is costly; and, like most of what are now recognized as "collective goods," absent individual possibilities of realization, it will not be supplied or often even demanded unless some sort of subsidy (at least in the form of advertising) is supplied by someone.[11]

To further clarify the issues involved in the decision to participate in collective action under uncertainty, Popkin et al. introduce their most striking idea—the notion that political action should be analyzed as *investment*, with "the simple act of voting" requiring at least an investment of time and attention as a limiting case.[12]

Now, this suggestion has many exciting implications—too many implications, indeed, for this paper to assess. Consider, for example, how non-Downsian it is at its core. Though Popkin et al. generally claim they are following Downs, conventional neoclassical exchange theories provide the basic framework for most of Down's work. While, as mentioned earlier, Downs pioneered the analyses of investment, he did not pursue the sweeping implications of his results. As a consequence, in his presentation investment enters largely as a further complication in a more detailed model of voter control. Because investment does not really emerge as a prominent theme in its own right, neither Downs nor later analysts who share his methodological bent have fully recognized the implications of their own theory. As Joan Robinson and other critics of neoclassical microeconomics have observed, even the simplest acts of investment imply change over time and accordingly are almost impossible to incorporate into the general equilibrium framework that Downs himself champions as an ideal (Robinson, 1971, Chap. 1). Similar logic also inspires John Roemer's insufficiently appreciated observation that much politically relevant behavior involves shattering the boundaries of what most microeconomic analysts too hastily identify as the "feasible set."[13]

For this paper, however, the chief importance of the investment analysis of Popkin et al. lies in the possibility of its consistent extension to political parties. In several passages strongly reminiscent of parts of Burnham's work, Popkin et al. (1976) sharply criticize the Michigan group for assuming that most individuals can normally afford to contest outcomes that are products of a whole system whose scale is many times that of the average voter.

> The SRC also assumed that the major barriers to participation were internal to the individual. In 1960 they stated "[t]he greater impact

of restrictive electoral laws on Negroes is, in part at least, a function of the relatively low motivational levels among Negroes." The increase of participation among black voters in the 1960's is, of course, a clear example of a situation where political participation as well as political interest and involvement, rather than being fixed expressions of individual motivation, responded instead to an increase in investment opportunities and a legal decision by Congress to reduce the cost (or more aptly, to provide subsidies to aid blacks in paying the costs) of voting. (p. 790)

In the investor voter model, interest, involvement, and participation depend on the voter's calculation of the individual stakes and costs involved in the election; included in this calculation are the voter's issue concerns and his estimates of his opportunities for participation. As a result, much of the stigma of "apathy" is transferred from the voter to the electoral system. (pp. 789–90)

Instead of arguing that irresponsible voters lead to irresponsible parties, we argue that a fragmented system with weak parties leads to information problems for the individual voter which make the best possible decisionmaking strategies less than ideal. (p. 795)

But despite their inspired and often very amusing beginning, Popkin et al. do not pursue their inquiry to its logical conclusion. Their analysis points out the vast disproportion between what the individual voter-investor can afford and the range of potential information and action in principle available to him or her, and exposes the flimsiness of much of the "spatial modeling" now popular in political science, but there it halts. Remaining content with an investment theory of *voting*, Popkin et al. refrain from taking the obvious next step. They do not broach the question that their study clearly implies: if ordinary voters can't afford to invest much in American political parties, then who can? And by virtue of their unique status, do not these "big ticket" investors automatically become the real masters of the political system?

Raising these questions, I think, transports one to the heart of the disastrous misunderstanding of the nature of political parties inscribed at the center of the Downsian approach to political parties (and its less formal ancestors). For what can be taken as the core proposition of the "investment theory of *political parties*" denies the validity of the Downsian treatment of parties as simple vote maximizers. Instead, the investment theory of parties holds that parties are more accurately analyzed as *blocs of major investors who coalesce to advance candidates representing their interests.*

As should momentarily become apparent, this proposition does not imply that such investor blocs pay no attention to voters. It does, however, mean that in situations where information is costly, abstention is possible, and entry into politics through either new parties or existing organizations is expensive and often dangerous (that is, in the real world in which actual political systems operate) political parties dominated by large investors try to assemble the votes they need by making very limited appeals to particular segments of the potential electorate. If it pays some other bloc of major investors to advertise and mobilize, these appeals can be vigorously contested, but—and this is the critical deduction which only an investment theory of parties can draw—on all issues affecting the vital interests that major investors have in common, no party competition will take place.[14] Instead, all that will occur will be a proliferation of marginal appeals to voters—and if all major investors happen to share an interest in ignoring issues vital to the electorate, such as social welfare, hours of work, or collective bargaining, so much the worse for the electorate. Unless significant portions of it are prepared to try to become major investors in their own right, through a substantial expenditure of time and (limited) income, there is nothing any group of voters can do to offset this collective investor dominance.

While the "principle of noncompetition" over the vital interests of all major investors constitutes the most important predictive difference between the investment and the Downsian theory of political parties, it is scarcely the only one. A whole series of contrasts can be drawn between them.

1. *Downsian theory privileges voters, who are said to exercise control over at least the broad shape of public policy. The investment theory holds that voters hardly count unless they become substantial investors. When the ranks of significant investors are limited to relatively small numbers of elite actors commanding disproportionate shares of politically mobilized resources, mass voting loses most of its significance for controlling public policy. Elections become contests between several oligarchic parties, whose major public policy proposals reflect the interests of large investors, and which minor investor-voters are virtually incapable of affecting, save in a negative sense of voting (or nonvoting) "no confidence."*

Because the claims made by the investment theory of parties can easily be misunderstood, the logic of the underlying argument is worth pursuing a bit further. Two points in particular require clarification: one relates to the potential role of voters according to the theory; the other, involving a rather complicated set of considerations growing out of the "rational choice" literature that Popkin et al. rely on, concerns the precise nature of some of the advantages large investors enjoy when they act politically.

In regard to voters, what the investment theory of parties does not say is every bit as important as what it does say. The theory does not deny the possibility that masses of voters might indeed become the major investors in an electoral system, or that, if they did so, conditions approximating a Downsian ideal of voter sovereignty might exist. As a later section briefly illustrates in discussing the expansion of unions during the New Deal, such conditions are conceptually very clear and empirically identifiable. To effectively control governments, ordinary voters require strong channels that directly facilitate mass deliberation and expression. That is, they must have available to them a resilient network of "secondary" organizations capable of spreading costs and concentrating small contributions from several individuals to act politically, as well as an open system of formally organized political parties. Both the parties and the secondary organizations need to be "independent," i.e., themselves dominated by investor-voters (instead of, for example, donors of revokable outside funds). Entry barriers for both secondary organizations and political parties must be low, and the technology of political campaigning (e.g., cost of newspaper space, pamphlets, etc.) must be inexpensive in terms of the annual income of the average voter. Such conditions result in high information flows to the grass roots, engender lively debates, and create conditions that make political deliberation and action part of everyday life. What the theory claims is merely that in the absence of these conditions a party system that is competitive in the relevant Downsian sense cannot prevent a tiny minority of the population—major investors—from dominating the political system. The costs that the voters must bear to control policy will be literally beyond their means.

A proper analysis of the reasons why large investors are likely to dominate political systems, however, need not rest with the observation—however weighty—that, to paraphrase Hemingway, the rich are different because they have more money. By pursuing several themes in the literature on economic theories of politics that Popkin et al. draw upon, we see that a more subtle picture emerges of the special position that large investors occupy in a political system.

There is first of all a point whose potential importance was clearly recognized by Downs, though I do not believe that he ultimately accorded it sufficient weight (Downs, 1957a, Chap. 13). This is the simple fact that much of the public policy–relevant information that voters must pay heavily in time or money to acquire comes naturally to businesses (i.e., major investors) in the daily course of operations.

Closely related to this edge that large investors enjoy in acquiring information are the advantages they usually command in analyzing it. Computers engaged to service customers, for example, easily perform all sorts of politically relevant tasks. Perhaps a little less obviously, the business contacts that an international bank maintains also constitute a first-rate foreign-policy network. And the sometimes thin line separating normal advertising from lobbying virtually disappears for many producers of major weapons systems.

In many cases vast economies of scale further enhance the position of large investors. What is for a voter an absolutely prohibitive expense a large firm can afford on a regular basis. As long ago as the eighteenth century, for example, large investors routinely consulted their lawyers before making major moves. Two hundred years later, these consultations are likely to be done in a committee which includes not only lawyers but also public relations advisers, lobbyists, and political consultants.[15] In sharp contrast to voters, for whom even jury duty can become an onerous burden, large firms also can easily afford to divert personnel to special projects.

Still other advantages armor what is sometimes cited as the Achilles' heel of large investors—their very size and frequent diversity of interests (Bauer, Poole, and Dexter, 1972). Modern management structure developed precisely to afford top executives the capacities for detailed command and control that they need to adjudicate conflicts within the firm and to optimize complex sets of interests.[16] Such organizational forms, along with the informal retinue of advisers large investors have always maintained, constitute uniquely institutionalized "memories" that dwarf the resources available to most voters.

Olson's well-known study *The Logic of Collective Action* demonstrates that, in addition to all these advantages, major investors also derive subtle but decisive benefits from certain general characteristics of the process of interest intermediation and articulation (Olson, 1971).* Both because several of the most significant consequences of Olson's argument have not as yet been integrated into empirical research and because his own applications of it to the business community were cursory and, in part, misleading, his analysis is worth retracing in some detail.

Its initial stages have been well summarized by Barry (1970, p. 24):

> Olson's argument is intended to apply wherever what is at stake is a "public good," that is, a benefit which cannot be deliberately restricted to certain people, such as those who helped bring it into existence. A potential beneficiary's calculation, when deciding whether

---

*Readers unfamiliar with this work and the issues it raises may wish to skim over the next few pages. Nothing essential will be lost, and the later historical sections of the paper should be readily intelligible.

to contribute to the provision of such a benefit, must take the form of seeing what the benefit would be to him and discounting it by the probability that his contribution would make the difference between the provision and the non-provision of the benefit.

In a world in which most collective goods can be safely assumed to be beyond the means of isolated individuals, Olson's formal theory of collective action follows directly from his judgment that the probability that one actor's decision to contribute will influence another's drops steeply with increases in the size of the group which will enjoy the collective good (see Olson, 1971, p. 44):

> In a small group in which a member gets such a large fraction of the total benefit that he would be better off if he paid the entire cost himself, rather than go without the good, there is some presumption that the collective good will be provided. In a group in which no one member got such a large benefit from the collective good that he had an interest in providing it even if he had to pay all of the cost, but in which the individual was still so important in terms of the whole group that his contribution or lack of contribution to the group objective had a noticeable effect on the costs or benefits of others in the group, the result is indeterminate. . . . By contrast, in a large group in which no single individual's contribution makes a perceptible difference to the group as a whole, or the burden or benefit of any single member of the group, it is certain that a collective good will *not* be provided unless there is coercion or some outside inducements that will lead the members of the large group to act in their common interest.

Now, this argument is of course subject to all the limitations of its premises, which include two that have frequently become targets for criticism: that human behavior is an exercise in rational calculation and that it is exclusively self-interested.[17] But it is doubtful if the criticism in this vein that Olson's argument has received makes much difference. It is possible to agree that strictly neoclassical approaches to political economy invidiously neglect ideology. One can therefore endorse the search for a more comprehensive theory of action. It is equally possible to reject Olson's implicit assumption that action is always a cost rather than a good in itself, and allow that the process of collective action can become a uniquely rewarding experience in its own right. And anyone can recognize that the assumption that humans are exclusively self-seeking may sometimes be a potentially serious distortion of reality even in a capitalist society.

But unless one is prepared to make truly heroic counter-assumptions, Olson's fundamental point is likely to stand. Expectations that large groups of people will voluntarily provide huge subsidies over long periods of time to projects that return no benefit to themselves (and may often be completely wasted) is unlikely to prove fruitful as an approach to most of human history—and particularly to the analysis of market societies. As rival accounts of collective action put forward by Olson's critics inadvertently illustrate when they initially posit the origins of collective action in attempts to escape misery and deprivation, reason (or history) may be cunning, but it is rarely philanthropic: much, probably most, collective action undertaken is straightforwardly instrumental and animated by perfectly ordinary passions.[18] Most of it, accordingly, should follow the basic logic of Olson's model.

But while his general analysis identifies an important reason for expecting small groups of large investors to display capacities for self-organization far beyond the capability of ordinary citizens, Olson's actual application of his model to the business community is perhaps the least satisfying section of his work.

In part this is almost certainly the consequence of an ambiguity in his original presentation that has a most important bearing on its implications for large investors. If Olson is correct, one would expect to find many instances in American history in which relatively small groups of major investors organized and bore most of the costs of political campaigns directed toward ends that greatly benefited themselves. Since in the United States most of what the state provides is formally provided for the benefit of the whole population, these investor groups would therefore supply collective "goods" to the rest of the country in the perhaps elongated technical sense that Olson employs the term.[19] And, indeed, though many contemporary social scientists often are unable to distinguish accounts of small groups of major investors efficiently providing themselves with public goods from outlandish and improbable "conspiracy theories,"[20] American history is replete with vivid examples of the fundamental asymmetry Olson's account suggests between the markets for collective action enjoyed by the rich and poor, respectively. Three of the greatest investors in the United States, for example, virtually financed the later stages of the War of 1812 all by themselves (Brown, 1942, p. 126; Hammond, 1957, pp. 231–32). Much of the money required for the force that quelled Shays's Rebellion came from a handful of very affluent (and very nervous) investors.[21] The original promoters of what eventually became the Brookings Institutions were a bloc of investors frankly hoping to reduce their taxes by curbing federal spending (by promoting the establishment of what became the Budget Bureau), while another group of millionaires bore the lion's share of the costs for the effort to repeal Prohibition with the no less bluntly declared aim of reducing their taxes through the taxation of liquor (which the poor would pay).[22]

Oddly, however, Olson discounts such cases as "empirically trivial" (1971, p. 48, no. 68). He does this because in addition to making his main argument (discussed earlier), which relates group size to the likelihood that individual action can decisively affect the provision of a collective good (for instance, by the influence of one's example on others), he also develops another line of thought. In this second account he tries to derive his proposition that large groups will not provide themselves with collective goods (absent coercion or selective incentives) directly from an analysis of how an individual's share of a collective good varies with group size.[23]

Now, this is an exceedingly dangerous way to make the case. For as Olson himself is well aware, the only calculation strictly relevant to deciding whether an individual will participate in collective action relates to the net advantage that accrues to that individual from that action. While there is no reason anyone who wishes to cannot relate this condition of the total gains to the group as a whole (by simply forming the appropriate ratios), additional formulations simply distract from this crucial point. And, as an examination of Olson's mathematical presentation shows, his efforts on this score led him into an error that has no consequences for his basic argument but which obscures the vitally important case of major investors who provide themselves and the country as a whole with collective goods.[24]

Olson's own discussion of the business community is very brief, and largely confined to underscoring the conclusion that industries in which only a small number of firms compete will find it easier to organize. Cursory and highly stylized, it makes no sustained effort to engage empirical material (1971, pp. 141–48).

Many of the most interesting implications of his findings are not discussed at all. For example, if one accepts Olson's arguments about the difficulties of achieving coordination in decentralized industries, then large merger waves, such as the United States experienced in the 1890s, 1920s, and more recent past, acquire potential political significance. Mergers, in effect, are a prime method by which actual businesses solve their collective action problems. Also, if Olson is correct, then the usual neoclassical dismissal of the importance of "aggregate" (in contrast to particular "industry") concentration is probably mistaken, for it is clear that the scope of rivalry among a few giant firms which can coordinate and trade off operations in many industries at once will be vastly different from highly atomized and decentralized competition.[25]

The most significant omissions in Olson's discussion of collective action within the business community, however, concern his neglect of the financial system and the potential role of coercion (even) within market systems. The former is important because the strategic position that leading financiers enjoy in many economies may at least partially solve free-rider problems among businessmen. Of course, the leverage banks can exert over other enterprises varies with many factors, including the secular trend of economic growth, the business cycle, and, obviously, the development of credit markets.[26] No less clearly, the interests being served in such cases may not be those of "business as a whole" or some similarly exalted abstraction, but primarily those of the banks themselves. But it is probably no accident that empirical studies of really powerful cross-sectoral business organizations like the Business Council or the Committee for Economic Development (CED)—neither of which Olson mentions—reveal the omnipresence of big banks.[27] And a long search I undertook of private records yielded direct evidence of pressure banks exerted on reluctant industrialists to enroll in the CED.[28]

Olson's analysis should also stimulate a re-evaluation of the role coercion plays among large investors. Both Olson and his critics dwell overmuch on the "voluntary" character of social interactions. When he discusses individual cases, Olson customarily breaks off the discussion after he reaches his conclusion that, while huge gains accrue to groups which succeed in organizing themselves, absent coercion or selective incentives this is quite unlikely.[29] By contrast, many of his critics, concerned either to reestablish the rationality of large group organizing efforts, or, more rarely, bothered that reality seems to provide more examples of successful collective action by large groups than theory predicts, often reply by tracing out arabesques of increasingly far-fetched reasoning which might lead a large group to come together voluntarily in its own interest. But of course, the real alternatives facing a group with free-rider problems frequently include options more lively than dialogue among the members to build up a perhaps irrational mutual trust (Offe and Wiesenthal, 1980), encouraging the probably mistaken realization that none can hope to advance independently of the others (Roemer, 1978), or even locally based federation (which, since it associates small groups, fits Olson's model as a part to collective action.) Specifically, it often is the case that the real "logic of collective action" for a large group with a vital interest at stake is the swift application (by some—perhaps self-appointed—subgroups) of coercion to erring members of the larger group.

Of course Olson, and his readers, are all perfectly well aware that coercion, force, violence, terror, and such practices are possibilities for social groups. The point, however, is that only in his discussion of labor unions does Olson energetically pursue the strategic trail in this direction (1971, pp. 66 ff.). Yet there is no reason to single out unions (or managements confronting unions). In general, any group of rational actors seeking to organize a large group will experience the same incentives—including major investors in the business community organizing various sorts of political coalitions.

American history is replete with examples of business groups and individual firms retaining vast arrays of military and paramilitary forces for long periods of time. In the nineteenth century many railroads kept private armies. The Pennsylvania Coal and Iron police ran their own *Obrigkeitsstaat* for decades. General Motors maintained the Black Legion; Ford sported a veritable *Freikorps* recruited by the notorious Harry Bennett; and any number of detective agencies, goon squads, "special consultants," and wiretappers have also been active.[30] That most of these—though clearly not all, for railroads often fought pitched battles with competitors—are usually said to have been directed at labor makes little difference. While this claim does underline the quasi-military character of many of the most important cases of collective action in American life, there is little reason to believe that it represents the whole truth. Force on such a scale potentially menaces competitors, buyers, and suppliers almost as much as it does workers.[31]

It is true that market forces place definite limits on the scope for coercion within the business community. But as the earlier reference to financial pressure on businesses should suggest, even an economy that might be reasonably competitive in the long run contains all sorts of imperfections and uncertainties that leave plenty of scope for direct pressure. Accordingly, it ought to surprise no one if, especially in times of extreme emergency, as, for example, during a war or strike wave, many businessmen turn rapidly to structures that contain strong elements of coercion—either by (some part of) themselves, emergency provisions in a liberal constitution, or, in truly dire emergencies, a Führer. And in less straitened circumstances political coalitions should be scrutinized carefully for elements of coercion as well as voluntary accord even within dominant groups.

2. *Inside political parties, Downsian theory focuses all the attention on professional politicians. Investment theory takes care never to confuse investors/employers with politicians/employees.*

The investment theory of politics does not deny that candidates and professional politicians have a great stake in their success, or indeed that they might have a greater interest than their major backers in winning at almost any price. But investment theories maintain that political organizations are (sometimes very complex) investments; that, while they need small amounts of aid and commitment from many people, most of their major endorsements, money, and media atten-

tion typically come as direct or indirect results of their ability to attract
heavyweight investors. As a consequence not even former presidents
with enormous personal popularity like Theodore Roosevelt could run
insurgent campaigns without support from investors like U.S. Steel or
investment banker George Perkins.[32] In addition, for all the attention
Downsian theorists focus on offices as the primary lure for candidates
and parties, the investment theory of parties expects that a fairly clear
distinction exists between routine lower-level appointments, with limited discretion and established formal and informal role expectations,
and top policymaking slots. These latter, the investment theory of parties anticipates, are often reserved for representative major investors
or their immediate designates (Ferguson, 1986).

3. *Downsian theory expects parties to move near the voters on important pol-
    icy dimensions and, indeed, often even "leapfrog" rivals in their haste to
    find the median voter. The investment theory expects very modest moves
    toward the public on all issues affecting major investors, rocklike stability
    toward the vital interests of these investors, and many efforts to adjust the
    public to the parties' views rather than vice versa.*[33]

The Vanderlip-McAdoo-Hilles deliberations regarding the Federal
Reserve System discussed earlier, or the many other examples American history offers of major party candidates who flatly refused to take
immensely popular steps opposed by almost all major investors (such
as abandoning a balanced budget to extend relief during major economic downturns)[34] should embarrass Downsian theory but scarcely
the investment theory of parties. On the contrary, if, for example,
George McClellan in 1864, Horatio Seymour in 1868, Rutherford
Hayes in the late 1870s, Grover Cleveland in the 1880s and 1890s,
Alton Parker in 1904, William Howard Taft in 1912, all major party
candidates in 1924 and 1932, Alfred Landon in 1936, Barry Goldwater
in 1964, Jimmy Carter in 1980, and any number of other presidential
candidates all expressly repudiated major factions of their party immediately ahead of closely contested elections, the investment theory just
looks for the investors who insisted on having their way.[35]

4. *Downsian theory anticipates competition between the parties on most is-
    sues; the investment theory of parties, on the contrary, expects that whole
    areas of public policy will not be contested at all, while on others the parties
    will differ like Ford and GM before the Japanese arrived.*

Downs hedged his original analysis of political dynamics with all
sorts of qualifications about single-peaked preferences, etc. Subsequent
commentators added a variety of other caveats, of which those concerning the number and types of issues contested were probably the

most important (Stokes, 1966). But neither Downs nor most of his critics ever indicated they believed that most major parties in advanced industrial societies would actually fail to compete on many important issues in which the interests of many citizens were fairly clearly defined, or could, through political campaigning, readily be defined. Nor, so far as I can discover, did anyone *ever* do more than glance at systematic pressures put on parties not to make issues out of certain questions of public policy or entertain the possibility that both major parties (in a two-party system) would regularly do precisely this. To the investment theory of political parties, of course, nothing is more natural. If all major investors oppose discussing a particular issue, then neither party is likely to pick the issue up—no matter how many little investors or noninvestors might benefit—not because of any active collusion between parties but because no effective constituency exists to force the issue onto the public agenda.

Also, the investment theory of parties would scarcely be surprised to discover that the major parties in party systems marked by great economic inequality or sharp swings in national income often confine almost all competition to noneconomic issues less threatening to elite investors. This does not, it should be observed, imply that political parties *generate* these noneconomic cleavages. It says merely that, if an emphasis on noneconomic issues protects major investors in all parties, then emphases on ethnic, racial, or cultural values will proliferate relative to economic appeals. And, the investment theory adds, studies of voting behavior that cite ethnocultural voting patterns congruent with such partisan appeals as evidence against older economic interpretations of U.S. political behavior are invalid in principle.[36] Without an analysis of party leadership and public policy output, the voting patterns cannot be interpreted.

The contrast between the Downsian and the investment theory of political parties could go on indefinitely and with endless refinement. But the implications for this paper on critical realignments should now be clear: for all its merit and intellectual interest, Downs's *An Economic Theory of Democracy* misspecifies the basic market in which political parties operate. Not voters but investors constitute their fundamental constituency.

Once this central point is clarified, a revised approach to the definition of party systems and critical realignments becomes immediately available. If, according to the investment theory of parties, political parties are constituted by "core" blocs of major investors interested in securing a small set of specific outcomes, then "party systems" are the systems of action organized by these major investment blocs. Depending on the relative strength of the contending blocs, several different types of "party systems" can be distinguished. In rare cases (such as the Era of Good Feeling after the War of 1812) virtually all major investors may be organized into one massive, utterly "hegemonic" bloc, so that national party competition literally ceases to exist. Similarly, even where competition between rival blocs has brought into being another party, one investment bloc may still strongly dominate the other. Where one bloc succeeds in controlling most outcomes and reducing its opponents to variations on its themes (as, for example, the Democrats did to the Republicans for years after the New Deal), it also makes sense to continue to refer to the dominant bloc as "hegemonic," though this case is clearly very different from instances where no organized opposition exists at all. Where no one party exercises hegemony, rival blocs will simply be "competitive." Since the identity of parties—and thus of a party system—depends on the blocs that make them up and not on whether some party happens to win or lose, it is perfectly reasonable to speak of a party system as decaying over time from hegemony to competitive status, or even as having a life cycle, provided that is understood as referring, say, to changes in the relative power of various elements composing a once-dominant bloc or to minor shifts between the parties. And, obviously, party systems also pass away. In theory this could happen by slow change of identity in an industrial equivalent of Key's "secular realignment" (which could lead to tedious definitional arguments).[37] In actual fact, however, for reasons adumbrated in the next section, all but the first American party system ended catastrophically in brief critical realignments that ushered in new and notably different party systems.

Also, in the spirit of the earlier analysis of the crucial role size differentials among coalition partners play in political coalitions, one would expect that a bloc that is hegemonic for any length of time might be—in Gramsci's famous phrase—"crowned" by a particularly outsized and active unitary (or near unitary) actor. Because of its disproportionate size relative to the rest of the coalition, and its relatively enormous stake in the system as a whole, this "hegemon" often becomes the final source of the emergency subsidies any political coalition sometimes requires. Its prominence within the system may also afford it some scope for coercion, which also will help keep the bloc together.

III. Testing the Investment Theory of Political Parties: Methodological and Operational Considerations

Many discussions of the methodological issues involved in testing highly abstract social science theories strongly resemble Sunday morning radio broadcasts. Inspired more by a desire to protect a license than by any audience demand for the information, they fill the air with a hodgepodge of pious cant and sententious banality that only rarely connects to real problems. At the risk of further blackening the good name of empirical social science, however, some discussion of methodology is indispensable in this paper, for it is perfectly obvious that any number of questions are likely to arise naturally in the course of operationalizing the theory just sketched. If, for example, blocs of major investors constitute party systems, then how should one distinguish "major" from "minor" investors? For that matter, just exactly who or what constitutes an "investor" in the relevant sense?

Assuming that these notions can be satisfactorily elucidated, what counts as evidence for claims that major investors "support" particular candidates, issues, and parties? Still more importantly, let us agree for the sake of argument that the evidence shows that powerful blocs of investors have actually massed behind different parties at different times. How can the *existence* and *stability* of such coalitions over the course of a whole party system be demonstrated? Without evidence on these points the investment theory of parties is vulnerable to the same sort of embarrassments that electoral theories endured when tests failed to reveal the stable voting blocs persisting through the "party systems" that they were supposed to define. And finally, of course, how does one recognize and deal with situations which the investment theory itself acknowledges, when major investors do not dominate a party system and something like effective mass democracy actually occurs?

Not all of these questions are equally urgent. The first, for example, sounds far more profound than it really is, and can be dealt with summarily. Essentially the investment theory of political parties postulates that a strong relationship exists between the extremes (or "tails") of two different distributions; the distribution of investors in political action and the distribution of investors in the circumambient economy. In testing the theory nothing important depends on the exact values of the cutoff points used to indicate "large" investors in each distribution—the top 5 percent, 10 percent, 12 percent, or whatever.[38] So long as both distributions actually are skewed, large investors can be meaningfully distinguished, though, of course, in any case study specific characteristics of a particular skewed distribution are almost certain to become important facts.[39]

The closely related question of who or what counts as an "investor" also sounds more penetrating than it really is. As the proliferating literature on managers, owners, and corporate control suggests, identifying the locus of working control in certain organizations can be difficult and time-consuming (Herman, 1981; Burch, 1972; Zeitlin and Norwich, 1979). In some cases, accordingly, unravelling the identity of the relevant "investors" may be tedious and complicated. But there is little point to pursuing such considerations here. The significant operational point is plain: depending on the historical period, the relevant investing units could be individuals, partnerships, firms, foundations, financial groups, or, in cases where the fortunes of particular families or individuals are centrally invested and controlled, a "fortune." In rare cases, a state agency or bureaucracy might also be considered a "major investor," as could the exceptional case mentioned earlier, of an autonomously acting division of a large firm going into business on its own. Beyond the jejune injunction that empirical inquiries into these questions need to be guided by the best available literature and techniques of the parts of business history concerned with them, nothing general can be said. What is at stake are complicated facts whose meaning is bound tightly to context and particular cases.

While puzzles about the identity of investors are therefore problems less for the investment theory of political parties than for other branches of the social sciences such as business history, the same cannot be said about the methodological problems involved in inquiries into which parties or policies a firm or a group of investors supports at particular moments. In the absence of a clear justification for these sorts of claims the investment theory of parties cannot hope to flourish.

Records of campaign contributions by major investors, of course, can provide important clues about who supports what. But while such evidence often yields important insights, it is most commonly marked by distinct limitations. The biggest problem is with the fragmentary character of the data for nearly all periods of American history. Analysts of campaign contributions are nearly unanimous in pointing to its inadequacies (Overacker, 1932; Thayer, 1973). Large numbers of pecuniary contributions were understated or never recorded at all. Cash paid in the form of excessive consultant, lawyer, and other third-party fees is rarely noticed and in-kind contributions almost never listed. "Loans" which are never repaid or are granted on preferential terms rarely attract notice. Neither do "gifts" to "friends."

Not surprisingly, almost every seriously pursued investigation of campaign contributions, from the Hearst-inspired attacks on Theodore Roosevelt and E. H. Harriman to the recent inquiries into corporate bribery conducted under the auspices of the Securities and Exchange Commission, has unearthed unreported contributions of astronomical magnitude. And there is reason to think the omissions have often followed systematic patterns. In an ingenious statistical comparison, Pittman has demonstrated that a series of striking and predictable differences exist between the original "public" campaign contribution lists of the 1972 Nixon campaign and the secretly maintained files that later court cases brought to light (Pittman, 1977). A good rule of thumb, accordingly, is to treat published campaign contributions (even after the recent changes in the law) as the tip of an iceberg, and be wary of any analysis that relies only on them.

This is less devastating to political analysis than it appears. Sometimes a fuller pattern of corporate contributions can be retrieved by careful archival work. Other cases can sometimes be clarified by thorough analysis of apparent patterns in corporate contributions: looking either at a sample of core actors that one has defined on other grounds as possessing a strong common interest, or checking carefully among the attorneys for major actors.

The beginning of real wisdom in these matters, however, occurs when one reflects that direct cash contributions are probably not the most important way in which truly top business figures ("major investors") act politically. Both during elections and between election campaigns, their more broadly defined "organizational" intervention is probably more critical. As the earlier discussion of free-riders suggested, such elite figures function powerfully as sources of contacts, as fundraisers (rather than mere contributors) and, especially, as sources of legitimation for candidates and positions. In particular, as I have sought to document elsewhere, the interaction of high business figures and the press has frequently been pivotal for American politics (Ferguson, n.d.). Merely for J. P. Morgan or David Rockefeller to make known his choice for president or his policy views to newsmen is to instantly confer substantial newsworthy reality to them—and to contribute an in-kind service whose value dwarfs most cash contributions.

This "organizational" influence is less conveniently available than national campaign committee records, but it is not impossible to obtain, and it has the virtue of being far more reliable than published single-figure dollar totals. While of course anyone can reel off a long list of their potential limitations,[40] private archival sources provide unparalleled access to this sort of evidence. If Thomas Lamont of J. P. Morgan & Co. in 1932 was writing intimate small-circulation letters to other New York bankers in support of incumbent President Herbert Hoover, and one can obtain these letters, that should settle the question of Lamont's choice for president, no matter how often American historians have asserted he was Franklin D. Roosevelt's friend (Ferguson, 1986, n.d.). Similarly, if the chairman of the General Electric Company was actively aiding New York Senator Robert Wagner in preparing the National Labor Relations Act, it is a fair conclusion that he favored it over alternatives (Ferguson, 1984, n.d.).

But published sources contain much more evidence than most scholars realize. Newspapers print ads with endorsements; obituaries often disclose a remarkable political history; and collating newspaper accounts of campaigns and campaign press releases often is enormously illuminating. Even biographies, institutional histories, and magazine profiles of businessmen sometimes contain important facts, while for figures active in the present and recent past, oral interviews can be hazarded.[41] In most cases, if one cannot come up with the full roster of a candidate's supporters, still one can generally identify a "core." When this is examined for internal consistency and structure (perhaps in the light of preexisting theory), very striking patterns often emerge.

Political appointments can also furnish important evidence. As several recent studies have shown, a systematic examination of these can be remarkably revealing.[42]

Complicating questions of evidence are instances in which industries or firms appear to be operating in both parties. These are often cited by analysts who wish to deny that businesses promote definite public policies or that they wield their influence to obtain these policies, so the logic of the situation is important to understand.

The first step in a realistic analysis is to focus sharply on the ways in which issues figure in political campaigns. Party politics in America most commonly displays only loose relations to issues. As a consequence, in practice, issue politics in America at a national level always implies a focus on a particular candidate. Right here, a fair number of cases of business bipartisanship become immediately intelligible.

In the nomination stage of election campaigns it is only common sense for many firms to float a candidate (or more) in each party. The chances of getting a winner are thus much enhanced. Similarly, different levels of government and different regions of the country may make useful mixed strategies of candidate support by one firm. Other forms of bipartisanship are no less intelligible but depend on different reasoning. The guiding principle is that selection of political parties is merely a special case of rational portfolio choice under uncertainty: one holds politicians more or less like stocks.

A firm cannot predict exactly who will win or know for certain exactly what policies will be implemented if a candidate or party is victorious. But, as the Vanderlip-Stillman exchange suggests, it has some useful knowledge of the candidates and parties. So it has to estimate its chances of advancing a particular policy and discount for the possibility it will lose. Some industries or firms find themselves wanting policies that the other party clearly could never accept. Having nothing to gain from bipartisan strategies, these industries (or firms) become the "core" of one party, as, for example, textiles, steel, and shoes were in the Republican Party after the New Deal because of labor policy, and chemicals because of trade (Ferguson, 1984, n.d.). Other industries or firms, differently situated, can try out both parties. But this is the crucial point: rarely equally. For everyone to find it in his or her interest to hold identical portfolios of parties is as outlandish as the case of everyone's attempts to buy and hold one stock, and for exactly the same reasons.

The chance of one candidate's simultaneously satisfying high- and low-tariff advocates, labor-intensive and high technology firms, or exporters and importers is zero. And, especially in large firms which have resources big enough to affect the outcome, some clarity about this can be shown to obtain.[43]

The underlying dependence of business bipartisanship on an incomplete articulation of issues is pointed up by critical elections like the one of 1936. That election had been preceded by several in which issues had not always been clearly defined. It was thus easy, and common, for many (not all) investors with a party identification (especially attorneys, whose position in the party depended on party regularity) to swallow their disappointment at one or another candidate they disapproved of and remain to support him in the general election. But the 1936 election showed that, as policy divergence between parties grew, the bipartisanship of firms disintegrated in a perfectly obvious and—it can be shown—predictable fashion (Ferguson, 1984, n.d.).

Once intensive research has produced data linking as many major investors as possible to particular candidates, issues, and parties, the focus of the inquiry turns naturally from the facts of "support" (or the "support network") to attempts to explain it. Now, the general thrust of the investment theory of parties on this question is straightforward: The political investments *of major investors* are governed by the same criteria that all their other investments are.[44] For this essay, where there is not space to consider the many rather obvious ways one can modify or qualify this postulate, this should be taken to *normally* imply an attempt to maximize wealth (relative, perhaps, to some level of risk) in whatever form existing institutional arrangements permit this to be augmented: revenues in a business, salaries in a bureaucracy, or whatever.[45] Accordingly, the investment theory of political parties predicts that the political investments of major investors can usually be related directly (if commonly more subtly than most "economic" theories of politics suggest) to their particular positions in the political economy.

Now, it should be clear that a general methodological analysis cannot hope to specify precisely how one defines the politically relevant aspects of these "particular positions in the political economy." Such analyses emerge only from a detailed analysis of specific historical periods.

Nevertheless, it is quite possible to identify a general method for handling most of the data that one usually encounters. Essentially a graphical analysis of political coalitions in terms of industrial (and, where necessary, agricultural) structures, this procedure has the happy property of providing a means for displaying the coherence of coalitions during a single election. In addition, a simple extension of the technique to several elections provides the answer to another of the questions raised earlier, viz., how it is possible to demonstrate the coherence and stability of entire party systems (as well as, of course, their eventual breakdown).

An application to industrial structures of spatial analysis techniques used for many years in many parts of the social sciences, this technique is perhaps most conveniently explained by outlining the steps one might take once one had finished acquiring information on the empirical pattern of "support," as discussed previously.

The procedure is straightforward. First one identifies what appears to be the major outcomes or issues involved in an election. As I have elsewhere observed (Ferguson, 1986)—and it should be obvious anyway—the identification of the relevant outcomes requires great care. The judgments involved (which may, and indeed commonly should, be justified as far as possible by reference to quantitative evidence) frequently rely on intelligent aggregation of cases, measures, and other particulars. They are therefore normally complex and sometimes delicate, making it very easy to overlook major policies that the analyst happens not to care about, that involve recondite or obscure facts (such as monetary policy), or which require reference to so-called nondecisions or subtle policy moves disguised as administrative measures.[46]

Once a plausible list of outcomes that brought the coalition together has been identified, the second and most important step becomes obvious. When compared with the objective facts of the actual economic structure, the issues define a multidimensional space. By simply plotting each major investor's position in this space, a "spatial" profile emerges that displays relationships between investors' policy positions and their economic situation. One can then see—sometimes at a glance—whether a logic exists within the business structure to a candidate's support "network" during an election or to a whole party system.

A concrete example (adapted and greatly simplified from an actual model conceptualized in an earlier essay) that illustrates the use of these techniques to analyze a party system as a whole may be helpful.

An inquiry into the sources of the monolithic policy cohesion exhibited by the Republican Party during most of the "System of 1896" suggested that a two-dimensional scattergraph of the contemporaneous American business structure might be quite revealing.[47] For present purposes let us regard the first dimension as referring to the "labor intensity" of an individual firm's production process. The second can then be described as a nationalist-internationalist dimension in which free-trading businesses opposed tariff-seeking protectionists.[48] When the nonfinancial sectors of the business community are scattergraphed along those dimensions and the financial community is then added in,[49] it is impossible to miss seeing the gigantic—indeed hegemonic—antilabor, intensely nationalist bloc of the system of '96 centered in quadrant 1 of figure 1.1

Unfortunately the varying quality and frequent gaps in available data require that an extensive commentary accompany all attempts to present scattergraphs of actual party systems in American history. So

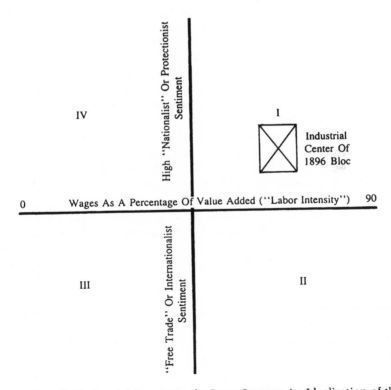

FIGURE 1.1. The Industrial Structure of a Party System: An Idealization of the "1896" Case

neither this nor the next section of the paper can undertake to estimate actual models.[50] These will have to be separately published. But even from the example under discussion, the general procedures for analyzing stability over time should be clear. While short-run issues and emergencies may briefly disrupt long-run politics, as long as the economy remains relatively the same, so will the basic coalitions.

But it should also be clear how the very act of plotting a coherent party system can uncover the model of its decay (a decline, incidentally, in which the generational decline of partisanship among the electorate need play no role whatsoever). Over time, and especially over a series of booms, cumulative changes in industrial structure occur. New fortunes, firms, and industries rise, older ones may decline, and any number of related changes begin to occur. As a consequence the distribution of major investors within the space begins to alter (i.e., the points representing major investors on the graph shift position). Without analysis of actual cases, one can only speak in the most general terms about the changes that ensue. As the sketches in the following sections suggest, what usually occurs first are some reshufflings within existing coalitions. Older alliances begin to break down, and signs of strain emerge. What happens next depends importantly on the overall level of economic activity as well as the specific sectoral, firm, and institutional patterns that real economies display. In theory waves of rapid growth could simply lead to the gradual disintegration of a political coalition. Depending on the facts of the case, a new one might arise (as when some new bloc gradually forms), or, of course, chaos might follow the disintegration of a previously hegemonic bloc. It is also possible that two previously warring blocs might merge and competition cease.

Commonly, however, the transition to a new party system is more complicated. As described in another essay (Ferguson, 1984), the economic growth that comes with long booms often leads to basic changes in an economy's overall pattern of development. Entire new sectors dominated by new elites, for example, may rise up in the course of a boom, or secular change may take place in the financial system. Such cases often force new issues to the fore and complicate the transition to a new party system.

The passage from one party system to another, in addition, is very often catastrophic. As pressures for change build up over a boom, a sharp downturn finally arrives. This can, of course, excite the (at that moment usually miserable) general population. But if, as occurred in every case save that of the New Deal, substantial numbers of people are unable to become significant political investors, then the character of the transition depends almost entirely on the changing alignments of major investors.

Typically major depressions rapidly reshuffle investors in several ways. First, they bring about waves of bankruptcies and (often defensive) mergers. If these are sufficiently extensive—as they were, for example, in the giant merger wave of the 1890s that literally created the System of '96 Republican bloc,[51] then the old party system may cease to exist. Economic downturns also have other effects that may lead to swift reorganization of investor blocs, however. Even if there is no general merger wave, depressions strengthen the position of the strongest investor groups relative to their rivals. As the dominant groups move to capitalize on their advantageous positions, very dramatic clashes often occur that may involve far-reaching changes in public policy—of the order of the New Deal's Glass-Steagall Act (Ferguson, 1984, n.d.).

Rapid changes in the world economy may provide impetus for other rapid reshufflings. Since many major American downturns are merely local manifestations of world economic crises,[52] the situation of American industrialists has sometimes been drastically affected by the strategies foreign competitors adopt to cope with their own problems. Some industries in the United States, for example, may not be able to face heightened international economic competition that accompanies a shrinking volume of world trade, or the export drives foreign manufacturers mount to make up for declining demand in their home markets. So their stances toward tariffs and related issues may change abruptly from what they have been all through the previous party system. And, as I have described in other works (Ferguson, 1980, 1984, n.d.), various pathological (in the sense of abnormal and transitory) phenomena that accompany steep downturns may also reshuffle older coalitions. Industrialists, for example, have on occasion dramatically split with financiers over the question of measures to stimulate the economy or whether to remain on the gold standard.

The transition from the Republican-dominated System of 1896 to the New Deal was of course affected decisively by the dramatic shift in the balance of power between management and labor that occurred during the New Deal. But the very clarity and vividness of this example—which involved the rapid spread of unionization and the mass mobilization of millions of ordinary Americans—draw attention to the close links between the analysis of party system stability over the long run and the final question posed at the opening of this section concerning the significance for an investment theory of parties of situations where millions of ordinary investors have in fact joined to contest control of the polity by major investors.

Now, the fundamental factors militating against control of public policy by ordinary citizens have already been discussed.[53] More light, in addition, will be shed on these issues in the next section, which briefly examines American trends in mass political mobilization. Nevertheless, because the question is so fundamental, and because even analysts who should know better often write as though they believe the only way they can defend the dignity of the victims of American history is to make them responsible for its outcomes,[54] a closer look is warranted at the conditions under which one might decide that ordinary voters are controlling public policy, and at how often they have done so in American history.

Perhaps the most obvious sign that major investor dominance is under challenge is public, visible indications of panic among major investors. Perhaps the best-kept secret of the endless discussions of community power that have marked recent American political science is that it is probably impossible to disguise a condition in which the community actually acquires power. At such times—as in the New Deal, or the (failed) Populist insurrection—the political atmosphere heats up enormously. As whole sections of the population begin investing massively in political action, elites become terrified and counterorganize on a stupendous scale. The volume—and acrimony—of political debate and discussion increase—so much so that the echoes reverberate for years afterward. And, invariably, elites openly begin discussing antidemocratic policy measures and more than usually exalt order and discipline as social goods.[55]

Some indicators that major investors in fact dominate policymaking are fairly obvious. Officially organized or sanctioned violence against large groups of the citizenry probably constitutes one telltale sign. While one can imagine situations in which a government represses a particular strike or protest demonstration to the cheers of the bulk of the electorate, the longer this persists and the broader the attacks, the less plausible this possibility becomes. Similarly, widespread cases of surveillance by police (abetted perhaps by private groups in a patron-client relationship to the gendarmes), the disruption of meetings, and formal and informal harassment of dissenters (such as their inability to find jobs) are scarcely compatible with citizen sovereignty.[56]

A close scrutiny of the substance of public policy, of course, should in principle disclose the interests it serves. In industrial societies, perhaps the single most important and obvious dimension to examine in this respect is state policy toward the "secondary" organization of the citizenry. By far the most important of such organizations, of course, are labor unions. Though most discussions of American "democracy" elide the often ugly facts, the truth is that if employers are allowed untrammelled rights to destroy organizations created by their laborers, then claims about "citizen sovereignty" are merely cynical rationalizations for elite investor dominance, whether in Poland in the 1980s,

Massachusetts in the 1850s, Pennsylvania before the New Deal, or much of the South and West today. Mutatis mutandis, the same is true of agricultural societies in which the state subsidizes organizations designed for large farmers while placing hurdles in the way of organizations (including cooperatives and credit unions) servicing small farmers, sharecroppers, tenants (urban or rural), and the permanently underemployed or poor.

Other dimensions of public policy are also important, of course. Perhaps the most urgently needed piece of research in American history is a set of reliable, quantitative estimates of the tax burdens borne by segments of the population at different points in time. Short of that ideal study, it is vital to attend as best one can to the shifting incidence of taxation, for until social services began to grow it may well have been the most important single issue in assessing the overall balance of power between large and small investors.[57]

Social services themselves are, obviously, another excellent indicator of how much control ordinary investors are able to exercise over public policy. It is, of course, true that demand for these varies over time and especially with the level of urbanization and spread of wage labor through society. Nevertheless, it is highly doubtful that a modest social security program, a minimum wage, savings guarantees, small agricultural credit programs, and well-funded relief programs during depressions would have been any less popular among the citizenry as a whole in 1840 than they were in 1940. (Certainly there was plenty of agitation for them in the 1840s.)

By making rough and, in this paper, necessarily informal estimates of the content of state policy on these and perhaps a few other issues (such as immigration), real empirical content can be infused into the often vacuous debate over who or whose interests historically have governed. It is perfectly easy, for example, to imagine a pattern of policy results, leadership, and mobilization that would support an "electoral sovereignty" model of nineteenth-century American politics. For instance, state policy *could* have promoted organizing and political activity among small farmers and labor, shortened the length of the working day, taxed the wealthy, and generalized social insurance at an early date. Leadership of political parties and voluntary organizations *could* have been virtually monopolized by ordinary citizens; and the most affluent Americans could have been least involved, active, and interested in the party system—but they were not.

Instead, as the following sketches suggest, not until the New Deal did any important segment of the mass population acquire much importance as political investors. Before that date, the major investors who defined the various American party systems consisted almost entirely of businessmen. As a consequence, critical realignments that resulted in hegemonic blocs before the New Deal marked elections in which a powerful new element within the business community ascended to power—in 1860, the railroads; in 1896, manufacturers; while in the New Deal, the biggest winners were not unions but the combination of international oil, investment, and commercial banking firms that I have elsewhere termed the "multinational bloc" (Ferguson, 1984). By contrast, party systems like those of the Federalist era, or the Jacksonian period, during which no clear hegemonic element emerged, marked periods of bitter competition within rival groups in the business community—in the former, between pro-British merchants, planters, and financiers on one hand, and pro-French merchants and planters on the other; in the latter, between regionally dispersed arrays of merchants, (some) planters, and state banks on one side, and most other sectors on the other.

IV. Party Systems in American History 1789–1984

Bearing in mind all these methodological considerations, it is possible to try briefly to summarize the major investment blocs that have constituted successive American party systems. It should of course be obvious that a single paper can at best present nothing more than a series of highly stylized and tentative sketches. As much a report on research in progress as anything else, such sketches necessarily neglect all sorts of significant details, and they cannot afford to do more than glance at alternative interpretations of the same events.[58] They serve mostly to identify problems and to suggest connections between outcomes which initially might appear unrelated. They also provide an indication of what traditional electoral-centered accounts of power in America have missed.

A. The First Party System: Federalists vs. Jeffersonian Republicans

Whether the Federalist-Republican clashes that began shortly after the ratification of the Constitution can be described as constituting a true "party system" in the conventional sense has sometimes been questioned.[59] But since politics in this period looked extensively like a party system—featuring more or less formally organized parties, recognized leaders, and substantial issue differences—and sounded like one, marked as it often was by bitter clashes and, as figure 1.2 shows, a steadily rising level of voter participation which peaked during the crisis of 1812—the first party system might as well be recognized as one.

But affirming reality is only the first step toward explaining it. Once one acknowledges that the first party system was no counterfeit, the successive stages of its often puzzling career still await explanation. Why did a political coalition fresh from its dazzling success in maneuvering the Constitution's acceptance break up so rapidly in the early 1790s? What was the connection between the gradual U.S. slide into war with Britain and the soaring rise in voter turnout? Perhaps most mysteriously of all, how could the intense partisanship of 1812 evaporate within a mere four years? And what miracle of political alchemy transformed the Jeffersonian Republicans from bitter opponents of Alexander Hamilton's schemes in support of the "Money Power" to ardent champions of tariffs and a Bank of the United States after 1816, when the Era of Good Feeling and a period of one-party government can be said to have begun?

The search for a solution to all these puzzles, I think, properly begins with an appreciation of the complex and rapidly changing nature of the American upper class of this period. As figure 1.2 suggests, all

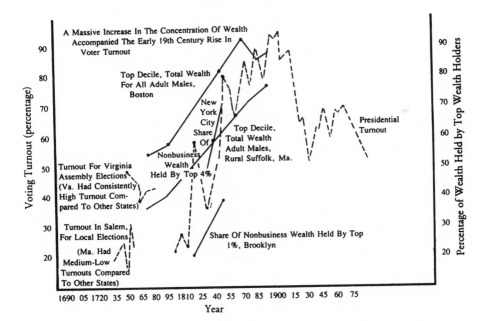

FIGURE 1.2. Voting Turnout and the Concentration of Wealth in the Nineteenth Century

Sources: Presidential turnout (Burnham): colonial turnouts (Dinkin 1977); wealth data (Williamson and Lindert, 1980).

Note: All data are discrete; lines represent conventional interpolations.

through the 1790s wealth in the United States remained far more equally distributed than it was a generation later. But while the social pyramid remained comparatively broad and low all through the first American party system, still its upper levels attained considerable height—and it was primarily this upper 10 percent to 15 percent of the population that first created that system and then, after the War of 1812, abruptly ended it.

The endless wrangling over the details of Charles Beard's famous analysis of the Constitutional Convention, for example, should not be allowed to obscure the critical point: that once the bulk of the upper class decided they wanted the Constitution, effective resistance was literally beyond the means of the mostly, though not entirely,[60] poor and provincial anti-Federalist opposition. Although, as Main and other recent analysts have observed, a majority of the population in many states probably opposed the new regime, the resources available to the affluent, well-educated, and cosmopolitan merchants, planters, large landowners, financiers, and lawyers who led the campaign for ratification dwarfed those of their opponents.[61] Especially after they made concessions on the Bill of Rights (which the reactionaries at Philadelphia had declined to include), their campaign ran roughshod—the words are carefully chosen—over all opposition and secured the adoption of the Constitution (Main, 1961).

But almost immediately this first hegemonic bloc of virtually all the big investors disintegrated. Backed by a huge interlocking and interrelated directorate of merchants, lawyers, financiers, and certain landowners who dominated a handful of key financial institutions (including Robert Morris and Thomas Willing's Philadelphia-based Bank of North America, the Bank of New York, and the Massachusetts Bank), Secretary of the Treasury Alexander Hamilton (co-founder of the Bank of New York, who married into one of the families that controlled it) put forward his famous fiscal program.[62]

Calling for federal government assumption of the foreign debts of the Revolution and Confederation, tariffs, federal assumption of state debts, the issuance of money, public securities, and a Bank of the United States, Hamilton's program struck directly at the vital interests of many planters. Many of the Southern states had already paid their debts; now they would be taxed to pay others. The Bank was not intended to aid agriculture, only commerce.[63] In addition, it soon became apparent that many prominent Federalists had been speculating on a rise in the value of existing securities, betting that Hamilton's program would pass and provide them with massive capital gains that the rest of the population would be taxed to pay for.

Not surprisingly, therefore, Thomas Jefferson, James Madison, and their planter associates almost immediately began mobilizing. Joining them in due course were a variety of business groups that resented Federalist attempts to limit banking competition by restricting the number of bank charters, which at that time had to be individually approved by the legislature (Hammond, 1957, pp. 146–47). Prominent among these were a bloc of businessmen, financiers, and landowners in New York City that included the Clinton family and Aaron Burr (who eventually organized the Bank of Manhattan to rival the Federalist Bank of New York).

Polarization increased as Hamilton expanded the scope of his tax program. His proposals laid only modest duties on goods imported by his merchant constituency. Instead, Hamilton wanted to raise much of the money necessary to pay off the government debt by taxes on slaves (owned by the planters) and whiskey produced by subsistence farmers in the West.

A widespread "tax revolt" began. Jefferson and other members of George Washington's cabinet without strong ties to the "Money Power" (as opponents dubbed the Federalist complex) resigned one by one. Aided by Washington's forcible suppression of the pathetic Whiskey Rebellion and later Federalist attacks on important emigrant leaders of the opposition, Jefferson's Republican Party gathered strength.

Had conflict between the Federalists and Republicans been limited to Hamilton's fiscal program, it is possible that the Federalists might have survived in power. Very shortly, however, the Federalist investors began to divide sharply over foreign policy.

Ever since the Revolution, relations between Britain and the United States had been poor. British regulations restricted U.S. trade with Britain and its dependencies; ships of the British navy frequently seized U.S. vessels, and British forts remained in the American Northwest, where they were frequently accused of stirring up the Indians to attack.[64]

Planter spokesmen such as Edmund Randolph, who succeeded Jefferson as secretary of state, favored harsh measures to deal with the British. Federalist financiers and merchants, dependent on Britain for trade and, more importantly, credit, strongly opposed this. After a series of intrigues involving both Britain and France, New York merchant John Jay negotiated a treaty with the British. Because it sacrificed almost all other American interests, including that of the planters (whose old debts to the British the treaty reconfirmed) to the merchants' desire for good relations with Britain, the treaty became very controversial.

Though the Federalists weathered the storm over the Jay Treaty, pro-French elements in the mercantile community, such as Philadelphia merchant banker Stephen Girard (whose attorney, Alexander J. Dallas, was closely associated with Albert Gallatin, Jefferson's chief financial spokesman),[65] began coming over to the party of "agrarian democracy."

Though this paper cannot afford to trace each quarrel in detail, subsequent battles between the Republicans and the Federalists virtually all reflect disputes along these same two dimensions of financial/fiscal policy and foreign relations.

The difference between earlier and later outcomes, which the Jeffersonians largely controlled, however, reflects the increasing strength of the anti-British party. Since the Revolution, American trade had been shifting away from Britain to other parts of Europe, the West Indies, Russia, and the Orient.[66] Over time, this significantly reduced the number of merchants dependent on the British. Jefferson's election as president in 1800, for example, hinged importantly on prodigious organizing efforts by the Bank of Manhattan (Hammond, 1957, p. 160). During the Napoleonic Wars pro-French merchants such as Robert Smith of Baltimore (Jefferson's secretary of the navy) and the Crowninshield and Story families of Salem, Massachusetts, supported Jefferson (Burch, 1981a, pp. 86, 90, and 110). No less importantly, expansion into the West created a new class of merchants, such as legendary fur trader John Jacob Astor (a close friend and supporter of Gallatin, after Gallatin became Jefferson's secretary of the treasury) with a strong interest in ejecting British rivals from the West. Many planters and large landowners who were openly planning to seize Florida from Spain, and drive the British from both the Midwest and Canada, also supported this goal.[67]

The mushrooming sentiment for war in the West alarmed the still largely proBritish elites of New England. With the pro-war party growing vigorously, increasingly frantic Federalists coalesced behind a peace-oriented ex-Republican from New York City. The vigorous campaign and high stakes brought out the enormous turnout that figure 1.2 shows.[68]

With the end of the war, and the temporary removal of the "British question" from the public agenda, the mounting elite strength within the party of "agrarian equality" made it perfectly natural that the Republicans should adopt "Federalist" policy measures.

Back in his first term, Jefferson had deliberately encouraged pro-French merchants like Salem's Joseph Story (whom Jefferson appointed to the Supreme Court) to found Republican banks.[69] These disproportionately Republican state banks had flourished in the decade before the charter of the First (Federalist) Bank of the United States came up for revision in 1811. Joined by Girard (who wanted to set up his own national bank), Astor, and others, these state banks blocked renewal of the first Bank's charter.[70] But subsequently Astor, Girard, and other businessmen purchased large amounts of government bonds to help finance the War of 1812. (It was, after all, their war.) When the bonds began dropping in value after the war, these major investors moved at once to secure their investments by establishing a bank that would support a market for the bonds.[71]

Having taken over the centerpiece of the old Federalist program, the Republicans also realized another Hamiltonian goal: a protective tariff. As soon as the war ended, British industrialists moved to recapture their former position in the American market. Hoping to destroy the manufacturing capacity that the war and British blockade had stimulated in the United States, the British began dumping goods in American ports. Virtually all sectors of the business community rose in angry protest. Even Southerners, who may have harbored hopes for industrialization themselves (at this moment when cotton's commercial success was still not assured), backed tariffs.[72] With almost no major issues now dividing American elites, party competition (and voting turnout) virtually disappeared. President James Monroe traveled to Boston and made gestures of reconciliation toward Federalist elites, who had only recently discussed secession at the Hartford Convention in 1814. An Era of Good Feeling commenced. Quite like Mexican elites a hundred years later, American investors for a time enjoyed the luxury of ruling an essentially one-party state under the banner of revolutionary democracy.

B. The Jacksonian Party System

As though to underscore the point that elite competition, rather then swelling mass political sentiments, would provide the driving force in nineteenth-century American politics, the Era of Good Feeling had just barely taken hold when the devastating depression of 1819 burst upon the scene. Though reliable statistics are lacking, there is little doubt that what could be identified as America's first modern business depression wreaked widespread havoc. Though the predominantly agricultural character of the economy perhaps mitigated the worst consequences, unemployment soared, perhaps topping 20 percent in some cities. Both business and farm bankruptcies soared, and demand for relief triggered riots and demonstrations all over the country.[73]

All the tumult, however, created barely a ripple in the placid waters of American national politics. While few members of the American upper class probably relished the Era of Good Feeling quite as much as

President Monroe (who, as long as he sat in the White House, enjoyed loans from Astor at concessionary rates),[74] none even bothered to contest the president's reelection in 1820. Instead they organized at the local level to oppose public relief and attempted to hold down private relief disbursements—when they were made at all—to well under 1 percent of the gross national product (GNP).

Cumulative economic changes during the 1820s, however, eventually accomplished what all the human misery of the panic of 1819 could not. The headlong expansion of the American national economy began redividing and reordering the business community. Whole new blocs of investors came into being. In this early stage of industrialization, major infrastructural projects could still be mounted by states and localities. Accordingly many big investors concentrated their efforts there. Turnout in local races often rose, party machinery developed, and any number of campaign techniques entered increasingly into general use.[75]

Over time, however, the process of capitalist development posed issues that could only be settled at the national level. For example, industrialization stimulated tariff agitation all through the 1820s. Organizing nationwide, industrialists perfected the technique (which the parties later took over) of turning out their work force for mass meetings around demands that preeminently benefited someone else.[76] They also subsidized scholars to promote protectionism (including Friedrich List, whose *Nationalökonomie* was perhaps the one foreign import appreciated by the Pennsylvania iron manufacturers who arranged his long visit here).

As revenues from tariffs piled up, what should be done with the money naturally became an issue. Several different proposals found support. Some suggested that all the money be applied to the national debt, others proposed that it be returned to the states, while Henry Clay put forward his famous program of internal improvements. A generally rising level of agricultural prices also stimulated demand for Western lands. Since the federal government controlled these, how they should be developed automatically became a national issue.

Perhaps the most important issues which came inevitably onto the political agenda during this period concerned the Bank of the United States and the question of territorial expansion. Both issues could be resolved only at the national level, and both attracted major blocs of investors. The basic dimensions of the Bank question were brilliantly spelled out a generation ago by Bray Hammond, and there is little to add to his treatment.[77] Throughout the 1820s, the Bank of the United States restrained (rival) state and private banks from circulating un or thinly backed bank notes by its ability to collect and then present large amounts of notes for redemption into hard money. With state banks proliferating at a prodigious rate, a head-on collision between the regulator and the involuntarily regulated became inevitable. Because Philadelphia capitalists dominated the Bank, New York and other city bankers and capitalists took the lead in the campaign to destroy it. Though Hammond did not mention it, it is possible that railroad rivalries between Philadelphia, Baltimore, New York, and other cities also played a role.[78]

Since several well-known Jacksonian scholars have flatly asserted the contrary, it is probably worth observing that the anti-Bank forces went about their business about as straightforwardly as any group ever has in American politics. Andrew Jackson's cabinet and advisers included many state bankers, who did not conceal their desire to smash the Bank (notably Attorney General Roger Taney, who not only served as a director of a state bank whose president hated the Bank, but was also a part-time legal counsel to the Baltimore and Ohio Railroad, which stood to gain from the injury the Bank's destruction would inflict on Philadelphia's capacity to raise railroad finances). The ranks of the Albany Regency, the political machine perfected by Martin Van Buren, a close associate of Jackson, included many important bankers, from both New York City and upstate.[79]

Subsequent battles over banking and finance legislation followed a similar pattern. The Loco Focos, whom two generations of historians have treated as virtual Jacobins because of their agitation against financiers, have recently been demonstrated to have won support from literally hundreds of New York City bankers and merchants, whose plans for "free banking" and other reforms could plausibly be passed off as "antimonopoly" measures.[80] Van Buren's controversial plan for an Independent Treasury arose in response to demands from these quarters. No less than Churchill Cambreleng, a longtime associate of John Jacob Astor, sometime railroad official and founding director of the Farmers Loan and Trust Co. (of New York City), pushed the plan on Van Buren, whose former law partner happened also to be a major (New York City) bank director.[81]

The other outstanding national issue during this period concerned the rate and timing of territorial expansion into what almost everyone referred to as the "inland empire." For decades many important American investors had dreamed of incorporating all or parts of Mexico and the Far West (including Oregon) and Canada into the United States. In the 1820s, Monroe, John Quincy Adams, Clay, and other business leaders encouraged Latin American countries to rebel, believing that this would remove European influence from the hemisphere and open these countries to U.S. trade.

As transportation improved, and profits from Southern cotton production soared, the question of territorial aggrandizement came increasingly to the fore. By 1828 proposals for the annexation of Texas (where many American businessmen from Boston, New York, Philadelphia, and the South were heavily invested, and where Sam Houston migrated after helping to run Jackson's campaign) had triggered a growing national debate. Involved were many issues—the balance between free and slave states within the Union, the risks of war with Mexico and Britain, a preference by some blocs in the United States for Oregon or California or Canada instead, etc.

Space limitations make it impossible to do more than trace the barest outlines of the ensuing controversies. But the broad outlines of the process which revived national party competition are clear enough.

Throughout the 1830s, issues involving the Bank, tariffs, and expansion became increasingly urgent. In rough proportion to the rising stakes followed major investor interest. Copying the political methods for recruiting turnout pioneered by the Albany Regency, more and more blocs of investors joined battle. A process of polarization ensued. With controversy increasing over the tariff and nullifications, Jackson destroyed the Bank. Almost immediately party alignments began to crystallize. Party cohesion in Congress leaped up and rival party identities became increasingly firm.[82]

The continuation of Jackson's bank policies under Van Buren sealed this process. The Democrats tended to oppose a strong federal role on everything except expansion: they opposed the tariff (after Jackson), the Bank, and extensive federal expenditures for anything except harbors. They favored vigorous expansion, especially toward Texas and Mexico (where conflict with Britain was less likely) and, of course, opposed efforts to regulate slavery. This program directly advanced the interests of their core constituencies: port city (especially New York City) bankers who financed trade and depended on British financing; many merchants (who controlled many of the largest fortunes in the country in this period); many railroads (which favored free trade and wished to import iron rails from Britain, and whose most successful units, such as Democrat Erastus Corning's New York Central Railroad, opposed federal aid to other transportation companies); expansion-minded planters (such as Robert Walker, treasury secretary under James Polk, whose heavy investments in Texas land and cotton made him the natural leader of the pro-Mexican War faction in the Democratic Party) [Burch, 1981a, p. 190]; plus farmers who favored trade agreements with European countries to permit their grain to enter those markets.

By contrast the Whigs emerged quickly as the party championing a strong federal role. While the rapid expansion of railroads gradually limited enthusiasm for tariffs even among the Whigs (since in the short run it reduced the capital going into manufacturing and created positive incentives to expand trade), the party did always stand for some protection; it also favored the Bank (until the spread of state banks rendered the issue moot) and more internal improvements and steamship subsidies. Many Whigs also tended to be less liberal in the terms they favored for the sale of public land. Though Whigs also favored expansion, they went about it more cautiously. Unlike the Democrats, they did not vigorously advance the Monroe Doctrine in this period, and when offered the chance most of the party tried to compromise over both Texas and Oregon. Their elite constituencies, of course, differed from the Democrats': the relatively small (except for textiles and iron) manufacturers; a substantial number of merchants and bankers oriented toward the home market or invested in manufacturing; many railroads, including the Pennsylvania Railroad (Sobel, 1977, p. 39) (which often did not support a tariff); many (but far from all) land speculators; some planters whose interests and identities have been extensively debated (Frescia, 1982, pp. 109 ff.), but who certainly included champions of the Bank; and overseas traders and fishermen, whose desire for California harbors led them to downgrade Texas, the top imperial priority of many planters, and who vigorously promoted Whig overtures to Japan and China.

But while merchants, planters, railroad men, and other major investors often found their investments in politics paid off handsomely, mass voters rarely did.

Bankruptcy legislation that reduced the chances that heavily indebted merchants and industrialists would languish in prison for nonpayment of debts undoubtedly aided ordinary Americans. And a more substantial part of the population doubtless derived some profit from all the canals, turnpikes, public schools, and other infrastructures built at least partly at their expense during this period. But the increasingly meaningless ritual "Repulicanism" that marked festivals and public occasions in this period marked the limits of official concern for the vital material interests of the bulk of society.

For example, though precise figures do not exist, the party system that witnessed the sharpest overall increase in both wealth and income inequality in American history (figure 1.2) probably also saw the largest proportion of ordinary people left to starve, beg, or steal during severe economic downturns. Virtually without exception, proposals for laws to shorten the length of the working day (to a mere ten hours) fell on deaf ears. Neither agricultural wage earners nor owner-occupied small farms received any significant assistance from public policy. Disability compensation (which would have benefited farmers no less than workers) or unemployment insurance was always rebuffed. Minimum-wage legislation was debated but never passed. Jackson himself became the first U.S. president to send troops to break a strike, while all levels of government largely declined to interfere with employers' "rights" to dismiss, spy upon, or blacklist any worker they chose. Rights for women (who had been disenfranchised in all states since the turn of the century)[83] were a cause of an unpopular minority, while the fortunes of blacks in this period need no comment.[84]

The rising voter turnout that marked the period is perhaps better analyzed as an effect of the high elite investment in new, cheaper technology of voter mobilization and as a sign of elite confidence that additional unorganized voters were incapable of posing severe threats than in terms of increases in the abilities of ordinary people to control the state. Though the unit costs of the means of popular mobilization were probably lower in this period than in any since, entry barriers remained prohibitively high, especially at the national level. Then, as today, most voters could not afford to take extensive time off from work to campaign and agitate. In addition, most lacked more than a rudimentary education; somewhere between 10 percent and 20 percent were illiterate, while many more were not fluent in English. While formal barriers to suffrage mostly fell away during this period, financial barriers did not—indeed, overall they doubtless increased. In a subtle touch insufficiently appreciated by later analysts, members of Congress received no regular salaries until 1856. While printing costs fell and newspapers were probably easier to start than ever since, the incomes of ordinary people were not sufficient to sustain papers reflecting their interests: out of more than 1,000 papers the Census estimated existed in America in the 1830s, not more than perhaps 50 were prolabor—and most of these folded in the panic of 1837.[85]

Even more important than these "passive" entry barriers were the active ones. While political machines of course had to deliver some benefits to voters, all the relief, Christmas turkeys, citizenship papers, and whatever else later analysts have celebrated them for probably amounted to less than 1 percent of GNP. In addition, the growth of the political machine destroyed all chances ordinary citizens had for exercising power. As social organizations, political machines were critically dependent on money—enormous streams of it. Without the cash, reason, discussion, or persuasion availed one nothing. Machines also made it easy to isolate segments of the electorate and to play endless games to divide and rule.[86]

The wealthy dominated most other voluntary organizations as well. Conspicuous in this regard were the churches. Gramsci once observed that in America there were many sects but only two parties (Gramsci, 1971, pp. 20–21). But, while entry barriers for churches were lower than for the major parties, the major denominations offered little beyond alms to the lower classes—indeed, they became the chief source of movements to remake the American working class from above, in the guise of "benevolence." In a seminal study, Paul Johnson has documented the overwhelming importance of manufacturers in launching the great revivals and temperance crusades of the 1830s— the prototype for the reform movements that convulsed middle-class life in this period (Johnson, 1979). Similarly, other studies have shown the impact of changing social class in nurturing the schisms and breakaway groups that have proliferated ever since (Singleton, 1975).

The only forms of social organization that might have afforded the work force an independent capacity to act in politics were denied them almost completely. While business elites almost always protected (and often encouraged) immigrant churches, they spared no expense to destroy unions—to such an extent that a smaller percentage of workers belonged to unions at the end of the period than at its beginning (Lebergott, 1972, p. 220). Though I have not been able to find any systematic studies of entry barriers within farm organizations in this period, there is little doubt that the network of "scientific" farm groups that sprang up after 1820 was controlled by the larger farmers, whose businesses were the only ones large enough to justify the expense of dues, travel, and meetings, and occasional subsidies for organizational experiments.[87] One might therefore suspect that in the case of single-family farmers, unlike that of labor, the adverse microeconomics of voter control, rather than more overt repression, defeated agrarian democracy.

C. The Civil War Party System

For years the epic highlight of many survey sources in American history and politics has been a detailed analysis of the ever-widening gulf that grew between the North and South in the years before the Civil War. By now the stars of this drama are so well known they scarcely need any introduction: tariff-seeking manufacturers in the North; Northern farmers and laborers who feared competition from slavery and wanted access to free land either for themselves or their children or because they hoped Western settlement would pull up wages in the East; and Southern planters who sharply opposed tariffs and were increasingly convinced that slavery had to expand or die.[88]

In recent years, however, this classic formulation of the Progressive interpretation of history has come under sharp attack. The importance attached to the tariff, for example, has been sharply questioned. In the early 1960s, several New Economic Historians argued that the South could actually have benefited from rises in tariffs. While this result now looks even more flimsy than some of the early quantitative work on railroads and the economics of slavery, the best recent assessments of how much the South lost from tariffs make it difficult to believe that the sums were worth secession in 1861.[89]

In addition, several studies have shown that the cotton textile industry, one of the largest and best-organized manufacturing interest groups, and one which presumably would have benefited from the Civil War tariffs, staunchly opposed Abraham Lincoln in 1860 out of anxiety for its supply of cotton (Foner, 1941; O'Connor, 1968).

Depending on their exact form, parts of the land argument also are shaky. Cotton planters worried about running out of land could always have developed some of the fields they later planted *within* the South after the Civil War—an area twice as great as in 1860. Older arguments that cotton destroyed the soil and thereby forced expansion are simply wrong: planters headed West to take advantage of much higher yields, not because their own lands were wrecked. Nor is it obvious that increasing cotton (or wheat) acreage would have helped farmers as a group in either the North or the South. As Lee and Passell have observed, assuming that demand did not change, prices of crops would drop, lowering an individual farmer's revenues from the same output (Lee and Passell, 1979, pp. 212–13).

Not surprisingly, therefore, recent treatments of the political economy of the Civil War increasingly resemble movies about the Titanic in which the iceberg melts away before it can come on camera. Several highly sophisticated analysts have simply thrown up their hands, while others have resorted to increasingly improbable devices, including suggestions that thousands of Southern planters were literally paranoid.[90]

From the perspective of the investment theory of parties, however, the giant forces that first polarized the nation and then broke it apart are easily identified.

Consider first the situation of major Southern investors. While Lee, Passell, and other New Economic Historians have greatly advanced the argument by bringing out more clearly the main economic issues in the dispute over expansion of slavery into the territories, they slip past the historically decisive point. Within any likely range of price declines, it simply does not matter if opening up new cotton lands might have slightly reduced the world price for cotton, or lowered the productivity of cotton acreage in general. These are *aggregate* effects spread out among all cotton growers. As the investment theory of parties suggests, what usually matters most in historical change is the position of the major investors. And here the situation is clear.

As the earlier planter invasions of Alabama, Louisiana, Texas, and Missouri illustrated, major cotton growers were highly mobile. They (or their agents and sons) moved rapidly to take advantages of any rich growing areas that opened up. Walling off these slaveholders from the territories by prohibiting slavery there would have reduced the rate of return on their investments, almost certainly to a significant degree. That less mobile or smaller groups would benefit if the major investors sacrificed profits and stayed home is irrelevant. One might as well expect major oil companies not to pump oil for the sake of the independents, or affluent farmers not to apply machinery and fertilizer, to increase everyone else's returns.

It could be replied that the territories opening up in the 1850s scarcely compared to Texas and Louisiana, and so could hardly have seemed widely attractive. But many reasons exist for thinking this was not the case. On and off the Senate floor in the period just before the Civil War, planters repeatedly demanded the right normally accorded capital in America to seek the highest possible rate of return by going anywhere it pleased.[91] In addition, both their words and some actions suggest that leading Southerners were making or projecting investments in southern California (then a very shaky free state), New Mexico, and perhaps Nevada—all areas whose status as slave or free remained unsettled in the 1850s.[92]

It is also doubtful if the more recent literature has been sufficiently sensitive to the impact the admission of increasing numbers of free states to the Union was making on the Southern position within the federal government. Many newer accounts pause only to nod at the traditional arguments about Southern fears of permanent minority status, especially in the Senate.

But this skepticism is unwarranted. One of the few real battles in the Era of Good Feeling came over the admission of Missouri into the Union—and the solution to the problem, involving the carefully paired admission of Missouri as a slave state and Maine as a free state, underscored the importance accorded regional balance.

Similarly, the annexation of Texas was delayed for years while debates raged over its impact on sectional power. Considering the heat these early fights generated, it is difficult to see why anyone would now doubt that the new conquests of the 1840s would inevitably raise the issue to a new level of interest, or that as Southerners watched California, Oregon, and other states enter the Union as free states, they would become increasingly fearful. Especially after the Kansas-Nebraska controversy undermined the painfully hammered-out Compromise of 1850, it is easy to see why Southerners believed that the loss of Kansas not only meant abandoning all hope for additional slave states in the Southwest but also threatened the status of vulnerable slave states like Missouri.[93]

A succession of Caribbean adventures in the 1850s showed just how alarmed Southern elites were becoming, as well as how the issue of control of the government was now transforming expansion from a unifying theme in the 1840s to a cause of breakdown in the 1850s. Planters and businessmen from New Orleans, a major center of agitation during the Texas controversy, launched an abortive attack on Cuba in 1851. Several groups of investors, led by one William Walker, organized ventures aimed at other parts of Central America in the mid-1850s.[94]

To dismiss these cases as essentially actions of private businessmen misses all the vital points. Walker's actions were widely hailed in the South. Because they promised control of territory that could later be brought into the United States, these ventures found wide support not only there, but in parts of the Southern-dominated Buchanan administration. Finally, as it became obvious that Northern Whigs and perhaps the Democrats were not about to support an attack on Cuba that the British (major investors in many Northern enterprises and the dominant power in the world economy) opposed, the Southern champions of expansion who had once opposed John C. Calhoun's increasingly strident attacks on the North now had no reason not to join him.[95]

Any remaining doubts about why Southerners became increasingly, and rationally, anxious should be stilled when the situation of major Northern investors in the later stages of the Jacksonian Party System is clarified.

As the New Economic History analysis misspecified the problems affecting the South, so it has failed to focus sharply enough on the critical power blocs in the North. That opening more lands along the Northern frontier (which at that time included parts of Indiana, Ohio, Michigan, and Illinois, as well as Wisconsin, Iowa, and Minnesota)[96] might lead to lower world prices for wheat or, perhaps, corn scarcely mattered to the investors chiefly responsible for promoting growth in these regions. While such considerations might eventually trouble farmers (though not if they believed that demand for their product was elastic or they sought a place for their children), and workers (who probably would still have preferred farms to factories), as well as later historians and social scientists convinced that it was these groups that provided the backbone of the Free Soil parties, major investors were certainly not trying to get rich by buying 160-acre farms.

Their efforts, by contrast, were directed at securing capital gains, for which "development" was essential. Most important, and fatefully, however, they were investing in railroads. Now, had they been differently circumstanced, it is exceedingly doubtful that the Eastern merchants, financiers, industrialists, and lawyers (such as the Forbes family of Boston, or the legendary "Associates" of the same city) who dominated major American railroads would have scrupled at carrying slave-produced cotton any more than their grandfathers had worried as their ships carried slaves between Africa and the United States.

In the world of the 1850s, however, cotton expansion could at best have helped a tiny minority of these major investors. Railroad growth and profits in states like Indiana, Ohio, Illinois, and Wisconsin depended on the expansion of family farms in corn, wheat, and related products (plus, of course, such infant or locally based industries as could survive). Even if the railroads hoped to postpone conflict, there was no chance the settlers they were feverishly recruiting (who certainly feared slave labor) would sit still.

The rapidly developing discussions about a transcontinental railroad lent additional urgency to the debate over national development. A sugarplum that danced in the visions of many major investment groups in both the North and the South in the 1850s, this venture absolutely required government assistance if it were to be feasible. And here was an unpleasant dilemma. Given the enormous expense, it was initially possible to build only one. No one had to be a New Economic Historian to see that the location of that one line would thereby become a major determinant of the whole course of national development, and thereby the balance of power between North and South. Not surprisingly, therefore, investors proposing to begin construction from various cites—Chicago, St. Louis, New Orleans—maneuvered all through the decade, and, no less unsurprisingly, essentially checkmated each other in the 1850s.[97]

The stupendous scale of railroads compared to all other enterprises of the period is difficult to imagine today. America's first true "big business" dwarfed every other institution in society in the 1850s. (One recent analysis has observed, for example, that as late as the early 1880s Carnegie Steel, a leading manufacturing corporation, was still capitalized at only $5 million, while at least 41 railroads had capital values of $15 million or more [Burch, 1981b, p. 16].)

As a consequence, the Western-oriented railroads would by themselves probably have sufficed to force the issue of North against South. Once the issue began to be joined, however, other investor interests could hardly afford to sit back passively.

Even textile manufacturers for example, whose attachment to "cotton" as opposed to "conscience" Whiggery is correctly observed by the studies cited earlier, probably could not afford to let the South ex-

pand at the pace Southerners wanted. If textile magnates like the Law-
rences of Boston tried to prevent war at the last moment by organizing
the Constitutional Union Party in the 1860 election, they still had to
make certain that Southern expansion into Cuba or the West did not
eventually render their tariff-protected manufacturing investments as
worthless as their heavy contributions to William Henry Harrison (who
died in office holding an interest-free loan from Abbot Lawrence before he could act on either the tariff or the Bank) (Burch, 1981a, p.
218, n. 26).

With partial exceptions among textile manufacturers, merchants,
and financiers in New York, Cincinnati, and other commercial centers
who were interested in trade with the South, leading figures in every
sector of the Northern business community played some role in the
abolitionist campaign of the 1850s, and indeed statistical studies have
demonstrated that they were far overrepresented among that campaign's leaders.[98]

Illinois Central Railroad attorney (and U.S. Senator) Stephen
Douglas, for example, destroyed the Compromise of 1850 by advancing a plan for the settlement of Kansas and Nebraska that was a cover
for a transcontinental railroad (Potter, 1976, pp. 145–76). When
"bleeding Kansas" began hemorrhaging, textile king Amos Lawrence
(who clearly tried to restrain the group to nonviolent efforts) joined
many merchants, lawyers, and industrialists to back the network of
Kansas Aid Societies that sprang up to funnel men and supplies to Free
Soilers. Contributing money, time, and his almost mythic name, Lawrence helped hammer out the plans for a land company that offered
shares to literally thousands of clergy in the New England and the mid-
Atlantic states and that eventually had large impact on public opinion
(Harlow, 1935).

Finally, transcontinental railroad promoter Samuel Ruggles (a New
York merchant and leader of the short-lived American Party), William
B. Ogden (a major developer of Chicago and agent for many Eastern
capitalists), and superlawyer William Seward (a leading abolitionist,
and member of a law firm that is today Cravath, Swaine and Moore,
which at that time represented Wells Fargo and many other leading
Western interests) all helped build the demand for a Northern-based
line that eventually achieved expression in the newly formed Republican Party (Russel, 1948, passim; Burch, 1981b, pp. 19–21; Boorstin,
1969).

The Whig Party had largely been built around the twin issues of
the Bank and the tariff. A series of booms in the late 1840s and early
1850s, however, undermined the constituency for both these issues
and led to the disintegration of the party. Headlong internal commer-

cial expansion and the spread of railroads both reduced pressures for tariffs—in part because they created interests oriented toward the moving (rather than the production) of goods, but also because many railroads wanted to import superior British rails for their own tracks. In addition, the rapid expansion of state and private banks further multiplied the natural enemies of a national bank, while privately developed schemes for guaranteeing bank soundness, such as Boston's Suffolk system for state-run bank examinations, partially satisfied backers of a "sound" money (Hammond, 1957, Chap. 17).

As the Whigs fragmented, the pieces of the old party looked around for new coalitions. For a few years in the early 1850s, when very high immigration rates created fertile ground for nationalist themes, various factions experimented with all sorts of appeals.

When the panic of 1857 arrived, bringing with it a wave of religious revivals, smashed unions, and, as always, thousands of starving unemployed left without relief by "their" political parties (Rezeck, 1942), the Jacksonian System was close to collapse. Prompted by Southerners within the party and by some New York businessmen fearful for their city's trade with the South, President James Buchanan vetoed homestead laws and steamship subsidies. He also lowered tariffs and halted all aid to railroads (Polakoff, 1981, pp. 170–90; Yarwood, 1967; Burch, 1981b, p. 23).

Under this dramatic stimulus a new historical bloc now began coming together. While almost none sought war, legions of Northern businessmen grew increasingly impatient with the developing national stalemate. In the early 1850s, railroad titan John Murray Forbes, the leader of the so-called Forbes group of (mostly Western-oriented) railroads, and his lieutenant James Joy, president of the Michigan Central Railroad (in which the Forbes group held a dominant position) had strongly promoted the short-lived Free Soil Party.[99] Subsequently, Joy, while working briefly for the Illinois Central (which was then controlled from New York) engaged Abraham Lincoln as an attorney. Lincoln continued to work intermittently for the Illinois line after Joy departed. He did not, however, become the favorite candidate of the railroad, which backed Stephen Douglas in the famous Senate race of 1858.[100]

What happened thereafter is complex and, despite all the attention the period has received from historians, not entirely clear in all particulars.

Still hoping to avoid war, many Northern businessmen dramatically increased pressure on the South by fanning abolitionist flames. Emulating earlier business support for the Kansas aid movement, Forbes and other top business figures contributed money to John

Brown, the noted abolitionist.[101] The Forbes group, which operated a string of Western railroads that eventually grew into the famous Santa Fe line, seems also to have supported Charles Sumner.[102]

As businessmen all over the country began uncoordinated, decentralized searches for a presidential candidate for the 1860 election, the panic of 1857 hit. Some railroads folded. Others, including several controlled by Forbes, and the Illinois Central itself, were hurt badly and barely escaped bankruptcy.

While many details remain obscure, it is clear that these developments enormously strengthened radical sentiments within the business community. Among the directors of the Illinois Central, for example, anti-Lincoln sentiment seems to have abated,[103] while elsewhere demand for more vigorous action mounted. By the time former Massachusetts Republican Governor Nathaniel Banks had become head of the Illinois Central, Forbes, Joy, and company were all backing Lincoln as the Republican nominee.[104] So were too many other railroad men to mention, including many with ties to the earliest stages of Lincoln's candidacy (Burch, 1981b, pp. 18–19). Joining them were a host of other major business figures, including Ogden, the leader of the Chicago business community (which stood to profit enormously from Northern transcontinental lines and the newly laid railroad connections to the East rather than South) and an associate of many powerful Eastern railroad interests;[105] Ohio Publisher Henry Cooke (who came bearing campaign contributions from his soon-to-become famous brother in the banking business, Jay); Cooke's friend, Cincinnati merchant and abolitionist leader Salmon Chase; and Western Union's Ezra Cornell.[106] Businessmen demanding both banking reform (which was widely blamed for the panic) and tariffs, notably Pennsylvania iron manufacturers led by Simon Cameron, all climbed aboard.[107]

As the Southern states seceded and the Civil War began, the legislative logjam gradually broke up. Tariffs soared, railroad grants proliferated, the Homestead Act sailed through, national banking legislation that chartered a whole new crop of pro-union financiers passed, and Jay Cooke and other financiers did a splendid business in government bonds.[108]

If the investment theory of political parties accounts well for the timing and policies of the hegemonic bloc that dominated the Civil War System, it also makes it very clear why that system's unity could not last and why a return to two-party competition was inevitable. Though space limitations make it impossible to offer more than the briefest outline, this process is so much less well understood than the dramatic events of the late 1850s that it merits brief notice.

A close look at how commerce and finance functioned within the hegemonic bloc of the system provides the key to virtually all later developments. Though the Union League clubs that quickly formed in most major cities in the North certainly enrolled a majority of major investors during the war, a substantial number of bankers and merchants remained opposed to the new Republican bloc. The core of this Democratic opposition consisted mostly of merchants and financiers with strong commercial ties to the South or overriding commitments to free trade (such as New York banker August Belmont). Also in this group were a handful of manufacturers who, because they dominated world markets for their products, favored free trade (such as Cyrus McCormick) and a few railroads (including the New York Central) with obvious interests in the return of Southern commerce.[109]

While Union defeats in the early part of the war created trying times for the Republicans, as long as the war lasted this rival bloc could offer only limited opposition. As soon as hostilities ended, however, it posed a more formidable threat.

For the end of the war immediately posed the question of what policy to pursue toward the South. This automatically raised the possibility of an alliance between the "War Democrats" and the elements of the Republican bloc that had a long-term interest in the revival of the cotton trade and New York City's traditional commercial ties, a lower tariff rate, and a speedy return to the gold standard abandoned at the start of the war.

Though this essay cannot trace the process in detail, precisely this alliance emerged in time to revive the Democratic Party. Backed by a massive coalition of bankers, merchants, and some (not all) important railroad men, President Andrew Johnson treated the South rather like another group of similarly connected business leaders treated Germany 80 years later, and began reinstalling the old leadership of the defeated country into power. He also pursued a highly conservative monetary policy designed to get the United States quickly back on gold, and laid plans to cut tariffs (Nugent, 1967; Coben, 1959).

All of these proposals generated powerful opposition. The Reconstruction, tariff, and monetary policies were sharply opposed by many industrialists, especially those in Pennsylvania and the Midwest, who complained bitterly about tariff cuts and deflation; some railroads, which did not want to have to pay off newly issued bonds in sound money; and many Republicans of all stripes whose overriding priority was the creation of a viable Republican Party in the South to secure the fruits of the Civil War. Johnson had to be rescued by superlawyer William Everts, attorney for the Astors and the New York Central, and barely escaped impeachment (Nugent, 1967; Coben, 1959; Burch, 1981a, pp. 26–32).

Over time the Republican bloc tended to melt away in a complicated and confusing pattern. "Liberal Republicans" pressed demands
for tariff and civil service reform (which almost always began with the
Customs House, the center of both party organizations and tariff
abuses). Led by Samuel Tilden, a New York bank attorney with the
closest possible ties to the big banks and many railroads, the Democrats
reorganized.[110] Though a complex bargain between the Pennsylvania
and several other big railroads, along with the more familiar agreement
to end the occupation of the South, deprived Tilden of the Presidency
in 1876, polarization between industry and finance continued.[111] In
Boston, bankers like Henry Lee Higginson joined John Murray Forbes,
and many merchants and attorneys such as Moorfield Storey, and split
loudly from the GOP. Similar events occurred in New York. Sometimes
referred to as Mugwumps, these groups pushed hard for lower tariffs,
maintenance of the gold standard, civil service reform, and a foreign
policy that limited American aggressiveness in the interest of close relations with Great Britain (the final source of credit for many in these
groups).[112]

A substantial number of railroads fell in line, either because the
financiers were coming to control them or because the program attracted them. Throughout most of this period the New York Central
and the Democratic machine that was closely associated with it continued to pour stupendous resources into efforts to mobilize high
turnouts.[113]

In 1884 the banks and their allies won with their favorite candidate, Grover Cleveland. By then the seesaw pattern of major party
competition that characterized the rest of the system was essentially
set. Industrialists (who often favored soft or "softer" money than financiers, though never free coinage of silver or unlimited issues of
greenbacks); some railroad magnates (who sometimes backed tariffs
for special reasons); many merchants; and (mostly inland and small)
bankers opposed the Democrats on the traditional GOP platform of
high tariffs, although a few major exporters sometimes were willing to
waive (someone else's) specific duties for very carefully circumscribed
"reciprocity" treaties that would get their own goods into another
country. They also expressed a willingness to subsidize the merchant
marine (which the Democrats opposed as contrary to free trade). In a
portent of things to come, the Republicans became increasingly strident in their calls for a naval build-up and foreign expansion in the
Caribbean. They also harshly criticized the Democrats for their friend-
ship with the British (Schirmer, 1972, Chaps. 1–3; Eiteman, 1930).

Neither party made any serious appeal to workers. Both watched
impassively while the panic of 1873 destroyed the unionization drives

of the late 1860s, which had enrolled 2.4 percent of the total work force by 1869 (Lebergott, 1972, p. 220). As related in more detail below, both parties also favored all necessary force to put down the strikes and riots that soared after the onset of early 1870s depression. Both opposed virtually all relief during the Great Depression. They both also exalted the role of the judiciary in checking relief measures passed by occasionally errant legislatures.[114]

The parties also ignored all but affluent farmers. Bankers and railroadmen typically dominated the newly created Department of Agriculture regardless of which party held power. Both parties also greeted farmers, clamoring for regulation of railroads, or much larger increases in the money supply than the industrialists would stand for, with proposals for increasing exports (Crapol and Schonberger, 1972) and, as the ethnocultural analysts remind us, with conservative religious appeals.[115]

D. The System of 1896

From the standpoint of the investment theory of political parties, the System of '96 is perhaps more satisfactorily treated in recent literature than any other U.S. party system. Lawrence Goodwyn and Michael Schwartz, for example, have written excellent studies of the emergence of organized protest among Southern and Western farmers in the 1880s.[116] While some mystery still surrounds the extent and precise nature of farm grievances in this period, these works demolish any lingering impression that farm protest was somehow "irrational." They also vividly convey the agonizing difficulties that confront any mass movement that seeks to transform ordinary voters into major political investors. A number of authors, of whom David Montgomery (1979) and Jeremy Brecher (1972) are perhaps the most notable, have also extensively analyzed the savage repression accorded organized labor after 1877, when the great railway strike and related upheavals heralded the arrival of a new and extraordinarily fierce stage of class conflict in American life. And Walter Dean Burnham's careful analysis of the striking drop in voter turnout that began around 1896 and his discussion of the System of '96 have explored the most important political efforts by industrializing business elites to insulate themselves from popular reaction at this time.[117]

Because this literature states the general problems so well, and because I hope shortly to publish a much longer analysis of the System of '96, this sketch will develop only a few major themes.[118]

It is convenient to begin by taking a closer look at the controversies engendered by Burnham's discussion of turnout decline during this period. At first glance, it is surprising that anyone would doubt that the sharp decline in turnout was related to industrialization. For as Montgomery and others have stressed, throughout the period industrial conflicts rose sharply. They burst forth in peaks of mass violence several times in the 1880s, in the Great Depression of the 1890s, and then again during World War I, when a stratospheric strike rate and widespread union agitation brought on the temporary destruction of most of organized labor through the combined effects of the great Red Scare, the Palmer raids, extensive deployment of federal troops, and something like civil war in parts of Pennsylvania affected by the great steel strike.[119] That these processes, not to mention the spread of Taylorism and "scientific" management in factories or the widespread destruction of craft unions that marked the period, could proceed in anything remotely resembling a democracy strains credulity.

Still, the Burnham-Converse controversy is well known. For more than a decade now, alternative theories that explain the turnout decline as an artifact of rural vote frauds or institutional changes unrelated to industrialism have been discussed and suggestions seriously voiced that Burnham was somehow a "conspiracy theorist" (Burnham, 1974; Converse, 1972 and 1974; Rusk, 1970 and 1974).

Rather than review the debates in detail in this paper, it makes sense to test the global hypotheses. If Burnham rather than Converse or Rusk is correct, turnout decline after 1896 should be proportional to the spread of industrialism within various states (outside the South).[120]

Now, this is a straightforward proposition to test. Measuring turnout decline by the drop in turnout between the 1890s and mid-1920s, and industrializaton by the growth of manufacturing value added per capita between 1880 and 1929, let us test for a relationship between vote loss and industrial growth. Figure 1.3 shows the remarkable result: save for three states with perhaps 3 percent of the population, industrialization and turnout decline stand in an almost linear relationship.[121]

A recent analysis of the spread of the Australian ballot after the late 1880s concluded that the "reform" was deliberately designed to weaken third parties like the Populists (Argersinger, 1980). Further evidence that the turnout decline of this period was no accident is visible in table 1.1, which summarizes the development of restrictive suffrage among the states from 1789 to 1940. It shows several interesting trends. After 1890 the nineteenth-century trend toward the elimination of the poll tax abruptly reversed. There is also a sharp rise in the number of states imposing other taxes on voters. Residence requirements stiffened, especially at the ward level, though at the state level

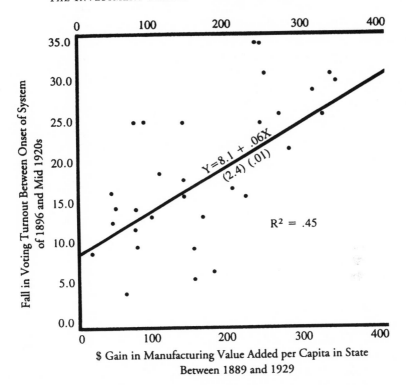

FIGURE 1.3. Outside the Southern States (and the Exceptions Noted in the Text), Voting Turnout Decreased in Proportion to the Growth of Manufacturing Within States

Note: Standard errors in parentheses; for sources and other comments, see text.

these had been tightening since the Jacksonian period. Registration requirements proliferated between 1890 and 1912, while educational requirements, almost unknown before the 1890s, became far more common, even in the North.[122] Most striking of all, however, a complete reversal of attitude took place toward the common mid-nineteenth century practice of allowing aliens who had declared their intent to obtain U.S. citizenship to vote.

Once industrial power is accepted as the final cause of the legal changes, extralegal pressures, party efforts to recruit voters, and the simple removal of many issues from politics that all combined to reduce voter turnout during the System of '96, plenty of other questions remain.[123]

One of the most urgent is very simple, but seldom asked: how

Chapter One

TABLE 1.1 Number of States with Selected Suffrage Limitations

Restriction	Date							
	1789	1800	1830	1860	1890	1912	1928	1940
Specific property	6	7	8	3	2	9[1]		5(+6)[2]
Taxes	6	7	12	8	11	16[3]	14	8
Residence—state								
2 Years	—	4	6	5	3	7	4	5
1 Year	3	2	10	19	28	29	35?	32
6 Months	—	—	1	4	9	11	8	11
4 Months	—	—	—	1	1	—	—	—
3 Months	—	—	1	2	2	1	1	—
Residence—township, city, etc.								
1 Year	5	5	4	2	2	6		3
6 Months	2	6	9	10	11	14		9
5 Months	—	—	—	1	1	1		1
4 Months	—	—	—	2	1	2		2
3 Months	—	—	2	2	6	6		9
2 Months	—	—	—	1	7	5		—
1 Month	—	—	—	2	5	10		6(+1)[4]
10 Days	—	—	—	3	2	1		—
Residence—ward, etc.								
90 Days	—	—	—	—	1	3(+4)[5]		4(+7)[6]
60 Days	—	—	—	1	2	3		4(+1)[7]
30 Days	—	—	—	1?	9	10		14(+2)[8]
10 Days	—	—	—	3	3	5		6
Oath	3	4	5	5	10	6		
Serious crime	—	1	11	24	37	39		41
Alien (allowed)	—	—	1	5	15	8	1	—
Pauper, dependent, etc.	—	1	5	16	33	47		44[9]
Indians	—	1	2	8	9	8		
Education	—	—	—	2	5	16	18	19
Registration	—	—	—	4	21	47	46	47

Sources: This table has been prepared from information supplied by many sources, including various state constitutions and statutes. But most of it comes from four large-scale surveys of state voting provisions: O. H. Fisk's *Stimmrecht und Einzelstaat in den Vereinigten Staaten von Nordamerika* (Leipzig: Verlag von Duncker & Humbolt, 1896); The Legislative Reference Bureau of the Rhode Island State Library's *General Constitutional and Statutory Provisions Relative to Suffrage* (Providence: Freemen, 1912); Richard Boeckel, *Voting and Non-Voting in Elections* (Editorial Research Reports, 1928); Council of State Governments, *Voting in the United States* (Chicago: Council of State Governments, 1940).

All summary efforts like these have problems stemming from minor variants among similar state laws and the occasional loopholes or special qualifications created by states. For example, in 1830 New York had a three-year residence requirement for the "man of color." Should New York figure in the table as a state with a residence requirement or not? My answer was no, on the grounds that this would be too specific a usage for a category that usually represents a far more universal disability. Similar problems attend some of the other categories, especially "serious crime" and "paupers." "Serious crime" is a catchall category that varies from state to state. Much state legislation barring the lowest classes from voting ("paupers") lumps them together with maniacs, alcoholics, or other types of "dependents."

TABLE 1.1 Number of States with Selected Suffrage Limitations (*continued*)

I have attempted to standardize among the sources by checking likely exceptions and cases that stand out as anomalous between them, so the figures here sometimes differ from any particular sources. Where exact details about individual states became important, however, recourse should be had to each source's notes and the state's consitution and statutes, for more exceptions exist than are noted here.

It should also be noted that several states' literacy requirements were waived for the occasional affluent illiterate: i.e., one could buy into the franchise if one could not pass the literacy test.

Note: Blank space = no information; — = zero as far as ascertainable.

1. Includes two states in which property owners alone could vote on special tax and debt issues and one state in which they alone could vote on expenditures.

2. The second figure (6) applies only to elections for bond issues.

3. Includes one state in which tax requirement applies for votes on taxation and one in which it is required at state and county levels for votes on council and expenditures.

4. One state required 40 days.

5. Three states required 90 days: two required 6 months; and two required 4 months.

6. Four states required 90 days; six required 6 months; one required a full year.

7. One state required 40 days.

8. Two states required 20 days.

9. Includes 12 states which specifically exclude paupers and 18 which declare their desire to exclude illiterates (not all these had literacy tests).

could the rise of manufacturing, a long-term process, possibly account for the sudden emergence of the System of '96, which required at most a few years?

To contemporaries the decisive factor in the alteration of the party system was obvious. It was the defeat of the Gold Democrats by the Free Silver and Populist forces and the subsequent move by most of the former into the Republican Party.

But while this accounts superbly for the timing of the realignment and certainly explains the intense unity the Republicans displayed in the 1896 campaign, it fails to provide any clues why many of the Gold Democrats became Republicans. We have no hints why some, but not all, of the Gold Democrats returned to the Democratic Party or why financiers who had regularly crossed party lines earlier became permanently enamored of the GOP.

The answer to this question comes only from a close scrutiny of the major investors in both parties. As previously suggested, after the 1870s, controversies over the tariff, gold, and foreign policy found many, almost certainly most, major bankers in the Democratic Party.

Grover Cleveland's efforts in his first term to lower tariffs, reform the Customs Service, extend civil service, and defuse tensions with Great Britain during the 1888 Venezuelan crisis provided the Gold Democrats' finest moments. In the 1890s, however, this internationalist drive began to slow down. Cleveland in his second term was only slightly less bellicose toward the British than the Republicans. William C. Whitney and other New York Democrats temporized on the tariff, and industrially oriented figures like Attorney General Richard Olney (a Pullman Co. stockholder who was responsible for Cleveland's dispatch of troops to break the strike at Pullman) received major appointments (Schirmer, 1972, Chap. 3; Burch, 1981b, pp. 96–103).

What was happening is perfectly obvious but rarely noted. The financiers were investing more and more in American industry. They were beginning to acquire some of the same interests in tariffs, aggressive foreign policies, and export drives against British competitors that the industrialists shared. In addition, their own rising sense of importance tempted them to claim a bigger role in world finance.

The climax of this process was the breathtaking merger movement of 1897–1901. Led by a handful of investment bankers, notably J. P. Morgan (whose law firm retained Cleveland between terms), this wave of mergers placed bankers on the boards of hundreds of corporations. Centralizing the economy as never before, the great merger wave created a series of gigantic new corporations in which the bankers had major influence. The perfect symbol of the new unity between banking and industry that the movement created was the biggest merger of all, United States Steel: Andrew Carnegie, the industrialist, sold out to Morgan, the investment banker.[124]

Parallel to the industrial merger movement was a massive consolidation of many increasingly shaky (often actually bankrupt) railroads (Kolko, 1965, Chap. 4). Superintended by Morgan and a handful of other bankers, this step essentially ratified the disintegration of the Civil War System's hegemonic bloc and further consolidated the new unity within the business community.

With manufacturing now playing a new pivotal role in the plans of the major investors in both banks and railroads, a switch of sentiment on the tariff was inevitable.

Though most leaders of these consolidations (like many big manufacturers) continued to press for highly selective "reciprocity" agreements with a few countries that would open particular export markets to goods their more successful corporations produced, their interest in "free trade" abruptly disappeared. They accepted protection in principle, and helped build the GOP around it. The ne plus ultra of this accommodation was probably reached in 1909, when Morgan fine-tuned a tariff bill by telegraph from his yacht (Wiebe, 1962, p. 107).

Other issues of foreign economic policy helped cement the developing unity between industry and finance. The gold standard, formally adopted in 1900 after discussions too complex to trace here, was obviously a foreign economic theme that united this Republican "national capitalist" bloc. So, too, was imperialism, though aggressive imperialists were concentrated in a few sectors: steel and munitions, obviously, some foodstuffs, and textiles, which collided head on with British and German competition in Latin America, the Far East, and elsewhere.[125]

But while an analysis of the GOP elites accounts perfectly for their behavior during the System of 1896, what explains their ability to carry if off so well, so long? For, after all, a substantial if only occasionally successful second party existed throughout the period. An explanation is required of why this party only rarely challenged the repressive character of the party system that is also consistent with the obvious fact that it remained another party.

The beginning of the answer has already been supplied in the earlier discussion of labor policy and class conflict. Outside of a few crafts, labor unions, socialist or nonsocialist, were victims of unremitting attack all during that period. In most industries they could not even get a toehold. The notion that workers who could not even organize their own industry could control a party structure that was now extended over the entire United States is utterly fantastic. It could be seriously entertained only by analysts who have not systematically examined differences in public policy between government structures with and without labor union participation.

The point can be reinforced by a glance at the state of mass politics in the Democratic Party. Lawrence Goodwyn has brilliantly depicted the organizing efforts of the People's Party which led up to the 1896 debacle. By comparison with any mass movement before or since, the Populists were incomparably better prepared to contest control of the state apparatus. They were solidly rooted in local organizations. They had their own press, speakers' bureaus, and festivals. That most of their forces were concentrated in one party provided them with yet another advantage over most groups seeking to influence the government (Goodwyn, 1976, Chap. 12).

But they were easily knocked over in the Democratic Party, not by the business community as a whole but by a single sector. In the mid-1890s silver companies poured resources into the party, hoping to secure government aid. As Goodwyn's work shows in detail, the farmers and their allies were no match for Anaconda, the Hearst interests (which owned not only newspapers but silver mines), and their allies.[126] In state after state, the silver companies picked off the Populist Party leaders one by one. The mining companies sealed their triumph by installing an editor of one of their newspapers, William Jennings

Bryan, as the party's nominee (Goodwyn, 1976, Chap. 13). *The largest, best-organized, and most cohesive mass political movement in American history could not compete with even a part of the business community.*

Since control of the national party was literally beyond the means of the Populists, and labor unions remained weak throughout the period, power within the Democratic Party passed virtually automatically to the only groups that could afford to exercise it: businessmen and affluent farmers.

These were rather more numerous than most references to "Republican business dominance" within the System of 1896 suggest. For most of the party system, they included a still-substantial bloc of investors who remained committed to free trade: Southern planters, of course, but also importers (who were concentrated in port cities); a handful of multinationals without major overseas competitors who wanted lower tariffs, like International Harvester; copper companies, whose American refineries could process foreign ores only if tariff rates were secure; many, though far from all, retailers; mercantile and financial elites who missed the 1890s' move into industry; some railroads (including the head of the Pennsylvania) and utilities (including the head of New York's Consolidated Edison); and last, if scarcely least, foreign multinationals, who promoted the party to get their wares through Republican tariff walls.[127]

Virtually all of these interests shared Republican views on the desirability of bureaucratic reform—reform of civil service, reform of the diplomatic service, reform of municipal government.[128] They were also as frightened of the mass populace as any Republican. Grasping intuitively the investment theory of political parties' principle of noncompetition across basic investor interests, they accordingly made few moves to stir the "Great Beast" (as Plato sometimes referred to the citizens of another democracy). Instead, they promoted their own version of Democratic Progressivism, which (along with many Republicans) gradually accepted women's suffrage and on occasion made a few gestures toward labor (chiefly in regard to disability compensation). When the Republicans split, or when crosscutting issues like the Federal Reserve temporarily disrupted normal politics, this was sometimes enough to win—in an electorate that grew smaller and smaller as a percentage of the potential electorate.

For about a decade after the turn of the century the issue of antitrust did create turbulence in both parties, and especially within the Democratic Party. Here again, however, the main forces at work exhibited only an indirect relationship to mass electoral pressures. As Alfred Chandler has observed, among the most powerful forces operating in favor of antitrust were the thousands of small-town wholesalers and distributors threatened by the growth of forward integration among manufacturers and the spread of major retailing concerns (Chandler, 1980). Other important support for antitrust measures came from the shoe industry, whose numerous firms directly confronted a giant trust, United Shoe Machinery, and from some importing merchants who feared the power of concentrated buyers. Independent oilmen, who proliferated after the new oil discoveries in Texas and elsewhere, also strongly favored vigorous antitrust enforcement.[129]

While partisan differences were slight, the Democrats tended to come down somewhat more strongly on this issue. Not only were the trusts to be busted headed by predominantly Republican businessmen, but several peculiar features of geography strengthened the party's commitment as well. In Boston the dense concentration of shoe companies, small savings banks, and merchants created a real basis for a thin "reform" stratum within the business community that helped sustain the heterodox opinions of Oliver Wendell Holmes, Jr. and Louis Brandeis. In the largely Democratic South and West, independent oilmen often constituted the wealthiest segments of the local business community. There the antitrust sentiment merged easily with sentiment for free trade and an income tax (paid largely by the affluent East) to form an aggressive small-scale capitalist ideology that has often been confused with mass-based populism.[130]

E. The New Deal System

Because I have recently published a formal analysis of the growth of the New Deal coalition out of the slowly disintegrating System of '96, and coauthored a lengthy analysis of the gradual dealignment of the New Deal System,[131] this paper's analysis of what might be termed the System of '36 will be even more summary than the preceding sketch of the System of '96.

Perhaps the most important point to stress concerns the precise nature of the New Deal coalition. To attain a clear view of the New Deal's uniqueness and significance it is necessary to break with most of the commentaries of the past 30 years, go back to primary sources, and attempt to analyze the New Deal as a whole.

As outlined in detail in the next essay, what stands out is the novel type of *political coalition* that Franklin D. Roosevelt built. At the center of this coalition, however, are not the workers, blacks, and poor that have preoccupied liberal commentators, but something else: a new "historical bloc" (in Gramsci's phrase) of high-technology industries, investment banks, and internationally oriented commercial banks.[132]

The origins of this bloc are most conveniently traced by beginning with World War I, which abruptly disrupted the tight relationship between industry and finance that defined the System of '96.

Overnight the United States went from being a net debtor to being a net creditor in the world economy, while the tremendous economic expansion the war induced destabilized both the United States and the world economy. Briefly advantaged by the burgeoning demand for labor, American workers also struck in record numbers and for a short interval appeared likely to unionize extensively.

Not surprisingly, as soon as the war ended, a deep crisis gripped American society. In the face of mounting strikes, the question of U.S. adherence to the League of Nations, and a wave of racial, religious, and ethnic conflicts, the American business community sharply divided.

On the central questions of labor and foreign economic policy, most firms in the Republican bloc were drawn by the logic of the postwar economy to intensify their commitment to the formula of 1896. The worldwide expansion of industrial capacity the war had induced left them face to face with vigorous foreign competition. Consequently they became even more ardent economic nationalists. Meeting British, French, and later German and other foreign competitors everywhere, even in the United States home market, they wanted even higher tariffs and further indirect government assistance for their export drives. Their relatively labor-intensive production processes also required the violent suppression of the great strike wave that capped the boom of 1919–1920, and encouraged them to press the notorious "open shop" drive that left organized labor reeling for more than a decade.

By contrast, the new political economy of the postwar world pressured a relative handful of the largest and most powerful firms in the System of '96's hegemonic bloc in the opposite direction. The capital-intensive firms that had attracted increasing attention since the beginning of the System of '96 and which had grown disproportionately during the war were under far less pressure from their labor force. The biggest of them also had developed by the end of the war into not only American but world leaders in their product lines. Accordingly, while none of them were pro-union (legislation along the lines of the Wagner Act would have struck them as incredible), they preferred to conciliate rather than to repress the work force. Those that were world leaders also favored lower tariffs, both to stimulate world commerce and to open up other countries to them. They also supported American assistance to rebuild Europe, which for many of them, such as Standard Oil of New Jersey and General Electric, represented an important market.

Joining the industrial interests of this second bloc were the international banks. Probably nothing that occurred in the United States between 1896 and the Depression was so fundamentally destructive to the System of '96 as the World War I–induced transformation of the United States from a net debtor to a net creditor in the world economy (Kindleberger, 1977; Ferguson, 1984, n.d.).

The overhang of both public and private debts that the war left in its wake struck directly at the accommodation of industry and finance that defined the Republican Party. To revive economically, and to pay off the debts, European countries had to run export surpluses. They needed to sell around the world, and they, or at least someone they traded with in a multilateral trading system, urgently needed to earn dollars by selling into the United States. Along with private or governmental assistance from the United States to start up when the war ended, accordingly, the Europeans required a portal through the Republican tariff walls that shielded U.S. manufacturers from the outside world.

For reasons of space this paper cannot trace in any detail how spiraling conflicts over labor and foreign policy between the older System of '96 group and the newer multinational bloc led increasingly to the disintegration of the Republican Party, so that by 1928 the partisan alignments of 1896 had disappeared altogether.

All that can be observed here is that the long-run trends in the world economy greatly favored the multinational bloc. With the notable exceptions of the big chemical and national oil companies, this bloc included the largest, most rapidly growing corporations in the economy. They were the recognized industry leaders with the best and most sophisticated managements. Perhaps even more importantly, they embodied the norms of professionalism and scientific advance which fired the imagination of large parts of American society in this period. The largest of them also completely dominated all major American foundations, which, during the System of '96, had come to exercise major influence on not only the climate of opinion but also the specific content of American public policy. And, while I cannot stop in this chapter to justify the claims, what might be termed the "multinational liberalism" of the internationalists was also aided importantly by the spread of liberal Protestantism; by a newspaper stratification process which brought *the* free trade organ of international finance, the *New York Times*, to the top; by the growth of capital-intensive network radio in the dominant Eastern, internationally oriented environment; and by the rise of major newsmagazines, which, as Raymond Moley himself observed while taking over at what became *Newsweek*, provided "Averell" [Harriman] and "Vincent" [Astor] "with a means for influencing public opinion generally outside of both parties."[133]

Not surprisingly, it was during the great boom of the 1920s that the representative capital-intensive, multinationally oriented American business firm ascended to the pinnacle of the economy: the giant integrated oil company (see table 1.2, which gives rankings of the thirty largest industrials from 1909 to 1948).

Space limitations also preclude this paper from doing more than asserting what I have sought to document in detail elsewhere: that between 1935 and 1938 this emergent bloc came together around Roosevelt's Second New Deal (Ferguson, 1984, n.d.).

Because these firms were mostly capital-intensive, the rise in the power of organized labor that the Wagner Act permitted and the very limited intervention in market-determined patterns of (lifetime) wage setting that Social Security represented posed less of a threat to them. And their dominant position in the world economy made them the leading beneficiaries and most ardent champions of the other part of the New Deal's reform package—Secretary of State Cordell Hull's famous reciprocal trade program, which broke decisively with the System of '96's protectionism. (Oil companies, in addition, profited handsomely from the Interstate Oil and Gas Compact legislation which established the framework that fixed the price of oil for a generation.)

But while the biggest investors in the New Deal—including the dramatic election of 1936—were the multinationals and their internationalist allies among domestic exporters, there is no point in denying the obvious. To many within this group, even the almost dormant American Federation of Labor (several of whose top officials had become enmeshed in a close patron/client relationship with the larger firms within this bloc)[134] represented a graver threat than they felt comfortable with. While, left to themselves, the firms in the multinational bloc might have sponsored company unionism and made less extensive use of the private armies and detective agencies than more labor-intensive firms, they surely would not have created the Congress of Industrial Organizations (CIO).

That independent industrial unionism emerged during the New Deal is primarily a result of one factor: that, for the first time in American history, masses of ordinary voters organized themselves and succeeded in pooling resources to become major independent investors in a party system. Their success in this decade contrasts vividly with their failures during previous party systems, and vividly underscores the investment theory of political parties' strictures on the importance of distinguishing between simple rises in voter turnout, such as characterized the Jacksonian Party System, and the real growth in the political power of mass voters that came with their effective organization.

In a longer analysis of the New Deal System, several stages could helpfully be distinguished within it. The rise in the power of labor, for

TABLE 1.2 Largest American Industrials at Various Points in Time (Ranked According to Assets)

1909

1. U.S. Steel
2. Standard Oil of New Jersey
3. American Tobacco
4. International Mercantile Marine
5. Anaconda
6. International Harvester
7. Central Leather
8. Pullman
9. Armour
10. American Sugar
11. U.S. Rubber
12. American Smelting & Refining
13. Singer
14. Swift
15. Consolidation Coal
16. General Electric
17. ACF Industries
18. Colorado Fuel and Iron
19. Corn Products Refining
20. New England Navigation

1919

1. U.S. Steel
2. Standard Oil of New Jersey
3. Armour
4. Swift
5. General Motors
6. Bethlehem Steel
7. Ford
8. U.S. Rubber
9. Socony Mobil
10. Midvale Steel and Ordnance
11. General Electric
12. International Mercantile Marine
13. International Harvester
14. Anaconda
15. Sinclair
16. Texaco
17. American Smelting and Refining
18. DuPont
19. American Tobacco
20. Union Carbide

1929

1. U.S. Steel
2. Standard Oil of New Jersey
3. General Motors
4. Standard Oil of Indiana
5. Bethlehem Steel
6. Ford
7. Socony Mobil
8. Anaconda
9. Texaco
10. Standard Oil of California
11. General Electric
12. DuPont
13. Shell
14. Armour
15. Gulf
16. Sinclair Oil
17. International Harvester
18. General Theater Equipment
19. Swift
20. Kennecott

1935

1. Standard Oil of New Jersey
2. U.S. Steel
3. General Motors
4. Socony Mobil
5. Standard Oil of Indiana
6. Ford
7. Bethlehem Steel
8. Anaconda
9. DuPont
10. Standard Oil of California
11. Texaco
12. Gulf Oil
13. General Electric
14. International Harvester
15. Shell
16. Sinclair
17. Koppers
18. Kennecott Copper
19. Swift
20. Armour and Co.

TABLE 1.2 Largest American Industrials at Various Points in Time (Ranked According to Assets) (*continued*)

1948

1. Standard Oil of New Jersey	11. Standard Oil of California
2. General Motors	12. Bethlehem Steel
3. U.S. Steel	13. Sears, Roebuck and Co.
4. Standard Oil of Indiana	14. Union Carbide
5. Socony Mobil	15. Sinclair Oil
6. Texaco	16. Westinghouse
7. DuPont	17. American Tobacco
8. Gulf Oil	18. International Harvester
9. General Electric	19. Anaconda
10. Ford	20. Western Electric

Source: A.D.H. Kaplan, *Big Enterprise in a Competitive Setting* (Washington, D.C.; Brookings, 1962), pp. 140 ff.

example, came to an abrupt halt during or soon after World War II. A massive campaign led by the National Association of Manufacturers pushed through the Taft-Hartley Act, and the Truman administration initiated the first of several security investigations of the left wing of the Democratic Party.

But while these and related measures halted labor's advance, they did not turn the clock back to the early 1920s. The rise in unionism merely halted and began a slow decline that has now lasted for almost a generation. Other legislative enactments, such as the 1959 Landum-Griffith Act, also incrementally trimmed labor's power, but did not fundamentally alter the status quo.[135]

More recently the flight of business to the Sunbelt, where labor is weak, and abroad, where it cannot go, and the failure of President Jimmy Carter's labor law reform initiative in the late 1970s have in combination with new organizing initiatives by the business community, such as the creation of the Business Roundtable, eroded organized labor's position.[136]

Rather more serious has been the deterioration of the network of community groups generated in the course of struggles over the rights of blacks, women, and the poor. Such groups flourished in the turbulent 1960s, when the economy was expanding and substantial financial assistance was available from the government and large foundations.[137] Since the recession of 1973–1974, however, their position has become increasingly precarious. Only the more conservative parts of the feminist and black movements continue to attract substantial funds from more liberal investors.

By contrast with the almost glacial pace of change with regard to labor policy, the other crucial policy outcome involved in the New Deal

alignment—its commitment to internationalism—has come under increasingly severe challenge.

Though this essay cannot elaborate on the point here, the shape
of things to come on this issue was clearly visible as far back as the
1936 election. After a bitter internal struggle, Republican nominee Alf
Landon repudiated Hull's reciprocal trade policies. Enraged, many
high-level businessmen in the party abandoned Landon's campaign
and endorsed Roosevelt (Ferguson, 1984). All through the 1940s similar controversies flared; they were especially bitter when issues like
the ratification of the International Trade Organization Treaty were
pending.

While proliferating opportunities for investment abroad strengthened many large firms' commitment to internationalism after World
War II, the revival of world economic competition in the 1950s sharpened protectionist tendencies in industries like steel, textiles, and
shoes. The predictable result was a growth of right-wing nationalist
sentiment within the Republican Party. Often strongly critical of the
United Nations, foreign aid, and the Rockefeller family, such groups
joined with many independent oilmen to provide most of the force
behind the Barry Goldwater candidacy in 1964. (Ferguson and Rogers,
1981, p. 12; Burch, 1973, pp. 120–21, n. 51). They have also weighed
heavily in Republican primaries ever since (Ferguson and Rogers,
1981, pp. 12 ff.).

By 1971, as imports from Japan surged into the United States and
the first absolute trade deficit in modern U.S. history appeared, nationalist sentiment within the business community was mushrooming. The
Nixon administration responded with its famous New Economic Policy,
with consequences too vast to be considered here.[138]

Thereafter, the international economic system, and thus American
party politics, lurched from one crisis to another. The Organization of
Petroleum Exporting Countries (OPEC) raised prices, raw-material
prices briefly surged, food prices soared, and bank loans to Third World
countries expanded immensely. By the mid-1970s it was clear that economic growth in the advanced countries was slowing down while in
parts of the Third World it was booming.

In time it is possible that these and other forces too complex to
consider here might produce a realignment in American politics. By
itself slow growth is likely to generate rising dissatisfaction among an
increasingly squeezed population. In addition a major crisis is brewing
inside the Democratic Party. While the New Deal transformed the party
into a historically unique coalition of capital-intensive, multinationally
oriented businesses and organized labor, almost every major trend in
the world economy now militates against that order. In the wake of

OPEC's price increases, the United States held down the domestic price of oil through a complex system of special price controls. The price of natural gas was also strictly regulated. The astronomical sums involved made these programs some of the largest income transfer programs in world history.[139] Not surprisingly, most oil and gas companies ardently supported lifting the controls. Because it struck so massively at labor, blacks, and the poor, however, such a move was almost impossible for most Democrats to sponsor. As a consequence, the oil industry, which had played a pivotal role in the emergence of the Roosevelt coalition and had longstanding ties to high levels of the Democratic Party, became almost monolithically Republican in the mid-1970s.[140]

Rising business interest in an increasingly unstable Third World has also operated to weaken the Democratic Party. While serious differences over the size of the total defense budget and specific weapons programs persist within the business community, interest in higher military spending still has tended to unite both nationalists and internationalists (Ferguson and Rogers, 1981, pp. 18–19). But economic stagnation now makes it impossible to fund both social welfare and higher defense budgets without higher taxes. Accordingly, the Democratic Party is coming apart, riven by struggles between the party's mass base, which needs more, not less, social welfare spending, and its elite constituency, which would prefer to reform the budget process, cut social spending, and raise defense expenditures. In addition, Japanese imports are surging, raising demands from labor for protection that collide head on with the internationalists' desire for an open world economy. How this struggle will be resolved is anyone's guess, but it is instructive to see what an investment theory of parties predicts. It will be recalled that turnover among the top thirty firms during World War I and the boom of the 1920s heralded the ascent of the multinational bloc within a new party system. Until recently, a list of these major investors would have reflected little change since the New Deal—the rise, mainly, of electronics firms, and a further decline of steel. The last few years, however, suggest that major turnover within these ranks may be imminent. A new merger movement among the giants, spectacular failures of once multinationally oriented firms like Chrysler, the wreck of the auto industry, and, most recently, a major decline in oil prices suggest that new realignments with new blocs of investors could be in the offing.

V. CONCLUSION

The early sections of this paper raised fundamental questions about conventional electoral theories of American politics. Virtually all subsequent discussion has concentrated on elaborating and testing alternative accounts of party systems and electoral competition. While all results remain preliminary and tentative, it is now appropriate to look briefly at what this effort to interpret American political history in industrial terms says that is new or, at least, distinctive.

Here, it seems to me, one conclusion stands out ahead of all others: that the "welfare effects"—the tendency to satisfy popular demands— that most liberal political analysis attributes to two-party competition have been greatly overstated. This does not mean that voters never influence public policy or even that they do not constantly do so. It does imply, however, that their influence on state policy is highly variable and uncertain. In a political system like that of the United States, the costs associated with control of the state effectively screen out the bulk of the electorate from sustained political intervention. Accordingly, as the last section's review of American party systems suggested, power passes ineluctably to relatively small groups of major investors. And political changes are usually—but not always—intimately involved with shifts in the balance of power among these large investors.

These fundamental points have vast implications. The potential significance of voter turnout, for example, changes abruptly. Many discussions of declining voter turnout implicitly link high voter turnout with effective democratic control of the polity. Now it is easy to understand why, for whatever can be imagined as a logically possible outcome, in the real world a political system that consistently serves the interests of a mass of nonvoting citizens is most improbable. But as the discussion of the Jacksonian period suggested, high voter turnout may indicate strong popular demands on the political system—or it may simply indicate that elites are willing to subsidize the cost of participation. To assess the meaning of voting in such situations, a hard look is vital at the resources available to individual voters to form and express an opinion—and above all to participate in secondary organizations. In this respect, I think, the American experience has been less than edifying.

Another common practice in American political science that this inquiry raises questions about concerns the conventional distinction between "foreign" and "public" policy. Few contemporary studies of American politics afford foreign policy questions the weight they deserve as factors in domestic party politics. From the Federalist acts of binary fission to the New Deal's controversial free trade policy, however, American parties have fought bitterly over foreign policy issues. Considering the peculiar monopoly that the national state enjoys in foreign policy, it is time to abandon the notion that "politics stops at the water's edge." Analysts of public policy should normally expect to find questions of the world economy, foreign policy, and transnational relations acting to divide political investors. And election analyses, if they purport to deal with reality, should normally explain how industrial blocs, campaign issues, and international relations affect electoral outcomes.

Finally, if one considers the basic meaning of what might be termed the "microeconomics of voter control" implied by the investment theory of parties, then certain forms of interventions to create really effective democratic structures can readily be envisaged. Once it is clear that most ordinary people cannot afford to control the governments that rule in their name, then the normative remedy is obvious: public participation must be subsidized[141] and the costs of its major forms made as low as possible.

This recommendation, however, must be understood in the context of this essay's earlier discussion of the social nature of information and action. The prerequisites for effective democracy are not really automatic voter registration or even Sunday voting, though these would help. Rather, deeper institutional forces—flourishing unions, readily accessible third parties, inexpensive media, and a thriving network of cooperatives and community organizations—are the real basis of effective democracy.

ACKNOWLEDGMENTS

This paper was originally part of a larger study which was divided and revised for publication. The first part of the longer paper, analyzing existing electoral theories of American politics and critical realignments, appeared as "Elites and Elections; Or What Have They Done to You Lately? Toward an Investment Theory of Political Parties and Critical Realignment," in Benjamin Ginsberg and Alan Stone, eds., *Do Elections Matter?* 1st ed. (Armonk, N.Y.: Sharpe, 1986). An appendix to the original paper which attempts to integrate the present essay's historical analysis of the relationship between business structures and American party systems with available statistical data on the law partners, business connections, and corporate affiliations of high federal officials has had to be dropped here, for reasons of space.

I should particularly like to thank Walter Dean Burnham, Gerald Epstein, Arthur Goldhammer, Robert Johnson, and Paul Zarembka for their comments on drafts of this essay. For important assistance with other parts of the study I am also grateful to Richard DuBoff, Benjamin Ginsberg, Lawrence Goodwyn, Duane Lockard, Samuel Popkin, Gail Russell, and Martin Shefter. Early discussions of Anthony Downs's work with Stanley Kelley, and of Mancur Olson's with Tim Scanlon and William Baumol, were also very helpful. Thanks also to Gavan Duffy, Cynthia Horan, and Lola Klein for additional assistance. It should not be necessary to add that readers and critics of a paper cannot be held responsible for its contents—only its author can.

NOTES

1. Frank Vanderlip to James Stillman, September 20, 1912, Frank Vanderlip Papers, Rare Book and Manuscript Library, Columbia University. On the controversy about the National City Co., the Taft and Wilson administrations' inaction, and subsequent developments in defining the relationship between commercial banks and the securities markets, see Ferguson (n.d.). I have added the comments in brackets to provide background for non-specialist readers.

2. The literature on realignments, voting behavior, and party systems is vast. Since Ferguson (1986) discusses much of it, and extensively references other discussions and bibliographies, this paper will not attempt another inventory of the literature. Also, the summary of critical realignment theory which follows sticks closely to the theory's "core" propositions, leaving aside many nuances and disputed points.

3. Some realignment theorists, including Burnham, Ginsberg, and David Brady, argue that effective popular control of public policy is most likely during critical realignments; at other times institutional obstacles to effective majorities inhibit the impact of voting on public policy. For a more extensive discussion see Ferguson (1986).

4. Note that with the possible exception of Lichtman (1980), whose closing chapters begin an analysis of the role of the business community which could lead toward an investment theory of parties, the critics of critical realignment theory draw few general conclusions about elections and the control of public policy. They largely concentrate on the facts of voting behavior during elections.

5. For example, Clubb, Flanigan, and Zingale (1980). Such efforts normally also propose intensive examinations of the content of public policy.

6. Ferguson (1986) summarizes the evidence on this score and makes use of data collected in Ginsberg (1982) to provide some quantitative evidence of the tenuous and unstable relationships between elections and public policy.

7. For example, Downs (1957a, pp. 247 ff.).

8. Some friendly critics of an earlier draft of this paper have suggested that Downs's work ultimately takes a more jaundiced view of the possibilities for voter control of the polity than suggested here. Now, if consistently maintained, the discussion of "producer bias" in the closing chapters of An Economic Theory of Democracy leads toward an investment theory of parties. Also, as I suggest elsewhere, other parts of Downs's work broach important lines of argument that could undermine "electoral control" theories. But these sections have been almost entirely ignored in the subsequent literature. Even Downs's own summary of his views (1957b) did not develop the "producer bias" arguments at all but instead presented his analysis as a more rigorous and modernized updating of quite traditional voting models of politics. It is therefore unsurprising that neither reviewers nor the author of an excellent general discussion of economic "influence" in politics (Bartlett, 1973) considered such efforts essentially "Downsian." See also the discussion later, on the principle of noncompetition and other quite non-Downsian consequences of the investment theory of parties.

9. It should hardly be necessary to observe that this brief discussion cannot hope to cover the nuances of the "socialization" approach or the differences that divide its exponents. For a more extensive discussion, see, *inter multa alia*, Campbell et al. (1960).

10. As discussed above; it is surprising that an application of Downs along Popkin and associates' lines took as long to arrive as it did.

11. Olson (1971, Chap 1) briefly summarizes the notion of a "collective good." See also the discussion of his work later in this paper.

12. Popkin et al. (1976, p. 786); the "simple act of voting" reference is to Kelley and Mirer (1974).

13. Roemer (1978); note that Roemer restricts his point here to what this paper refers to as "major investors."

14. This is technically incorrect. Party competition takes place until investors in both parties feel their overall losses from mobilizing voters through appeals that lead to sacrifices of vital investor interests exceed the gains that might come from control of the state. But since what is at stake are *vital* interests—such as labor legislation, or perhaps even the existence of private property itself—virtually any erosion along these dimensions results in massive investor losses. Virtually no investors, accordingly, finance campaigns that involve such appeals, and so practically no competition occurs along these dimensions.

15. For a somewhat untypical case, see the description of the organizational structure established to help manage the Rockefeller fortune in P. Collier and D. Horowitz's book *The Rockefellers* (1976). It should be noted here that this discussion of the advantages business enjoys in acting politically cannot be exhaustive. Nor, perhaps more importantly, is it intended as a contribution to the growing theoretical literature on the relationship of the state and market. Most of the considerations advanced in works like Lindblom (1977) are taken for granted here, where the concern is much more concrete.

16. For the evolution of modern management structures, see Chandler (1977) and also DuBoff and Herman (1980). While they make their argument cautiously, Bauer et al. (1972) come close to asserting that large firms do not have reliable cost data—a point which, I venture, will find little support in the mass of business history writings.

Several other observations about this frequently urged position are probably also worth making here. First of all, no one denies that lower-level bureaucrats occasionally escape from the control of their supervisors in the manner described in Allison (1971) (though later analysis suggests his examples may not have been well chosen), or that personality differences and other disputes are not endemic in large business organizations. The point, however, is that management structures have been continuously redesigned to reach and enforce a working policy consensus in the face of such obstacles. When internal divisions over basic policy surface in an important case, their consequences are fairly easy to observe: there will be visible signs of turmoil in the organization and, often, clear attempts by higher-level executives to deliberately take back control.

My own studies of internal documents and memoranda relating to corporate decision making on major public policy issues during the New Deal turned up only a few cases in which major issue-related differences persisted inside corporate managements. Where they did, the usual procedure was to call a committee meeting to hammer out policy. In this connection, see also William Baumol's observations on the use of operations research after World War II to put such decision-making procedures even more firmly in place [quoted in Walsh (1970, p. 113)].

17. Strictly speaking, as Olson himself notes, his account of collective action also covers altruistic behavior (1971, p. 64). But many politically relevant applications of the theory probably require the stronger assumption of self-interest.

18. See, e.g., Roemer (1978), which rather clearly assumes that fairly concrete issues of work, distribution, and such are sources of frustrations that lead to collective action.

19. Many of these cases, including perhaps most of those discussed here, should perhaps be more properly described as private transactions which have important external effects on the rest of the population. But Olson himself continues to refer to "the group" provision of "public goods" in such cases (see, e.g., p. 48, n. 68), and this chapter will follow that usage.

20. After more than two decades of work on game and coalition theory, it is rather surprising, and cause for some alarm, that this sort of thing continues to happen. Even the most elementary acquaintance with the "prisoner's dilemma" or oligopoly pricing theories should make it clear that "perfect competition" in a neoclassical sense is a wholly inappropriate assumption for the analysis of many important social outcomes. Like the Justice Department's claim about the American antiwar movement in the 1960s, a confusion of such "imperfectly competitive" or interdependent situations with conspiracies reveals more about the speaker's goodwill and clarity of mind than the merits of any actual case.

It is, after all, a sad day for social science when, for example, Morris Fiorina's *Congress: Keystone of the Washington Establishment* (1977) has to perform a virtual ritual dance of purity in the introduction merely to advance the suggestion that congressmen vote for spending programs in part because they want to be reelected.

21. Personal communication from Lawrence Goodwyn, who has extensively researched this incident.

22. For more details see Ferguson (1984, n.d.) which relies on extensive primary sources.

23. See Olson's (1971) discussion, pp. 24–25, especially n. 42, and p. 48.

24. This is apparent even from the example Olson uses in presenting his formal analysis. He considers the case of a group of property owners lobbying for a property tax rebate. Then he sets up the following model.

T = the rate at which the collective good is supplied;

S_g = the "size" of the group, "which depends not only upon the number of individuals in the group, but also on the value of a unit of a collective good to each individual in the group" (p. 23).

The "group gain" $(S_g T) = V_g$. Now, $V_i/V_g = F_i$, the "fraction" of the collective good an individual obtains; the total gain to an individual therefore is $F_i S_g T$.

For an individual to act, a positive advantage (A_i) must accrue to him or her.

To use the model to discover how much of the collective good will be supplied, Olson therefore analyzes how A_i varies with T.

Since the first order condition for A_i to be at a maximum is $dA_i/dT = O$, Olson evaluates

$$\frac{dA_i}{dT} = \frac{dV_i}{dT} - \frac{dC}{dT}$$

Now, because

$$V_i = F_i S_g T,$$

the right-hand side becomes

$$\frac{d(F_i S_g T)}{dT} - \frac{dC}{dT}$$

For an individual to act,

$$F_i S_g > \frac{dC}{dT}$$

Now, all of this is well and good. But what Olson does next is to argue that, because increases in the size of the group drive down F_i, individuals in large groups will not be able to meet this condition, which defines situations under which it is rational for individuals acting by themselves to bear the whole cost of collective action and, by their action, benefit the group as a whole. So, here is a reason, Olson concludes, why large groups will not be provided with collective goods.

But there is clearly something wrong with this analysis. As more than one real estate group in recent American history has discovered to its delight, rewriting a proposed tax rebate to include half or more of the potential electorate does not automatically reduce benefits to itself. Despite Olsons claim that increasing the size of the group should decrease individual benefits, such a strategy is often precisely the high road to success.

In terms of Olson's discussion on pp. 22–23 of his book, this is to say that F_i does not necessarily change as additional property owners are added. Of course, whether collective action occurs depends on more than the maintenance of the F_i's, but they, at least, need not pose a problem in a large group.

Note, however, the differences between this example and the Cournot market case Olson discusses on pp. 26–27. In the latter, the demand curve limits total sales, so that increases in individual F_i's really do take directly away from someone else. This distinction is clearly recognized by Olson in the next section, which distinguishes between "inclusive" and "exclusive" groups (pp. 36–43), but the original claim that increases in group size lead directly to lower probabilities of collective action because of changing F_i's is repeated thereafter.

It may also be worth observing that the point at issue here differs from the criticisms of Frohlich, Oppenheimer, and Young (1971). Their main argument centered on the possibility of introducing marginal cost-sharing arrangements (pp. 146–48).

25. This is, of course, far from the only problem with the neoclassical approach to "aggregate" concentration.

26. A good discussion of the U.S. experience in this respect is in Kotz, (1979), though its discussion of the New Deal should be supplemented by Ferguson (1984, n.d.).

27. For evidence on the CED see Burch (1979); among many sources on the Business Council see Collins (1981, passim). The only study known to me that failed to

confirm the special significance of large financial institutions in major business organizations is Useem (1980). But this study included organizations like the National Association of Manufacturers (NAM) that formally prohibit financiers from being on the board in the sample it analyzed, thus imparting a downward bias to its estimate of the importance of financiers. Of course, the NAM is not without significance, but as Burch (1973) observed, the NAM only occasionally has represented really large firms. As Ferguson (n.d.) argues, when, as in the 1930s, the NAM's national significance increases, it is because a core of large firms has subsidized organizational growth.

28. See Carle Conway to Thomas Lamont, Dec. 2, 1943; Lamont to E. T. Stannard, Dec. 3, 1943; Conway to Lamont, Dec. 15, 1943; Lamont Papers, Baker Library, Harvard University. Conway, the president of Continental Can and a CED activist, asked Lamont to intervene with Kennecott Copper. The famous Morgan partner did, and Kennecott increased its contribution.

29. See Olson (1971), e.g., Chap. 4.

30. For extensive discussion and references see Bernstein (1950), Fusfeld (1980), Goldstein (1978), Ferguson (1984, n.d.), and Zilg (1976, pp. 327–30). What appears to have happened to Zilg's excellent study after its publication underscores this essay's general analysis of the role major investors play in American life. See the chilling discussion in Sherrill (1981).

31. A close examination of smaller business support for Pennsylvania's "Little New Deal," I suspect, would be very revealing in regard to the abolition of the Coal and Iron Police.

32. See the discussion in Mowry (1946, pp. 225, 249, and 292–93); and Kolko (1963, Chap. 8). A few details of Kolko's interpretation of the Perkins-J. P. Morgan links perhaps are mistaken, though there is no space here to discuss the question.

33. For the "leapfrog" reference, see Downs (1957a, Chaps. 8 and 9); and Barry (1970, pp. 118 ff).

34. See the discussion of relief in section 4 and the references cited there.

35. For the individual cases just mentioned, consult any detailed history of political parties and election campaigns, e.g., Polakoff (1981); for Carter in 1980, see Ferguson and Rogers (1980, pp. 28 ff).

36. Though not all analysts using an ethnocultural framework have claimed their results refute explanations of American politics that rely chiefly on economic arguments, many have. See, e.g., Bogue (1980), who cites Kleppner, Formisano, and Jensen to this effect. In fact, however, all but strong formulations of the "ethnocultural synthesis" are entirely compatible with this essay. And the strong formulations are clearly wrong. Almost none of the best-known studies in this tradition have employed adequate controls for economic factors, not have they tested analyses relying on sophisticated economic theories. Where sensible economic controls have been tried, the results show significant and powerful direct economic effects on voting behavior even in cases where ethnocultural theories should show to best advantage. See, for example, Lichtman's (1980, Chap. 8) striking discussion of voting in the 1920s (whose analysis, especially when read in the light of his final chapter's remarks on the utility for business elites of race and other noneconomic appeals, is highly compatible with this essay's analysis) and Williamson's (1981) study of Kansas in the 1890s.

Ethnoculturally oriented voting analysts have also made life easy for themselves by avoiding any detailed analyses of class structure and the churches (as is briefly discussed later, in section 4). Nor does it help the cause of either theory or clarity when Morris Fiorina, in his analysis of *Retrospective Voting in American National Elections* (1981), adopts a definition of "economic" influence on voting that excludes cases in which workers who have lost their jobs in a world recession accept Jesus Christ as their savior and then come out vigorously in favor of, for example, aid to Taiwan, South Africa, or the B-1 bomber (not to mention "right-to-work" laws).

37. See the discussion in Key (1959).

38. As Ferguson (1984, n.d.) suggests, often the best and most practical way to define "large" investors makes reference to (whoever controls) the largest corporations and banks in the country, and as many large individual fortunes as data can be gathered for. Also, as Ferguson (1986) observes, in this sort of work, as in other parts of the social sciences, missing data often represent a hazard which is to be worked around as best as one can.

39. It is obviously absurd to think that some fixed percentage of major investors somehow exercise an unvarying amount of influence at all moments in the life of a national economy. Any serious attempt to analyze concrete cases has to recognize that relations between large and small investors are dynamic and historically ever-changing. That said, it remains true that large investors are uniquely important to analyze within any given historical circumstance—even on the rare occasions in which many small investors become politically active and the level of class conflict rises.

40. It is obvious, for example, that many existing archives are missing any number of potentially important documents, including not only many which were inadvertently destroyed or mislaid but also many that were deliberately suppressed or which still exist but continue to be withheld by interested parties or their descendants. Material that has been recovered sometimes contains errors and can also mislead simply because it must sometimes be interpreted without a complete understanding of the context. More subtly, the kinds of material one examines most frequently can bias one's conclusions. Excessive concentration on readily available government agency records, for example, makes it easy to exaggerate the importance of bureaucrats in historical events; the same is potentially true, mutatis mutandis, with all other kinds of records, including those in private business archives.

Memoirs and eyewitness accounts of major historical events contain additional sources of bias as well. Most kings, presidents, ministers, and such are prone to exaggerate their own roles in key decisions. Such sources also contain all sorts of other confusions, good-faith mistakes, and occasionally outright fraud.

It should also be obvious that no one has done more to damage the historical record than Alexander Graham Bell, and that written documents help little where the groups and persons concerned do not write at all or rarely articulate their views extensively.

41. Oral interviews, however, are probably the least useful and reliable of all possible sources. It is probably no accident, for example, that virtually all accounts of the business community that cast doubt on its general political skills and power rely extensively on oral interviews for their "facts." For some striking comparisons of what high business and political figures told interviewers about their behavior in the New Deal and what archival evidence revealed about their actual behavior, see Ferguson (n.d.).

42. See the discussion of recent literature on appointments and the analysis of political power in Ferguson (1986).

43. For example, the analyses in Ferguson (n.d.).

44. Note the restriction of this condition to major investors. While it probably fits most other investors to varying degrees at different points in time, this paper is not basically concerned with how to analyze mass politics. It is important to note, however, that a special interest in profit maximization does not derive from any unusual deductive powers unique to large investors. Their behavior, in this respect, faces constraints that may not operate evenly on the rest of the population. As is not the case for lesser investors, in many situations the resources available to major investors ensure that what they do matters, visibly, tangibly, and often immediately. An error, or inaction, accordingly, imposes real costs.

45. In this paper there is little point in taking a turn on the income/wealth/maximization/optimization/satisficing/time horizon/discount rate carousels. Nor is there time to do more than pause ritually to acknowledge that, of course, the role profits play in capitalist economies is unique and not at all comparable with other sources of income.

Nor is there space to discuss how this analysis of wealthy investors relates to current discussions of cultural and ideological factors in social development. While these will have to wait for another occasion, it may be noted here—as it should be plain from parts of section 4—that investments in "culture" and information represent a major share of all politically relevant investments by major investors.

46. For the notion of a nondecision, see Bachrach and Baratz (1970). All these cautionary remarks, of course, provide no excuse for endorsing vacuous searches for "perfect" or "comprehensive" indicators. One point in favor of careful working procedures in the social sciences is that they permit cumulative improvement. See also the remarks in Ferguson (1986) on so-called thick description as a social science strategy for advancing knowledge.

47. For the original, more complex models, and many more details and references to the literature on the System of '96, see Ferguson (1984, n.d.).

48. Which means that, unlike the first, this dimension is not continuous, but takes only two values. It also, of course, oversimplifies the relation of firms to the international economy.

49. It is perfectly sensible to plot the financial system on these graphs, as in Ferguson (1984). But financial markets are often highly decentralized and individual banks are frequently tied to very specific sectors and regional economies. Depending on the issues involved, accordingly, banks may simply support their borrowers. For example, it was surely not their own labor problems, but concern for labor problems that afflicted their investments ("borrowers") that persuaded most nineteenth-century bankers to support government policy actions against labor. The assignment of the financial sectors to spaces on graphs like those discussed here is, therefore, more complicated than it appears at first sight. It is perhaps also worth noting that membership on boards of directors and trusteeships can often provide important evidence for further analysis by this scattergraph method. Note, however, that in such cases, the directorships merely function as data to support or negate a theory whose explanatory force depends upon the model of the underlying political economic relationships implicit in the dimensional analysis of the coalition. "Networks" by themselves explain nothing; their significance derives entirely from the demonstration they can provide that certain actors really are interacting in accordance with a theory of how they should act. I mention this point because previous (informal) statements of the methods discussed in this paper have been misunderstood as advocating "network analysis," or as suggesting that the mere discov-

ery of some sort of social tie between actors counts as definite evidence of joint, effective action. Obviously, it does not, and, a fortiori, it is substantive considerations of political economy, not the abstract fact of a "network," that explains political outcomes.

50. It should not, however, be too difficult to form an impression of what these will look like when published. The sketches of various party systems which follow all clearly label outcomes and principal actors, and discuss the broad dynamics of the various transitions. It is perhaps also worth noticing that nothing in this analysis prejudices the possibility that a normally stable party system could be briefly disrupted by some intensely but briefly contested issue unrelated to other elections within the period. In that case, graphs for one election would be scrambled, requiring an extra dimension useless for analyzing the system as a whole. But if the basic long-run industrial alignment is not disrupted, then the "exceptional" character of such an election will be evident.

51. See section 4.

52. Now a major theme of much work inspired by Immanuel Wallerstein's research.

53. See section 2.

54. Perhaps in reaction to the last generation of "consensus historians," many recent studies of American history make a determined effort to discuss the often very painful daily-life experiences of ordinary people. This research has produced many significant works that amount to a powerful indictment of conventional pluralist theories of American politics. But while I am totally in sympathy with efforts to "assert the dignity of work," "reveal the thoughts and actions of the rank and file," or show ordinary people as "active, articulate participants in a historical process," and similar aims, I am very skeptical about this literature's frequent unwillingness and inability to come finally to a point. That ordinary people are historical subjects is a vital truth; that they are the primary shapers of the American past seems to me either a triviality or a highly dubious theory about the control of both political and economic investment in American history.

55. See, for example, Goldstein (1978, passim).

56. Except in specialist works like that of Goldstein (1978), such cases are normally neglected by all varieties of "consensus" historiography.

57. See, e.g., Ratner (1967). Taxes, of course, always remain one side of a problem whose other face is expenditures, though this essay cannot afford more than the briefest consideration of either.

58. "Ethnocultural" histories have produced much work on particular periods and elections, but no synoptic interpretations of American critical realignments. Perhaps the closest approach to one, though it scarcely represents a "pure" example of the genre, is Polakoff (1981). See also the works cited in Bogue (1980) and for a view that stands between these works and this paper, Shefter (1978).

A few other reservations may also be noted here for the record. First, because this is a paper and not a book, the sketches which follow pass over any number of major events in American history, from the political adventures of John C. Calhoun to the Vietnam War. This is unfortunate, but there is no alternative. Second, similar limitations of space preclude much discussion of the role of "intellectuals" and ideas in the realignment movements discussed here. I hope to return to this theme in the separate studies of the party systems I expect to publish in the future. For the time being, it must suffice to note that virtually all the major business figures discussed here maintained close, often intimate, relations with channels for the dissemination of ideas. Third, while a few of the most obvious and outstanding facts that bear on the daily life of average Americans are discussed here as crude benchmarks, an enormous amount of demographic, statistical, and personal facts have had to be left out. Only the barest details of how women, minority groups, or even workers as a whole fared [as well discussed, for example, in Gordon, Edwards, and Reich (1982)] can be put into an essay that must concentrate on the process of bloc formation among major investors. Finally, this essay has to focus on broad trends at the national level, without regard to differences between levels of government.

On many of these topics, however, an industrially sensitive analysis could contribute much. In regard to the progress of the movement for women's rights, for example, it surely mattered a great deal that two of the biggest and fastest-growing sectors in the early stages of industrialization—textiles, and the brewing and liquor sectors—were dead set against women's suffrage. One was opposed because initially women's suffrage would likely have led to a stronger political position for its own workforce (which included many women and children); the other because of the leading roles women played in the Temperance campaign. Nor was it accidental that the final successful campaign for women's voting rights coincided with World War I, when public hysteria and official investigations had virtually immobilized the heavily German-oriented brewers.

The gradual passage of laws giving women the right to hold property in their own names in the nineteenth century also had major consequences once the trust movement appeared. Combined with the somewhat misnamed "managerial revolution" (which enabled shareholders to control large blocks of shares without having to actively manage the enterprises), this development led directly to the ironic fact that some women (e.g., Mrs. Russell Sage) ended up in command of enormous fortunes upon the deaths of their husbands. They could then redirect (some of) the money to social causes. But more of this another time.

59. For example, the discussion in Formisano (1981); Ferguson (1986) discusses some of the ramifications of taking positions on this question.

60. Elbridge Gerry and his allies, for example, were certainly not poor, provincial farmers.

61. In this and most of the remaining notes in this paper, it would be easily possible to reel off a plethora of references. But there is simply not enough space for this. Accordingly, subsequent references are strictly limited to the minimum number necessary to support the argument and make no attempt to index even a minimally adequate list of major works on each period.

62. See the excellent summary of Hamilton and other Federalist leaders' wealth and kinship ties in Burch (1981a, Chap. 2); this source also has a brief summary of Hamilton's fiscal program.

63. See the discussion of banking practices in regard to loanable assets in Hammond (1957, pp. 74–75).

64. Among many discussions see, e.g., Polakoff (1981, Chap. 2), La Feber (1972), and Van Alstyne (1972).

65. Burch (1981a, p. 88) is most illuminating. Dallas himself represented Stephen Girard on several occasions. His very close associate Jared Ingersoll regularly represented Girard. Dallas seems also to have served as a sort of courier between Philadelphia's Republican business community and the administration.

66. Reliable trade figures showing the dramatic reorientation of American trade after the Revolution away from Britain have only recently become available. See Robertson and Walton (1979, pp. 126–28). For John Jacob Astor and the other Republican merchants, see Burch (1981a, p. 88).

67. Hammond (1957, pp. 145–461); Van Alstyne (1972); and Burch (1981a, Chap. 3). Note that Joseph Story did not support Jefferson's embargo policies. For the Western movement, see Van Alstyne (1972); for background, La Feber (1972). Paying for the weaponry necessary for this imperial venture, however, was a contentious issue in both Jefferson's and Madison's regimes.

68. A word about the significance of this brief increase in turnout may be advisable here. There is no reason in principle why the dream of conquering the West, or Canada, or Florida, should not also have captured a large mass of voters, as well as the elites this paper dwells on. Indeed, it almost certainly did. But the very steep decline in turnout in the elections following, as well as the considerations advanced below, in the discussion of the Jacksonian era, make it difficult to claim that voters were determining policy in general. On the contrary, the rise in turnout probably testifies to massive mobilization by sharply divided elites.

69. Hammond (1957, pp. 146–47); for Story, see Burch (1981a, p. 110). In this paper it is not possible to pursue the question of how the Supreme Court relates to the various party systems discussed here. Burch's discussion of Supreme Court appointments (1980, 1981a,b) suggests, however, a variety of ways this issue can be approached that have so far not been widely explored, even in the growing literature on so-called critical legal studies.

70. Hammond (1957, Chaps. 6 and 8) is a superb discussion. For Girard's plans, see Brown (1942).

71. Brown (1942) and Hammond (1957, Chap. 9) have excellent discussions. See also Burch (1981a, pp. 99–100).

72. The origin of Southern support for tariffs in this period has been debated extensively. For references and a perhaps less than wholly convincing analysis, see Preyer (1959).

73. For a vivid account of the distress that accompanied the depression of 1819, see Rezeck (1933). The 20 percent unemployment figure (in some cities) is a guess. It assumes that the figures for particular locations mentioned in Rezeck (1933, pp. 29–31) are exaggerations and that the panic of 1819 probably was not as severe as later depressions, such as those in the 1890s or 1930s.

74. See Burch (1981a, p. 100 and p. 122, n. 69). Astor evidently did not seek repayment of principal until after Monroe left the White House.

75. Shade (1981), which is an exceptionally interesting essay; McCormick (1960); and Polakoff (1981, Chap. 4). Note that local rivalries in this period remained intense. For some of the tensions associated with this development, see Welter (1960).

76. Taussig (1964), and Pincus (1977) are sources on the early tariffs. See also a fine and very stimulating study by Chase-Dunn (1980), which, however, attaches more importance to manufacturing during the period before 1860 than its weight in the economy warranted and greatly underestimates the significance of railroads.

77. Hammond (1957); compare the reception accorded this book with the earlier study of Schlesinger (1945) which Hammond had brilliantly reviewed (Hammond, 1946). Hammond, perhaps, could have made a bit more than he did of the support the

Bank commanded among some large state banks (including some in New York City), though he was aware of it and indeed briefly discusses it most intelligently.

78. See Burch (1981a, p. 171, n. 126) and Sobel (1977, pp. 8 ff. and 26). For Philadelphia's crucial role in finance during this period, see Chandler (1954).

79. Hammond (1957, Chaps. 12–14); but see especially Burch (1981a, p. 147), which demonstrates major errors of fact in earlier criticisms of Hammond by Remini (1967) and especially by F. O. Gattell (1966).

80. See the discussion in Haeger (1981, pp. 138 and especially 139), which is a nice case study of what American "radicalism" is frequently all about. Hammond made the same point in general but not in detail. On New York parties in general, see Bridges (1982).

81. See the discussion in Trimble (1919, pp. 410–11); for Cambreleng's business ties, see Burch (1981a, p. 152, p. 170, n. 119 and 123, and p. 171, n. 126).

82. Compare the indications of increasing party cohesion in, e.g., Russel (1972). On the basis of a wealth of data, Shade (1981) argues convincingly that national parties properly "emerged" only toward the end of the 1830s. This is also the present essay's argument; but I am somewhat puzzled why Shade believes this development is difficult to explain, or how relabeling capitalist development as "social mobilization" advances the inquiry. Nevertheless, his broad argument is compelling and merits a wide readership.

83. Evans, 1981, p. 34.

84. A good survey of the American experience with laws regulating wage and hours is Ratner (1980). See also Dankert, Mann, and Northrup (1965). David and Solar (1977) summarize trends in real wages and the cost of living. Williamson and Lindert (1980) provide a comprehensive analysis of wealth and income differentials over the course of American history. The minuscule nature of relief (less than 1 percent of GNP) all through the nineteenth century is clear in Peterson (1935) and can be directly estimated from what are probably reliable data for the 1890s in Mills (1894). Note that Peterson suggests that relief was much better organized in the 1890s than previously. It is also probably worth noting that relief expenditures ran highest in the largest American cities.

85. The illiteracy figures are taken from Cremin (1980, pp. 490–91), who cautions that variations in census procedures affected results at different points and that blacks' illiteracy rates ran far higher than whites'. The 1854 Census estimates of newspapers show 852 papers in the United States in 1828, 1,631 in 1840, and 2,526 in 1850. The estimate of prolabor papers comes from Sumner (1936, p. 286) and is for the years 1828–1832—years before the panic of 1837, which wrecked unions across the country.

86. I have not been able to find any reliable estimates of the economic value of the output of political machines in this period. For slightly later dates, Yearly (1970, passim, but especially pp. 265–66) is suggestive. Much of the literature on political machines in America is highly romantic. A more accurate and less sentimental treatment seems now to be emerging, however; see, for example, Shefter (1976) or Erie (1980).

Note that a few voting analysts have raised questions about the reliability of the figures for voting turnout in this and later periods. In particular, it is sometimes suggested, the U.S. Census population reports might induce important errors. This chapter does not have space for a full consideration of such arguments, but it should be pointed out that Burnham, who is the most frequently cited source of turnout figures, made important use of state rather than federal censuses whenever he believed the federal government's figures could be improved upon. Accordingly, calculations of errors based on experience with the U.S. Census miss the point; and the Burnham estimates, which were very carefully done, are probably as good as any that will ever be produced.

87. See, e.g., the discussion in Cremin (1980, pp. 338 and 341 ff.); this source perhaps exaggerates the number of actively involved farmers who did more than read papers or magazines.

88. The literature is immense, but see, for example, Beard and Beard (1934, Chaps. 15 and 17).

89. See the review of these various studies in Lee and Passell (1979, Chap. 10).

90. For references and a discussion of these theories, see Lee and Passell (1979, pp. 214–18).

91. For example, Robert Toombs, in a speech to the Senate, in the *Congressional Globe* (Jan. 7, 1861), pp. 270–71; though this is quoted in Lebergott (1972, p. 214), its point seems not to have been taken up in the subsequent literature, although Lebergott himself makes it clearly.

92. See the discussion in Polakoff (1981, p. 165), although he perhaps underestimates the pro-Southern sentiment that grew in parts of southern California. Note also that further settlement was certain to follow a successful transcontinental railroad, which many Southerners promoted.

93. Jones (1970) is one of many discussions.

94. For Walker, see LaFeber (1993, pp. 28–30); for Cuba, see, e.g., Jones (1970, pp. 66, 69).

95. Expansion into Mexico, for example, virtually required that the states remain united. Not surprisingly, therefore, many early Southern supporters of territorial expansion, such as South Carolina's Joel Poinsett, opposed efforts to bring North-South conflicts to a head. See also Draughton (1966) on the role played by Sam Houston's brother George in sparking opposition to Calhoun in the late 1840s.

96. Note also that parts of several of these states fell well below the Mason-Dixon line, the traditional dividing point between North and South.

97. See, among many sources, Russel (1948, passim). Jefferson Davis, future president of the Confederate States of America, was a major player in some of these struggles.

98. See Sorin (1970) for a statistical study of leading New York abolitionists. A leading abolitionist, New York's Gerit Smith, was for some years probably the largest landowner in the United States. Lewis Tappan, another abolitionist leader, founded the firm that is today Dun & Bradstreet.

99. "James F. Joy," *National Cyclopedia*, XVIII, p. 121; Forbes (1900, p. 171).

100. "James F. Joy," *National Cyclopedia*, XVIII, p. 121; Dodd (1911, p. 787); Stover, (1975, p. 90).

101. Edelstein (1968, pp. 216–17). Forbes had earlier helped ship guns to Kansas. Gerit Smith also contributed to Brown. See "Gerit Smith," *National Cyclopedia*, XVIII, p. 332.

102. See, e.g., Forbes (1900, p. 186).

103. Dodd (1911, p. 787) identifies several prominent New York Democrats as controlling the Illinois Central in this period. But while Dodd may be correct, neither the *United States Railroad Directory for 1856* nor *Low's Railway Directory for 1858* records any of the men Dodd discusses as serving on the board. These directories do, however, show

clearly that Dodd was right in claiming that New York interests maintained a dominant position on the board. The next directory I have been able to locate dates from 1861. This shows a continued heavy representation of New Yorkers, but also some turnover, including the removal of one director listed as living in Chicago, and the arrival of Nathaniel Banks. The seriously incomplete accounts of Lincoln's relationship to the Illinois Central in Sunderland, (1955, pp. 24 and 39) and Corliss (1950, pp. 108, 117 ff., and 121) are consistent with the view that the Central's top officers and directors were far more favorably inclined to Lincoln in 1860 than in 1858. It should also be observed that railroads in certain areas (like the Baltimore & Ohio, which ran through border states) were not at all enthusiastic about either Lincoln or conflict with the South.

104. Forbes (1900, p. 182); "James F. Joy," *National Cyclopedia,* XVIII, p. 121.

105. While the full network of ties between all the principals in the Lincoln campaign is too dense to discuss here, for Ogden's business relations with Thomas Scott of the Pennsylvania Railroad, see *Burgess' Railway Directory* (1861), p. 88. Note also that most of these men still hoped to avoid war with the South.

106. For Cornell, see Dorf (1952, pp. 199 and 227); for Chase and Cooke, see Burch (1981b, pp. 20–21).

107. Almost all accounts of Lincoln's election mention Pennsylvania and the tariff; for banking reform, see Rezeck (1942) or Hammond (1957, Chaps. 21 and 22). See also Burch (1981b, p. 22).

108. The literature on these matters is immense; see, e.g., Polakoff (1981, pp. 196 ff.) for a brief account.

109. Of many accounts, see e.g., the discussion of McClellan's candidacy in Burch (1981b, p. 55, n. 70). In this period many railroads also shifted back and forth among the parties in a complex pattern that defies summary here.

110. Polakoff (1981, Chaps. 6 and 7); Burch (1981b, pp. 74–75).

111. For the railroad and other bargains in the Compromise of 1877, see Burch (1981b, p. 74). See also Josephson (1963) for many of the events of this period and Goodwyn (1976) or Schwartz (1976) for the subsequent nightmares Southern elites visited upon their subject population.

112. Schirmer (1972, Chap. 2). For civil service reform in this period see especially Roy (1981); for Forbes, see "John Murray Forbes," *National Cyclopedia,* XXXV, pp. 331–32.

113. For the New York Central and the Democrats, see inter alia, Shefter (1976); for the turnout efforts in this period, see Polakoff (1981, pp. 232–33). In the 1880s the New York Central drew closer to the GOP.

114. I am presently preparing a study of "The System of '96: A Reconsideration," which attempts a rough quantitative evaluation of these trends.

115. See the sensitive discussion in Polakoff (1981, pp. 249 ff.); note his discussion of the importance of distinguishing among levels of government.

116. Goodwyn (1976) presents a wealth of new and very important information on the origins of Populism and the dynamics of its ascent. Schwartz (1976) adds important information on the Populist press, which Goodwyn also discusses, and has a penetrating discussion of some of the larger background reasons for the Populists' eventual demise and the emergence of a racist planter-industrialist coalition in the South.

117. For example, Burnham (1970, 1974, 1981).

118. See Ferguson (n.d.).

119. Montgomery (1979) and Brecher (1972); the best strike statistics are those presented in Griffin (1939).

120. Where everyone admits that blacks and poor whites were deliberately pushed out of the electorate; I regret that space limitations preclude my discussing these developments in any more detail. Note, however, that Northern elites were very deliberate parties to this scheme. Northern bar associations and law reviews, for example, worked overtime thinking up reasons why the courts should not hear suits brought by disenfranchised Southern blacks.

121. Turnout dropoff is figured by averaging each states' turnout in 1888, 1892, 1896, and 1900, then subtracting from this figure the average of the turnouts in 1920 and 1924. The turnout data came from Walter Dean Burnham and incorporate a minor correction for Delaware that he has not yet published. The figures for manufacturing value added per capita come from Kuznets, Miller, and Easterlin (1960, p. 131). For each state I have subtracted value added per capita in 1889 from the same category for 1929, yielding the difference per capita that appears in the graph on the X axis. The three exceptional states (which are not included in the calculations for the regression line drawn on the scattergraph) are Maryland, Rhode Island, and Wyoming. (Arizona and several other states not then in the Union also had to be eliminated since they provided no totals for 1888–1896 to compute.)

In all three cases, the special circumstances that produced the original low turnouts are too obvious to require elaborate analysis. Maryland was simply the northernmost state to have adopted the Southern system of voter disenfranchisement (around 1907). (It should be recalled that if the Battle of Antietam had gone the other way, Maryland would probably have made the transition much earlier.) Rhode Island in the nineteenth century was less a political jurisdiction than the name of America's largest company town, as the elites of this early industrializing textile center, lacking any rural smallholders to strike alliances with, installed a succession of fantastically restrictive suffrage laws that at times excluded as much as 75 percent of the white male population of voting age from participation. (They also had to put down a series of revolts against their new order, of which Dorr's Rebellion, in 1842, is perhaps the best known.) And Wyoming, for much of the System of '96 the least populated state in the Union, probably eluded mass disenfranchisement for the same reason that Andorra escaped occupation by the Nazis during World War II—some places with more sheep than people are not worth the trouble of taking them over.

The full statistics for the regression equation are as follows. The equation itself is $Y = 8.104 + .057x$, $R^2 = 0.45$.

The standard errors for the first and second terms, respectively, are (2.426) and (0.0118); t-values are (3.34) and (4.81); $F(1/28) = 23.231$. These are all significant results, and tests did not suggest significant heteroscedasticity.

All regressions of this sort face various pitfalls. Spatial autocorrelation, for example, is a possibility. But with the limited number of cases there is little point in testing. Since the Southern states are not in the equation at all, the most obvious source of spatial autocorrelation is not a problem; nor does there appear to be a problem with the other states. Omitted variables, of course, are another possibility, but any discussion of particular candidates would be very lengthy; I believe there are good reasons for cautiously accepting the equation as is.

122. See Ferguson (n.d.) for more details.

123. Note that there is no reason to assume that changes in election laws *by them-selves* necessarily produced the total turnout decline. All the factors mentioned in this paragraph doubtless played a role. At some point, also, "negative bandwagons" would doubtless form, pushing turnout much lower as voters realized that such incidents as the wholesale fraud that defeated Henry George in the New York mayoralty race of 1887 meant that they would never be permitted to assume power.

124. For the basic statistics and an excellent discussion of the merger wave, see Edwards (1979, Chap. 3) and Reid (1976, pp. 66–68).

125. See the discussion in my "System of '96."

126. Goodwyn (1976, Chap. 13); for Hearst's copper (and, thus silver) interests, see Lundberg (1937, p. 65).

127. See the longer discussion in my 1984 and n.d. papers. Note that rivalries with European companies sometimes complicated the partisan choices of the copper companies in ways too complex to discuss here.

128. Ibid.; Weinstein (1968); and Kolko (1963). For reasons of space no further discussion of the Progressive era is possible here.

129. See Kolko (1963); but especially Ferguson (n.d.).

130. Oil imports, where they became an issue, of course ended demands for totally "free" trade by independent oilmen.

An outstanding review of the relations between big business and the press in this period is Debouzy (1972), pp. 153–56; see also pp. 210–22 on the relations of business to the churches and universities. Analyses of mass politics that slide past the facts discussed so well in this French study are unlikely to produce anything except confusion in regard to such topics as "rational expectations."

131. Ferguson (1984, n.d.) and Ferguson and Rogers (1981). As originally published, the next few paragraphs of this chapter borrowed liberally from the brief summary in Ferguson (1984); the 1984 essay was also indicated as the appropriate source for details and references. In this book, a revised version of the 1984 essay follows immediately. Removing the paragraphs, however, seemed likely to significantly impair the unity and pedagogical value of the overview of American history presented here. I therefore left them in.

132. Virtually all the discussion which follows is based on Ferguson (1984, n.d.), so more specific references will be kept to a minimum. Both of these papers present a formal model of the processes discussed here along the lines discussed in section 3.

133. The quotation comes from an entry in Raymond Moley's *Journal* for June 13, 1936, now in the Moley Papers, Hoover Institution. Astor and Harriman were major owners of the publication.

134. To such an extent that when a bank with ties to top union officials failed in the Depression, Standard Oil of New Jersey and other large companies raised a fund for its recapitalization. See Ferguson (n.d.) for details.

135. Ferguson and Rogers (1980, pp. 267–75; 1981, pp. 20–26).

136. Ibid.

137. See, e.g., Goulden (1971, pp. 257 ff.) for a striking example.

138. See the discussion in Ferguson and Rogers (1981, pp. 13 ff.).

139. Kalt (1981) presents convincing estimates of the size of these transfers.

140. This subject merits more discussion than it can be given here. I hope in the near future to consider it at greater length and with extensive documentation.

Note that the aggressive fundamentalism displayed by many elite Texas churches in the 1970s has a powerful "elective affinity" for decontrol because of its emphasis on individual action.

141. No single institutional change can possibly undo the effects of a whole system of influences. Still, consider the likely consequences of a federal campaign spending reform that established individual tax credits for contributions to political campaigns instead of guaranteeing money to the nominees of the two major parties. If these contributions were allowed up to, say, $100, then masses of ordinary voters would have resources that really counted. Some quite striking developments in the American party system would probably occur as these pools of money found their way to new candidates and parties, and as venturesome candidates discovered that even nonvoters now had resources worth pursuing.

REFERENCES

Allison, G. (1971), *The Essence of Decision,* Boston: Little Brown.

Argersinger, P. (1980), "A Place on the Ballot." *American Historical Review* 85 (April 1980).

Bachrach, P., and Baratz, M. (1970), *Power and Poverty,* New York: Oxford University Press.

Barry, B. (1970), *Sociologists, Economists, and Democracy,* London: Collier-Macmillan.

Bartlett, R. (1973), *Economic Foundations of Political Power,* New York: Free Press.

Bauer, R., Poole, I., and Dexter, L. (1972), *American Business and Public Policy,* Chicago: Aldine.

Beard, C., and Beard, M. (1934), *The Rise of American Civilization,* New York: Macmillan.

Benson, L., Silbey, J., Field, P. (1978), "Toward a Theory of Stability and Change in American Voting Patterns: New York State, 1772–1970." In Silbey, J., Bogue, A., Flanigan, W. eds., *The History of American Electoral Behavior,* Princeton: Princeton University Press.

Bernstein, I. (1950), *The New Deal Collective Bargaining Policy,* Berkeley, Calif.: University of California Press.

Bogue, A. (1980), "The new Political History in the 1970s." In Kammen, M. (ed.), *The Past Before Us,* Ithaca: Cornell University Press.

Boorstin, D. (1969), "The Businessman as an American Institution." In A. Callow (ed.), *American Urban History,* New York: Oxford University Press.

Brecher, J. (1972), *Strike!,* San Francisco, Straight Arrow Books.

Bridges, A. (1982), "Plutocracy and Politics in Antebellum New York City." *Political Science Quarterly,* spring 1982.

Brown, K. (1942), "Stephen Girard, Promoter of the Second Bank of the United States." *Journal of Economic History* II (November).

Burch, P. (1972), *The Managerial Revolution Reassessed,* Lexington: Lexington Books.

Burch, P. (1973), "The NAM as an Interest Group." *Politics And Society* 4 (fall).

Burch, P. (1979), Unpublished manuscript on the core firms in the CED.

Burch, P. (1980), *Elites in American History,* Vol. III, New York: Holmes & Meier.

Burch, P. (1981a), *Elites in American History,* Vol. I, New York: Holmes & Meier.

Burch, P. (1981b), *Elites in American History,* Vol. II, New York: Homes & Meier.

Burgess' Railway Directory (1861), New York: Wilbur & Hastings

Burnham, W. D. (1970), *Critical Elections and the Mainsprings of American Politics*, New York: Norton.

Burnham, W. D. (1974), "Theory and Voting Research: Some Reflections on Converse's 'Change in the American Electorate.'" *American Political Science Review* 68 (Sept.).

Burnham, W. D. (1981), "The System of 1896: An Analysis." In Kleppner, P., *et alia* (eds.), *The Evolution of American Electoral Systems*, Westport, Ct.: Greenwood Press.

Campbell, A., Converse, P., Miller, W., Stokes, D. (1960), *The American Voter*, New York: Wiley.

Chandler, A. (1954), "Patterns of American Railroad Finance, 1830–50." *Business History Review* XXVIII.

Chandler, A. (1977), *The Visible Hand*, Cambridge: Harvard University Press.

Chandler, A. (1980), "Government Versus Business." In Dunlop, J., (ed.), *Business and Public Policy*, Cambridge: Harvard University Press.

Chase-Dunn, C. (1980), "The Development of Core Capitalism in the Ante-Bellum United States." In Bergessen, A., ed., *Studies in the Modern World System*, New York: Academic Press.

Clubb, J., Flanigan, W., Zingale, N. (1980), *Partisan Realignment*, Beverly Hills: Sage.

Coben, S. (1959), "Northeastern Business and Radical Reconstruction." *Mississippi Valley Historical Review* XLVI (June).

Collier, P. and Horowitz, D. (1976), *The Rockefellers*, New York: Holt, Rinehart, and Winston.

Collins, R. (1981), *Business Response to Keynes*, New York: Columbia University Press.

Converse, P. (1972), "Change in the American Electorate." In Campbell, A. and Converse, P. (eds.), *The Human Meaning of Social Change*, New York: Russell Sage.

Converse, P. (1974), "Comments on Burnham's 'Theory and Voting Research.'" *American Political Science Review* 68 (Sept.)

Corliss, C. (1950), *Main Line of Mid-America: The Story of the Illinois Central*, New York: Creative Age Press.

Crapol, E., and Schonberger, H. (1972), "The Shift to Global Expansion, 1865–1900." In Williams, W. A. (ed.), *From Colony to Empire*, New York: Wiley.

Cremin, L. (1980), *American Education*, New York, Harper.

Dankert, C., Mann, F., Northrup, H. (1965), *Hours of Work*, New York: Harper.

David, P., Solar, P. (1977), "A Bicentenary Contribution to the History of the Cost of Living in America." In *Research in Economic History*, Vol. II.

Debouzy, M. (1972), *Le capitalisme sauvage aux Etats-Unis 1860–1900*, Paris: Editions du Seuil.

Dinkin, R. (1977), *Voting in Provincial Elections*, Westport, Ct.: Greenwood Press.

Dodd, W. (1911), "The Fight for the Northwest, 1860." *American Historical Review* XVI (July).

Dorf, P. (1952), *The Builder, Ezra Cornell*, New York: Macmillan.

Downs, A. (1957a), *An Economic Theory of Democracy*, New York: Harper.

Downs, A. (1957b), "An Economic Theory of Political Action in a Democracy." *Journal of Political Economy* LXV, No. 1.

Draughton, R. (1966), "George Smith Houston and Southern Unity, 1846–1849." *Alabama Review* (July).

DuBoff, R. and Herman, E. (1980), "Alfred Chandler's New Business History: A Review." *Politics and Society* X, No. 1.

Edelstein, T. (1968), *Strange Enthusiasm: Thomas Wentworth Higginson*, New Haven, Ct.: Yale University Press.

Edwards, R. (1979), *Contested Terrain*, New York: Basic Books.

Eiteman, W. (1930), "The Rise and Decline of Orthodox Tariff Propaganda," *Quarterly Journal of Economics* 45 (November).

Erie, S. (1980), "Two Faces of Ethnic Power." *Polity* 13 (Winter).

Evans, J. (1981), "USA." In Lovenduski, J. and Hills, J. (eds.), *The Politics of the Second Electorate*, London: Routledge.

Ferguson, T. (1980), "Von Versailles zum New Deal." In *Amerika: Traum und Depression 1920/40*, Catalogue essay for the Neue Gesellschaft für Bildende Kunst Exhibit of American Art, Berlin and Hamburg, 1980.

Ferguson, T. (1983), "The System of '96: A Reconsideration," manuscript.

Ferguson, T. (1984), "From 'Normalcy' to New Deal: Industrial Structure, Party Competition, and American Public Policy in the Great Depression." *International Organization* (winter).

Ferguson, T. (1986), "Elites and Elections; Or What Have They Done to You Lately? Toward an Investment Theory of Political Parties." In Ginsberg, B. and Stone, A. (eds.), *Do Elections Matter?* (1st. ed.) pp. 164–188, Armonk, NY: Sharpe.

Ferguson, T. (n.d.), *Critical Realignment: The Fall of the House of Morgan and the Origins of the New Deal*, New York: Oxford University Press, forthcoming.

Ferguson, T. and Rogers, J. (1980), "Labor Law Reform and Its Enemies." In Green, M. and Massie, G. (eds.), *The Big Business Reader* (1st ed.), New York: Pilgrim Press.

Ferguson, T., and Rogers, J. (1981). "The Reagan Victory." In Ferguson, T. and Rogers, J. (eds.), *The Hidden Election*, New York: Pantheon.

Fiorina, M. (1977), *Congress: Keystone of the Washington Establishment*, New Haven, Ct.: Yale University Press.

Foner, P. (1941), *Business and Slavery*, Chapel Hill, N.C.: University of North Carolina Press.

Forbes, S. F. (1900), *Letters and Recollections of John Murray Forbes*, Boston and New York: Houghton Mifflin.

Formisano, R. (1981), "Federalists and Republicans: Parties, Yes—Systems, No." In Kleppner, P., *et al.*, (eds.), *The Evolution of American Electoral Systems*, Westport, Ct.: Greenwood Press.

Frescia, G. (1982), "Contradictions of the American Party System: An Explanation of Party Reorganization During the Nineteenth Century," Ph.D. Thesis, University of Massachusetts.

Frohlich, N., Oppenheimer, J., Young, O. (1971), *Political Leadership and Collective Goals*, Princeton: Princeton University Press.

Fusfeld, D. (1980), *The Rise and Repression of Radical Labor U.S.A.*, Chicago: Charles H. Kerr.

Gattell, F. (1966), "Sober Second Thoughts on Van Buren, The Albany Regency, And the Wall Street Conspiracy." *Journal of American History* LIII (June).

Ginsberg, B. (1982), *The Consequences of Consent*, Reading, Mass.: Addison Wesley.

Goldstein, R. (1978), *Political Repression in Modern America*, New York: Schenkman.

Goodwyn, L. (1976), *Democratic Promise*, New York: Oxford University Press.

Gordon, D., Edwards, R., and Reich, M. (1982), *Segmented Work, Divided Workers*, New York: Cambridge University Press.

Goulden, J. (1971), *The Money Givers*, New York: Random House.

Gramsci, A. (1971), *Selections From the Prison Notebooks*, (eds.), Hoare, Q. and Smith, G., New York: International Publishers.

Griffin, J. (1939), *Strikes*, New York: Columbia University Press.

Haeger, J. (1981), *The Investment Frontier*, Albany, N.Y.: State University of New York.

Hammond, B. (1946), "Schlesinger's Age of Jackson." *Journal of Economic History* VI (May).

Hammond, B. (1957), *Banks and Politics in America*, Princeton, N.J.: Princeton University Press.

Harlow, R. (1935), "The Rise and Fall of the Kansas Aid Movement." *American Historical Review* XLI (October).

Herman E. (1981), *Corporate Control, Corporate Power*, New York: Cambridge University Press.

Johnson, P. (1979), *A Shopkeeper's Millenium*, Berkeley, Calif.: University of California Press.

Jones, G. S. (1970), "The Specificity of U.S. Imperialism." *New Left Review* 60 (March-April).

Josephson, M. (1963), *The Politicos*, New York: Harcourt.

Kalt, J. (1981), *The Economics and Politics of Oil Price Regulation*, Cambridge, Mass.: M.I.T. Press.

Kelley, S., and Mirer, T. (1974), "The Simple Act of Voting." *American Political Science Review* LXVIII (June).

Key, V. (1959), "Secular Realignment and the Party System." *Journal of Politics* 21 (May).

Kindleberger, C. (1977), "U.S. Foreign Economic Policy, 1776–1976." *Foreign Affairs* (Jan.).

Kolko, G. (1963), *The Triumph of Conservatism*, New York: Quadrangle.

Kolko, G. (1965), *Railroads and Regulation*, Princeton, N.J.: Princeton University Press.

Kotz, D. (1979), "Bank Control of Large Corporations in the United States," Ph.D. Thesis, University of California, Berkeley.

Kousser, J. (1980), "History QUASSHED, Quantitative Social Scientific History in Perspective." *American Behavorial Scientist* XXIII (July/August).

Kuznets, S., Miller, A., and Easterlin, R. (1960), *Population Redistribution and Economic Growth*, Vol. II, *Analyses of Economic Change*, Philadalphia, Pa.: American Philosophical Society.

La Feber, W. (1972), "Foreign Policies of a New Nation." In F. W. A. Williams (ed.), *From Colony to Empire*, New York: Wiley.

LaFeber, W. (1993), *Inevitable Revolutions: The United States in Central America*, New York: Norton.

Lebergott, S. (1972), "The American Labor Force." In Davis, *et al.* (eds.), *American Economic Growth*, New York: Harper.

Lee, S. and Passell, P. (1979), *A New Economic View of American History*, New York: Norton.

Lichtman, A. (1976), "Critical Election Theory and the Reality of American Presidential Politics, 1916–40." *American Historical Review* 81 (April).

Lichtman, A. (1980), *Prejudice and the Old Politics*, Chapel Hill, N.C.: University of North Carolina Press.

Lichtman, A. (1982), "Critical Elections in Historical Perspective." California Institute of Technology Social Science Working Paper #420.

Lindblom, C. (1977), *Politics and Markets,* New York: Basic Books.

Lows Railroad Directory (1858), New York: Wynkoop, Hallenbeck & Thomas.

Lundberg, F. (1937), *America's 60 Families,* New York: Vanguard.

Main, J. (1961), *The Anti-Federalists,* Chapel Hill, N.C.: University of North Carolina Press.

McCormick, R. (1960), "New Perspectives on Jacksonian Politics," *American Historical Review,* LXV (January).

Mills, C. (1894), "The Relief of the Unemployed in the United States During the Winter of 1893–94." *Journal of Social Science* XXXII (November).

Montgomery, D. (1979), *Workers Control in America,* New York: Cambridge University Press.

Mowry, G. (1946), *Theodore Roosevelt and the Progressive Movement,* Madison, Wisc.: University of Wisconsin Press.

Nugent, W. (1967), *The Money Question During Reconstruction,* New York: Norton.

O'Connor, T. (1968), *Lords of the Loom,* New York: Scribners.

Offe, C., and Wiesenthal, H. (1980), "Two Logics of Collective Action: Theoretical Notes on Social Class and Organizational Form." *Political Power and Social Theory,* Vol. 1.

Olson, M. (1971), *The Logic of Collective Action,* Cambridge: Harvard University Press.

Overacker, L. (1932). *Money In Elections,* New York: Macmillan.

Peterson, F. (1935), "Unemployment Relief." In Commons, J. (ed.), *History of Labor in the United States,* Vol. III, New York: Macmillan.

Pincus, J. (1977), *Pressure Groups and Politics in Antebellum Tariffs,* New York: Columbia University Press.

Pittman, R. (1977), "Market Structure and Campaign Contributions." *Public Choice* 32 (Fall).

Polakoff, K. (1981), *Political Parties in American History,* New York: Wiley.

Popkin, S., Gorman, J., Phillips, C., and Smith, J. (1976), "Comment: What Have You Done for Me Lately? Toward an Investment Theory of Voting." *American Political Science Review* 68 (Sept.).

Potter, D. (1976), *The Impending Crisis 1848–61,* New York: Harper.

Preyer, N. (1959), "Southern Support of the Tariff of 1816: A Reappraisal." *Journal of Southern History* (August).

National Cyclopedia of American Biography, Various vols.

Ratner, R. (1980), "The Social Meaning of Industrialization in the United States." *Social Problems* 27 (April).

Ratner, S. (1967), *Taxation and American Democracy,* New York: Wiley.

Reid, S. (1976), *The New Industrial Order,* New York, McGraw Hill.

Remini, R. (1967), *Andrew Jackson And The Bank War,* New York, Norton.

Rezeck, S. (1933), "The Depression of 1819–22, A Social History." *American Historical Review* 39 (October).

Rezeck, S. (1942), "The Influence of Depression upon American Opinion." *Economic History* II (May).

Robertson, R., and Walton, G. (1979), *History of the American Economy,* New York: Harcourt.

Robinson, J. (1971), *Economic Heresies,* New York: Basic Books.

Roemer, J. (1978), "Neoclassicism, Marxism, and Collective Action." *Journal of Economic Issues* 12 (March).

Roy, W. (1981), "From Electoral to Bureaucratic Politics." *Political Power and Social Theory,* Vol. 2, Greenwich, Ct.: JAI Press.

Rusk, J. (1970), "The Effect of the Australian Ballot Reform on Split Ticket Voting: 1876–1908." *American Political Science Review* 64 (December).

Rusk, J. (1974), "Comment: The American Political Universe: Speculation and Evidence." *American Political Science Review* 68 (September).

Russel, D. (1972), "The Major Political Issues of the Jacksonian Period and the Development of Party Loyalty in Congress, 1830–1840." *Transactions of the American Philosophical Society,* LXII (May).

Russel, R. (1948), *Improvement of Communication with the Pacific Coast as an Issue in American Politics,* Cedar Rapids, Mich.: Torch Press.

Schirmer, D. (1972), *Republic or Empire,* Cambridge: Schenkman.

Schlesinger, A., Jr. (1945), *The Age of Jackson,* Boston: Little, Brown.

Schwartz, M. (1976), *Radical Protest and Social Structure,* New York: Academic Press.

Shade, W. (1981), "Political Pluralism and Party Development." In Kleppner, P. *et alia* (eds.), *The Evolution of American Electoral Systems,* Westport, Ct.: Greenwood Press.

Shefter, M. (1976), "The Emergence of the Political Machine." In Hawley, W. and Lipsky, M. (eds.), *Theoretical Perspectives on Urban Politics,* Englewood Cliffs: Prentice Hall.

Shefter, M. (1978), "Party, Bureaucracy, and Political Change in the United States." In Maisel, L. and Cooper, J. (eds.), *Political Parties,* Beverly Hills: Sage.

Sherrill, R. (1981), "The Nylon Curtain Affair: The Book That DuPont Hated." *The Nation,* Feb. 14, 1981.

Singleton, G. (1975), "Fundamentalism and Urbanization." In Schore, L. (ed.), *The New Urban History,* Princeton, N.J.: Princeton University Press.

Sobel, R. (1977), *The Fallen Colossus,* New York: Weybright and Talley.

Sorin, G. (1970), *The New York Abolitionists,* Westport, Conn: Greenwood Press.

Stokes, D. (1966), "Spatial Models of Party Competition." In Campbell, A., Converse, P., Miller, W., and Stokes, D. (eds.), *Elections and the Political Order,* New York.

Stover, J. (1975), *History of the Illinois Central Railroad,* New York: Macmillan.

Sumner, H. (1936), "Citizenship." In Commons, J., *et al.* (eds.), *History of Labor in the United States,* New York: Macmillan.

Sunderland, E. (1955), *Abraham Lincoln and the Illinois Central Railroad,* New York: Privately Printed.

Taussig, F. (1964), *The Tariff History of the United States,* New York: Capricorn Books.

Thayer, G. (1973), *Who Shakes the Money Tree,* New York: Simon and Schuster.

Trimble, W. (1919), "Diverging Tendencies in the New York Democracy in the Period of the Locofocos." *American Historical Review* 24 (April).

United States Railway Directory, 1856, New York: Homans.

Useem, M. (1980), "Which Business Leaders Help Govern?" *Insurgent Sociologist,* IX (Winter).

Van Alstyne, R. (1972), "The American Empire Makes Its Bow on the World Stage, 1803–1845." In Williams, W. A. (ed.), *From Colony to Empire,* New York: Wiley.

Walsh, V. (1970), *Introduction to Contemporary Microeconomics,* New York: McGraw-Hill.

Weinstein, J. (1968), *The Corporate Ideal in the Liberal State,* Boston: Beacon Press.

Welter, R. (1960), "The Frontier West as an Image of American Society." *Mississippi Valley Historical Review* (March).

Wiebe, R. (1962), *Businessmen and Reform,* Chicago: Quadrangle.

Williamson, J. (1981), "Economics and Politics: Voting Behavior in Kansas." *Explorations in Economic History* (July).

Williamson, J., and Lindert, P. (1980), *American Inequality,* New York: Academic Press.

Yarwood, D. (1967), "Legislative Persistence." *Midwest Journal of Political Science* (May).

Yearly, C. (1970), *The Money Machines,* Albany, N.Y.: State University of New York.

Zeitlin, M., and Norwich, S. (1979), "Management Control, Exploitation, and Profit Maximization in the Large Corporations." *Research in Political Economy,* Vol. 2, Greenwich, Ct: JAI Press.

Zilg, G. (1976), *DuPont,* Englewood Cliffs, N.J.: Prentice-Hall.

PART TWO

Studies in the Logic of Money-Driven Political Systems

CHAPTER TWO

From 'Normalcy' to New Deal:
Industrial Structure, Party Competition, and American Public Policy in the Great Depression

IN OCTOBER 1929, only weeks after Yale economist (and investment trust director) Irving Fisher publicly announced that "stock prices have reached what looks like a permanently high plateau," and virtually on the day that J. P. Morgan & Co. partner Thomas W. Lamont reassured President Herbert Hoover that "there is nothing in the present situation to suggest that the normal economic forces . . . are not still operative and adequate," the New York Stock Exchange crashed.[1] Over the next few months the market continued dropping and a general economic decline took hold.[2] As sales plummeted, industry after industry laid off workers and cut wages. Farm and commodity prices tumbled, outpacing price declines in other parts of the economy. A tidal wave of bankruptcies engulfed businessmen, farmers, and a middle class that had only recently awakened to the joys of installment buying.[3]

While the major media, leading politicians, and important businessmen resonantly reaffirmed capitalism's inherently self-correcting tendency, havoc spread around the world. By 1932, the situation had become desperate. Many currencies were floating and international finance had virtually collapsed. In part because of the catastrophic fall in income and in part from mushrooming tendencies toward consciously pursued policies of trade restriction, world trade had shrunk to a fraction of its previous level. In many countries one-fifth or more of the workforce was idle. Homeless, often starving, people camped out in parks and fields, while only the virtual collapse of real-estate markets in many districts checked a mammoth liquidation of homes and farms by banks and insurance companies.[4] As a new *spiritus diaboli*, Fascism, joined the old specter, Communism, to haunt Europe and the world, conflicts multiplied both within and between nation states.

In this desperate situation, with regimes changing and governments falling, a miracle seemed to occur in the United States, the country that, among all the major powers in the capitalist world economy, had perhaps been hit hardest. Taking office at the moment of the greatest financial collapse of the nation's history, President Franklin D. Roosevelt initiated a dazzling burst of government actions designed to square the circle that was baffling governments elsewhere: how to enact major social reforms while preserving both democracy and capitalism. In a hundred days his administration implemented a series of emergency relief bills for the unemployed; an Agricultural Adjustment Act for farmers; a bill (the Glass-Steagall Act, also sometimes referred to as the Banking Act of 1933) to "reform" the banking structure; a Securities Act to reform the stock exchange; and the National Industrial Recovery Act, which in effect legalized cartels in American industry.[5] Roosevelt suspended the convertibility of the dollar into gold, abandoned the gold standard, and enacted legislation to promote American exports. He also presided over a noisy public investigation of the most famous banking house in the world: J. P. Morgan & Co.

For a while this "first New Deal" package of policies brought some relief, but sustained recovery failed to arrive and class conflict intensified. Two years later, Roosevelt scored an even more dramatic series of triumphs that consolidated his position as the guardian of all the millions, both people and fortunes. A second period of whirlwind legislative activity in 1935 produced the most important social legislation in American history—the Social Security and Wagner acts—as well as measures to break up public-utility holding companies and to fix the price of oil. The president also turned dramatically away from his earlier economic nationalism. He entered into agreements with Britain and France informally to stabilize the dollar against their currencies and began vigorously to implement earlier legislation that empowered Secretary of State Cordell Hull to negotiate a series of treaties reducing U.S. tariff rates.[6]

After winning one of the most bitterly contested elections in American history by a landslide (and giving the coup de grace to the old Republican-dominated System of 1896), Roosevelt consolidated the position of the Democrats as the new majority party of the United States. He passed additional social welfare legislation and pressured the Supreme Court to accept his reforms. Faced with another steep downturn in 1937, the Roosevelt team confirmed its new economic course. Rejecting proposals to revive the National Recovery Administration (NRA) and again devalue the dollar, it adopted an experimental program of conscious "pump priming," which used government spending to prop up the economy in a way that foreshadowed the Keynesian policies of demand management widely adopted by Western economies after 1945. This was the first time this had ever been attempted—

unless one accepts the Swedish example, which was virtually contemporaneous.[7]

Roosevelt and his successive New Deals have exercised a magnetic attraction on subsequent political analysts. Reams of commentary have sought to elucidate what the New Deal was and why it evolved as it did. But while the debate has raged for over forty years, little consensus exists about how best to explain what happened.

Many analysts, including most of those whose major works shaped the American social sciences and historiography of the last generation, have always been convinced that the decisive factor in the shaping of the New Deal was Franklin D. Roosevelt himself.[8] They hail his sagacity in fashioning his epoch-making domestic reforms. They honor his statecraft in leading the United States away from isolationism and toward Atlantic alliance. And they celebrate the charisma he displayed in recruiting millions of previously marginal workers, blacks, and intellectuals into his great crusade to limit permanently the power of business in American life.

Several rival accounts now compete with this interpretation. As some radical historians pose the problem, only Roosevelt and a handful of advisers were farsighted enough to grasp what was required to save capitalism from itself.[9] Accordingly, Roosevelt engineered sweeping attacks on big business for the sake of big business's own long-run best interest. (A variation on this theme credits the administration's aspirations toward reform but points to the structural constraints capitalism imposes on any government as the explanation for the New Deal's conservative outcome.)

Another recent point of view explains the New Deal by pointing to the consolidation and expansion of bureaucratic institutions. It deemphasizes Roosevelt as a personality, along with the period's exciting mass politics. Instead, historians like Ellis Hawley single out as the hallmarks of the New Deal the role of professionally certified experts and the advance of organization and hierarchical control.[10]

Some of these arguments occasionally come close to the final current of contemporary New Deal interpretation. This focuses sharply on concrete interactions between polity and economy (rather than bureaucracy per se) in defining the outcome of the New Deal. Notable here are the (mostly German) theorists of "organized capitalism," several different versions of Marxist analysis, right-wing libertarian analysts who treat the New Deal as an attempt by big business to institutionalize the corporate state, and Gabriel Kolko's theory of "political capitalism."[11]

These newer approaches provide telling criticisms of traditional analyses of the New Deal. At the same time, however, they often create fresh difficulties. "Organized capitalism," "political capitalism," or the libertarian "corporate state" analyses, for example, are illuminating with respect to the universal price-fixing schemes of the NRA. But the half-life of the NRA was short even by the admittedly unstable standards of American politics. The historic turn toward free trade that was so spectacularly a part of the later New Deal is scarcely compatible with claims that the New Deal institutionalized the collective power of big business as a whole, and it is perhaps unsurprising that most of this literature hurries over foreign economic policy. Nor are more than token efforts usually made to explain in detail why the New Deal arrived in its classic post-1935 form only after moving through stages that often seemed to caricature the celebrated observation that history proceeds not along straight lines but in spirals. It was, after all, a period in which the future patron saint of American internationalism not only raised more tariffs than he lowered but also openly mocked exchange-rate stability and the gold standard, promoted cartelization, and endorsed inflation.[12] Similarly, theorists who treat the New Deal chiefly as the bureaucratic design of credentialed administrators and professionals not only ignore the significance of this belated opening to international trade in the world economy, but they also do less than full justice to the dramatic business mobilization and epic class conflicts of the period.

Nor do any of these accounts provide a credible analysis of the Democratic Party of the era. Then, as now, the Democratic Party fits badly into the boxes provided by conventional political science. On the one hand, it is perfectly obvious that a tie to at least part of organized labor provides an important element of the party's identity. But, on the other, it is equally manifest that no amount of cooptation accounts for the party's continuing collateral affiliation with such prominent businessmen as, for example, Averell Harriman. Why, if the Democrats truly constituted a mass labor party, was the outcome of the New Deal not more congruent with the traditional labor party politics of Great Britain and Germany? And, if the Democrats were not a labor party, then what force inside it was powerful enough to contain the Congress of Industrial Organizations (CIO) and simultaneously launch a sweeping attack on major industrial interests?[13] These analyses also slip past the biggest puzzle that the New Deal poses. They offer few clues as to why some countries with militant labor movements and charismatic political leaders in the Depression needed a "New Order" instead of a New Deal to control their workforce.

Nor has theory, especially economic theory, figured significantly in most of these studies. The centrality of issues like the money supply, international finance, and macroeconomic policy has failed to come into focus. Important theoretical discussions (like debates over Federal Reserve policy during the period) echo only faintly, or not at all, in more general writing, while neoclassically inclined economists have thus far ignored all aspects of the New Deal that create difficulties for their particular theoretical viewpoint.[14]

In this chapter I contend that a clear view of the New Deal's world historical uniqueness and significance comes only when one breaks with most of the commentaries of the last thirty years, goes back to primary sources, and attempts to analyze the New Deal as a whole in the light of explicit theories about industrial structure, party competition, and public policy. Then what stands out is the novel type of *political coalition* that Roosevelt built. At the center of this coalition, however, are not the workers, blacks, and poor who have preoccupied liberal commentators, but something else: a new "historical bloc" (in Gramsci's phrase) of capital-intensive industries, investment banks, and internationally oriented commercial banks.

This bloc constitutes the basis of the New Deal's great and, in world history, utterly unique achievement: its ability to accommodate millions of mobilized workers amidst world depression. Because capital-intensive firms use relatively less direct human labor (and that often professionalized and elaborately trained), they were less threatened by labor turbulence. They had the space and the resources to envelop, rather than confront, their workforce. In addition, with the momentous exception of the chemical industry, these capital-intensive firms were world as well as domestic leaders in their industries. Consequently, they stood to gain from global free trade. They could, and did, ally with important international financiers, whose own miniscule workforce presented few sources of tension and who had for over a decade supported a more broadly international foreign policy and the lowering of traditionally high American tariffs.

In the first part of this chapter I develop a formal theory of industrial partisan preference as the joint consequence of class conflict and the differential impact of the world economy on particular businesses. I also relate the theory to the V. O. Key–Walter Dean Burnham–(Michigan) Survey Research Center (SRC) discussions of party systems and critical realignments, arguing that transformations of elite industrial coalitions lie behind the phenomena voting analysts have for so long tried to analyze. This section also presents an explicit account of the dynamics of the transition from the System of 1896 to the New Deal.

In the second part I outline the major elements of the coalition that triumphantly came together during and after Roosevelt's Second New Deal—the coalition that, in its successive mutations, dominated American politics until Jimmy Carter. Employing the first part's theoretical framework, I sketch the systematic, patterned disintegration of the System of '96 and the simultaneous emergence of another New Deal bloc, whose interests and ideology shaped what can conveniently be termed "multinational liberalism."

1. Party Competition and Industrial Structure

My principle argument divides conveniently into two subordinate parts. The first, what might be called the "static theory of industrial partisan preference," builds on recent work by James Kurth, Peter Gourevitch, and Douglas Hibbs, among others.[15] Introducing first the "labor constraint" and then issues in international political economy, I present an abstract, basic model of partisan choice by particular industries and firms exhibiting differential sensitivity to class conflict and foreign economic policy issues. Following two earlier articles, I show how the policy—and hence, partisan—choices of these firms define the durable party systems extensively discussed by analysts of mass voting behavior.[16] I also demonstrate a method for the measurement and graphical analysis of these political coalitions.

The second spells out the dynamic implications of the static model. It investigates how major changes in the level of national income (i.e., long booms or major depressions) affect party systems and political coalitions. Major spurts of economic growth and protracted economic decline, runs the argument, destabilize political coalitions in quite specific, predictable ways. By tracing how steadily rising or falling income affects a given industrial structure, one glimpses the logic by which earlier coalitions, built around increasingly obsolescent combinations of trade and labor, decay, while new coalitions arise. One also comes to understand how booms and depressions characteristically generate brief but intense conflicts over certain issues, notably money and finance, which can enormously complicate transitions from one party system to another. By examining in detail how such forces affect the basic model of the System of '96's partisan cleavages, I provide an account of the dynamics of the New Deal—one that explains not only the long-run evolution of the System of '96 into the New Deal but also the complex sequence of apparently contradictory policy changes through which the New Deal evolved before it assumed its classic Second New Deal form.

The Static Theory

The basic argument connecting industrial structure to political parties and public policy is uncomplicated. It follows from two widely acknowledged facts. The first can be summarized as the ubiquitous and enduring presence of social class conflicts within the electoral systems of virtually all countries permitting at least moderately free elections and modestly competitive political parties. As one careful quantitative study of the cross-national evidence recently observed, "Although the importance of socioeconomic status as a basis of electoral cleavage varies substantially across party systems, the mass constituencies of political parties in most advanced industrial societies are distinguished to a significant extent by class, income, and related socioeconomic characteristics."[17] The second merely highlights the policy consequences of the first: the actual influence of labor and the working classes on public policy varies substantially over time, both within and across countries.[18]

Thus, as a long and distinguished tradition of social theory emphasizes and evidence from some, but not all, countries suggests, it might well be the case that labor's ability to dominate a political party—and, when that party is in power, government policy—is such as to threaten gravely the institution of private business itself or at least to strike deeply at the prerogatives and earnings of all employers. In these instances, other things being equal, the whole business community will rush into opposition and establish one or more political parties of its own.

But if labor's social position is weak, if it cannot organize its own political party, what happens? Most social scientists and historians recognize that in such circumstances labor enters into a coalition, appearing as one among several interest groups within a party or government. Most do this implicitly, in the course of narratives or analyses that record the historical facts. A few substantially improve upon this practice and try deliberately to spell out what the artless language of modern game theory often refers to as the "payoffs" to each partner in particular political coalitions in various countries at different times.[19]

Viewed in the light of industrial structure, however, a more general logic to political coalitions involving labor becomes plain. For what is at stake in these coalitions is the exact "price" that businesses seeking to coalesce to advance their own ends must "pay" to obtain support from the workforce. If one could specify in detail which firms or industries could most easily afford this price, one would have developed a predictive model of party competition. Such a perspective might cast light on the strange character of the Democratic Party in the United States and, perhaps, some of the tamer social democratic parties in postwar Europe.

Such an assessment of abilities to "afford the price" is not beyond the reach of current interpretative capability. Two polar cases make the essential points transparent. Consider the hypothetical case of a business that employed absolutely no labor, one that relied entirely on robots. Such an enterprise would have an exceedingly remote interest in most of the issues historically disputed between business and labor.[20] Other things being equal, it could quite easily afford to support what looked to the unaided and untheoretical eye like a "labor" party, or at least practice consistent bipartisanship. By contrast, industries that rely on masses of un- or semiskilled labor, for whom national labor issues are highly salient, would enjoy far less freedom of maneuver. Unlike the fully automated firm, they could not afford higher social insurance, could not pay higher wages, could not accept a union. Where the workforce was already organized, they could not resist the pressure to attempt to undermine it. And a legislated minimum wage would usually constitute a direct threat to them. In Europe, such firms would most likely bulwark a conservative party; in America, they would have no alternative but to become rockribbed Republicans.

Of course, some level of class conflict always exists beyond which all industries retreat to a single business party (a case more common in Europe than in the United States). But short of that point, different industries featuring differential sensitivities to what can be termed the "labor constraint" can seize the opportunity to govern through the votes of their laborers.

The rule of "minimal accounts of labor" obviously needs to be modified in many cases.[21] But, as the allusion to robot-run factories suggests, in general a business that relies less on workers than it does on, for example, capital should properly be considered less "labor-sensitive" than one that does the reverse. Accordingly, industry statistics for variables like "wages as a percent of value added" provide rough quantitative estimates of an industry's ability to afford a coalition with labor and make it quite easy to order industries and firms along this dimension.

The firms *least* likely to undertake such an effort (and thus *most* likely to support the "business party") are, obviously, low-wage labor-intensive firms like those commonly found in the textile industry. Thereafter, using 1929 estimates from the *Census of Manufacturers* of wages as a percentage of value added, we can identify:

textiles (cotton goods)	52 percent
steel and iron	47
boots and shoes	44
automobiles	41
copper	38
meat packing	37

rubber (tires and inner tubes)	37 percent
agricultural implements	36
electrical machinery	34
chemicals	23
oil (petroleum refining)	22
tobacco (chewing and smoking)	8

Then come two industries—commercial banking and investment banking—whose labor costs measured in this manner are almost irrelevant, since their costs are overwhelmingly the costs of borrowed money (paid to depositors or whomever); and, finally, real estate (local only).[22]

Combining an industry's "labor sensitivity" with the known facts of class conflict yields a simple, comparative static model of industrial structure and party competition, which can summarized visually (see figure 2.1). On the horizontal axis runs a continuous variable representing a proxy (which can be as complex as the analyst desires) for the degree of class conflict, or its equivalent, the balance of power between labor and capital actually struck in terms of public policy over some stretch of time.[23] On the vertical axis is an estimate of an indus-

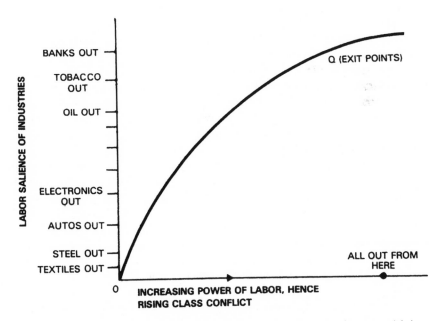

FIGURE 2.1. The Labor Constraint: Industries Vary Widely in Their Sensitivity to Labor

try's sensitivity to the labor constraint (as derived from the above listing). In a simple model, where taxes or international issues do not
induce complications, this establishes the value of a probability function Q, the "exit point" at which labor's ability to define public policy
in its interest makes it useless for the industry to extend any support
to the "labor" party.[24] At successively higher levels of class conflict
(equivalent to a move out along the horizontal axis), more and more
industries drop out of the labor party, until at length none are left and
the system passes from an American "pluralist" type to a classic, highly
polarized "European" party system.

Formidable problems naturally stand in the way of attempts to
apply a scheme such as this to any event as complex as the New Deal.
For example, empirically ascertaining which parties or policies a firm
or an industry is supporting at a particular point can be very labori-
ous.[25] It is also clear that some industries can afford to extend at least
some support to both parties (though both logic and history suggest
that this support will not be offered equally). But already some clearly
testable propositions can be generated that have obvious relevance to
the New Deal. For example, one would not expect that a relatively
labor-intensive economy, dominated by textiles, steel, and shoes,
would find it easy to accommodate mass movements for unionization.
By contrast, if it turned out that in the decade immediately preceding
the New Deal the characteristic modern American form of capital-
intensive enterprise, the giant integrated, multinational petroleum
company, ascended to the pinnacle of the American industrial structure, an important clue to the historical uniqueness of the New Deal
has probably been located. Similar reasoning might explain why other
countries, like Germany, seemed able to transplant the New Deal in
the 1950s but not in the 1930s, or why deradicalized labor parties in
Europe were often able to cooperate more closely with big business
after World War II than before it.

But if characterizing parties—and, by extension, party systems—
according to their labor sensitivity illuminates the politics of advanced
capitalist countries, it is by itself obviously not enough. Class conflict,
after all, scarcely exhausts the sources of political turbulence. Accordingly, the single-dimension, simple class-conflict model needs to be
supplemented if it is to have much predictive value. In principle, the
number of complicating supplementary issues could be infinite, dashing all hopes for parsimonious explanation and making analyses impossibly difficult.

During most of the period that concerns me here, comparatively
few issues that were not broadly labor-related were potent enough to
stir major, persisting conflicts within the generally laissez-faire Ameri-

can political system.[26] Accordingly, while references to other dimensions are sometimes necessary for detailed discussion of particular cases and are required for an analysis of the actual transition from the System of '96 to the New Deal, the most general (or "normal") case needs but a single extra dimension—one that summarizes the competitive positions of various firms and industries within the world economy. Thus I divide firms into "internationalists," whose strong position vis-à-vis international competitors leads them to champion an open world economy with minimal government interventions that would hinder the "free" market–determined flow of goods and capital; and "nationalists," whose weakness in the face of foreign rivals drives them to embrace high tariffs, quotas, and other forms of government intervention to protect themselves (see figure 2.2).[27] Combining this line of cleavage with the class-conflict dimension yields an analysis in which each firm or industry as a whole can be located at two coordinates: one summarizes the characteristics of its production process with respect to the workforce; the other, its situation in the world economy.

A party system as a whole can now be characterized in these terms. If most elements of the industrial structure cluster tightly together in one or another "quadrant" of figure 2.3, political conflict within the system is likely to be muted.[28] Assuming that the workforce can be contained, the conditions are satisfied for the stable hegemony of a

PETROLEUM (POST-RED LINE NEGOTIATIONS)	COPPER (PRE-DEPRESSION)			PETROLEUM (PRE-RED LINE NEGOTIATIONS)
ELECTRICAL MACHINERY	PAPER			STEEL
FARM IMPLEMENTS	TOBACCO			SHOES
PACKING (?)	ALL OTHER AUTO COMPANIES			RUBBER
FORD				CHEMICALS
				TEXTILES
				COPPER (POST-DEPRESSION)
INCREASING INTERNATIONALISM			INCREASING NATIONALISM	

FIGURE 2.2. International Competitive Status of Selected U.S. Firms and Industries in 1929 and 1935

Source: Based on M. Wilkins, The Maturing of Multinational Enterprise (Cambridge: Harvard University Press, 1974), and sources cited in note 27.

Notes: In several cases notable intra-industry differences are not reflected here, especially in petroleum. There is no significance to the distance between categories, only to the ordering.

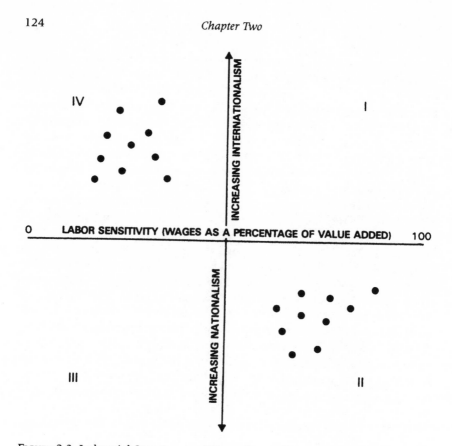

FIGURE 2.3. Industrial Structure and Party Competition: A Stylized Two-Party Case

particular historical bloc. In sharp contrast, should class conflict and the world economy combine to scatter large firms and major industries among all the quadrants, the party system would be incoherent. Similarly, figure 2.3's sharp division between two diagonally opposed quadrants yields a rather stable, fairly well-balanced, two-party system in which the less labor-intensive bloc, by allying with labor, might well achieve hegemony.

From the Statics of Party Competition to the Dynamics of Party Systems

The account of partisan choice and party systems presented here is static in the sense that it applies to actions and events at a single moment in time. Yet, as the earlier allusion to the rise of the major oil companies during the Roaring Twenties suggests, the static theory can be extended to cover dynamic issues. It thereby renders possible a fresh explanation of the oft-debated and still not entirely resolved puzzles surrounding the timing and sequence of the major New Deal policy initiatives.

Perhaps the most convenient way to begin is to refer again to figure 2.3. Instead of the diagonally opposing clusters of firms it shows, however, imagine the figure's space as representing the American political system around 1900. In that case, nearly all the dots will cluster tightly in quadrant 2, indicating the power bloc defined by the almost monolithically Republican business community of that period, whose component firms were nearly all strongly protectionist and labor-intensive.[29]

If the figure were drawn a quarter-century later it would exhibit substantial differences. In the interval, major cumulative changes in industrial structure have occurred. World War I and the boom of the 1920s have spurred the mechanization of production. Large, science-based corporations have become far more prominent. The war has also transformed the United States from a net debtor to a net creditor in the world economy. Textiles have withered away in the Northeast, meat packing and steel have declined relative to oil, and so forth. Virtually all these developments affect the distribution of firms in regard to labor and trade policy, and thus, to some degree, transform the party system. In terms of the graphical analysis many dots have begun to migrate. New ones—representing firms in developing industries—have suddenly appeared in new places while some old dots, marking marginal firms in dying industries, have disappeared.

In the United States after World War I, the analysis implies, a new bloc of big, capital-intensive firms that increasingly dominate the world market for their products is beginning to grow in quadrant 4, diagonally opposite the old System of '96 bloc. It is obvious that such a party system is headed for trouble, with or without a major depression. As firms increasingly move into the other quadrant, the old bloc will clearly come under strain. As it disintegrates and the new bloc, which will dominate the next party system, is born, policy fights and transaction costs associated with public policy-making will rise. Political stalemates are likely to increase and the sense of a vacuum forming will probably spread, as traditional political alliances evaporate and surprising new ones emerge.

The exact form the transition from one party system to another will take, however, depends critically on the level of national income. National income is important for two different reasons. First, over time it exercises what might be termed "direct effects" on the location of business firms on the two "primary" dimensions of labor and international economic policy. Second, and much less obviously, major fluctuations in the trend of national income roil the transition to a new party system by temporarily forcing certain characteristic kinds of new issues to the fore, issues that supplement or even momentarily replace labor and international economic policy as pivots for the system.[30] The nature of these "secondary" tensions ("secondary" in contrast to the "primary" issues of labor and trade, not in the sense of having lesser importance) is perhaps best spelled out by tracing how they combine with the "direct effects" of changes in national income to define two distinct, idealized models of the transition path from one party system to another.

Transition via Prolonged Boom. In the first transition path, national income sustains a high rate of growth for a substantial period of time. The prolonged boom consequently exerts powerful "direct effects" on the party system's primary defining axes of labor and trade by rapidly transforming productive techniques and the operation of firms. In the boom of the 1920s, for example, some firms and sectors experienced high rates of technical change and mechanization, and consequently changed their position on labor policy. With the major exception of the chemical industry, which still lagged behind the Germans, they commonly changed position on international economic policy as well. New leading sectors also appeared, of course, while some older industries slowly disappeared.

If growth were sustained, successive scattergraphs of the party system would show a continuous, gradual migration of more and more firms or sectors from one quadrant to the other as the new bloc gained strength and the older one declined. Parallel to these shifts, political histories would probably chronicle a widening sense of dislocation, followed by increasingly intense polarization and, at last, the emergence of a distinctly new ruling bloc. But for all the conflict such an account might record, moments of high drama would be few and far between. As a whole the process would be protracted and, in principle, straightforward. Marked by an absence of complicating issues and identifiable turning points, this sort of change would by itself pose comparatively few puzzles for political analysis.

Even a transition of this kind, however, would probably be complicated by at least two sorts of "secondary" tensions generated by the process of growth itself. A sustained boom, for example, is highly likely to bring about the rise of new firms and sectors. If older business elites do not succeed in entering these fast-growing sectors, whole new groups of entrepreneurs will emerge. While most major battles between what are commonly advertised as "new" and "old" elites turn out to involve clashes between different sectors on primary issues of labor and trade policy (and thus call for no special interpretative apparatus), the rise of new entrepreneurs can in itself generate a certain degree of tension. Or, as has often happened in American history, a major boom scrambles existing financial markets. As financial innovations proliferate to meet historically unprecedented demands for finance from whole new regions, sectors, and firms, competition heats up. Older market shares become unbalanced, and pressures build for regulatory change. While such "secondary" cleavages normally lack the permanence of the "primary" conflicts (since, after all, new elites eventually mature, and large-scale uncertainty resulting from long-term developmental pressure in the financial system typically results in "landmark" legislation that resolves whole ranges of issues), such conflicts confuse the transition to a new party system.

Transition via Economic Depression. The most dramatic complications of the transition from one party system to another, however, arise from the simple fact that the history of the American political economy is far from a chronicle of continuous growth and progress. Along with the booms and growth spurts that help build and destroy political coalitions come cyclical instability and, often, deep and protracted depressions. These catastrophic events define the second transition path.

The statistical record of depressions and party realignments demonstrates that even a very steep downturn will not by itself suffice to wreck an entrenched party system.[31] But if, as in 1837, 1857, 1893–94, and the 1930s, the party system is already decaying because of a previous boom, then a shattering depression is likely to generate a variety of new pressures that will further complicate the transition to a new party system.

Several distinct sorts of pressure are likely to emerge. First of all, the "direct effects" of deep depressions are frequently very dramatic. While a depression, unless it persists for many years, will not greatly affect the labor intensity of an economy's production processes (though, of course, speedups and spreading anxieties about unemployment can deeply color work relations, particularly in labor-intensive sectors), it will certainly produce abrupt changes in different firms' preferred international economic policies. When an American depression coincides with a world economic collapse, for example, many American industrialists are drastically affected by the strategies their foreign competitors adopt. If the volume of world trade shrinks, and export drives proliferate as domestic demand collapses, economic nationalism is certain to grow within the business community. If the depression persists, even many previously successful "internationalists" will be forced to change colors. In terms of the scattergraphs of the System of

'96, this implies a swift and substantial reshuffling of positions along the nationalist-internationalist axis—in a direction that in the short run dramatically reverses long-term trends working in favor of an open economy.

The collapse of political blocs favoring internationalism is, however, only one (direct) effect of prolonged drops in the level of national income. Such periods also typically lead to a whole series of uniquely "pathological" (in the sense of non-normal and transitory) secondary tensions. Sustained economic decline, for example, normally intensifies economic rivalries, leading to waves of bankruptcies and defensive mergers. Appearing on the scattergraphs as abrupt disappearances and sudden relocations of dots, these, if sufficiently numerous, can redraw the shape of the whole party system almost overnight. Even if no general merger wave occurs, the positions of the largest firms in the system often change dramatically as the strongest surviving business groups attempt to capitalize on their positions and take control of other, momentarily undervalued, assets.

A prolonged depression is also likely to trigger two further sorts of "secondary" conflicts (or, perhaps more precisely, sets of secondary conflicts), which, when they suddenly burst forth, are likely to mystify observers used to thinking in terms of categories derived from the preceding boom.

The first of these additional tensions can be readily identified: it is a dramatic rise in the importance of the money supply as a political issue. Whereas during most boom periods money is fairly readily available at a reasonable real cost—and thus as a political issue is unlikely for most businesses to bulk as large as labor and international economic policy—persisting economic declines will eventually generate powerful movements for lower interest rates and an increase in the money supply. This process, of course, takes time to start. In the early stages of a depression, for example, most firms react by cutting production, laying off workers, and, in the less oligopolistic parts of the economy, cutting prices. But while firms may briefly welcome reductions in the level of economic activity—because they cool off demands for wage increases and make the labor force more tractable—no one is likely to remain enthusiastic if the downturn persists and cuts deeply into profits. Nevertheless, for a while the bulk of the business community, or at least those in it not facing immediate bankruptcy, put up with the deflationary adjustment process, since generations of academic economists have persuaded most of them that deflation is the path to revitalization.

In all modern economies, however, it has eventually become clear that deflation does not always restore the conditions for profitable accumulation at a price most of the business community can afford. As this lesson dawns, and losses mount even among the rich, firms and sectors begin to divide over measures for reflation—either an increase in the money supply, which, of course, carries with it the prospect of abandoning the gold standard or other international mechanisms regulating the volume of money in circulation; or higher government expenditures, which almost irresistibly expand the money supply as the government deficit is financed; or both. On one (deflationary) side are firms that want above all to preserve the value of financial assets, to retain foreign deposits (which they will lose as the currency devaluation consequent upon the abandonment of gold takes hold), and, perhaps, to protect what they believe to be the long-run best interests of the international financial system. Chief among the proponents of deflation are big international banks, insurance companies, and bond holders. Opposed to them is nearly everyone else for whom the overriding priorities increasingly become the maintenance of any degree of purchasing power, escape from increasingly heavy fixed charges, devaluation to shore up fading international competitiveness, or some combination thereof. This latter camp includes many prominent industrialists and retailers, as well as farmers and ordinary people.

While many accounts of deflationary periods stress the misery they have brought to farmers, an industrial sector analysis of this transition's pathology highlights the role of certain types of industries, namely those with large amounts of fixed capital. Because their capital is fixed, these firms take enormous losses as the depression persists and they have to run far below capacity for long periods. Many will have borrowed heavily in the preceding boom to finance expansion and thus feel pressure from financiers; but even where debt service is light, the opportunity costs of underutilized fixed capital still remain enormous. Firms enjoying very strong oligopolistic positions may be able to cope by keeping prices up; many others that are heavily dependent on bank financing may not dare to protest the deflation. These two exceptions notwithstanding, the logic of the demand for reflation yields an unambiguous prediction of which industries will lead the "emergency reflation" coalition "for national economic recovery": giant, capital-intensive industries whose prices are breaking and that are relatively independent of banks (large oil companies in the Depression, for example).

Once the forces of national recovery begin to march (and since by that moment most of them have become ardent economic nationalists and many are also labor-intensive, they do indeed march), a final kind of secondary conflict is likely to break out within the financial sector.

It is, of course, quite possible—and it certainly was the case in the

1930s—that segments of the banking community may already be at
one another's throats for various "secondary" reasons mentioned earlier: because rising entrepreneurs challenge older elites who happen
to be bankers; because of competitive pressures derived from secular
changes in the financial structure, changes that the previous boom
brought about; or because powerful financial groups come into conflict
as they try to aggrandize their own relatively strong positions as everyone else's asset values are collapsing.

As economic disaster continues unabated and pressures mount for
"national recovery," however, fragmentation within the financial community is for several reasons likely to increase enormously. First, the
spiraling collapse of the international economy increasingly calls into
question older political alliances premised on a growing national income (and volume of trade). At length even some financiers will begin
to break ranks. Obviously, defectors are most likely to come first and
in the greatest numbers from among investment bankers with the
smallest stakes (though their stakes may still be substantial by comparison with other sectors') in the business of international banking and
commercial bankers with the strongest ties to those parts of domestic
industry which are up in arms over reflation—for example, the oil
industry. Once this fragmentation gets under way it is likely to pick up
momentum as it becomes enmeshed in debates over financial reform
stimulated either by the previous boom or by the increasingly urgent
monetary debates of the economic crisis.[32]

Together with the direct effects of falling national income, these
accumulating secondary tensions will immensely complicate the conflicts over labor and trade generated by the preceding boom. What during the period of prosperity (the first transition path) had seemed so
clear—the rapid growth of a powerful bloc of internationally oriented,
capital-intensive firms with their own distinct interests in more liberal
trade and labor policies—now appears hopelessly confused. The development of the internationalist bloc first slows, then ceases altogether.
As income continues to fall, history almost appears to be running backward. Economic nationalism spreads like wildfire. As older alliances
premised on a growing international economy break down, "secondary" tensions and pathologies characteristic of depressions get full play
and further scramble previous alignments. At length, even big banks
begin openly to attack one another and investment banking is riven
by dissent. A "national recovery" coalition comes to power as the internationalists scatter.

In the short run, the strange new package of public policies that
holds this coalition together appears only tangentially related to the
primary tensions that had dominated the system for so many years.

For, given a sufficiently deep contraction of the international economy, this transition coalition inevitably takes a strongly nationalist form, thus flying in the face of previously dominant trends that favored increasing international integration. But this impression is an illusion; it derives entirely from the special circumstances of the colossal decline in national income. As soon as recovery starts and other transition issues (such as monetary and banking reform) begin to be resolved, the old lines of cleavage over primary issues reappear. The national recovery coalition blows apart over labor and foreign economic policy, and the long-run trends evident in the preceding boom reassert themselves.

In the latter part of this article I trace how a distinct multinational bloc first emerged in the United States after World War I. Gaining coherence during the boom of the 1920s, it virtually fell apart in the early 1930s, until national income began very slowly to rise again, during FDR's "Second New Deal." It was only then that a fresh party system, crowned by a new historical bloc, could emerge.

2. High Cards in the New Deal

I begin with a brief analysis of the System of '96 as it looked in its pre-World War I "stable phase."[33] After identifying the institutional basis of the period's well-known Republican hegemony in the relative unity of most industry and major finance, I turn to the system's crisis at the end of World War I. By tracing how the dislocated world economy combined with existing social tensions to divide a business community that until then had been solidly Republican, it becomes clear how the older hegemonic bloc of the System of '96 began breaking into two— one part intensely nationalist, protectionist, and (with a few notable exceptions) generally labor-intensive; the other oriented to capital-intensive production processes and free trade.

A newer multinational bloc rose to power during the New Deal. In accord with my earlier discussion of variations in national income and the two distinct paths of transitions between party systems, I distinguish three stages in the new bloc's ascent. The first includes the period immediately following World War I and the great boom of the 1920s. In this interval of generally rising national income (the first transition path), the leading firms of the emergent multinational bloc began to articulate their interests on labor and trade separately from the rest of the business community. Along with several secondary cleavages that the boom generated and a feature peculiar to American society in the 1920s (Prohibition, discussed below), the efforts this bloc made to alter American policy toward labor and the rest of the world created considerable turbulence in American politics. By the 1928 election, the accumulating tensions had "dealigned" the existing structure of U.S. politics.

The second stage of the new bloc's rise to power occurs after the great crash of 1929 and major events associated with it, including the East Texas oil field discoveries and the British abandonment of the gold standard. In this interval, the political coalition that had dominated the United States for a generation collapsed completely, setting off a scramble for power. However, as I will show, the wreck of the System of '96 amid frightful deflation (the second transition path) did not immediately bring the multinational bloc to power. Instead, with the collapse of the international economy, Hoover's determination to remain on the gold standard at all costs sharply divided the business community, including the multinational bloc.

Out of these tensions, by sequential stages, came the American political world we now know: first, a gradual massing of nationalist and inflationist business groups (and farmers); second, the rapid emergence of increasingly bitter divisions within the financial community as heretofore "secondary" disputes over the control and future shape of the financial system escalated, and older alliances based on a growing economy lost their *raison d'être;* third, the temporary coalescence during the First New Deal of the nationalists and inflationists with a famous group of financiers who sought to challenge the preeminence of the House of Morgan; and, finally, as soon as decline was arrested and the long-run logic of the first transition path could assert itself, a slowly improving economy that began spawning epic class and trade conflicts, leading to the triumphant reemergence of the multinational bloc during the Second New Deal.

A Boom and a Bloc: The First Transition Path, 1918–1929

At the center of the Republican Party under the System of '96 was a massive bloc of major industries, including steel, textiles, coal, and, less monolithically, shoes, whose labor-intensive production processes automatically made them deadly enemies of labor and paladins of laissez-faire social policy.[34] While a few firms whose products dominated world markets, such as machinery firms, agitated for modest trade liberalization (aided occasionally by other industries seeking specific export advantages through trade treaties with particular countries), insistent pressures from foreign competitors led most to the ardent promotion of high tariffs.[35]

Integral to this "national capitalist" bloc for most of the period were investment and commercial bankers. These had abandoned the

Democrats in the 1890s when Free Silver and Populist advocates briefly captured the party. The financiers' massive investments in the mid-1890s and after, in huge trusts that combined many smaller firms, gave them a large, often controlling, stake in American industry, brought them much closer to the industrialists (especially on tariffs, which Gold Democrats had abominated), and laid the foundation for a far more durable attachment to the GOP.[36] Most financiers also shared the industrialists' enthusiasm for aggressive foreign policies directed at the other great powers, especially in Latin America, though they were sometimes less willing to challenge the British, whose capital (in many senses) remained the center of world finance.

World War I disrupted these cozy relations between American industry and finance. Overnight the United States went from a net debtor to a net creditor in the world economy, while the tremendous economic expansion induced by the war destabilized both the U.S. and the world economy.[37] Briefly advantaged by the burgeoning demand for labor, American workers struck in record numbers and for a short interval appeared likely to unionize extensively.[38] Not surprisingly, as soon as the war ended a deep crisis gripped American society. In the face of mounting strikes, the question of U.S. adherence to the League of Nations, and a wave of racial, religious, and ethnic conflicts, the American business community sharply divided.

On the central questions of labor and foreign economic policy, most firms in the Republican bloc were driven by the logic of the postwar economy to intensify their commitment to the formula of 1896. The worldwide expansion of industrial capacity the war had induced left them face to face with vigorous foreign competitors. Consequently, they became even more ardent economic nationalists. Meeting British, French, and later German and other foreign competitors everywhere, even in the U.S. home market, they wanted ever higher tariffs and further indirect government assistance for their export drives. Their relatively labor-intensive production processes also required the violent suppression of the great strike wave that capped the boom of 1919–20 and encouraged them to press the "open shop" drive that left organized labor reeling for the rest of the decade.

However, this response was not universal in the business community. The new political economy of the postwar world pressured a relative handful of the largest and most powerful firms in the opposite direction. The capital-intensive firms that had grown disproportionately during the war were under far less pressure from their labor force. The biggest of them had by the end of the war also developed into not only American but world leaders in their product lines. Accordingly, while none of them were pro-union they preferred to conciliate rather than to repress their workforce. Those that were world leaders favored lower tariffs, both to stimulate world commerce and to open up other countries to them. They also supported American assistance to rebuild Europe, which for many of them, such as Standard Oil of New Jersey and General Electric, represented an important market.

Joining these latter industrial interests were the international banks. Probably nothing that occurred in the United States between 1896 and the Depression was so fundamentally destructive to the System of '96 as the World War I-induced transformation of the United States from a net debtor to a net creditor in the world economy. The overhang of both public and private debts that the war left in its wake struck directly at the accommodation of industry and finance that defined the Republican Party. To revive economically and to pay off the debts, European countries had to run export surpluses. They needed to sell around the world, and they, or at least someone they traded with in a multilateral trading system, urgently needed to earn dollars by selling into the United States. Along with private or governmental assistance from the United States to help make up war losses, accordingly, the Europeans required a portal through the tariff walls that shielded Republican manufacturers from international competition. (Following the procedures described earlier, Figure 2.4 estimates as closely as possible the shape of both blocs. They are defined—somewhat arbitrarily—to include the top thirty firms [ranked according to assets], the big banks, and cotton textiles, by far the largest American industry characterized by small firms.)[39]

The conflict between these two groups runs through all the major foreign policy disputes of the 1920s: the League of Nations, the World Court, the great battles over tariffs, and the Dawes and Young plans. Initially, the older, protectionist forces won far more than they lost. They defeated the Leagues, kept the United States out of the World Court, and raised the tariff to ionospheric levels. But most trends in the world economy were against them. Throughout the 1920s the ranks of the largely Eastern internationalist bloc swelled.[40]

Parallel to the multinational bloc's increasing numbers was its growing unity of interest. In 1922, the British opened negotiations to admit Standard Oil interests into Iraq. A milestone in the integration of the world economy, this step and related developments also removed a major obstacle to concrete forms of cooperation among the internationalists.[41] Indeed, it had been a split between big oil and big banks over the specific terms of the peace treaty that was pivotal in defeating the League of Nations. The original American champions of the League, as Massachusetts Senator Henry Cabot Lodge's correspondence reveals he was vividly aware, were international financiers lo-

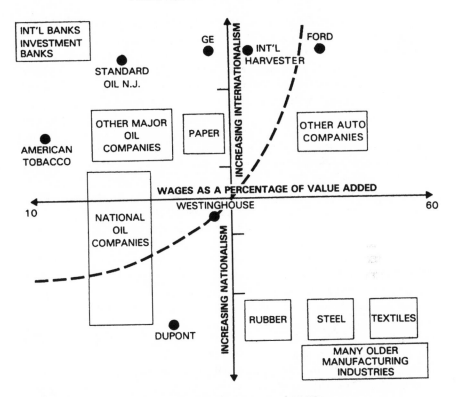

FIGURE 2.4. The New Deal Coalition, ca. 1929 and 1935

Notes: Vertical axis is ordinal, as in fig. 2.2. Companies and industries located left and above the dashed line were far more likely to favor the New Deal; the line thus encloses the leaders of the capital-intensive free trade bloc in the 1920s and 1930s. Between the late 1920s and the mid-1930s the copper industry changed position. In the 1920s it belongs near "other auto companies"; in the 1930s, near "steel." See note 27.

cated mostly in port cities; free-trading merchants like Edward A. and A. Lincoln Filene; and the relative handful of American industrialists who favored either low tariffs (e.g., Phelps Dodge's Cleveland Dodge, a major supporter and close friend of Woodrow Wilson) or direct foreign investment. By contrast, the League terrified most American manufacturers who feared, as the American Tariff League expressed it, that "the League of Nations is simply a rally ground for free traders and all who are opposed to the doctrine of 'adequate protection' for the industries and labor of the United States."[42]

Led by groups like the American Tariff League, the Boston Home Market Club (a long-time political base of Lodge's, "the Senator from Textiles"), and the League for the Preservation of American Independence—dominated by upstate New York industrialist Stuyvesant Fish and Louis A. Coolidge, a close friend of Lodge's and treasurer of the giant Boston-based United Shoe Machinery (which was probably seeking to protect its clientele among U.S. shoe producers)—these "Irreconcilables" launched a powerful counterattack.[43] Their success came only because of a fatal split among the internationalists. At the climax of the struggle over the League of Nations, the Standard Oil companies, which had already come out for tariff reform, were locked in a bitter struggle with the British over control of Middle Eastern and Latin American oil reserves. Because of the advantages the League was thought to afford British interests, Rockefeller, Standard Oil policy adviser and Rockefeller family associate Charles Evans Hughes, and other dedicated internationalists allied with petroleum producers were able to endorse the League only "with reservations."[44] Their opposition, added to that of Lodge's "Irreconcilables" and many other protectionist spokesmen, helped doom Wilson's original plan. Warren Harding's subsequent plan to resubmit a compromise measure, endorsed in principle by all the internationalists, was shelved after it was bitterly attacked by the nationalists; and after the multinational bloc discovered it could achieve its immediate foreign-policy objectives by working unofficially around Congress with key executive-branch functionaries and New York Federal Reserve Bank officials.[45]

Along with its increasing internal homogeneity, the multinational bloc enjoyed several other long-run advantages, which helped enormously in overcoming the new bloc's relative numerical insignificance vis-à-vis its older rival. The multinational bloc included many of the largest, most rapidly growing corporations in the economy. Recognized industry leaders with the most sophisticated managements, they embodied the norms of professionalism and scientific advance that in this period fired the imagination of large parts of American society.[46] The largest of them also dominated major American foundations, which were coming to exercise major influence not only on the climate of opinion but on the specific content of American public policy.[47] And, while I cannot pause to justify the claims in this article, what might be termed the "multinational liberalism" of the internationalists was also aided significantly by the spread of liberal Protestantism; by a newspaper stratification that brought *the* free-trade organ of international finance, the *New York Times*, to the top; by the growth of capital-intensive network radio in the dominant Eastern, internationally oriented environment; and by the rise of major news magazines. These last promised, as Raymond Moley himself intoned while taking over what became *Newsweek*, to provide "Averell [Harriman] and Vincent

[Astor] . . . with a means for influencing public opinion generally outside of both parties."[48]

Closely paralleling the business community's differences over foreign policy was its split over labor policy. Analysts have correctly stressed that the 1920s were a period of violent hostility toward labor unions. But they have largely failed to notice the significant, sectorally specific modulation in the tactics and strategy employed by American business to deal with the labor movement.

The war-induced boom of 1918–19 cleared labor markets and led to a brief but sharp rise in strikes and the power of labor. A White House conference called by Wilson to discuss the situation ended in stalemate. John D. Rockefeller Jr. and representatives of General Electric urged conciliatory programs of "employee representation" (company-dominated, plant-specific works councils). Steel and other relatively labor-intensive industries, however, rejected the approach. Led by Elbert Gary, head of U.S. Steel, they joined forces, crushed the great steel strike of 1919, and organized the American-plan drives of the 1920s.[49]

Rockefeller and Gary broke personal relations. Rockefeller supported an attack on the steel companies by the Inter-Church World Movement, an organization of liberal Protestants for which he raised funds and served as a director. Later he organized a consulting firm, Industrial Relations Counsellors, to promote nonconfrontational "scientific" approaches to labor conflict. For a while the firm operated out of his attorney's office, but eventually it acquired space of its own. It continued to receive grants from the Rockefeller Foundation and to involve Rockefeller personally.[50]

Industrial Relations Counsellors assisted an unheralded group of capital-intensive firms and banks throughout the 1920s—a group whose key members included top management figures of General Electric, Standard Oil of New Jersey, and partners of the House of Morgan. Calling themselves the "Special Conference Committee," this group promoted various programs of advanced industrial relations.[51]

Industrial Relations Counsellors worked with the leading figures of at least one group of medium-sized firms. Perhaps ironically, they were organized in the Taylor Society, once the home of Frederick Taylor's well-known project for reorganizing the labor process. Two types of firms comprised this group: technically advanced enterprises in highly cyclical (hence, in the 1930s, highly depressed) industries like machine tools, and medium-sized "best practice" firms in declining sectors. Mostly located in the Northeast, these latter firms hoped that the introduction of the latest management and labor relations techniques

would afford them cost advantages over burgeoning low-wage competitors in the South. A sort of flying buttress to the core of the multinational bloc, most of these firms strongly favored freer trade, while
several future New Dealers, including Rexford Tugwell and Felix
Frankfurter, worked with them.[52]

The leading figures in Industrial Relations Counsellors and their
associates (who included, notably, Beardsley Ruml, head of the Spelman Fund, a part of the Rockefeller complex that began funding the
first university-based industrial relations research centers) played important roles in virtually all major developments in labor policy across
the 1920s. These included the campaign that forced the steel industry
to accept the eight-hour day (which Herbert Hoover led in public); the
milestone Railway Labor Act; and the increasing criticism of the use of
injunctions in labor disputes (a legal weapon that was an essential element of the System of '96's labor policy) that eventually led to the
Norris-La Guardia Act.[53]

Under all these accumulating tensions the elite core of the Republican Party began to disintegrate. The great boom of the 1920s exacerbated all the primary tensions over labor and international relations
just described, while it greatly enhanced the position of the major oil
companies and other capital-intensive firms in the economy as a whole
(see table 2.1). Though their greatest effects came after the downturn
in 1929, secondary tensions also multiplied during the boom. One,
which affected partisan competition even in the 1920s, concerned investment banking. A flock of new (or suddenly growing) houses
sprang up and began to compete for dominance with the established
leaders: the House of Morgan and Kuhn, Loeb. In time these firms
would produce a generation of famous Democrats: James Forrestal of
Dillon, Read; Averell Harriman of Brown Brothers Harriman; Sidney
Weinberg of Goldman, Sachs; John Milton Hancock and Herbert Lehman of Lehman Brothers. Because many (though not all) of these
bankers were Jewish, the competition with Morgan almost immediately assumed an ugly tone. J. P. Morgan Jr. quietly encouraged Henry
Ford's circulation of the notorious *Protocols of the Elders of Zion* in the
early 1920s, and later his bank forbade Morgan-Harjes, the firm's Paris
partner, to honor letters of credit from Manufacturers Trust, a commercial bank with strong ties to Goldman, Sachs, and Lehman Brothers.[54]

In commercial banking, rivals also began to contest Morgan's position. The Bank of America rose rapidly to become one of the largest
commercial banks in the world. Though the competition did not yet
take partisan form, the bank bitterly opposed Morgan interests, which
attempted to use the New York Federal Reserve Bank against it. Mor-

TABLE 2.1 Largest American Industrials, 1909–1948 (Ranked by Assets)

Company	1909	1919	1929	1935	1948
U.S. Steel	1	1	1	2	3
Standard Oil of New Jersey	2	2	2	1	1
American Tobacco	3	19			17
International Mercantile Marine	4	12			
Anaconda	5	14	8	8	19
International Harvester	6	13	17	14	18
Central Leather	7				
Pullman	8				
Armour	9	3	14	20	
American Sugar	10				
U.S. Rubber	11	8			
American Smelting & Refining	12	17			
Singer	13				
Swift	14	4	19	19	
Consolidation Coal	15				
General Electric	16	11	11	13	9
ACF Industries	17				
Colorado Fuel & Iron	18				
Corn Products Refining	19				
New England Navigation	20				
General Motors		5	3	3	2
Bethlehem Steel		6	5	7	12
Ford		7	6	6	10
Socony Mobil		9	7	4	5
Midvale Steel		10			
Sinclair Oil		15	16	16	15
Texaco		16	9	11	6
DuPont		18	12	9	7
Union Carbide		20			14
Standard Oil of Indiana			4	5	4
Standard Oil of California			10	10	11
Shell			13	15	
Gulf			15	12	8
General Theater Equipment			18		
Kennecott Copper			20	18	
Koppers				17	
Sears Roebuck					13
Westinghouse					16
Western Electric					20

Source: A.D.H. Kaplan, *Big Enterprise in a Competitive Setting* (Washington, D.C.: Brookings, 1962), pp. 140 ff.

gan also was hostile to Joseph Kennedy and other rising financial powers.[55]

The cumulative impact of all these pressures became evident in the election of 1928. Some of the investment bankers, notably Harriman, turned to the Democrats. Enraged by the House of Morgan's use of the New York Fed to control American interest rates for the sake of its international objectives, Chicago bankers, led by First National's Melvin Traylor, organized and went to the Democratic convention as a massed body.[56]

Most sensationally of all, elements of the arch-nationalist, previously rockribbed Republican chemical industry went over to the Democrats. A more vivid illustration of how primary and secondary tensions generated by the boom were dealigning traditional elite alliances could scarcely be found. For more than a generation, the chemical industry had been solidly Republican. Industry spokesmen and publications never ceased observing that only the GOP tariff walls stood between them and ruin at the hands of foreign, especially German, competitors.[57] Before 1928 it would have been unthinkable for DuPont or some Union Carbide executives openly to support a national Democrat.

Behind this dramatic reversal is a political evolution that has three main parts. The special situation of the DuPont family in relation to other great fortunes in American society of that period constitutes the point of departure. Such statistics as are available indicate that the bulk of the truly colossal fortunes in America were made prior to World War I. (Not that a great amount of money has not been made since, but few newer fortunes have been generated to match those of Rockefeller, Morgan, or Henry Ford.)[58] The rise of the DuPonts, however, began with their profits from World War I explosives sales and continued with their investment in General Motors.[59] By comparison with most of the American superrich in the 1920s, the DuPonts' ratio of wealth to income was considerably below average. Consequently, while all the rich were strongly in favor of reduced taxes, which had risen as a consequence of the war, the DuPonts had a bigger incentive than most.[60]

Their spectacular success in the 1920s rendered the situation even more urgent. Not only did their General Motors investments and the DuPont corporation grow, but so did their position in United States Rubber and other large companies. By about 1925 Pierre DuPont had decided that reduced income taxes would require finding another source of revenue for the government. Consequently he, his brothers Irénée and Lammot, and several close associates, including John J. Raskob, took over the Association Against the Prohibition Amendment

(AAPA). They campaigned throughout the country, opening contacts with hundreds of newspapers, aiming to encourage a repeal of national Prohibition and then to levy taxes on liquor. At the start, the campaign was bipartisan: "As our average tax collections for the years 1923–26 from individuals and corporations were $1,817,000,000 resulting in a considerable surplus, it is fair to say that the British liquor policy applied in the United States [i.e. the legalization of liquor] would permit the total abolition of the Income Tax both personal and corporate. Or this liquor tax would be sufficient to pay off the entire debt of the United States, interest and principal, in a little less than fifteen years."[61]

The enormous departure this program represented from previous norms of the American upper class merits some attention. For over a century prohibition had been a cause not only of rural drys but, more importantly, of major manufacturers.[62] Large fortunes like the Rockefellers', together with some big retailers like J. C. Penney, had been lavish contributors to the Anti-Saloon League and other proponents of liquor restrictions.[63] Their opposition to liquor was rationalized on religious grounds, although it was certainly also rooted in their desire to control unruly lower-class behavior.[64] DuPont, however, represented the cutting edge of science-based industry, the most powerful secularizing force in history.

But the DuPont interests had more concrete objectives than witnessing the cultural transformation of modern capitalism. Friction was increasing between this newly ascendent group and other large American fortunes—in particular with the House of Morgan, which had a strong, though minority, position in General Motors. After several unpleasant encounters, including a dispute over how much DuPont enterprises should pay for Morgan financing, the DuPonts made a bid for a share of Morgan's own U.S. Steel. After DuPont began a massive purchase of U.S. Steel stock, the Federal Trade Commission began an investigation (on a few hours' notice), forcing DuPont to back off.[65]

Meriting separate mention as a cause of the "dealignment" of the party structure was an aspect of the rivalry with Morgan that related directly to the great foreign economic policy dispute that marked the 1920s but has so far been virtually unappreciated: American attempts to aid the reconstruction of Germany. American officials had seized German patents in the chemical and other industries during the war. Though the peace agreement (the United States, of course, did not ratify the Versailles Treaty) with Germany acknowledged the U.S. right to the patents, a Homeric struggle quickly broke out over what was to be done with them. Internationalists wanted to return at least some of them so that the Germans could build up an export capacity and pay off war debts. The chemical industry wanted to keep them.[66]

At first, the chemical industry prevailed. The Chemical Foundation was established to hold and license the patents. DuPont held about one-third of the stock, and the rest was held by other concerns. The foundation became the battleground for internationalist and protectionist forces. German chemical company agents worked with American bankers and government officials, including senators and President Harding himself, to get the patents back. To keep track of these efforts, the Chemical Foundation's able head, Francis P. Garvan, engaged private detectives. The surviving reports from these men, who were probably former Federal Bureau of Investigation (FBI) agents, can be partially verified from other sources and vividly testify to the tensions that quickly developed.[67]

The banks and their allies could not overcome protectionist opposition. Former Attorney General Harry Daugherty was indicted for taking a bribe to help return German assets.[68] J. Edgar Hoover, a close political ally of Chemical Foundation attorney A. Mitchell Palmer and Garvan, was appointed, and removed suspected German agents from the FBI. And the government lost the suit it brought to force the Chemical Foundation to return the patents—in Wilmington, Delaware.

Continuing strains on the world economy intensified the pressure to aid Germany and heightened the antagonism between DuPont and the multinationals. Allen Dulles and other high officials in the U.S. Department of State attempted to stop American munitions exports that competed with the Germans; meanwhile, the Chemical Foundation was actively encouraging French resistance to Allied plans to put Germany back on its feet.[69] As American bankers helped organize huge loans to the Germans and looked on while most of the German chemical industry consolidated into one gigantic combine—I. G. Farben—tensions mounted.[70]

Although the DuPont Co. had repeatedly explored (and would continue to explore, without much success) possibilities for coming separately to terms with the Germans, Pierre's brother Irénée, the president of the company, hand-delivered a stiff note protesting American loans for potential German competitors to Secretary of Commerce Herbert Hoover.[71] The Chemical Foundation and other industry leaders joined in the campaign, but their efforts drew strong opposition. When the newly established Institute of Economics in Washington, D. C., prepared a skeptical report about foreign loans, the banks intervened and threatened its grants. Shortly thereafter the institute merged with another organization (creating the modern Brookings Institution).

I learned yesterday, confidentially but reliably, that the continued existence of the Institute of Economics in Washington . . . is threatened. The Institute lives off a yearly grant of $150,000.00 which the Carnegie Corporation of New York awarded for ten years. In the next few days the Carnegie Corporation will decide whether this grant will be paid beyond 1932. In the heart of the Corporation strong opposition has risen. The leader of the opposition is [Russell] Leffingwell, a member of the Morgan firm, who has for a long time been angry at the publications of the Institute, especially the books over Germany and France, because they depict the economic situation of these lands skeptically, and therefore influence the prospects for the bringing of the loans to these lands on the American market. It is clear that Leffingwell as a banker doesn't like such books. Also, [Garrard] Winston from the Treasury Department who in previous years had been friendly to the Institute is said in the most recent days to have turned and labeled the publications of the Institute "simple propaganda."

Whether under these circumstances the plan of the Institute to write a new book on Germany and [the] Dawes plan can be carried out, or whether [Harold] Moulton [the Institute's head], who now fears the anger of the bankers, can find the courage to publish such a book is questionable.[72]

As the presidential election of 1928 loomed, all sides organized. The DuPont Co., for example, bought more than two dozen memberships for its top officials in the American Protective Tariff League, which had until then been declining.[73] The Chemical Foundation repeatedly sought to dissuade financiers from making additional foreign loans.

In early 1928 these conflicts came to a head. Anxious to secure support from leaders of the internationalist bloc, Secretary of Commerce Hoover sent emissaries to Thomas Lamont at the House of Morgan. While not as rousing as it might have been, Lamont's response suggested that he and other internationalists might be open to persuasion:

The ground swell for Hoover seems to be rolling up. Within the last two weeks, Hoover sent first Norman Davis [a close associate of Lamont's and formerly Woodrow Wilson's undersecretary of state], then Julius Barnes to me, complaining that our partners—he mentioned you as a former one, and Tom Cochran—had been working against him and for Dawes [who later dropped out]. Barnes wanted to know what our real attitude was. I told him that there was no attitude as attaching to the firm in the whole matter. Each member of the firm, Republican or Democrat, as the case might be, had his own particular preferences. I said that we had always felt very friendly here toward

Hoover. . . . I said that if Hoover were the nominee of the Republican Party we should all expect to support him loyally. With this Barnes expressed himself as very well satisfied and said that what he feared was that even if Hoover were the nominee the prejudice of some members here against him was so great as to lead them to work against him. I reassured him on that point.[74]

A tense and complex process of accommodation now began between Hoover and most of the multinational bloc. First, Wall Street lawyer John Foster Dulles, Lamont's old associate at the Versailles Conference and (because he was widely recognized as the leading American expert on Germany) already deeply involved in the advance planning for what eventually became the "Young Plan" revision of the older Dawes Agreement, crossed party lines—Dulles had backed Democratic candidate John W. Davis in 1924—and jumped aboard Hoover's bandwagon.[75] Warning German newspaper correspondents about the sensitivity of German reconstruction questions, Dulles quickly emerged as an important Hoover adviser. As Dulles joined his campaign, Hoover called a conference attended by representatives of most of the major American chemical companies, in part to discuss American policy toward I. G. Farben. Then he left town while a top operative in his preconvention campaign, Assistant Attorney General William ("Wild Bill") Donovan, addressed the group. Basing his decision in part on material supplied by I. G. Farben (through the German embassy), Donovan announced that the I. G.'s practices did not violate American antitrust laws.[76]

Almost simultaneously, long-running negotiations to divide parts of the world market for various products between DuPont, I G. Farben, Britain's ICI, Allied, and other big chemical companies stalled. So did other talks aimed at wider agreements between DuPont, I. G. Farben, and ICI. Standard Oil of New Jersey formed its notorious "cartel" with I. G. and, together with the National City Bank and others, began preparing to establish American-I. G. Farben.[77]

As secretary of commerce, Hoover had acquired an immense reputation as the champion of American domestic industry. Right up to convention time, accordingly, important internationalists persisted in discreet attempts to renominate Coolidge. But as it became clear that the president could not be persuaded to run for what was generally reckoned to be a third term, more and more of them moved toward Hoover. After Democratic candidate Al Smith rejected an internationalist foreign-policy plank drawn up by an attorney for J. D. Rockefeller Jr. and Hoover declined to accept a platform plank, proposed by top executives of many chemical concerns and the Chemical Foundation, that condemned American capital exports to foreign competitors, the trend in favor of Hoover sharply accelerated.

With Hoover taking the side of the internationalists and receiving support from almost all the major figures of multinational liberalism, DuPont bolted. After a row on the General Motors board (where the House of Morgan, the Fishers, and other interests were aghast) John J. Raskob, an official of both General Motors and DuPont and a longtime associate of Pierre DuPont, assumed leadership of Al Smith's campaign. This created a sensation. But with Smith running for president against Prohibition on the only high-tariff platform in the history of the Democratic Party, the Democrats divided. Some Southerners deserted the party. Meanwhile, in New York, Franklin D. Roosevelt ran a gubernatorial campaign that clearly established distance between himself and Smith.

Though Smith's loss left a vacuum inside the Democratic Party, the strength of his urban support suggested that the next nomination could be worth a great deal. Raskob and DuPont moved to secure their control by establishing the modern form of the Democratic National Committee.[78] They pumped thousands of dollars into the party, for the first time giving it the means to hire permanent staff between campaigns. They also waged a vigorous propaganda war against Hoover.

The Path to Catastrophe: Falling Income and "National Recovery"

The onset of the Great Depression opened a new phase in the decay of the now creaking System of '96. As the Depression grew worse, demands for government action proliferated. But Hoover, who gradually became so in thrall to the big banks that he concealed Morgan's crucial role in initiating his famous European debt moratorium of June 1931 by deliberately faking entries in a "diary" that he left historians (one of whom years later cited it as evidence for the independence of Hoover, and the American state from the bankers), opposed deficit-financed expenditures and easy monetary policies.[79] After the British abandoned the gold standard in September 1931 and moved to establish a preferential trading bloc, the intransigence of Hoover and the financiers put the international economy onto a collision course with American domestic politics. Increasingly squeezed industrialists and farmers began clamoring for government help in the form of tariffs even higher than those in the recently passed Smoot-Hawley bill; they also called for legalized cartels and, ever more loudly, a devaluation of the dollar through a large increase in the money supply.

Concerned, as Federal Reserve minutes show, at the prospect that the business groups and farmers might coalesce with angry, bonus-marching veterans, and worried by French gold withdrawals and fears that not only farmers and workers, but leading bankers, might go bankrupt, the Fed briefly attempted to relieve the pressure by expansionary open-market operations. But after a few months, the policy was abandoned as foreigners withdrew more gold and bankers in Chicago and elsewhere complained that the drop in short-term interest rates was driving down interest rates on short-term government debt (and thus bank profits, which, given the scarcity of long-term debt and the disappearance of industrial loans in Federal Reserve districts outside of New York, now depended directly on these rates).[80]

Exactly as the earlier discussion of the effects of deflation on political coalitions suggested, Hoover's commitment to gold began driving inflationist, usually protectionist businessmen out of the GOP to the Democrats. Their swarming ranks (which, as will become evident below, came to include several major oil companies) triggered a virtual identity crisis among party regulars. As familiar rules of thumb about the growth of the world economy grew increasingly anachronistic, the mushrooming sentiment for monetary expansion and economic nationalism scrambled the calculations of the contenders for the Democratic nomination.

The developing situation called for the highest kind of political judgment from aspiring presidential candidates. At this point a legendary political operative came out of retirement to advise Franklin D. Roosevelt. Colonel Edward House had been a longtime adviser to Woodrow Wilson, normally an ardent champion of low tariffs and the League of Nations; but, perhaps most important for the First New Deal, he was now closely associated with Rockefeller interests.[81] Along with the more famous Brain Trust, which functioned largely as a transmission belt for the ideas of others, including, notably, investment bankers from Lehman Brothers, House helped chart Roosevelt's early path.[82] It was calculated to blur his image and make him acceptable to all factions of the party. Making overtures to William Randolph Hearst and other like-minded businessmen, Roosevelt repudiated his earlier strong support for the League of Nations, talked rather vaguely of raising tariffs, and began showing an interest in major revision of the antitrust laws.[83]

The tactics were successful. Roosevelt's supporters were able to defeat Smith and turn back an eleventh-hour effort led by Morgan, the National City Bank (which feared Roosevelt might abandon gold), and many public utilities (whose leader, Wendell Wilkie, helped organize a telegram blitz of the convention) to nominate Cleveland bank attorney Newton D. Baker.[84]

Coming into office at the very darkest moment of the Depression, with all the banks closed, Roosevelt moved immediately to restore business confidence and reform the wrecked banking structure. The real significance of this bank reform has been misperceived. With the world economy reeling, the shared interest in a liberal world economy that normally (i.e., when the economy was growing) bound powerful rivals together in one political coalition was disappearing. In this once-in-a-lifetime context, what had previously been secondary tensions between rival financial groups now suddenly came briefly, but centrally, to define the national political agenda. With workers, farmers, and many industrialists up in arms against finance in general and its most famous symbol, the House of Morgan, in particular, virtually all the major non-Morgan investment banks in America lined up behind Roosevelt. And, in perhaps the least appreciated aspect of the New Deal, so did the now Rockefeller-controlled Chase National Bank.

In the eighteen months previous to the election, relations between Rockefeller and Morgan interests had deteriorated drastically. After the crash of 1929, Equitable Trust, which Rockefeller had purchased and in the late 1920s sought to build up, had been forced to merge with the Morgan-oriented Chase National Bank. The merger caused trouble virtually from the beginning. Lamont and several other banking executives allied with Morgan attempted to block the ascent of Winthrop Aldrich, the brother-in-law of John D. Rockefeller Jr., to the presidency of the Chase. Their efforts, however, proved unsuccessful, and Aldrich quickly, if apparently rather tensely, assumed an important role in Chase's management. But when Rockefeller attempted to secure a loan for the construction of Rockefeller Center (which threatened [Pierre] DuPont and Raskob's Empire State Building, already under construction and unable to rent all its space with the collapse of real-estate values), the bank seems not to have gone along. The chief financing had to come instead from Metropolitan Life. An old dispute between two transit companies, one controlled by the Morgans and the other perhaps by the Rockefellers, also created problems.[85]

Though sniping from holdover employees continued for several years, operating control of Chase passed definitively out of Morgan hands in late 1932. With longtime Chase head Albert Wiggin retiring, Aldrich was announced as the next chairman of the bank's governing board, and plans were made to reorganize the board of directors.

In the meantime, East Texas oil discoveries dropped the price of oil to ten cents a barrel. It was a development that, among other things, ruined the cost calculations underlying the Standard-I. G. Farben schemes for massive synthetic oil production and removed that issue from the political agenda. But it also brought the entire oil industry to the brink of disaster. Becoming more interested in oil and domestic recovery, and less in banking, Rockefeller interests urged a substantial relief program on Hoover, who brusquely rejected it. Almost simultaneously top Rockefeller advisor Beardsley Ruml, then still at the helm of the Spelman Fund and a prominent Democrat, began promoting a complicated plan for agricultural adjustment. At Chicago the Roosevelt forces accepted some of its basic concepts, just ahead of the convention.[86]

Only a few days before the 1932 presidential election, Morgan discovered that high Chase officials were supporting Roosevelt.[87] House's daughter was married to Gordon Auchincloss, Aldrich's best friend and himself a member of the Chase board. During the campaign and transition period, House and Vincent Astor, Roosevelt's cousin and also a member of the reorganized Chase board, passed messages between Roosevelt and Chase.[88]

A few days after Roosevelt was inaugurated, Chase and the investment bankers started their campaign, both in public and in private, for a new banking law. Aldrich made a dramatic public plea for the complete separation of investment and commercial banking. Then he began personally to lobby Roosevelt and high administration officials: "I have had a very interesting and refreshing conversation with Mr. W. W. Aldrich. . . . I also suggest that you consider calling in, when convenient to you, Senators Glass and Bulkley and Mr. Aldrich to discuss the advisability and necessity for dealing not only with the divorcement of affiliates from commercial banks but the complete divorcement of functions between the issuance of securities by private banks over whom there is no supervision and the business of commercial banks. We feel that this suggestion should be incorporated in the Glass Banking Bill."[89]

Aldrich also joined the ancestral enemies of the banks—William Randolph Hearst, Samuel Untermeyer, South Dakota Senator Peter Norbeck, and others promoting Ferdinand Pecora's investigation of J. P. Morgan & Co. He cooperated fully with the investigation, promoted "reforms," and aided investigators examining the Wiggin era at Chase.

> Winthrop Aldrich, President of the Chase National Bank, got in touch with me yesterday through Gordon Auchincloss. I found Aldrich sympathetic to the last degree of what the President is trying to do, and I advised him to tell the Banking Committee the whole story. He is prepared to do this, and has gone to the country today to write his proposed testimony in the form of a memorandum, a copy of which he is to send me tomorrow morning. He intimated that if there was any part of it that I thought should be changed he would consider

doing so. . . . He tells me that his Board is back of him and some few of the leading bankers. However, most of them are critical and many are bitter because of what they term his not standing with his colleagues.[90]

These efforts came to fruition in the Glass-Steagall Act. By separating investment from commercial banking, this measure destroyed the unity of the two functions whose combination had been the basis of Morgan hegemony in American finance. It also opened the way to a financial structure crowned by a giant bank with special ties to a capital-intensive industry—oil.

With most of the (Morgan-dominated) banking community opposed to him, Roosevelt looked toward industry for allies. By now an uncountably large number of firms, for reasons discussed earlier, were actively seeking inflation and, usually, an abandonment of the gold standard. For more than a year, for example, Royal Dutch Shell, led by Sir Henri Deterding, had been campaigning to get Britain, the United States, and other major countries to remonetize silver. At some point— it is impossible to say exactly when—Deterding and his American financial advisor Rene Leon began coordinating efforts to secure some kind of reflation with James A. Moffett, a longtime director and high official of Standard Oil Co. of New Jersey and a friend and early supporter of Roosevelt.[91]

While they campaigned to expand the money supply, a powerful group of industrialists, large farm organizations, and retailers organized separately for the same general end. Led by Bendix, Remington Rand, and Sears Roebuck, they called themselves "The Committee for the Nation." As Roosevelt took over in the spring of 1933, contributions from Standard Oil of New Jersey and many other industrial firms were swelling this committee's warchest.[92] The committee was vigorously pushing the president to go off the gold standard.

Working closely with sympathizers in the Treasury Department, the banks fought back. Federal Reserve Bank minutes show the Executive Committee of the System Open Market Committee distinguishing between "technical" and "political" adjustments of the money supply, with the political adjustments designed to head off demands for reflation.[93] But the industrialists could not be denied. Moffett and Leon found legal authority for Roosevelt to go off gold during the banking crisis, when even the banks conceded the step to be briefly necessary. Later the same pair teamed up to reach Roosevelt at the crucial moment of the London Economic Conference and persuaded him to send the famous telegram destroying the hopes for informal agreements on currency stabilization devoutly wished for and almost achieved by James P. Warburg and other international financiers.[94] Still pressured by the Committee for the Nation and the oil companies, Roosevelt embarked on his famous gold-buying experiments in the autumn, driving most of the banks to distraction. Roosevelt also continued with the National Recovery Administration, whose name wonderfully symbolized the logic of a political coalition built around protectionist industrialists (whose ranks had been swelled by the collapse of world trade, and with whom even major oil companies desperate for price controls could at least cooperate), farmers, and the handful of major bankers whose distinctive trait was an absence of ties to Morgan and, in the most important case, a special relationship with the oil industry.

When the first treasury secretary, William Woodin, had to resign because of ill health, Henry Morgenthau Jr., the Committee for the Nation's candidate to replace him, received the job.

> I noted with a great deal of pleasure the appointment of Mr. Morgenthau as Assistant Secretary of the Treasury, which I assume put him in charge of the Treasury Department during Mr. Woodin's illness. If that illness continues, I trust that Mr. Morgenthau will become his successor. There is a certain group of men in this country, who opposed your nomination and your election, and who have opposed the great majority of the policies you have put into effect and who are preparing for the final fight against your monetary policy. In every possible way they are putting out a barrage to interfere with the fulfillment of that policy. You are fortunate in having a man like Mr. Morgenthau who will have the strength and courage to carry out that monetary policy.[95]

The Phoenix Rises: Economic Upturn and the Return of the Multinational Bloc

But as part 1's analysis suggested as to how recovery threatens political coalitions built around the relief of monetary emergencies, this first New Deal was desperately unstable. Once the worst phase of deflation ended and the economy began slowly to revive (table 2.2), industries with good long-term prospects in the world economy would start exploring ways to resume profitable overseas business. In time, this search would necessarily bring them back in the direction of the international banks, which (with the obvious exceptions noted above) generally opposed the NRA, and away from the economic nationalists for most of whom the NRA initially represented the promised land. In addition, the NRA's half-hearted and incoherently designed attempt to supplement price mechanisms with administrative processes for the

TABLE 2.2 National Income by Quarters, 1929–1936 (in 1972 $billions)

1929-1	317.7	1932-1	244.3	1935-1	268.8
-2	321.2	-2	228.8	-2	265.5
-3	321.6	-3	217.1	-3	278.8
-4	312.3	-4	222.2	-4	287.7
1930-1	300.2	1933-1	199.7	1936-1	279.1
-2	292.0	-2	223.8	-2	294.5
-3	280.9	-3	242.4	-3	302.8
-4	274.9	-4	227.0	-4	317.3
1931-1	282.7	1934-1	239.7		
-2	284.4	-2	244.4		
-3	266.2	-3	235.4		
-4	254.4	-4	241.6		

Source: Figures for "actual real GNP" from Robert J. Gordon, unpublished data appendix to "Price Inertia and Policy Ineffectiveness in the United States, 1890–1980," Journal of Political Economy 90, 6 (1982), pp. 1087–1116. Numbers rounded.

allocation of resources bitterly divided its natural constituency of protectionist businessmen.

Not surprisingly, therefore, the NRA began to self-destruct almost from the moment it began operations. Freer traders fought with protectionists; big firms battled with smaller competitors; buyers collided with suppliers. The result was chaos. The situation was especially grave in the biggest industry of all, the oil industry. There the majors and the smaller independent oil companies stalemated in the face of massive overproduction from the new East Texas fields.[96]

As the industries fought, labor stirred. A bitter series of strikes erupted as the ambiguous wording of the National Recovery Act's 7A clause, guaranteeing employee representation, came to be interpreted as securing "company" rather than independent trade unions.[97]

With the pressure beginning to tell on Roosevelt, he looked around for new allies. He sponsored an inquiry into foreign economic policy conducted by Ruml, which recommended freer trade. Simultaneously he allowed Secretary of State Hull to promote reciprocal trade treaties in a series of speeches. The prospect of a change in U.S. tariff policy drew applause from segments of the business community that had mostly been hostile to Roosevelt. The Council on Foreign Relations sponsored a symposium in which journalist Walter Lippmann declared that freedom itself could probably not be maintained without free trade.[98]

As the first New Deal coalition disintegrated under the impact of inter-industrial and class conflicts, Roosevelt turned more definitely toward free trade. He pushed through Congress a new bill (bitterly opposed by steel, chemicals, and other industries) giving Hull the authority to negotiate lower tariffs and then let him build support for the trade treaties.

The rest of the New Deal's program stalled. With their public support already eroded, the NRA and other measures were declared unconstitutional by the Supreme Court. Largely out of ideas, Adolph A. Berle and other administrators anxiously eyed the activity of the Left; the prospect of strikes, especially in the steel industry; and sporadic urban disorders.

> Mr. Berle stressed the need for prompt action in any program of economic security. He dreads the coming winter. While the City of New York has gotten along better in the past months than was to be expected, the City's finances are near the exhaustion point. Mr. Berle also stated that the 'market' was 'jittery' about the credit of the federal government. Another complete financial collapse is distinctly possible if 'Wall Street' should decide to 'dump' U.S. bonds, which Mr. Berle thinks it might be foolish enough to do. The Communists are making rapid gains in New York City and the one thing that can save the city is very prompt action which will give the people out of work something better than they now have. The fiscal situation is such that the total costs of taking care of these people cannot be increased. The prompt enactment of an unemployment insurance bill and, if possible, old age pension legislation would have a very wholesome effect. Mr. Berle believes that the unemployment insurance system should be a national one, but with regional differentials, but he thinks that something like the regional organization in the Federal Reserve Bank system might well be used for unemployment insurance. Mr. Berle apparently was not familiar with the Wagner-Lewis bill but when this was explained to him he felt that it might prove a way out. Any unemployment insurance system adopted should be put into operation at once, both to give new hope to the unemployed and to bring in new revenue badly needed to take care of the large numbers of people to be cared for at this time. . . . [99]

In this, the darkest point of the New Deal, at the moment in which other countries had terminated constitutional regimes, the first successful capital-intensive–led political coalition in history began dramatically to come together.

As national income continued its gradual rise, John D. Rockefeller Jr. and his attorney, Raymond B. Fosdick, voted a special grant from the Spelman Fund to pay staff of the Industrial Relations Counsellors while they worked on social welfare legislation within federal agencies. Then the capital-intensive big business members of the Commerce Department's Business Advisory Council, led by Walter Teagle of Standard Oil and Gerard Swope of General Electric, joined leaders of the Taylor

Society on an advisory committee whose task was the preparation of the Social Security Act. Backed by Aldrich, Harriman, Thomas Watson of International Business Machines, George Mead of Mead Paper, the Filenes, and a huge bloc of retailers and other corporations, the group subcontracted preparation of the bill to Industrial Relations Counsellors (where Teagle and Owen D. Young, the board chairman of General Electric, were, or within months became, trustees). With slight changes, that bill, with its savagely regressive tax on payrolls, became the law of the land.[100]

Almost simultaneously, the decisive legislative struggle over the Wagner National Labor Relations Act came to a climax. Throughout 1934 strikes and work stoppages had mounted. In June 1935, the National Recovery Act was due to run out, threatening to leave the country without any machinery for processing class conflicts.[101]

As Armageddon approached, the conservative American Federation of Labor (AFL) was becoming increasingly desperate. Roosevelt had fairly consistently sided with business against it, and the federation was increasingly divided and rapidly losing control of its own membership. AFL memoranda of the period show that top union officials were convinced that without a new labor relations law they were going to be destroyed.[102]

But while many big business executives were sympathetic to the strongly conservative union's plight (Alfred P. Sloan, for example, wrote frankly that the AFL had to be preserved because it constituted a bulwark against Communism),[103] they adamantly opposed any extension of the legal rights of unions. Caught between the warring groups, Robert Wagner, the senator from New York, the most perfectly representative capital-intensive state in America, began searching for compromise while Edward Filene's Twentieth Century Fund opened a special inquiry. Working closely together, the fund and Wagner began considering alternatives. Shown drafts of a proposed bill, the general counsels of U.S. Steel and most other industries shifted into open opposition. Teagle and Swope, however, began meeting with Wagner. What happened next is too complex to be fully described here. All that can be said is that attorneys for the AFL pressed the Twentieth Century Fund for a stronger bill; Wagner took some amendments Teagle and Swope proposed to the sections defining unfair labor practices; a number of mostly Northeastern textile and shoe firms, which were hoping to stop the flow of jobs to the South, promoted the legislation; and Twentieth Century Fund trustees (which included not only Edward Filene but important members of the Taylor Society and several other major business figures) joined Mead, several tobacco executives, probably Swope, and perhaps Teagle, in endorsing the bill. The fund then assisted the lobbying effort, arranging testimony and helping to defray some of the costs Wagner was incurring.[104]

Almost at the same instant, Roosevelt turned sharply away from the proposals for more inflation and stronger federal control of banking advanced by the Committee for the Nation and major farm groups. For some time the administration had been buying silver (to the great satisfaction of Western senators from silver-producing states, Shell, and silver speculators the world over) but holding the dollar firm against the pound. After ferocious infighting, the administration now accepted a compromise Federal Reserve Act of 1935.[105] The measure contained provisions (ardently promoted by Chase President Aldrich, who played a key role in the final negotiation) reconfirming the separation of investment from commercial banking. It also confirmed the supremacy of the board of governors in Washington over the New York Federal Reserve and the other regional banks, as the Bank of America and other leading non–New York banks (including the chain controlled by Fed Chairman Marriner Eccles) had long desired.

Only days later, as Democratic Party leader James Farley collected cash contributions from oil companies, Roosevelt overruled Interior Secretary Harold Ickes and established a compromise oil price control scheme. With its implementation, the most important American capital-intensive industry achieved near-complete price control for a generation.[106]

The powerful appeal of the unorthodox combination of free trade, the Wagner Act, and social welfare was evident in the 1936 election. A massive bloc of protectionist and labor-intensive industries formed to fight the New Deal. Together with the House of Morgan (which had reasons of its own to oppose Roosevelt), the DuPonts recruited many of these firms into the Liberty League. They were joined by some firms hoping to find a Republican candidate to run a milder New Deal.

But Standard Oil could not abide Alf Landon, who had once been in the oil business as an independent in Kansas. On the eve of the Republican Convention, Standard Oil dramatically came out against him.[107] In addition, a furious battle raged in the Republican camp over Hull's reciprocal trade treaties. Landon, who was at that moment surrounded by advisers from major banks, including James Warburg and figures from both Chase and Morgan, originally favored them. But the Chemical Foundation and many industrialists were bitterly opposed. At the Republican convention the latter group prevailed during the writing of the platform. For a few weeks thereafter, however, it appeared that the free traders would nevertheless win out. Landon repudiated that part of the platform and ran as a free trader.[108]

But the protectionists did not give up. Organizing many businesses into the "Made in America Club" and backed by Orlando Weber of Allied Chemical and other top executives, Chemical Foundation President Garvan and journalist Samuel Crowther, author of a book called *America Self-Contained* who enjoyed close ties with many businessmen, began kamikaze attacks to break through the cordon of free-trading advisers who were attempting to wall off Landon. Eventually they succeeded in getting their message through:

> On the foreign trade and gold, Landon was extremely interested and he gave no evidence of ever before having heard of either subject. [Olin] Saxon had not gone into the gold question and, in a general way, seemed to size up like the ordinary economist—that is, as having learned nothing that was not in his textbooks. However, [Chemical Foundation advisor and farm leader] George Peek went back and forth over this subject, in terms of Landon's own business, and Landon seemed thus to get a grasp of what it was all about. Saxon also wanted to go a great deal further into it. Peek hammered the subject of the tariff and of our whole foreign trade program and, although he could not say positively that Landon accepted it as his paramount issue, he did believe that by the time he left, Landon had begun to realize something and that he would go further. He was not so certain as to Saxon, who is more or less of the orthodox economic type, but he felt there had at least been an awakening. Saxon agreed that, whatever the merits of stabilization, the first movement must be to get at American money and not to take an excursion into international stabilization.[109]

Though Warburg and the other bankers repeatedly warned him against it in the strongest possible terms, Landon began to waver. In mid- and late September his campaign began to criticize Hull's treaties.

His attacks alienated many multinationalists, who had watched with great interest Roosevelt's effort to stabilize the dollar. When, after speeches by First National's Leon Fraser and others, Roosevelt opened negotiations with Britain and France, the New Deal began to look like a good deal to them. It became still more attractive when the Tripartite Money Agreement was announced in September and after the Roosevelt administration raised reserve requirements on bank deposits, as many bankers had been demanding. As Landon's attacks on the trade treaties increased (but, be it noted, while many of his polls were holding up, including the *Literary Digest's*, which had never before been wrong), a generation of legendary American business figures began backing out of the Republican campaign. On active service in war and peace, Henry Stimson, who had already backed the treaties, refused to support Landon and withdrew from the campaign. On October 18, as spokesmen for the Rockefeller interests debated issuing a veiled criticism of the Liberty League, came the sensational announcement that James Warburg, who since his noisy public break with FDR two years before had waged unremitting war on the New Deal and frequently advised Landon, was switching to Roosevelt out of disgust with Landon's stand on the trade treaties. Only a couple of days after Warburg released his rapturous public encomium to Hull, Dean Acheson, Warburg's friend and former associate at the Treasury Department, did exactly the same thing. So did cotton broker William Clayton, who also resigned from the Liberty League.

On October 29,

> at a mass meeting in the heart of the Wall Street District, about 200 business leaders, most of whom described themselves as Republicans, enthusiastically endorsed . . . the foreign trade policy of the Roosevelt Administration and pledged themselves to work for the President's reelection.
>
> After addresses by five speakers, four of whom described themselves as Republicans, the Meeting unanimously adopted a resolution praising the reciprocal trade policy established by the Roosevelt Administration under the direction of Secretary of State Cordell Hull. . . . Governor Landon's attitude on the reciprocal tariff issue was criticized by every speaker. They contended that if Landon were elected and Secretary Hull's treaties were revoked, there would be a revolution among conservative businessmen.[110]

While the Republicans switched, the Democrats fought. The Bank of America and New Orleans banker Rudolph Hecht, who was just coming off a term as president of the American Bankers Association, bulwarked the "Good Neighbor League," a Roosevelt campaign vehicle. Lincoln and Edward Filene supported the president to the hilt, as did sugar refiner Ellsworth Bunker, a major importer from the Caribbean. Weinberg of Goldman, Sachs came back into the campaign and raised more money for Roosevelt than any other single person. Behind him trailed a virtual Milky Way of non-Morgan banking stars, including Harriman of Brown Brothers Harriman; Forrestal of Dillon, Read; and probably Hancock of Lehman Brothers.

From the oil industry came a host of independents, including Sid Richardson, Clint Murchison, and Charlie Roesser; as well as Deterding, Moffett of Standard Oil of California, W. Alton Jones of Cities Services, Standard Oil of New Jersey's Boris Said (who helped run Democratic youth groups), and M. L. Benedum of Benedum-Trees. Top executives of Reynolds Tobacco, American Tobacco, Coca-Cola, International Harvester, General Electric, Zenith, IBM, Sears Roebuck, ITT, United Fruit, Pan Am, and Manufacturers Trust all lent support.

Prodded by banker George Foster Peabody, the *New York Times* came out for Roosevelt, as did the Scripps-Howard papers.[111]

In the final days of the campaign, as Landon furiously attacked social security, Teagle of Standard Oil of New Jersey, Swope of GE, the Pennsylvania Retailers Association, the American Retail Federation, and Lorillard tobacco company (Old Gold), among others, spoke out in defense of the program. Last, if scarcely least, the firm that would incarnate the next thirty years of multinational oil and banking, the Chase National Bank, loaned the Democratic National Committee one hundred thousand dollars.

The curtain fell on the New Deal's creation of the modern Democratic political formula in early 1938. When the United States plunged steeply into recession, the clamor for relief began again as it had in 1933. Pressures for a revival of the NRA also mounted. But this time Roosevelt did not devalue the dollar. With billions of dollars in gold now squirreled away in the Fed, thanks to administration financial policies and spreading European anxieties, early 1930s' fears of hoarding and runs on gold had vanished. As a consequence, reflation without formal devaluation or a revival of the NRA became a live option. Rockefeller adviser Ruml proposed a plan for deficit spending, which Roosevelt implemented after versions won approval from Teagle and nearly all the important bankers, including Morgan. Aldrich then went on NBC radio to defend compensatory spending from attacks, as long as it was coupled with measures for free trade (to the great annoyance of the DuPonts). Slightly later, the State Department, acting in secret with the Chase National Bank, and in public with the Roman Catholic cardinal of Chicago and high business figures, set up a committee to promote renewal of the Reciprocal Trade Act in the wavering Corn Belt.[112] They were successful. National income snapped back and the multinational bloc held together. As it would be through most of the next generation, the national Democratic Party was now committed: it was the party of the "people"—and of internationalism and free trade.

CONCLUSION: THE TRIUMPH OF MULTINATIONAL LIBERALISM IN AMERICA

In a longer analysis it would be desirable to distinguish various stages in the transformation of the Second New Deal into an organizing principle in American politics—through World War II, the "Fair Deal," and the Cold War, for example. It would also be important to analyze more extensively how class conflicts rose and ebbed during this period, as well as how some of the secondary tensions discussed earlier, notably

those involving investment and commercial banking, were finally resolved. One would also want to look more carefully at the vicissitudes
of Hull's trade policy, especially in regard to cotton textiles, the fate of
agriculture, and the changing role of the Supreme Court (where the
chief justice chanced to be Standard of New Jersey's former top policy
adviser). Nevertheless, even this abbreviated presentation establishes
several important points of both substance and method.

First of all, it should make plausible the claim that by at least late
1938 all the elements of what deserves recognition as a distinct System
of '36 were, at least provisionally, in place—social welfare, oil price
regulation, free trade, even "Keynesianism." Though all of these measures except the fixed price for oil still drew massive, well-financed
opposition, the logic of their combination into a powerful and immensely popular political coalition was now apparent.

No less important, this analysis specifies far more precisely the role
labor (and a few radicalized farm and professional groups) played in
shaping the New Deal. While the "labor constraint" analysis that is part
of the static theory of industrial partisan preference does not pretend
to explain surges in labor militancy (note that the model says nothing
at all about why these occur), its implicit cost-benefit framework
allows one to understand—indeed, anticipate—differential responses
to these challenges by various industries. It thereby becomes a formal
way of integrating independent initiatives by labor, such as those well
described in Piven and Cloward's *Poor People's Movements,* into a more
complex model of divisions within the business community.[113]

Also, of course, the analysis indicates the inadequacy of traditional
approaches to the politics of business. To understand the New Deal, I
have argued, one must thrust aside the hoary models of "big vs. small"
business (or "monopoly vs. competitive" capital). One has to recognize
that related but distinct lines of cleavage ultimately divided big business in that period: the division between labor- and capital-intensive
industries on one hand, and between nationalists and internationalists
on the other. And the financial system's sometimes very complex effects on political coalitions have to be elucidated in detail, as one must
also be wary of the sometimes dramatic effects of big swings in national income.[114]

Finally, this study has implications for many working procedures
in contemporary politics. First, it should suggest how much material
about political events remains to be discovered in archives. The New
Deal is one of the most extensively discussed phenomena in American
history. Yet plenty of gaps have remained about who exactly did what
precisely when. When these gaps begin to be filled in, quite a different

picture emerges of what once seemed the "facts" of legislative drafts-manship and political initiative.

Political analysis can benefit from a more thoroughgoing integra-tion with economic analysis. This does not, of course, imply acceptance of the view that most people maximize income (or wealth), or that cultural factors do not importantly affect political outcomes.[115] It does demand, however, that the analyst try to trace in detail how industrial structures link to society and politics, and how factors like falling in-come might explain what he or she is interested in. Otherwise one is likely prematurely to invoke one of the various *dei ex machina* now fashionable in the more affluent parts of comparative politics, such as "autonomous" (which often means "inexplicable") state bureaucrats, nebulous "national" interests, or "thick descriptions" of irrelevant facts. And one will thus miss the sovereign reality of the New Deal's "multi-national liberalism": that the decisive support for a political coalition that strongly accented "comparative advantage" came from the ranks of the comparatively advantaged.

ACKNOWLEDGMENTS

This chapter summarizes part of the argument of my *Critical Realignment: The Fall of the House of Morgan and the Origins of the New Deal* (New York: Oxford University Press, forthcoming) and sharpens considerations advanced in "Von Versailles zum New Deal," a catalogue essay in Neue Gesellschaft für Bildende Kunst, *Amerika: Traum und Depression 1920/40* (Berlin and Hamburg: 1980), pp. 436–50. To reduce documentation to manageable proportions, I have strictly limited references to no more than are absolutely necessary for precision of ar-gument.

The same space limitations make it impossible to acknowledge all who have aided my research. For very helpful comments on drafts of this chapter, how-ever, I should like to thank Lawrence Goodwyn, Charles Kindleberger, James Kurth, Mira Wilkins, the members of Harvard University's Economic History Research Seminar, and the editors of *International Organization*. I am also very grateful to Alfred Chandler both for comments and for affording me a look at two unpublished papers on the evolution of big business ("Global Enterprise: Economic and National Characteristics—An Historical Overview," and "The M Form—Industrial Groups, American Style").

For providing me with unrestricted access to his personal papers and unique insights into the New Deal, I am grateful to a leader of the independent oilmen in Texas during the New Deal, Mr. J. R. Parten, now of Madisonville, Texas. For other assistance in securing material I also thank Mr. and Mrs. Everett Case, Anthony Garvan, Mr. and Mrs. John W. Coolidge Jr., Herbert Gintis, Charles Harvey, and Mrs. Rene Leon. Other valuable assistance came from Walter Dean Burnham, Bruce Cumings, Gerald Epstein, Henry Farber, Peter

Gourevitch, Robert Johnson, Lola Klein, Duane Lockard, Martin Shefter, Peter Temin, and more librarians than can be named here.

NOTES

1. See, among many other comments on Fisher's unfortunate pronouncement, John Kenneth Galbraith, *The Great Crash* (Boston: Houghton Mifflin, 1961), p. 75. The Irving Fisher Papers at Sterling Library, Yale University, contain many references to his service on boards of investment companies and Remington Rand, a major manufacturer. Fisher's later role in New Deal monetary controversies made these ties an object of extensive comment. The final copy and various drafts of Lamont's letter to Herbert Hoover of October 19, 1929 are in the Lamont Papers, Baker Library, Harvard University. (Most archives used in this project are adequately indexed; box numbers are provided for the readers' convenience only where confusion seems likely.)

2. For a review of debates on the stock market's contribution to the Depression, see Peter Temin, *Did Monetary Forces Cause the Great Depression?* (New York: W. W. Norton, 1976).

3. For a good summary of the Depression's effects on the economy, see Lester Chandler, *America's Greatest Depression* (New York: Harper, 1970).

4. Ibid. For the Depression in comparative context, see Charles Kindleberger, *The World in Depression* (London: Allen Lane, 1973).

5. The 1933 Banking Act, also commonly referred to as *the* Glass-Steagall Act, should not be confused with a 1932 bill that bore the names of the same senator and representative but dealt with different financial issues. The Emergency Banking Legislation, rammed through Congress in a matter of days in March 1933, was also a different bill.

6. The first of several New Deal reciprocal trade measures passed rather early in Roosevelt's first term, but, as explained in this chapter, it had virtually no immediate effect on the administration's essentially protectionist trade policy.

7. The role of Keynesian public finance versus a bulging export surplus in leading the Swedish revival of the mid- and latter-1930s has been extensively debated; the weight of the evidence suggests that the Swedish government did not vigorously implement the advanced monetary and fiscal proposals that were undeniably in the air. In view of this paragraph's clear distinctions and exact datings of the New Deal's "Keynesian turn," I find inexplicable the recent claim by M. Weir and T. Skocpol that my essay "mistakenly conflates the labor regulation and social insurance reforms of 1935–36 with Keynesianism." See their "State Structures and the Possibilities for 'Keynesian' Responses to the Great Depression in Sweden, Britain, and the United States," in P. Evans, D. Rueschemeyer, and T. Skocpol, eds., *Bringing the State Back In* (New York: Cambridge University Press, 1985), p. 154.

8. See, for example, Arthur Schlesinger Jr., *The Age of Roosevelt*, 3 vols. (Boston: Houghton Mifflin, 1957–60); William Leuchtenburg, *Franklin D. Roosevelt and the New Deal* (New York: Harper, 1963); and Frank Freidel, *Franklin D. Roosevelt*, 4 vols. (Boston: Little, Brown, 1952-). Erwin Hargrove observes how images of Roosevelt and the presidency derived from such works have dominated postwar political science, in his *The Power of the Modern Presidency* (New York: Knopf, 1974), chap. 1.

9. See, for example, Barton Bernstein, "The New Deal: The Conservative Achievements of Liberal Reform," in Bernstein, ed., *Toward a New Past: Dissenting Essays in American History* (New York: Pantheon, 1968), and Ronald Radosh, "The Myth of the New Deal," in Radosh and Murray N. Rothbard, eds., *A New History of Leviathan* (New York: Dutton, 1972), pp. 146–86.

10. See, for example, Ellis Hawley's "The Discovery and Study of a Corporate Liberalism," *Business History Review* 52, 3 (1978), pp. 309–20. In contrast, his classic *The New Deal and the Problem of Monopoly* (Princeton: Princeton University Press, 1962) does not emphasize these themes. See also Alfred Chandler and Louis Galambos, "The Development of Large Scale Economic Organizations in Modern America," in E. J. Perkins, ed., *Men and Organizations* (New York: Putnam, 1977). It appears that Weir and Skocpol's "Keynesian Responses," and other recent essays in the "state managers" vein, represent something of a synthesis of this view and the older "pluralist" approach—with the conspicuous difference that the state manager theorists rely mostly on secondary sources.

11. For a review of the German work, see H. A. Winkler, ed., *Die Grosse Krise in America* (Göttingen: Vandenhoech & Ruprecht, 1973); perhaps the finest of the libertarian writings are those by Murray Rothbard—see his "War Collectivism in World War I," and "Herbert Hoover and the Myth of Laissez-Faire," both in Radosh and Rothbard, eds., *New History of Leviathan*; for Kolko's views, see his *Main Currents in Modern American History* (New York: Harper & Row, 1976).

12. Some commentators, such as Elliot Rosen in his very stimulating *Hoover, Roosevelt and the Brains Trust* (New York: Columbia University Press, 1977, hereafter *Brains Trust*), have questioned the existence of "two New Deals." These doubts, however, are difficult to sustain if one systematically compares the policies pursued during each period.

13. Sidney Verba and Kay Schlozman's recent suggestion that American workers remained captivated by the "American dream" all through the New Deal does not constitute an answer. The "American dream," before the 1930s, had not included mass unionization or social security—the term is elastic. See their "Unemployment, Class Consciousness, and Radical Politics: What Didn't Happen in the Thirties," *Journal of Politics* 39, 2 (1977), pp. 291–323.

14. See the discussion in Milton Friedman and Anna Schwartz, *A Monetary History of the United States* (Princeton: Princeton University Press, 1963); Temin, *Monetary Forces;* Karl Brunner and Alan Meltzer, "What Did We Learn from the Monetary Experience of the United States in the Great Depression," *Canadian Journal of Economics* 1, 2 (1968), pp. 334–48; Elmus Wicker, "Federal Reserve Monetary Policy, 1922–33—A Reinterpretation," *Journal of Political Economy* 53 (August 1965), pp. 325–43, and later writings.

15. Kurth, "The Political Consequences of the Product Cycle: Industrial History and Political Outcomes," *International Organization* 33 (winter 1979), pp. 1–34; Gourevitch, "International Trade, Domestic Coalitions and Liberty: Comparative Responses to the Crisis of 1873–96," *Journal of Interdisciplinary History* 8, 2 (1977), pp. 281–313; Hibbs, "Political Parties and Macroeconomic Policy," *American Political Science Review* 71, 4 (1977), pp. 1467–87.

16. I build here on my "Elites and Elections; Or What Have They Done to You Lately? Toward an Investment Theory of Political Parties and Critical Realignment," in Benjamin Ginsberg and Alan Stone (eds.), *Do Elections Matter?* (1st ed.; Armonk, N.Y.:

Sharpe, 1986); and "Party Realignment and American Industrial Structure: The Investment Theory of Political Parties in Historical Perspective," in chapter 1 of this volume.

17. Hibbs, "Political Parties," p. 1470.

18. For representative cross-national data on some of the large differences see ibid., and Edward Tufte, *Political Control of the Economy* (Princeton: Princeton University Press, 1978), chap. 4.

19. See, for example, Kurth, "Political Consequences"; Gourevitch, "International Trade"; and David Abraham's *The Collapse of the Weimar Republic* (2nd ed.; New York: Holmes & Meier, 1986); Abraham's "Introduction to the Second Edition" should be consulted on the long controversy. The honored ancestors of this general approach include Alexander Gerschenkron, *Bread and Democracy in Germany* (Berkeley: University of California Press, 1943); Eckhart Kehr, *Battleship Building and Party Politics* (Chicago: University of Chicago Press, 1975); and Arthur Rosenberg, *Democracy and Socialism* (New York: Knopf, 1939).

20. Taxes, for example, might be one issue that would not disappear entirely.

21. Indeed, many exceptions exist; for example, firms whose hazardous working conditions are more likely to be detected by a union (which can bear the detection costs) than by unorganized individuals (who may never realize the danger) will resist unionization far more fiercely than one might expect from the role wages play in their value added. Ability to pass through wage increases and, consequently, a firm's location in the flow of production will also affect concessions vs. opposition to labor. Nevertheless, as a first testable approximation, the rule is probably the best available.

22. The (rounded) data for all but chemicals and copper come from the 1929 *Census of Manufacturers* as presented in Charles A. Bliss, *The Structure of Manufacturing Production* (New York: National Bureau of Economic Research, 1939), appendices, especially p. 214. My "automobiles" category is a weighted average of two of Bliss's categories (parts and assembly). The chemicals figure has been calculated as per note 39, below. The copper data, for 1929, have been calculated from the 1963 *Census of Mineral Industries* (Washington, D.C.), vol. 1, 10C-10, table 1 (the figure is for "copper ores"). The "refining and smelting" part of the industry shows up in the 1929 *Census of Manufacturers* (Washington, D.C.), vol. 2, p. 1085. The most reasonable method of weighting and combining all the data yields a corrected estimate of 36.2 percent; but the difference in terms of this article are meaningless. Note that all figures are for industries; data for individual firms are not available, causing problems for estimates of individual firms (see note 39, below). Note also that the estimates for petroleum probably greatly understate the industry's capital intensity. Finally, industries are listed on the chart if at least one firm in the top 20 as listed in table 2.1 did substantial business in them in both 1929 and 1935. I have also added textiles, by far the largest industry in terms of employment during most of this period, and shoes, as a representative "old" industry also with substantial employment.

23. The assumption that vectors of class conflict indicators and public policies can be treated as scalers is not strictly necessary to this analysis. But it is in accord with both ordinary language and many social science treatments of "rising" or "falling" social strife and labor activity. Note also that while, as suggested in this chapter, this analysis scarcely adds up to a theory of the labor movement and while this essay focuses on the business community, labor is not being treated as a passive element—note carefully the horizontal axis on figure 2.1, which reflects changing levels of social class *conflict*.

24. I choose this language carefully, to cover instances where a business firm sup-

ports both parties. Such instances are much less common or important than generally believed. As I argue at greater length in my "Party Realignment," chapter 1, no more in politics than in the stock market can *everyone* profit by buying into the same stock. No less important, most cases of apparent "bipartisanship" rest on undiscriminating evidence—usually public campaign expenditure records. In most cases, more institutionally subtle behavior signals a preference for one or the other candidate.

25. For this, obviously, archival evidence has a privileged position. See, however, my "Party Realignment" chapter 1, for a discussion of the whole question of "evidence." My experience with corporate records convinces me that the single most important form of business influence on American politics is not the actual transfer of money but the power major businessmen have to influence associates and cultural institutions, especially the media.

26. As with all modeling in the social sciences, of course, more dimensions become necessary the finer the context. "Broadly" labor-related issues include most "social welfare" policies.

27. On these definitions, note 1) the "free" market may well be an oligopoly maintained by a few firms; 2) "internationalists" often have to live in a world full of nationalists and accordingly modify their behavior; 3) occasionally "nationalism" and "protectionism" are not equivalents; 4) occasionally "internationalism" could helpfully be broken down into several dimensions; 5) "internationalism" is usually a matter of degree—any number of firms oriented toward international competition in an open world economy have been happy to welcome government aid where that would not upset a larger equilibrium.

To use this dimension for a real economy requires some impression of the positions of the various industries and firms. I use an independent source: with one exception noted in this essay, subsequent scattergraphs rely largely on summaries of the changing world economic positions of major American businesses presented by Mira Wilkins in her *The Maturing of Multinational Enterprise* (Cambridge: Harvard University Press, 1974). Based on a judgment about which policies objectively advanced the interests of firms as Wilkins depicts them (where "interest" is equated with profitability), I have placed firms and industries into one of five arbitrarily defined, ordinally ranked spaces along the nationalist-internationalist dimension. Some argument about particular cases is to be expected, especially with General Motors in the '20s, where most analysts have underestimated the pressures from GM's major owner, DuPont, to limit its overseas commitments and the importance of the so-called "rubber war." However, nothing of importance here is sensitive to this imprecision; indeed, the ordinal scale is of some advantage. On the copper industry I follow James Ridgeway, *Who Owns the Earth?* (New York: Macmillan, 1980), p. 106.

28. Because only one of these axes has a true metric the definition of a "quadrant" is arbitrary: what is at issue is proximity in the defined spaces. Here, however, it is convenient to speak of "quadrants."

29. See the discussion in my "Party Realignment," which also contains a longer and more general statement of the "scattergraph" approach to the analysis of American party systems applied in the present article, a detailed justification for concentrating on big business in the analysis of political change, and some qualifications—unimportant in this article but of considerable significance in general—on the treatment of the financial sector in such graphs.

A word should probably be added about how agriculture figures into the analysis presented here. While reasons of space make it impossible to justify the claim, the politics of farm policy in the New Deal has received more attention than it deserves; while agriculture constituted an important part of Roosevelt's coalition, most of what defined the New Deal derived from other constituencies. Furthermore, agriculture, like industry, is marked by both class and sectoral conflicts, and its political behavior can be analyzed on lines analogous to those for industry.

30. Complicating issues do not, of course, only appear during transition to a new party system, I simply claim that additional issues sometimes complicate such transitions.

31. See the discussion in my "Elites and Elections." Severe but brief downturns, like that in 1920–21, do not last long enough to generate the processes described below in other than feeble, symptomatic form.

32. Because of this "cumulative" role played by past financial and other secondary cleavages, the actual sequence of historical events makes a real difference even in the model.

33. This expression refers to a party system before decay. See, for example, Paul Kleppner, "Critical Realignments and Electoral Systems," in Kleppner et al., *The Evolution of American Electoral Systems* (Westport, Conn.: Greenwood Press, 1981), pp. 1–33.

34. See my "Party Realignment," section 4. The shoe industry was singular because in contrast to most other charter members of the Republican bloc, its firms directly confronted a giant trust, United Shoe Machinery. As a consequence, they were far more likely to harbor doubts about the wisdom of "big business" and often went over to conservative Democrats.

35. This discussion neglects a modest movement for very limited trade liberalization promoted by several sectors in the pre-1914 period.

36. For the merger movement of the 1890s, see my discussion in "Party Realignment." Railroad mergers, organized by leading financiers, were also a part of the consolidation of this bloc.

37. For World War I's major financial consequences for the U.S. economy, see Charles Kindleberger, "United States Foreign Economic Policy 1776–1976," *Foreign Affairs,* January 1977, pp. 395–417.

38. For the period's labor turmoil, see Jeremy Brecher, *Strike!* (Boston: South End Press, 1977), chap. 4.

39. For rankings along the "internationalism" dimension see above, note 27. Because data for wages as a percentage of value added are available only for industries as a whole, I have assigned specific large *firms* the value of the industry mean, thus eliminating intra-industry differences. While these may sometimes be significant, they are miniscule by comparison to the variations across industries. I have assigned the firms to particular three-digit industries by comparing their main lines of business with "Manufacturing Industries with Large Scale Operations, 1929," (Bliss, *Manufacturing Production,* p. 214); and, where possible, checking my industry code assignments against those in the Harvard Business School Project data presented in the Chandler papers "Global Enterprise" and "The M Form." In this period only the calculations for General Electric, which moved in the 1920s into consumer durables while continuing its older lines of business in electrical machinery, raised questions about the need to weight two very different Standard Industrial Classification three-digit codes to get one number for the

whole. Because the size of the consumer durables segment of GE's business (with its relatively low wages as a percentage of value added) seemed too small to affect the overall firm average, I did not refine the data for "electrical machinery." However, Westinghouse, which had not yet moved into consumer durables in this period, always seems to lag slightly behind GE's political efforts in the New Deal, in a direction one would predict from knowing the firms' labor sensitivities. (The two firms also differed sharply in the degree of overseas involvement.)

In the case of chemicals, I used a slightly different procedure. As Walt Rostow, *The World Economy* (Austin: University of Texas Press, 1978), p. 278, observes, the industry is markedly heterogeneous. Accordingly, in preparing figure 2.4's estimate of "wages as a percentage of value added" for DuPont, I used the Chandler data's list of the three-digit codes relevant for the firm in 1930. The codes were matched as closely as possible with particular branches of the industry for which statistics were available. On the basis of the 1931 Commerce Department *Biennial Census of Manufacturers*, pp. 564–83, "wages as a percentage of value added" was estimated for each three-digit industry in which DuPont operated. (In some cases categories had to be combined, using various weighted averages.) Since no better weights were available, an average was taken of wages as a percent of value added for all these three-digit figures and is used in figure 2.4. Because a large paper company placed among the top 30 industrials only in 1935, there should strictly speaking be no entry for the sector. I have added it because of my later discussion of the role played by the Mead Corp. in the Second New Deal. Note, finally, that many older industries dominated by small firms, such as shoes, would show up in the same area as textiles and steel if they were plotted.

40. Further footnotes are devoted to primary references or important amplifying facts, which will necessarily be stated in summary form.

41. These long-running negotiations culminated in the Achnacarry Accord of 1928, which cartelized the world oil market outside the United States. It scarcely exaggerates to say that the problem of oil policy during the New Deal was to find a viable domestic complement to this international cartel.

42. For Lodge's views on the League of Nations and international finance see his extensive correspondence for 1919 and 1920, now in the Henry Cabot Lodge Papers, Massachusetts Historical Society Library, Boston. The most complete collection of papers of the League's supporters is in the files of Harvard President A. Lawrence Lowell, now in the Pusey Library, Harvard University. The American Tariff League's denunciation of the League of Nations (one of many) is from its *American Economist*, March 21, 1919, p. 190. I am grateful to John W. Coolidge Jr. for permission to examine additional correspondence of Louis A. Coolidge (beyond that in the Lodge Papers) in his family's files; and to Carl Kaysen of M.I.T. for comments on United Shoe's interest in the U.S. market.

43. The literature on the League of Nations debate is extensive but short on specific details of exactly who supported what compromises. A few later analysts have questioned whether Lodge should be numbered among the "Irreconcilables," though everyone concedes his pivotal role in the final outcome. Correspondence from all sides persuades me that Lodge was, indeed, irreconcilably opposed to the League and intended to destroy it all along.

44. Hughes's intimate connections to Standard and the Rockefellers have been extensively overlooked, and actually denied by several biographers. Files of the Standard Oil Co. of New Jersey, now in storage at Tulane University Library, New Orleans, list him

as the corporation's chief foreign policy adviser; in 1917–20, Hughes served as an attorney for both Standard of New Jersey and the American Petroleum Institute, and was a trustee of the Rockefeller Foundation. He was also active in the newly organized (and liberal) Northern Baptist Church, whose interlocking ties to the Rockefeller complex were very close. Carl Parrini's *Heir to Empire* (Pittsburgh: University of Pittsburgh Press, 1973) gives an excellent summary of the clash between Standard and the British, and the role of the League in this context. See especially pp. 58 and 138 ff.

45. As is often emphasized, a stronger executive was fundamental to the New Deal.

46. The division between the old and new blocs in the business community, however, is certainly not equivalent to one between traditional and modern management or between firms with and without formal personnel programs. The multidivisional management structures described by Alfred Chandler and other analysts were slowly diffusing through both blocs. Most of the more advanced firms, however—DuPont is the most notable exception—were multinationally oriented.

47. A summary of the overwhelming Eastern bias in the control of U.S. foundations in this period, as well as their growing expenditures for studies of foreign affairs, is Eduard C. Lindeman's long-ignored *Wealth and Culture* (New York: Harcourt, 1936), especially pp. 44 ff. For the interaction of big business and the professions, see, among others, David Noble, *America by Design* (New York: Knopf, 1975).

48. For the *New York Times*, see below; the Moley quotation is from a 13 June 1936 entry in his Journal, now in the Moley Papers, Hoover Institution, Stanford, Calif. Astor and Harriman were the most important of the magazine's owners. Moley later moved much further to the right.

49. Cf. Brecher, *Strike!* chap. 4, among other sources.

50. The sources for this and the following paragraphs are mostly papers scattered through several archives, including the Rockefeller Archive Center at Tarrytown, N.Y.

51. Industrial Relations Counsellors seem to have coordinated the meetings of the group for most of the 1920s. Not every firm was capital-intensive. For the dominance of Standard Oil and General Electric within the group, cf. J. J. Raskob to Lammot DuPont, November 26, 1929, Raskob Papers, Eleutherian Mills–Hagley Foundation, Wilmington, Del.

52. Several (Northeastern) textile executives played leading roles within this group, which produced the otherwise inexplicable sight of a handful of textile men supporting Franklin D. Roosevelt during the Second New Deal, and which for a brief period generated some interesting, if ultimately unimportant, wrinkles in the Hull-Roosevelt trade offensive in the mid-1930s. Boston merchant E. A. Filene, who established (and controlled) the Twentieth Century Fund and who ardently championed what might be labeled the "retailers' dream" of an economy built on high wages and cheap imports, was deeply involved with this group. The small businessmen of the Taylor Society differed very slightly with their big business allies on two entirely predictable issues: antitrust and financial reform. Supreme Court Justice Louis D. Brandeis, who is usually credited as a major inspiration for many New Deal measures, had once served as Filene's attorney and remained closely associated with him and his brother, A. Lincoln Filene.

53. Ruml's activities in this regard have been well chronicled in James Mulherin, "The Sociology of Work and Pattern of Development" (Ph.D. diss., University of California, Berkeley, 1979).

54. For the astonishing and complicated Morgan-Ford interaction, see, for example, Henry Ford to J. P. Morgan Jr., May 7, 1921, and Morgan to Ford, May 11, 1921, Ford Archives, Henry Ford Museum, Dearborn, Mich. Surrounding correspondence and an oral history memoir at the archives indicate that a larger group of New York WASP businessmen was also involved and that one Charles Blumenthal, who had a definite though obscure connection to Morgan, subsequently helped out with articles in Ford's Dearborn *Independent*. For the Manufacturers Trust incident, cf. Thomas Lamont to V. H. Smith at Morgan Grenfell, January 10, 1929, Box 111, Lamont Papers.

55. A large mass of correspondence in the Lamont Papers testifies to the increasing bitterness within investment banking. Cf. Gordon Thomas and Max Morgan-Witts, *The Day the Bubble Burst* (Garden City, N.Y.: Doubleday, 1979).

56. This episode was reported in *Time*, July 30, 1928, p. 23.

57. For the chemical industry's commitment to tariffs, see Gerard Zilg's remarkable *DuPont* (Englewood Cliffs, N.J.: Prentice-Hall, 1974). Zilg's study deserves a much wider audience; for a brief analysis of some extra-intellectual factors affecting the book's reception, see Robert Sherrill, "The Nylon Curtain Affair: The Book That DuPont Hated," *The Nation*, February 14, 1981, pp. 172–76.

58. This discussion draws on a still-unpublished review of top American wealth holders by Philip Burch of Rutgers University.

59. Cf. Zilg, *DuPont*, chap. 9.

60. A striking confirmation of the role of late-developing large fortunes in the tax revolt of the '20s is the behavior of the chief representative of the one other truly gigantic American fortune that, while considerably more mature than the DuPonts', nevertheless still remained in its "takeoff" phase during the decade: Andrew Mellon, leader of the Republican move to cut taxes.

61. A circular sent by Pierre DuPont to other wealthy Americans during the AAPA campaign, quoted in Fletcher Dobyns, *The Amazing Story of Repeal* (New York: Willett, Clark, 1940), p. 20. This study grasps the dynamics of the Repeal Movement far better than David Kyvig's *Repealing National Prohibition* (Chicago: University of Chicago Press, 1979).

62. See in particular the penetrating and splendidly detailed study by Paul Johnson, *A Shopkeeper's Millenium* (New York: Hill & Wang, 1979).

63. For Rockefeller, in particular, cf. Raymond Fosdick, *John D. Rockefeller, Jr.* (New York: Harper, 1956), pp. 250 ff.

64. Cf. Johnson, *A Shopkeeper's Millenium*, for an excellent discussion of the early period.

65. A crucial letter establishing that the DuPonts were in fact seeking a seat on the board of U.S. Steel is Irénée DuPont to John J. Raskob, March 31, 1926, in the Raskob Papers, File 677, Eleutherian Mills–Hagley Foundation Library; see also Zilg, *DuPont*, pp. 230 ff, on the broader divisions of interest, and several perhaps impolitic statements by Raskob; but note especially the bitter exchange on financing charges between Morgan partner Edward Stettinius and Lammot DuPont, after which the DuPonts appear to have withdrawn part of their business from Morgan (Edward Stettinius Sr. Papers, University of Virginia, Charlottesville). Pierre DuPont's own unhappiness with the frequently tense GM situation, even while its massive dividends were piling up, is clear; see, for example, Pierre DuPont to T. Coleman DuPont, April 9, 1924, Pierre DuPont Papers, Eleutherian Mills–Hagley Foundation.

66. Most of what follows is based on the Chemical Foundation Papers in the Library of the University of Wyoming, Laramie.

67. For example: "B. says he, (B.) first discussed the Chemical Foundation matter with [New Hampshire Senator] Moses some six months ago and that Moses immediately went directly to President Harding and laid the matter before him. B. claims the entire credit for Harding's recent move [to help compensate the Germans]." From a detective report to Francis P. Garvan of the Chemical Foundation dated July 4, 1922, now in the personal possession of Dr. Anthony Garvan. Francis Garvan was closely associated with J. Edgar Hoover both before and after Hoover became head of the FBI. A few surviving letters now in a file belonging to the Garvan family in New York City show that the pair exchanged sensitive intelligence information. The Chemical Foundation papers suggest that the detectives were probably ex-FBI men. I have made intensive efforts to verify the contents of these reports and am persuaded that they constitute good evidence. For German efforts to secure the return of the patents, see also Joseph Borkin, *The Crime and Punishment of I. G. Farben* (New York: Free Press, 1978), pp. 170 ff, in particular the discussion of John Foster Dulles.

68. Note that this case had nothing to do with the "Teapot Dome," the scandal for which the Harding administration is best remembered.

69. Dulles's efforts came to light as a result of a congressional investigation years later. See U.S. Senate, Special Committee Investigating the Munitions Industry, *International Munitions Control*, 37th Congress, December 4 and 5, 1934, pp. 2254 ff, which reproduces minutes of a meeting between Dulles and the arms exporters.

70. The German chemical companies had, of course, worked closely together before the amalgamation of the mid-1920s.

71. See Irénée DuPont to W. F. Huntington, March 6, 1926, Box 26, DuPont Co. Papers, Eleutherian Mills–Hagley Foundation, for a full account of the visit to Hoover; see Irénée DuPont to Herbert Hoover, March 6, 1926; and Hoover to Secretary of State Kellogg, March 12, 1926 (the original letter is missing from the Hoover Papers, Hoover Presidential Library, West Branch, Iowa, but is plainly referred to in the letter to Kellogg that Hoover attached with it. (A copy of the original letter is in accession no. 1662, part of the DuPont Co. Archives.) In the light of later events, it is interesting that Hoover's response to these overtures was sympathetic but largely pro forma.

72. Translated from a confidential report to the German ambassador in Washington, November 5, 1926. The microfilm of this and related exchanges with Erich Warburg (nephew of Institute of Economics Trustee Paul Warburg) are now on National Archives Microfilm T 290 no. 27.

73. See, for example, J. Laffey, DuPont General Counsel Office, to P. S. DuPont et al., March 8, 1926, DuPont Co. Papers, written two days after Irénée met with Hoover.

74. Lamont to Dwight Morrow, December 16, 1927, Lamont Papers.

75. For Dulles' activities, in particular, see Hoover to Dulles, March 12 and 24, May 31, and June 16, 1928; together with Dulles to Hoover, March 2, May 29, and June 13, 1928; all now in the Dulles Papers at Princeton University. See also R. W. Preussen, *John Foster Dulles* (New York: Free Press, 1982), pp. 92–96. It was Dulles who seems first to have supplied the Germans with a copy of the government's brief in its suit against the Chemical Foundation.

76. See von Knieriem to Ritter, February 2, 1928, National Archives Film T 290, no. 27, and the surrounding cables. Donovan's speech virtually quotes the I. G.'s formula

as relayed in these cables; see the reprint of his address, "Foreign Cartels and American Industry," in *Chemical Markets*, March 1928, p. 281. Donovan's position can usefully be contrasted with what he had defended only a few months before in "The Antitrust Laws and Foreign Trade," a speech delivered to the National Paint, Oil, and Varnish Association on October 28, 1927 (copy in Box 183 of the Hoover Commerce Department Papers at the Hoover Presidential Library).

77. See the discussion in Borkin, *I. G. Farben*, chap. 2; at this time Farben was supporting the liberal Weimar government. Not until the East Texas oil discoveries ruined the market for synthetic petroleum did it make its fateful switch. For the inability to reach agreement in the wider talks, see W. J. Reader, *Imperial Chemical Industries: A History* (London: Oxford University Press, 1975), 2, pp. 47–49.

78. Cf. Zilg, *DuPont*, pp. 267 ff.

79. In her *American Business and Foreign Policy* (Boston: Beacon Press, 1971), pp. 137–38, Joan Hoff Wilson cites a Hoover "diary" in the Hoover Presidential Library as the authority for an account in which Hoover worked *against* the bankers. Box 98 of the Lamont Papers contains transcriptions of the telephone conversations to which the "diary" refers. The transcriptions not only refute every detail of Hoover's account but actually record Lamont's specific instructions to the president to conceal the origins of the moratorium. (As Lamont signed off from the first conversation: "One last thing, Mr. President . . . if anything, by any chance, ever comes out of this suggestion, we should wish to be forgotten in this matter. This is your plan and nobody else's.") A mass of supporting correspondence in the file confirms the authenticity of the transcripts, while being grossly inconsistent with what Wilson reports about the "diary." (Hoover often harbored private misgivings about both his policies and his advisers—but he never consistently acted upon these doubts.)

80. See Gerald Epstein and Thomas Ferguson, "Monetary Policy, Loan Liquidation and Industrial Conflict: The Federal Reserve and the Open Market Operations of 1932," chapter 3 of this volume, and Epstein and Ferguson, "Answers to Stock Questions: Fed Targets, Stock Prices, and the Gold Standard in the Great Depression," *Journal of Economic History* 51, no. 1 (March 1991), pp. 190–200.

81. The House Papers, now at Yale University, contain many letters between House and important figures in the Rockefeller complex. See, e.g., the discussion below, especially the main text to note 90.

82. Rosen, *Brains Trust*, p. 113, argues that House's influence on Roosevelt ebbed after March 1932. But the aging House could scarcely be expected to provide the daily memoranda and speeches that Roosevelt then needed. There is a sense in which House and all of Roosevelt's early advisors were supplemented, and in part supplanted, by many other forces then coming to life in the Democratic Party; however, House always remained a major actor in the New Deal.

83. See Rosen, *Brains Trust*, among many other works on the 1932 campaign.

84. The Newton Baker Papers now at the Library of Congress, Washington, D.C. and the Franklin D. Roosevelt Papers at the Roosevelt Library in Hyde Park, N.Y., have a mass of material on the primary and convention battles (e.g. the letters between Baker and Ralph Hayes in the Baker Papers). Rosen, *Brains Trust*, chaps. 9 and 10, presents considerable detail on the business opposition to FDR's nomination, and is very good on the stop-Roosevelt forces' manipulation of the press.

85. For Lamont's dramatic bid to block Aldrich, see Aldrich interviews, Chase Man-

hattan Bank Oral History Project, November 29, 1961, now in the Winthrop W. Aldrich Papers, Baker Library, Harvard University; for apprising me of the Rockefeller Center financing controversy I am grateful to Robert Fitch, whose own work on urban development and American political structures involved a lengthy period of work in the Rockefeller Archives. For the subway battle, see the *New York Times,* July 31, 1932; August 27 and 31, 1932; as well as Cynthia Horan, "Agreeing with the Bankers: New York City's Depression Financial Crisis," in Paul Zarembka (ed.), *Research in Political Economy* (Greenwich, Conn.: JAI Press, 1986), vol. 8, pp. 201–232. (Exactly who controlled the Manhattan Elevated, one of the parties in the urban transit dispute, is unclear, though the *New York Times* indicates that the Rockefellers did. Aldrich had certainly represented the line in the late 1920s, when one of several bitter disputes with a Morgan-controlled subway was in litigation.)

86. Agricultural economist M. L. Wilson is normally identified as the author of the adjustment plan. For Rockefeller's role in financing Wilson's early work, see Rosen, *Brains Trust,* p. 180; see p. 178 for Ruml's role in the famous Wilson-Rexford Tugwell meeting on the eve of the convention.

87. See the crucial letters of Thomas W. Lamont to various business associates and attached memoranda in Box 123 of the Lamont Papers, and my discussion of them in "Elites and Elections."

88. Some of these are in the House Papers, others in the Aldrich Papers. See, e.g., the House-Auchincloss correspondence in the former.

89. Secretary of Commerce Daniel Roper to Franklin D. Roosevelt, March 28, 1932, Roosevelt Library. This is one of many documents relating to Aldrich's vast lobbying efforts; other aspects of this legislation involved fairly heated exchanges between the Bank of America and the National City Bank of New York. While not as enduringly significant as the separation of investment from commercial banking, these conflicts persisted for some years and complicated the position of the National City Bank during much of the New Deal.

90. House to Roper, October 21, 1933, House Papers.

91. The chief source for most of what follows are the personal papers of Rene Leon, copies of which are now in my possession. See also the correspondence between Walter Lippmann and Leon, now in the Lippmann Correspondence at Yale, and between Raymond Moley, Leon, and Deterding in the Moley Papers, Hoover Institution, Stanford, Calif. Moffett later joined Standard of California.

92. The Frank Vanderlip Papers at Columbia University, New York City, contain the financial records of the Committee for the Nation during this period. The Standard Oil contributions are plainly listed there.

93. See, for example, the Minutes of the Executive Committee of the Open Market Committee, September 21, 1933; these are in the George Harrison Papers at Columbia University and available at the Federal Reserve Bank of New York. Copies also appear in the Minutes of the Directors Meetings of the Federal Reserve Bank of Boston for October 4, 1933, and other dates.

94. When Mrs. Rene Leon originally told me of her husband's efforts to block the efforts of Warburg and the other financiers at the London Conference, she could not remember the name of the businessman who had assisted him. The Leon Papers make it obvious that Moffett was the man as, independently, Mrs. Leon subsequently wrote me. A copy of what is perhaps the urgent telegram sent to warn FDR against Warburg's

efforts, which Mrs. Leon remembers her husband dispatching, can be found in Raymond Moley's papers relating to the London Conference. When that telegram came into Moley's hands is not clear; but this and other files in the Moley Papers contain numerous messages from Leon and even Deterding himself.

95. Robert Wood to Franklin D. Roosevelt, November 16, 1933, Robert Wood Papers, Herbert Hoover Presidential Library. Wood was president of Sears Roebuck, and a leader of the Committee for the Nation.

96. See, among others, Norman Nordhauser, *The Quest for Stability* (New York: Garland, 1979), chap. 8. I have profited greatly from the material in the J. R. Parten Papers.

97. See, for example, Sidney Lens, *The Labor Wars* (Garden City, N.Y.: Doubleday, 1973), pp. 288 ff.

98. See Walter Lippmann, "Self-Sufficiency: Some Random Reflections," *Foreign Affairs*, January 1934.

99. "Memorandum on the Views Relating to the Work of the Committee on Economic Security Expressed by Various Individuals Consulted," National Archives Record Group 47, Public Record Office, Washington, D.C. The interviews reported in this memo were taken "on a trip to New England and New York on August 19–21, 1934." I am grateful to Janet Corpus for bringing this memo to my attention.

100. It is impossible to inventory all of the relevant citations here, but see the material in Record Group 47 of the National Archives and, especially, the material in Box 31 of the Ralph Flanders Papers, Syracuse University Library, Syracuse, N.Y.

101. Some authors suggest that because strike rates went from ionospheric in 1934 to merely stratospheric in 1935, the Wagner Act cannot have been adopted in response to pressure from labor. In fact, the expiration of the NRA determined when the soaring overall rate of class conflict would affect the statutes. The Supreme Court decision declaring the NRA unconstitutional came only days ahead of the law's lapse. Obviously, what follows on the origins of the Wagner Act hardly suffices as a treatment of the rise of labor during the New Deal. I largely discuss elite responses to mass protest; I do not pretend to be offering a theory of the labor movement.

102. See, for example, Charlton Ogburn to William Green, January 7, 1935, Box 282, W. Jett Lauck Papers, University of Virginia.

103. See Sloan's remarkable letter to J. J. Raskob, October 23, 1934, Raskob Papers.

104. In the Twentieth Century Fund deliberations, some railroad leaders, noting the Wagner bill's similarity to the Railway Labor Act, supported its passage; Industrial Relations Counsellors opposed some of its key provisions; while nearly all the businessmen sought an equivalent "unfair labor practice" provision applying to unions. AFL attorney Charlton Ogburn, however, won out. Some aspects of New Deal tax policy (which was certainly not radical) should probably also be viewed as evidence of labor's rising power.

105. Morgan had sought to repeal Glass-Steagall. Aldrich blocked this, but had to accept a shift of power within the Fed from the New York bank to the board of governors in Washington, which the Bank of America and other non-New York bankers championed. The almost simultaneous legislation aimed at breaking up public utility holding companies drove another nail into the coffin of the House of Morgan, for that bank totally dominated the industry, especially after Samuel Insull's bankruptcy.

106. The Parten Papers, along with those of Interior Secretary Ickes at the Library of Congress and Texas Governor James Allred, now in the University of Houston Library,

Houston, Texas, contain large amounts of material on oil issues. See, as one example, Franklin D. Roosevelt to Governor E. W. Marland of Oklahoma, May 17, 1935 (copy in the Allred Papers).

107. See Bernard Baruch to Eugene Meyer, May 20, 1936, Baruch Papers, Seeley Mudd Library, Princeton University. Meyer was at that time helping to run the Landon campaign. Note that in autumn 1935 Standard had helped turn aside Hoover's bid for the '36 nomination (see Herbert Hoover to Lewis Strauss, September 23, 1935, Lewis Strauss Papers, Hoover Presidential Library).

108. The Chemical Foundation Papers contain much material on Francis P. Garvan's efforts to promote protectionism around the time of the convention. See especially Garvan's correspondence with F. X. Eble and Samuel Crowther, in Box 11-2.

109. Samuel Crowther to Francis P. Garvan, July 18, 1936, Box 11-2, Chemical Foundation Papers.

110. *New York Times*, October 29, 1936, p. 10.

111. The details of all the high-level switches around the trade issues and the complex positions of some large interests (such as the Rockefellers) cannot be discussed here for reasons of space. Note, however, George Foster Peabody to A. H. Sulzberger of the *New York Times*, December 5, 1935, on the importance of good coverage for FDR and Sulzberger's accommodating reply of December 12, both in George Foster Peabody Papers, Box 50, Library of Congress. Peabody held a large demand note on Roosevelt's Warm Springs, Ga., Foundation.

112. For some documentation on the trade committee, cf. Aldrich Papers, Box 67. For Ruml's role in the deficit spending plan, cf. Robert Collins, *Business Response to Keynes* (New York: Columbia University Press, 1981), pp. 69 ff.

113. Francis Fox Piven and Richard Cloward, *Poor People's Movements* (New York: Vintage, 1976).

114. "Ferguson," write Weir and Skocpol in "Keynesian Responses," p. 114, "[is] unmistakably a writer in the peculiarly American 'Beardsian' tradition" who attributes "magical powers" to business. Who could complain about a comparison with the greatest of all American political analysts (who, we now learn, was basically right about the founding fathers; see Robert Maguire and Robert Ohsfeldt, "Economic Interests and the Constitution: A Quantitative Rehabilitation of Charles A. Beard," *Journal of Economic History* 44 [June 1984]: 509–19)? Serious readers of this essay, however, will recognize that the only "magical" power possessed by the New Deal's business supporters is their ability to remain invisible to historians.

Thomas Ferguson and Joel Rogers, *Right Turn: The Decline of the Democrats and the Future of American Politics* (New York: Hill & Wang, 1986), analyze at length the movement of various industrial groups in and out of the party during the decline of the New Deal. The explanation put forward there can usefully be contrasted with, for example, Thomas Byrne Edsall, *The New Politics of Inequality* (New York: W. W. Norton, 1984), which continues to portray the GOP as the party of big business, while analyzing the Democrats mainly in demographic terms.

115. See the discussion in my "Party Realignment," especially notes 44 and 45, chapter 1 in this volume, and the appendix, "Deduced and Abandoned."

Monetary Policy, Loan Liquidation, and Industrial Conflict:
The Federal Reserve and the Open Market Operations of 1932

GERALD EPSTEIN AND THOMAS FERGUSON

... in the United States the fear of the Member Banks lest they should be unable to cover their expenses is an obstacle to the adoption of a wholehearted cheap money policy.

J. M. Keynes, September 1932[1]

IN THE SUMMER of 1929, output and employment in the American economy began falling. After the stock market crashed in late October, the decline turned into a catastrophic rout. By mid-1930, the United States, along with many other countries, was clearly sliding into deep depression. Yet the Federal Reserve System, widely trumpeted in the 1920s as the final guarantor of financial stability, did very little to offset what soon developed into the greatest deflation in American history.

For two long years the Fed maintained its posture of Jovian indifference. On occasion the New York Fed promoted very modest increases in liquidity; discount rates were lowered and flurries of open market purchases occurred, but nothing more.

In the spring of 1932, however, the Fed abruptly came to life. Following passage of a new banking law, the Glass-Steagall Act of 1932, which liberalized collateral requirements for Federal Reserve notes, the Fed seemed poised for a dramatic effort to break the deflationary cycle.[2] As one eyewitness, who enjoyed special access to top Fed officials during this period, recalled many years later:

> The Federal Reserve Bank's experts, meanwhile, attempted their own cure by monetary controls aimed at expanding the supply of money. The strategy of "open market" purchasing of bonds by the Federal Reserve Banks had been used earlier; but now it was employed on a gigantic scale by [New York Fed Governor George L.] Harrison, who

headed the Open Market Committee for the country's twelve Reserve Banks. Under the new banking rules, he had one billion dollars more in gold available. With these funds he began to buy $100 million in U.S. government bonds every week during ten successive weeks up to May, 1932, by which date a hoard of $1.1 billion in bonds was accumulated. These transactions, of a size unequalled in the history of any central bank, put cash in the hands of the Reserve's member banks and were expected to form the basis for the expansion of loans or investment in the ratio of 10 to 1.[3]

But the campaign ended almost as quickly as it began. In the summer of 1932, the Fed effectively abandoned the new policy. A few months later, like millions of other Americans, Herbert Hoover lost his house. Soon thereafter another wave of bank failures began. Eventually the entire financial system of the United States collapsed completely.

Ever since those dark days, debates have raged over the Fed's policies.[4] Little of this new work, however, has analyzed the Federal Reserve System's shortlived attempt in early 1932 to reflate the economy through open market operations. Yet, as we will demonstrate, a reconsideration of the Fed's actions in the period raises searching questions about the most widely accepted explanations of the Fed's behavior in the Depression. We highlight the potentially disastrous consequences of one of the Fed's most basic structural characteristics: its dual responsibility for both the health of the member banks and the welfare of the economy as a whole.

THE ROLE OF THE FED: PREVIOUS VIEWS

Among the recent works addressing the question of what the Fed thought it was doing are those by Friedman and Schwartz; Wicker; and Brunner and Meltzer. Their accounts of the 1932 episode can be compared by contrasting the answers each provides to three questions. Why did the Fed wait so long to begin its reflation program? Why did the campaign begin when it did, in early 1932? Why was the effort hastily abandoned the following summer?

Friedman and Schwartz offer explicit answers to each of these queries. Three reasons, they believe, explain why the Fed was reluctant to move against the Depression before 1932. The first is the untimely death in 1929 of the Fed's dominating personality, New York Federal Reserve Bank Governor Benjamin Strong. What made his demise so significant were the other two factors Friedman and Schwartz stress: the Fed's weak, decentralized organizational structure and the absence within the Federal Reserve System (save for the New York Fed) of a broad "national" point of view. "Parochial" and "jealous of New York," the regional banks were "predisposed to question what New York proposed." Their reluctance to cooperate increased turmoil in the Fed and made bold action impossible.[5]

Flatly denying that most Fed officials harbored any desires to reflate on their own, Friedman and Schwartz argue that pressure from Congress explains the timing of the open market operations of 1932. The close of the congressional session, they suggest, freed the Fed from these pressures and accounted for the tapering off of the program in the summer of 1932.

Wicker's account is less clearcut. In different parts of his work he mentions various factors, including a failure by most of the Fed's directors and officials "to understand how open market operations could be used to counteract recessions and depressions," and a concentration on short-term rates "to the neglect of member bank reserves and the money supply."[6] Unlike Friedman and Schwartz, who downplay international considerations, Wicker refers frequently to the Fed's anxiety about the international gold standard and, at least occasionally, free gold. Although Wicker does not focus on what caused the Fed to begin the open market operations, he is clear on why the Fed abandoned them: Fed officials misinterpreted the meaning of the accumulation of excess reserves, and considered monetary policy easy.[7]

Brunner and Meltzer do not specifically discuss the 1932 reflation and, as discussed below, large-scale open market purchases are precisely what their theory of Fed behavior does *not* predict. But if their account thus affords no answer to the second of our three questions (why the open market operations began), it is easy to reconstruct implicit answers to the other two questions from their general account of the Fed in this period. Their discussion focuses on the latter point mentioned by Wicker, the misinterpretation of excess reserves and short-term rates. They argue that the severe deflation of the early 1930s made nominal interest rates unusually poor guides to real interest rates.[8] With severe deflation, low nominal rates represented a comparatively high real rate. During much of the Depression, and particularly in the summer of 1932 when nominal rates were quite low, the Fed may simply have misinterpreted conditions in the money market; it believed real rates were low, when they in fact were high.

Brunner and Meltzer also argue that the reigning Fed doctrine on open market operations, referred to as the "Riefler-Burgess-Strong framework," led the Fed astray. The doctrine, they assert, not only failed to distinguish nominal from real rates, but also upheld the "real bills" theory, according to which bank lending for actual trade (real bills) represented the only acceptable asset for rediscount by central banks.[9]

Each of these accounts clarifies vital points. But we cannot accept any of them as definitive. For example, all place heavy weight on policy errors, mistaken theories, and, in the case of Friedman and Schwartz, and Wicker, personalities. Yet, not only the Fed, but virtually all other central banks failed to move vigorously against the Depression.[10] How far can one press an argument that a deceased Benjamin Strong was responsible for all of this?

The assumptions and claims in the literature about targets and indicators relied upon by the Fed during this period are also problematic. The claim of Brunner and Meltzer, and Wicker that the Fed did not understand the difference between real and nominal rates relies on an implication that is difficult to believe: that bankers were unable to see that real interest rates were high but that the industrialists, who joined them on the boards of the Federal Reserve banks, were. (That is why they did not borrow, according to the argument.) References to the real-nominal distinction among top bankers, economists, and leading members of the Federal Reserve System were also far more common than the work of Brunner and Meltzer suggests. Material in the Fed's archives indicates that, at least in the 1930s, neither Burgess nor Riefler subscribed to the doctrines bearing their names.[11]

Direct evidence of a relationship between real bills and Fed behavior is also weak. Our own statistical tests failed to confirm earlier views of the influence of short-term interest rates on Fed policy, while a continuation of Meltzer's own table relating changes in the gold stock, member bank borrowing, and interest rates on three-month to six-month notes to Fed decisions on open market operations past his mid-1931 cutoff point shows that the Fed repeatedly ignored the signals sent by member bank borrowing.[12]

Friedman and Schwartz's account of the making of monetary policy in this period raises other questions. It emphasizes domestic concerns and underestimates the role international economic considerations, especially a concern for protection of the gold stock and maintenance of the gold standard, played in the making of policy throughout most of the period of 1929 to 1932. As we will explain below, although Friedman and Schwartz are correct in claiming the passage of the Glass-Steagall Act of early 1932 temporarily alleviated the free gold problem for the Federal Reserve System as a whole, they are mistaken in dismissing both gold and the international economy as constraints thereafter.

To see how the international economy affected Fed policy after the

Glass-Steagall Act of 1932, however, it is necessary to break with the tradition of analyzing the Fed's actions in terms of their effects on broad categories, such as the total gold stock, the balance of payments, or the national income. One must look in detail at the microeconomics of the banking sector to identify how various actions of the Fed potentially affected bank profitability at different points in time. If, following Stigler, Posner, and other recent analysts of the symbiosis of regulator and regulated, one gathers evidence on the policy preferences of private bankers and their interaction with the regulators, we find a ready answer to our three central questions about the Fed's open market program of 1932.[13]

WHY DID THE FED WAIT SO LONG?

Our principle concern is the behavior of the Federal Reserve System between January and July 1932, and thus we concentrate on answering the last two of the three questions. Responding to the first query, why the Fed waited so long to act, however, requires a glance backward at Fed policy in earlier stages of the Great Contraction.

Between October 1929 and April 1931, industrial production fell by 26 percent, while the monetary base declined by 90 million dollars. In the period it is clear that the Fed did not pursue an activist policy to revive the economy, but some differences occasionally developed in the approaches various reserve banks took to manage the deflation.

Immediately after the stock market crash, for example, the New York Fed purchased $160 million of government securities and encouraged the New York banks to discount freely. During the next year and a half, the New York Fed pressed for reductions in discount and acceptance rates. Opposition from the board of governors and the other reserve banks, however, generally delayed or reduced the impact of these measures.[14]

But, if the New York Fed generally favored easier money than the rest of the Federal Reserve System, it did not advocate large-scale reflation. New York Fed Governor Harrison's report of the open market policy conference to the governor's conference on April 27, 1931, for example, clearly repudiated the notion of an active countercyclical policy.[15]

Why was the New York Fed more expansionary than other reserve banks, and why did no one seriously try to revive business? The answer to the first question surely relates to the important connection between the New York commercial banks and the stock market (or perhaps, the banker directors of the New York Fed, many of whom were later shown to have been in some distress in this period).[16]

The reasons for the lack of interest in more expansionary policies are more interesting and can be pieced together from primary sources and our statistical investigation. Archival sources make a point which is obvious in retrospect, but which later accounts do not take seriously enough: Conventional doctrine among businessmen, bankers, and economists in the period held that occasional depressions (or deflations) were vital to the long-run health of a capitalist economy. Accordingly, the task of central banking was to stand back and allow nature's therapy to take its course. As one well-known voting member of the Fed's board of governors, Treasury Secretary Andrew Mellon, expressed it, the way out of a depression consisted of a sustained effort to "liquidate labor, liquidate stocks, liquidate the farmers, liquidate real estate." [17] In private discussions among bankers, economists, and Fed officials, the need to compel liquidation was a common topic of conversation. Reasons given included correcting the mistakes of businessmen, curbing the excessive spending of governments, and especially, reducing the wages of labor. [18]

Among industrialists and high government officials, faith that wage reductions would eventually revive prosperity was less strong than among bankers. After the stock market crash, for example, President Hoover made several highly publicized efforts to promote work sharing and discourage wage cuts. His efforts were backed strongly by a number of major industrialists in predominantly capital-intensive industries, including the heads of Standard Oil of New Jersey and AT&T. In the end, however, the campaign did not amount to much. Petering out as the Depression grew worse, it failed to move the Fed. [19]

Their inability to move the Fed led the industrialists either to give up and join the bankers in calls for wage reductions or to influence Congress in favor of legislated directives for monetary expansion. Hoover, who left to himself would probably have moved more vigorously against the Depression than has been presumed, in practice gave in to pressures from the banks, especially J. P. Morgan & Co., and the Treasury. [20]

Though Friedman and Schwartz argue that in the period free gold and the gold standard were not major concerns of the Federal Reserve Board, we believe they are mistaken. Their narrative, for example, alludes to a memorandum from a January 1931 meeting of the Federal Reserve Board. Yet at the conference, many participants were deeply concerned with gold. Fed economist E. A. Goldenweiser, for example, reports that "There was a good deal of discussion about free gold. Anderson had made a statement that free gold was down to $600,000,000, and we were, therefore, nearer to the time when credit policy would have to be guided by the availability of gold." To which

A. C. Miller of the Federal Reserve Board bluntly replied that "purchases of securities by diminishing free gold are a dangerous procedure."[21]

Although convertibility remained axiomatic to everyone in the banking system, real bills did not. Some top Fed officials seem to have subscribed to this doctrine.[22] But many Fed officials and bankers (especially in New York) actively promoted the removal of the extra constraints on free gold imposed by existing limitations on the definition of the "eligible paper" acceptable as backing for Federal Reserve notes. Goldenweiser observed to the Federal Reserve Board in early January 1930, "My own view is that collateral provisions are obsolete and unnecessary."[23] His statement counts heavily against Brunner and Meltzer's argument on the importance of the real bills doctrine as an explanation of Fed behavior. The collateral provisions associated with the definition of free gold were one of the major embodiments of the real bills doctrine in the Federal Reserve System.

The desire to force wages down, intermittent anxiety about gold, and (to a lesser extent) the belief of some in real bills, probably account for most of the Fed's inactivity until the fall of 1931.[24] An event then occurred which explains the Fed's inaction throughout the rest of 1931 and the timing of its belated reflation efforts in early 1932. That event was the British abandonment of the gold standard in September 1931.

THE DECISION TO REFLATE

Friedman and Schwartz, who deemphasize international factors in their account, agree that the desire to remain on gold controlled Fed policy in the next few months. The run on the dollar that followed Britain's announcement that it was leaving gold resulted in a heavy gold loss for the United States. From September 16 to September 30, 1931, the U.S. gold stock declined by $275 million. In October it decreased by an additional $450 million. The losses just about offset the net influx during the preceding two years.[25]

For a brief time Harrison and the New York Fed hoped to avoid a sharp rise in the discount rate, but experience in the first few weeks persuaded everyone in the Federal Reserve System that the time had arrived to apply the classic remedy for halting a run on gold. In two weeks the Fed raised the rate by 2 percentage points, the sharpest rise in such a brief period in the Fed's history. It also halted all expansionary open market operations.

The benefits of this policy were predictable: The run on the dollar halted; gold outflows ceased and then began to reverse. But its costs were no less obvious and foreseeable: There were massive new waves of deflation, business bankruptcies, and bank failures.

The chorus of voices demanding reflation swelled, and calls for public works expenditures, veterans' benefits, government-sponsored cartelization of industry, and other forms of market intervention proliferated. As Friedman and Schwartz suggest, many of the new pressures found expression in Congress, where bills mandating various forms of monetary expansion, including one coauthored by Irving Fisher, were introduced.[26]

All the tumult certainly worried the Fed and the banking community at large. The banks, however, had major worries of their own. The rise in the discount rate sent bond prices plunging, even triple-A bonds. The collapse of bond prices threatened the solvency of many banks.[27]

With many large banks facing the potential of trouble, many leading bankers joined veterans, industrialists, and farmers in calling upon the Fed for action. A few financiers, including several Morgan partners, advocated expansionary monetary policies explicitly for macroeconomic reasons.[28] Most bankers, however, appear to have been dubious or uncomprehending about the macroeconomic case for reflation. But at this juncture it hardly mattered, for with runs on banks, hoarding, and other threats to deposits developing, most banks had a desperate need for action by the Federal Reserve to revive the almost defunct bond market and to restore liquidity.[29]

Unable for several months to do anything with monetary policy (because their sovereign commitment to gold left them no choice but to support discount rate increases), leading bankers began consultations with Hoover's Treasury Secretary Ogden Mills (who had replaced Andrew Mellon), Fed Chairman Eugene Meyer, and other top officials. Led by Thomas W. Lamont of J. P. Morgan & Co., they evolved a plan for a private "National Credit Corporation." The NCC, however, had one drawback: It was "National" in name only. Actually, it functioned as a bank bailout fund, operating on capital privately supplied by leading bankers, which exposed them to possible losses. As soon as the run on gold abated in the last couple of months of 1931, Lamont, other private bankers, Hoover, Mills, and high Fed officials gradually evolved new and different plans.[30]

The new program was represented to the open market policy conference in early January 1932. Standard accounts of the Fed in this period accurately present five of the six points in the plan "to stop deflation and encourage some credit increase." These five are: (1) passage of the Reconstruction Finance Corporation, (2) Federal Reserve and member bank cooperation with the Treasury program, (3) the buying of bills when possible, (4) the reduction of discount rates, and

(5) the purchase of governments. The remaining point is usually reported as "support for the bond market." In the minutes it reads "organized support for the bond market predicated upon railroad wage cuts."[31]

Thus a major goal of the program was to revive railroad bond values, of which major New York banks held $200 million, comprising a third of their private bond portfolios in December 1931, and bond prices in general. Private bankers and the Federal Reserve saw wage cuts as a necessary condition to reviving those values. By reviving the bond market the Federal Reserve hoped to regenerate the savings and investment process and revive the banks.

Another component of the program, hidden in the January minutes, appears in a memorandum from W. Randolph Burgess to Harrison: "most of the points of our January program have now been achieved: rail wages have been reduced, the administration had made a definite commitment on balancing the budget, the Reconstruction Finance Corporation is in operation, and the bond pool has been operating—though feebly. Everybody else has done the tasks assigned to him, but the reserve system. . . ." Burgess adds, "there was a very good reason for not doing so, and that was the limited amount of our free gold in the face of European gold withdrawals."[32]

Though Friedman and Schwartz discount it, Fed memoranda during the period show that free gold did handicap the Federal Reserve System for several months. After massive lobbying by the Fed and private bankers, however, Congress passed the Glass-Steagall Act.[33] The new law permitted government securities to be used as backing for Federal Reserve notes, thus freeing additional gold for export.

Keeping careful watch on critical variables (the gold stock, excess reserves, free gold, foreign balances, and bank suspensions), the Fed commenced open market operations.[34] In a memorandum prepared for an April 5 meeting of the executive committee and the board of governors, Harrison reported that "the program . . . has been even more successful than could well have been hoped for at that time, as member bank indebtedness has been reduced by more than $200,000,000."[35]

At that meeting, Harrison "reviewed the current economic situation, the continued decline in prices, the increase in the pressure of debts, the increase in bankruptcies, and the threat of radical action in Congress. . . . After extended discussion of these questions it was moved and carried that purchases of government securities be continued at a rate of $25,000,000 a week.[36] The mention of "the increase in the pressure of debts" after "the continued decline in prices" suggests that, contrary to Brunner and Meltzer, Harrison was aware of the effects of falling prices on the real value of debt. Harrison's allusion to congressional pressure also confirms Friedman and Schwartz's suggestion that this factor was a concern at the Fed. But the reference also sets this factor in its proper context as but one among several figuring in the decision to reflate.

At an April 12 meeting, Treasury Secretary Mills, Fed Chairman Meyer, Miller of the board, and Harrison urged the Fed's Board of Governors to approve a major increase in the scale of open market purchases. Mills asserted that "[f]or a great central banking system to stand by with a 70% gold reserve without taking active steps in such a situation was almost inconceivable and almost unforgiveable." Harrison explained the delay in moving toward an expansion program after the passage of the Glass-Steagall Act as the effect of "[t]he uncertainty as to the budget and bonus legislation [which] had constituted obstacles to inaugurating such a program, but he believed that the outlook in these directions was hopeful, and that it would not be possible or necessary to wait until these questions were completely solved."[37]

THE PROGRAM ABANDONED

By this time, however, serious opposition to the program had surfaced among the reserve banks and on the board of governors. Governor J. B. McDougal of Chicago had strongly opposed it virtually from the beginning. In this pre–New Deal period, when authority for open market purchases was not as yet vested firmly in the board of governors, McDougal's opposition was very important, for his bank was, with the exception of New York, the most important in terms of its influence within the Federal Reserve System and in terms of the number of securities it could buy.[38] Often, however, Governor Roy Young of the much smaller Boston bank supported him, at least to the extent of speaking against the program before committing his bank to participating.[39]

At the April 12 meeting McDougal and Young questioned the program again, and a revealing exchange with Harrison occurred. Objecting that as the program continued, reserves would pile up in reserve centers, Young allowed that "he was skeptical of getting the cooperation of the banks . . . and was apprehensive that a program of this sort would develop the animosity of many bankers." Harrison replied, most meaningfully, that in "the present situation the banks were much more interested in avoiding possible losses than in augmenting their current income, and that their attitude had changed gradually since last year in the face of the shrinkage in values."[40]

This exchange between governors provides one of the first clear hints of the importance of one of the three major factors that eventually led to the abandonment of the whole program. We call it the "loan liquidation effect."

By the middle of the Great Contraction, bank portfolios in many Federal Reserve districts were beginning to assume a curious shape. Either because bankers were becoming very wary or because good lending opportunities were difficult to find, loans were falling off catastrophically. The loan liquidation effect then took hold. As loans and many bonds became increasingly risky, bankers looked around for ways to maintain earnings. In due course, they began to purchase larger and larger amounts of the safest asset that remained available in large quantities—short-term government securities. Tables 3.1 and 3.2 indicate the dimensions of this change. Whereas in 1929 investments made up less than 30 percent of member bank earning asset portfolios, by the end of 1933 they made up almost 50 percent (see table 3.1). A large percentage of the increase took the form of increases in holdings of government securities.

TABLE 3.1. Ratio of Investments to Loans and Investments For Selected Member Banks

Year	All Member Banks	New York Central Reserve City Banks	Chicago Central Reserve City Banks	All Reserve City Banks	Boston Reserve City Banks
1929					
October	.2715	.2217	.1711	.2529	.1867
December	.2723	.2383	.1759	.2447	.1462
1930					
December	.3152	.2837	.2783	.2956	.2109
1931					
March	.3423	.3142	.3195	.3372	.2512
June	.3569	.3380	.3211	.3543	.3043
October	.3689	.3674	.3127	.3559	.3136
December	.3700	.3615	.3164	.3535	.2937
1932[a]					
March	.3888	.4066	.3152	.3689	.3215
June	.4076	.4517	.3140	.3842	.3492
October	.4322	.4933	.3733	.4067	.3913
December	.4465	.5171	.3962	.4161	.4213
1933[a]					
March	.4639	.5186	.4351	.4442	.4380

Source: Board of Governors of the United States Federal Reserve System, Banking and Monetary Statistics (Washington, D.C., 1943), pp. 72, 74, 80, 86, 92, 696.
[a]Call dates except for March 1932, 1933, which are linear interpolations since there were no call reports for those dates.

TABLE 3.2. Ratio of Bills and Notes to Total Investments
For Selected Member Banks

Year	All Member Banks	New York Central Reserve City Banks	Chicago Central Reserve City Banks	All Reserve City Banks	Boston Reserve City Banks
1929					
October	.1057	.1422	.1182	.1288	.0773
December	.0786	.1071	.0712	.0870	.0573
1930					
December	.0777	.1544	.2259	.0611	.1205
1931					
March	.1035	.1585	.3716	.1045	.1667
June	.1077	.1899	.3712	.0989	.2117
October	.1053	.2025	.4202	.0739	.1502
December	.0991	.1665	.3979	.0793	.1943
1932[a]					
March	.1137	.2152	.4022	.0815	.2354
June	.1284	.2638	.4065	.0836	.2765
October	.1830	.3615	.4157	.1341	.3302
December	.1993	.3911	.3357	.1446	.3951
1933[a]					
March	.2322	.4146	.4039	.1828	.4306

Source: Board of Governors of the United States Federal Reserve System, *Banking and Monetary Statistics* (Washington, D.C., 1943), pp. 77, 84, 90, 96, 700.

[a]Call dates except for March 1932, 1933, which are linear interpolations since there were no call reports for those dates.

These shifts had important consequences for bank earnings. The net return on investments tended to be lower than that on loans.[41] In addition, table 3.2 indicates the banks, especially the reserve city banks, bought a sharply rising percentage of short-term securities.

With expansionary open market operations and reductions in nominal income moving short-term rates to extremely low levels (rates on three-month to six-month Treasury notes and certificates plunged from 3.4 percent in November of 1929 to 0.34 percent in June of 1932), a squeeze on bank earnings developed.[42] Unable to obtain capital gains because of the shortness of their portfolios, banks had to face diminished earnings as they turned over portfolios and as rates on short-term governments fell.

Of course, rate reductions would not have impaired current earnings if rates on the money banks borrowed and other expenses had fallen just as rapidly. But while rates on borrowed money did decline, there were pitfalls here. In 1932, banks still paid interest on demand deposits. As rates paid approached zero, it would become increasingly difficult to hold deposits, especially if a run materialized.[43] Even worse, the banks still had to pay expenses, and these, especially payments for salaries and wages and "other expenses" (which included fees for directors and advisory committees), failed to decline as much as earnings in 1932 (and several other years). Accordingly, net earnings, *before losses*, fell more or less steadily after 1929. But earnings after losses on loans and securities plunged steeply in 1932 and 1933, leading to $-\$0.89$ and $-\$1.42$ in net profits per $100 of loans and investments in 1932 and 1933.[44]

These developments led to growing opposition to the open market campaign in a straightforward manner. Although loan liquidation ultimately spread to banks in all Federal Reserve districts, some districts were hit much harder than others in 1932. Banks that stood to lose the most from declining rates were those with a relatively high percentage of short-term debt in their portfolios. Table 3.2 indicates that Chicago's central reserve city banks, the city's larger banks, had a much higher proportion of bills and notes in their portfolios than all member banks or all other reserve city banks, and that Boston's reserve city banks were adding short-term governments to their portfolios at a breakneck pace between October 1931 and June 1932. (Note that Chicago central reserve city banks had double the percentage of bills and notes than those in New York through 1931, with New York catching up only in the last quarter of 1932 after the open market purchases were abandoned; while between October and December 1931, reserve city banks in Boston and central reserve city banks in New York changed the composition of their portfolios in virtually opposite directions.)

These portfolio changes had important consequences for net earnings of member banks by Federal Reserve district. Since earnings on the overall portfolios reflected the interest rates on assets accumulated in previous months, current security rates would have their major effects on portfolio earnings some months after they were purchased. So, for example, returns in December of 1932 would reflect the interest rates on securities purchased in the summer of 1932. There were great reductions in net earnings facing banks in the Chicago district in the half-year ending December 1932, reflecting the earlier decline in interest rates. Their net margin (earnings per $100 of loans and investments) fell to $0.23 from $0.43 in the period six months earlier, which translates into a substantial drop in total profits. New York bank earnings margins, on the other hand, still held up comparatively well even at this late date, falling only from $0.62 to $0.54. The rates for other districts (generally of less significance within the system than Chicago or New York) were scattered.[45]

That the governors of the Boston Fed and, especially, the Chicago Fed should be early critics of the reflation program is therefore no mystery.

Opposition on the other grounds was soon registered in minutes and memoranda. A memo on open market purchases, April 5, 1932, reported that between March 2 and April 6, the Fed had bought $130 million of securities. But only four reserve banks participated in the open market purchase program directly. Moreover, the Federal Reserve Bank of Kansas City had discontinued its participation on March 23, "owing to its free gold position."[46]

This reference points to a second reason for the eventual termination of the program, what might be termed the growing problem of "gold distribution." As Friedman and Schwartz emphasize, especially after the passage of the Glass-Steagall Act, both the Federal Reserve as a whole and the New York Fed had more than enough gold to meet any conceivable run. But Federal Reserve banks in each district still had to maintain a 40 percent gold cover for their notes. And here an acute problem began shaping up. The Federal Reserve was, after all, only a federal reserve. A series of unresolved controversies in the 1920s had led to debates about the Federal Reserve Board's legal authority over individual reserve banks. Though it is difficult to be sure, since the issue eventually was settled not in court but by New Deal banking legislation, it is doubtful that individual reserve banks would have surrendered their gold without struggle. (Indeed, under far graver conditions a year later, the Chicago Fed flatly refused the New York Fed's desperate request for emergency rediscounting assistance and made the refusal stick.)[47]

As a consequence, not only the total amount of gold but its distribution among the Federal Reserve banks became important. As individual banks lost gold and approached the legal limit for their gold cover, they would have to stop participation in the reflation program. Over the next few months this happened: Not only Kansas City but other reserve banks became more and more nervous about running out of *their* gold. As their nervousness increased, they stopped supporting reflation.[48]

The last of the three major factors which induced the Fed to abandon its open market program also concerned gold. Like the question of distribution, however, it has not figured significantly in the literature. The problem, at its starkest, was this: At the time the open market program began, foreign balances held by American institutions amounted to more than $1.2 billion. These sums were not distributed evenly throughout the system's districts, but were heavily concentrated in New York (with, probably, lesser amounts in Boston and one or two other reserve centers).[49] Difficulty arose because the French (and toward the end, British and other interests) withdrew large sums, and the British threatened to withdraw still more. That the Federal Reserve System as a whole had reserves that more than covered the foreign deposits was all very well. To the big New York banks, however, this was academic. It was *their* deposits that were leaving, to the detriment of *their* earnings and safety.

In a theoretically perfect world, of course, the deposit loss might have been neutralized by continued open market operations. But America in 1932 was not a theoretically perfect world. First of all, for reasons already discussed, the whole open market program was acutely controversial. No New York bank could be sure how long it would continue or what the purchases would amount to. In addition, the magnitude of foreign deposits involved was large—almost equal to the projected total of open market purchases for the system as a whole. There was also the possibility that Americans would look at the foreign withdrawals and themselves begin fleeing from the dollar, especially as the battle over the budget climaxed.

From the beginning of the open market program, private bankers and Fed officials sought ways to minimize losses of foreign gold. It is uncertain whether Prime Minister Pierre Laval pledged to maintain French deposits when he visited the United States in the fall of 1931, but, in any case, the Banque de France soon compelled the Fed to agree to their withdrawal. With the faint hope of persuading the French to change their minds. Thomas Lamont of J. P. Morgan & Co. made a special trip to France in the early spring. For a while, Lamont and other bankers believed these efforts might succeed. But events gradually proved them mistaken. Encouraged by a series of widely discussed articles by H. Parker Willis, an economist well known for monetary orthodoxy that criticized the Fed's program as "inflationary," the Banque de France and other foreign interests continued withdrawing deposits from the Fed and other banks.[50]

Though Fed officials and bankers worried privately about the lost deposits, for a while the losses were bearable. The French withdrew most of their deposits, but under Harrison's leadership the Fed continued with the program. In late spring, however, the British threatened to emulate the French.

As early as March, the Bank of England had indicated that it did not want to let sterling appreciate in response to an expansionary program in the United States. At that time, however, the Bank of England

was pursuing a modest "cheap money" policy of its own (with the enthusiastic support of the British Treasury, which urged the Bank of
England to proceed even more vigorously.)[51] With sterling declining
about as much as the dollar, there was no necessary conflict between
the policies of the two central banks for several months. But while
little overt conflict existed, concern on both sides led the two central
banks and the Morgan bank to begin a round of discussions.

As they negotiated, influential New York bankers, including Morgan partners who supported monetary expansion, complained about
their lost foreign deposits:

> loans and deposits of the New York banks have fallen almost perpen-
> dicularly. . . . The loss of French and other foreign deposits, particu-
> larly since sterling went off gold, has fallen principally upon New
> York. Not only actual withdrawals of balances from America to
> abroad, but transfers of balances from banks to the Federal Reserve
> Bank have taken place. This loss of deposits has forced the New York
> banks to realize on assets.
>
> I question whether the Federal Reserve Banks' liberal purchases
> of bills and governments have even so much as kept step with the
> member banks' losses in deposits and *stillhaltungs* [sic]. Such pur-
> chases cannot begin to have an affirmative effect on the general price
> level until they have exceeded the amount of the frozen credits and
> withdrawn deposits.[52]

In late spring the Bank of England (though not the British Treasury) became concerned that sterling would drop too far. By May 26,
the New York Fed was receiving cables that the Bank of England was
selling dollars.[53] Pressure on the dollar mounted. Whereas French deposits in New York banks had been falling for a number of months,
British funds plunged between May and August by over a third. Withdrawals of the remaining French deposits also accelerated.

The continued loss of gold and deposits put many New York banks
in an increasingly uncomfortable position. As the difficulties associated
with the pursuit of an independent monetary policy in a context of international capital mobility and a managed exchange rate were expressed
in their balance sheets and income statements, the banks were faced
with a dilemma. If interest rates rose, they would encounter losses on
their bond portfolios that might lead to bank runs and insolvency. If interest rates fell, foreigners would withdraw deposits, forcing the banks
to liquidate bonds and therefore realize losses on their bond portfolios
due to the inelasticity of demand for bonds at the time of the forced sale.

Not surprisingly, the New York financial community began sending
mixed signals. Many complained that the reflation program had "de-
moralized money and exchange markets."[54]

Adding to the turmoil was the climax of the long-running battle over the national budget in early June. Harrison believed that the gold outflow would slow down once France removed its gold. But that did not prevent him from joining with leading businessmen in using the preservation of the gold standard as an argument in an ultimately successful fight for a sales tax and a balanced budget and against the reflation bills being debated in Congress.[55]

For these reasons—the loan liquidation effect, the problems of gold distribution with the Federal Reserve System, and the problem of withdrawal of foreign balances—opposition to "inflation" intensified within the Fed and among bankers in the early summer. At various meetings complaints were voiced above the slowness with which monetary policy seemed to be working. Extensive discussion about the need to find borrowers and to coordinate investments and loan applications took place. Private bankers, Fed officials, and prominent industrialists laid plans for officially sponsored "banking and industrial committees." Rather clear evidence that the proponents of monetary expansion were losing strength, these committees were shortly announced with a great flurry of public attention.[56]

In June, just as optimistic Fed staffers and some private experts were announcing that the worst of the gold crisis had passed, the Bank of England asked the Fed to earmark more gold. Discussions between the Bank of England and the Fed continued into July; there are indications that these concerned sterling/dollar exchange rates. In any event, various Fed minutes and official documents refer quite explicitly to the anxiety felt in the New York district about the loss of foreign deposits (which now totaled almost half a billion dollars, since the first of the year—half the size of the reflation program for the system as a whole).[57]

At the June 16 meeting of the executive committee of the open market policy conference, even Harrison declined to press for increases in the open market program. Something had changed. He suggested the Fed aim to ". . . maintain the excess reserves of member banks at a figure somewhere between $250,000,000 and $300,000,000 until there was some expansion of credit which would make it desirable to reconsider the program."[58] Harrison's decision to place the target in these terms probably reflects the increasing difficulty in getting more expansionary policies passed as much as a desire to use excess reserves as a target. It probably does not reflect confusion over the role of excess reserves, as Wicker maintained. Support for this view is found in the same minutes where "it was pointed out that a number of the [Federal Reserve] banks were limited by relatively low reserve percentages from taking their full quota of participation in System purchases."

At the beginning of July, the coup de grâce to the program came
from Chicago (which was then recovering from a staggering wave of
bank failures and where bank margins were being desperately
squeezed). As McDougal bluntly wrote Harrison in a letter: "We are
of the opinion that no additional purchases should be made by the
system. . . . While purchases by the system for the purpose of offsetting
gold exports were probably justified, we believe that the additional
purchases made were much too large and have resulted in creating
abnormally low rates for short-term government securities."[59]

By the end of the month, open market operations were virtually
stopped. At the July 14 meeting of the open market policy conference,
"The Governors of a number of banks pointed out that with their reserve percentages not far from 50 percent their directors were reluctant
to participate much further in open market purchases, particularly unless the operations were a united system undertaking." Expressing
hope that the banking and industrial committees would secure better
results, the Fed and the bankers effectively abandoned the experiment
as well as another privately financed bond pool announced in June.[60]

STATISTICAL TESTS

Our evidence thus far has been mainly archival, and statistical tests
would provide further confirmation. An ideal test of our underlying
hypothesis, that the Federal Reserve policy in the Great Contraction
responded primarily to the needs of the larger banks, would relate Fed
behavior to the profits of large banks, controlling for the influences of
other relevant variables in the economy. This test, however, is very
difficult to perform because of the existing bank profit data. Most published sources report only semiannual figures for all banks by Federal
Reserve district.[61] Several different kinds of statistical problems, requiring a variety of more or less plausible assumptions for their solution,
must also be faced.[62] Within these limits, however, it is possible to estimate the determinants of the Federal Reserve Board's monetary policy
to see whether statistical evidence supports our explanation of the
1932 open market operations.

Consider first the dependent variable. Most of our sources suggest
that the policy variables usually manipulated by the Federal Reserve
were the amount of securities bought plus the amount of bills bought
in its open market operations. (The open market committee made decisions about security purchases while the New York Federal Reserve
had more control over the amount of bills bought, which it could
affect by altering the rate offered on bills.) The larger the amount

of securities and bills bought (*OMO*), the more expansionary is the monetary policy.

Our analysis implies that several sets of independent variables are relevant. One involves various domestic influences on bank profits, and another reflects international constraints. A third group relates Federal Reserve reactions to pressure from industry, while a final set tests miscellaneous variables related to the structure of financial markets as well as other factors suggested in the literature.

The first "domestic" variables include, for example, real wages. The Fed wanted to reduce real wages, hoping that lower wages would help restore bond prices by reestablishing industrial profitability and lowering inflationary expectations. Thus, when real wages increased, the Fed should have reacted by tightening the money supply, giving an expected negative sign on the real wage variable, *RWAGE*.

When bond prices fall, our hypothesis is that monetary policy would become more expansionary. Triple-A corporate bond prices (*CORP*) are measured in absolute terms. Another variable to measure direct responses to bond prices is the difference between the long-term and short-term interest rates (*DIFF*). A widening difference might be a sign that the riskiness of long-term bonds was increasing, which would lead the Federal Reserve to attempt to expand the money supply to reduce the spread.

Archival evidence suggests that alterations in the portfolios of non–New York large banks from loans and long-term assets to short-term assets led these banks in 1932 to pressure the Federal Reserve to tighten monetary policy in order to raise their profit margins. To measure the loan liquidation effect on non–New York banks, we have constructed a measure, *RATM*, which is the ratio of loans and long-term assets to total assets of non–New York large banks. As *RATM* falls these banks should have put pressure on the Fed to tighten monetary policy, implying a positive influence of *RATM* on *OMO*.

International variables include free gold, foreign deposits, and currency sent abroad. Archival evidence indicates that the Federal Reserve was constrained by the availability of free gold, Friedman and Schwartz's claims to the contrary. Free gold captures both the international and the domestic constraints imposed by the gold standard. The Federal Reserve was forced to maintain gold and collateral as backing for notes; even after Glass-Steagall, it still had to keep gold for cover. When the United States lost gold internationally the Fed was less willing to expand. If free gold was a constraint, then when more free gold became available, the Federal Reserve could more freely engage in open market operations. We have constructed a measure of free gold (*FGOLD*) which includes the freeing up of gold with the Glass-Steagall Act of 1932. We expect a positive coefficient on the *FGOLD* variable.

As U.S. banks lost foreign deposits, the Federal Reserve became concerned about the effects on bank liquidity and profits. This suggests that as foreign deposits fell, monetary policy would become tighter, in order to protect the deposits. Our proxy for "deposits" is foreign deposits held at the New York Federal Reserve Bank. As an earlier quotation from Russell Leffingwell indicates, deposits were being taken out of the New York commercial banks and placed in the New York Federal Reserve. This loss of deposits to the New York banks would not be picked up in our data. With this caveat, we would expect a positive coefficient on the foreign deposit variable (*FB*).

Our archival research also indicates that in crises the Federal Reserve was concerned that U.S. currency hoarded by American and foreign holders could be liquidated for gold or foreign assets. Data collected by the Fed on currency sent to and from abroad by New York banks can be used to estimate such occurrences. In crises currency tended to be sent to New York banks from abroad, apparently reflecting a previous hoarding of U.S. currency that was sent abroad and sold for foreign assets and gold; the currency then returned to New York banks for redemption.[63] We expect the Federal Reserve to tighten monetary policy when the flow of currency from abroad to New York (*CURAB*) is positive, indicating a threat to U.S. gold reserves.

By January 1932 bankers and the Fed could not entirely ignore the effects of monetary policy on industry, if for no other reason than that industrial production affected loan demand and the profits of the banks. Thus, one might expect the Federal Reserve to conduct countercyclical monetary policy as suggested by Carl Snyder and other staff members of the New York Fed. This leads us to test for a third major type of independent variable, one that could be called "industrial," based on the industrial production index (*IP*). Open market purchases by the Fed might be expected to increase when *IP* decreased.

Finally, Wicker, Brunner and Meltzer, and others have hypothesized that the Federal Reserve mistakenly used excess reserves as an indicator of monetary policy. When excess reserves were high, they argue, the Federal Reserve stopped expanding the money supply. This hypothesis would suggest that when excess reserves (*EXRE*) went up, the Federal Reserve contracted the money supply, implying a negative relationship between *EXRE* and *OMO*.

It might also be expected that, given the function of the Federal Reserve as a potential lender of last resort, the Fed might try to reduce bank failures. In this case, when there was an increase in failures (*FAIL*), monetary policy would become more expansionary.

The equations we estimate are in double log form and the coefficients are the elasticities. All independent variables have been lagged by one period, and the results have been corrected for first-order serial correlation by using the Corchrane-Orcutt technique. The time period, from February 1930 to February 1933, was chosen to avoid the effects of the stock market crash in October 1929 and the banking panic of March 1933. All data are monthly. Definitions and sources are given in appendix 3.1.

Three of the coefficients in table 3.3, industrial production, real wages, and free gold, are uniformly of the hypothesized sign and are significant at least at the 10 percent level and usually at the 1 percent level for a one-tailed test. During this period, the Fed tightened money when real wages or industrial production rose and when free gold fell.

TABLE 3.3. Explaining Open Market Operations Monthly Data, February 1930 to February 1933 (Dependent variable: securities plus bills bought)

	1	2	3	4
Constant	25.87	35.44	28.88	36.48
	(3.30)	(4.35)	(3.50)	(4.38)
IP	-2.36	-2.90	-1.90	-2.40
	(4.99)	(-7.10)	(-3.20)	(-6.00)
RWAGE	-3.99	-3.40	-3.18	-4.1
	(-2.90)	(-2.12)	(-2.07)	(-2.72)
FGOLD	.11	.13	.08	.09
	(1.80)	(2.30)	(1.38)	(1.60)
CORP	2.21	3.16		2.1
	(1.99)	(3.25)		(2.40)
RATM	2.55	1.95	1.50	3.2
	(1.98)	(1.47)	(1.14)	(2.54)
EXRE	.10		.10	.10
	(2.22)		(1.90)	(2.38)
FB	-.01		.10	
	(-.10)		(.69)	
DIFF			.21	
			(1.28)	
FAIL				.02
				(1.20)
CURAB				-.004
				(-1.72)
$\bar{R}^2$	.77	.61	.67	.76
Durbin-Watson statistic	1.90	1.95	1.50	1.75
ρ	.63	.78	.71	.68

Source: See text.

Note: t-statistics are in parentheses.

The loan liquidation variable (*RATM*) is also of the hypothesized sign and is usually significant at least at the 10 percent level. This variable indicates that, other things being equal, as the loan-liquidation effect took hold (that is, as banks become more dependent on bills and security investments for their earnings), Fed policy became less expansionary, as our hypothesis implies.

The bond risk variable (*DIFF*) also has the correct sign and is almost significant at the 10 percent level. But an alternative measure of the capital loss variable (*CORP*) has the wrong sign, and the coefficient is significant, although *RATM*, which is significant, may already reflect this capital-loss effect. The explanation of the coefficient on *CORP* is not clear and calls for further analysis.

Among the international variables, the free gold variable (*FGOLD*) has the predicted sign, as does "currency sent to and from banks abroad" (*CURAB*). Alternative foreign deposit variables, however, do not show up as well, perhaps because the data for foreign balances include balances held at the New York Fed. Results for deposits of failed bank (*FAIL*) indicate that the Federal Reserve was unconcerned about all banks.[64]

Finally, excess reserves are indeed significant determinants of Fed policy during this period, but the coefficient is the opposite sign of that implied by the Brunner-Meltzer hypothesis. The Federal Reserve seemed to have reinforced excess reserves rather than worked against them; other variables remain unchanged.

In summary, the results on the main domestic and international variables appear consistent with our major hypotheses, and the Brunner-Meltzer hypotheses are not supported.

THE FEDERAL RESERVE AND THE PROBLEM OF BANK REGULATION: CONCLUDING REMARKS

We have argued that conflicts of interest within the Federal Reserve System, and between it and the rest of the economy, help account for the Fed's notorious failure to arrest the Great Contraction. Although our findings are tentative, we believe we have established a prima facie case that previous accounts of the Fed in this period are mistaken in several important respects. There were, for example, real international constraints on the Fed throughout the period 1929 to 1932. Free gold was a problem until early 1932; thereafter, the loss of foreign deposits in private banks and the need to maintain the 40 percent gold cover on Federal Reserve notes constrained the Fed. As a consequence of what we termed the loan liquidation effect, bitter conflicts arose within the Fed concerning yields of short-term government securities.

By ignoring or abbreviating consideration of these factors, the existing literature has failed to come to grips with important historical questions and major theoretical points. Viewed in terms of our analysis, most of the mystery evaporates about two controversial issues in the later financial history of the Depression: the final disastrous run on the banks that led to the "bank holiday" of early 1933 and all the subsequent worries within the system about inflation after 1935. Both of these are almost unintelligible in terms of the standard historiography. That the Federal Reserve System largely sat on its hands as the entire American financial structure collapsed seems unbelievable. That anyone could fear "inflation" in 1935 to 1936 is not any more comprehensible.

In our view, of course, neither of these issues poses a problem. At the January 4, 1933, meeting, before the final banking crisis and after Governor Meyer observed that "at no time since the war has the relation between the open market policy of the Federal Reserve System and the general economic situation been so important," Governor George Norris of Philadelphia aptly summarized our thesis. "Further increases in excess reserves," he noted, "would adversely affect bank earnings, and incur the risk of disturbance which might arise from eliminating interest on deposits."[65]

As the Depression deepened, the loan liquidation effect proceeded apace. By the mid-thirties, the position of *all* the Federal Reserve banks had come to resemble the position of Chicago in 1932. With their earnings tied directly to rates on the government securities they now widely held, most bankers, not surprisingly, favored the increases in reserve requirements that the Fed eventually awarded them. They were less concerned with the effects these might have on the rest of the economy.[66]

Previous research has failed to reckon with the possibility of what might be termed a "supply-side liquidity trap." As Keynes alone seems to have recognized (see the headnote), the capitalist organization of finance implies that interest rates may fail to drop low enough to revive an economy because bank earnings might not permit it in an acute depression. Moreover, contemporary students of money and banking have not reconciled a fundamental problem of the current system of bank regulation: that the Federal Reserve System is charged with performing two often incompatible tasks—that of advancing the interests of a specific industry while simultaneously overseeing the protection of other businesses and the public at large.

APPENDIX 3.1

A Note on Sources

Specification of all the variables used in this paper is contained in appendix 1 of our "Monetary Policy." Most data came from the Board of Governors of the Federal Reserve System, *Banking and Monetary Statistics* (Washington, D.C., 1943), hereafter *BMS*. Other variables, not drawn from that source or indirectly derived from figures in it, follow. *CURAB*, shipments of currency abroad from New York banks in thousands of dollars: *Federal Reserve Bulletin*, January 1932, p. 9, and February 1933, p. 103. Figures do not reflect outflows of currency from non–New York banks. *FAIL*, deposits of suspended banks (in $ thousands): *Federal Reserve Bulletin*, September 1937, p. 909. Figures are monthly, and cover all banks. *RWAGE*, M. Ada Beney, *Wages, Hours, and Employment in the United States, 1914–36*, National Industrial Conference Board Study No. 229. (New York, 1936), p. 50. *FB*, monthly data for total short-term foreign liabilities reported by banks in the United States (in $ millions): *BMS*, pp. 574–80, and subtract out French foreign balances after January 1932, since the Fed had reached an agreement with the French Central Bank concerning removal of the balances, and monetary authorities proceeded in the expectation they would be removed. *FGOLD*, free gold: February 1930 to January 1932: *BMS* as described in *Federal Reserve Bulletin*, March 1932. See also H. Villard, "The Federal Reserve System's Monetary Policy in 1931 and 1932," *Journal of Political Economy*, 45 (December 1937), 734. February 1932 to February 1933, *FGOLD* is represented by bank excess reserves, to take account of Glass-Steagall. The data are from Annual Report of the Federal Reserve Board, 1933 (Washington, D.C.), p. 94, Table 9. *IP*, manufacturing and mining production, seasonally adjusted: Board of Governors of the Federal Reserve System (Washington, D.C., 1960), pp. 150–151. *OMO*, bills purchased plus government securities purchased, from *BMS*. *RATM*, the ratio of loans and long-term bonds to total assets for non–New York reserve city banks and Chicago central reserve city banks, has been converted to monthly data by linear extrapolation from quarterly data in *BMS*.

ACKNOWLEDGMENTS

Earlier versions of this chapter were read at the Annual Conferences of the Southern Economics Association and the American Historical Association. The authors are especially grateful to Richard Sylla and Peter Temin for extensive comments on several drafts. For other assistance, they should also like to thank

Carl Backlund, Samuel Bowles, James Crotty, Richard Duboff, Michael Edelstein, Barry Eichengreen, John Garrett, Brian Gendreau, Stephen Goldfeld, Ellis Hawley, Edward Herman, Robert Johnson, Charles Kindleberger, Stanley Lebergott, Richard Nicodemus, Leonard Rapping, Juliet Schor, Barrie Wigmore, David Weiman, and the editors and referees of the *Journal of Economic History*. This essay was in every sense joint work, and the alphabet was therefore allowed to determine the order of the authors' names. The essay has also benefited liberally from the discussion of the American political economy of the late 1920s and early 1930s in Thomas Ferguson, *Critical Realignment: The Fall of the House of Morgan and the Origins of the New Deal* (New York, Oxford University Press, forthcoming). For further discussion of the issues in this paper see Epstein and Ferguson, "Answers to Stock Questions: Fed Targets, Stock Prices, and the Gold Standard in the Great Depression," *Journal of Economic History*, 51, 1 (March 1991), 190–200.

NOTES

1. Keynes's remark is in his "A Note on the Long Term Rate of Interest in Relation to the Conversion Scheme," *Economic Journal*, 42 (September 1932), 421–22.

2. This Glass-Steagall Act should not be confused with a law passed a year later, bearing the names of the same two legislators, that mandated the separation of investment from commercial banking.

3. Mathew Josephson, *The Money Lords* (New York, 1973), p. 101. Josephson was then in fairly close touch with top Fed officials. See his *Infidel in the Temple* (New York, 1967), p. 21.

4. See Milton Friedman and Anna Schwartz, *A Monetary History of the United States 1867–1960*, (Princeton, 1963); Karl Brunner and Allan H. Meltzer, "What did we learn from the Monetary Experience of the United States in the Great Depression," *Canadian Journal of Economics*, 1 (May 1968), 334–48; Meltzer, "Monetary and Other Explanations of the Start of The Great Depression," *Journal of Monetary Economics*, 2 (1976), 455–71; Peter Temin, *Did Monetary Forces Cause the Great Depression?* (New York, 1976); Elmus R. Wicker, "Federal Reserve Monetary Policy, 1922–33: A Reinterpretation," *Journal of Political Economy*, 73 (Aug. 1965), 325–43; and *Federal Reserve Monetary Policy, 1917–33* (New York, 1966). See also the essays in K. Brunner, ed., *The Great Depression Revisited* (Boston, 1981), and Paul Trescott, "Federal Reserve Policy in the Great Contraction: A Counterfactual Assessment," *Explorations in Economic History*, 19 (July 1982), 211–20.

5. Friedman and Schwartz, *Monetary History*, pp. 411–18; the quotations are from p. 415.

6. Wicker, *Reserve Policy*, pp. 195, 171.

7. Ibid., p. 195.

8. Brunner and Meltzer, "What Did We Learn," p. 343; Meltzer, "Monetary and Other Explanations," p. 468.

9. See for example, Meltzer, "Monetary and Other Explanations," p. 465.

10. Charles Kindleberger, *The World in Depression* (London, 1973) surveys international responses to the Depression.

11. Our discussion here summarizes the more detailed analysis in our "Monetary

Policy, Loan Liquidation, and Industrial Conflict: The Federal Reserve and the Great Contraction," available from the authors.

12. Meltzer's table is presented in his "Monetary and Other Explanations," pp. 465–67. Our continuation of the table is available from either of us.

13. See George Stigler, "The Economic Theory of Regulation" in his *The Citizen and the State* (Chicago, 1971), and Richard Posner, "Theories of Economic Regulation," *Bell Journal of Economics*, 5 (autumn 1974), 335–58. For one attempt at applying the economic theory of regulation to the Federal Reserve System, see Gerald Epstein, "Monetary Instability and the Political Economy of the Federal Reserve," in Alan Stone, ed., *The Political Economy of Public Policy* (Beverly Hills, 1983). Pressures from other sectors strongly affect the treatment of the Fed as a creature of a single industry. Note that Wicker, and Friedman and Schwartz, though they did considerable research in archives, gathered very little material on the private sector. Of course, what the Fed needs to do to raise bank profits depends on the state of the economy and, as we discuss later, on the condition of bank portfolios. In regard to the latter question, see Lawrence Fisher and Roman L. Weil, "Coping with the Risk of Interest Rate Fluctuations: Returns to Bondholders from Naive and Optimal Strategies," *Journal of Business*, 44 (October 1971), 408–31; and Mark Flannery, "Market Interest Rates and Commercial Bank Profitability: An Empirical Investigation," *Journal of Finance*, 36 (December 1981), 1085–1101.

14. The previous two paragraphs primarily rely on Friedman and Schwartz, *Monetary History*, pp. 363–71. Note that opposition to the New York Fed's initiatives helped lead to a reorganization of the open market committee.

15. See Harrison, "Report of the Chairman of the Open Market Policy Conference to the Governors Conference" of April 27, 1931, for a review of policy up to then. This and the other Harrison papers quoted can be found in the George L. Harrison Papers, Rare Books and Manuscript Library, Columbia University. The papers there are often said to be duplicates of those in the Federal Reserve Bank of New York archives.

16. The stock market crash initially threatened banks in New York to a greater extent than those in other districts. Almost 50 percent of the loans of central reserve city member banks in New York were loans on securities, over a third of them to brokers and dealers in New York City. This compares to less than 40 percent for all member banks with only 10 percent of those to dealers and brokers in New York. Moreover, much of the pressure of withdrawals of bank deposits following the crash was concentrated in New York banks. See Board of Governors of the Federal Reserve System, *Banking and Monetary Statistics* (Washington, D.C., 1943), p. 76, 83; in regard to the directors see the quotation in Meltzer, "Monetary and Other Explanations," p. 463.

17. Andrew Mellon, quoted in David Koskoff, *The Mellons* (New York, 1978), p. 265; Koskoff in turn is quoting from the report in Hoover's memoirs.

18. See the sources discussed at greater length in our "Monetary Policy."

19. For Hoover's efforts, see the entry in the Henry Stimson diary for April 4, 1931 (which discusses the policies Hoover implemented soon after the crash), Henry Stimson Papers, Sterling Library, Yale University, and Murray Rothbard, *America's Great Depression* (Princeton, 1963). See also Martin Baily, "The Labor Market in the 1930s," in James Tobin, ed., *Macroeconomics, Prices and Quantities* (Washington, D.C., 1983).

20. Thomas Ferguson, "From 'Normalcy' to New Deal: Industrial Structure, Party

Competition, and American Public Policy in the Great Depression," (chapter 2, this volume).

21. E. A. Goldenweiser, Meeting with Federal Reserve Board, January 3, 1930 from Goldenweiser Papers, Library of Congress, Box 1, quoted in Friedman and Schwartz, *Monetary History,* p. 401. For other evidence on how seriously the Fed viewed the gold question, see Minutes of Meeting of The Open Market Policy Conference, April 29, 1931, in the Harrison Papers.

22. Miller, for example, clearly relied on real bills in his statement cited in the preceding paragraph of the text. The true meaning of real bills during this period is complicated by the Fed's enthusiasm for liquidation. During much of the early Depression the brunt of deposit withdrawals, runs, and suspensions fell on smaller, generally state-regulated banks. As a consequence, deposits had a discernible tendency in some Fed districts to leave such banks for larger ones regulated by the Fed. Because a bank that gained deposits probably had less need to borrow from the Fed and real bills advocates frequently relied on such borrowing to gauge how tight policy was, a plea in favor of real bills by larger banks was equivalent to a request for a policy that transferred the assets of their marginal competitors to them. Note that our regression results, reported in the last part of this chapter, indicate that for the Depression as a whole, the Fed did not respond to bank failures and that the Fed was frequently criticized in this period for its alleged hostility to small banks.

23. E. A. Goldenweiser, Memorandum on Meeting with Federal Reserve Board, January 3, 1930, Goldenweiser Papers. Harrison's forceful advocacy of the reduction of collateral requirements mentioned in this chapter shows that he agreed with Goldenweiser, and is incompatible with a real bills doctrine. In 1932 when the Glass-Steagall Act passed, Thomas W. Lamont of Morgan was also openly attacking older, restrictive notions of "elegibility." See Lamont to Walter Lippman, Memorandum, dated February 11, 1932, Lippman Papers, Sterling Library, Yale University.

24. Certain brief, anomalous aspects of Fed behavior during 1931 cannot be considered here.

25. Friedman and Schwartz, *Monetary History,* p. 316.

26. Ibid., p. 322; they also note Hoover's interest in other assistance for banks.

27. U.S. Board of Governors of the Federal Reserve, *Banking and Monetary Statistics* (Washington, D.C., 1943), pp. 468, 475, 478. Lower grade bonds had plunged earlier. Note that actual failures continued to be concentrated among smaller banks.

28. See the striking letter of Morgan partner Russell Leffingwell to Senator Carter Glass, Jan. 8, 1932; Leffingwell Papers, Box 3, Yale University, Sterling Library. Leffingwell's views had been very different only a few months before, and he now emerged as a leading lobbyist for the program.

29. The portfolio changes discussed here can also be expressed more technically as an analysis of changes in the "duration" of bank assets and liabilities as, for example, in Paul Samuelson, "The Effect of Interest Rate Increases on the Banking System," *American Economic Review,* 35 (March 1945), 16–27.

30. See the discussion in Ferguson, *Critical Realignment.*

31. Minutes of the Meeting of the Open Market Policy Conference, Washington, D.C., January 11 and 12, 1932, p. 7; Harrison Papers. Friedman and Schwartz do mention the issue of railroad wage cuts, p. 383, but do not indicate its importance. Wicker

does not mention it. The report of an official communication (New York Federal Reserve, January 20, 1932, from J. E. Crane to Confidential Files, Bank of France telephone conversation; report on talk of Harrison with Lacour-Gayet) underscores the importance of the railroad wage cuts.

32. Letter from Burgess to Harrison, February 16, 1932, Federal Reserve Board of New York archives (hereafter FRBNY). This memo is also an excellent indication that Burgess has abandoned (if he ever held) the "Riefler-Burgess-Strong" doctrine.

33. See Ferguson, *Critical Realignment.*

34. See the Eugene Meyer and Ogden Mills papers at the Library of Congress; and "Selected Monetary and Banking Series," in the Presidential Papers—Subject—Financial Matters, Gold & Silver, Herbert Hoover Presidential Papers, Hoover Presidential Library, West Branch, Iowa.

35. Preliminary Memorandum for Executive Committee of The Open Market Policy Conference, April 5, 1932, Harrison Papers.

36. Preliminary Draft, Minutes of Meeting of the Executive Committee of the Open Market Policy Conference, April 5, 1932, Harrison Papers.

37. Meeting of Joint Conference of the Federal Reserve Board and The Open Market Policy Conference, April 12, 1932; Washington, D.C., Harrison Papers. Note that even Miller, previously a champion of real bills, supported reflation.

38. All issues of the *Federal Reserve Bulletin* in this period present comparative data for the various Federal Reserve banks. In the 1920s controversies between the Chicago and New York Federal Reserve banks had been acute; for a particularly striking example, see Ferguson, 'From Normalcy to New Deal,' chapter 2 of this volume.

39. McDougal and Young, for example, had opposed the program at a February 24 and 25 meeting of governors. See Minutes of the Meeting of Governors held at Washington, D.C., February 24 and 25, 1932, Harrison Papers. Minutes of the Boston Fed, for various dates in 1932, now held in the Federal Reserve Bank at Boston, indicate that the Boston bank, nevertheless, sometimes bought securities.

40. Meeting of Joint Conference, April 12, 1932, Harrison Papers, p. 21. Harrison's answer indicates what he thought was animating the critics and seems to rule out an appeal to belief in real bills as an explanation for their behavior. After questioning the program as "inflationary," McDougal finally voted with the majority. No significance should be attached to this move, however. Both before and after this meeting, McDougal, whom Harrison later described as "always a reluctant follower" of the reflation program, vigorously attacked open market expansion. (See Harrison's comments at the June 23, 1932, meeting of the directors of the New York Fed, Binder 50, Harrison Papers.) Note also that bureaucratic pressures, to close ranks once the outcome of a decision was clear, were very strong and led losers to say frankly on several occasions that they would vote formally against what they lacked the strength to halt.

41. See the figures for the period in *Federal Reserve Bulletin* (February 1938), pp. 123–24.

42. The Federal Reserve volume *Banking and Monetary Statistics* actually has a record of negative values for short-term interest rates in October 1932, p. 460.

43. By 1933 some banks were refusing deposits because they were losing money on them. See *Commercial and Financial Chronicle* (February 11, 1933).

44. The data on net earnings are from *Federal Reserve Bulletin* (February 1938), p. 119. Table 3 of our "Monetary Policy" breaks down bank expenses for salaries and

wages and other categories during the early 1930s. The data for this table, on which our discussion here is based, are from various issues of the *Federal Reserve Bulletin*.

45. These figures are drawn from table 4 of our "Monetary Policy" paper, which calculates net margins for banks in each Federal Reserve district from 1927 to 1932. The data come originally from various issues of the *Federal Reserve Bulletin*. Net margin equals interest earned less interest paid less other expenses per $100 of loans and investments. Note that margins vary considerably over the whole five-year-period.

46. Report of Open Market Operations to Meeting of the Executive Committee of the Open Market Policy Conference Held at Federal Reserve Bank of New York (FRBNY) on April 5, 1932, Harrison Papers.

47. F. Cyril James, *The Growth of Chicago Banks*, (New York, 1938), vol. 2, pp. 1062–63. After the declaration of the banking moratorium, when it was too late, the Chicago bank finally did agree to rediscount for the New York Fed.

48. For statistics on each bank's notes and gold holdings, see *Federal Reserve Bulletin* for 1932 and 1933, various issues; remember that each bank desired a safety margin. Note also that opponents of reflation soon began arguing that the system-wide nature of the program was very important, if it were to be done at all, while the New York Fed feared the wrath of the provinces if it tried to go it alone.

49. Board of Governors of the Federal Reserve System, *Banking and Monetary Statistics*, p. 574.

50. For statistics of the gold loss, see ibid. The much-disputed question, whether French Prime Minister Laval made a promise to President Herbert Hoover, is discussed in Ferguson, *Critical Realignment*.

51. See Allan Sproul (E. M. Despres) to Crane and Burgess, June 8, 1932 (a retrospective on gold in recent months), in FRBNY archives. For Fed–Bank of England communications in this period see the file for the Bank of England in the Archives of the Federal Reserve Bank of New York. For the Bank of England's efforts to lower interest rates in the spring of 1932, see the *Monthly Newsletter* of the National City Bank of New York, May 1932, p. 69; see also Susan Howson, "Sterling's Managed Float," *Princeton Studies in International Finance* (Princeton, 1980) concerning the conflict between the British Treasury and the Bank of England.

52. R. Leffingwell, Memorandum, April 2, 1932, Box 3, Leffingwell Papers, Yale University.

53. Federal Reserve Bank of New York, May 26, 1932, telephone conversation with Cariguel, Banque de France. From L. W. Knoke, reporting on a call from Cariguel to Crane of the staff of the New York Fed. See also Howson, "Sterling's Managed Float," p. 15, which suggests that the Bank of England had been buying dollars in May, but was selling them in June and July; and Goldenweiser, untitled memo for June 10, 1932, Goldenweiser Papers.

54. Woodlief Thomas to Sproul; Subject: "Gold Movements and System's Open Market Policy," June 9, 1932, reporting the comments of several investment bankers, FRBNY archives. Note that many, perhaps most, lower-ranking New York Fed officials supported the reflation program.

55. Harrison to Confidential Files, from Governor Harrison, June 2, 1932, Subject: "The Dollar in England, President's meeting May 30, balancing budget, etc., "Harrison Papers, which discusses a meeting with various industrialists and a U.S. senator to put pressure on Hoover and the leaders of Congress.

56. See Ferguson, *Critical Realignment*. Among primary sources, see especially the Charles Hamlin diary for May and June 1932, at the Library of Congress. It is also worth mentioning that currency hoarding worried some Fed officials, as did the prospect that this could develop into a domestic gold run.

57. For example, the memoranda referenced in n. 54. In May and June some Fed staffers who supported reflation had attempted to minimize the significance of the gold outflow. But the bankers who were losing the deposits and the high Fed officials responsible for policy took a more serious view of the situation. Gold cover problems in individual Fed banks also continued.

58. Minutes of the Meeting of the Executive Committee of the Open Market Policy Conference, June 16, 1932, Harrison Papers.

59. J. B. McDougal to Harrison, July 9, 1932, FRBNY archives. Note that falling interest rates could, and in districts like Chicago where many banks were already collapsing, almost certainly did increase chances that depositors would withdraw their funds.

60. The "pool" was a corporation in which different financial groups could buy shares. See Ferguson, *Critical Realignment*, and contemporary references such as the *Journal of Commerce and Finance*, (June 8, 1933), 780.

61. Our "Monetary Policy" reports a regression on bank stock data indicating that falling prices of bank stocks, but not industrial production, influenced the Fed. We have only limited confidence in this equation, however, and so do not discuss it here.

62. See, for example, S. Goldfeld and A. Blinder, "Some Implications of an Endogenous Stabilization Policy," *Brookings Papers on Economic Activity*, 3 (1972), pp. 585–640. The problem of "selective attention" is particularly worrisome.

63. See the literature on currency substitution, for example, L. Girton and D. Roper, "Theory and Implications of Currency Substitution," *Journal of Money, Credit, and Banking*, 13 (February 1981), 12–30, and the discussion in the *Federal Reserve Bulletin* (January 1932).

64. Given the traditional posture of central banks and discussions of the time, one might expect that the Fed would respond to inflation. We found, however, in our statistical work that the Fed did not respond to inflation in this period, contrary to conventional wisdom.

65. Minutes of the Meeting of the Open Market Policy Conference, Jan. 4, 1933, Harrison Papers. McDougal of Chicago also expressed a desire to "make open market money rates firmer." Epstein and Ferguson, "Answers to Stock Questions," presents further documentation in regard to the squeeze on bank earnings.

66. See Ferguson, *Critical Realignment*.

Industrial Structure and Party Competition in the New Deal:
A Quantitative Assessment

[At] a mass meeting in the heart of the Wall Street District, about 200 business leaders, most of whom described themselves as Republicans, enthusiastically endorsed yesterday the foreign trade policy of the Roosevelt Administration and pledged themselves to work for the President's reelection ... the Meeting unanimously adopted a resolution praising the reciprocal trade policy ... Governor Landon's attitude on the reciprocal tariff issue was criticized by every speaker. They contended that if Landon were elected and Secretary Hull's treaties were revoked, there would be a revolution among conservative businessmen.
The New York Times, October 29, 1936

INTRODUCTION

THE NEW DEAL'S curiously elusive political formula—at once daringly radical and venerably conservative—has perplexed analysts for almost two generations. "From 'Normalcy' to New Deal" (originally published in 1984; chapter 2 of this volume) sought a fresh approach to the puzzle. Relying extensively on primary sources, the essay traced how an entirely new kind of political coalition—one dominated by capital-intensive, multinationally oriented businesses—rose to power during the stormy days of the Second New Deal of 1935–38.

Because they were predominantly capital-intensive, these enterprises were not seriously jeopardized by the epochal welfare measures that they and Franklin D. Roosevelt's administration collaborated in preparing. And because they were internationally oriented, these enterprises were the primary beneficiaries of the administration's historic turn to free trade after 1934.

The essay also outlined how the 1936 election figured in this triumph of multinational liberalism. As the administration prepared to sign the Tripartite Money Agreement and raise bank reserve requirements (as many financiers were demanding), Republican nominee Alf

Landon came under fierce pressure from his party's base of protection-ist, mostly labor-intensive (the chemical industry was an exception) manufacturers to repudiate Cordell Hull's trade treaties. For a while the Kansas governor resisted. Eventually, however, he buckled.

Wall Street financiers publicly rallied to attack Landon while enough multinational luminaries to fill a future Democratic president's cabinet left the GOP campaign, including cotton broker Will Clayton (who also resigned from the American Liberty League), banker James Warburg, and superlawyer (and former Treasury Undersecretarty) Dean Acheson. Meanwhile, a phalanx of famous non-Morgan invest-ment bankers (including more future Democratic cabinet appointees, e.g., James Forrestal and Averell Harriman) joined (imported) sugar refiner Ellsworth Bunker and many oil executives in raising funds for FDR's campaign. The outgoing president of the American Bankers As-sociation and the head of American Locomotive (a large would-be ex-porter) endorsed the president's reelection. The Rockefeller-controlled Chase National Bank and Manufacturers Trust each loaned the Demo-cratic National Committee $100,000 (an amount equivalent to slightly less than one million 1991 dollars), while the Bank of America lobbied on behalf of the president.

In the campaign's final days, Landon began to attack the Social Security Act. As fainter hearts from the previous year's special advisory committee on social security recoiled from embroilment in electoral politics, the presidents of the Standard Oil Co. of New Jersey and Gen-eral Electric (whose own chair stated flatly to intimates that he favored the president's reelection) publicly rebutted Landon's criticisms. The *New York Times* endorsed FDR, while tobacco companies and retailers distributed literature defending social security.[1]

Several historians have plainly stated their own prizewinning work on American foreign policy confirms "From 'Normalcy' to New Deal"'s findings (Hogan 1987, pp. 11–12, 1986, p. 365; Cumings, 1990, pp. 18, 90–91). Economists of markedly different viewpoints have also published confirming evidence that, in at least one case, they initially disbelieved (Magee, Brock, and Young, 1989, pp. 179–201; Borchardt, 1991, p. 15).[2] It is also fair to say that critics of an essay (chapter 3 of this volume) I coauthored on the Federal Reserve in the early 1930s, whose arguments are integral to my main work on the New Deal, fared poorly in a recent exchange (Epstein and Ferguson 1984; Coelho and Santoni, 1991; Epstein and Ferguson, 1991).

Webber (1991), however, claims to refute my account of the New Deal. He also asserts that his paper invalidates my broader investment theory of party competition (Chapter 1 [originally published in 1983] of this volume; Ferguson 1986).

On first reading, his analysis appears highly plausible. The apparently stark evidence presented, e.g., table 9, "Campaign Finance Contributions of $100 or More of Officers and Directors in Key Firms Named by Ferguson to Illustrate His 'Investment Theory of Politics,'" appears precise and, accordingly, convincing.

His evidence, however, is flawed. While claiming to test my theories, Webber ignores my discussions of how quantitative data can be used to test my views (see my essay, originally published in 1989, in chapter 5 of this volume; along with chapter 1 and Ferguson, 1991; Ferguson and Rogers, 1986; appendix) and puts forward a statistical design of his own that is desperately vulnerable. His sample, for example, is defective: it includes many people it should not and excludes many others who should be reckoned in, including many prominent Texas oilmen. His effort to test my views by reporting percentages of top officials and directors contributing is wrong in principle, since it excludes large cash payments made to the Democrats during the 1936 campaign by such firms as Standard Oil of New Jersey and General Electric, as well as the loans that Chase and other banks bestowed on the Democrats. The method also is insensitive to cases in which a single executive dominated the political activities of firms. And the campaign finance data he relies upon are also far less complete than he implies, while his statistical methods are hopelessly defective. Indeed, because he only occasionally compares percentages across industries, he fails to notice the clues in his own study that support my argument about the distinctive political behavior of capital-intensive industries during the New Deal.

However, to show that Webber is wrong about the New Deal does not prove that I am right. Thus, after critically reviewing Webber's findings, this essay will present results of direct statistical tests of the central claims of "From 'Normalcy' to New Deal." Based not only on the parts of Overacker's data files that Webber relied on—those concerning individual contributions—but on the rest of her files as well, which record direct corporate contributions, and based on my own work in many other archives, the tests strongly support "From 'Normalcy' to New Deal"'s analysis. They also demonstrate that the pivotal notion of my investment theory of political parties—that competition within the business community is central to the American electoral process—is a straightforward proposition to test empirically.

THE NEW DEAL AND THE INVESTMENT THEORY

In regard to this latter, broader, point, one initial clarification is in order. Though Webber claims that his results embarrass my investment theory of political parties, he nowhere addresses that theory directly. Indeed, he virtually ignores the essay (chapter 1) in which I advanced the investment account of parties—an essay that was written after, although published before, "From 'Normalcy' to New Deal."[3] His presentation creates the impression that my analysis of the New Deal is largely coextensive with this investment theory of parties, and that by attacking the one he can strike fatally at the other.

But this is not possible even in principle. The investment theory essay presents a general case: pressures of time, limited information, financial constraints, and transaction costs (including many imposed by political systems, such as direct repression) are more burdensome to ordinary voters than classical democratic theorists allow. As a consequence, political parties in countries such as the United States

> are not what . . . most American election analyses . . . treat them as, viz, . . . the political analogues of "entrepreneurs in a profit-seeking economy" who "act to maximize votes." . . . Instead, the fundamental market for political parties usually is not voters . . . most of these possess desperately limited resources and—especially in the United States—exiguous information and interest in politics. The real market for political parties is defined by major investors, who generally have good and clear reasons for investing to control the state. . . . Blocs of major investors define the core of political parties and are responsible for most of the signals the party sends to the electorate (chapter 1, p. 22).

In such investor-driven systems, the meaning of political competition is very different from its analogue in classical democratic theory:

> political parties dominated by large investors try to assemble the votes they need by making very limited appeals to particular segments of the potential electorate. If it pays some other bloc of major investors to advertise and mobilize, these appeals can be vigorously contested, but . . . on all issues affecting the vital interests that major investors have in common, no party competition will take place. Instead, all that will occur will be a proliferation of marginal appeals to voters— and if all major investors happen to share an interest in ignoring issues vital to the electorate, such as social welfare, hours of work, or collective bargaining, so much the worse for the electorate. Unless significant portions of it are prepared to try to become major investors in their own right, through a substantial expenditure of time and (limited) income, there is nothing any group of voters can do to offset this collective investor dominance (chapter 1, p. 28).

In terms of the spatial models of voter behavior now so fashionable in the social sciences, this principle of noncompetition has a striking implication: the general failure of control by the "median voter" (the voter whose strategic position exactly in the middle of a distribution of voters guarantees a candidate one more vote than he or she needs to defeat all comers). For example, consider a world in which labor-intensive textile producers (3 percent of the voting population) command virtually all pecuniary resources beyond those necessary for ordinary wage earners to live (a world, that is, characterized by the "classical savings function" popularized by Kalecki, Kaldor, and Robinson). Suppose, further, that an election is being staged in which everyone recognizes that the only issue is passage of a law that is likely to lead to 100 percent unionization of the work force. All wage earners agree that the law is desirable. All textile magnates vehemently disagree. What stance do the political parties adopt? If money matters importantly to the campaign, no party can afford to take up the median voter's position in figure 4.1—a position at the right-hand peak (marked "97%") that indicates the views of the vast majority—even though no one is being fooled about anything. Because all parties depend on textiles for funding, they must comply with the industry's demand for a union-free environment, or else they cannot afford to compete at all. Conversely, if a second party dependent on capital-intensive industries that do not object to, say, a scheme for 20 percent unionization can raise enough funds to offer

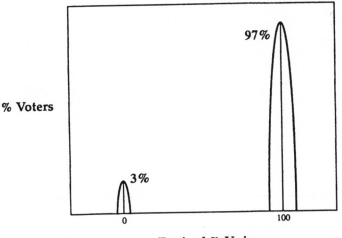

FIGURE 4.1. An Overwhelming, but Unsuccessful Majority for Unionization—An Idealized Example

another deal—a New Deal, that is—then the populace may get a chance to vote for the latter; still, the median position is never attained.[4]

Webber, accordingly, can scarcely claim to invalidate my investment theory of parties by attacking my account of the partisan breakdown of American business during the New Deal. That would simply beg the question of what underlay a Democratic coalition that, after all, admitted to spending more than $5 million during the depths of the greatest depression in world history in order to retain the presidency (a sum that attracted less attention than it should have, since the Republicans spent even more). This question cannot be escaped by pointing, as Webber does toward the end of his essay, at the fact that ordinary people voted for Roosevelt and the Democrats. If he wants to refute the investment theory, Webber needs to show not that people voted for the Democrats, but that the party did not need money to campaign to get those votes. (Or, perhaps, that organized labor, which contributed about $770,000 to FDR's campaign, or some other segment of the severely cash-strapped general electorate, could somehow have increased its contributions by 700 percent had business funds not been forthcoming [Overacker, 1946, p. 50]).

But, of course, even Roosevelt had to raise large sums to be reelected. And this brings us to the data that Webber presents to refute "From 'Normalcy' to New Deal."

Objections

His point of departure appears so naively reasonable that one might hesitate to challenge it: "By framing the argument in terms of large firms and industrial segments, Ferguson makes it possible to test his claims by examining the campaign contributions of the top officers and directors of such firms" (Webber, 1991, p. 477).

To test my theory, Webber should not ignore the various papers I have written on how to do so, particularly those that set out the methods I believe are appropriate for analyzing campaign finance data.

It is best to begin with the problem's most general aspect. Webber claims that ". . . Ferguson places great emphasis on the importance of campaign finance contributions in his analysis of the New Deal" (1991, 474). But this is so only in a far more equivocal form than his paper suggests. I certainly believe that social scientists and historians have neglected campaign finance. I am also convinced that intelligent appraisals of the meager data that survive yield important insights into how the American (and every other) political process really works. Indeed, this is precisely what I believe I have demonstrated in my series of quantitative papers on recent elections (chapters 5 and 6; Ferguson, 1991) and my coauthored book (Ferguson and Rogers, 1986).

But reliance on the "Golden Rule" as an initial working hypothesis has never tempted me to suppose that the principal political use of money is for campaign contributions. The truly general notion employed explicitly in the "Investment Theory" and "From 'Normalcy' to New Deal" chapters concerns "support" for policies or politicians. "Support," however, includes much more than simply funnelling cash to politicians at election time:

> The beginning of real wisdom in these matters . . . occurs when one reflects that direct cash contributions are probably not the most important way in which truly top business figures ("major investors") act politically. Both during elections and between election campaigns, their more broadly defined "organizational" intervention is probably more critical . . . such elite figures function powerfully as sources of contacts, as fundraisers (rather than mere contributors), and, especially, as sources of legitimation for candidates and positions. In particular . . . the interaction of high business figures and the press has frequently been pivotal for American politics . . . [this is] an in-kind service whose value dwarfs most cash contributions (chapter 1, p. 41).

Webber criticizes "From 'Normalcy' to New Deal" for resting its case in part on "diaries, letters, and newspapers of the period." Yet these are precisely the kind of evidence that the "Investment Theory" essay identified as particularly appropriate for assessing facts (and thus theories) about business support.

A recent essay of mine also issues two other caveats to analyses of politics and money that take campaign finance as their principal focus. One is the fact that lobbying expenditures vastly exceed total spending on campaign finance. The other is the less manifest reality that "the most important modern use of money in politics" is the "subsidization of information through think tanks and policy research institutions, and the closely related emergence of private foundations as a major source of support for research on public policy" (Ferguson, 1992).[5] "From 'Normalcy' to New Deal" discussed both foundations and research organizations; any serious effort to test its account must do so as well.

If, in contrast to Webber, one observes these qualifications, an inquiry into campaign finance is perfectly sensible. But the methodology needs to be very carefully designed.

As my "Investment Theory" essay cautioned, the ways in which politically relevant money is hidden are almost limitless:

Large numbers of pecuniary contributions were understated or never recorded at all. Cash paid in the form of excessive consultant, lawyer, and other third-party fees is rarely noticed and in-kind contributions almost never listed. "Loans" which are never repaid or are granted on preferential terms [which, from the standpoint of economic theory, include virtually all political loans, since most would never measure up to an honest bank examiner's standards] rarely attract notice. Neither do "gifts" to "friends." Not surprisingly, almost every seriously pursued investigation of campaign contributions, from the Hearst-inspired attacks on Theodore Roosevelt and E. H. Harriman to the recent inquiries into corporate bribery conducted under the auspices of the Securities and Exchange Commission, has unearthed unreported contributions of astronomical magnitude. . . . A good rule of thumb, accordingly, is to treat published campaign contributions . . . as the tip of an iceberg, and be wary of any analysis that relies only on them (chapter 1, pp. 40–41).

These elementary facts guarantee that Webber's strategy of displaying percentages of top officers and directors reported by one source as having personally contributed at least $100 to either party is likely to go astray. Consider, first of all, a pair of procedural decisions he made to construct his data set:

All company and institutional contributions, such as those made by various labor unions, were excluded, so that only individual contributions were included in the final compilation. (p. 479) . . . loans, and illegal or returned contributions were not included (Webber, 1991, p. 480).

These decisions have major implications. The first excludes a host of large donations from giant firms that are central to "From 'Normalcy' to New Deal"'s claims. Through precisely the sort of stratagems that the "Investment Theory" essay warned about, these firms *as firms* directly gave the Democrats amounts *far larger than the $100 minimum that qualifies individuals for inclusion in Webber's tables.* Among these were *all* of the capital-intensive/internationalist firms his table 9 singles out to refute my views—General Electric ($2,500), Standard Oil of New Jersey ($2,500), International Harvester ($2,500), American Tobacco ($2,500)—as well as many more businesses of obvious relevance to testing my views, such as Phillips Petroleum ($2,500), Signal Oil ($3,500), Ohio Oil ($1,000), R. J. Reynolds (more than $3,000), Liggett & Meyers ($2,500), Lorillard Tobacco ($500), Eastman Kodak ($625), Boeing ($2,500), Grumman ($2,500), Ford Motor ($4,000), Crown Zellerbach ($1,500), IBM ($2,500), United Fruit ($5,000), and American Radiator and Standard, the multinational giant (at least $10,000). Yet none of these contributions—which had, incidentally, virtually no counterparts on the Republican side—figure in his tables, since they were not contributed by individuals.[6]

In addition, Webber's procedure makes the Chase National Bank and its legendary owners disappear, as well as Manufacturers Trust, which shows up in his tables as a bank that inclined toward the Republicans due to a handful of contributions worth, all told, a tiny fraction of the bank's aid to the Democrats. This is a consequence of his excluding loans—even those as large as $100,000, and on which, some five months after the election, the campaign still owed each bank $60,000 (Overacker, 1937, p. 497).

Further Difficulties

Webber's "individual percentage" strategy has another defect. Prior to the mid-seventies' legislation that placed (still very elastic) limits on individual contributions to presidential candidates, firms had no particular incentive to spread out campaign contributions among several officers. Depending on circumstances, one person could easily superintend the political equivalent of the one-stop shop. Or, more commonly, a particularly well-placed person handled most of the serious political negotiations while handing out the lion's share of the cash, even if other executives also contributed.

James A. Moffett provides an instructive example. Judging from the entry in his table 6 for Standard Oil of California—which indicates no aid to the Democrats—Webber appears unacquainted with the case. But, if one wants to assess the relation of the oil industry to the New Deal, one dares not neglect him.

Moffett served for years as a high official and director of Standard Oil of New Jersey. By 1932, the entire oil industry was in crisis. Moffett, in the meantime, had become a friend and very early supporter of Roosevelt for president. On the basis of an interview and many documents which I obtained from the widow of a close associate, "From 'Normalcy' to New Deal" related the story of how Moffett and an American contact of Sir Henri Deterding, the head of Shell Oil, teamed up to help push the United States off the gold standard and persuade FDR to send his famous message that wrecked the London Conference. But Moffett did not then disappear; for a while he served Roosevelt as an oil administrator. Later, after a major disagreement with Walter Teagle, who headed Jersey Standard (and whose celebrated fondness for hunting and fishing enabled him to periodically dispatch fresh fish or game to the White House), Moffett left Jersey Standard. But he did not thereby leave the "family": Standard Oil of California immediately hired him as a senior vice president. Over the next few years, Moffett shuttled back and forth, sometimes working formally for FDR and sometimes formally for Socal. In 1935, he negotiated the fateful lease with the Saudis that led to the creation of Caltex, a joint subsidiary of Socal and Texaco (which he soon headed) and, a decade later, to the formation of the ultimate American multinational: Aramco.

Neither the Lonergan Committee records nor the Overacker data contain any entries for contributions from Moffett during the 1936 campaign. There is, nevertheless, absolutely no doubt that he was deeply involved in the campaign: still serving as a Socal vice president, he was showcased in public as a member of the executive advisory committee of the Democratic National Campaign Committee. The archives of the Roosevelt library also testify to his easy, indeed, almost casual, access to the White House.

Similarly, Montana's J. Bruce Kremer, for decades a member of the Democratic National Committee, was notorious for his close relations with the Anaconda Copper Co. that long dominated his state (Malone, 1975, pp. 243–245). Should he, a regular party contributor, who donated in 1936, be counted in any effort to assess Anaconda's political contributions that year? (It begs the question to reply that his relation with the local power company was almost equally infamous.)[7]

With omissions like these, the only "systematic" aspect of tables reporting the proportion of executives contributing $100 or more is that they may often be systematically wrong as a guide to what happened. Yet even the counts of the contributions cannot be accepted at face value.

First, there is the problem that many of the wrong people are being counted. Webber tabulates the contributions from both directors and top executives of the firms in his sample. The tables group together contributions from both without distinguishing between them.

Again, while this procedure appears eminently reasonable, it is open to grave objection. The role that directors play in the modern corporation has been the subject of vigorous debate. Some analysts view them as virtual pawns of the management. Others dispute this "managerial control" thesis, arguing that owners of large blocks of stock still wield decisive power. Also, it is sometimes suggested that banks, either because they hold large amounts of stock in trust, or simply because they provide vitally needed liquidity, exercise plenary power in most modern corporations (Kotz, 1978; Chandler, 1990; Burch, 1972).

This discussion has important implications for campaign finance studies, but space limitations make it impossible to review the various arguments. Here I can only state that my own work in archives and experience as a consultant to very large firms convinces me that the bank control thesis is untenable. In economies like those of Britain and the United States (since at least World War I), with fairly deep financial markets and relatively open securities emporia, bank power is distinctly limited, although it surely varies over the business cycle.

If one dismisses the bank control argument, then the exact view one takes about the managerial revolution—the case for which I consider overstated, especially for the 1930s, but also as identifying a real tendency even then—is less important, but with this qualification: it is essential to draw a clear distinction between "inside" directors (those who serve in the firm's management), directors who represent large, presumably controlling, blocs of shares, and "outside" directors, whose interest—irrespective of pious legal injunctions about fiduciary duty—is basically aligned with their own firms.

In assessing political contributions, those of the first two classes of directors can reasonably be aggregated with donations from a firm's other top managers, but the third type should not be. *Otherwise, one will in effect be sampling the rest of the economy instead of the firm in which one is interested.* Bank boards, for example, frequently contain many outside directors from other large firms. These outside directors normally do not run the bank—indeed, Chase and some other banks threw large numbers of them off their boards during the New Deal. The practice of keeping them on the board was defended, then and now, in terms of attracting potential business customers, not in terms of recruiting potential controlling interests, and there is certainly no reason to assume that outside directors, in making political contributions, generally do not look principally to their primary interests.

In my own quantitative work I have tried to weed out the outside directors (an arduous task for almost every period save the 1930s, when the famous Temporary National Economic Committee (TNEC) study provided unrivalled data about stockholders). Webber does not draw any distinctions. Accordingly, since no one has ever suggested that most big businessmen supported Roosevelt, his tables surely inflate the numbers of Republican sympathizers.

Additional Data and Sample Problems

Webber's methodology also excludes a second class of actors that I called attention to in my own work on operationalizing the investment theory: the very wealthiest private investors. The logic in favor of their inclusion is as follows: the investment theory is concerned principally with "large investors" (in the sense [chapter 1] of major economic actors, rather than the idiosyncratic meaning of someone who happens to invest heavily in one particular race). Webber takes this to mean the largest firms in each industry. This is, fundamentally, perfectly sensible. It is essentially equivalent to the first steps I take in constructing samples for my own quantitative studies. But one has to realize that lists of large firms (which, when they are based on *Moody's* or, more recently, *Fortune Magazine* and similar sources, also typically exclude some very large privately held firms) are only part of the solution. A substantial number of individual investors exist whose vast resources are comparable to firms on at least the middle-to-bottom rungs of any rank ordering of large firms. Some way has to be found to take such individuals into account. For contemporary research, someone undertaking the task of estimating wealth holdings would probably adapt *Forbes's* annual list of the richest Americans. There are no perfect sources for the thirties, but, as indicated below, it is possible to find ways to cope.

If one does not, the consequences are likely to be serious. The oil industry is perhaps the most important of all modern American capital-intensive industries—and its behavior in the New Deal was a major focus of "From 'Normalcy' to New Deal." Webber believes that he can refute my analysis by sampling various sizes of oil companies listed in *Moody's*. But this notion is wrong. We have already discovered that his treatment of Standard Oil of New Jersey, Phillips, Socal, Ohio Oil, and other firms that donated directly to the Democrats is hopelessly misleading. But it is also deeply significant that many of the greatest fortunes in modern America—such as those amassed by Clint Murchison, Sid Richardson, H. L. Hunt, and others—began their exponential growth in the oil fields of East Texas. And many of this group were strong backers of the New Deal until well past 1936. Typically, these operators shuffled small, usually privately held, often even unincorporated, companies around like so many playing cards. Such concerns will not appear, except by accident, on any list of firms compiled from standard business sources. But if they are omitted, it is idle to generalize about oil and the Democrats.

Omissions of this sort are one reason Webber's discussion of the oil industry misses what "From 'Normalcy' to New Deal" brought into focus for the first time. But there are other problems with his discussion as well.

My analysis of the oil industry's relation to the New Deal, for example, drew heavily on primary sources, including the personal papers of a leading New Deal oilman. One cannot delve very deeply into such sources, however, before the inadequacies of existing campaign finance data become apparent. Yet, in sharp contrast to the methodological canon quoted earlier from my "Investment Theory" essay—"a good rule of thumb . . . is to treat published campaign contributions

. . . as the tip of an iceberg, and be wary of any analysis that relies only on them"—Webber scarcely raises any questions about missing data. Not once does he consider whether one reason he disagrees with me is that I might have uncovered some facts not reflected in his limited data.

But "letters, diaries, and newspapers of the period" almost always repay careful attention. It is easy to show that both the Lonergan Committee's public report and the larger data set Overacker valiantly rescued (which together constitute Webber's sole source) are seriously incomplete. Indeed, this is precisely why I did not undertake a statistical analysis of the data in the original committee report.

The 1925 law Webber mentions in his brief discussion of his data was never seriously enforced—Sorauf suggests that not one person or corporation was ever prosecuted under it—and was clearly honored mostly in the breach, so that reported funds represented a mere fraction of the funds actually deployed in campaigns (Sorauf, 1988, pp. 28–33; Ferguson, 1992). Large amounts of money were raised locally, by county and precinct committees, by special local and state funds, and by any number of other imaginative vehicles, with exiguous or no records kept.

County committees around New York, for example, raised prodigious amounts of funds quite independently of the national committees. These funds came essentially from New York business groups, including, notably, the House of Morgan, which could and often did make transfers to other states and regions, or to the national committee itself, without ever accounting for where the money came from (Ferguson, 1992). The Overacker records Webber relies upon contain many references to transfers from groups such as the Democratic State Committee of New York, the Nassau County (Long Island) Republican Finance Committee, etc., with no notation as to who gave how much.

The Lonergan Committee's own surveys of contributors did little to lift this veil of darkness. While it did attempt to gather data on the principal state party funds, the committee decided at the outset not to issue any subpoenas. (Not surprisingly, the committee's final report complained that some state committees ignored its queries.) The committee also decided not to pursue county and precinct data at all, nor did it even try to identify "innumerable" "emergency committees and organizations" that "ostensibly function independently of the regular national party organizations" at both the national and state levels, whose cumulative impact on the campaign was acknowledged to be "tremendous in scope and financial import" (U.S. Congress, 1937, p. 25).

Its much-touted survey of large contributors amounted to scarcely more than the mailing of questionnaires to large contributors asking for information about additional contributions they might have tendered. While the committee alluded to the legal obligation to respond, it is obvious that many recipients took this in the same spirit with which they had approached compliance with earlier regulations, such as the 1925 act itself.

The results were a travesty. In Houston, Texas, for example, the county-level campaign for Roosevelt was actually led by an attorney for Humble Oil, the giant (it was larger than all but a handful of firms in the industry) affiliate of Standard Oil of New Jersey, while other Humble executives contributed to the Democratic campaign. My own statistical analysis, discussed below, confirms that oil was indeed overrepresented among industries that contributed to the Democrats. This analysis, however, includes at least some of the organizers (e.g., Murchison, Richardson, and others, who acted in concert with a substantial number of major oil companies) of a scheme to channel oil money from Texas to FDR's campaign through dummy organizations in other states.[8]

The oil industry is not the only place where data missing from Webber's particular source could lead one erroneously to conclude that "From 'Normalcy' to New Deal" is in error. A raft of other, virtually certain, Democratic contributors to FDR's campaign are missing from both the public Lonergan Committee report and Overacker's private files. Among them are Joseph P. Kennedy (who is mentioned for a loan in Overacker's records, but who clearly contributed large funds); Vincent Astor (who may well have had a role in obtaining the Chase loan, since he owned a large bloc of stock and served as a director of the bank); and Bernard Baruch. Investment banker Sidney Weinberg appears to have raised more money for FDR than anyone else, yet he never made the Lonergan report, and is listed in Overacker's private archive as making one contribution of $250. Nor do Webber's tables give any suggestion that Sir Henri Deterding, the head of Shell Oil, ardently admired Roosevelt (though his influence on the president had passed its peak); or that investment banker Clarence Dillon was a "Roosevelt backer" in 1936 (Knolige and Knolige, 1978, p. 252).[9]

On the Republican side, data on major contributors are also egregiously missing. Neither the Lonergan Committee nor Overacker record Thomas W. Lamont of J. P. Morgan & Co. as contributing to the GOP. Yet careful archival work demonstrates that Lamont was deeply involved in the campaign as both contributor and fundraiser. (Indeed, his office at 23 Wall Street probably qualifies as the most important of all the centers of Republican power in that notably polycentric GOP campaign.) Other Republicans who indisputably gave large sums to help defeat Roosevelt, including John J. Raskob, a founder of the American Liberty League, also contrived to keep out of both the Lonergan Committee report and Overacker's files.[10]

Webber's published tables also show no contributions from some very important Roosevelt supporters who actually are listed in Overacker's private files. Some of these provide confirmation of the case made in "From 'Normalcy' to New Deal," such as the executives from Mobil and Tidewater Oil who contributed (the latter included John Paul Getty, who probably controlled the firm even then), or A. P. Giannini, head of the Bank of America (whose bank's archive contains copies of several long campaign telegrams of the Democratic National Committee that confirm "From 'Normalcy' to New Deal"'s analysis of the bank's strong support of FDR, despite Webber's table indicating a Republican tilt for it). It is, of course, true that identifying people from unpublished listings can be extremely tricky and mistakes are inevitable. However, Webber should have indicated that his identifications might be in error, particularly where "From 'Normalcy' to New Deal" plainly indicated strong pro-Roosevelt partisanship, as in the Bank of America case, and where it was so public (Giannini's name was prominently displayed on the letterhead of the Good Neighbor League, a Roosevelt campaign vehicle).

I will conclude the general critique of Webber's claims by addressing a question whose final resolution is importantly affected by missing data: how best to test, in statistical terms, "From 'Normalcy' to New Deal"'s assertion that capital-intensive, internationally oriented businesses were disproportionately favorable to the New Deal.

Webber reduces this question to a hunt for industries close to "100%" in favor of the New Deal. These, he claims, do not exist. Again, this is simply wrong. Overacker (1937, p. 486) long ago concluded, and my analysis confirms, that the capital-intensive, export-oriented tobacco industry was lopsidedly Democratic.[11] So, as we shall see, were several other major industries. The vital point, however, is that the whole question is a red herring. A sensible alternative is easy to find— once again, in my own essays on how to test the "investment" approach.

When I wrote "From 'Normalcy' to New Deal" and "Investment Theory," perhaps the most fashionable argument on the relation between money and politics was that business normally supported both major political parties. Accordingly, "From 'Normalcy' to New Deal" was carefully worded to permit an interpretation according to which the rising power of labor gradually made a bipartisan strategy infeasible as more and more businesses found it impossible (i.e., unprofitable) to "extend any [more] support to the 'labor' party" (chapter 2, p. 122).

A note to that discussion also suggested that "most cases of apparent 'bipartisanship' rest on undiscriminating evidence—usually public campaign expenditure records. In most cases, more institutionally subtle behavior signals a preference for one or the other candidate."

"Investment Theory" analyzed the bipartisan case at length, trying to explain when such a strategy made sense and when it did not. For present purposes, its crucial claim was that

> Some industries or firms find themselves wanting policies that the other party clearly could never accept. Having nothing to gain from bipartisan strategies, these industries (or firms) become the "core" of one party, as for example, textiles, steel, and shoes were in the Republican Party after the New Deal because of labor policy, and chemicals because of trade . . . Other industries or firms, differently situated, can try out both parties. But this is the crucial point: rarely equally. (chapter 1, pp. 42–43).

This passage implies that not one but a whole family of statistical distributions are potentially useful in testing the investment theory. But one empirical regularity was especially illuminating:

> In analyzing the modern Democratic [P]arty . . . one does well to recognize that comparatively few firms and industries of any size give anything to the party, and then focus sharply on those who do (Ferguson, 1991, p. 254, n. 26).

The fact that the business community is so heavily Republican can, in practice, simplify problems of missing data for large data sets: since reliable figures for total expenditures are rare (and more institutionally subtle information resists quantification), precise quantitative estimates of "how much" most firms in a large sample prefer Democrats or Republicans are likely to be spurious. Accordingly, one does well to try to avoid the problem in the statistical design. Instead, assess, for example, how many investors in some bloc of firms of interest (an industry, for example) contribute any money at all (above some threshold, perhaps) to the Democrats. This virtually always produces a clearly bi- or tri-modal distribution, in which some set of firms, industries, or whatever units towers over or sinks beneath the rest (i.e., some are also clearly especially inhospitable). In such cases, the best statistics to use are often the simplest, such as tests that a particular industry or set of firms in fact has a rate of contribution significantly above (or below) the rest of the sample's mean.[12]

This solution has another point in its favor. There is a powerful argument for the proposition that the question of "how much" a firm favors either candidate in an election when it contributes to both is often the wrong question to ask. That the money arrives at all may be the overriding fact, and, even if the amount is less than that donated to someone else, it may still be influential. (Indeed, at the margin, it may well be more influential.) Certainly, the prospect of losing such resources can influence a candidate's behavior. Or a candidate, if he can count on money from a powerful, if perhaps scattered, minority of the business community for his stance might gain the means to launch a strong campaign that would otherwise be hopeless.

In terms of "From 'Normalcy' to New Deal," the appropriate question thus becomes not whether some industry was virtually 100 percent Democratic, but whether the percentage of capital-intensive, internationally oriented firms supporting FDR and the Democrats was significantly higher than the proportion in labor-intensive, protectionist industries.

Webber does not systematically compare results across industries, nor does he conduct any tests of statistical significance.[13] Still, his results suggest the possibility that the oil industry had a markedly higher rate of Democratic support than, say, steel or textiles. But we have also seen that his sample, methods, and over- and under-counts of many contributors make it impossible to interpret the results. (In addition, it is likely that many of the "smaller" oil firms that happen to be on his list—taken, as he says, from *Moody's*—were either dependent upon or even partially owned by some of the "larger" firms, so that it is not at all clear how distinct the two lists really are, or who was truly giving the money.) Nor did he even try to test "From 'Normalcy' to New Deal"'s claims about orientation to the world economy.

There is one way to address the issue: build a new database of major investors consisting both of large firms and the wealthiest individual investors that incorporates all political contributions in whatever form they were made (loans, corporate contributions, individual donations, etc.). Then conduct the appropriate statistical tests using "wages as a percent of value added" (probably the best overall measure of firms' sensitivities on the labor question) and some indicator of a firm's position in the international economy.

A Fresh Quantitative Analysis

Ever since "From 'Normalcy' to New Deal," I have been working on just such a study. The database and its sources are described in appendix 4.1. For now, it must suffice to observe that the sample has been constructed along the lines of my other quantitative studies: a basic list of the very largest firms and investors (taking special care to include the largest—mostly Texas-based—oil fortunes), supplemented in this instance, because textiles, still very important in the 1930s, were dominated by small firms, with a special list of firms in that industry (I used my replication of Webber's study). The campaign contribution data includes every contribution known to me from any reliable source, including not only the individual contribution data from the Lonergan Committee and Overacker's files that Webber drew upon, but also Overacker's invaluable inventory of corporate contributions, along with all contributions I have succeeded in uncovering in private archives.

One final issue merits brief mention, before considering the light the data shed on the multinationals and the New Deal: the question of the time period relevant to collecting data on contributions. Webber analyzed contributions that were made between the November 1936 presidential election and the previous congressional election. For testing "From 'Normalcy' to New Deal," however, this time frame is too generous: the Second New Deal does not date from earlier than 1935. It was, moreover, not an event, but a complex process that certainly was not completed before the scales fell from the eyes of Acheson, Clayton, Warburg, et al., in the final weeks of the campaign. (In a deeper sense, perhaps, it did not assume its final form until after the wave of strikes and the recession of 1937–38). As a practical compromise, I set May 1, 1935, as a cutoff date. This marked a period after the tumultuous United States Chamber of Commerce meeting, came long after the birth of the Liberty League, and was the month in which it became clear that the Wagner Act would become law with a (reluctant) presidential blessing.

Now let us consider what the data say. The critical question is easily and compactly answered: capital-intensive, multinationally oriented industries clearly supported Roosevelt at rates disproportionately higher than the rest of American business.

Consider first the top of table 4.1, which reports the average level of contributions to each party for the entire group of 405 "investing units" (hereinafter "firms," where this is specifically extended to embrace the great private fortunes). The figure for the Democrats is 32 percent, while the figure for the Republicans is almost twice that at 58 percent. Clearly, there are no surprises here: American business as a whole supported the GOP in 1936.

Genuine illumination begins with the next section of table 4.1, in the entries that compare how the Democrats fared across industries. The data on industries, arrayed in rough order of capital intensity (i.e., low ratio of wages to value added), confirm the pattern predicted by "From 'Normalcy' to New Deal." The first cluster of industries (in which wages as a percent of value added all average well under 30 percent)—tobacco, food, oil, chemicals, and "media"[14]—tells a striking tale: all but heavily protectionist chemicals are far (and significantly)

TABLE 4.1. Average Level of Contributions to Each Party (Figures for
Particular Industries)

Democrats			
Food and beverages	59% (.00)	Textiles	17% (.09)
Tobacco	88% (.00)*	Mining	0% (.01)*
Media	80% (.00)*	Coal	0% (.16)*
Oil	49% (.01)	Steel	36% (.77)*
Chemicals	8% (.07)*	Heavy industry	13% (.02)
		Machinery	40% (.51)
Banks	40% (.45)	Autos	40% (.60)*
Investment banks	36% (.61)	Railroads	23% (.27)
Largest banks & Investment		Utilities	8% (.00)
Banks	45% (.09)	Retailing	47% (.15)
Republicans			
Food and beverages	59% (.97)	Textiles	42% (.09)
Tobacco	25% (.05)*	Mining	73% (.23)
Media	30% (.07)*	Coal	75% (.50)*
Oil	35% (.00)	Steel	100% (.00)*
Chemicals	83% (.07)	Heavy Industry	83% (.00)
		Machinery	73% (.23)
Banks	85% (.01)	Autos	70% (.45)
Investment banks	73% (.08)	Railroads	47% (.18)
Largest Banks & Investment		Utilities	56% (.72)
Banks	78% (.00)	Retailing	73% (.16)

Sources: See text.

Notes: N = 405 firms, as defined in the text. (Based on contribution data from 1,872 individuals)
Republicans—.58; Democrats—.32. Level of significance for difference from party's average level of
contribution is in parentheses.

*Expected value of cell in chi-square less than 5—warning of low power.

above average in supporting the Democrats. Clearly, this was friendly
territory for FDR. Chemicals, by contrast, are far below average in their
level of support.[15]

Most of the other results for separate industries simply reflect what
we already know: American industry mostly disliked Roosevelt and
the Democrats. Textiles (many of which are in the South) are significantly below average (which, it should be borne in mind, is already
very low); the separate parts of what can plausibly be regarded as
heavy industry (coal, steel, mining) are below average, but the differences are not statistically significant. This is, however, mostly a consequence of sample size: recoding the three as one industry ("heavy industry") immediately yields a highly significant result. Virtually all the
other industries did not differ significantly from the mean in their lack

of affection for the Democrats, including glass, aluminum, etc. I have, accordingly, dropped them from the table. Note, however, that the electrical industry and machinery, both export-oriented, along with some other product lines (some export-oriented capital goods sectors) have important Democratic representation: there simply are not enough cases in many of these industries to yield reliable results. One way to get around this problem is to collapse categories, so that the totals become large enough to be reliable. But this strategy only rarely makes sense: there is too much variation among most industries for this to mean much. In addition, industry by itself is frequently a poor predictor: variation within some industries in regard to labor and trade practices is large. A much better idea, realized below, is to aggregate them all and test differences between political party contributors for both labor sensitivity and international position.

Some questions about individual industries do arise, but they are mostly secondary, and can be neglected here.[16] Two results that are interesting concern utilities, where Roosevelt is unsurprisingly abominated, and retailing, which was friendly to the New Deal's efforts to stimulate consumption, at least until the upsurge of unionism.[17]

Also of great interest are the results for investment and commercial banking. Both are above average in their support for the New Deal, but the results are not statistically significant. On examination, two factors appear to account for this. One is the usual sample size problem. But the other seems to be connected with features of the industry. "From 'Normalcy' to New Deal" stressed how the first New Deal's historic Glass-Steagall Act exacerbated tensions within the banking community that had arisen during the boom of the twenties. Based on many primary sources, the essay identified banking rivals of the House of Morgan, particularly the Chase Bank, as the principal forces behind that bill's separation of investment from commercial banking (as applied even to private banks, such as Morgan). The essay also outlined other aspects of the various New Deals that struck at the Morgan interests, notably the 1935 act breaking up utility holding companies, and the Federal Reserve Act of the same year, in which Chase President Winthrop Aldrich and a coalition of other bankers once again stepped into the breach, to block the repeal of Glass-Steagall that Morgan and its allies had sought.

Not surprisingly, although the Morgan bank generally supported the administration's monetary policies and clashed sharply behind the scenes over trade policy with the protectionist industrialists that were now firing up the GOP, it and its large number of clients and allies enlisted in the campaign against the New Deal and, eventually, in favor of Landon.

These facts suggest that a closer look at the data for both invest-ment and commercial banking might be appropriate. Nothing in "From 'Normalcy' to New Deal" implies any particular hypotheses about which percentage of either industry does what—only that a clear Mor-gan vs. non-Morgan split exists, and that the Morgan faction was and remained enormously influential. The Morgan bank had been the leading "brand name" in both industries for many years, and vast por-tions of each were used to doing business with it. This suggests that contracting the sample to include only the largest firms in commercial and investment banking might actually increase the proportion of con-tributions to the Democrats, for many of the lower-ranking firms on both lists had fairly obvious ties to Morgan. This was particularly plain in the case of the investment houses. My sample included, along with all those on Webber's list, the large firms formed out of Glass-Steagall's mandated divestiture of investment banking affiliates from commercial banks. Morgan's continued influence within these firms—if not neces-sarily its remote "control" of them—was well documented by various congressional investigations. So was their rather plainly stated collec-tive hope of repealing Glass-Steagall (TNEC, 1940a). I also suspected that the largest banks would be more willing to run the risk of breaking ranks with Morgan.[18]

Reducing the sample size, of course, decreases reliability. The way around this is to pool data for the ten largest commercial banks and the investment banks in Webber's sample (thus dropping the other houses mentioned above, though of course retaining the few large private in-vestors in these fields)—creating a special group that might be termed the "largest financiers." As the table entry "largest financiers" indicates, polarization does rise, and this time there is no question about its statis-tical significance. The largest investment and commercial bankers clearly contribute to the Democrats at disproportionate rates compared with business as a whole. (When the same test is performed on Repub-lican contributors, on the other hand, the rate does not rise, a hint that simple bipartisan strategies are not being implemented.)

The results for the Republicans are less consequential for assessing "From 'Normalcy' to New Deal." These findings testify to a vast busi-ness coalition, with particularly deep veins of support within heavy industry, chemicals, manufacturing as a whole (which would certainly emerge as statistically significant if the data were pooled), and com-mercial and investment banking. Textiles also show a high rate of GOP support, but at a level somewhat below the rest. This may reflect some real trend, but is probably due largely to the conservative way in which missing data are recorded (and suggests that the industry may still be undersampled, or, perhaps more likely, that its mostly small firms concentrate their contributions on local party committees, and thus are less likely to show up in tabulations of national campaign spending).

On the other hand, in the most capital-intensive sectors, the absolute rate of contributions to the GOP is essentially the same as to the Democrats in the food industry, and actually below the rate of contributions to FDR's campaign from tobacco, media, and the oil industry.

The Critical Test

These findings do not yet add up to conclusive proof that capital-intensive, multinationally oriented industry disproportionately backed the New Deal. For that one would ideally want measurements on both the Democratic and Republican coalitions as a whole with respect to both labor sensitivity and trade.

Such tests, however, are not difficult. Wages as a percent of value added are a real number that can be averaged for both coalitions. If the Democrats come in lower, "From 'Normalcy' to New Deal" is correct; is not, it is wrong. Similarly, the trichotomous classification used in categorizing firm orientation to the world economy—"protectionist" (or, if one is willing to live with some ambiguity, "nationalist" [chapter 2, p. 163, n. 27]; "internationalist" (export-oriented or multinational); and a middle category for cases where the distinction is irrelevant or unclear—can easily be ordered and assigned numerical values (e.g., protectionist = 0; the middle category = 1; multinationals and exporters = 2).[19]

It is then a simple matter of averaging each party's contributors, thereby obtaining the other global measure of the difference between Republican and Democratic contributors required to test the theory.

Table 4.2 shows the result: in both cases, the *t*-test for differences between means (with the conservative assumption of separate rather than common variances) is significant. As "From 'Normalcy' to New Deal" predicted, contributors to the Democrats are indeed much less labor-intensive than those who donated to Republicans, and they are also far more internationally oriented.

These findings demonstrate a major premise of the investment theory of political parties: that it is possible to analyze investor coalitions in precise ways that relate directly to policy. Before concluding, however, it is appropriate to comment on how sensitive these conclusions might be to coding errors or to other problems.

Coding errors undoubtedly exist, but almost certainly not enough to change the results. A conservative classificatory strategy was employed which, in several instances, led to decisions not to exploit prob-

TABLE 4.2. *T*-Tests for Differences in Means of Labor Intensity and Internationalism Between Democratic and Republican Contributors—1936 Election

	Mean	Standard Error	*T*-Value	Degrees of Freedom	Significance (Separate variances) (2-tailed)
Sample Including Banks and Investment Banks					
Internationalism					
Democrats	1.69	.07	6.75	155.56	(.00)
Republicans	.93	.08			
Labor					
Democrats	24.09	1.53	−3.38	145.07	(.00)
Republicans	31.47	1.55			
Banks and Investment Banks Deleted					
Internationalism					
Democrats	1.66	.08	8.79	129.49	(.00)
Republicans	.65	.08			
Labor					
Democrats	25.12	1.57	−5.46	123.68	(.00)
Republicans	37.06	1.53			

Sources: See text.

abilities that seemed likely to favor the main hypotheses (as in the case of retailing, mentioned above, which probably implies an understatement of the Democratic contributors' international orientation). These figures are, after all, averages of large aggregates. In addition, the magnitude of the differences, particularly on the internationalism dimension, is impressive.

Nor are these results due to regional effects. Though Domhoff (1990, p. 234) has claimed that "From 'Normalcy' to New Deal"'s analysis is vulnerable in this respect, he is mistaken: statistical tests for South/non-South and other likely regional contrasts all failed to turn up significant differences, whether performed for all industries at once, for oil, textiles, and tobacco separately, or for various combinations of them.[20]

But there is a final consideration. An implication of "From 'Normalcy' to New Deal" was that the 1936 election set off a struggle between two factions for the control of the GOP. One faction consisted of the Morgan (and some Rockefeller) interests and their allies. This group was frequently difficult to tell apart from the Democratic multinational liberals who endorsed Roosevelt in 1936, although the Morgans, in particular, had historic ties to very old parts of the industrial structure, such as U.S. Steel and many coal companies. The other faction was a coalition of heavy industry and protectionist chemical companies.

The latter group's vision of America's place in the world, and of Americanism as an ideology, differed significantly from that of their "allies" in the rest of the party in 1936. In most of the United States, however, this group constituted the real core of the GOP. It is noteworthy that, as table 4.2 testifies, the gap between the GOP and the Democrats widens appreciably when the *t*-tests are run with the data for investment and commercial banks removed.

It was this gulf, I think, that Acheson, Harriman, Clayton, Warburg, and their allies sensed when in 1936 they contemplated what the Democratic administration had wrought—social security, the Wagner Act, and the tax and other measures—only to conclude that a consistent application of the principle of comparative advantage led finally to the judgment that the New Deal was the best deal for them, the comparatively advantaged.

APPENDIX 4.1

Sources of Data

Two hundred largest nonfinancial firms as of Dec. 31, 1937, from TNEC (1940, pp. 346–47); Humble also was included, as an integral part of Standard Oil of New Jersey. Two rosters of banks, as explained in the text, were used. Shorter list of top 10 banks for 1940, prepared from *Moody's Bank and Finance Manual* from Burch (1980, p. 17); longer list of "the leading commercial banks valued over $100 million according to company balance sheets in 1936" from Webber, 1991, table 5. Textile firms from "leading cotton textile companies valued over $10 million" from Webber (1991, table 1) and "cotton textile companies valued between $1–10 million according to company balance sheets in 1936" (Webber, 1991, table 2). Shorter list of investment banks from "major investment banks in 1936" (Webber, 1991, table 4). Longer list adds J. S. Bache; Stone and Webster; Halsey, Stuart; Paine Webber; Harris Upham; Field, Glore; E. A. Pierce, firms prominently discussed in TNEC 1940a, part 22, plus Otis, which emerged as a feisty competitor. Six largest insurance companies for 1940 from Burch (1980, 17). (Note that a clear break exists between the six and the rest of the industry.) Director information came almost entirely from *Poor's* (1936), though a few firms not listed there had to come from elsewhere, including company archives, TNEC listings, or the 1937 *Poor's*.

Procedure was to select the top (first) six officers listed for all firms;

if by so doing, one was forced into a column or row of vice presidents, then all the vice presidents were included, although if among the top six officers, the vice president title was supplemented by others (e.g., vice-president and treasurer), then the regular vice presidents would not be included. This procedure cannot be used for all banks because of the enormous number of vice presidents; in these cases, the list of top officers had to be cut at whatever seemed a reasonable point in the organizational chart after at least five officials. (For the investment houses all partners were included; though I should prefer to weight them by their shares of the business, data limitations make this impossible.) All inside directors of whatever position were included, along with owner-directors. Ownership data (to eliminate outside directors and retain owner-directors) generally follows Burch's review of the TNEC data (Burch, 1972, appendix A) with very minor changes based on my own work. In a very few cases where the owner was clearly influencing the company although not on the board, he or she was included (the outstanding case is Eugene Meyer at Allied Chemical). Also, the relatively few people who served on more than one board were treated as separate observations on their respective "investor units" ("firms," as the text explains); the same was true for the handful of directors who overlapped with the separately prepared list of large investors.

List of large investors: compiled from (Lundberg, [1938] 1946, pp. 26–27), which drew in part from federal tax data for 1924; after long review of various possible changes discussed in sources analyzed in Lundberg (1968) and Burch (n.d.), three changes made in list of families: Harriman added; Lundberg's own portmanteau "Standard Oil group" of various lesser investors in the old company (not including Rockefeller or Harkness) deleted, save for Bedford; J. P. Morgan Jr. replaced Lundberg's "Morgan inner group"). Because this list dates from the early twenties, it misses the effect of the boom, the Depression, and, especially, the East Texas oil discoveries. A partial correction for these omissions is to add the names on the list of "Taxpayers with Largest Net Income, 1941" (from unpublished Treasury documents) in Brandes (1983, table I); a few spouses that appeared as two entries were consolidated into one. Also, where Brandes indicated a definite company as a primary source of a person's income, contributions from that company were also checked where appropriate in light of the connection indicated. (Note that the list strongly supports Lundberg's earlier assessments; and that the observation in Brandes [1983, p. 310] that Sid Richardson, although the third largest taxpayer in 1941, may not have reported any net income in 1936 is almost surely an artifact—independent oilmen very commonly ran [and still run] paper "losses" for several years in a row.) This list of only 100 people, however, is for the United States as a whole, and thus still fails to catch most of the Southwest titans. I hoped briefly that Texas Railroad Commission data might fill the gap, but the Commission claims not to have the requisite records. Recalling that the New Deal oil kings first reached general attention in the early 1950s, and that the statistically critical imperative is to avoid biasing the list, not that of finding an exactly contemporary roster, I added the oil-related names from two early *Fortune* (1957, p. 177; 1968, p. 156) lists of the largest American fortunes, along with the revisions for that industry only suggested by two critics of the *Fortune* efforts that I consider particularly well informed: (Lundberg, 1968, p. 42–44, 68–78) and Burch (n.d., appendix C and chart). The latter I have tried to use with the caution befitting an excellent study that has not been revised for publication.

Data for "wages as a percent of value added" follow the discussion (chapter 2) and are subject to all the qualifications entered there. The essential problem is that figures are available only for industries, not for firms. A further problem is that the 1929 *Census for Manufacturers* uses a different industry code from later censuses, thus the very valuable and convenient study from which I drew virtually all of the data for manufacturing (Bliss, 1939, appendices) is sometimes difficult to correlate with later analyses of firms by industry code (as in Chandler [1990], although a preliminary set of the Chandler data were kindly made available to me; and I have used this data to refine estimates for a few firms where it was unclear in which of Bliss's industry categories they belonged). Bliss, however, very helpfully distinguishes large plant industries, which is a valuable indicator of the presence of large firms. Non-manufacturing data are from diverse sources, and are probably less reliable because many mineral industries engage in both extraction and refining, thus mixing industries in a way that is difficult to sort out. In addition, the mining industry commonly shed labor massively in the Depression, dramatically altering the way several industries functioned. Figures for wages as a percent of value added in mining for all but copper (which follows the table in chapter 2, p. 120) and the one firm that produced sulphur (where the figure for refining in Bliss required consideration) come from the appropriate Depression-era entries in the *1967 Census of Mineral Industries* (1970). Where a large change in the labor dimension appeared, I interpolated between the figures for 1929 and 1939 on a straight-line basis, so that the former would not make the firms look more labor-intensive than they were (i.e., so that my main hypothesis would not be too easily confirmed). I have been unable to locate useful calculations of wages as a percent of value added for utilities or railroads. A rough but usable estimate for retailing in 1929 can be derived from (Barger, 1960, p. 330): The data in his table 3 might reasonably be adjusted in various ways; my procedure was to add a (conservative) 20 percent of his figure for "unincorporated profits" to his estimate of "employee compensation" to arrive at a final figure for "wages" (which is then divided by the same table's figure for value added). Wages as a percentage of value added are rarely calculated in the financial sector: the largest item of expense is usually interest costs, and wages make up only a fraction (in investment banking, a particularly minute fraction) of total compensation costs, which often include part of what should properly be accounted profits. Available statistics for the thirties, however, present special problems. First, the earnings and, especially, the costs that banks reported in the standard Federal Reserve sources were greatly influenced by tax and regulatory considerations (e.g., write-offs of securities) that if anything were becoming even more important as asset values collapsed. Second, as interest rates fell over the course of the Depression (chapter 3; Epstein and Ferguson, 1991) the structure of bank income statements and balance sheets became peculiar indeed, so that one can produce a wide range of figures for wages as a percent of value added by simply varying the year. In these circumstances, the most sensible thing to do is to settle on a value that could reasonably be taken to represent the "normal" case that could guide behavior in the long run: for investment banking, this implies perhaps a value of 10 percent; for commercial banking, with its larger labor force, perhaps 15 percent. But how to treat insurance, with its flock of agents, was obscure, and I made no assignment for it. (This imprecision makes no difference to the statistical results reported in the text. Institutions in the same industry are counted the same for both parties, and, as table 4.2 indicates, removing the financial sector actually widens the differences in labor intensity between the parties.)

The coding of firms' orientation to the world economy again follows "From 'Normalcy' to New Deal" closely, with that essay's warnings and qualifications underscored. This time, however, the effort was simplified. Firms were classified into one of three categories. The first contained those that seemed clearly protectionist or, perhaps, "inward looking" in the sense of Galbraith (1989); the second, its polar opposite, contained successful "outward" oriented multinationals and exporters favoring free(r) trade. In the middle were classed firms for which these classifications either made little sense or were heavily attended with uncertainty. No standardized databases exist that are usable; no alternative exists but to investigate firms using whatever data are at hand. Two works, however, were very helpful: Chandler (1990) and Wilkins (1974) for cases in which not enough other sources existed. (Note, however, that the latter's tables of "multinationals," while perfectly sensible for her treatment, cannot be used here without major modification: they include many firms that simply control mineral deposits abroad, often out of defensive motivations, and that were often prominent champions of the tariff). It is also important to assess carefully the implications of the various cartels that filled the interwar period—for some firms in cartels (e.g., General Electric) qualify as "multinationals" in the relevant sense of this essay. Others—as in most of the chemical industry—definitely do not. The turn in the copper industry (chapter 2, n. 27) in the thirties is of significance: I believe similar changes in sentiment affected virtually the entire class of minerals producers. Finally, it should not be necessary to say that a degree of uncertainty and disagreement about how cases are classified is only to be expected and that classifications of firms at different points in time even in the Depression sometimes changed sharply as the economy rose or fell (chapter 2).

The cutoff for contributions was $100, though, as the text indicates, many contributions ran far above that. Scarcely anyone in the sample was recorded as giving less than $100 in total, incidentally. Loans were also included. Of course, the observations in the text about known contributors in the 1936 campaign who are missing from Overacker's files refers to the time period for contributions defined in the text; other parts of the files cover 1932 and other years, but are irrelevant for this paper.

ACKNOWLEDGMENTS

The author gratefully acknowledges the very kind assistance rendered him by Herbert Alexander and the staff of the Citizens Research Foundation at the University of Southern California and other aid from Edmund Beard, Gerald Epstein, and Richard Freeland. The John W. McCormack Institute of the University of Massachusetts, Boston, provided modest, but very timely, financial support. Special thanks to Benjamin Page, for reading a draft under trying conditions, and Goresh Hosangady, for invaluable assistance with the statistics.

NOTES

1. Most of these details are taken from Ferguson (1984, pp. 89–92), supplemented by material collected from various archives for my full-length study of the New Deal (Ferguson, n.d.).

2. Initially, Magee, who had read my essay (1984), was skeptical about the historical relation between Democrats and low tariffs; the skepticism disappeared after he and his coauthors produced their own evidence in favor of the proposition. Magee, Brock, and Young (1989, pp. 185–201) provide additional evidence supporting my point about

the connection between the post-New Deal Democrats and multinationals, but their in-genious model linking tariff rates, unemployment/inflation tradeoffs, and the party re-verses the actual historical relations: Hull's tariff revisions and the Wagner Act preceded macroeconomic stabilization efforts. And their suggestion that my account is incomplete because "it does not explain why Democratic presidents would support free trade when this works counter to the interests of blue collar and much union labor" (1989, pp. 194–195) is true only if one cannot bring oneself to accept the obvious conclusion: that my account explains why blue-collar workers and unions do not, in fact, control the party.

Borchardt's essay originally appeared in German in 1984; he was responding to Fer-guson (1980).

3. Ferguson (1983) and (1986) were originally written as one paper and had to be divided for initial publication. Ferguson (1984) was completed long before any work had commenced on either, save for slight revisions inserted as it went to press. Ferguson (1989a) is largely an abridgement of the 1984 article, save for several footnotes.

4. It should not be necessary to caution that this example is discussed only infor-mally. But the thrust of the argument should be abundantly clear—as also why the objections brought against my essay by some "rational expectations" enthusiasts (e.g., McKelvey and Ordeshook, 1986) fail. The investment theory essay's fundamental criti-cism of the economic theory of democracy is that most people are not wealthy enough to control government, *not* that they are uninformed. At the same time, it should be observed that in all real political systems, problems of the flow and processing of infor-mation are extremely important. Accordingly, the basic reply to McKelvey and Ordes-hook (1986) is that information systems rapidly become politicized in episodes of major social conflict, so that traditional cues (including polls, which frequently are very poor or deceptive) used by voters become very unreliable. This process was clearly visible in the 1936 election, during which many Republicans cited a wide variety of poor indica-tors of sentiment, including the famous *Literary Digest* poll, in hopes of influencing public perceptions of momentum. See the appendix to this book.

5. I disagree with the view that these organizations exist outside of partisan politics. Actually, they have a very complex relation to political parties—as was true in the New Deal.

6. Most of these contributions, and those of many other corporations (including a few that, at first sight, are not consistent with "From 'Normalcy' to New Deal") are plainly grouped together in a little over a box and a quarter of Louise Overacker's papers, now housed at the Citizen's Research Foundation at the University of Southern Califor-nia. Overacker coded a variety of information about the contributions she (and the Lon-ergan Committee—see U.S. Congress [1937]) studied. But the code is not difficult to decipher; it is clear that some of these contributions were those involved in what became a major controversy at the time: paid advertisements in a *Book of the Democratic Convention of 1936*, which was later sold in several versions, including a deluxe "edition bound in leather and autographed by the President" (Overacker, 1937, p. 480). Others took the form of bulk purchases of these various editions.

Such efforts (whose true dimensions become plainer when one multiplies by just under 10 to translate the 1936 amounts into current 1991 dollars, as indicated at the opening of this essay) provided a way around laws against direct payments by corpora-tions to political parties. They could also be defended (and were, by corporation officials and Democratic Party operatives, when the GOP complained) as ordinary advertising, though no firm would have paid such rates to commercial media. (There was, of course, no plausible defense for the practice of buying copies in bulk.) From the standpoint of testing the investment theory, all such payments belong in the database, and in the analysis below, they are, though, of course, not all the companies that contributed are part of my sample.

I was unable to check the original data at the National Archives because analysts with the Record Group that Webber names could not locate the material. I do not read much into this; many libraries, like individuals, frequently have less than perfect recall. I have a great deal of confidence in Overacker, whose records were clearly painstakingly compiled and meticulously maintained. There are some mistaken individual identifications, but not many. In some individual cases, notes indicate that her totals differ from those of the Lonergan Committee; I infer that this usually arises because she continued working on the data after the report was published.

7. My answer, in regard to the statistical tests below, ultimately was "no," since a committed lobbyist like Kremer, who also doubles as a party official, may simply not be in a position to follow his patron's each and every turn, especially around a turning point like the New Deal.

8. The existence of such a scheme is plausibly asserted in Roosevelt and Brough (1975, p. 133), and a great deal of supporting evidence exists for their claim, though I cannot deal with the question in this essay. Nor can I sort out the question of the relations among independent, national, major, etc., oil companies any further.

9. Weinberg was assistant treasurer of the Democratic National Committee in both 1932 and 1936; Baruch's biographer, Schwarz (1981, p. 314), says flatly that Baruch contributed in 1936 though he is unable to determine how and when. After reviewing the archival evidence, I concur. On Astor, a variety of sources are available. Though caution is necessary because of its author's strained relations with FDR, Raymond Moley's diary, now with Moley's papers at the Hoover Institution at Stanford, makes it plain that Astor (who was then in business with Harriman) was working—and spending—to reelect the president. Kennedy (who is not in my sample) has been discussed by innumerable analysts and the facts are not in doubt. In cases such as these or such as Texas oilman Roy Cullen—who was openly attacking the New Deal in many forums and who should clearly be counted against "From 'Normalcy' to New Deal"'s case—or the "Liberty League" Republicans discussed in this essay—where the evidence appears dispositive even though no precise date or form of payment can be pinned down, the individual has been counted in the data set as a contributor. (Such cases number fewer than 10 out of 1,872 individuals appearing in my data set; they should not be confused with cases like that of Thomas W. Lamont—discussed in note 10—where archival sources contain receipts or letters acknowledging otherwise unrecorded contributions.) I also examined the (public) listings of the national executive committee and the national advisory council of the American Liberty League, since it appears that recruitment for these bodies was linked to a willingness to contribute. In the end, however, this search brought forth only three names, for two of which other evidence exists that is very strong indeed (Raskob and William Knudsen), while the third seems quite definite (S. Bayard Colgate).

10. Evidence of Lamont's activities in the 1936 campaign can be found in many archives. But Box 123 alone, in his own papers, now at the Baker Library at the Harvard Business School, establishes conclusively that Lamont was a lavish contributor and ma-

jor fund-raiser—though the unwary are cautioned that the range of Lamont's efforts is only imperfectly represented in these papers. In a striking warning of the incompleteness of the Lonergan data and the Overacker files, there is even a formal receipt from the New Jersey Republican National Finance Committee for one particular contribution of $2,500. This is especially interesting, because this organization appears actually to have been covered by the committee's report. Yet, somehow, while Lamont's son (also at Morgan) made it into the document (U.S. Congress, 1937, p. 84), the best-known banker of the age did not. Nor was he included in Overacker's files.

11. Domhoff (1990, pp. 232–235) claims repeatedly that Webber's work disproves "From 'Normalcy' to New Deal" thesis in the course of a lengthy discussion of *Right Turn* (Ferguson and Rogers, 1986). He adds that Webber's results show "conclusively" that the evidence discussed in "From 'Normalcy' to New Deal" that *Right Turn* cited in regard to business support for the New Deal is an "artifact of regional differences" (1990, p. 234). Webber is more circumspect in his paper on this point. This is fortunate, for, as shown in this chapter, New Deal business support is not an artifact of regionalism, not even in the case of tobacco (where by no means all firms were based in the South). Domhoff's own discussion contains other methodological errors. See my comments in chapter 6 of this volume, n. 37.

Almost everything that has been said about the shortcomings of Webber's discussion applies also to Allen (1991) save that Allen does at least attempt to incorporate an analysis of large investors. (Though I lack the space for detailed comment, I do not consider his choice a happy one, not least because it takes virtually no account of the Texas oil producers.) On p. 683, for example, he describes his sample as consisting of "589 individuals who were among the most powerful members of the capitalist class during the New Deal," or less than a third the size of my sample. Alas, however, he indicates that he took over only the individual contributions from Overacker's data set, and makes no allowance (or mention) of corporate contributions or loans. This, of course, is guaranteed to produce nonsense, particularly if one also mistakenly believes that the Overacker data represent an accurate count of "all campaign contributions of $100 or more received during calendar year 1936 at the state and local level by party organizations and other political organizations . . ." (p. 683). From his other descriptions of his sample and procedures, it is sometimes difficult to know for sure what he is doing. I cannot, for example, tell if the subsample of 110 industrial corporations—all that he relies on to test my views about labor intensity—include oil companies or not, or how many there were. But his subsample here is so minute and selective that it is something of a minor miracle that it nonetheless produces evidence that I am right after all ("labor intensity does have a modest negative effect on contributions to the Democratic Party").

Other claims he makes in the paper that run counter to my work are so easily falsifiable that one can only shake one's head. On p. 687, for example, he explains that "corporate elites from investment banks contributed nothing to the Democratic [P]arty." But this is ridiculous, as anyone who is willing to take the time to inspect the Lonergan Committee or the Overacker data in person will readily discover. (Consider, for example, such Roosevelt contributors as Averell Harriman, Paul Mazur, James Forrestal, or—as previously discussed—even Sidney Weinberg—all of whom appear in one or the other or both of these sources that he claims to have relied upon.) And his "explanation" for this nonfact only makes it obvious that he does not understand the issues in the Glass-Steagall Act. Otherwise, all his paper has to contribute is some unintended humor, as when he respectfully cites another study on p. 681 that found evidence that "the New Deal coalition included a 'power bloc' . . . [of] representatives of capital-intensive corporations with international markets," while failing to realize that this (waiving details) is the central argument of my 1984 paper that so vexes him.

The evidence about the industrial basis of Roosevelt's coalition, of course, is quite counter to the "state managers" or "independent state apparatus" views of essays such as Weir and Skocpol (1985). Precisely what distribution of campaign contributions claims such as theirs entail is, perhaps, not altogether clear. Perhaps most plausible on the basis of their premises would be a completely random distribution of contributions between the parties. If one were willing to beg certain fundamental questions, perhaps one could also argue that the traditional view of Roosevelt as lacking important business support (and the GOP as the party of "business") should show up in the statistics. But no matter what one's views, it is clear that my findings are not what such theories predict.

12. In such instances, chi-square tests are obviously appropriate, though so are others. Such testing can, however, involve some subtle questions of hypothesis testing. Many common statistical tests rely on exclusive partitions of the data. The question must be framed to allow for cases where contributions are made to both parties, e.g., test for differences between those who gave at least one contribution to Party X from those who did not.

What should not be done is equally clear, I think—regressions on totals are to be avoided. (No one, I think, who has ever read coal magnate Edward J. Berwind's remarkable letter to Thomas W. Lamont of October 31, 1932, in Box 123 of the Lamont papers on the Berwind companies' "normal" level of political contributions in the many states where they had interests is likely to succumb to this temptation.)

13. Both my sample and Webber's are technically forms of systematic rather than pure random probability samples. But, as long as the reader is duly warned about the nature of the sample, in problems of the type we are concerned with here, it makes perfect sense to treat such samples as though they were probability samples. See, for example, Stone (1971) for a vigorous defense and the subsequent discussion in Floud (1973, pp. 177–178). (Note that the work Stone is defending makes liberal use of confidence intervals.) The use of significance tests in such cases is now virtually universal in econometric history, though not always appreciated outside of it. The dubious are invited to consider that even comparatively large samples—such as those Webber and I each constructed—surely contain random variation that will affect one's best estimate of differences among investor blocs in their support or opposition to the New Deal. If, for example, I had taken the top 190 firms instead of the top 200, etc., as discussed in appendix 4.1, some minor differences in my results are to be expected.

14. My portmanteau term for an industry that embraces a few of the largest fortunes based in newspapers, but mostly magazines and film companies, both of which have a substantially lower labor intensity.

The significance values reported in table 4.1 are for the (2×2) Pearson chi-square test, with instances where the expected frequency in a cell falls below 5 flagged for the reader. In such cases, many analysts prefer to report results for Fisher's Exact Test (Jarausch and Hardy, 1991, p. 109). For the Democrats, the relevant two-tailed Fisher test results are as follows: Tobacco (.00); Media (.00); Chemicals (.11); Mining (.00); Coal (.31); Steel (.75); Autos (.73). For the Republicans, the cases where the test is relevant are Tobacco (.07), Media (.10), Coal (.64), Steel (.00). The analysis in the text is, clearly, not affected by the choice of significant test.

15. Note that these figures report the percentage of firms contributing to the Democrats as a percentage of all firms. All of my empirical papers have used this conservative approach (otherwise, missing data/no contribution entries would swell the Democratic percentages). The Republican comparisons discussed later are reported the same way—but, in these cases, one can be much more confident that a lot of the missing data were really Republican contributions that happened to be lost.

16. The evidence for the auto and rubber industries (plus a part of the steel industry too small to add up to anything in the aggregate) contains an interesting twist that may shed some light on the "process" character of the Second New Deal. These firms collectively show in the data as average. But I believe there is a deeper meaning here. To see it, however, it is necessary to reject a serious misreading of "From 'Normalcy' to New Deal" that Webber makes. He cites automobiles as an example of a capital-intensive, internationalist industry, and claims that his inability to locate contributions to the Democrats is evidence against my views.

The automobile industry is conventionally considered to be a classic example of an internationally oriented sector. But my essay specifically observed that I had doubts about General Motors, where there is clear archival evidence that its major owners, the DuPonts, exerted pressure on the company not to internationalize as much as it could have (Ferguson, 1984, p. 54). But let this, and the complicated question of Opel, pass for now. The real response to Webber is that he has forgotten about the automobile workers. Contrary to what he says, I have always designated the industry as "labor-intensive"; indeed, at the time I wrote (1984) I used to tease the author of an outstanding essay on European politics and industrial structure that by his "leading sector" argument, Alfred P. Sloan should have been the greatest of New Dealers (Kurth, 1979).

In reality, the case of autos is even more complicated. Among the firms listed in the Overacker data as providing various forms of financial assistance to the Democrats in 1936 are Ford ($4,000), Chrysler, and Chevrolet, a part of GM ($2,000). Provided one takes seriously the injunctions given earlier on the use of institutionally subtle evidence, these cases are less mysterious than they look. First, it is necessary to remember that the strike wave had not yet occurred. Also, the automobile companies had been particularly successful before in pressuring FDR into ruling in their favor in moments of crisis. On the other hand, it is clear that GM worked hard for a Republican victory—spending large sums in the process. Ford, the most multinational of the auto companies, and Chrysler, for which exports probably mattered a great deal, present less clear-cut cases. Henry Ford and most of the Ford management were strongly for Landon. Ford's son Edsel, however, who had a real role in the management of the firm, backed FDR strongly. Chrysler, I think, initially was sympathetic to Roosevelt, but then clearly moved away. After 1936, virtually all of Detroit moved massively against the New Deal.

The picture is of an industry trying to control events, and then being forced by its inability to coalesce with labor to move completely into the enemy camp. The same is true for the handful of steel and rubber companies that also donated to the president's campaign. Already very hostile and suspicious, they had not quite reached the fork in the road in 1936. They campaigned for Landon, but a few (we are, after all, dealing with a decided minority) were still willing to hazard comparatively small sums on the Democrats.

17. I suspect, but am not yet prepared to assert as a fact, that Roosevelt's tariff stand also attracted retailers, who probably wanted access to the lowest-priced merchandise. But there are various stumbling blocks to this conclusion; as a consequence, retailing, save for a few genuine multinational chains, is coded as neutral (intermediate) in this analysis. This will probably turn out to be too cautious, but it strengthens my confidence in the conclusions.

18. Webber criticizes my associating Herbert Lehman with investment bankers, saying that he had left the firm. This, of course, is true. But an important principle of realistic political economy is that family wealth should normally function as a touchstone of assessments of individual social and economic locations. I do not believe that a serious analysis of Lehman's subsequent political career can sustain a claim that he did not derive continuous, basic advantages from his ties with the family investment bank—any more than Harriman or Nelson Rockefeller did not from their respective enterprises. Indeed, there is perhaps a better than even chance that someone in the Lehman orbit helped arrange the Manufacturers Trust loan to FDR's campaign. Nor is there any reason to become vexed about the Lehman partners in 1936. Mazur is on the record as a contributor, while it seems plain that the obvious place for the others to contribute is to the Lehman campaign (or are we to believe they had nothing to do with their former partner?)—and this was very closely coordinated with the Roosevelt campaign.

A last point: Frank Altshul's papers, now open at Columbia University, record his efforts to gather contributions from investment bankers for Landon, particularly at the start of the campaign, before Landon attacked Hull's treaties. He certainly raised some money, but I am struck by how little. Some Dillon, Read partners and Lehman partners appear to have contributed (one such episode raised but $1,500). By comparison, Forrestal, by then clearly the dominant figure at Dillon, Read (after Dillon himself) alone gave at least $7,500 to FDR.

19. Exactly how one ought to code insurance, railroads, and utilities is unclear. Free-traders, of course, stress that they should favor free trade—because that would make for a higher rate of economic growth. But while this argument is popular today (and was then—among communicants), it ignores the fact that many business groups at that time defended what amounted to a dependency-reversal argument, akin to those popular until recently in the Third World, that stressed the role of the tariff in protecting nascent industries. Some studies I have undertaken of nineteenth-century business views reinforced my view that this is a potentially serious problem. Accordingly, I did not try to code the three industries for this analysis; they are not included in the calculations that follow, nor are a few private investors for whom I simply could not find enough data to allocate them.

How to code Texas oil and other "national" oil concerns was another thorny problem. The difficulty arose because these producers usually opposed imports in their industry, but strongly favored free trade everywhere else. The import issue did flare in the industry until approximately 1935, when it faded away, in no small part because Standard and other producers in South America rerouted oil shipments away from the United States as the Second New Deal's oil price support program got under way. My solution was to try to keep this issue—which after all only affects a portion of the industry—from having a major impact on results. These producers were coded a neutral 1.

As explained in appendix 4.1, I was unable to locate usable wage data for insurance, railroads, and utilities. These industries accordingly had to be dropped from the apposite *t*-test. This exclusion surely cannot affect the basic results—the differences are simply of too large a magnitude.

The results of the *t*-tests reported here differ very slightly from those reported in my original essay. No point of substance is involved—purely statistical considerations are at issue. The original essay reported results for *t*-tests in which contributors to both parties remained in both groups. I adopted this procedure because I feared (correctly, it turned out) that many readers would interpret my results in terms of an idealized clash between representative industries, such as "steel" vs. "oil," and one's estimate of which bloc is near what would be greatly affected by dropping the cases. Retaining these contributors, however, adds to the number of cases, thus changing the statistics reported. I regret that my written caution about this point was not included in the published version—a fact I did not learn until I saw the article in print.

In this essay, accordingly, I have reverted to the preferred alternative of dropping all the joint contributors—the econometric equivalent of testing between laboratory-pure samples of Democrats and Republicans. As will be evident when these results are compared with those in the original paper, my central hypotheses are confirmed no matter how one does the tests.

20. In the form raised by Domhoff (1990), the regionalism question is jejune; the very meaning of the term is unclear, when, for example, a Southern textile firm is controlled by executives who live in New York, Southern utilities are run from the Midwest or the East, and oilmen come to Texas from Pennsylvania to add to their fortunes. Moreover, it is perfectly obvious to all but perhaps some elite theorists that many of these industries operate in a world market, no matter where they are located. This was certainly the case with the textile industry, for example, which was badly hit in the 1930s by imports from Japan.

On the other hand, if one is not trying to explain away the effects of the world market and related economic forces, there may well be a role for some interpretation in terms of regional effects, including ones of a cultural nature. Here I would mention two results that I consider too tentative for the main text, but worth mentioning since I have not yet, despite much effort, found an inconsistent pattern.

Reasoning that a failure to find regional effects might derive from an antecedent failure to control for major economic influences, I explored how controlling for international position affects the results. Two results turned up. First, in the South, Democrats (only) who are located at either extreme on the free trade-protection axis appear not to be influenced by any regional variable. But Democrats in the middle position—where, perhaps, the clues of industry are less clear—appear to be somewhat more Democratic than they otherwise would be. Outside the South, this finding is reversed, but only for Republicans—save that it occurs for all levels of international position. These results—evaluated by chi-square values—are all statistically significant. I continue to analyze these results, but cannot refrain from observing that they are perfectly consistent with conventional views of the political culture of the (expiring) political System of 1896: a strong Southern culture organized around the Democrats and free trade, while outside the South a powerful Republican culture is pervasive.

One last point. Webber (1991) raises the question of the Council on Foreign Relations (CFR). This question arises not because of anything I wrote, but because other writers, who do not work from primary sources, mention it. My view is that the council did not become truly important until the end of the decade, around the time of the so-called

"Century group." Before then, I am inclined to think that it overrepresented the Republican internationalists, particularly those close to the Morgan interests. There certainly were prominent Democrats within the group, but I can think of no reason why it should overrepresent Democratic, as opposed to Republican, internationalists in 1936. It would be news, on the other hand, if the council were proven to be full of protectionists. But this is someone else's problem.

REFERENCES

Allen, Michael Patrick. 1991. "Capitalist Response to State Intervention: Theories of the State and Political Finance in the New Deal." *American Sociological Review* 56:679–89.

Barger, Harold. 1960. "Income Originating in Trade, 1869–1929." Pp. 327–333 in *Trends in the American Economy in the Nineteenth Century, Studies in Income and Wealth*, vol. 24, National Bureau of Economic Research Conference on Research in Income and Wealth. Princeton: Princeton University Press.

Bliss, Charles A. 1939. *The Structure of Manufacturing Production.* New York: National Bureau of Economic Research.

Borchardt, Knut. 1991. *Perspectives on Modern German Economic History and Policy.* Translated by Peter Lambert. New York: Cambridge University Press.

Brandes, Stuart. 1983. "America's Super Rich 1941." *The Historian* 45:307–323.

Burch, Philip. 1972. *The Managerial Revolution Reassessed.* Lexington, MA: D.C. Heath.

———. 1980. *Elites in American History, Vol. III.* New York: Holmes & Meier.

———. n.d. "Appendix C, with Table A" [Review of Studies of the Very Wealthiest Americans]. Unpublished manuscript.

Chandler, Alfred D., Jr. 1990. *Scale and Scope: The Dynamics of Industrial Capitalism.* Cambridge, MA: Harvard University Press.

Coelho, Philip and G. J. Santoni. 1991. "Regulatory Capture and the Monetary Contraction of 1932: A Comment on Epstein and Ferguson." *Journal of Economic History* 51:282–289.

Cumings, Bruce. 1990. *The Origins of the Korean War: Volume II: The Roaring of the Cataract.* Princeton: Princeton University Press.

Domhoff, G. William. 1990. *The Power Elite and the State.* New York: Aldine De Gruyter.

Epstein, Gerald and Thomas Ferguson. 1984. "Monetary Policy, Loan Liquidation, and Industrial Conflict: The Federal Reserve and the Open Market Operations of 1932." *Journal of Economic History* 44:957–983.

Epstein, Gerald and Thomas Ferguson. 1991. "Answers to Stock Questions: Fed Targets, Stock Prices, and the Gold Standard in the Great Depression." *Journal of Economic History* 51:190–200.

Ferguson, Thomas. 1980. "Von Versailles zum New Deal" Pp. 436–450 in *Amerika: Traum und Depression 1920/40*, catalogue essay for the Neue Gesellschaft für Bildende Kunst Exhibit of American Art. Berlin and Hamburg.

———. 1983. "Party Realignment and American Industrial Structure: The Investment Theory of Political Parties in Historical Perspective." Pp. 1–82 in *Research in Political Economy: Volume VI*, edited by Paul Zarembka. Greenwich, CT: JAI Press.

———. 1984. "From 'Normalcy' to New Deal: Industrial Structure, Party Competition, and American Public Policy in the Great Depression." *International Organization* 38:41–92.

———. 1986. "Elites and Elections: Or What Have They Done to You Lately? Toward an Investment Theory of Political Parties." Pp. 164–188 in *Do Elections Matter?* edited by Benjamin Ginsberg and Alan Stone. First edition. Armonk, NY: Sharpe.

———. 1989a. "Industrial Conflict and the Coming of the New Deal: The Triumph of Multinational Liberalism in America." Pp. 3–31 in *The Rise and Fall of the New Deal Order 1930–80*, edited by Steve Fraser and Gary Gerstle. Princeton: Princeton University Press.

———. 1989b. "By Invitation Only: Party Competition and Industrial Structure in the 1988 Election. *Socialist Review* 19:73–103.

———. 1991. "An Unbearable Lightness of Being—Party and Industry in the 1988 Democratic Primary." Pp. 237–254 in *Do Elections Matter?* edited by Benjamin Ginsberg and Alan Stone. Second edition. Armonk, NY: Sharpe.

———. 1992. "Money And Politics." Pp. 1060–1084 in *Handbooks to the Modern World: The United States*, vol. 2, edited by Godfrey Hodgson. New York: Facts on File.

———. n.d. *Critical Realignment: The Fall of the House of Morgan and the Origins of the New Deal.* New York: Oxford University Press. Forthcoming.

Ferguson, Thomas and Joel Rogers. 1986. *Right Turn: The Decline of the Democrats and the Future of American Politics.* New York: Hill & Wang.

Floud, Roderick. 1973. *An Introduction to Quantitative Methods for Historians.* London: Methuen.

Fortune Magazine. 1957. "The Fifty-Million-Dollar Man." November:177.

———. 1968. "America's Centimillionaires." May:156.

Galbraith, James. 1989. *Balancing Acts.* New York: Basic Books.

Hogan, Michael. 1986. "Corporatism: A Positive Appraisal." *Diplomatic History* 10:365.

———. 1987. *The Marshall Plan: America, Britain, and the Reconstruction of Western Europe 1947–52.* New York: Cambridge University Press.

Jarausch, Konrad and Kenneth Hardy. 1991. *Quantitative Methods for Historians.* Chapel Hill: University of North Carolina Press.

Knolige, Kit and Fredericka Knolige. 1978. *The Power of their Glory.* New York: Wyden Books.

Kotz, David. 1978. *Bank Control of Large Corporations in the United States.* Berkeley: University of California Press.

Kurth, James. 1979. "The Political Consequences of the Product Cycle." *International Organization* 33:1–34.

Lundberg, Ferdinand. [1938] 1946. *America's Sixty Families.* New York: Citadel.

———. 1968. *The Rich and the Superrich.* New York: Lyle Stuart.

Malone, Michael P. 1975. "The Montana New Dealers." Pp. 240-268 in *The New Deal, Volume II: The State and Local Levels*, edited by John Braeman, Robert Bremner, and David Brody. Columbus, OH: Ohio State University Press.

Magee, Stephen, William Brock and Leslie Young. 1989. *Black Hole Tariffs and Endogenous Policy Theory.* New York: Cambridge University Press.

McKelvey, Richard and Peter Ordeshook. 1986. "Information, Equilibrium, and the Democratic Ideal." *Journal of Politics* 30:909–937.

Overacker, Louise. 1937. "Campaign Funds in the Presidential Election of 1936." *American Political Science Review* 31:473–498.

————. 1946. *Presidential Campaign Funds.* Boston: Boston University Press.

Poor's Register of Directors of the United States and Canada. 1936. New York: Poor's Publishing Company.

Roosevelt, Elliott and James Brough. 1975. *A Rendezvous with Destiny.* New York: Putnam.

Schwarz, Jordan. 1981. *The Speculator.* Chapel Hill: University of North Carolina Press.

Sorauf, Frank J. 1988. *Money in American Elections.* Boston: Scott Foresman/ Little, Brown.

Stone, Lawrence. 1971. "Lawrence Stone and the Manors: A Rejoinder." *Economic History Review* 24:115–116.

Temporary National Economic Committee. 1940a. *Hearings before the Temporary National Economic Committee.* 76th Congress, 2nd Session. Part 22: *Investment Banking.* Washington, DC: U.S. Government Printing Office.

————. 1940b. Investigation of Concentration of Economic Power. Monograph 29. *The Distribution of Ownership in the 200 Largest Nonfinancial Corporations.* Washington, DC: U.S. Government Printing Office.

U.S. Bureau of the Census. 1970. *U.S. Census of Mineral Industries: 1967, Industry Series.* Washington, DC: U.S. Government Printing Office.

U.S. Congress. Senate. 1937. *Report of the Special Committee to Investigate Campaign Expenditures of Presidential, Vice-Presidential and Senatorial Candidates in 1936.* 75th Congress, 1st Session 1936, S. Rept. 151.

Webber, Michael. 1991. "Business, the Democratic Party, and the New Deal: An Empirical Critique of Thomas Ferguson's 'Investment Theory of Politics.'" *Sociological Perspectives* 34:473–492.

Weir, Margaret and Theda Skocpol. 1985. "State Structures and the Possibilities for 'Keynesian' Responses to the Great Depression in Sweden, Britain, and the United States." Pp. 107–163 in *Bringing The State Back In,* edited by Peter Evans, Dietrich Rueschemeyer, and Theda Skocpol. New York: Cambridge University Press.

Wilkins, Mira. 1974. *The Maturing of Multinational Enterprise: American Business Abroad from 1914 to 1970.* Cambridge: Harvard University Press.

CHAPTER FIVE

By Invitation Only:
Party Competition and Industrial Structure in the 1988 Election

THE EARLY YEARS of the "Reagan revolution" witnessed one of the great public relations campaigns in U.S. history. From almost every quarter of American public life, not only obviously interested parties—the White House, the Republican Party, or most big business circles—but also virtually the entire press, many social scientists, and even many prominent Democrats rushed to proclaim that the U.S. electorate had shifted dramatically to the right.

It was a long time before these claims were subjected to quantitative testing by the normal methods of public opinion analysis. When they were, however, the results were startling. By simply lining up time series data, it was easy to show that the U.S. public had not made a "right turn." On the contrary, the basic structure of postwar political opinion remained remarkably stable. Most voters continued to shy away from the "liberal" label, but they were still very suspicious of "big business" and supportive of government intervention in the economy and many areas of social life.

New Deal issues continued to attract them. Most opinion changes were quite gradual, and often, in a broadly liberal direction. Opinions on taxes and some social welfare issues occasionally suggested that the electorate was skeptical of new initiatives, but there was no popular support for laissez faire. Above all, Ronald Reagan was far from being the most popular president of modern times. Nor was he uniquely beloved by people who disagreed with his policies.[1]

The modern theory of critical realignments in U.S. politics is a flexible, even protean, system of thought. But there is no place in its conceptual apparatus for a smashing loss of the Senate by the party that is identified as triumphantly ascendant. For a while, therefore, it was possible to hope that the tidal wave of Democratic Senate victories in 1986, including a spectacular victory in Georgia by a biracial coalition much concerned with economic issues, might function in U.S. politics a bit like the famous eclipse observations of 1919 did in the debates over Einstein's theory of relativity.[2]

But political commentators in the United States can often resist anything except temptation. While many post-election analysts drew attention to the opaque, almost "issueless" character of the 1988 campaign, a second wave of Reagan realignment studies is beginning to crest.

The best known of these are flimsy indeed. The postelection revival of the myth of Reagan's overwhelming popularity, for example, is easily refuted by the simplest arithmetic: the Great Communicator's average popularity falls 16 percentage points below Franklin D. Roosevelt's, 14 points below Dwight D. Eisenhower's, and 18 points below John F. Kennedy's. It is even 2 points below Lyndon Johnson's average, and a bare 5 points above the much despised Jimmy Carter's.

Another claim widely touted in the latest Reagan revival, that non-voters preferred George Bush to Michael Dukakis, is also almost certainly wrong. What is probably the best instrument for directly ascertaining the opinions of nonvoters, the Gallup poll's final pre-election surveys of who is likely to vote, indicates that in 1988, as in most elections since the New Deal, substantially more nonvoters than voters preferred the Democrats.[3] Nor is there much evidence for the common claim that young voters are becoming the avant garde of tomorrow's Republican majority. In the 1988 election, voters between 18 and 29 years of age gave fewer votes to Bush than any other age group except those over 60.[4]

More serious efforts attempt to locate a mass basis for Reaganism in either the revival of fundamentalist Christianity or racial antagonisms. Close readers of even the very best of these studies, however, will notice a striking fact: that direct evidence of the importance of either race or fundamentalism in anyone's voting decision is scarce indeed.[5]

Though space limitations make it impossible to pursue the point here, when voters' decisions are analyzed properly, with a method that allows alternative bases for the voting decision, the new views turn out to be as chimerical as the old. It is not race, or the flag, (or the "L-word," or foreign policy) that is killing the Democratic Party at the presidential level. Instead, since Carter, the Democrats have forfeited their ancestral identification as the party of prosperity. With its continuing flirtation with austerity and raising taxes, while refusing to challenge the GOP on important New Deal issues, the party has had little to say to ordinary Americans on many issues that matter most to them.[6]

But if voters were not responsible for the eerie silence that left many of them more anxious about Dukakis's economic policies than Bush's, or for what even the media recognized as "the mysterious disappearance of issues" during the primaries (Jesse Jackson obviously aside), then who or what was? And what does Bush, the man who left no tracks in the primaries, stand for?

These are the questions I propose to tackle in this chapter. Relying on the investment approach to party politics developed in earlier essays and using data from the Federal Election Commission and other sources, I attempt to apply the "Golden Rule" to the 1988 presidential election: To see who rules, follow the gold.[7]

FROM REAGAN TO BUSH: A TALE OF TWO BLOCS

It is convenient to begin with the Republicans, for the divisions that surfaced within the business community over the 1988 election follow immediately from policy dilemmas that emerged as a direct consequence of decisions taken in the earliest days of the Reagan revolution. At that time, the height of what might be termed the laissez-faire revival, the incoming Republican administration sought sweeping changes in both U.S. society and the world order. In the name of restoring domestic economic growth, it sought major cuts in taxes on high incomes and corporations, rollbacks in environmental and safety regulations promulgated in the seventies, major reductions in federal ownership and spending, and a broad deregulation of the economy, including major changes in the administration of the National Labor Relations Board (NLRB).

Its ambitions, however, did not stop at the water's edge. It planned to make not only the United States, but the world, safe for free enterprise (which it equated with "economic growth"). To reverse what it claimed was a decline in U.S. power around the globe, the administration commenced the largest military build-up in history, with a particular focus on the navy. It heated up the cold war, pressuring Europe and Japan to rearm and restrict exports to the Soviet bloc. It also sought to roll back the tide of state-owned enterprise in the Third World and to pressure other countries to deregulate their own markets, especially in finance. It also aggressively intervened in various Third World trouble spots in favor of regimes it preferred.[8]

The almost millenarian frenzy with which the administration approached these labors in its early days invited analysts—friends and critics alike—to view it as a political formation sui generis. Critics, in particular, tended to treat Reaganism as the political program of a newly unified business community.

For a few months of 1980 to 1981, this line of thought is not misleading. A global analysis of Reaganism in these terms, however, courts serious misunderstanding. It makes it impossible to understand the dynamics of the two Reagan terms with the abrupt switch toward détente and inter-allied economic cooperation during the second term, or to analyze the forces now bearing on the Bush administration.

The truth is that the Reagan coalition always had a huge seam running down its middle. That seam, the consequence of living in the world economy, divided the Reagan camp into two distinct blocs (each of which, in turn, was crisscrossed by other seams too complicated to discuss now). The policies of the Reagan administration served, or appeared to serve, the interests of major parts of both. Each, however, had a somewhat different interpretation of what it thought was really happening, and the two basically disagreed about where the policies were supposed to lead. In effect, the Reagan revolution was a giant banner, under which two columns marched in different directions.

The first "bloc" might be referred to as the "protectionist" bloc.[9] As the label suggests, this bloc, centered in old industries long tied to the GOP, like textiles or steel, saw the Reagan revolution largely as political and economic Alka-Seltzer: Relief from imports, from labor, from hated government regulators, and, perhaps, from endlessly menacing Communists was only a jubilant swallow away.

In sharp contrast, the second bloc, or more precisely, its leading spokespersons, were thinking far more expansively (and they were indeed thinking, in the sense that all through this period they were making major investments in policy-oriented research published through a wide variety of think tanks and research institutions).

To sum up the views of this second, multinational, bloc in a few pithy sentences inevitably invites caricature and risks exaggerating the degree of centralization and consensus within it. Nevertheless, with due allowance for these pitfalls, its thinking can be analyzed as the polar opposite of the now fashionable "imperial overextension" critique of Reaganism brought to public attention most forcibly by the historian Paul Kennedy in his recent *The Rise and Fall of the Great Powers.*[10]

It is not that the business leaders (organized in such groups as the Committee for the Present Danger) who in 1980 were calling for a 600-ship navy, worldwide "horizontal escalation" in the event of war with the Soviet Union, major new weapons modernization programs, and an end to the "Vietnam syndrome" necessarily shrank from analogies with the Dutch, French, or British empires. It is that they saw and, with some qualifications, continue to see the comparison differently.

In their view, the overriding issue in the world was whether the three great economic areas (the Pacific Basin, the Americas, and Western Europe) were going to develop "cooperatively" into one essentially "worldwide" multinational market, or whether these areas would go their own ways, each under the influence of a regional hegemon. How this issue was resolved would shape development in the Third World, and in the long run perhaps even in the Second.

From this standpoint, the vast U.S. expenditures on military force and foreign aid that critics of imperial overextension feared would bankrupt the United States actually represented major investments in free trade and an integrated world economy committed to a dollar standard.

Not only would these investments help stabilize the Third World (and thus lower the target rate of return a multinational required before deciding to invest), but the military build-up, in addition, was a vital U.S. bargaining chip with the other major allied governments. Only the United States could afford the fabulous costs of the conventional and nuclear guarantees that provided the social overhead capital for the postwar recoveries of Japan and Western Europe. And only the United States could project enough force into the Middle East to protect the oil supplies of the allies.

As long as the United States maintained its military dominance, therefore, European governments had little incentive to try to go their own way, and many reasons to cooperate. So did the Japanese, a fact which by 1980 had become of towering significance to many U.S. businesses, which were increasingly convinced that exclusion from the Pacific implied banishment from the next century's fastest-growing region.

In the late seventies, after the West German refusal to reflate in tandem with the United States and Japan wrecked the Bonn summit, most members of the second bloc, which included multinational manufacturers and financiers, but also many exporters, high-tech firms, oil companies, and weapons producers, became convinced that only dramatic unilateral action by the United States could break the economic deadlock that was developing in the "triad" (today's buzzword) or "trilateral" (yesterday's) world and avert the drift toward state-owned enterprises in the Third World. With increasing talk of repricing internationally traded raw materials (read: oil) in another currency as U.S. rates of inflation raced ahead and the dollar depreciated, these businesspeople also became convinced that only truly draconian monetary policies could end inflation and save the dollar.

The atmosphere of intensifying crisis enormously advantaged the only political party for which massive social expenditure cuts were thinkable: the GOP. Multinationals which had been perfectly prepared to support Democrats during the New Deal era abruptly cut off their support, or intensified their commitments to Republicans. At the same time, so did the traditional protectionist bloc. Not surprisingly, the first result was confusion, as all sorts of "New Right," "Old Right," and "neoconservative" cultural and political entrepreneurs competed to tap the rivers of cash that rapidly began flowing.

Under the inflexible pressure of political deadlines, however, a more or less articulate compromise emerged within the Republican Party. Candidate Reagan struck a formal agreement with South Carolina Senator Strom Thurmond on behalf of the textile industry, and appears to have made promises to several other industries, including steel, while publicly trumpeting the merits of free trade. The prospective general revision of the General Agreement on Tariffs and Trade (GATT) ardently desired by the free traders was put off until after the administration had some time to force restructuring on the rest of the world, while powerful industries were promised piecemeal protection in the meantime.

By temporarily removing the divisive trade issue from the agenda, this deal (which was struck by Reagan rather than by Bush, the first choice of many multinationalists in the "Eastern establishment") opened the way for the "golden horde" that financed the GOP's sweeping triumph in the fall of 1980. Once the decision to raise interest rates was taken by Federal Reserve Chairman Paul Volcker during the Carter administration, for example, what multinational would object to domestic restructuring? And, while contemplating the promised import relief, what protectionist would object to a new cold war? From this vantage point it is easy to see the logic that drove the Reagan administration first to foreswear G5 (later G7) cooperation and noisily to denounce the "evil empire," and then, in early 1985, as James Baker took over at the Treasury, dramatically to reverse both policies.

As it came to power, the administration faced a set of decisions that could easily split its coalition apart. Not surprisingly, it moved very cautiously. To the disgust of Secretary of State, Alexander Haig, it declined to make a major issue of Central America at that time. To the dismay of social conservatives, it placed social issues on the back burner.

The Reagan administration concentrated instead on economic issues that sent broad rivers of cash flowing to all its supporters in the business community: the military build-up, deregulation, personnel changes at the NLRB, and the centerpiece of its economic program, the famous tax cuts. After some fits and starts, the Reagan administration fell in line with Volcker's high interest rate policies.[11]

The result, from the administration's standpoint, was a series of striking successes. Along with its new labor policies and deregulation, the high interest rates triggered a sweeping reorganization of the workforce. Unions lost ground and wage growth slowed, as many firms took advantage of the huge rise in unemployment to make major cuts in staffing and changes in work rules. As other central banks transmitted the interest rate rises to their countries (and, pushed by the Reagan administration, promoted deregulation of their own economies), a worldwide movement toward laissez faire gained steam. The growing climate of austerity, in turn, encouraged further cuts in social spending and taxes everywhere, while the rise of the dollar reestablished its position as the world's currency, and started an export boom in Europe and Japan that helped undo the damage caused by the "evil empire" rhetoric.

The policies, however, could not be sustained forever. The price of the interest rate rise was the deepest recession of the postwar era. In the Third World, growth ceased absolutely, while in the United States imports flooded in and business bankruptcies mounted, bringing friction with Japan and calls for import relief. Although they went along with the intermediate-range nuclear forces (INF) deployment, Europeans resented the administration's efforts to discourage business with the Soviets. And, as it seems clearly to have foreseen, the administration failed to get enough spending cuts to offset the tax reductions, leading to an enormous rise in the budget deficit.

Political opposition emerged on both the left and the right of the business community. On the left, the Democrats revived. A breakdown of 1984 Democratic campaign financing, done along lines of that presented for 1988 below, shows clearly how real estate interests in (primarily) the Northeast and Midwest moved to defend federal grants for urban infrastructure and mass transit from the burgeoning claims of the defense budget. (Statistical tests showed that the real estate bloc, but not the other industries that also featured high levels of Democratic contributions, only supported liberals—precisely what one would expect if competing claims on the budget were the issue.)[12] And as the deficit mounted, many investment bankers (and some insurance industry figures) joined them.[13]

On the right, Jack Kemp emerged as a champion of a "supply-side" economics that was essentially Reaganomics with low interest rates. For business, its key claim was that if interest rates were pushed low enough, the United States could grow its way out of the deficits without any new taxes.

How the administration rode out this heavy weather bears close analysis for the light it can shed on what the Bush administration might do. To defuse protectionist sentiment, it deployed a three-pronged strategy: To the biggest and most powerful industries, notably steel and autos, it afforded continued piecemeal protection. To agriculture and some exporters, it offered limited export subsidies, either in the form of direct loans, or, in the case of some high-tech industries, funds for basic research. Finally, it pressed other countries, particularly in East Asia, to open their markets to U.S. products.

Faced with the need to hold together two blocs pulling in different directions, the administration also made a set of fundamental choices on the deficit. Because the tax cuts were so attractive to both blocs, but particularly to the protectionists, who were, after all, fated to be submerged in the long run, they provided the perfect issue over which to make a stand. Still hoping that ballooning deficits would eventually force spending cuts, the Administration proceeded, loudly and publicly, to draw a line in the sand.

To finance the deficits in the meantime, the administration devised a two-track strategy. First, it accepted "revenue enhancements" that did not threaten the sacrosanct position of the top brackets, including a steep rise in highly regressive social security taxes, which over time were intended to help close the deficit. Then, in a truly momentous decision, it elected to let foreign capital finance the deficit.

From the standpoint of the multinational bloc as a whole, this move had a compelling logic. By worldwide standards, direct investment in the U.S. economy was quite low. Direct investment, in sharp contrast to portfolio investment, is reasonably stable. Here, accordingly, was a chance to square the circle. Provided no one moved to prohibit foreign takeovers, capital could flow into the United States for years. As it did, it would support the dollar, while helping mightily to finance both the trade and the government officials. As it did these things, it would also create a more powerful lobby in the United States in favor of free trade and an integrated world economy, while also giving major foreign interests compelling reasons to let U.S. multinationals continue operating in their home territory.

As interest rates fell in the wake of the Mexican debt rescue and defense spending began to pull the economy out of its slump in classic Keynesian fashion, the administration had the satisfaction of watching its new policies pay off. The economic revival and foreign buying led to a tremendous boom in the stock market. The new wave of mergers and takeovers, in turn, further restructured industry while creating a substantial number of new fortunes in finance and commodities markets with a stake in Reaganomics.

The boom, an ingredient of the largest political business cycle since the Depression, carried the administration safely through the 1984 elections. The continued strength of the dollar, however, fueled protectionist sentiment, further inflaming relations with Japan and the Asian

NICs (newly industrializing countries). By early 1985, it was obvious that something had to be done, or the whole postwar structure of multinational trade might unravel as the U.S. Congress moved to retaliate.

The administration moved on several fronts at once. First, it added wrinkles to the strategy it had employed for defusing relations with Japan in 1983–1984. It pressed the Japanese to open markets for a handful of the most impatient sectors whose support it was counting on to head off a protectionist upsurge, including telecommunications, electronics, forest products, medical instruments, and pharmaceuticals.

Next, as an alternative to "industrial policy," the administration joined many Republican big business leaders in talking up "competitiveness," that is, the notion that improved macro policy and some broad structural changes (such as improvements in education) that involved little direct market intervention might alleviate the overseas challenge.

Then, largely through the Pentagon (but mostly outside "Star Wars"), where, by a miracle of nomenclature, "defense"-related production direction is not reckoned as a violation of the principles of free enterprise, it announced a spectacular program of subsidies, again mostly to "swing" industries dominated by multinationals in, or potentially in, the coalition. Among these projects, which continued to be announced as Bush geared up to run for the presidency, were a $4-billion supercollider project, a five-year $1.7-billion program in computing, a dramatic new "superconductor" initiative, contracts for a fabulously expensive space station (the announcement called attention to the benefits the project would produce for the pharmaceutical and electronic industries), "Sematech," a join venture between the government and high-tech companies, as well as other initiatives in robotics, computer-aided manufacturing, and materials science. And while the administration was taking these little-publicized moves that might someday transform the Pentagon into an American equivalent of the famous Japanese Ministry of International Trade and Industry (MITI), it moved at last to bring the dollar down.

Here, with Baker at the Treasury, a new and more delicate phase of relations with the allies began that leads directly to the policy dilemmas Bush now faces. In effect, the administration was seeking what might be termed a "kinder, gentler" dollar decline. For this to happen, the cooperation of the allies, and particularly of Japan and West Germany, was essential. Specifically, if the dollar were to decline (thus reducing the imbalance in the U.S. current account), the Japanese and Germans would not only have to agree to let their export surpluses shrink, but they would also have to expand their domestic economies to avoid a decline in total world demand. They would, in addition, have to cooperate in guarding the relative exchange rates of the major currencies, or there would be massive flight from the dollar.

Neither country was anxious to do any of this. Both had grown rich in the postwar period by pursuing strategies of export-led growth, and both now feared that an expansion of internal demand might well disequilibrate carefully struck balances of power between labor and management.

Baker, however, had several powerful incentives of his own. First, in the background there remained always the United States' trump card, its overwhelming comparative advantage in defense. By pushing the allies to do more or, sometimes, by upping the ante of what "security" required, the United States could exercise real leverage by threatening to raise costs on the allies.

Second, there was Baker's well-advertised policy of negotiating bilateral trade treaties with particular countries. (The most significant of these is the recent agreement with Canada, which is shortly to be expanded to embrace Mexico.) By suggesting that the U.S. might go it alone with a handful of carefully selected partners, these deals acted as a check on allied intransigence.

In the end, however, Baker's most potent threat proved to be the simplest: the United States could simply threaten to let the exchange rate drop unilaterally if the allies would not agree to an orderly decline. Though in October 1987 this strategy of brinkmanship took the world to the edge of the abyss, when Baker and other Treasury officials publicly admonished the Germans for provoking an upcoming fall in the dollar and crash in the market, in the end it worked. After bitter internal debates, Japan expanded internal demand substantially, and dismantled a few trade barriers. Germany made rather feebler efforts to expand. The dollar continued coming down until the summer of 1988, as foreign central banks built up massive dollar reserves, in effect subsidizing (as several acute critics noted) a vigorous political business cycle for Bush to run on.[14]

Animated not only by its growing concern for allied harmony, but also by the unyielding pressures of the budget deficit and the plain fact that the West Germans would sell to the USSR if the United States wouldn't, the administration abandoned its strident anti-Soviet posture. Led by new Commerce Secretary William Verity, food companies, capital goods exporters, and several business organizations, the administration began to explore avenues for increasing trade. It also, of course, negotiated the INF accord and a Soviet withdrawal from Afghanistan.

In electoral terms, there can scarcely be any question that the policy package Bush and Baker were gradually fashioning for the vice president to run on—peace and prosperity—was highly plausible, particularly if one refrained from asking awkward questions about the long run. As an early *Fortune* poll of top executives indicated, and the astonishingly high level of contributions revealed in my statistical study confirms, their agenda commanded the loyalty of most mainline multinationals.[15]

But multinationals (and allied financiers) are far from the only business groups active in the GOP. Moreover, major veins of dissatisfaction exist within the multinational bloc itself, particularly in regard to détente.

As the 1988 campaign approached, ominous signs of dissatisfaction began to appear on the right of the GOP. New York Congressman Kemp, who during most of President Reagan's tenure in office had usually been counted Bush's strongest prospective opponent for the nomination, stridently denounced the INF Treaty and began running furiously against détente and the "sellout" of freedom fighters around the globe.

Donald Rumsfeld, once Gerald Ford's hawkish secretary of defense and then chief executive officer of G. D. Searle, a large pharmaceutical concern, began scouting a run, and also looking rightwards. So did another card-carrying multinational cold warrior, Haig. Pierre DuPont, a one-time moderate Republican governor of Delaware, announced his candidacy on a platform that would have warmed the heart of the elder Pierre DuPont, who as head of the family's chemical company during the New Deal was one of FDR's sharpest critics. Televangelist Pat Robertson also declared, on a platform that on defense and many other topics was well to the right of Attila the Hun. And, to the surprise of practically everyone who does not closely follow the political economy of the GOP, Kansas Senator Robert Dole finally came down well to the right of the Bush campaign.

Not all of these candidates were equally formidable. Kemp, for example, was strongly identified as the partisan of supply-side economics. In years past, he had also drawn important supporters from aerospace and defense enterprises for whom the deficit functions first of all as an entry in the profits column, and who clearly welcomed Kemp's insistence that détente was a dangerous illusion. But, as earlier observed, the practical meaning of supply-side doctrines for the average business was lower interest rates. By early 1988, however, Baker had been bringing the dollar down for almost three years. With exports booming, and the economy beginning to bump up against what most business economists reckoned was full capacity (whatever the numbers of discouraged workers who no longer figured in the unemployment statistics), what was the point of a new monetary experiment? And despite the intra-party row over détente, the vice president was obviously a plausible standard bearer for defense in the fall campaign against the Democrats.

Not surprisingly, few of the Republican business leaders who had in years past been attracted to Kemp's "exciting new ideas" were still excited by them. When Kemp unfurled the banner of aggressive free enterprise, salutes came from only a comparative handful of deregulation enthusiasts (e.g., Dow Chemical's Paul Oreffice), anointed keepers of the supply-side flame, such as Lewis Lehrman, and as table 5.1 indicates, a fair number of PACs or executives from savings banks, utilities, and transportation companies, plus the handful of real estate contribu-

TABLE 5.1. Industry Contributions to Candidates by Party

REPUBLICANS		
Bush (*N*=436: 69%)	Kemp (*N*=60: 10%)	Dole (*N*=324: 51%)
Oil (.11)	Utilities (.16%)*	Services (.10)
Computers (.06)*	Savings Banks (.16)*	Real Estate (.06)
Investment Banking (.13)	Transportation (.12)*	Insurance (.01)
Utilities (.13)*	Beverages (.01)*	Investment Banking (.02)
	Real Estate (.05)*	Autos (.15)
		Private Hospitals (.15)
		MNOC-MIC (.01)
DuPont (*N*=112: 18%)	Haig (*N*=13: 2%)	
Chemicals (.01)	Aircraft (.01)*	
Commercial Banking (.01)*	MNOC-MIC (.07)*	
Investment Banking (.01)	Real Estate (.15)*	
DEMOCRATS		
Babbitt (*N*=31: 13%)	Gore (*N*=93: 38%)	Hart (*N*=18: 7%)
Real Estate (.08)*	Utilities (.15)*	Investment Banking (.06)*
		Retailers (.03)*
Biden (*N*=33: 14%)	Jackson (*N*=10: 4%)	Dukakis (*N*=117: 48%)
Chemicals (.08)*	Food/Grain (.01)*	Computers (.04)*
Real Estate (.01)*	Commercial Banking (.02)*	Media/Communication (.06)
Investment Banking (.01)		Real Estate (.01)
		Investment Banking (.10)
Gephardt (*N*=89: 37%)	Simon (*N*=47: 19%)	Schroeder (*N*=3: 1%)
Services (.05)*	Food/Grain (.01)*	Media/Communication (.01)*
Autos (.11)*	Electronic (.12)*	
Aircraft (.02)*	Real Estate (.01)	
Utilities (.12)*		
MNOC-MIC (.05)*		

Source: Based on FEC data, but including soft money; see text.

Note: (The universe of comparison is each party's respective contributors.) Numbers in parentheses by each industry are significance levels, not strength. They indicate only positive differences from the candidate's average-industry figures.

*Expected value of cell in chi-square less than 5, which is warning that the test has low power.

tors probably attracted by the future housing and urban development secretary's emphasis on "enterprise zones". The rest, sometimes after pausing respectfully, moved on.[16]

In all probability, DuPont really had his eye on either the vice presidency or on 1992 or 1996. However, save for the press (which kept hailing his iconoclasm and "courage" in tackling the sacred cows of farm subsidies and social security), the family circle (which includes a dazzling number of the Forbes 400 wealthiest Americans, who, because they are concentrated in one industry, skew table 5.1's portrait of the chemical industry), and a surprising number of top financiers and bank executives (who, as the people most concerned with the future of the dollar in the 1990s, were perhaps making small votive offerings in honor of that "courage"), he failed to attract much support from business or anyone else.

Neither did Haig, whose appeal as a right-wing internationalist overlapped that of the later Dole or DuPont, but who also had to live down a reputation as an unguided missile. (Perhaps appropriately, the aircraft industry and a specially defined bloc of superhawks discussed below in reference to the Dole campaign backed him at a statistically significant level compared to other Republicans.) Rumsfeld, after contemplating what it now costs to run for president, thriftily called off his effort, as did Nevada Senator Paul Laxalt.

And Robertson's campaign, for which the media and many scholars had been predicting a heavenly future, staggered under two deadly blows. First came the collapse of oil prices, which badly hurt some of his major financial backers (such as Bunker Hunt) in the sector that had over the years probably invested more in fundamentalist politics than any other. The coup de grâce to his campaign as a serious national

TABLE 5.2. Party and Industry in the 1988 Election ($N = 1,380$)

Percentage of total sample contributing to	
at least one Republican	46%
at least one Democrat	17%
Industries significantly above the mean in support of Democrats	
Beverages	50%*
Investment banking	40%*
Real estate	39%*
Computers	32%†

Source: Based on FEC data, as in text.

Note: The universe of comparison is all investors in the sample.

*Statistically significant below .01.

†Statistically significant below .07.

threat, as distinct from an annoying party presence, came with the disastrous news of apparent devilish doings in Charlotte, North Carolina, by Jim and Tammy Bakker, and an unorthodox form of witness practiced in Louisiana motels by the Reverend Jimmy Swaggart.

That left Dole as the person with the best chance of stopping Bush. As all the world knows, he came within a hair of doing precisely that. Because of the light it sheds on the potential opposition the Bush presidency now faces, it is exceedingly instructive to see how he did it.

It is possible that a few people who eventually hopped on the bandwagon did so simply because they believed that Dole might run a stronger race than Bush, who was then viewed by many in his party the way many Democrats now regard Dukakis. Such cases, however, should be scattered randomly, and not be concentrated in particular sectors, and certainly not in sectors where prominent industrialists are openly campaigning for one or the other particular issue. Though my data are not perfectly adapted for this task, it is easy to show statistically that while Dole and Bush did have partially overlapping appeals, Dole very clearly succeeded in tapping sectors (and parts of sectors) with a plausible grievance against Bush.

Dole's initial campaign impressions, for example, derived mostly from the record he had compiled as Senate Republican leader. In that role, he had pressed hard on the deficit, much harder than Bush. Indeed, as table 5.1 shows, among Republican contributors, Dole's appeal to investment bankers and insurance executives—sellers and buyers, respectively, of long-term bonds—stands out compared to Bush's. (For both candidates, statistical tests of significance suggest each had above-average support from investment bankers, but the results for Dole are much more impressive, whereas the results for Bush are borderline.)

As Dole kicked off his campaign, he was also known as a friend of Israel, whereas Bush's credentials on that score, while scarcely negligible, were suspect in some quarters. Dole's campaign contribution list also suggests a certain closeness with the commodities markets, and the Kansas senator was in any event a hero to large export-oriented farmers. The veteran member of the Senate Finance Committee also seems to have attracted support from some private hospital chains and parts of the service industry.

All this, however, provided a rather narrow base. Dole tried developing the deficit issue into a call for "burden sharing" by the European allies. This would have freed up resources for some domestic spending, which Dole pointedly observed had been neglected under Reagan. Table 5.1 suggests that some real estate magnates either got (or, more likely, sent) the message. But the rest of the business community hung back. For all the talk about how the compassionate, yet fiscally responsible Dole would make a stronger candidate against the Democrats, the plain fact was that Bush's campaign was rolling ahead.

So, after hesitating almost interminably, Dole made a fateful choice. In a complex maneuver, in which he came out for the INF Treaty, but positioned himself as a stern critic of the other treaties the administration was talking up, he allied with the right and center-right opponents of détente. He also spoke out strongly on the importance of the American position in the Persian Gulf.

The result was a political coalition that leaves little trace in my regular industry analysis, but which shows up spectacularly when one defines a very special universe of comparison: the very largest multinational oil companies (all of them among the top twenty industrials on the 1987 *Fortune* list) except Occidental and Chevron (which both had major deals in progress with the USSR) plus the subset of firms in the aircraft industry whose principal business is producing major warplanes and missiles. This "industry" (or better, world-historical force), shown in table 5.1 as the MNOC-MIC "multinational oil, military-industrial complex" bloc, now swung massively for Dole.[17] As Dole now rushed in on Bush, top executives and political action committees from companies such as Lockheed, General Dynamics, Northrop, and Rockwell all contributed. Henry Kissinger, the living incarnation of prudent multinational skepticism about détente, began to confer with him.[18] And a remarkable number of executives from big multinational oil concerns also began donating. It is doubtful that oil-policy differences between the candidates accounted for this. Bush and Dole did not differ greatly in regard to oil policy, though as the race heated up Dole made some half-hearted and not particularly convincing noises about an oil tariff which many independents, but not most majors, supported. Along with gold, however, oil and natural gas are the principal balancing items in East-West trade. Many Europeans, indeed, take it for granted that the primary limit on how much they can sell the Soviets in the short run is how much gas Moscow can sell back to them. With oil prices already down, it is unlikely that most major oil companies not involved in deals with the Soviets relished the prospect of large-scale sales into the West any more than they did in the 1920s or 1950s, when this issue spurred major agitation in the industry.[19]

Preston Tisch, the brother and close business associate of Lawrence Tisch, who had recently acquired CBS, resigned as postmaster general, returned to his family's business interests, and declared for Dole.[20] Then, as the center-right criticism of Bush reached a crescendo just

ahead of the Iowa primary, Dan Rather, who had previously created a
stir by briefly slipping into Afghanistan, conducted a highly publicized
interview with Bush about his role in the Iran-Contra affair.

Though analysts debated who won that exchange, no one disputed
that Dole defeated Bush in Iowa, or, as Haig, Rumsfeld, and other multinational cold warriors came out for Dole, that he seemed on the verge
of knocking the vice president out of the race. In New Hampshire,
however, the Bush forces were led by Governor John Sununu, who,
like Bush himself, was an ardent proponent of nuclear power (witness
table 5.1's suggestion about the utilities) and the licensing of the controversial Seabrook, New Hampshire, nuclear plant. Sununu, whose
political rise began with the encouragement of a lobbyist for Westinghouse, had taken great care to organize the state. Aided by enormous
infusions of cash, Bush's campaign eked out victory there.[21]

As the campaign headed south, Dole then tried a classic maneuver.
At least three times in the past twenty years, a right-wing candidate
confronting a strong free-trader has cemented the alliance of the center
with the right by explicit commitments to textiles and other protectionist industrial sectors. Now Dole came out in public for protection.
Top executives from Bethlehem and USX, the automobile industry,
some figures from the electronics industry almost certainly worried
about the Japanese, and prominent textile leaders, including Roger
Milliken (a prominent advocate of "buy American" policies) contributed to his campaign. Dole, like Richard Nixon and Reagan before him,
struck a formal arrangement with Thurmond, the long-time champion
of the textile industry.[22]

Now, however, the devastating long-term effects of the high dollar
showed. After seven years of imports, and the gradual transformation
of the Southern industrial structure from a heavy reliance on textiles
to finance, services, and electronics, the old Southern protectionist industrial base was hollowed out. The Bush machine's multinational jug-
gernaut rolled over Dole, effectively destroying his candidacy.

Bush had won, and turned to face the Democrats. As usual, the
situation in that party appeared confusing until one analyzed competition within the power bloc.

Paying for a Party No One Came To

A flashback to 1984 is a convenient place to begin. In that election, it
will be recalled (indelibly by many), Walter Mondale ran on a program
that eschewed many traditional Democratic verities. Instead, he promised to raise taxes to close the deficit, and—a bit less clearly—uphold

"fairness" by trimming the military budget to protect some traditional, often extensively urban-oriented, social programs.

Although many in the media and academia subsequently blamed the ensuing disaster on Mondale's capitulation to the "special interests" of labor, blacks, and women, these groups were certainly not responsible for the disastrous tax pledge or the related rejection of bold proposals for tax simplification. Instead, the Democrats' campaign strategy matched the interests of the two major components of Mondale's business bloc. These were investment bankers, who as sellers of long-term bonds were in white heat about the ballooning deficit, and real estate magnates (mostly in the Northeast and Midwest, plus San Francisco and a few other places outside the Rust Belt), whose building projects depended on continuing federal aid for infrastructure and mass transit.

Because funds for the cities competed dollar for dollar with military spending, the real estate interests genuinely could not afford to back conservative Democrats inclined to indulge the defense establishment. As a consequence, in 1984 the real estate bloc was greatly underrepresented among contributors to conservative Democratic presidential candidates and overwhelmingly concentrated on relatively "liberal" presidential candidacies. (Many, indeed, had earlier helped to finance the antinuclear movement.) These same interests, of course, would have lost heavily had tax simplification removed the tax code's special treatment for real estate. (Eventually, it did, and they were hit with enormous losses.)[23]

A notable advantage the U.S. political system affords large investors is that most of the risk accrues to the politicians who take the cash rather than to the investors who disburse it. The 1984 landslide accordingly buried Mondale, but not the investment bankers and developers. They remained available, indeed, tirelessly active, as tables 5.1 and 5.2 indicate. The task facing Democratic presidential aspirants in 1988, therefore, was to find strategies that promised to bring these blocs on board while, if possible, broadening their appeal.

In 1987, this did not appear easy, though it was certainly less difficult and risky than attempting to run with less money and trying to revive the party's traditional bases of mass support. Investment bankers like Roger Altman (previously Carter's assistant secretary of the treasury; in 1984 at Lehman Brothers; and by 1988 a top executive of the Blackstone Group, an elite new house organized by Peter Peterson, well-known as a critic of the deficit) and Goldman, Sachs' Robert Rubin, who had both flown out to Minnesota to press Mondale on the budget, still had deficit reduction as a top priority. Increasingly prepared to tolerate limited forms of government intervention on behalf of "competitiveness," such financiers retained an abiding interest in free trade and the future flow of investment capital from Japan to the United States. Most also retained a deep fear of inflation (and thus of monetary ease) while preserving an attachment to one legacy of the New Deal: the Glass-Steagall Act, which prevents commercial banks from entering investment banking.[24]

Few of these issues had any mass appeal, however. Accordingly, Democratic candidates had little choice but to focus on U.S.-Soviet relations or the military budget, if they expected to have anything to offer the electorate (and the real estate bloc) at all.

Here, too, however, would-be candidates faced powerful constraints. Although many financiers and other business groups sympathized with détente (indeed, a few strong critics of the Reagan administration's Soviet policy, such as IBM's Thomas J. Watson, had supported Mondale in 1984) and were openly organizing to cut the military budget, the top priority of most remained deficit reduction and, usually, dollar stability. In addition, most members of this bloc—in addition to many defense contractors that retained powerful positions within the party's right wing (contributing to such groups as the newly organized Democratic Leadership Council [DLC])—certainly appreciated the role military force plays in U.S. calculations vis-à-vis Japan, the Third World, the Middle East, and Europe, as well as the USSR.

Not surprisingly, more than one prospective candidate contemplated the alternatives, and then decided that discretion was the better part of valor. New Jersey Senator Bill Bradley, for example, was enormously popular on Wall Street. But, as Morgan Stanley's Richard Fisher and other investment bankers talked up his candidacy, Bradley backed off. Similarly, Mario Cuomo, advised by a virtual Milky Way of international financial stars, including Anthony Solomon, Peterson, Felix Rohatyn, and James Robinson, also drew back, after what appears to have been a policy clash with at least some of the real estate bloc. And Georgia Senator Sam Nunn, a champion of military spending, resisted a vast media buildup (in which CBS played a prominent role) and prudently took himself out of contention.

As the campaign wore on, other, perhaps less perspicacious, candidates probably wished they had emulated the trio of reluctant dragons. Even before the monkey business on the *Monkey Business*, for example, it was apparent that Gary Hart's 1988 campaign—which prominently featured a call for an oil import fee—was failing to attract much business support outside of the oil-producing states (where multimillionaire Texas Lieutenant Governor William Hobby had endorsed him, as did several prominent oilmen) and a handful of investment bankers (table 5.1) and venture capitalists enthusiastic about his detailed and rather far-reaching proposals for combining industrial policy with an open world economy.[25]

Similarly, former Arizona Governor Bruce Babbitt positioned himself as the campaign's enfant terrible, but to little avail. Reeling off a host of ideas that the media kept calling "exciting," Babbitt succeeded in attracting contributions from some very well-placed supporters (including David Rockefeller, a leading figure on the Trilateral Commission, on which Babbitt himself had served). Table 5.1 suggests also that he had some appeal to real estate. Although the significance level just fails to make the table, it is interesting to note that firms in the category I call "media/communications" contributed disproportionately to Babbitt. Strikingly, he also benefited from what one statistical study of campaign coverage concluded was more favorable press coverage than any other candidate received.[26] But the public was less entranced by the value-added tax and other notions that Babbitt put forward than was this rather thin slice of big business, and Babbitt's vigorous, frequently very amusing, campaign failed to catch fire. By the Iowa primary, Babbitt's fund-raisers had obtained commitments for major new funds, provided that he finished at least fourth. When he just barely failed to do so, his campaign collapsed.

The structural dilemmas of how to retain support from both investors and voters also destroyed the candidacy of Illinois Senator Paul Simon. Announcing himself an unreconstructed New Deal Democrat, Simon initially attracted support from leading developers—the only segment of the business community (aside, obviously, from the very special case of defense) where the notion of federal spending was still popular. He also got some support from concerns in the food and grain business—where advocates of friendlier relations with the USSR have often found friends in recent years.[27] To this base, he added many American friends of Israel, Jews and Gentiles alike. (Simon was co-sponsor of a resolution to expel the United Nations office of the Palestine Liberation Organization from the United States.)

It is interesting to speculate what might have happened had Simon persevered in his support of the New Deal and economic equity. Possibly, his candidacy might have taken off like Jackson's. But he did not. Although polls show that more than three-fifths of the public favor a federal job guarantee, and the balanced budget multiplier is a standard result in orthodox economic theory, the media and more conservative Democrats ridiculed Simon's program for full employment. Virtually questioning his intelligence, they patronized him, and frequently implied that the program would fatally swell the deficit.[28] Instead of striking back vigorously, Simon elected to keep raising money from essentially conservative real estate magnates like Donald Trump, from the Chicago commodities exchanges, and from similar sources. He toned down his campaign, running mainly on symbols like the bow tie. Probably only a fraction of the population figured out what he stood for before his candicacy ran out of money.

By then, however, Missouri Congressman Richard Gephardt was on center stage and alarm bells were ringing from New York to Tokyo. A founder of the conservative DLC who had voted for the 1981 tax cuts and championed military spending, Gephardt originally appeared to be just another member of the growing bloc of "neoliberal" congressmen who wanted to move the party to the right.

The high dollar, however, devastated agriculture and much of industry in middle America. After the collapse of oil prices in the late winter of 1985–1986, many congressional Democrats whose districts were not sharing in the relative prosperity of what many were then referring to as the "bicoastal economy" began casting about for a program. Stimulated at least in part by Jim Wright, the new House speaker, whose Texas district faced severe economic dislocation, this group gradually began to evolve a program.

This program had three main planks. The first was a plan for cartelizing farm prices. Trumpeted as a means of saving the family farm, the program in fact had broader objectives. By guaranteeing product prices, it would halt the erosion of real estate prices and provide more income for distressed farm regions. This, in turn, would stabilize conditions for lenders in the region, many of which were facing bankruptcy.

A second part of the program was a tariff on imported oil, which would accomplish for the oil patch what the farm program would do for the farm states.

The third part of the program was the famous "Gephardt amendment," added by Wright and Gephardt to the pending trade bill. The amendment required countries, such as Japan and Korea, which consistently export more goods to the United States than they buy from it, to reduce those trade surpluses by 10 percent per year, or their goods would be subject to new penalty duties designed to force the adjustment.

From the moment it was introduced, the measure was a lightning rod for free-traders, who insisted that it represented a modern version of the notorious Smoot-Hawley tariff and a capitulation by the Democrats to the AFL-CIO.

The latter charge, at least, was simply not true. The bill was in fact a shrewdly designed measure to attract back to the Democrats a part of the business community that seemed, in 1986–1987, to be potentially movable. Part of a series of other congressional Democratic initiatives that included a major report on the status of American high-tech industries and studies highlighting what was said to be a growing disparity of incomes within the workforce, the amendment appears actually to have been promoted by lobbyists for companies that were worried about the Japanese challenge, such as Motorola, or that wanted to force open the Japanese market, such as Monsanto (located in the same city as Gephardt's district, it donated a set of silicon wafers to Gephardt for distribution to House members as an attention-getting device in the days before the vote). Obviously, some protectionists did support the bill: Lee Iacocca was certainly not hoping to pry open the Korean market to $48,000 Chryslers when that corporation came out for the bill, nor were the United Auto Workers.[29]

Exceptionally well conceived in its early stages, the movement to make Gephardt president got under way early. Long before he declared his candidacy, many businesses—especially agricultural creditors, including a striking number of insurance companies, along with various manufacturers—had contributed to his PAC. Then the congressman distributed the money to his colleagues running for reelection in 1986 and after. When Gephardt finally declared, an impressive phalanx of his House colleagues then turned around and endorsed him.

The campaign itself also raised considerable money from manufacturing concerns that had not recently—or, probably, ever, in some cases—aided a Democratic presidential candidate. Monsanto, Ralston-Purina, NCR, and other companies (or their executives) contributed. It is interesting to note that although Gephardt did comparatively little talking about military spending, he was the only Democrat who attracted any significant support from the defense industry (see the entry in table 5.1 for "aircraft"). A number of prominent auto industry figures contributed, including not only executives from General Motors but Iacocca himself. In a nice regional touch, Detroit Edison executives also contributed.

Save for a handful of concerns that hoped to use the bill as a wedge to open up Japan, however, the multinational community was terrified by Gephardt's trade policy. Not surprisingly, according to statistical studies of the campaign, the most multinational of all American industries, the prestige media, flayed Gephardt.[30]

Blasted by the press and cut off because of his support for trade restriction from most major sources of funds, Gephardt radicalized his appeal. He began carrying around a copy of a book highly critical of the Federal Reserve's relations with large banks, William Greider's *Secrets of The Temple*, and he started to denounce an unfeeling "establishment."

Popular response to his campaign was phenomenal. But perhaps because of the blurred image he had on defense issues, he was not able to break through to one big constituency in particular that perhaps might have shared his new interest in "populism"—real estate—and he faced increasing difficulty raising money.[31] When the campaign turned South and for the first time faced an expensive multistate media buy-out, it began to disintegrate. For a while it coped by aggressively soliciting from corporate lobbyists. But it simply could not find the funds to compete all over the South.

Tennessee Senator Albert Gore had earlier entered the race upon the entreaties of (mostly Northern) businessmen who had previously failed to persuade Arkansas Senator Dale Bumpers to take the plunge. Subsequently Gore had allied himself with the champions of military spending and the Likud party's interpretation of Israeli security. Although hyped by much of the media as a uniquely Southern candidate, in fact the former liberal's conservative *volte-face* and alliance with local machines and utilities (table 5.1) did not sit well in his own region.

With polls taken shortly before "Super Tuesday" raising the possibility that the only Southern feature of his campaign might be that it would soon be gone with the wind, Gore did not stand on principle. Making timely use of Yankee lucre, he was born again at the last minute as a populist à la Gephardt. Connoisseurs who treasure the memory of H. L. Mencken will regret that no polling agency thought to ask how many Southern voters in fact thought they were voting for the elder Gore, a famous New Deal senator who now graced the board of Occidental Petroleum, but the switch in the nick of time saved Gore, and it almost certainly helped put Gephardt out of the race.[32]

Either because it was almost uniquely short-sighted or, perhaps, always represented less a real campaign than a device for tying up the convention for someone else's benefit, the Gore campaign had never bothered to organize most areas outside the South. As a consequence, aside from New York state, where his campaign famously allied itself with Mayor Edward Koch, Gore swiftly disappeared as a factor in the race, turning the campaign into a two-man contest between Jackson and Dukakis.

One could analyze this, the most dramatic part of the campaign forever—but from the standpoint of political economy, the broad pattern is cut and dried. In 1984, Jackson's campaign received minor assistance from a few American multinationals that do business in the Third World, and which have historically cultivated ties with parts of the African-American community. (Atlanta-based Coca-Cola is perhaps the outstanding example.) It also received some aid from some multinationally oriented foundation personnel (e.g., David Rockefeller Jr.), some prominent Americans who have long advocated a change in U.S.

policy toward the Middle East (e.g., former U.S. ambassador to Saudi Arabia James Akins), and many African-American business figures.[33]

As important as this support undoubtedly was, however, the plain fact is that it did not add up to much. Even if one reckons in the controversial grants to Operation Push from the Arab League, Jackson's 1984 campaign was far underfunded by comparison with that of virtually every other major candidate.

The same was true of the 1988 campaign, particularly in its crucial early stages. Here, again, it is clear that some money arrived from Arab-Amerians and others concerned with changing American policy toward the Middle East,[34] as well as from two distinguishably different African-American business groups: professionals who have risen to responsible positions within American big business, and entrepreneurs, whose companies tend to be much smaller. But in 1988, support from foundations or major corporations appears to have amounted to even less than in 1984. The campaign's organizational base was essentially elsewhere—in what remains of the civil rights movement, and part of organized labor.[35]

Later, the Jackson campaign clearly did receive some support from parts of Wall Street (where there is considerable sympathy for Jackson's plea for more attention to the Third World, if not for other parts of his message, and where there is some evidence that his relative silence on the role of the Federal Reserve and high interest rates was noted). That part of the American establishment that favors a shift in American policy toward the Middle East also, at least intermittently, talked up Jackson's role in the party—once it was clear that he could not be nominated.

Virtually everyone else in the party, however, quickly closed ranks against Jackson, in favor of his remaining opponent: Dukakis.

This was no accident of circumstance. Standing originally in the shadows of Bradley, Cuomo, and Senator Joseph Biden, Dukakis shared their appeal to investment bankers worried about free trade and budget deficits. In due course, many of the leading Democratic stars of Wall Street began contributing: Not only Rubin and Altman, but also John Gutfreund, chair of Salomon Brothers, and Rohatyn, among many others. As supporters befitting a candidate who took public transit to work every morning, many real estate developers also pitched in, including several members of the Dunfey family who had prominently backed the early antinuclear movement, and Alan Leventhal. (Compare, in table 5.1, the striking similarities between Biden and Dukakis in their overlapping appeals to both investment banking and real estate, if not the chemicals industry—Dukakis was not, after all, a senator from Delaware.)

To this base (and the Greek entrepreneurs beloved of so many newspaper "analyses" of the Dukakis campaign) reminiscent of Mondale, however, Dukakis quickly began adding other sectors. In sharp contrast to Mondale, who by no means succeeded in unifying the Minneapolis business community around him in 1984, Dukakis won support from many of the most influential concerns in the Boston area, including the fabled "Vault" of major banks and most of the Massachusetts High Tech Council.[36]

Indeed, his campaign strongly attracted high tech and computer firms.[37] Hale & Dorr attorney Paul Brountas, who conducted the vice presidential search for Dukakis and is usually numbered among his closest friends, is widely recognized as a leading specialist in high-tech law, and has long been close to the leadership of the High Tech Council, as well as to many of its individual firms, such as Analog Devices.

Promoting the kind of (limited) business-government-academe partnership that these threatened sectors now find so attractive, Dukakis's fund-raisers ranged over the entire country. Aided by the head of Prime Computer and others, the campaign made early inroads into California's Silicon Valley. There, Regis McKenna, a leading public relations consultant to the industry, who in 1984 had aided the Hart campaign, became an early donor.

Uniquely among the white candidates, Dukakis also began a major campaign around health issues. Although one is not used to thinking of this sector as part of the high-technology economy, in fact medical instrument companies, research hospitals, and biotechnology concerns are as much a part of high tech as any defense contractor. Dukakis's best-known initiative on this front, a bill to phase in universal health insurance in Massachusetts, was attacked by doctors but supported by other parts of the health industry, including hospitals after they were released from most cost controls. Other supporters of the bill hailed it as part of a long-term effort to shore up the state's position in the increasingly hot competition for world leadership in biotech industries.

Throughout his campaign, Dukakis periodically called for a national version of the Massachusetts plan. While this figured to attract voters, for whom a long stay in the hospital often means bankruptcy, it also had plenty of powerful, well-funded business support. Even a cursory glance at FEC records of Dukakis's swelling campaign chest shows an outpouring of donations from at least some personnel in parts of the insurance industry,[38] notably Blue Cross companies from around the country. Dukakis himself owned a small amount of stock in a company controlled by a high-tech industrialist whose foundation has made major efforts to place health care on the national agenda.

The campaign's efforts to tap parts of what might be termed the "medical-industrial complex," however, along with its commitments to housing and mass transit (if not, perhaps, to "cities" on the scale of the old federal programs) greatly narrowed its room for maneuver in regard to the issues and sectors that often make or break presidential campaigns: defense and military spending.

Not surprisingly, Dukakis moved very cautiously in this area. Early in the campaign, precisely as one would expect from a candidate with his business base, he appeared skeptical of military spending. Not only did he sharply criticize aid to the Contras, but he also came out against additional testing of virtually all new strategic weapons systems. He also attacked "Star Wars" and opposed both the proposed single-warhead Midgetman missile and the Reagan administration's own version of mass transit—the famous, and fabulously expensive, scheme to base the MX missile on underground railway cars. No less predictably, representatives of the defense (aircraft) industry in my sample refrained disproportionately from contributing to Dukakis's campaign.

In the latter stages of the race, this led to heavy criticism from the party's right wing, as well as some scarcely veiled hints in the *Wall Street Journal* and elsewhere that Dukakis consider the virtues of emulating Kennedy's 1960 campaign (which famously highlighted a bogus missile gap) and tack to his right, perhaps by selecting Nunn as his running mate.

In a series of slow steps, the Dukakis campaign proceeded to do precisely this. Coming out flatly against Jackson's demand for major cuts in defense spending, Dukakis announced his determination to hold defense spending steady in real terms over the next few years— a position that distinguished him from the hard right, but which was in fact rather close to the position Defense Secretary Frank Carlucci pursued after taking over from Caspar Weinberger. In a critical signal of his intentions on military spending, Dukakis ruled out fast-track arms negotiations with USSR President Mikhail Gorbachev—a position that was then being embraced by a wide range of establishment figures, from Cyrus Vance to Kissinger, and which briefly plunged German-American relations into crisis after the election. In negotiations over the Democratic platform, Dukakis also surprised the Jackson forces by backing off his earlier positions against the Contras. He also strongly opposed Jackson's resolution on the Middle East, which, along with Dukakis's declaration that the United States should recognize Jerusalem as the capital of Israel and assiduous work by several members of his finance committee, helped bring over to him many supporters of Gore.

In a major speech to the Atlantic Council, Dukakis also vigorously promoted a new conventional defense initiative—and "conventional" here meant "high tech," since no U.S. defense planner contemplated trying to go one-on-one with Soviet forces. Perhaps not surprisingly, Raytheon, the giant, Boston-based defense contractor whose chief contributed to the campaign, later told the *Boston Globe* that it expected few problems if Dukakis were elected, while other electronics industry spokespersons in New England openly predicted that the stress on conventional weapons would lead to new business.[39]

And of course, Dukakis eventually selected as his running mate Texas Senator Lloyd Bentsen, champion of a bristling national defense, the Contras, oil import levies, the 1981 tax bill, the MX, and the B-1, and a representative of a state whose business elite has been self-consciously modernizing around high tech and biotechnology. Because Bentsen could hardly fail to look good next to Dan Quayle, his selection as vice presidential candidate was never really scrutinized, nor did many connect the choice to the disastrously muted tone of the Democratic campaign. Nevertheless, as the cleanup began from the bash at the Democratic Convention celebrating the historic Boston-Austin axis cosponsored by America's largest natural gas pipeline concern, it was already clear that the candidate would have nothing to say to the electorate in the fall. Like Carter and Mondale before him, admission to the real party was by invitation only—and invitations were only going to major donors; voters needed not apply.

Not surprisingly, the electorate was less than entranced. The Dukakis campaign had already puzzled and angered many of its supporters within the Democratic party by its insulting treatment of Jackson, its coolness to organized labor, and its repeatedly expressed disdain for traditional Democratic verities. Now to almost everyone's surprise, the Massachusetts governor declined to counterattack when challenged by the GOP. Day after bewildering day, neither he nor anyone else in the entourage had anything to say. Flinching at the very mention of what rapidly became known as the "L-word" ("liberal"), the campaign disdained to defend its standard bearer's patriotism, and backed away from an earlier commitment to Jackson to vigorously register new voters.

While top campaign officials warned about the dangers of pandering to electoral passions that might win votes, the governor's camp turned a deaf ear to widespread pleas to spotlight economic issues of concern to average voters, such as international trade or mounting evidence of growing disparities in income. Instead, until a fortnight before the election, the candidate and the party held firmly to Aesopian rhetoric about "values" and "competence." The eleventh-hour rediscovery of the New Deal sent the Massachusetts governor's poll ratings up smartly, but by then it was too late. Whereas in the spring, people who believed the economy would remain "about the same" mostly preferred Dukakis to Bush, by November the reverse was true—even though only a third of this pivotal middle group asserted they were voting to continue the Reagan legacy. (Those who had managed to persuade themselves that the economy would be better were voting overwhelming Republican; those who believed the economy would be worse, Democratic.) Dukakis lost, as voter turnout in many regions of the country fell to levels not witnessed since the 1820s, when property suffrage restrictions were in force.[40]

ACKNOWLEDGMENTS

Early versions of this paper were presented to the Seminar on International Political Economy of the University of Chicago, the Johns Hopkins University's School of Advanced International Studies at Bologna, and also at Bard College, Hobart and William Smith Colleges, Colgate University, New York University, Bentley College, the Boyden Seminar of the University of Massachusetts, Boston, a plenary session at the 1989 Annual Meeting of the Midwest Political Science Association, and several conferences in Bonn and West Berlin organized by the Friedrich Ebert Stiftung. I am grateful to a number of the participants in these sessions for helpful comments. It is also a pleasure to acknowledge special debts to Stanley Kelley, John Geer, Walter Dean Burnham, Ben Page, Rick Pullen, and Paul Perry, for data or other assistance; to Erik Devereux, John Havens, and particularly Goresh Hosangady for advice on statistical methods; and to Bruce Cumings, James Kurth, Robert Johnson, David Hale, Alain Parguez, Joel Rogers, and Sherle Schwendiger for many discussions.

NOTES

1. On the "myth of the U.S. public's turn to the right" under Reagan, see Thomas Ferguson and Joel Rogers, *Right Turn: The Decline of the Democrats and the Future of American Politics* (New York: Hill & Wang, 1986), chap. 1; Stanley Kelley, "Democracy and the New Deal Party System," in A. Guttman, ed., *Democracy and the Welfare State* (Princeton: Princeton University Press, 1988) demonstrates the persistence of New Deal issues.

Right Turn was not alone in reaching the conclusions about opinion trends that it did. Tom Smith of the National Opinion Research Center, Vicente Navarro, and a number of other analysts have all argued rather similarly, while some students of comparative politics made similar observations about the Margaret Thatcher regime in Britain. Recently the whole question in regard to the United States was reexamined by Benjamin Page and Robert Shapiro, who, after reviewing an enormous number of polls, concluded in their *The Rational Public* (Chicago: University of Chicago Press, 1992) once again that "Ferguson & Rogers are correct, therefore, in arguing that the policy right turn of the Reagan years cannot be accounted for as a response to public demands." (pp. 169–70).

In his *The Changing American Mind* (Ann Arbor: University of Michigan Press, 1992), William Mayer claims that *Right Turn* was mistaken. Mayer's argument, however, is tendentious in the extreme. Early in his book he concedes that he does not disagree with our claims about opinion trends after 1980 and even suggests that our way of proceeding makes perfect sense. (Cf. p. 125: "Given [Ferguson and Rogers'] interests, their [emphasis on the 1980s] is a perfectly appropriate procedure; as will become clear, their verdict on these years agrees with my own . . .") His subsequent discussion of opinion trends in the '80s, however, takes no account of our discussion and slips past the key question of the relation of policy to opinion. In other parts of his book, he picks quarrels with our analyses of the pre-1980 data. A very close reading, however, shows that he consistently backs away from critical points, even as he suggests that somehow our evidence is flawed. Thus, for example, we noted a number of opinion trends that moved in a conservative direction before 1980, including opinions on crime, taxes, and military spending. These, we thought, scarcely added up to an explanation of the sweeping policy changes that occurred under Reagan, and we attempted to place them in the framework of our general argument. Mayer acknowledges that we noted these trends, but then carries on as if we were somehow careless about the data, rather than simply disagreeing with us about the meaning of the data. (p. 125 ff.) This is remarkable, particularly given his later caution that in fact, he is *not* arguing that any of the shifts he and we noticed in fact explain the election results of 1980. (See his p. 123, n. 20.)

Mayer also makes several statements that are simply absurd. Although a fairly large number of researchers were reviewing the same polls we were and coming into general agreement with us, he accuses us of "selectively" choosing data. It is of course true that we did not report every poll ever taken. But *Right Turn* looks at a great many polls and highlights a number of areas that don't fit the general pattern it suggests exists. Nor, as anyone can see, do we in fact "demonstrate a consistent, and highly questionable preference for data from the Harris poll, whose surveys are often tilted in a liberal direction." (p. 126) Even a simple count of sources will show far more citations to polls by the *Los Angeles Times, CBS/New York Times,* ABC, Gallup, etc. Indeed, the Harris data could be removed entirely without affecting our general argument. He also claims (p. 125, n. 24) that part of our argument about military spending is based on a "factual error." I believe that one poll (out of literally dozens discussed) confused data that had excluded residual categories with results that included answers such as "don't know." But that one poll is immaterial to the argument we make that most of the shift in favor of more military spending occurred late in the seventies (as the cold war heated up and the Soviets invaded Afghanistan). We cite a series of polls for this conclusion, and our argument is correct (and confirmed in Mayer's table 9.2). (Further sometimes quite amusing comments on Mayer's very facile discussion are in a memorandum of November 8, 1992, made available to me by Joel Rogers.)

I conclude that Mayer's footnoted caution about the implications of his work is fully justified, and that public opinion trends cannot explain the changes in American public policy wrought by the Reagan administration—exactly as *Right Turn* argued.

2. See Thomas Ferguson, "Lessons from a 'Meaningless' Election," *Texas Observer,* December 5, 1986.

3. Gallup has kindly made its unpublished data for 1980, 1984, and 1988 available to me. For 1988, the last Gallup pre-election survey showed that among registered voters, 53.3 percent of those who were likely to vote favored Bush, 41.6 preferred Dukakis, and 5.1 percent were undecided. On the other hand, of those who were unlikely to vote, only 46.1 percent favored Bush, 42.3 percent liked Dukakis, and fully 11.6 percent were undecided. Note that this would not guarantee victory for the Democrats if everyone

voted, but it would certainly make for a qualitatively different strategic situation, and probably a very different campaign. This Gallup survey, in contrast to former practice, is restricted to registered voters. A survey of those who were not registered might well show up even better for the Democrats. The Reagan popularity figures in the previous paragraph came from Thomas Ferguson, "F.D.R., Anyone?" *The Nation*, May 22, 1989.

4. For the 1988 voting results, see the *New York Times*, November 10, 1988.

5. See, for example, Walter Dean Burnham, "The Reagan Heritage," in G. Pomper, et. al., *The Election of 1988* (Chatham, NJ: Chatham House, 1989) who argues that a "traditional decay-revitalization cycle" provided a significant mass underpinning for the Reagan revolution. Thomas B. Edsall, "Black vs. White in Chicago," *New York Review of Books*, April 13, 1989, is one of many statements of the case on race. Neither, however, examines any opinion data.

6. What is perhaps the best general approach to voters' decisions is laid out in Stanley Kelley, *Interpreting Elections* (Princeton: Princeton University Press, 1983). An important consequence of this view is that hardly anyone appears to be a one-issue voter, such as Burnham's revitalization view would predict. Using Kelley's general methods, John Geer has produced several important papers (see his "The Electorate's Partisan Evaluations: Evidence of a Continuing Democratic Edge," *Public Opinion Quarterly* 55; no. 2, pp. 218–31, and "New Deal Issues and the American Electorate, 1952–88," *Political Behavior* 14, pp. 45–65). The former shows convincingly that, contrary to many studies (e.g., E. Carmines and J. Stimson, *Issue Evolution* [Princeton: Princeton University Press, 1989]), race presently plays a secondary role in American politics as a whole (though obviously not in particular localities); he also shows that this was not true in the sixties. On the basis of Kelley and Geer's results, I broke down changes in the net pull of various issues that affect public attitudes toward the Democratic Party. For reasons of space, this had to be detached from this chapter.

7. This formulation, of course, is deceptively simple. For a full discussion of methods and pitfalls, including the "obvious" objections, cf. Ferguson, "Party Realignment and American Industrial Structure" (chapter 1 of this volume). The analysis of 1988 campaign contributions set out below is premised on this essay. One implication, perhaps, needs to be noted here: the particular focus on top investors—the very largest, richest firms and individuals. It is obvious that a great deal of money in politics arises from outside this sector. But as the essay argues, large investors have unique advantages (including, collectively, the fact that they own the media); they in addition—and certainly in the 1988 campaign—do much of the organizing that brings in the rest of the money.

The actual data analysis closely follows the procedure described in the statistical appendix to *Right Turn* (including the reliance on 2×2 chi-square tests, with the industry being tested separated from the rest, and inclusion within the sample of both PACs and individual top investors, top executives of all large firms, and members of the Forbes 400), with the notable exception that the sample is much larger. The industry divisions, except where noted, generally follow the industry codes used in the *Fortune* lists of large firms, with the obvious exceptions that, for example, investment banking does not have its own code there, as it certainly does in my analysis; and that the *Fortune* category "diversified financial company" makes little sense in my context. Its separate firms have therefore been located in other appropriate industries (e.g., Morgan-Stanley is classified with the investment banks). I should add that I doubt very much that any conclusion of this paper is at all affected by any of these decisions—this data set is truly large. But because it includes far more contributors than just PACs, it differs a great deal from all other studies known to me of campaign financing. I should also note that while virtually all the data are drawn from the Federal Election Committee (and are complete through at least mid-September 1988, when the parties officially go to the public trough), I have added in the donors for both the GOP and Democratic soft money lists, as disclosed after the election in a much-publicized series of articles in the *Washington Post.* (These lists, in fact, add virtually no information to my sample; the absence of good information about totals is precisely why I avoid regression, and other ratio or interval-levels tests, in favor of chi-square and other less presumptuous approaches).

8. Much of what follows is discussed at length in many works on Reagan, including Ferguson and Rogers, *Right Turn,* ch. 3, and my "Who Bought Bush, and Why," *International Economy,* (January/February 1989), pp. 68–75.

9. One almost hesitates to employ the expression "bloc," since this group, in sharp contrast to the second, exists largely in a reactive mode, defined preeminently by what it opposes, and since the 1930s, when it lost its dominant position in U.S. society, has never succeeded in articulating a well-developed alternative point of view. Neither are its views well represented in the major media.

10. Paul Kennedy, *The Rise and Fall of the Great Powers* (New York: Random House, 1978).

11. Rejecting the advice that Herbert Stein, Walter Wriston, and other analysts were giving not to make the ritual promise to avoid fighting inflation by means of unemployment, the administration's earliest economic projections envisioned only a short recession. See Ferguson and Rogers, *Right Turn,* p. 118.

12. See the statistical appendix to Ferguson and Rogers, *Right Turn,* pp. 221–27, especially tables 1 and 2 on p. 225.

13. Other business groups complained about the deficit, of course. But they did not leave the party over it; nor, though the point cannot be pursued here, were they always serious. That was, after all, the point of hammering away at the deficit to build pressure on social programs. And a few firms, notably defense, certainly had other priorities. See *Right Turn,* p. 154.

14. See David Hale, "Accounting for the Dollar Glut," *Wall Street Journal,* April 18, 1988.

15. These are overwhelmingly represented in the sample. U.S. textiles firms have fallen so far that they are no longer well represented in this data, and their political behavior has to be separately analyzed. For the *Fortune* poll, see the issue of February 15, 1989.

16. The table also registers disproportionate support from the beverages industry. One might well ask why. The sample suggests a fairly obvious answer: For Kemp, the "cola wars" combine with support from some right-wing beer barons to drive the numbers up. Note also that the table compares each party's candidates with regard to all contributions within the party, so that pockets of industrial support for particular candidates can be assessed. Table 5.2 compares industries with statistically above-average rates of contributions to each party, where the universe of comparison is all investors. The findings for the GOP showed a high mean of .45 across more than 20 industries. The industries with rates of contributions to the Democrats significantly above average (.17) for the entire sample are unsurprising; computers (.32, at the .07 level); investment banking (.40, .01); real estate (.39, .01) and beverages (.50, .01 level). Finally it should

be obvious that many important political cleavages show up inside industries. Indeed, this chapter alludes to several rifts at various points. But I know of no mechanical way to statistically test for these. One must instead proceed case by case, as I do in the discussion of Dole, for example.

17. Because of my grave doubts about reported spending totals, I am skeptical of comparing percentage rates of contributions, especially when reporting within blocs in each party, as in the present table. I think it makes more sense to think in terms of a bloc of industries that all prove significantly above the mean (always, of course, assuming that the mean is not impossibly small, as in the Haig case). For what it is worth, however, Dole's absolute rate for this bloc is actually higher than Bush's—a remarkable indicator of sentiment, considering that Bush collected far more contributions. The list of defense firms is adapted from James Kurth, "The Military Industrial Complex Revisited," in J. Kruzel, ed., *American Defense Annual, 1989–90* (Lexington, MA: D.C. Heath, 1989).

18. See, for example, the *New York Times*, January 20, 1988. The *Boston Globe* ran somewhat fuller notices around the same time.

19. From this standpoint, it is scarcely surprising that the first days of the Bush administration witnessed a sharp rise in world oil prices that the Soviets abetted, and an influx of Kissenger protégés. In effect, the most powerful potential opposition to the administration was being coopted. Nor is it surprising that this led almost at once to indecision on détente, and a crisis in German-American relations. Subsequent events, notably the Gulf War and the collapse of the Soviet Union, complicated matters in ways too complex to analyze here.

20. The *New York Times*, January 11, 1988. Preston Tisch at the time indicated that he was normally a Democrat.

21. For Sununu and Westinghouse, see the *Boston Globe*, January 16, 1989. The other industries in table 5.1 for Bush might merit a word. Recall the previous discussion on government support for the computer industry in negotiations with Japan. Oil needs no comment, in general; nor do the (multinational free-trading) investment bankers, who barely make the grade anyway. I strongly suspect interindustry differences play a role here, for in the Bush camp are representatives of several firms that have prominently championed financial deregulation and are actively lobbying to expand into the role of nonbank banks. Many other investment bankers have strongly opposed this, and this industry was one of those most likely to back Democrats in the 1988 election.

22. See, for example, "Presidential Campaign Hotline," February 23, 1988. For past textile commitments inside the GOP, see Thomas Ferguson, "The Right Consensus? Holsti and Rosenau's New Foreign Policy Belief Surveys," *International Studies Quarterly*, 30 (1986), p. 414.

23. See Ferguson and Rogers, *Right Turn*, chap. 6, but especially the statistical tables in the appendix on campaign contributions; for the antinuclear movement, see pages 150–54.

24. For most of what follows on the Democrats, see Ferguson, "Private Money and Public Policy," *International Economy* (September/October, 1988); useful also is Fran Hawthorne, "Playing Politics," *Institutional Investor* (April, 1988).

25. While consistent with Hart's orientation toward free trade, the table's indications of support from retailers may well be a statistical artifact. The table warns plainly that the power of the test is low, but it is worth noting here how exiguous the result really

is: it rests on two contributions that are significant only because the *N* is so small for Hart. I report the result only because I do not favor tailoring data presentation to a priori theories.

26. See S. R. Lichter, D. Amundson, and R. Noyes, *The Video Campaign* (Washington, DC: American Enterprise Institute, Center for Media and Public Affairs, 1988), p. 76.

27. What table 5.1's suggestion in regard to electronics is worth is not clear. The finding is marginal to begin with, both statistically and in regard to strength (it concerns two firms, both highly regulated). One might guess that it relates to issues before a Senate committee, but I simply do not know.

28. For representative polls and a useful overview of the media reaction to Simon, cf. the FAIR (Fairness and Accuracy in Reporting) newsletter *Extra*, March/April, 1988.

29. For more on the Gephardt amendment's real origins and purposes, cf. Thomas Ferguson, "Have the Democrats Really Gone Protectionist?" *Baltimore Sun*, May 10, 1987.

30. See Lichter et al., *Video Campaign*, p. 115. On p. 104, the authors briefly attempt to absolve the networks of responsibility for the tone of coverage toward Gephardt, claiming that they simply carried the attacks of other candidates. But their argument is flimsy indeed—deciding which candidate attacks to carry is a primary power of the media. Jackson, for example, criticized many of the other candidates. But the data of Lichter et al.—which confirm that issues simply were not featured in most coverage— imply that most of these attacks were never aired. After the Iowa primary, the best way to hurt Gephardt was surely to publicize the flip-flop and special interest charges leveled at him by Dukakis, while failing to notice the arrant hypocrisy of the affluent Dukakis campaign's claims that Gephardt's PAC money uniquely branded him a "special interest" candidate.

31. As discussed above, the 1984 data revealed a clear relation between candidates' liberalism and support from the real estate bloc. In 1988, there was no outstanding liberal candidate—if for the moment one excludes Jackson as at least partly sui generis. So partitioning the candidates makes little sense. But it is still possible to demonstrate structural incompatibility within coalitions. One very striking result is that any Democrat whom the aircraft industry disproportionately favored is disproportionately unfavored by real estate, and vice versa. The rule works for all candidates, who, like Gephardt and Dukakis, have sizable contributions. But the effect is significant for candidates with small numbers of contributions, also. (Two cases of really minuscule contributions raise doubts about significance levels, but do not contradict this.) It is always unwise to invest any single data analysis with too much significance. But reality, I think, is trying to tell us something.

32. How the well-financed, but derivative and often very unstable appeals financed by the investor blocs discussed here were translated by voters is a subject that this essay simply does not have room to treat in detail. From the present standpoint, however, most ordinary electoral analyses are technically misspecified in that they neglect, for example, Gephardt's running out of money, as well as many other factors that influence candidate appeals in a systematic manner. They also fail to discuss, or even to raise, questions about the way money functions to make sure certain questions are not asked in public, as the investment theory notes. While I, therefore, cannot follow its treatment of the campaign, see for some analysis of the voting patterns, Bruce Cain, I. A. Lewis, and Douglas Rivers, "Strategy and Choice in the 1988 Presidential Primaries," Social Science Working Paper 686 (Pasadena: California Institute of Technology).

33. See Ferguson and Rogers, *Right Turn*, pp. 176–79.

34. In this category I would place the commercial bank contributions recorded in table 5.1. Although they were few, they are statistically—and probably politically—significant.

35. On the Jackson campaign, see also the *New York Times*, April 17, 1988, and April 15, 1988. The latter provides some indication of how wide Jackson's support among regional and local labor leaders was—an important corrective to the view espoused by much of the media and some academic analysts that Jackson's white support was concentrated among upper-income and white-collar groups. Jackson was clearly not the choice of the AFL-CIO or the UAW but his effort definitely would not have gotten off the ground without the support it received from a minority of (mostly white) trade unionists.

On May 9, 1988, the *Washington Post* published a *Post*/ABC poll claiming to show that Jackson had brought few new voters to the polls during the primaries. Being rather surprised, I phoned the *Post*, where a man, identifying himself as one of the authors of the story, flatly refused to make available to me any part of the survey. Neither would ABC. This was the first time this had ever happened to me, and it was a marked departure from the usual practice of reputable polls. Because they would not release details of the survey, it is impossible to say for sure how they arrived at this implausible conclusion. Examining the story, however, suggests they fell victim to a classic blunder: taking the word of the respondent as evidence that he or she voted. It is well known that people overreport voting. As a consequence, the survey would turn up many people claiming to have voted in 1984, who in fact were new 1988 voters. But it is possible to do better than this. I. A. Richards of the *Los Angeles Times* poll kindly made available to me an unpublished survey taken during the New York primary which is sorted by whether the respondent admitted to not voting in 1984 or not. While this is not perfect either, it is very likely that most people who admitted to not voting in 1984 in fact did not. Among these 1988 voters, 64 percent voted for Jackson—a very striking rate of new voter attraction, if every there was one.

36. On Dukakis's campaign, see especially Ferguson, "Private Money"; also helpful for this and the rest of this section are Hawthorne, "Playing Politics"; also the *Boston Globe*, April 12, 1988, June 22, 1988, and May 12, 1988. Dukakis's stock holding in Automatix, Inc., founded by Philippe Villiers, is mentioned in the *New York Times*, July 6, 1988. Enron's cosponsorship of the Boston-Austin link is noted in the *Austin American-Statesman*, July 22, 1988; one hint in the *Wall Street Journal* on running to the right can be found on April 29, 1988. The media talk about "small regional donors" misses the main point that is, perhaps, a little easier to see now that the Democratic list of major soft money donors has become public—that such a structure is one way people in the elite sample I analyze actually manifest clout.

37. Some friendly readers of a draft of this essay wondered whether they should worry about industries that contributed to both parties. In my view, the answer is no, for reasons that are discussed in my "Party Realignment" (chapter 1 in this volume), and "From 'Normalcy' to New Deal: Industrial Structure, Party Competition, and American Public Policy in the Great Depression," (chapter 2 in this volume). Bipartisanship happens; it is not a universal phenomenon, but is limited, as these data show again, to certain industries. In analyzing the modern Democratic Party, therefore, one does well to recognize that comparatively few firms and industries of any size give anything to the

party, and then to focus sharply on those who do. I should also note that intra-industry factors are certainly at work here in many cases (this is particularly obvious in the case of investment banking, where the interest of the bond houses in the deficit and Glass-Steagall is openly avowed, in contrast to, for example, sellers of retail stocks); I have not yet discovered a method to reveal this kind of cleavage, however, without constructing a catalogue of cases.

38. These are not in the sample of "large" investors analyzed here. In the general election, the Democrats also received substantial funds from various trial attorneys, who were organizing against Bush's anticipated restructuring of the legal rules on liability in response to a demand by major segments of his business constituency.

39. The *Boston Globe,* May 24, 1988.

40. Most of the scenes in the Democrats' 1988 passion play are so well known that specific references are redundant. But one or two aspects of this quite carefully written description might raise questions. See in particular, on the broken commitment to Jackson and the Dukakis campaign's hostility to voter registration (aside from a few states where local leaders insisted), the excellent reporting of Andrew Kopkind in the *Nation* and James Ridgeway in the *Texas Observer* and the *Village Voice;* on Dukakis and labor, cf. the *Boston Globe,* September 4, 1988. I personally know of one case in which a top Dukakis campaign operative declined—late in the campaign—to make any use of excellent data suggesting growing U.S. inequality. And one well-known Cambridge academic acknowledged to be very close to the campaign was telling some business groups that the governor had placed most discussion of Japan and the trade deficit off limits—which should be obvious to anyone who followed the campaign.

The surveys cited come from the CBS/*New York Times* poll; see the discussion in Barbara Farah and Ethel Klein, "Public Opinion Trends," in G. Pomper, et al., eds., *The Election of 1988* (Chatham, NJ: Chatham House, 1989). The turnout data come from Walter Dean Burnham, personal communication. Note that among modern elections, 1924's overall turnout certainly ranked lower—but that was in an era in which Southern turnouts were carefully held down.

'Real Change'?
'Organized Capitalism,' Fiscal Policy, and the 1992 Election

THROUGHOUT 1992's marathon race to the White House, candidate Bill Clinton and his surrogates kept chanting one word like a mantra: "change." The morning after the election, however, signals switched dramatically. Suddenly the president-elect and his spokespersons began warning that bringing about real change would be a long and difficult process.

Soon the people who had won the election by focusing single-mindedly on "the economy, stupid," abruptly changed the subject—to the issue of gays in the military. After a few days, they dropped it like a hot potato. Over the next few weeks, the bond market rallied euphorically, while the man who promised that his cabinet would "look like America" announced an economic team that looked like Wall Street, a foreign-policy team that resembled Jimmy Carter's, and a raft of other appointments that looked, if not exactly like the Business Council (still a white male bastion), then perhaps the affluent clientele of some exclusive spa or ski resort.

Nor was this all. Only days after the election two major unions, the United Auto Workers (UAW) and the American Federation of State, County, and Municipal Employees, pulled the rug out from under the coalition for Canadian-style ("single payer") health insurance—a step that both common sense and well-connected insiders indicated was related to the ascent of the new chief executive.[1]

At the celebrated two-day economic summit in Little Rock in December 1992, more strange new signals started flashing. Clinton advisers encouraged John White, who originally had put together Ross Perot's deficit plan before defecting to the Arkansas governor, to repackage data that *they had possessed for months* to emphasize the impression that the deficit was growing faster than anyone suspected. Shortly afterward Clinton, who all through the campaign had pilloried Perot for targeting the deficit instead of economic growth, told the *Wall Street Journal* that reducing the deficit now had to be his top priority.[2]

In the midst of this dramatic about-face came another less heralded but very revealing vignette. In Little Rock, Massachusetts Institute of Technology economist Rudiger Dornbusch (and others) urged a quick devaluation of the dollar against both the Japanese yen and the other dollar-linked Asian economies that have year after year racked up enormous trade surpluses against the United States. The president-elect himself responded by declaring that "I'm for a strong dollar," while Robert Rubin, the Goldman, Sachs executive whom Clinton named to head his newly created National Economic Council, worried out loud about "business confidence and long-term bond yields." Immediately after the conference, Clinton aides put out word to the press that Fred Bergsten, an economist widely thought to be sympathetic to a lower dollar, had damaged his standing with the new administration by his comments in Little Rock. Subsequent press reports also indicated that doubts about the commitment of other potential candidates to a high dollar had played a role in the decision to appoint Harvard economics professor (and World Bank President) Lawrence Summers to the bellwether post of undersecretary of the treasury for international affairs.[3]

The Clinton Economic Plan

In mid-February 1993, after an embarrassing series of missteps over appointments and the question of gays in the military, the president at last unveiled his economic plan. Addressing a joint session of Congress and a nationwide TV audience, the president boldly repudiated the Reaganomics of his immediate predecessors. He called for higher income taxes on the very wealthiest Americans and a rise in the corporate tax rate. He also proposed a new, broad-based tax on energy that would be phased in over several years. In the next breath, the president put forward a series of sweeping new spending initiatives (including tax credits) totalling some $169 billion by 1997, while proposing cuts of $247 billion over the same period. Taken as a whole, his package aimed to reduce the deficit—then running at about $319 billion a year and projected to rise, if nothing were done, to about $346 billion by 1997—to about $200 billion per year (approximately 3 percent of GNP) in the last year of his first term, though the White House emphasized that continued progress on deficit reduction would also depend on passage of the president's forthcoming health-care plan.[4]

Although the earliest polls suggested that the public's initial reaction to the speech was favorable, within days the administration's splendid new coach began turning into a pumpkin. From the start the media highlighted complaints by wealthy Americans about the proposed increases in taxes in the very highest brackets. Over time this line of criticism hardened into a cliche: Republicans, conservative Democrats, Perot, and many business groups accused the administration of underestimating how much the president's plan would cost average Americans. Spending, they argued, should be cut by far more than the president proposed.

One disaster after another began piling up for the administration. Even though the economy was creeping along at a snail's pace and polls indicated that jobs rather than the deficit were by far the public's top priority, the Senate brusquely rejected the President's request for a tiny fiscal stimulus program (initially some $30 billion, later reduced to $16 billion).[5] Insurance companies, doctors, pharmaceutical concerns and the rest of the medical-industrial complex besieged task forces drafting the health-care proposals. The administration also became bogged down in battles with Congress and the Pentagon over the question of gays in the military; debates over intervention in Somalia, the Balkans and Haiti; and conflicts over taxes (especially energy taxes) and appointments.

Amid growing popular concern about the "jobless recovery," the president began sliding in the polls. In March, the president's approval ratings, according to a CBS/*New York Times* poll, stood at 55 percent. Two months later, his approval rating was around 40 percent and falling. Comparisons of Clinton to Carter and talk of a possible one-term presidency started seeping into the major media. At the end of May, a desperate White House responded dramatically by naming David Gergen, White House director of communications under Ronald Reagan, and a major architect of the policies Clinton was pledged to reverse, counselor to the President.[6]

Though the president's poll rating did not move a jot, the media showered praise on Gergen. Amid a blizzard of exuberant press notices hailing the president's return to the "middle of the road," the wrenching sense of imminent collapse faded. At the price of additional spending cuts and a wholesale retreat on energy taxes, the White House secured passage of its deficit plan. It also began scaling back its highly touted plan for overhauling the nation's health-care delivery system, and started gearing up to pass the North American Free Trade Agreement (NAFTA).

In a society already filled with foreboding about the future, these moves triggered a riot of speculation and criticism. But while the torrent of commentary undoubtedly heightened many Americans' sense of desperation, it did little to clarify what all the shouting was really about.

In public, everything appeared very simple, at least until Gergen's appointment. As William Kristol and many other Republicans charged, the rise in income taxes in the highest brackets and the increase in corporation tax rates suggested an abrupt declaration of "class war." The Democrats, it seemed, must be returning to their New Deal roots, reclaiming a heritage everyone thought they had abandoned. From this perspective, the new spending programs outlined by the president were entirely predictable: more tax and spend, spend and tax.

But as so often in American politics, appearance and reality diverge. From the standpoint of social equity, it can scarcely be doubted that the initial version of the Clinton fiscal program differed drastically from anything ever contemplated by Presidents Reagan and George Bush.

Still, the notion that even the original plan amounted to class war is absurd on its face. Sometimes one picture is worth a thousand words. Such, perhaps, was the case with the television shots of Federal Reserve Chair Alan Greenspan and Apple Computer CEO John Sculley sitting next to Hillary Rodham Clinton during the president's speech to Congress. Nor can one easily imagine Lloyd Bentsen, Rubin, or Roger Altman in the role of Lenin or Trotsky; or forget the millions of dollars in soft money that flowed to the Democrats in 1992 (not to mention the almost frivolous "plan" put forward by the president to curb the influence of lobbyists and political money in the same speech).[7]

As the introduction to this book observed, the administration's flamboyant, "hot button" appeals to particular liberal constituencies in its first months—the appointment of Robert Reich to head the transition team, the nominations of several liberals to second-tier positions in various government agencies (none were offered a major position), the highly publicized search for the perfect "politically correct" cabinet—were really quite misleading. Not only every top-level appointment in the areas of economics, foreign policy, and defense, but the whole trend of the new regime's macroeconomic policies ran in thoroughly center-right directions, to the extent that the administration made a special point of calling attention to how closely some of its budget proposals resembled Perot's.

In addition, even the original budget plan (to say nothing of the far more conservative bill that finally passed) was relatively modest. For all the wailing in the upper brackets, the increase in tax rates initially requested scarcely added up to a reversal of Reaganomics: All of 5 percentage points for households with incomes of $180,000 or more, with an additional surtax of 10 percent on incomes over $250,000 (adding, perhaps, 3 more percentage points to the effective tax rate on this most affluent of groups). Familiar tax shelters, including the exemption for interest earned on tax-free government bonds, escaped untouched. The rise in the corporate tax rate initially requested (and eventually enacted) amounted to exactly 2 percentage points. And a substantial share of the new spending proposed was earmarked for business, including various tax credits and a wide variety of new subsidies, sometimes masked by such labels as "defense conversion" or "research."[8]

To say this is not to condemn the program—I have already indicated that from an equity perspective, it is probably the best we are likely to see. But it is to warn, urgently, that much more is going on here than anyone has suggested in public.

And, alas, it is to raise another yellow caution flag as well. In replacing the campaign's emphasis on spurring economic growth with Perot's focus on the deficit once the election was over, the president appears to have fatally compromised the whole effort.

Asked to choose between reducing the deficit and spurring economic growth, Americans overwhelmingly indicate to pollsters that their priority is growth. If, as the polls also indicate, many average Americans were also willing to indulge the president's new concentration on the deficit, it is surely because most were persuaded that eliminating the deficit would guarantee a return to rapid economic growth.

But they are almost surely mistaken, as is discussed in more detail in the latter parts of this essay. One symptom of the problem is the anemic $30 billion in new spending initially proposed by the president to stimulate the economy. As Robert Eisner, Paul Davidson, and others have pointed out, in a trillion-dollar economy the amount is derisory. Yet the administration abandoned the whole effort at the first sign of trouble, without any effort to explain to the public what the real stakes were.[9]

In the context of the administration's commitment to a high dollar (save against the yen), the result is likely to be real trouble a year or so down the road. In the presidential campaign, candidate Clinton repeatedly objected that Perot's "cold turkey" approach to cutting the deficit would strangle the economy by fatally constricting total demand. Perot, however, did have a partial answer. The economic simulations that were run to check out his plan's overall impact assumed a substantial devaluation of the dollar. By raising exports as government spending contracted, this would have partially compensated for the fall in total demand.[10]

Now, however, the Clinton administration has taken over much of Perot's deficit plan, but not his devaluation. (It has pressured the Japanese to revalue the yen, but, as is discussed below, this step poses major political risks to the ruling political coalition in Japan, since it implies a sharp break with the Japanese economy's traditional orientation toward exports rather than domestic consumption. It also bypasses the equally compelling problem of the smaller Asian "tigers", which have year after year piled up enormous trading surpluses against the United States.) As a result, the administration's economic plan rests almost entirely on optimistic hopes that deficit reduction will quickly and durably bring down long-term rates of interest as the Fed cooperates and investors shed their fears of inflation.

Despite the Dionysian revels accompanying the bond-market rally that began soon after the new president defined his course, this is unlikely. Not that interest rates will not come down—for a while. Or that spending for capital investment will not respond—at least to the extent of triggering yet another wave of "America is back" flag-waving. But in the longer run, as exports fail to rise enough to offset the reductions in aggregate demand occasioned by a shrinking budget deficit, the resulting rates of growth are likely to be disappointing.

This will not, however, be the only serious consequence of the administration's decision to court financial markets so ostentatiously. In the 1990s, alas, those who live by financial markets are all too likely to die from them. A consistent focus on retaining Wall Street's confidence will require the president to concede the Federal Reserve extensive freedom over interest-rate policy. Given the virtual paranoia about inflation that now dominates world financial markets, the result is predictable: At the first sign of a recovery, the Fed will move to choke off "inflation" by raising short-term interest rates.

The clamor for a rise in interest rates will be all the stronger if, as is likely in the early stages of even the Clinton program, the U.S. rate of economic growth runs ahead of that of most of its trading partners. Imports into the United States will then be rising faster than American exports. This will swell the already huge U.S. current account deficit with the rest of the world, and put downward pressure on the international value of the dollar. Just as in the Carter years, financial markets are certain to respond by calling for higher rates, both to make dollars more attractive to hold and also to reduce imports by slowing the economy's rate of growth. The trade deficit would then slowly shrink, simply as a result of the United States growing less rapidly than other parts of the world.

Such policy packages are precisely what the millions of Americans who elected Clinton voted *against*, and what they believed they were avoiding by supporting his plan to reduce the deficit. It is not difficult to imagine their reactions as they discover, over the next several years, that they were wrong. As the now well-documented squeeze tightens on their wages, pensions, and medical benefits, dashing their hopes for recovering the "American dream," these voters' sense of desperation is likely to increase.[11] Particularly if they become convinced that the "liberal" or "left" alternative has demonstrably failed, many such people are likely to explore drastic alternatives: One or the other Republican supply-sider, Perot, or perhaps someone still in the shadows—anyone who can plausibly embody fading ideals of economic growth and American preeminence (while raising the millions of dollars required to run).

Such thoughts may remind us that while Hollywood has easy access to the Clinton White House, a happy ending to the current imbroglio is not guaranteed. But what, therefore, ever impelled the president to become a born-again deficit hawk in the first place? Could this belated metamorphosis have been predicted by a careful observer of the 1992 campaign? Why, with unemployment so high, was the proposed economic stimulus so feeble? What about the quite sizable investment component of the administration's program and its widely touted initiatives in favor of various businesses? And why is the administration so concerned with the level of the dollar and the bond market?

In an age when even major media figures decry the replacement of news by entertainment, there is little to be gained by rounding up and interrogating yet again the usual suspects from the press or the academy. Instead the task is to put the investment approach to party competition, outlined earlier in this book, to work on what are rather obviously the three main questions about the 1992 election: First, how did Bush, who appeared invincible throughout virtually all of 1991, ever contrive to lose? Above all, why didn't he stimulate the economy, as virtually everyone expected? Second, what enabled Clinton to outlast all the other entrants in the crowded Democratic field, so that he rather than someone else became the all but inevitable alternative to a regime that vast numbers of Americans were coming to detest? Third, why did Perot, the 1992 campaign's unidentified flying object (and walking incarnation of the investment theory of political parties), really break with the Republican Party and what did he (does he) really stand for?

RUNNING ON EMPTY

During most of 1991, Bush seemed destined for a reelection triumph of overwhelming—indeed, historic—proportions. Amid the world-shattering upheavals of his first term—the fall of the Berlin Wall and the reunification of Germany; the collapse of Communism, first in Eastern Europe and then, shockingly, in the USSR itself; Iraq's invasion of Kuwait and the Gulf War—the man whom opponents formerly derided as a wimp now appeared to most Americans like Shakespeare's Julius Caesar, someone who "doth bestride the narrow world like a colossus." At times his Gallup ratings were the highest ever recorded for any president, higher than Dwight D. Eisenhower's, above John F. Kennedy's, even briefly surpassing Franklin D. Roosevelt's. As the joke went round that in 1992 the Democrats were planning to nominate Bush for president and Bentsen for vice president, many of the strongest potential Democratic candidates drew back from even making the race.[12]

Now, of course, the irony is almost vertiginous. But there is more than irony: there is an abiding puzzle. If any proposition commanded universal assent from commentators on all shades of the political spectrum as the 1992 election approached, it was that Republican strategists lucidly understood the importance of the political business cycle to getting reelected; and that in 1992 they would, as they had in 1984 and 1988, make sure that the economy was headed firmly up.

In the end, however, Bush compiled the worst economic record of any president since the end of World War II. The economic upturn that finally materialized was anemic by comparison with past cyclical recoveries. Indeed, down to the very eve of the election, it was all but invisible to the naked eye. For the first time since Carter, arguments that the United States economy faced structural crisis and secular decline became plausible to the average man and woman in—sometimes literally—the street.

On election night, with exit polls showing that the economy far outpaced all other issues as a factor in voters' decisions, virtually everyone could agree that the election was less a triumph for Clinton than a stunning repudiation of Bush.[13] But no very satisfying answer emerged as to why the president's economic record was so uniquely disastrous.

Perhaps the most commonly expressed view was that somehow "George Bush just didn't get it," that he had spent too much time in Washington isolated from voters and real life. More economically sophisticated analysts tried to account for the bungled campaign by pointing to an array of problems allegedly overhanging the economy. Among the most commonly mentioned were the credit crunch, brought on, depending on who was talking, by the comptroller of the currency and other overzealous bank regulators, the Basel Accords regulating bank capitalization standards among the G7, or hypercautious bankers; high import leakages that lower the multipliers from government or consumer spending and thus held down national income; cuts in defense spending; and reluctance by consumers and businesses to borrow while tunneling out from under the mountains of debt run up in the 1980s. Some analysts have also argued that Bush, like Martin Van Buren or Herbert Hoover, who also inherited their mantles from popular incumbents of the same party, was too much the prisoner of a winning political coalition to be able to change course when disaster loomed.[14]

None of these views is foolish. All throw some light on the debacle. But they also abstract seriously from the historically specific concatenation of events and forces that wrecked the administration's hopes for a political business cycle.

The fundamental problem was indeed inherited from Reagan. But unfortunately for public understanding of the 1992 election, no investor bloc, hence no candidate (or, indeed, any commentator within earshot of average Americans) could bring himself or herself to pronounce in public what might be called the "FR" words—"Federal Reserve." Accordingly, only select business and financial circles ever understood the dilemma—or even realized there was one.

The basic difficulty was this: To restrain inflation and force adjustment to a changing world economy both at home and—this was less commonly admitted—abroad, the Reagan administration encouraged Paul Volcker to continue the high interest-rate policy he had inaugurated under Carter. Subsequently, as the gridlock over fiscal policy developed and the budget deficit ballooned, this reliance on monetary policy (code for high-interest rates that crushed aggregate demand) became almost complete.

With the rest of the world growing more slowly than the United States, the high U.S. interest rates attracted enormous inflows of foreign capital and drove up the value of the dollar.[15] This, in turn, made overseas purchases by Americans cheaper and sales to foreign markets more expensive. The already rising tide of imports into the United States swelled enormously while exports fell way off. Because the growing trade deficit put additional crushing pressures on ordinary workers to make concessions to employers if they wanted to work at all, and because the administration hoped to link the rest of the world's economies more closely to the United States (but especially Asia's, whose rate of integration was historically lower), the Reaganites initially not only tolerated but welcomed the trade deficit.

In the long run, however, the trade deficits generated strong protectionist pressures and complaints from exporters. In 1985, the Reagan administration dramatically reversed its celebrated policy of "benign neglect" of the dollar's value. It began cooperating with the rest of the G7 countries to bring down the dollar and reduce the trade imbalances.

From the standpoint of the Reagan-Bush political coalition, however, this amounted to a transit from Scylla to Charybdis. Because dollar devaluation implies a drop in purchasing power, and thus in living standards, it runs a serious risk of igniting struggles in the workplace over wage increases, and thus of "importing inflation." The combined impact of the "double hammer" of high interest rates and growing imports was driving down workers' wages and squeezing unprecedented bargaining concessions from employees, but financial markets, Fed policymakers, and most of the business community warned unceasingly about the dangers of "reigniting" inflation.[16]

Helped mightily by the Japanese Ministry of Finance, which informally pressed Japanese insurance companies and other large bond buyers to keep purchasing (and thus keep the dollar from crashing), Fed Chair Greenspan slowly walked the dollar down in advance of the 1988 election. As it became clear that the recovery would continue through the fall (which was clear long before final campaigning began, because of the long lags through which monetary policy works), Greenspan tightened up again.[17]

Throughout 1989 and 1990, with financial markets as anxious as ever about the slowly falling dollar, Greenspan held rates up to weaken aggregate demand. This tended to moderate the dollar's decline and also to restrain wage demands by tilting the balance of power between labor and management still more in favor of management. In due course, however, the economy slid into recession. As the situation became increasingly tense, a very traditional minuet began between the administration, the Fed, and the business community. As the miserable population fretted and fumed, Greenspan said nothing, Bush said little, and the media reported a jumble of impressions incomprehensible to all but specialists.

The shell game worked, as it usually does in an investor-dominated system. Attention was diverted from the Fed, to the extent that outside of very special circles, accounts of the 1992 election are likely to contain more references to Martin Van Buren than Alan Greenspan.

If it hoped to get the economy moving by 1992, however, the Bush administration knew that it eventually would have to do something to give the Fed more room to ease. In early 1990, it decided to take the bull by the horns. As yet another extension of the Federal debt ceiling loomed, Bush and his advisers moved at last to rein in the ever-swelling deficit.

This issue, like the high dollar, was another characteristic legacy of the Reagan years. Republican administrations had cut civilian spending massively and sought constantly to shift the burden of federal programs to states (which could not afford them, and thus, in the end, would end up killing them or scaling them back). Yet they never succeeded in obtaining reductions on the scale they wanted. Urban real estate interests in the Northeast, Midwest, and a few other areas broke with the administration and helped rally enough Democrats with congressional clout to preserve major spending programs.[18]

The Republican coalition's commitment to military spending, however, was intense. Even multinationals that boasted about the irrelevance of national borders to their businesses entered no such claim about the military force that backed up America's global 911 service. For the dwindling ranks of nationally oriented businesses in the Republican Party that were finding "America First!" an increasingly seductive appeal, the military was also virtually a religious cause. And for the military-industrial complex, itself, of course, "double-entry bookkeeping" had acquired an entirely new meaning: figures representing the federal deficit were simultaneously entries in its profits column.

Accordingly, as the gridlock over the budget deepened in the 1980s, Republican administrations just borrowed and spent. Eventually, they fretted, a day of reckoning would come. Civilian spending would succumb to growing financial pressures. In the meantime, buying weapons helped keep their political coalition together.[19]

Not long after President Bush took over, however, the unbelievable happened: the enemy began to vanish. Though in public the Republicans jubilated, and claimed credit, in private both they and many Democrats worried about pressures for reductions in military spending. Though the response of some of the armed services was truly ingenious—the navy at one point floated the idea of using carrier task forces in the Caribbean for drug interdiction—by 1990 not even the Bush administration could pretend that the United States needed all the military forces it had.

Hoping to open the way for Federal Reserve rate cuts, the administration proposed a budget that included a modest (2.1 percent) reduction in military spending in fiscal 1991 and projected further declines of 2 percent a year in real terms over the next five years. It also suggested further slashes in civilian expenditures. With memories still fresh of Democratic wavering on the issues the year before, the president also pushed for a reduction in capital gains taxes.

Although many administration supporters considered the capital gains issue a matter of the very highest priority, misgivings also ran deep, in and out of the White House. By now it was becoming acutely obvious that more than a decade of Republican economic programs had engineered one of world history's great upward redistributions of income and wealth. Even some stouthearted conservatives were beginning to recall the story of King Midas. On Wall Street there was anxiety about eroding the tax base in the face of continuing high deficits, while some large banks and insurance companies with portfolios full of declining real estate feared a new round of sell-offs by investors who wanted to take their tax gains and run.

Ever since the celebrated "feeding frenzy" that accompanied the first Reagan tax cut, many congressional Democrats, and particularly their leaders, had embraced large parts of the Republican agenda. While sometimes verbally denouncing America's "right turn," most had been more than happy to tap into the streams of cash that all through the 1980s coursed through Washington with almost Gilded Age brazenness. Over the decade, for example, Illinois Congressman Dan Rostenkowski, whose Ways and Means Committee had jurisdiction over tax bills, collected fantastic sums in PAC contributions alone.[20]

1990—A Taxing Problem

Particularly after the 1988 debacle, this richly rewarded acquiescence attracted some notice. Even investment bankers occasionally complained that the Democratic Party no longer stood for anything. Senate Democratic Leader George Mitchell and House Speaker Tom Foley, accordingly, experimented with new tactics. In a preview of the 1992 race itself, they continued unchanged their basic policy of conservative, bipartisan cooperation with the administration—to such an extent that they became the first Democratic leadership team since the New Deal to fail to put forward a jobs program during a major recession. To attract disenchanted Democrats, however, they announced with great fanfare a series of legislative initiatives. Among these were bills mandating unpaid leave for child care and upholding abortion rights, plus a measure forbidding companies to replace striking workers. After sparring with the president and Republican congressional leaders, they would then symbolically try to pass the bills. If they succeeded, the bills would then go to the White House, where they would be vetoed, amid great publicity. Then, somehow, despite lopsided Democratic majorities in both houses, negotiations to pick up enough support to override would fail.[21]

As the administration pushed on the capital gains tax, an almost comic sequence of events handed the Democratic leadership a stunning symbolic victory. Congressional Democratic leaders were known to be sympathetic to reducing capital gains. But when they tried to go along with the president, the rank and file in the chambers rebelled; 134 House Democrats, for example, sent a letter to the speaker insisting on raising taxes on the rich. As a result, positions hardened on all sides.

When the president signalled a willingness to deal by indicating that he might accept a tax increase, his right wing rebelled. In the meantime, the Democrats were slowly waking up to the power of rhetoric about fair taxes. In July, even the conservative Democratic Leadership Council held a press conference to urge a more progressive tax code.

With a Gramm-Rudman deadline for agreement nearing (which would automatically bring across-the-board cuts in spending to meet the deficit reduction act's targets), and the economy sliding into recession, pressures were strong for some kind of agreement on the budget. Democratic leaders and the president reached a compromise that the mass membership on both sides of the aisle disliked for different reasons. Amid cries of treason from every side, the House rejected the measure.

Encouraged by Treasury Secretary Nicholas Brady and Budget Director Richard Darman, President Bush then accepted another compromise bill. This measure gave his political coalition several things that were very useful to it, notably separate budget ceilings for military, international, and domestic spending. By preventing congressional Democrats from shifting between these categories for three years, the provision gave the military a grace period to develop a strategy and organize support to resist budget cuts. But there was a price: not only abandonment of capital gains reduction, but acceptance of a modest rise in taxes that contravened the president's famous "read my lips: no new taxes" pledge at the 1988 GOP Convention.

Conservative contributors raged. House Republicans, led by Newt Gingrich, who had deserted on the earlier budget compromise, sputtered angrily. In the meantime, Democratic leaders, who had first been pushed left by their members and then discovered that they liked it, gleefully pounced. They accused Republicans of trying to wage class war. In the midterm elections, Bush took what was generally regarded as a drubbing.

Ever since, any number of interested parties have found it in their interests to promote the view that the president's breach of his fiscal promise all but sealed his fate in 1992. This is pure propaganda. Only 14 percent of voters polled in the 1992 presidential election selected taxes as the leading issue in deciding whom to vote for. To most of the electorate, other economic issues—notably, growth—mattered far more at a time when the economy was doing poorly indeed. A great deal of other evidence also suggests that while Americans do not like taxes, particularly increases in taxes to pay for what they perceive to be government programs that do not work, the tax issue can only dominate voters' calculations if the opposition party allows it to do so by default—generally by failing to make any kind of counterappeal. (It was just such a counterappeal, of course, that the conservative investor blocs that dominated the Democrats in the 1980s would not permit.)[22]

Considering the 1990 recession—and the president's reluctance to do anything but deplore it—it was no surprise that the electorate in the off-year congressional elections registered acute dissatisfaction. This would have occurred with or without the violation of the "no new taxes" pledge. Indeed, from a purely electoral viewpoint, Bush's elephantine efforts to cut capital gains taxes probably turned off at least as many voters as the duties finally slapped on liquor, tobacco, motor fuel, yachts, etc. in the budget compromise. The shallowness of the whole episode in the face of policy success became obvious a few months later, as the president broke all records for popularity in the wake of the Gulf War.

From Bush's own perspective, accordingly, there was no reason to consider the wound mortal. Limits on the deficit, which the 1990 Budget Enforcement Act appeared at the time to have provided, were a precondition for easing by the Fed in time for the 1992 election. The coast, it could reasonably be believed, was now clear.

What, then, went wrong?

It is doubtful that the usual litany of potential factors contribute much to answering this question. Whatever the causes—shrinking money and credit multipliers; lower spending multipliers; oil prices; war worries; and anomalous economic statistics arising from the Gulf War, or from cuts in defense spending—such factors could not fail to be noticed, given the long stretch of time (more than a year). Indeed, they eventually were noticed, triggering a torrent of anxious discussion. So were the deleterious effects on American exports of the ill-fated European effort to maintain parities in the European Exchange Rate Mechanism after German Chancellor Helmut Kohl's decision to conceal the true costs of German reunification from German voters.

Of course, the Fed almost certainly was taken by surprise at the slowness with which the economy responded. Everybody was. But with time to collect their thoughts, many critics saw what needed to be done. So did Greenspan. And while he always remained constrained by the problems of a depreciating currency—which in its last stages may have included modest threats of a flight from the dollar—he did bring rates steadily down, albeit in almost imperceptible steps. In December 1991, he sent the man who had recently reappointed him a handsome present, cutting the discount rate a full point just before Christmas.[23]

By then the White House, and many others, knew there might be a problem. And they responded. To make sure reluctant consumers had the wherewithal to buy, Bush issued an executive order reducing for one year the amount of income taxes withheld. He also accelerated spending on federal projects. Then he challenged Congress to enact a new budget package within two months that included a cut in capital gains, a tax break for first-time homebuyers, higher tax exemptions for children, and even some spending increases. Though the president also sought long-term cuts in the deficit, it is clear what was on the White House's mind. The package as a whole would surely have provided a short-run stimulus.

It was here that the campaign came fatally apart, for reasons that had far more to do with investor blocs within the GOP than any straight calculation about votes in the fall. Just as they had in 1990, Democratic leaders demanded that the president pay for a stimulus by increasing taxes on the affluent. This time, however, Bush dared not even contemplate such a step. Not because he would gain votes by sticking to his guns (particularly after the Democrats had had time to "educate" voters, capital gains reductions in particular certainly figured to be a net vote loser, though a first-time credit for homebuyers might have been a winner from the standpoint of both politics and economics), but because the political situation had changed drastically. Whereas in 1990 the president could afford to bypass the angry conservatives of the GOP, now the massive bloc of conservative investors prepared to go to the wall over this issue (including investment banker Theodore Forstmann, supply-side guru Jude Wanniski, and any number of other stalwarts at the Heritage Foundation and other policy organizations) had someone else to throw their money and organizational resources behind.

That someone was not Pat Buchanan, who appears to have attracted only a handful of really major investors, but Ross Perot, of whom more shortly.[24] For the present it is necessary only to round off the fatal details. Forced to stand firm, the president did. So did the congressional Democrats, who offered a "middle-class" tax cut of their own in time for Bush's March deadline. This the president vetoed. Thereafter, he would not—because he could not—accept the congressional Democrats' proposals, and they had no reason to budge on his. Thus ended all hope of fiscal stimulus.

In the late spring of 1992, another heavy blow jolted the president's reelection campaign. As any number of studies have observed, all through the eighties (and, of course, long before), the Republicans had shrewdly used racial appeals to help split a minority of white middle- and working-class voters—mostly males—away from the Democrats. (Few of these studies, however, acknowledge that to work, this strategy required that investor blocs in the Democratic Party veto strong cross-cutting economic appeals. Most also exaggerate the number of voters actually so influenced.)[25] Bush's nomination of the exiguously qualified Clarence Thomas to the Supreme Court the previous year suggested that in 1992 the Republicans would be up to their old tricks.

At the end of April, however, long-smoldering racial and ethnic frustrations burst into flames amid the collapsing California economy. Following the acquittal of four police officers who had been videotaped beating black motorist Rodney King, a genuinely multiracial riot broke out in Los Angeles. Over the next few weeks, disturbances flared in many more cities. While there were signs of a backlash, in the main the public response was exactly what most studies of race and politics would *not* have predicted: For all the clashing perceptions about the incidence of discrimination and attitudes toward integration, most of the public, regardless of race, recoiled from the videotape of the beating. They considered the verdicts unjust, and generally favored action to improve race relations and conditions in cities. Most also considered jobs more important than more police for coping with the problem.[26]

Though the president did his best to make subliminal appeals, Perot, if not Clinton, was highly critical of Bush's lack of leadership and unwillingness to take responsibility. The media and many other audiences were also antagonistic to the president's feeble response. In the new climate, Willie Horton ads no longer were socially acceptable. Bush had lost perhaps his most important remaining electoral card.

By then, anyone could see that the Bush campaign was in difficulty. Gradually, what no one would have believed a year before was becoming plausible: that George Bush might be pushed from power before Saddam Hussein was.

Many commentators—indeed, probably most of them—remained dubious, however. They could not really bring themselves to believe what they were seeing—and there was plenty to justify their skepticism. The likely Democratic nominee was actually running third in the spring polls, and he appeared extraordinarily vulnerable to one of the Republican Party's patented "character" assaults. And though Perot increasingly loomed as a real threat, the consensus was that he, like John Anderson before him, was destined to wilt in the summer's heat. In the meantime, Bush remained the incumbent, able to shape events, dispense patronage, and raise campaign funds.

In regard to raising campaign funds, at least, the president was as yet in no trouble at all. At that time, the great bulk of American business, in particular a cross-section of America's multinational giants, still remained firmly behind him. Analyzed systematically, as in table 6.1, the extent of the president's support across an entire sample of major contributors was breathtaking: 55 percent of all the firms contributed—and this method of counting leaves noncontributors in. Much of this money came in very early. Indeed, in a special survey of early money (received before December 31, 1991) that I undertook in the spring of 1992 (not shown here), almost a fifth of the sample had already contributed to Bush's reelection campaign—a truly remarkable rate, considering that far and away the most money piles up as the primaries actually get under way. No other candidate was even close. Clinton, who clearly came next in the affections of this group of major investors, then trailed far behind, while Buchanan—the president's opponent in the GOP primaries—barely registered.[27]

To most members of this "golden horde"—top executives in oil companies (such as Exxon, Amoco, Chevron, Arco, Occidental, Pennzoil and many Texas independents), international banks (Chase, Chemical/Manufacturers Hanover), many investment houses (Morgan Stanley, Merrill Lynch, Nomura Securities, Shearson) and a long list of manufacturing, food and defense companies (General Electric, IBM, Motorola, Rockwell, Corning, Texas Instruments, Martin Marietta, Coca-Cola, Pepsico, Johnson & Johnson, AT&T, McDonnell Douglas, GM, and—this was after all, late spring—Ford and even Chrysler), plus many utilities and service companies—the president's goals remained the right ones: global integration of markets for goods, capital, and, much more quietly, people; and preserving America as sole superpower and principal leader of the "new world order", with only the most modest tempering of laissez faire at home.

Firms in sectors facing a variety of quite specific problems were also generous contributors. Among these were companies and executives in the insurance and pharmaceutical industries, where the threat of national health care was urgent, as well as those in the chemical industry, where environmental pressures were acute.[28] To top executives from these and many other firms in the spring of 1992, Bush may no longer have looked like a certain bet, but he still looked like their best one.

TABLE 6.1. Party and Industry in the 1992 Election ($N = 948$)

Percentage of Firms Contributing to	
Bush Campaign	55%
Clinton Campaign	21%

Source: Calculated from data from Federal Election Commission.

Note: Includes individual contributions, soft money, and PAC donations through the last week of October 1992.

A VERY EXPENSIVE PARTY

To understand the 1992 Democratic campaign and the new Clinton administration, it is essential to realize that the *Nightly Business Report's* "handwriting on the wall" episode (discussed in the introduction to this book) was a culminating moment in a process that stretched back over a decade: the effort by center-right business groups to remake the party in the wake of the triumph of Reaganism. Though the first stirrings of this effort trace back to the Carter years, the most striking shifts occurred after the 1980 debacle.[29]

At that time—and subsequently, for this "right turn" had to be reconfirmed at every election—Democratic leaders could have tried to rally the millions of middle-class and poor Americans who were about to suffer the economic reverses that the party, in a vastly different context, was at last willing to discuss in the 1992 campaign. They could have tried, for example, to explain to voters what Reaganomics was really all about: the years of high interest rates and austerity that the President's policies would entail; the massive export of American jobs that loomed; the steady deterioration of schools, roads, and services that would ensue; the demoralization, crime, and drugs that would mushroom in big cities and, eventually, in whole regions; the true costs of deregulating not only savings and loans, but airlines and the banking system; or the swelling tide of money that would corrupt all levels of government and overwhelm other forms of political participation.

For the most part, Democratic Party leaders did not even try to sound these warnings. Instead, as they contemplated the real estate boom around Washington and the skyrocketing compensation of America's corporate managers, they decided to compete with the Republicans for funds. Amid much flatulent oratory about finding a "third way" between New Deal and Great Society liberalism (whose programs and formulas certainly needed updating), and facing what was then a newly self-confident Republican conservatism, the entire spectrum of respectable discussion in the party lurched to the right.[30]

In 1984 and 1988, the Democratic Party's strategy for the presidential race turned on the pursuit of investor blocs disenchanted by one or another feature of Reaganomics: In 1984, investment bankers critical of the deficit (led, among others, by two New Yorkers named Robert Rubin and Roger Altman, who flew out to Minnesota to press Walter Mondale on the issue shortly before his ill-fated pledge to raise voters' taxes) and of Reaganite talk of abolishing or weakening Roosevelt's Glass-Steagall Act (which separated investment from commercial banking) flocked to the party. So did urban real estate interests (centered mostly in the Northeast and Midwest), whose needs for continuing federal aid for mass transit and the infrastructure put them at log-gerheads with the Pentagon over a share of the budget.[31]

In 1988, this conservative, business-led, but not Republican coalition widened appreciably, as the investment bankers and real estate interests were joined by many high-tech and other businesses still in favor of free trade but increasingly edgy about administration policies that allowed the Japanese to run massive trade surpluses year after year.[32]

At the same time, the party was also restructuring its relations with its (former) mass base. The most critical of these efforts involved its ties with organized labor. In the early 1980s, Democratic National Committee Chair Charles Manatt worked out an understanding with the AFL-CIO that guaranteed labor continued representation within the DNC apparatus. Despite criticism from some business elements in the party, this arrangement survived. In due course came another momentous shift. Congressional Democrats, with timely bipartisan assistance from influential Republicans, applied an old tactic—business and government subsidies to amiably inclined elements of the labor movement—on a grandiose scale. Through the National Endowment for Democracy and other government agencies, enormous subsidies flowed to union leaders for foreign activities associated with the cold war. By the mid-1980s, the AFL-CIO was spending over $40 million a year on foreign activities, a sum almost equal to its total domestic budget. Approximately 90 percent of this money came from the U.S. government. Revenues on this scale virtually ensure that AFL-CIO membership losses can continue for decades before the leadership will have to face the problem, in sharp contrast to the thirties, when declines in dues-paying members helped squeeze several reluctant union leaders to split from the rest of the moribund and corrupt AFL and organize the CIO.[33]

The party leadership also confirmed a long-standing pattern of trying to organize other potential mass political constituents—African-Americans, Hispanics and Latinos, women, even environmentalists—along almost Balkan lines. An earlier coauthored work traced in some detail how in the late seventies, these emerging social movements restructured in response to the combined pressures of financial exigencies, selective press coverage, and political patronage. What had started out as grassroots social movements were now developing more complex organizational structures. At the top were legally incorporated, hierarchically structured institutions dependent for their functioning on expensive lawyers, foundation grants, and steady political patronage. Increasingly tending to define the very real problems of their constituencies in conservative, market-oriented terms, the leaders of most of these institutions rarely even considered strategies such as attempting to raise the incomes of the vast majority of underpaid African-Americans, Latinos, or women by unionizing them. Instead they sought to function as junior partners, or often even paid advisers, to businesses and the Democratic Party. Frequently they refrained from even verbal condemnations of the party's commitment to economic austerity.[34]

Given the party's decision to pursue money, there was no chance of developing a message that would excite a mass audience. The formally organized constituency groups, accordingly, were of immense value to the party. By selectively doing business with their leaders, the Democrats could practice a sort of symbolic mass politics. By drawing on the energies of their core members, the party would acquire an ersatz mass base to replace the millions of voters it was abandoning.

There was a downside: Because the leaders of these groups held back from criticizing the party's conservative macroeconomic policies, their own demands for more access and positions could easily be made to look purely self-interested (which, when divorced from any critical stance toward common problems, they often were). In the money-driven American political system, public attacks by rival financial groups partake of the logic of a nuclear exchange between superpowers. They are, accordingly, rare, and "proxy" wars or symbolic political struggles between the respective "mass" clientele groups fill most of the political universe. As a consequence, Republicans and right-wing Democrats could fan immense resentment by talking as though, for example, the clientele groups, rather than the party, were breaking all records for fundraising or had pushed Mondale to make his fatal promise to raise taxes. Also, to the extent that any of these groups preserved any real links with their base, they remained a potential obstacle that could, on occasion, prove startlingly inconvenient. Still, a party had at least to look like it wanted a mass base, and these groups were all the Democrats had. If the party was to advance the cause favored by its less conservative business leadership, organizing anything else normally ran too many risks, even promoting voter registration, as opposed to promoting carefully targeted drives to get out the vote of the already registered.

In the wake of the 1984 election, many of the party's business interests reckoned that the cost of dealing with several of these groups—notably organized labor (whose pre-primary endorsement, along with those of many business groups, of Mondale upset many conservatives), Jesse Jackson's "rainbow coalition," and various defense and foreign policy groups (including some which intermittently claimed strong business support)—was still too high. They, accordingly, organized a new group to push the party even further to the right. Calling itself the Democratic Leadership Council, the group was led in public mostly by Southern politicians. No one, however, should be fooled: it was financed extensively from New York—not least by investment houses—and by defense concerns and utilities.[35]

The subsequent rise of Clinton has focused a great deal of attention on the DLC. While easy to understand, this impulse is perhaps misleading. In all probability, the thunder and lightning—such as the practice of in effect auctioning off places at its convention to corporate lobbyists—drew more attention to the storm than it deserved. As the 1988 race quickly demonstrated, there were few, if any, real conflicts of interest between the national party and the DLC. Not only had the national party long been self-consciously moving right, but in the mid-1980s, the wonderful world of "soft money" opened up for it. Soft money—donations given nominally to state and local parties for purposes unconnected to federal races, but that are in fact closely connected to national parties and particularly to presidential campaigns—was completely unregulated at the federal level until 1991. At that time, the Federal Election Commission (FEC) decided that whatever was spent had to be reported. State regulation was, as ever, minimal. Not surprisingly, affluent Americans and corporations quickly seized on this loophole to eviscerate laws regulating the size of campaign contributions. Contributions of $100,000 or more were common. The result was evident in the 1988 election. Michael Dukakis selected as his running mate Lloyd Bentsen, whose fundraising prowess qualified him as the six-million-dollar-man of American politics—and ran essentially even with the fabled Bush money machine in total funds raised.

Following the 1988 loss, Ron Brown took over the DNC. Dissolving the doubts of skeptics, who initially suspected the Patton, Boggs & Blow partner of sharing Jackson's goals, Brown worked closely with congressional Democratic leaders and business groups to help raise millions of dollars for the party, and many millions more in soft money.[36]

These efforts coincided with a series of economic changes that had major effects on one of the Democrats' core constituencies in the 80s: real estate. Such changes included the collapse of real estate values in some parts of the country, the increasingly hopeless conditions of many major cities, and the lagged effects of 1986 Tax Act, which eliminated several important real estate tax breaks. Amid signals by the Bush administration that it might be open to restoring some of the tax breaks and moves by leading American developers into Europe (which assuredly changes their calculation regarding the potential role of military force and the optimal configuration of U.S. budget), major real estate interests began backing out of the party. As those interests were the heart of the Democrats' "fairness" coalition, all mention of this virtue vanished from the Democratic Party vocabulary, along with most references to the poor or to cities.[37]

THE 1992 CAMPAIGN

Though an almost invisible seam perhaps remained in regard to organized labor, by 1992 the biggest remaining difference between the DNC and the DLC may well have been the middle initials. Ron Brown had an easy time (and many allies) in persuading Jackson not to run. No Democratic leader rose to rebuke him for his harsh attacks on Jerry Brown's criticisms of money's role in American politics. On at least some occasions, the party appears also to have sought to charge poor farm groups for the right to address the Democratic platform committee.[38]

The collapse of the real estate constituency within the Democratic Party (note that the discussion is in reference to interests comparable to those on the Forbes 400 list of richest Americans; smaller fry are of course scattered everywhere among the FEC contributor lists) explains why the truly sophisticated response to Nebraska Senator Bob Kerrey's celebrated retort in the primaries to Jerry Brown—"Are you saying that I am bought and paid for?"—might well be, in the end: "No—and so much the worse for your campaign."

Of all the Democratic primary candidates, Kerrey's pattern of contributions from the sample of top business figures I analyzed most resembles Mondale's or Dukakis's: knots of urban real estate magnates, investment bankers (including, according to one newspaper account, Volcker, by then at J. D. Wolfensohn & Co.), a handful of oilmen, plus some Hollywood figures. There just weren't enough of these types, however, to float a mild center-left campaign with a serious thrust on health care—an issue guaranteed to bring down on the head of anyone who raised it a mass of well-financed objurgation. As a consequence, Kerrey looked around hastily for other issues to emphasize, and made the fatal choice of international trade. While also popular with voters, who at that time favored restricting imports of foreign consumer products by such margins as 71 percent to 22 percent (with 7 percent having no answer or no opinion), the issue was a core concern of multinational industry and finance in both parties.[39] Amid another fusillade of bad press notices, Kerrey began flailing. On some days he dramatized himself as a quasi-protectionist hockey goalie; on another, a free-trader (who lets the puck go by?), and so on. The campaign collapsed, leaving behind a large debt.

Iowa Senator Tom Harkin's campaign appears to have been another that suffered from the collapse of the realtors' bloc within the party. In the very earliest stages of the race, prominent developers within the party touted his candidacy. Their support, however, never materialized (one initially vocal developer whose contributions I made a special effort to trace turned up as a contributor to Massachusetts Senator Paul Tsongas and Clinton, raising the question of whether the true aim of the early talk about Harkin was not to weaken New York Governor Mario Cuomo by tempting another perceived liberal into the race).

Harkin compounded his difficulty by making two grave mistakes. First, as some critics promptly noted, while the Iowa-based head of one of the largest insurance companies in the United States and other industry executives contributed to the campaign, Harkin dodged the health-care issue that Senator Kerrey so bravely raised.

Second, the candidate and his staff confused running a campaign with holding a seance. That is, in 1992, it was simply not enough to invoke the shade of Roosevelt (or, more precisely, of "traditional Democratic values"), or even to assure voters what a study of Harkin's career readily confirms: that, save perhaps on insurance-related issues, the Iowa liberal was indeed "on the side of" average Americans. To reach an increasingly jaundiced electorate requires not indirect discourse, symbols, etc., but plainspoken efforts to pound away on the handful of major issues that really matter to people—as, in different ways, Jerry Brown, Tsongas, and Perot all did later in the campaign.

Harkin, however, usually confined himself to an inside game increasingly dependent on the official union movement, which is now widely unpopular even with its own members. The PAC support that Tsongas criticized him for in the early primaries never amounted to much, with the result that Harkin had almost no money to transmit his unstable and somewhat Aesopian message. (It cannot have helped that the first primary outside of his home state occurred in one of the most strongly anti-union states in the country.) Around the time he withdrew, 75 percent of the population were telling pollsters that they didn't know enough about him to have an opinion.[40]

Running out of money, by contrast, was one problem that Clinton never had to face. Like Dukakis four years before, but unlike Mondale, the Arkansas governor began the race with strong support from businesses in his own state, including Tyson Foods, Murphy Oil, Wal-Mart (where his wife Hillary sat on the board and whose owners, the Walton family, were almost all campaign contributors); giant Beverly Enterprises, a large private provider of health care; and the investment banking, oil, and gas interests associated with the Stephens family.

It may be sheer coincidence that back in 1976 the latter were also close to Carter as he began his run for the White House. But the Clinton campaign's striking resemblance to the earlier Carter effort—in which a moderate conservative (former) member of the Trilateral Commission with some well-disciplined center-left humanitarian impulses ran from the periphery of America, supported by internationally oriented investment bankers and their allies in Wall Street, Washington, and the press—was certainly not accidental.

In 1992, however, most of American business was far more conservative than it had been in 1976, when, it should be recalled, the much more liberal Morris Udall could find important business supporters in addition to his labor backing. As a consequence, Clinton's candidacy centered far more on investment bankers than Carter's did.

Partners from giant Goldman, Sachs, for example (which, with the cloud that settled over Salomon Brothers now ranks as probably the strongest of all the investment houses), were among the earliest to begin raising funds for Clinton. Members of the firm—whose leading figure, Rubin, once compared the Glass-Steagall Act to the Magna Carta, only half in jest—contributed far more than $100,000 to the campaign (while, of course, raising many times that). Another early fund-raiser among investment bankers was Altman, vice chair of the Blackstone Group, who had known Clinton in college and who is reported to have renewed ties after encountering Hillary Rodham Clinton on the board of the Children's Television Workshop, producer of the highly acclaimed *Sesame Street*. Peter Peterson, chair of Blackstone (and husband of Joan Cooney, chair of the executive committee of the Children's Television Workshop), was another early contributor. So were many other prominent investment bankers from Greenwich Capital Resources and other large houses.[41]

With the obvious, though very important, exception of Glass-Steagall and related financial regulatory legislation, such interests differ only marginally from the internationalists at the core of the Bush coalition with respect to either foreign or domestic policy. More than a few, including Goldman and Blackstone, have Japanese partners (though Sumitomo, Goldman's partner, holds only a minority stake). Together with the myriad of Washington lobbyists for U.S. and foreign multinationals who contributed heavily to the campaign (and honeycombed the campaign organization), these interests virtually guaranteed what in any case rapidly became obvious: that the Clinton campaign accepted free trade and an open world economy as its fundamental strategic premise.

Though only someone aware of Georgia Senator Sam Nunn's early endorsement of Clinton's efforts, or paying close attention to the striking contributions rolling in from aircraft and other defense producers could be sure of the fact at the time, the campaign also fully accepted what the foreign policy community likes to call the "responsibilities" that go with being the world's only superpower.[42] (Indeed, by convention time, the Clinton camp was actually leapfrogging the Republicans in this regard, with volleys of neo-Wilsonian rhetoric suggesting that the Bush administration, which after all, averaged an armed intervention nearly every 12 months or so in office, was not aggressive enough in promoting freedom, human rights, and democracy around the world.)

THE CLINTON DIFFERENCE

What, then, distinguished the Clinton effort from the multinationally oriented Bush administration? At first glance, the response seems clear: Not much. But this is too clever by half. If one examines the data presented in table 6.2's analysis of sectors contributing disproportionately to the Clinton campaign in the light of the campaign's rhetoric and proposed policy initiatives, an interesting pattern emerges. With one exception, the sectors that disproportionately backed Clinton appear to share several characteristics. On one hand, like the mainline multinationals that dominated the Bush coalition, they support an open world economy. On the other hand, in contrast to the "borderless world" celebrants on the Republican side, they all have some direct, crucial tie that links them closely to the American state. The aircraft companies clearly depend on the government in an almost unique way; but almost equally apparent are the ties to government of the investment houses (whose Glass-Steagall privileges are currently up for grabs in the negotiations over foreign banking rights that are part of the ongoing GATT negotiations); the oil and gas industry (note, however, that this was one campaign that probably ran on gas, rather than oil: Clinton's Texas campaign managers were openly promoting the "clean-burning" fuel, and the candidate himself had a fairly long record on this point);[43] transportation; and tobacco (where the sample size is very small).

One might well ask about the utilities industry, which is not listed in the table, but which certainly has a peculiarly strong dependence on the state. Here reality may be sending a message: By conventional standards, the results for utilities (29 percent and $N = 31$, with a .28 level of significance) just miss qualifying for the table. This is one industry that may in fact be affected by the data in the FEC's final report, which has been delayed, and will not be available for some time. As a practical matter, I have reckoned it as a part of Clinton's coalition at least since he added Al Gore to the ticket. In my 1988 study, support for

Gore's presidential bid from this sector was strong, and the Tennessee senator has long been identified with technological issues of concern to the telecommunications industry and utilities.[44]

The one instance where the question of state dependence appears to break down, what table 6.2 refers to as "capital-intensive exporters" (my portmanteau term for an industry which includes Xerox, Honeywell, Kodak, and similar firms), is an exception that proves the rule. These are clearly firms that in several cases (Xerox, Kodak) have made strenuous and sometimes noisy efforts to reinvent themselves in the face of foreign (usually Japanese) competitors. They are rather obviously looking for an ally in the Clinton administration to help with both subsidies and market penetration problems.

All of this is to say that the Clinton coalition is exactly what several of the executives interviewed on the *Nightly Business Report* indicated it was: a bloc of businesses that are prepared to countenance a cautious public rejection of laissez faire because they need the American state to work. Given the exceptional dependence of their businesses upon that state, they cannot simply go somewhere else if the relative decline of the United States in the current world economy continues unabated.

In the best-known cases of industrial support for Clinton, calculations along these lines were clearly operative. Because table 6.2 refers to large firms and relies on sectoral assignments that are derived from

TABLE 6.2. Industries Significantly Above the Mean in Support of Clinton (for the mean, see table 6.1)

Tobacco $N=4$	50% (.20*)
Oil and gas $N=65$	28% (.18)
Capital-intensive exporters $N=7$	43% (.17*)
Aircraft $N=13$	54% (.00*)
Computers $N=16$	38% (.12*)
Transportation $N=33$	33% (.08)
Investment banking $N=50$	46% (.00)

Source: Computed from FEC data; see text.

Notes: Figures in parentheses are significance levels. Note text caution about utilities industry (not shown above).

*Expected value of cell in chi-square less than 5 is warning of low power. Significance levels reported in such cases are results of Fisher's Exact text.

the Commerce Department's standard industrial classification series, it does not contain an entry for "high technology." Thus no statistics in the table directly reflect the collective endorsement of Clinton by John Young of Hewlett-Packard, Sculley of Apple Computer, and other leading figures in the industry. (The entry for computers assures us that we are not seeing ghosts, but the fit is not perfect.) These business executives expressly rejected claims by critics in and out of the Bush administration that all would be well if everything were left to the invisible hand. Indeed, in the mid-eighties, after the Reagan administration declined to press ahead on recommendations for a more active role for the government in what has come to be known as "industrial policy," Young, who had chaired a special blue-ribbon President's Commission on Industrial Competitiveness, complained. When the administration still declined to move, Young and like-minded chief executive officers established their own privately funded Council on Competitiveness to promote their ideas for change in business-government relations. (One of the consultants they hired was Ira Magaziner, viewed by most of the business community as a virtual Jacobin, and a prominent supporter of Clinton for President. Eventually, of course, a large section of the high-tech industry came noisily over to the cause of the Arkansas governor.)[45]

The Clinton campaign's now-celebrated interest in "managed trade" and in more aggressive efforts to pry open foreign markets echoed proposals recently advanced by many of these firms.[46] Certain parts of the computer industry are thoroughly transnational, to the point of agitating against national actions in favor of the industry. But other sections of it and related industries, including (portions of) semiconductors and most of the software industry, have concerns that only coordinated action on a truly large scale can relieve. Many firms, for example, view themselves as pitted against "Japan, Inc." Up against what they perceive as the resources of an entire country, these producers strongly champion the view that laissez faire is obsolete. Many, in addition, believe that timely government action (for example, on education) would also assist their industries by widening their markets or improving the skills of their workforce. As is discussed later, software producers, in addition, are acutely aware that the position of English as a worldwide second language (and thus the world's premier software language) is bound up with the long-term position of the United States in the world economy.

In sharp contrast to firms in older industries such as steel or textiles, however, most of these firms actively import components. Often they also sell abroad, so that they continue to distrust high tariff policies. At the Little Rock economic summit in December 1992, for example, Sculley, a strong promoter of both Clinton and "competitive-ness" initiatives (as such industrial policy initiatives are now frequently styled), flatly ruled out protectionism.[47] But with the continuing growth of the Japanese trade surplus and the persisting over-valuation of the dollar relative to the rest of Asia, these firms and many others increasingly have come to accept the practical necessity for managing trade with the export-oriented economies of that re-gion, especially Japan's. They also want what the Clinton campaign promised to give them: substantial programs of government subsidies through existing cabinet departments, and a civilian counterpart to the Defense Department's Defense Advanced Research Projects Agency (DARPA).

As far back as 1984, carefully superintended programs along these lines were winning acceptance from prominent Democratic invest-ment bankers. By now, few on the top rungs of American business, or in the military, dispute that economics is as vital to national security as any defense treaty or military base. Within the part of the business community that was sympathetic to Clinton (and a few other candi-dates who raised similar issues), there is also curiosity about the advan-tages of "organized capitalism" on (what is imagined to be) the German or Japanese model. To these groups, Clinton's promise of an "economic security council" (as the new National Economic Council was referred to during the campaign) on a par with the National Security Council appeared about as dangerously radical as the program to restructure the U.S. military advanced by Clinton's early champion, Nunn. And the celebrated Clinton tax proposals, calling for a small rise in their taxes, looked more like political cover for new programs that would benefit them, first and foremost.[48]

Few Americans, however, are familiar with the strong, top-down state structures evolved by foreign business groups to catch up with their more advanced rivals in the Anglo-Saxon countries. As a conse-quence, all many Americans could see in these and similar proposals was the break with laissez faire.

To hard-pressed voters, who knew little and understood even less about Greenspan or the Fed, but who were increasingly anxious about the maddeningly slow pace of the economic recovery and saw all around them signs that the United States was secularly declining in the world economy, all this meant only one thing: relief, something at last that would benefit the average person.

This was a perception that the Clinton campaign fanned assidu-ously by all sorts of devices. In the campaign it put out front not Rubin or Altman, but a flock of liberal former Vietnam-era protesters destined for second-tier slots in the administration (or no positions at all). For a long time the Clinton camp also talked around the fact that their candidate had flatly rejected a proposal advanced by more than 100 economists for a temporary two-year job creation bill, while excitedly promising that the candidate would boost economic growth in the long run by increasing public investment in education, the infrastructure, and the environment. (Eventually, as even some bond traders began calling for a modest stimulus, Clinton relented. The issue was used with telling effect against Bush in the fall campaign. After the election, as already noted, it was scaled back almost to the vanishing point and then defeated in the Senate.)

The candidate and his economic advisers put out an economic plan filled with optimistic figures suggesting that Clinton could halve the deficit in his first term while implementing a tax cut for the middle class. They also promised to somehow reform the health-care system, while, as is discussed below, collecting substantial campaign contributions from parts of it. And—very quietly—the Clinton campaign lined up with trial attorneys, whose campaign to stop tort reform is now running in high—and very expensive—gear.

This set of appeals was probably the most brazen conflation of electoral *Dichtung* and investor bloc *Wahrheit* since "read my lips," but it worked. In the beginning, when he trailed far behind, for example, Jerry Brown in the Gallup polls, Clinton was built up massively by most of the press.[49]

In Clinton's one moment of maximum danger—the Gennifer Flowers scandal—the combination of money and favorable press coverage, along with the Clintons' own TV performance, saved the day. With their candidate on the ropes, investment bankers from Goldman and other houses organized a gigantic dinner at the Sheraton in New York only a few days before the New Hampshire primary. The affair raised more than $750,000. No less importantly, as one investment banker observed, "that dinner signaled to a lot of people that some very smart money was behind him. It was critical to Clinton's campaign."[50] In sharp contrast to the treatment meted out to Gary Hart, all but the yellow press put the story behind it, while proclaiming that a second-place finish would keep Clinton viable.

Clinton's strategy for winning the Democratic primaries ultimately came down to a financial counterpart of the Russian strategy that turned back Napoleon: Just keep spending, until your opponents run out of money.

Sometimes, the resulting irony was almost painful. Tsongas, for example, entered the race as a self-declared "pro-business liberal." If one wanted a tag line for this effort, one could do worse than to sum it up as the Route 128 view of American politics. Both the campaign's definition of America's economic problems and the most controversial parts of its proposed solutions (along with much of its early money that wasn't raised from ethnic Greek businesses) originated from around the famous high-technology highway.

Tsongas himself had served as a director of a number of major New England concerns. Among these were Boston Edison and several high-tech firms, including Wang Labs and one subsidiary of the highly regarded Thermo Electron, founded by George Hatsapoulos, the Greek-American MIT graduate who was then serving as vice chair of the American Business Conference.

Hatsapoulos has produced a stream of papers (some coauthored with Summers and Paul Krugman of MIT) on the cost of capital as a factor in U.S. economic growth. In the campaign, Tsongas said often enough that he took the capital problem very seriously. A capital gains tax cut for long-term holdings was the remedy he proposed, along with a further tilt by government in the direction of business, a sharp reduction of the federal deficit, and sweeping education reforms.

By the usual standards of American politics all this should have resulted in a shower of money for his campaign. But it did not, for the simple reason that Clinton had already cornered the market. After what was usually said to be a surprise victory in New Hampshire (although Tsongas had been campaigning in the state for almost a year and, by concentrating his funds on a neighboring state where he was already well known, was not badly outspent), his campaign coffers were almost empty. Though some money streamed in, he had to scramble to line up TV in the big multistate media buyouts in the South and Midwest. Clinton, with most party organizations already behind him, in the meantime unrolled the mighty bankroll. As donations from major investors in my sample poured into his campaign, the Arkansas governor denounced Tsongas in almost populist tones as unsympathetic to ordinary Americans, an enemy of social security, and an advocate of a regressive gas tax. Tsongas's efforts collapsed, and turnout generally declined. Those blue-collar workers, African-Americans and lower-income voters who did vote cast ballots for their "champion," Bill Clinton.[51]

That left only Jerry Brown. To the amazement of virtually everyone, Brown, whose refusal to take donations larger than $100 was driving party leaders to distraction, gamely hung on.[52] In Michigan, the leadership of the United Auto Workers union (though not all locals) lined up behind Clinton, who favored the North American Free Trade Agreement that the union opposed. Brown, who opposed the pact, pointed up the hollowness of Clinton's populism and did well. In Connecticut, he briefly panicked the establishments of both parties by winning.

The showdown came in the New York primary. Here Clinton's money afforded him almost complete domination of the airwaves. This turned out to be decisive when Brown began promoting a regressive "flat tax" plan that he appears to have hoped would win him plaudits on the right. Instead, Clinton focused his attack on the plan, thus positioning himself once again to Brown's left. The media played along. While the *New York Times* did eventually affort Brown's plan some less than dismissive notice, that mostly came long after the primary. Before the primary, however, the *Times* had very little good to say; indeed, it had surely been many years since the *New York Times* had been so solicitous about the progressivity of income taxes.[53]

Clinton's victory in New York effectively clinched the nomination. Almost up to convention time, however, rumors ran rife that one or another Democrat was considering an eleventh-hour challenge. By then, however, the big story was no longer the Democratic opponent to George Bush but the astounding emergence of a serious new challenger. In the most remarkable development of all in a year of surprises, an overwhelming historical force—$3.5 billion—had suddenly materialized from out of the Southwest.

A Truly Private Party

Not surprisingly, conventional political analysts, face to face with the truly unconventional, have had trouble coming to terms with Ross Perot. Most have repeatedly seized on almost any excuse to avoid taking him seriously. In July of 1992, when he first pulled out of a race he had never officially entered, many wrote him off as a lightweight with a heavyweight bankroll, a gadfly with no staying power. Others took him more seriously—but only as a threat: as Ross Peron, the man who would be king; Hercule Perot, P.I.; or simply (as one veteran Pentagon official delicately phrased it), a "Fascist."[54]

As he reentered the race in October, with his poll ratings in single digits, most pundits laughed. After he stole the show in the debates and finished with 19 percent of the total vote (after Theodore Roosevelt in 1912, the strongest showing by a third-party candidate in the twentieth century) analysts suggested it really hadn't mattered, since polls indicated that Perot voters split their second choices almost evenly between Clinton and Bush. Many election watchers also predicted that Perot would quickly fade into the woodwork, a claim they rushed to repeat as his poll ratings dipped once again after his celebrated tussle with Vice President Gore over NAFTA.

In a serious analysis of the 1992 election this obviously is not good enough. As is discussed below, it is in fact not easy to pin down precisely how Perot influenced the mass politics of the 1992 election. But there is evidence that it was he, rather than Clinton, who first cut Bush down to life size after Bush's Gulf War triumph. By focusing sharply on the economy, the Texan almost certainly made it easier for Democrats to attack Reaganomics, and he surely was in part responsible for the emergence of the deficit as a major national issue. By timing his pullout to coincide with the opening of the Democratic National Convention, Perot also helped Clinton become the cynosure of the nation at a truly critical moment. The reappearance of the fireball from the Lone Star in October, in addition, appears to have considerably increased voter interest in the race.

Particularly from an investment theory perspective, however, much more can be said about Ross Perot's Coney Island–like traversal of the American political landscape. In recent years, brief, sizzling appearances on the national political stage by charismatic business tycoons promising national renewal have become almost as common in world politics as reported appearances of the Virgin Mary have in world religion: Something recognizably akin to the "Perot phenomenon" emerged during elections in Poland, Bulgaria, South Korea, and Italy.

The secret, it appears, is leaking out. Given the contemporary political economy of mass communications, when the show becomes unbearable to many in the audience, the time is ripe for a special guest appearance from The Sponsor. What historically could be dismissed as a fantastic projection of the investment approach to analyzing politics is now cold, sober reality: A single super-rich investor can create a "party" of his or her own and bypass the antique trappings of mass political parties altogether.

Such candidacies, of course, are largely unintelligible if examined only from the mass political side. Absent more, and more searching, survey evidence than is publicly available as this essay goes to press, there is little to do save underscore what the 1992 race made obvious: that significant portions of the electorate are deeply anxious about the future and dismayed with conventional politics. Here, as in so many other cases in 1992, real answers to most of the interesting questions— why Perot, a public supporter of Richard Nixon, Reagan, and other generally conservative political figures, split so noisily from the Republicans; why he so evidently disliked Bush; and why he was so determined to run a campaign independent of both parties—come only from a careful analysis of the byzantine intersections between business and American politics.

A COMPLICATED STORY

In Perot's case, this requires a major research effort, for whatever the media stereotypes, the Texan is no cardboard cutout. He is a very complex figure whose thinking has clearly evolved over time and defies summary classification. Though his single-minded focus on the deficit in what must perforce be styled his "second coming" often made it difficult to see, Perot in his public statements over the last decade had begun to elaborate a serious if, in my opinion, incomplete, critique of American economic policy and practice. In contrast to both Bush and Clinton, he was willing to tackle the sovereign reality of American life today—the fact, manifested most strikingly in the divorce of top management compensation from corporate performance, of persisting and pervasive mismanagement *in the private sector.* Unlike the "free market" ideologues who dominated the Bush administration (and, with certain qualifications that should now be evident, control policy in the Clinton administration), Perot was prepared to look seriously at the "organized capitalism" of Japan or West Germany for ideas on how to restructure the American economy. Virtually alone among major figures in the U.S. business community, he was also prepared to break publicly with the free trade orthodoxy that has dominated American public policy since the New Deal once he became convinced that headlong pursuit of that ideal placed the domestic American economy at risk. That dangers attach to such efforts goes without saying; nor, it should hardly be necessary to add, does it follow that Perot was the ideal person for the job even if he offered more to think about on such issues than anyone else.

The Texan's inchoate and incomplete views about how to restructure the U.S. economy developed out of his experiences as a major innovator in the computer service and software industry. (His one conspicuous failure came in the early seventies, on Wall Street.) His earliest ideas focused on internal business organization. His thinking, however, was radicalized by his experiences on the front lines of the declining American empire—once in Iran, in 1979; and then again at General Motors in the mid-1980s. This GM encounter, in turn, intersected fatefully with a dark legacy of that greatest of all cases of imperial overextension, the war in Vietnam: specifically, the question of whether American prisoners of war had been left behind in Indochina. As Perot became increasingly involved in the uniquely acrimonious prisoner of war/missing in action (POW/MIA) issue, he became far more critical of Republican economic policies. The accumulating tensions led the Texan to become increasing dissatisfied with the structure of decisionmaking in the U.S. national security state. Eventually a bitter personal breach developed between Perot and Bush, whom the Texas billionaire clearly regarded as the incarnation of cautious bureaucratic managerialism.

The Evolution of a Center-Right Pragmatist

Seeing all this, of course, requires attention to topics that analysts of American elections rarely bother with. It also demands a clear-sighted acknowledgment of Perot's formidable business skills. Though these clearly impressed many voters, there were certainly many who scoffed during the campaign at the "welfare billionaire." But this charge is just close enough to the truth to be seriously misleading.

Despite tunnelling through a mass of documents and studies from the late sixties and early seventies, I have not been able to pin down the average costs of Electronic Data Systems, Perot's company, compared to the rest of its industry.[55] But the broad pattern is clear and all too familiar. A market innovator really does build a better mousetrap, which (until rivals catch up—a process that often takes much longer than orthodox economic theory wants to recognize) allows him (or rarely, her) to catch mice far more cheaply and efficiently than anyone else. As a result, he can consistently underbid competitors while still making vast profits and retaining the goodwill of customers, who are delighted to watch dead mice pile up while paying less. In due course the whole begins adding up to more than the sum of the parts, as overhead costs (like politics and lobbying) are spread over the growing volume of business, and other economies of scale emerge.

In the ideal world where dedicated state managers had both the knowledge and the motivation to adjust contract specifications to firms' real costs, the state could recapture some of these profits for taxpayers by altering the bidding process, perhaps after a decent interval to reward innovation. But neither we nor Perot live in an ideal world.

The widely touted organization of work at EDS was clearly related to the nature of its product. The company did not sell hardware—that was IBM's territory. Instead, building on his knowledge that most IBM customers had only very hazy ideas about what the great whirring machines could really do, Perot formed a software and service company that could teach them or, ideally, do the work for them.

Here he ran into a classic problem: how to motivate and monitor the workforce. The nature of work in computer services does not easily lend itself to any of the classic solutions to these dilemmas. Pay by piece, for example, rarely makes sense, nor does a flat wage always suffice to inspire the sustained application required over long periods. Perot's solution, which other parts of American industry are now experimenting with as they confront the broader crisis in work relations, produced the better mousetrap. Essentially, he made individual financial rewards dependent on the firm's success as a whole, tying total compensation to the stock price.

Trying to make a virtue out of his inability to measure individual output very reliably (this is the real point about all the stories of the fabulously long working hours, night shifts, etc., that characterized life at EDS), Perot also heavily stressed teamwork and joint activity. Investing heavily in worker training (an investment Perot sought to protect by having workers who left the firm commit to repaying), EDS consciously sought to envelop its employees in a thoroughgoing firm "culture" or "ideology." (This is the principal reason Perot was always hiring ex-military types, I think, rather than any attempt to build up a private covert activity capacity, though his affinity for covert action is obvious.)[56]

In the early seventies, a wave of investigations and bad publicity hit EDS, but the obituaries for both Perot and EDS were premature. Initially Perot tried expanding overseas. First he won a contract with the Saudis to set up an urgently needed data processing system for a new university on a crash basis. Then came the famous contract with Iran, reputedly one of the largest computer contracts ever. While this experience led Perot to pull back temporarily from the international arena, the domestic end of the business thrived. EDS continued to win government contracts, but it also gained substantial business from private firms. Perot's detractors sometimes attribute the EDS revival to Morton Meyerson, whom Perot had put in day-to-day charge of the firm. If one credits this analysis, then, in the spirit of the business historians who hailed Pierre DuPont as a business genius because he hired Alfred P. Sloan to run General Motors, the only sensible response is to ask who hired Meyerson.

Eventually, of course, General Motors acquired EDS and inadvertently provided Perot with a lesson no business school ever teaches about behavior at the top of the American corporate hierarchy. GM was seeking to diversify, but also to revitalize itself in the face of persistent losses of market share to rivals, especially the Japanese. The prospect of turning around the most conspicuous example of America's economic decline clearly fired Perot's imagination. Soon after going on the GM board, he began poking among the dealerships, talking to the UAW (becoming appalled at GM's labor relations) and talking excitedly about eventually exporting cars to Japan.

Quickly, however, the merger soured. Perot and GM Chief Executive Officer Roger Smith battled constantly over how EDS and GM would relate to each other, and the auto giant's management resented Perot's efforts to turn the company around. Though Perot has been much criticized for his tactics, the plain fact is that he was basically right, and usually was the only person on the GM board willing to rock the sinking boat. After all, the Japanese were selling millions of cars in the United States. But after more than twenty-five years of steady Japanese inroads, GM still could not make a car that was as good or nearly as cheap.

Perot, who in other contexts has referred scornfully to the impact on the workforce of low educational standards and easily available drugs, did not shrink from pointing the finger at the decisive fact about the decline of the auto industry in America: that for all the noise about unions or the decline of the work ethic, plenary responsibility for the shrinkage of the industry obviously lay with management. As he remarked in 1987,

> We have unfairly blamed the American worker for the poor quality of our products. The unsatisfactory quality and appearance of many of our products is the result of poor design and engineering—not poor assembly. . . . If you take a car made in Japan by Japanese workers and place it alongside a Japanese car made in a U.S. plant by U.S. workers (led by Japanese executives) there is no difference in quality. The Honda cars made in this country by U.S. workers are of such high quality that Honda intends to export them.
>
> Obviously the American worker is not the problem. The problem is failure of leadership.[57]

Zeroing in on the institutional structure that sustained this destructive pattern, Perot became one of the first to discuss corporate America's best-kept secret: that when corporations function efficiently and deliver products people want at a price they can afford, they make large profits, out of which the management is handsomely rewarded. But when they don't function efficiently, produce junk that few people want to buy, and end up garnering only small profits or even run at a loss for long periods, principally the workers, and secondarily, the shareholders, pay the price: Corporate compensation, voted on by interlocking directorates whose members rely on each other not to make waves, rises anyway, while the plants go overseas and shareholders fret. As Perot observed in a famous speech to the Economic Club of Detroit a few days after exiting the company, "If you go to war, you feed the troops before you feed the officers. You can't look the troops in the eye and say, 'It's been a bad year, we can't do anything for you,' but then say, 'By the way, we're going to pay ourselves a $1 million bonus.'"[58]

The climax of the struggle between GM and Perot came in the fight over the acquisition of Hughes Aircraft. Perot opposed it, warning that the firm was too dependent on a few large defense contracts. While time has vindicated his judgment, the board was not interested. Some accounts actually claim that no one said a word in response to Perot's carefully prepared objections.[59] A year later GM greenmailed him out of the firm for $700 million. Perot took it, after publicly giving GM time to withdraw an offer that both Jesse Jackson and T. Boone Pickens denounced, for different reasons.

His criticism of GM led the press to declare Perot a "populist." Of course, comparisons to the old Farmers' Alliance are silly, but Perot's economic and political views were beginning to evolve in strikingly unorthodox directions that would have major ramifications in 1992.

If EDS taught Perot about innovation and work relations, Iran taught him about the limits of the American government abroad, and GM taught him about inefficiency and the crisis in corporate management, then it was Perot's particular position in the Texas business class that encouraged him to breach the limits of laissez faire. In the early '80s, Perot was part of a group of Texas businessmen who wanted to diversify the state away from its traditional reliance on oil and into high technology, computers, biotechnology and other science-based industries. This group—whose members could be found in both parties, so that it could by turns be reasonably denominated as bipartisan, independent, or nonpartisan—can fairly be described as very conservative in regard to basic property relations. But it cannot sensibly be characterized as reactionary. Well aware of projections that Texas would eventually have a majority of non-Anglos, Perot and other members of this group were strong patrons of, for example, Henry Cisneros, then mayor of San Antonio and now Clinton's secretary of housing and urban development. Though scarcely champions of affirmative action in any of that protean term's common senses, many, including Perot, also strongly supported minority businesses and flatly opposed (overt) racial discrimination. They also accepted at least in principle the hiring and sometimes the promotion of women.

It can be said of this group of Texas business leaders that like their fathers and grandfathers before them, while they preached free enterprise, they practiced "creative federalism"—the highly political project of using state power to create not only economic infrastructure, but also to provide start-up capital for especially risky investments.

But this facile judgment masks a subtle new influence of the contemporary industrial structure on politics. As already observed, the

computer industry—really a congeries of several different industries—
is thoroughly multinational. The number of alliances across national
borders is increasing rapidly and muddying the whole question of national identities. At the same time, government intervention (and in
many countries, deliberate targeting) is truly massive, so traditional
free-enterprise, free-trade rhetoric is simply too hollow to sustain.

The service and software ends of the industry, Perot's niche, face
in addition a special problem in international trade: while it is perfectly
possible to process data for a shah, big contracts abroad often depend
on political standing and thus, like it or not, on the U.S. government's
ability to exert influence.

It is also possible to write software and sell services in countries
whose language is not English—but here even the most dedicated
group of monoglot ex-marines confronts a real obstacle as it faces off
with the locals. It is therefore unsurprising that all over the United
States, software and computer service firms show up in the vanguard
of campaigns to shore up the economy (through at least the minimal
move of promoting education) and preserve the position of U.S.-based
production in the world economy, which is closely bound up with the
viability of English as the world's universal second language.

So it makes sense that in Texas, Perot was a leader in the effort
that brought the Microelectronics and Computer Technology Corp.
(MCC) to Austin. And that Meyerson, who now runs Perot Systems
and who helped direct Perot's presidential campaign, served for a time
as chair of the support committee for the superconducting supercol-
lider, and that when he stepped down, he was succeeded by Tom Luce,
Perot's longtime attorney, and another principal figure in the presidential campaign. And that a host of Perot philanthropies, such as his vast
gifts for biomedical research at the University of Texas Southwestern
Medical Center at Dallas, fit clearly into this long-term project. (Many
of these benefactions come with various strings attached, a pattern of
doing good and doing well that marks U.S. business as a whole).

Perot's most celebrated political initiatives from the early 1980s—
the Texas war on drugs, which he declared more or less unilaterally
following his appointment to a state commission that was expected
to do very little; and the remarkable campaign he waged in favor of
improving education (and, if necessary, raising taxes to pay for it)—are
most easily understood against the background of Perot's professional
interest in American stability and competitiveness and his growing
anxiety about the direction of public policy.[60]

By the mid-1980s, Perot was generalizing his software experience
into a broad approach to industrial renewal. In a series of speeches that
were completely ignored by analysts in the 1992 campaign, he laid

out a vision of a U.S. economy transformed by the intelligent use of computers to replace middle management, restructure work, improve industrial design, and restore manufacturing.

His GM experience, however, dashed these hopes for swift success. Though many analysts have ruefully observed how American companies, especially in management and the broader service sector, have astoundingly little to show for their massive investments in office automation, Perot was clearly surprised when he ran into a brick wall of entrenched management and long-established social relations. In sharp contrast to most critics, however (who, in the case of at least one well known *business* critic of corporate compensation trends, have had columns canceled by magazines after corporate advertisers complained), Perot was a billionaire.[61] The world's most affluent mouse decided to roar.

THE BREAK WITH BUSH: MIA AND CIA

At the very moment Perot began to step forward as a critic of corporate America, however, he was sliding into another controversy that would eventually put him—the famous champion of America's armed services—on a collision course with virtually the whole national security and foreign policy establishment. Because in the 1992 campaign, the press repeatedly failed to ask certain very simple questions and instead published a selectively leaked "official story," this fateful episode has never emerged clearly.[62] It can now, however, be treated with some precision thanks to a striking new document made public late in the campaign to virtually no publicity. This is the sworn deposition Perot gave to Massachusetts Senator John Kerry's Select Committee on POW/MIA Affairs after he famously refused to testify in public before it in June of 1992.[63]

At issue is the long dispute over whether the American government left prisoners behind in Indochina in 1973. Since this question is uniquely inflammable, some advance disclaimers are in order. I myself have always regarded reports of POW sightings as on par with the many apparitions of Elvis, save that in the latter case no powerful organized interests have encouraged and circulated the claims for clearly political ends. With some qualifications that will momentarily become apparent, this remains my view: no substantial numbers of U.S. troops were left behind in Vietnam in 1973. But to come to grips with the Bush-Perot clash one has to make a deliberate effort to see the world as it is seen by others who start from different premises and view the evidence differently.

Many sighting reports were (and are) in complete good faith.

Though a fair number of charlatans—and penniless refugees dependent on official U.S. goodwill—have clearly moved into what quickly became an attractively remunerative field, there is no point in impugning the motives of most people who believe they saw, or heard, American POWs in Southeast Asia. Any number of Americans are likely to turn up in Indochina for perfectly comprehensible reasons. Not only was the wartime desertion rate phenomenal, but the United States waged a long, secret war in Laos that it generally refused to acknowledge. Though American prisoners in Laos were supposed to be turned over in the wake of the 1973 accords, both the United States and the Vietnamese pretended that the Pathet Lao was not officially party to the accord—as indeed, formally it was not.

Though U.S. pilots who came down in Laos were rescued at higher rates than those shot down over North Vietnam, the question of prisoners taken in that pre-1973 secret war on the ground is murky. Judging from a much-quoted but very cryptic remark by General Vernon Walters, some American covert forces may also have been captured in Cambodia. And a wide variety of governmental and private missions have operated on the ground since. Adding to the turmoil, Chinese intelligence is widely believed to have promoted reports of prisoner sightings to prevent a rapprochement between the United States and Vietnam, with which China has been intermittently at war.[64]

The recent hearings before the Kerry committee clouded this already turbid picture still more. Some stunning testimony indicated that American officials suspected back in 1973 that some prisoners might be missing, but did not want to talk about it. (It should be borne in mind that a host of perfectly sensible reasons exist for the discrepancies between reported captures and actual apprehensions and that the number of people unaccounted for in Vietnam was usually low compared to other conflicts. The U.S. government has also deliberately and repeatedly run together the inevitably large number of MIAs whose demise are virtually certain, but who fail the stringent requirements for being officially reported as killed in combat, with POWs, thus grossly inflating the number of potential POWs.)

A particularly striking portion of the testimony in June 1992 helps illuminate Perot's views about the controversy. The interlocutors are committee Chair Kerry and Roger Shields, formerly a Pentagon official in charge of the Nixon administration's efforts to account for MIAs.

THE CHAIRMAN: You recall going to see [then Deputy] Secretary of Defense William Clements in his office in early April [1973] ... correct?

DR. SHIELDS: That's correct.

THE CHAIRMAN: And you heard him tell you, quote, all the American POWs are dead. And you said to him, you cannot say that.

DR. SHIELDS: That's correct.

THE CHAIRMAN: And he repeated to you, you did not hear me. They are all dead.

DR. SHIELDS: That's essentially correct.[65]

The Kerry committee's efforts have produced a flood of new documents indicating that, for years, the government was shockingly uninterested in pursuing any evidence that did stray in. Indeed, officials were actively discouraging such investigation. For example, one previously classified memorandum by a naval officer in charge of the Pentagon's investigation in the mid-1980s (Thomas A. Brooks, who retired as a rear admiral) spoke of "a mindset to debunk" POW reports, along with a basic failure to employ "some of the most basic analytic tools such as plotting all sightings on a map to look for patterns, concentrations, etc."[66]

It should now be easy to understand the rage that built up in relatives of the MIAs, government officials, military personnel, and reporters who tried to take these reports seriously. Those who persisted were ridiculed, retired, passed over for promotion, etc. If they were reporters—even an Emmy Award–winning reporter for CBS's *Sixty Minutes* like Monika Jensen-Stevenson, or her husband William Stevenson, author of the well-known *A Man Called Intrepid*—they were harassed, intimidated, and rebuffed by various government officials. In the case of Jensen-Stevenson and her husband, a copy of their unpublished manuscript (eventually published as *Kiss The Boys Goodbye*) somehow ended up in the government's hands. Nor is it surprising that reporters like the Stevensons—whose honesty in reporting what they themselves saw and heard I do not doubt, although, as I have indicated, I weigh the evidence about POWs rather differently—eventually began talking to America's most famous champion of the Vietnam POWs, Ross Perot.[67]

Perot himself, according to his recently released deposition, had long been persuaded that the United States had left prisoners behind in Laos and perhaps Cambodia. But whatever his private suspicions, for a long time his public posture reflected skepticism. In 1981, for example, when a Perot encounter with one adventurer who claimed knowledge of POWs briefly made news, Perot's spokesperson emphasized that, while "deeply interested in the subject," Perot "doesn't believe there are any MIAs or POWs left back in the bush or in the jungle camps." He added: "We went through this issue in the 1970s and were satisfied in our minds that there were no more Americans over there."[68]

Though in the deposition Perot testified that the question never directly came up between them, it is of more than passing interest to note that on the board of EDS shortly before its sale to General Motors was the very same William Clements (then between terms as governor of Texas) whose role in defining the official U.S. position we have just examined.

Eventually, however, the long wagon train of skeptics alleging the government's bad faith appears to have moved Perot. In the mid-1980s, he began to raise the issue with Reagan administration officials. (For part of the '80s, Perot served on the president's Foreign Intelligence Advisory Board, which required a high-level security clearance.)

In his deposition, Perot related how then Vice President Bush phoned him one day in early 1986 to ask his assistance in obtaining a tape that was said to show American prisoners held captive somewhere in Indochina. The tape was said to be in possession of someone then held in jail in Singapore, who was asking $4.2 million for it. According to Perot's sworn testimony, Bush asked him to buy it and promised that if the tape proved to be authentic the government would reimburse the Texan. Later, however, as Perot was about to strike a deal, Donald Gregg from Bush's staff allegedly called to say that policy had changed and that Perot would not be reimbursed. When Perot persisted, federal agents attempted to apprehend the man claiming to have the tape upon his arrival in the United States.[69]

Perot also testified that in the late spring of that same year, he tried to persuade Bush to reconsider the government's handling of the so-called "Tighe Report." This was an inquiry headed by an Army general into the POW situation that top officials sought to soft-pedal, and then ordered classified. When he learned that officials were planning a briefing for reporters at which Lt. General Eugene Tighe would not be present, Perot protested. Eventually he went to Bush, who, according to Perot, decided to do nothing.[70]

The apparently arbitrary handling of the "Tighe Report" created waves in the small enclosed world of those in a position to know about it. Soon afterward, Perot was approached about making one last, final search through the files to close the issue. Perot, according to his deposition, accepted after receiving personal assurances of full cooperation and access to the files from both President Reagan and Vice President Bush. Perot testified, however, that not all records turned out to be open.[71] Nevertheless, in the fall of 1986, Perot personally—no one else had the requisite security clearances—spent vast amounts of time in Washington, poring over files.

Though reliable evidence is scanty, his investigation appears to have stirred up a hornet's nest. In *Kiss The Boys Goodbye*, Jensen-Stevenson and her husband report that Perot, the investigator, was himself being investigated by someone during a trip to Washington to gather and review evidence.[72] For this telling detail, one must accept the Stevensons' word, since other sources are not talking. But other facts they supplied to a *Nation* researcher who contacted them (at my suggestion) in Bangkok during the summer of 1992 check out.

The Stevensons are the most specific and detailed, but no longer the only, source for what seems to have happened next. As the struggle over GM raged, Perot, the man who identified drugs with American economic decline and had spent vast sums of money fighting the scourge in Texas, came upon something unexpected in his POW investigation: drugs. As most reliably documented by University of Wisconsin historian Alfred McCoy (whose work, upon its publication twenty years ago, became the object of a disgraceful official disinformation campaign, and which has recently been revised and updated as *The Politics of Heroin: CIA Complicity in the Global Drug Trade*), some American intelligence officials appear to have long been involved with the drug trade. Others have assuredly tolerated it for a variety of "national security" reasons.[73]

The Stevensons relate what happened when Vice President Bush inquired how Perot's inquiry was going:

> "Well, George, I go in looking for prisoners," said Perot, "but I spend all my time discovering the government has been moving drugs around the world and is involved in illegal arms deals. . . . I can't get at the prisoners because of the corruption among our own covert people."[74]

The deposition tells essentially the same story, under oath:

> Q[uestion to Perot by the Committee Counsel]. You are quoted in that book as having said: Every time I look for POWs, I bump into CIA agents running guns or drugs or words to that effect. Do you recall ever making a statement like that?
>
> A[nswer by Perot]. Not that exact statement, no. I basically said as you do a study all these things keep popping up unsolicited—just like this one.
>
> Q. To whom did you make that statement?
>
> A. To the lady writing the book.
>
> Q. Did you make a statement to that effect to George Bush?

A. Again, yes, I did make that statement to him.
Q. Was that in a face—
A. I don't remember the date. Yes.[75]

In early 1987, an obviously unhappy Perot gave a public interview to *Barron's*. There he poured out his frustration over GM, takeovers, and the stock market (which, months before the October crash, he insisted had lost touch with reality). He also, however, made one striking observation that should have led someone in the press to inquire.

> There are things going on in Washington around this whole Iran arms deal-[C]ontra thing. We should have been able to see that coming. . . . long before Reagan was even in the White House. . . . It is the same team of beautiful people selling arms around the world. This is not a new experience for them to be selling arms at a profit. I mean, some of them got caught once, in Australia [a reference to the collapse of the Nugan Hand Bank, which led to a major investigation by the Australian government]. They got caught again in Hawaii. Edwin Wilson got put in jail. And if you go back and follow the trail, these guys have been working together since the Bay of Pigs. And yet now, suddenly, it is all coming into focus. And we will clean it up.[76]

But the bulk of the press did not inquire. Soon thereafter, Perot—now out of GM—embarked on his celebrated trip to Vietnam and pursued a lengthy battle with Richard Armitage, a longtime Pentagon official.[77] He also gave a few speeches that suggested to some onlookers that he was weighing a (1988) presidential bid of his own. But of course, he did not run—then.

LIVING THE INVESTMENT THEORY

From the standpoint of an investment theory of party competition, the two Perot campaigns of 1992 are a milestone in the history of American political parties: It is perfectly obvious who paid for them and who ran them at every moment in time. Nevertheless, the social organization of the campaigns differed considerably, in ways that may still matter for American politics.

I am inclined to accept the story that not even Perot's immediate family anticipated his February 20, 1992, bombshell on the *Larry King Show* that he would consider running. But whatever Perot was thinking or saying before then, it is a fact that in late 1991, as George Bush sank lower and lower in the polls, Perot was making the rounds at rallies sponsored by groups protesting the congressional pay raise and, commonly, higher taxes. Perhaps the best known of these efforts was one organized by Jack Gargan, a Florida retiree, called THRO—Throw the Hypocritical Rascals Out.[78] Though Perot himself had several times advocated raising taxes, the response to his polished, well-delivered speeches at these gatherings was enthusiastic. Encouragement to run was also coming from other quarters, including a handful of business-oriented Southern Democrats previously known for various "populist" noises (as the much more mainstream DLC assuredly is not).[79]

Perot's decision to become an undeclared candidate generated widespread excitement. What appear to have been quite genuine grassroots campaign vehicles sprang up around the United States (though mostly outside the deep South). Crowds were big, mostly enthusiastic, and, it may be worth underscoring, quite orderly and respectful, with no trace of paramilitary stirrings.

Early polls suggested that Perot's appeal cut across the normal political spectrum, but fell off sharply among poorer Americans. Women, African-Americans and Jews tended to be skeptics. But the polls also suggest that next to either Bush or Clinton, the plainspoken Perot looked larger than life. By projecting an image of forceful initiative— and after the Los Angeles riots, when Perot was the only candidate who immediately criticized both the verdict and the president, the reality of forceful initiative—he appears to have diminished the aura of "leadership" that, however irrationally, clung to Bush after the Gulf War. By explaining in simple terms how the Reagan-Bush policies were damaging the economy, Perot also probably increased popular interest in the race. He also surely altered the terms of the debate between the major parties by vigorously attacking Bush at a time when Clinton looked weak indeed, and, as he withdrew, by backhandedly endorsing Clinton and the "new Democrats'" efforts to dramatize themselves as fresh, forward-oriented moderates.[80]

To most Americans, however, Perot himself was an unknown quantity. Though I know of no poll that ever inquired, I suspect that a fair number of voters initially confused him with one of his Dallas neighbors from the Hunt family. Coupled with the Texan's almost insouciant dismissals of details, which in fact differed little from Bush's or Clinton's airy generalities, but inevitably attracted more notice, this "blank slate" aspect to his candidacy implied that his public image was weakly anchored.

Eventually the White House, the Democrats, and Perot's foes in the media found this weakness and moved to exploit it. A series of selective leaks keyed to his scheduled appearance before the Kerry committee at the end of June sent his negative ratings soaring. Perot, whose commitment to racial equality (under free enterprise) is clear-cut and long-standing, also blundered badly in a famous address to the NAACP by appearing to patronize his audience. Because similar "dirty tricks" are now well attested to, I must say that I do not doubt Perot's testimony that Republican campaign operatives may also have been contemplating appalling schemes to embarrass him.[81]

As the second campaign proved, the damage to his image could have been repaired, given money and time. But while Perot did not lack for the first, in the early summer the second was becoming scarce indeed.

As far back as the Nixon period, Perot had fiercely resisted assimilation into conventional political labels.[82] His 1992 effort was entirely in this spirit. But if one looks closely, Perot, who scorned both political parties in the campaign, had in fact been carefully waging a struggle that was less antipartisan than bipartisan. What was clearly emerging as a "Noah's Ark" strategy of deliberate, simultaneous bridge building to both left and right aimed to balance off Republican endorsements with Democratic pledges of allegiance, overtures to one side with openings to the other, and so forth. Most obviously visible in the famously nonidentical twins he hired to advise (they thought: "run") his campaign—Ed Rollins and Hamilton Jordan—such tactics were in fact the campaign's hallmark.

The problem, which was acute by the time of the Democratic convention, was that the strategy was failing. Some business figures with fairly clear associations with the Democrats made widely touted moves in Perot's direction: A. C. Greenberg of Bear, Stearns; Felix Rohatyn (who was very coy about whether he would actually support the Democratic ticket); Richard Fisher (whose praises as Perot's foreign policy coordinator were sung by no less than Robert Hormats of Goldman, Sachs); and Thomas Barr of Cravath, Swaine and Moore. Lee Iacocca and Mortimer Zuckerman, who reportedly were talking up the Texan, might also qualify under this rubric.

But most, though not all, of these figures had past ties to Perot. Rohatyn formerly sat on the board of EDS; Fisher had married into a prominent Dallas family with Perot in attendance; Greenberg was another outspoken and longtime admirer of the Texan. Cravath represented Perot.[83]

Other nationally prominent Democratic leaders with valuable organizational ties hung back: Jackson, with whom Perot had been involved before in foreign policy ventures and the GM affair; several union leaders; Boston Mayor Raymond Flynn; and various other liberal Democrats. Just before the Democratic convention, Perot had an extended conversation with Tsongas. Their meeting produced praise for Perot from the former Massachusetts senator, but no endorsement.[84]

In sharp contrast, supply-side Republicans disenchanted with Bush flocked to Perot's standard, including Theodore Forstmann and Wanniski (who was touting a sharp rise in the Dow Jones industrial average if Perot won). Rollins also hinted broadly that a number of former top Reagan advisers were only awaiting the proper moment to make an endorsement.

That the campaign was striving to lift off the ground on only one wing was certainly responsible for much of the turbulence that rocked it in its final days. Judging from his public positions after he reentered the campaign, Perot was sympathetic to the supply-siders' opinions on capital gains tax reduction, if not on the rest of their tax policy. He also assuredly agreed that gigantic spending cuts were required to balance the budget.

On the other hand, his key insight into the need to make corporate managers responsible for corporate performance, though echoed in some recent "shareholder rights" proposals, is not an idea supply-siders promote, especially in public. Neither, obviously, are tax hikes and additional government investment in industries or infrastructure, not to mention the whole notion of "organized capitalism," which clearly intrigued Perot.

Nor were Perot's stances in favor of allowing banks to take equity positions in other companies and opposing NAFTA positions that would endear him to supply-siders, though at the time some were confident that they could eventually turn him around on the trade issue. The supply-siders were correct, however, that Perot's preferred forms of government intervention did not usually include tariffs as a first resort. In 1987, he had specifically cautioned against the penalty duties slapped on Toshiba. At several points in the campaign, he also declined to run against the Japanese when it would have been easy to pick up some of Buchanan's support by doing so. Influenced by Pat Choate, a prominent critic of Japanese and other lobbying, however, when Perot promised to tighten laws on foreign lobbying, he undoubtedly meant it.[85]

When another maverick billionaire, Howard Hughes, discovered the seaplane of his dreams, the famous *Spruce Goose*, couldn't stay airborne for more than a few minutes, he flew it to a nearby dock. There he left it moored, never to fly again. Perot, whose comparative advantage as a leader rested on the creation of effective teams (as he said repeatedly to skeptical auditors nervous about his bull-in-a-china-shop reputation), and who for twenty-odd years had aspired to reach out beyond a single party, was now coming to grips with the fact that society is not like a firm, which can recruit selectively.

No doubt all these factors weighed heavily on Perot. As he prepared to release an economic plan calling for draconian (and in my judgment, quite uncalled-for) budget cuts and contemplated a fledgling political movement that was maturing with only one wing, but that would still drain off at least $90 million more in campaign expenses, it is easy to understand why he decided to park his *Spruce Goose* and walk away.

But Perot was not, in fact, another Howard Hughes. His reentry into the race—with his poll ratings in single digits and amid all sorts of assurances from any number of the conventionally acclaimed "best and the brightest" pundits that "third parties always fade"—began one of the most remarkable comebacks in American political history. He was probably the winner of two of the three debates,[86] and was a striking innovator in campaign techniques. (His celebrated "infomercials" sometimes placed higher in the ratings than the programs they replaced—in defiance of expert opinion on the mass public's alleged lack of interest in technical economics and details of public policy.) He even survived another bout with CBS News in the last week of the campaign.[87] By election night, he had turned around his favorable/unfavorable ratings even with many people who had decided not to vote for him—a warning, perhaps, against taking any of his poll ratings since the election too seriously.

Shapes of Things to Come

As a political coalition, the new Clinton administration rather strikingly resembles the Seattle Space Needle. At the top are well-appointed, indeed luxurious, quarters nominally open to all, but in fact occupied by those who can afford them. (Though exactly what its figures refer to is not clear, the Associated Press claims that there are more millionaires among Clinton's top advisers than among Reagan's or Bush's.)[88] Below the glittering top rungs, however, the supporting structure is almost terrifyingly skimpy. Only a modern marvel of political engineering sustains it.

Within the business community, the Clinton base essentially consists of the relatively small group of firms that are prepared to experiment with slightly wider definitions of the role of the state and that are prepared to pay very modestly to see this happen. Alongside these firms, whose personnel directly control most of the levers of economic policy in the administration,[89] are grouped the remnants of the now heavily subsidized official labor movement, and the various constituency organizations that the Democrats have cultivated over the last couple of decades. The electoral foundation, as many have noted, is exiguous: Clinton was elected with just 43 percent of the total vote— the third-lowest winning total since 1828, when something like a modern system of presidential selection began evolving. Another way of putting the point is even more revealing: In terms of the winning candidate's percentage of the total potential electorate (i.e., including nonvoters), 1992 ranks at the very bottom, along with the election of 1912.[90]

Though no one should have been surprised, it is clear that the new regime's repeated stumbles in its first hundred days caught off guard both the public and most political commentators. Indeed, this shock was so severe (polls on the eve of the inauguration suggested that the public's hopes were soaring, with optimism among African-Americans at record levels) that the full meaning of what has happened probably has yet to sink in.[91]

Now that the administration has succeeded in getting a budget through and has at least temporarily stabilized itself, one must wonder about the future. Put bluntly: Can the Clinton administration recover?

The answer, I think, depends on precisely what one means by "recover." As the introduction to this book indicated, the administration may well succeed in muddling through until 1996 without suffering a fatal policy reversal at home or a disaster abroad. In the event its efforts to reform health care are crowned with success, it could even regain some of its lost luster. As long as its opposition remains divided (i.e, if the balance among Republicans, the followers of Perot, disaffected Democrats of various stripes, and the millions of nonvoters remains about where it was in the fall of 1992), then a strong political business cycle—which will require considerable help, witting or unwitting, from abroad—might suffice to pull the president narrowly through again.

But if by "recover" one means anything else, I fear the answer is not encouraging. All signs suggest that the world economy's long time of troubles is far from over, and that the U.S. political system, like that of so many other countries, is now slowly disintegrating. Amid the continuing turmoil, political infighting and leadership turnover are all but certain to increase.

In his public speeches during the 1992 campaign, then-candidate Clinton indicated that he understood the critical point for fashioning policy responses: that the American economy's fundamental problems relate to growth and productivity, and not simply to the deficit. But even then it was perfectly obvious that most of the investment bankers and other business figures lining up behind him remained committed partisans of the austerity policies the United States has pursued since the late seventies. And on numerous occasions, including some I witnessed firsthand, it was equally clear that—to put it charitably—the candidate or his spokespersons were carefully signalling elites that his public line was less a serious policy proposal than an aspiration.

No sooner was he in office than the president threw his campaign caution to the winds and settled on deficit reduction as his number-one priority. Any thought of serious economic stimulus was abandoned. At the first sign of heavy weather, the administration stopped paying even lip service to the concept.

Now that Clinton's deficit reduction plan is in place, however, the American economy is locked into a disconcerting course. Bringing down the deficit implies a reduction, year by year, in the proportionate amount the government spends over and above what it receives in revenues. While in theory total government spending could rise anyway as taxes go up even more, this interpretation of the president's plan was a fantasy his opponents encouraged to whip up public opposition to the rise in taxes on the rich. In fact, spending by the government is slated to taper off significantly as a percentage of total GNP.[92]

Were the drop in government demand promptly offset by an expansion of demand from the private sector, there would be no problem. One could sit back and cheer on the invisible hand as it brushed aside America's economic problems. But unfortunately, as the post-Keynesians among us have warned from the start, the invisible hand is now, in fact, mostly waving goodbye to vast numbers of ordinary Americans. Despite all the noise about how cutting the deficit is the key to restarting economic growth, this is simply not true. Cutting the deficit will for a time reduce interest rates. Consumers and businesses will, accordingly, borrow more. They will, therefore, spend more. And yes, this new spending will lead to some additional jobs and still further rounds of spending. But as California and many other parts of the United States are already discovering, total spending is unlikely to rise enough to offset the lost demand from government. The net effect of the Clinton budget package will be mildly contractionary: It will depress, not stimulate, the economy's rate of growth, for years.[93]

When he put forward his original deficit plan, Perot recognized this. Though the issue was never discussed in public, his scheme assumed a substantial fall in the dollar. Assuming world demand did not collapse—an "if" that is not unreasonable for a one-time-only development—the result would have been a rise in U.S. exports. This would have cushioned the big drop coming in government spending.[94]

But as the opening of this paper observed, Clinton's advisers, as they entered office, ruled out a devaluation of the dollar against the part of the world where the U.S. trade imbalances are most lopsided (Asia, aside from Japan, where they did encourage a sharp rise in the yen). Given what a falling dollar implies for dollar-denominated capital flows, the role investment bankers play in Clinton's political coalition, and the fact that promoting a devaluation against the rest of Asia amounts to asking the many U.S. firms which have relocated production there to devalue against themselves, one can be confident that this policy will not be lightly discarded.

This, however, leads to a problem: the United States has now embarked on a more equitable variant of Perot's deficit plan, but not the devaluation that was integral to it. By itself, this implies a slower rate of economic growth than anyone but market professionals are now talking about in public.

It also leaves the Clinton administration with several dilemmas to face in regard to economic policy. The most important of these involves the delicate question of relations with the Federal Reserve, whose chair, Greenspan, was of course appointed by the Republicans. Without Fed cooperation, there is no chance that the Clinton strategy of lowering long-term interest rates by "credible" deficit reduction can work. Both law and tradition, however, make the Fed notoriously refractory to presidential steering. To have any hope of getting his way, a president needs to mount subtle political campaigns over long periods of time while being very careful indeed about his own nominees to the board of governors. If anything is clear about the Clinton administration, however, it is that its processes for selecting and promoting nominees to all types of positions are near-fatally flawed by excessive caution and indecisiveness. This characteristic—which surely reflects the brittleness of its political backing as much or more than sloppy White House procedures—could prove very damaging indeed where the Fed is concerned. For the logic of the administration's position implies that, in regard to macroeconomic policy, what financial markets want, financial markets should get. (If they are unenthusiastic about long-term prospects, the whole process of interest-rate reductions grinds to a halt, as cautious investors pull back from buying long-term bonds.) If in the White House there is no will to advance a distinctive policy, there is no way it can happen by default.

Now an outstanding feature of contemporary financial markets is their almost Proustian sensitivity to the "specter" of inflation. It is therefore likely that long before the United States reaches anything approaching full employment, many parts of the financial community will be clamoring for the Fed to raise short-term rates to prevent "overheating." This the administration should oppose, with at least as much energy and determination as, say, John F. Kennedy's did in roughly similar circumstances.[95] Such a step, however, runs flatly against the main thrust of policy, so that it is hard to imagine the Clinton administration ever finding the courage—to say nothing of the political constituency—to do it.

Nor is this the administration's only problem with the Fed. Growth rates in the United States have been modest indeed for a long time. But outside of Asia and a few other developing countries, much of the rest of the world had frequently grown even more slowly. Though Europe will eventually start to grow again, it is improbable that the inflation-averse governments of Europe will suddenly become markedly less inflation-averse, or will cast aside their growing anxieties about their ratios of public debt to GNP. Accordingly, save perhaps in election years, their absorption of U.S. goods will be correspondingly reduced. Because of the overvaluation of the dollar and local trade restrictions, the more rapid pace of growth in Asia does rather less for the domestic U.S. economy than it does for the U.S. companies producing in the region. Depending on precisely what happens in Latin America—which certainly figures to absorb some U.S. exports—at times in the 1990s, as was true in much of the 1980s, the slow-growing United States may still find itself sometimes wanting to grow faster than the rest of the world. Unlike in the eighties, however, the United States cannot go on running up enormous trade deficits.

America can, of course, continue to finance its trade deficit by selling off not only financial, but real, assets. That option, however, is meeting increasingly stiff resistance in both the business community and the mass populace. Here, probably, is one more reason the administration, despite its public commitment to free trade, will find it convenient to manage trade with Asia, especially with Japan.[96] Because European markets are far more open to American firms than those of Asia, the administration is also likely to press the European Community to absorb still more U.S. exports—and in the process, to create still more trade friction. It will also try to shoehorn more American exports into what used to be called the Third World.

But if the rest of the world does not grow fast enough, then the United States can grow only at the price of increasing its already ballooning trade deficit. Eventually, however, it may well run into the same wall that the Carter administration, and several British governments before it, collided with: as the trade deficit rises unsustainably, the dollar will weaken. At that point, the United States would be virtually back to where it was in the late seventies.[97] Yet another Democratic financier—named Volcker, or a clone—would take over as Fed chair again, with consequences for the mass public and the Democratic Party that require no further discussion.

Long before this, however, the Fed and financial markets (well represented, of course, in the administration) would have called a halt to the "expansion" by raising rates. Or, in the happier version of the story that the administration is clearly hoping for, German interest rates will fall enough to restart growth in Europe, while the Japanese pursue some combination of rate cuts, market-opening initiatives, and fiscal stimulus, and Latin America expands smoothly. With the rest of the world growing again, the United States can keep on (slowly) expanding—though even here there is a risk that capital might begin fleeing a very slowly growing United States as other parts of the world take off, leading the Fed to hold rates up.

Regardless of how well or how poorly international economic policy coordination goes among the G7, the administration faces another towering problem. As it has repeatedly observed, the deficit cannot be brought under control without reining in health-care costs.

Here the problem is very large—and, in no small part, of the administration's own making. Earlier, I noted the impressive support Bush garnered from much of the health industry. But while my statistical survey of contributions largely fails to catch them—because most of these firms are not large enough individually to qualify for inclusion in my sample—even a visual inspection of the FEC data indicate that one Democrat succeeded in attracting important contributions from parts of the health-care industry: Clinton.[98]

As this essay goes to press, the administration is finally unveiling its long-awaited (and several times postponed) blueprint for overhauling the nation's health-care delivery system. Already, however, some of the costs of this strategy—to strike deals with as much of the existing health-care industry as possible, instead of pushing for a simple and economical "single payer" ("Canadian style") system—are plain. While the package of benefits and universal coverage the plan promises is carefully thought out and at least modestly appealing, the plan is fantastically complicated and not easy for ordinary voters to evaluate. The full costs of the network of oligopolies that the plan will create are being hidden, and savings are being claimed that are almost certainly not there.[99] The basic design is heavily weighted in the direction of the large insurers and several other parts of the health-care industry, including teaching hospitals. A few years down the pike the financing system proposed may well create strong pressures to curtail benefits or skimp on care.

Because the current U.S. health-care "system" is so bad, many people, myself included, are likely to feel that the Clinton plan is nevertheless a marked improvement. But it is important to note the broad pattern of what is occurring: in the midst of an economic crisis, the United States is (perhaps) moving toward universal coverage within an extremely high-cost system that is certain to unleash fierce and highly political regulatory struggles among vested interests after it is up and running.

The debate over the medical plan, perhaps, can serve as a metaphor for what is coming in the nineties. Here, as in so many other cases, a real "day of reckoning" may lie ahead. But this reckoning has less to do with discharging the modest burdens of the public debt than the tensions between voters and investors in the American electoral system. The plain fact is that the economy of the United States is failing an increasing percentage of its people. With slight differences (depending on the time period and precisely how one measures), hourly wages, total compensation (i.e., including benefits), and similar individual economic benchmark data have drifted down or even fallen steadily for almost two decades, even though productivity has slowly risen.

This is definitely not because the American people are becoming lazy: for those lucky enough to have jobs, working hours have risen dramatically. Nevertheless, virtually every year another small percentage of the population slides out of the middle class, while the decline of public services, the pressures on families, and polarization of society continue.[100] Yet because political action is so fantastically expensive in the United States, not only elections but public deliberation itself follows the "Golden Rule": those with the gold influence deliberations. Everyone else watches on TV.

Not surprisingly, all this contributes to a public atmosphere of cynicism and mistrust accompanied by all sorts of pathological phenomena (crime, bizarre cults, exotic murders, etc.) as individuals break down one by one under the unrelieved stress. It also reduces politics to subsidized debates over third-, fourth-, or even fifth-best alternatives. Now that Ross Perot's performance in the 1992 campaign has at last let the great secret out—that, with enough money, candidates can pole vault over the whole rotting structure of party politics in America—it will be surprising indeed if the firm bipartisan consensus in favor of macroeconomic austerity does not lead to what might be termed the "great compacting" of American public life and, perhaps, to considerable social turmoil.[101]

ACKNOWLEDGMENTS

For very helpful discussions on parts of this essay I am grateful to David Hale, Robert Johnson, Benjamin Page, and Alain Parguez. I should also like to thank Walter Dean Burnham for showing me a draft of his own manuscript on the 1992 election, and the members of seminars at York University, Toronto, and Swarthmore College, who patiently endured early versions of the paper. Goresh Hosangady provided invaluable help with the statistics. The staff of the Federal Election Commission, as ever, was unfailingly helpful, as were Ellen Miller and the staff of the Center for Responsive Politics. Max Holland and Jeri Scofield also supplied valuable material.

To save space in what follows, I have tried to collect as many notes as possible at the end of paragraphs in the text.

NOTES

1. This episode has not received the publicity it merits. The only written reference known to me is an editorial in *The Nation*, December 7, 1992, p. 1; complaints from the ranks of organizations affected by this development were sharp, but no one could afford to speak for the record.

2. On the fact that Clinton and his aides were well aware of the problem during the campaign, cf. the *Boston Globe*, January 10, 1993, and the *New York Times* of the same day. For the *Wall Street Journal* interview, see that newspaper for December 18, 1992.

3. See *Financial Times*, December 16, 1992; the quote is from that paper's description of Rubin's own comments. Note that against many European currencies, the U.S. dollar might well have been slightly undervalued in January of 1993. For Dornbusch, see his "The U.S. in the World Economy," n.d., which indicates that it is an expanded and edited version of his remarks before the Little Rock conference. For Summers, see *Boston Herald*, January 9, 1993, which also discusses the reception of Dornbusch's suggestions in Little Rock. For the aides' comments on Bergsten, see the *Boston Globe*, December 17, 1992; note, however, Bergsten's subsequent role in the yen/dollar contretemps.

Since many opponents of devaluation are fond of erecting scarecrows, it should be noted that no one advocated a policy of continuous or regular devaluation. Dornbusch, for example, compared the case for a one-time devaluation against Asia to the early-seventies devaluation against Europe, which adjusted for the more rapid growth in productivity as these economies revived after the war.

4. See Office of the President of the United States, *A Vision of Change for America*, February 17, 1993.

5. For the truly overwhelming poll numbers on jobs vs. the deficit, see e.g., William Schneider, "The President's 'Call to Arms': What Answer?" *Boston Herald*, February 19, 1993, p. 23. On various occasions, Dr. Schneider has indicated polite disagreement with my views on the role of public opinion in the making of public policy. I look forward to his explanation of how this article can be reconciled with the fate of the stimulus proposal.

6. See, e.g., the series of *New York Times*/CBS polls on the president's approval rating recorded as part of the press release on their poll fielded June 1–3, 1993. This shows a 53 percent approval rating in February, rising to 55 percent the following month, and then a steep plunge to 38 percent in June.

7. The original campaign-finance proposal failed to regulate most of the major ways in which big money influences elections. After sharp criticism, the White House advanced another plan which sounded better, but which would still permit very large sums of money—up to, I believe, about the median value of soft money contributions in the 1992 race—to flow as before. See, e.g., Ellen Miller, "The Senate's Sham Reform Plan," *Washington Post*, June 28, 1993.

8. However, the program as finally passed by Congress did significantly increase the earned income tax credit for the working poor. It also eliminated the ceiling on earnings subject to the social security-medicare tax, which had shielded richer Ameri-

cans from this levy. For the affluent, this step represented an additional tax bite of perhaps 2.9 percent.

9. See Paul Davidson, "Clinton's Economic Plan: Putting Caution First," *The Nation*, March 1, 1993, pp. 260–62; and especially Robert Eisner, *The Misunderstood Economy*, Boston: Harvard Business School Press, 1994. It is instructive to compare the behavior of some prominent economists on the stimulus question with their behavior during the Gulf War, when many rushed to reassure us that the United States could easily afford an extra $100 billion or so for a small war.

10. See the discussion of Perot's plan in James Galbraith, "A Two-Track Growth Program," *Challenge*, January-February 1993, p. 5.

11. The behavior over time of various measures of earnings, hourly pay, income, working hours, and other common indicators of economic welfare have been the object of much discussion. For a devastating review, see Lawrence Mishel and Jared Bernstein, *The State of Working America, 1992–93*, Armonk, N.Y.: M. E. Sharpe for the Economic Policy Institute, especially chapters 3 and 4.

12. Compare the graph on p. 256 of H. W. Stanley and Richard Niemi, *Vital Statistics On American Politics*, Washington: Congressional Quarterly Press, 1990, with the various figures summarized for Bush in, e.g., the press release to the *New York Times* poll of July 8–11, 1992.

13. Gary Langer, "Clinton Reclaims the Center—But It Remains Wary," ABC News briefing paper: The 1992 Exit Poll, November 18, 1992—update of November 6, 1992, reports that 42 percent of voters identified the economy as the most important issue in their vote. The next two choices named by large numbers of voters, the deficit (named by 21 percent) and health care (named by 20 percent), are obviously economic in a broader sense intended in note 11, above.

See also my discussion of Ray Fair's well-known economic model (and my prediction that it would be wrong, as, indeed, it was) in "George Bush as Lazarus: On Presidential Comebacks," The *Texas Observer*, September 18, 1992, p. 9. Recently proposed revisions of the GNP accounts for President Bush's term do nothing to ease the Fair model's situation: the revisions are in the wrong direction. (Nor, incidentally, do the revisions shake the conclusions about the poor performance of the economy under Bush compared to other post–World War II presidents.)

14. Some analysts also suggest that the Gulf War confused the Fed by complicating the interpretation of economic statistics. As discussed in this chapter, this is plausible for a few months, but no more.

15. For much of what follows, see the discussion in Thomas Ferguson and Joel Rogers, *Right Turn: The Decline of the Democrats and The Future of American Politics*, New York: Hill & Wang, 1986, chapter 4; and Thomas Ferguson, "By Invitation Only: Party Competition and Industrial Structure in the 1988 Election," chapter 5 of this volume.

Following Davidson's post-Keynesian analysis in his "Is Free Trade Always The Right Policy?" pp. 238–40 of *The Collected Writings of Paul Davidson, Vol. II: Inflation, Open Economies & Resources*, New York: New York University Press, 1991, I would now stress the difference in relative growth rates rather than the fact of the overvalued dollar as the driving force. But the dollar mattered, too.

16. On the Fed and Bush, see especially James Galbraith and Michael Mandler's, "Overview: Economic Policy," pp. 19–28, and James Galbraith's "Monetary Policy," pp. 88–99, in Mark Green, ed., *Changing America*, New York: New Market, 1993. Also helpful

is Gary Dymski, Gerald Epstein, James Galbraith, and Robert Pollin, "Report Card on the Greenspan Fed," Economic Policy Institute briefing paper, February 1992.

17. Discussions by David Hale and others of the Japanese contribution to the Bush reelection effort attracted some public attention in 1988; but see the startlingly direct admission by a former Bank of Japan official in the *New York Times*, January 21, 1994: "We asked life insurance companies to continue to buy U.S. bonds, especially right before the election." There was, he said, "a lot of administrative guidance." After the election, when the market turned, many of these firms suffered large losses.

18. For real estate interests in 1984, see Ferguson and Rogers, *Right Turn*, p. 150 and the appendix, which uses statistical evidence to rule out some alternative hypotheses. For 1988, see Ferguson, "By Invitation Only." This analysis indicates that Democratic primary candidates who received disproportionately high rates of donations from real estate received disproportionately low rates of donations from aircraft companies, and vice versa—striking evidence, indeed, that these constituencies were at cross-purposes.

19. Note, for example, that Caspar Weinberger was among the large group of (highly partisan) dissenters who collectively ensured the failure of the bipartisan National Economic Commission in early 1989—a body which had surely been created to give the president political cover to act on the deficit as he came into office.

20. For Rostenkowski, cf. the entry for one short period of time in Larry Makinson's highly instructive *Open Secrets*, 2nd ed.; Washington, D.C.: Congressional Quarterly, pp. 168–69, 1044–45. For the Democrats in general, see the discussion in this chapter.

21. This Democratic strategy tended to push up the percentage of party-line votes in Congress, leading some political analysts to conclude, rashly, that party differences were sharpening at that time. What was actually happening is a good deal more complex, and is a warning against the use of simple-minded quantitative indices. Party differences sharpened, but against a background of increasing conservative consensus on many public policy issues among the leadership of both major parties. (Not that the parties are identical, as the debates over health care and social security attest.) The party polarization evident in the early months of the Clinton administration was similar—Clinton is both a center-right Democrat and different from Reagan and Bush.

22. For voters' lack of interest in taxes and far greater interest in growth in 1992, see Langer, "1992 Exit Poll." Also note the insignificant (3 percent) number of voters who responded with the answer, "taxes," to an open-ended query in a *New York Times* poll of October 2–4, 1992 about what it was that most bothered them about reelecting George Bush to a second term. On voter views of taxes in general, see Benjamin Page and Robert Shapiro, *The Rational Public*, Chicago: University of Chicago Press, 1991, chap. 4, which indicates how variable views about taxes have been, but also the analysis in Louis Ferleger and Jay Mandle, *No Pain, No Gain*, New York: Twentieth Century Fund, 1992, pp. 22–33. I do not, accordingly, see any reason to modify the views expressed on the question in Ferguson and Rogers, *Right Turn*, chapter 1.

It is difficult to believe that if, for example, the Clinton administration succeeded in substantially raising the rate of growth and improving the level of public services that it would fail in a reelection bid because of a moderate tax increase. Indeed, 1992 exit polls, cited above, show that most voters who voted for Clinton disbelieved his promises that he would not raise taxes on most Americans.

On the blocking of cross-cutting appeals by Democratic elites in the 1980s, see, e.g., Ferguson and Rogers, *Right Turn*, pp. 185–86, 189.

23. See Galbraith and Mandler, "Economic Policy," p. 21.

24. On prominent supply-siders' attraction to Perot, see, e.g., the references to Forstmann and Wanniski in the *Boston Globe,* July 12, 1992; though the best way to follow the supply-side romance with the Texan was in Wanniski's newsletter during the campaign. A particularly detailed discussion by Wanniski of his and Forstmann's relations with Perot appeared in an issue of his newsletter of late June 1992. (The date on a fax copy indicates June 26, 1992.) After Perot withdrew and Bush held the line, Forstmann came back into the Bush campaign and helped raise substantial sums.

25. The best known of these is perhaps Thomas Edsall and Mary Edsall, *Chain Reaction,* New York: Norton, 1991, apparently written to explain in advance why George Bush would win the 1992 election. A certain amount of wry amusement can be gleaned by tracing subsequent efforts in the *Washington Post* to explain away what happened. See, e.g., Thomas Edsall's article of October 8, 1992, which, despite the wave of urban unrest, isolates a "new breed" of big-city mayor, who is described as able to transcend the racial and ethnic divisions that only a few months before the book had identified as crucial to the success of the GOP.

Some Democratic analysts have claimed that Clinton's celebrated rebuffs of Jesse Jackson played a major role in his victory. While a full discussion of this issue will require reference to the National Election Survey for 1992, I believe what really happened is already evident. First, there is no question that Clinton and his advisers went out of their way to reject Jackson. That was a message they wished to send. Second, there is also no question that some voters liked, or could be induced to like, that message. It is improbable, however, that many votes changed as a result of that message.

Little reliable quantitative evidence has been offered on how many votes are actually affected by calculations of this type in national (as opposed to particular state or local) elections. (Reliable evidence can be defined as the sort that meets objections of the type Stanley Kelley advances against conventional approaches to the role of the economy in the 1980 election in his *Interpreting Elections,* Princeton: Princeton University Press, 1983, chapter 9). Mostly we are given various results plucked from forced choice or other closed-ended questions, with little or no effort to investigate whether the considerations discussed actually affected voters' decisions. That voters had heard of the rebuff of Jackson, for example, or even whether they approved, is simply not sufficient. When a properly designed analysis is performed, as for example, by John Geer, in his "The Electorate's Partisan Evaluations: Evidence of a Continuing Democratic Edge," *Public Opinion Quarterly* 55, no. 2, summer 1991, pp. 224–26, the results are disastrous for the claim that race is a uniquely crucial stumbling bloc to Democratic victories. Race is revealed to play a role, but not a very large one. Indeed, its influence appears to have been stronger in the 1960s, when Democrats were winning elections. I doubt that any of the obvious objections to Geer's results (which parallel Kelley's) are valid and I believe it is possible to rule out, for example, the perfectly reasonable suggestion that the open-ended questions seriously mismeasure the effect prejudice has on voting decisions in national elections. Given the economic conditions of 1992, any plausible Democratic challenger had an excellent chance of defeating Bush with or without Jackson—and I believe that once the survey data becomes available, this will become a (retrospectively) testable hypothesis that can be approached in explicit quantitative terms.

See also the interesting analysis in Alan Abramovitz, "Issue Evolution Reconsidered: Racial Attitudes and Partisanship in the American Electorate," a paper prepared for delivery at the annual meeting of the Southern Political Science Association, Atlanta, Georgia, November 5–7, 1992.

26. On long-run trends in opinion toward race, see e.g., Page and Shapiro, *Rational Public*, chapter 3; for opinion following the unrest, see the various CBS/*New York Times* polls, e.g., the press release for their poll fielded May 6–8, 1992.

27. Table 6.1, like table 6.2, has been compiled along the lines of my "Industrial Structure and Party Competition in the New Deal," chapter 4 of this volume; the statistical appendix to *Right Turn;* and "By Invitation Only," chapter 5 of this volume. As in the 1988 statistical study, however, the sample size is vastly larger than that for *Right Turn:* It includes 1,945 individual entries from 948 firms. Readers seeking more detailed discussions of the methodology for constructing the sample should also consult my review essay on "Money and Politics" in Godfrey Hodgson, ed., *Handbooks to The Modern World— The United States*, vol. 2, New York: Facts on File, 1992, pp. 1060–84, which attempts to indicate the limitations of existing data on campaign finance.

In contrast to virtually all other election studies, my research attempts to include not only contributions from political action committees, but individual contributions and soft money as well. (For Bush and Clinton in 1992, PAC contributions were relevant only as sources of soft money, which is channeled through the parties, since each made the grand but empty gesture of refusing PAC donations to their formal campaign accounts.) I compile a systematic sample of top officers of firms at the apex of the American economic pyramid—the largest 200 *Fortune* industrials, top 20 commercial banks, 15 largest insurance firms, etc., from the *Fortune* service list, but also the largest firms on Wall Street, which do not necessarily appear on these other lists, and the Forbes 400 list of richest Americans for the year preceding the election. Then, by hand (the only way it can really be done) the individual and soft money contributions are pulled out of the Federal Election Commission files, along with contributions from their firms.

These data are then analyzed; typically the procedure is to identify industries (or other groupings, including sets of firms) which are disproportionately aiding various candidates. The typical test involves chi-square tests in which particular industries are tested against the rest for statistically significant differences in rates of contribution to particular candidates. As discussed in "Industrial Structure and Party Competition in the New Deal," the results need to be carefully interpreted; in particular, I would call attention to the facts that noncontributors are left in to avoid an impression of inflated (primarily Democratic) totals, and that some firms give to both sides.

At the time this analysis was completed, the Federal Election Commission still had not released its (delayed) final report on the 1992 election. Accordingly, the tables in the essay provide figures for individual, soft money and PAC contributions from the individuals and firms in my sample to the Bush and Clinton campaigns (including soft money given to the parties in Clinton's case after March 21, 1992, when he was incontestably the most likely nominee; and in Bush's case, all GOP soft money) reported by the FEC through late October, 1992. This includes the great bulk of all money ever taken in by the two chief candidates, and is thus unlikely to require major revision. Note, however, that the tables do not record contributions to the other primary candidates. My discussion also draws on a survey of early money I prepared in the spring of 1992, but aside from the principal candidates, small numbers of contributions make statistical generalizations hazardous. I accordingly have not sought to present a statistical treatment of the primaries now, and the remarks in the text about the primaries (other than for Bush and Clinton) should be interpreted as preliminary.

Two other points require mention. My 1984 and 1988 studies reported results for individuals within industries. As explained in "Industrial Structure and Party Competition in the New Deal," this procedure makes sense where there is reason to believe that corporations have an incentive to spread donations among more than one individual, as they did when the FEC limits on individual contributions still meant something. The enormous growth of soft money, however, has rendered this point moot. This was not a problem in 1984, and, after checking, I believe my 1988 results do not require significant correction. By 1992, however, the raising of soft money was formalized and endemic, incorporated into everyone's political strategies and reported to the FEC. Accordingly, I revert to the practice of reporting results by firms, as in my study of 1936. This has one bad consequence: by reducing cases, it decreases reliability. Since I use 2×2 chi-square tests, when the expected values in any of the cells goes below 5, I report the results of Fisher's Exact Test for the level of significance and mark it with an asterisk to call attention to it in table 6.2. (Here I follow K. H. Jarausch and K. A. Hardy, *Quantitative Methods For Historians,* Chapel Hill: University of North Carolina Press, 1991, p. 109).

28. For reasons of space, I have not analyzed the Buchanan campaign here. My impression, based on the incomplete survey of early money I performed in the spring of 1992, is that his campaign was built around an unstable coalition of two distinct constituencies. The first was the (protectionist part of) the American textile industry, to which the notion of putting America first is as attractive in the nineties as it was in the thirties. The second—undoubtedly larger—group, by contrast, might be termed not the "America First" but the "Me First" constituency. This group consists of a broad array of conservative, very well-heeled private investors (who nevertheless rarely show up on the Forbes listings) and second-tier figures (virtually none occupy top slots) working in firms in all sorts of industries, from finance to services. Dissatisfied with the "Tory Wet" caution that increasingly marked the Bush administration, they appear to have wanted two things above all: another big cut in capital gains taxes, and, of course, still further cuts in domestic spending.

Various newspaper stories during the later stages of the 1992 campaign suggested that big business began turning to Clinton in large numbers only very late in the campaign. Because I divided my data on soft money to the Democrats as described in note 27 above, I can compare how the sample behaved toward the Clinton campaign before and after the spring of 1992. It is plain that a marked turn toward Clinton occurred well before the highly publicized problem of the Bush campaign during and after late summer.

29. See, e.g., the sources cited in note 15.

30. Once again, see, e.g., the sources cited in note 15.

31. See Ferguson and Rogers, *Right Turn,* pp. 150 and the appendix; for Rubin and Altman's visit, cf. pp. 185–8.

32. See Ferguson, "An Unbearable Lightness of Being—Party and Industry in the 1988 Democratic Primary," in Benjamin Ginsberg and Alan Stone, eds., *Do Elections Matter?* 2nd ed.; Armonk, New York: M. E. Sharpe, 1991, pp. 237–54, and Ferguson, "By Invitation Only".

I lack the space to analyze the direct responses of voters in 1984 or 1988, but these do not appear to have been very complicated. As discussed in the appendix to this volume,

"Deduced and Abandoned: Rational Expectations, the Investment Theory of Political Parties, and the Myth of the Median Voter," I essentially accept the analysis of actual voters' reasons for casting their ballots developed in Kelley, *Interpreting Elections*, and "Democracy and the New Deal Party System," in Amy Guttmann, ed., *Democracy and The Welfare State*, Princeton: Princeton University Press, 1988, and by John Geer, who has continued Kelley's work in a notable series of recent papers. See Geer's "The Electorate's Partisan Evaluations: Evidence of a Continuing Democratic Edge," *Public Opinion Quarterly* 55, no. 2, summer 1991, pp. 218–31, and "New Deal Issues and the American Electorate, 1952–88," *Political Behavior* 14, no. 1, 1992, pp. 45–65.

Their analysis of the electorate's behavior in these two elections, particularly the stress they both lay on the way the Democrats forfeited their ancestral identification as the party of prosperity, is entirely consistent with my analysis of the changing business base of the Democratic Party. The investment approach explains why the party kept offering only conservative economic messages—which the voters kept rejecting. (Note that Mondale in 1984 offered little but a tax rise, while Reagan at least talked about growth and was riding a huge political business cycle.) As mentioned earlier, the Democrats' lack of a strong economic message (memorably summarized in 1988 as an emphasis on "competence" rather than "ideology") also helps to open the space for Republican racial and religious appeals.

33. See the discussion in Ferguson and Rogers, *Right Turn*, pp. 63–66, chapter 5, and pp. 198–200; the budget figure is on p. 142. See also Ferguson and Rogers, "Corporate Coalitions in the 1980 Campaign," Ferguson and Rogers, eds., *The Hidden Election*, New York: Pantheon, 1981, pp. 21–24.

Interestingly, along with its highly touted program of subsidies to high tech (discussed in this chapter), the Clinton administration has also announced special programs to aid two very highly unionized sectors: automobiles and construction. See the *Frankfurter Allgemeine Zeitung*, February 24, 1993, p. 15.

34. Ferguson and Rogers, *Right Turn*, pp. 53–57, 70–73. I fear that most writing on "new social movements" in both the United States and Europe fails to recognize that the unwillingness to agitate against austerity is a major factor in accounting for the acceptability of such groups within the political establishments of various countries.

35. A good study of the DLC is William Crotty, "Who Needs Two Republican Parties?" in J. M. Burns, et. al., *The Democrats Must Lead*, Boulder, Colo.: Westview, 1992, pp. 66–70. On the Northern financing, see, inter alia, Paul Starobin, "An Affair to Remember?" *National Journal*, January 16, 1993, pp. 120–22.

36. See Lawrence Longley, "The National Democratic Party Can Lead," in Burns, et. al., *Democrats Must Lead*, pp. 29–55.

37. Compare the percentages for 1984 in Ferguson and Rogers, *Right Turn*, appendix, and for 1988 in Ferguson, "By Invitation Only," this volume, table 5.2, with the nonentry for real estate in 1992 in table 6.2 of this essay. As explained above, note 27, this last table reports results for "firms," where that term refers both to individual and corporate entities. But in fact, for all three years, all the real estate entries are for individuals (or families, where the kin work together), and all come from the Forbes 400 lists. They may, accordingly, be compared directly with one another.

In chapter 9 of his *The Power Elite and The State*, New York: Aldine, de Gruyter, 1990, G. William Domhoff claimed that an analysis of campaign contributions in the 1936 election by one of his students ran counter to my work on the New Deal. He also argued that *Right Turn*'s analysis of 1984 data, according to which real estate and investment banks disproportionately supported the Democrats, confounded ethnic and economic factors. In both these sectors, he suggested, Jewish Americans were represented in large numbers, and these tend to favor Democrats.

But my "Industrial Structure and Party Competition in the New Deal" (chapter 4 in this volume) showed in detail that his claims about my New Deal work were untenable and that the campaign finance data for 1936 strongly confirm my earlier conclusions. In regard to the 1984 case, his analysis of individual contributions slipped past our point that our conclusions rested upon an analysis of both individual and PAC contributions from investment houses; the latter cannot possibly be written off as purely individual, or, accordingly, ethnically based, since the large houses in question, while unlikely to be mistaken for model equal opportunity employers, now draw partners from many different backgrounds.

The real estate results for 1992, in addition, are powerful, and quite devastate views that the industry's politics were ethnically driven. The Bush administration's relations with American Jews were rocky indeed, far more so than Reagan's. Yet real estate fell out altogether from the ranks of industries disproportionately supporting the Democrats. While I am sure the industry changed between 1988 and 1992, no plausible "circulation of elites" can account for this; the industry really changed its politics.

While I think these new results are dispositive for the cases at issue, I should note that there is no reason why weak ethnic effects, along the lines of the second-order regional effects my New Deal study identified, should not also sometimes be present. But—as the varying percentages of industry contributions across elections and candidates should caution us—slow-changing factors like ethnicity are unlikely to drive free enterprise economies. They are more likely to register strongly in the mass electorate, though even there I believe most voting analysts underestimate the influence of economics, because they so rarely test directly for economic influences other than social class.

The most obvious place for regional effects to show in the 1992 data is in the contributions to Clinton. I therefore tested for South/non-South differences, and found none at all. This underscores the point made earlier about Northern support for the DLC.

38. The source for this information was a top aide to a leading Democratic governor, who complained about this at a small meeting around the time of the Democratic convention.

39. See e.g., the breakdown reported in the press release for the *New York Times* poll of June 17–20, 1992 for the import question. The *Times* poll of July 8–11 indicates that 55 percent of the respondents described the trade agreement with Mexico as a "bad idea," versus 27 percent who thought it was a "good idea." In the course of the campaign to promote NAFTA as this book goes to press, it is to be expected that such numbers will bounce around. See also the discussion in the appendix of this volume.

For what follows on the primary (aside from the discussion of Clinton), see my "The Democrats Deal for Dollars," *The Nation*, April 13, 1992, pp. 475–78; the newspaper account linking Volcker (and Warren Buffett) to Senator Bob Kerrey's campaign comes from the *Boston Globe*, February 16, 1992. Note that Kerrey, in response to his critics, took pains to say that he generally favored an open economy.

As note 27 cautioned, the statistical results reported in the tables are for the Clinton-Bush race only, and *not* other primary candidates.

40. See Ferguson, "Democrats Deal for Dollars."

41. For Altman, Hillary Rodham Clinton, and the Children's Television Workshop, see *Boston Globe*, Jan. 10, 1993.

42. For Nunn's early endorsement, see Starobin, "An Affair," p. 121. The subsequent history of relations between the Clinton White House and Senator Nunn raises the question of what went wrong. One might reasonably suggest that the move toward a more hawkish position on the deficit accounts for at least some of the later difficulties. The additional tilt in the direction of Wall Street, in other words, ultimately cost Lockheed and the rest of the defense industry.

43. For Clinton and natural gas in Texas during the campaign, see *Christian Science Monitor*, November 23, 1992.

44. The utilities reference is mostly to, for example, telephone companies, rather than power stations. While it is equally feasible to break down the GOP contributors along the lines of table 6.2, there is little point in doing so, because of the very high overall mean. See the discussion in Ferguson, "Industrial Structure and Party Competition in the New Deal," chapter 4, this volume.

45. See, e.g., for high tech in general, *Washington Post*, September 17, 1992; for specific quotations and a discussion of high-tech executives' meetings with Clinton, see the *New York Times*, October 29, 1992; note that Sculley said he still thought of himself as a Republican; for Magaziner and the Council on Competitiveness, *Boston Globe*, November 15, 1992, which adds more details.

46. See e.g., *Boston Globe*, November 15, 1992; or the discussion in Susan Dentzer, "Clinton's High-Tech High Wire Act," *U.S. News and World Report*, March 29, 1993, p. 44.

47. For Sculley, see *New York Times*, December 15, 1992. The push for a yen revaluation is not costless. Because most other Asian currencies peg to the dollar, running up the yen lowers the costs of overseas Japanese acquisitions in that region. It may also open a rift with Wall Street, since Japanese holders of American bonds will be tempted to sell.

48. An example of the vogue in some circles for "organized capitalism," complete with higher tax rates in the upper brackets, is the interest in Michel Albert's *Capitalism vs. Capitalism*, New York: Four Walls Eight Windows, 1993. This American edition of a study by a French insurance executive who now serves on the board of the new, independent Banque de France carries a foreword by Felix Rohatyn of Lazard, Frères.

49. A very illuminating discussion of the early efforts by the *Washington Post* and the *New York Times* to puff Clinton is Tom Rosenstiel, *Strange Bedfellows*, New York: Hyperion Books, 1993, pp. 47ff. Rosenstiel, a *Los Angeles Times* reporter, notes how the major media used candidates' abilities to raise large sums of early money as a cue for intensive coverage. This point is particularly interesting, given the virtual noncoverage of financing in the press.

The media's differential coverage of Clinton and Bush in 1992 has stimulated considerable interest. Everett Ladd, for example, suggests that while "the press had no master plan to elect Clinton . . . a majority of journalists simply felt closer to the Democrats' stands than to those of the Republicans." See his "The 1992 Election and the Clinton Administration," special [supplementary] chapter for his *The American Polity*, New York: Norton, 1993, p. 18. This suggestion inevitably raises doubts. For example, what about the publishers? To whom did they feel close? More importantly, are we to suppose that the reporters' feelings suddenly changed after the election, when they finally began to cover Whitewater?

Though for reasons of space the question cannot be pursued here, it would probably be more fruitful to analyze the media explicitly in investment theory terms, as for example, Erik Devereux has done for the 1964 election. See his quantitative study of "Media Coalitions in the 1964 Campaign: A Political Investment Analysis," Working Paper 92-38, H. J. Heinz School of Public Policy and Management, Carnegie-Mellon University. From this standpoint, much of the media, and especially the elite newspapers—which can hardly abandon their respective metropolitan areas—strikingly resemble many other firms that supported the Clinton campaign. While they favor an open world economy, they nevertheless have no realistic prospects of moving substantially offshore.

Unlike Ladd's approach, such a view is not weakened by subsequent coverage of Whitewater. There is no reason all or even most such businesses need to sign on to the specific version of the Clinton health plan, which, it may plausibly be argued, occasions the virtual hysteria within the Beltway over a set of business transactions that pale beside Watergate or Iran-Contra. No less importantly, a realistic, investment-oriented account of the press would expect that business mobilizations as broad and intense as that triggered by the Clinton health-care proposals (which, as indicated in this essay, do have some influential business support) would inevitably gain far more sympathetic access to free enterprise–oriented media than, say, movements for increasing the minimum wage.

50. Starobin, "An Affair," p. 123. The presence of so many investment bankers so early around the Clinton campaign, along with the statistical results on his campaign's financing reported in this chapter, provide powerful support for subsequent denials by the White House that President Clinton had somehow been lately converted by Fed Chair Alan Greenspan to the cause of fiscal austerity. This interpretation had gained currency following publication of Bob Woodward's *The Agenda* (New York: Simon & Schuster, 1994).

51. For the social composition of the voter in the Southern primaries see the *New York Times*, March 11, 12, 1992. Note that turnouts in most of the Democratic primaries were low. Not surprisingly, the Clinton campaign's periodic reports on fundraising, filed with the Federal Election Commission in Washington, show total donations to the campaign rising sharply in this period.

52. Party chairs normally strike a neutral pose in primaries with no incumbent running. But not Ron Brown, who repeatedly attacked Jerry Brown. See, e.g., the *New York Times* of March 27 or March 28, 1992. Jerry Brown, for his part, raised hackles by frequently challenging Clinton to agree to abide by the Brown campaign's $100 limitation on individual campaign contributions. Backers of Clinton and Tsongas eventually struck a deal just before the Democratic convention with the aim of denying Brown much media exposure. See *New York Times*, July 15, 1992.

53. For a striking review of press coverage of the Brown campaign, see Fairness and Accuracy in Reporting's *Extra*, June, 1992, p. 14. This suggests that "no presidential candidate in recent memory has been more tarred and feathered with media putdowns and epithets than Jerry Brown." Cf. also the *New York Times* articles of March 26 and March 27, 1992, on the flat tax.

54. What follows on Perot draws in part on an earlier essay I wrote on Perot during the campaign. The *Nation* magazine assisted me in defraying some of the costs for what became a large-scale review of documents in presidential libraries and vast numbers of previously published articles. The *Nation* published a shortened version of my essay on August 17/24, 1992, pp. 168–76; the longest version ran in The *Texas Observer* of August

7, 1992, pp. 1–9. Since the earlier pieces are readily available, I have reserved the foot-notes below for new material and specific references of particular interest. Richard Armi-tage's pithy description of Perot appeared in the *Washington Post,* July 15, 1992.

An example of how leading conventional political analysts could miss major trends in 1992 is the ill-timed study by Raymond Wolfinger, et. al., of *The Myth of The Indepen-dent Voter,* Berkeley: University of California Press, 1992.

55. Most of these documents came from presidential libraries and papers, though several reports on EDS from various government agencies were also consulted. The *Texas Observer*'s back files on Perot were also very helpful and contain valuable articles on Perot's early career. Robert Fitch's "H. R. Perot: America's First Welfare Billionaire," in *Ramparts,* November 1971, pp. 42 ff. is another excellent early piece, though from the perspective of two decades I rate Perot's business performance much more highly than he does.

56. Perhaps the best review of the evidence on Perot and the Nicaraguan Contras is Joseph Albright's for the Cox News Service, *Austin American-Statesman,* May 15, 1992; Perot himself says he turned down requests to help the Contras. I examined the declassi-fied parts of Oliver North's diary, but this has so much material blackened out that it is useless.

57. *Washington Post,* October 25, 1987.

58. Perot, speech to the Economic Club of Detroit, December 8, 1986, quoted in Tony Chiu, *Ross Perot In His Own Words,* New York: Time Warner, 1992, p. 41. Some apologists admit the abuses Perot analyzes, but claim that more active institutional in-vestors can cure the problem. I think it is already clear that this counter-tendency is too weak.

59. On Perot and GM, see the contrasting accounts of Todd Mason, *Perot: An Unau-thorized Biography* (Homewood, Il: Dow Jones-Irwin, 1990) and Doron Levin, *Irreconcil-able Differences: Ross Perot versus General Motors* (Boston: Little, Brown, 1989).

60. It is only fair to note that Hillary Rodham Clinton's performance as head of a group charged with reforming the Arkansas education system was roughly comparable, and that it was her husband who appointed her.

Robert Fitch, "How Perot Made a Quarter Billion Dollars by Running for President," *The Perot Periodical* 1, no. 1 fall, 1993, p. 1 ff. links the large holdings of bonds disclosed on Perot's financial disclosure form for the Federal Election Commission to his concen-tration on the deficit. While his piece is characteristically insightful, I would not accept his implication that Perot was less interested in industrial restructuring or restarting eco-nomic growth than he claimed. Both his campaign statements and the admittedly con-servative portfolio, in my judgment, reflect Perot's anxiety about the future of the United States and his oft-repeated doubts about the overvalued U.S. stock market. If driving up bond values had been his chief concern, it would have been simple enough to have financed agitation on the deficit, or even invested in Clinton's campaign, as a number of prominent Wall Street deficit hawks actually did.

61. The reference is to the celebrated case of Graef S. Crystal, in years past probably the leading consultant on compensation questions to American businesses. See the *New York Times,* February 25, 1992.

62. Perot complained repeatedly during the campaign that his opponents leaked material to the press. At least some such leaks certainly occurred. The text of his now-famous letter to President Reagan reporting on his talks with the Vietnamese about nor-

malizing relations, for example, was assuredly highly classified until the day it broke in the *New York Times*. See the *New York Times*, July 5, 1992.

63. See "Committee Confidential, Deposition of H. Ross Perot, Wednesday, July 1, 1992," for the U.S. Senate Select Committee on POW/MIA [Prisoners of War/Missing in Action] Affairs, Dallas, Texas. This transcript was made available by committee staff in October 1992 and handed out to, it appears, anyone who asked for it.

No one should have been surprised when Richard Fisher, Perot's foreign policy coordinator, trumpeted the need for a radical rethinking of U.S. foreign policy and restructuring of decision-making structures. Toward the end of the first campaign, Perot's foreign policy emerged as an issue when Paul Nitze, famous as the principal author of NSC 68, raised questions. See *Washington Post*, July 15, 1992.

64. Probably the best discussion of the long controversy and what appear to be the facts is H. Bruce Franklin, *M.I.A. or Mythmaking in America*, New York: Lawrence Hill, 1992. Note that on p. 7, Franklin does not dismiss the possibility that a "few dozen at the very most" may have remained behind. From newspaper reports, this appears to be a conclusion supported by new material unearthed by the Kerry committee; it does appear that Laos and perhaps Cambodia were the suspected sites. For Walters' comment, see Monika Jensen-Stevenson and William Stevenson, *Kiss the Boys Goodbye*, New York: Penguin, 1990, p. 3.

65. This exchange appears in my essay in The *Texas Observer*, p. 6; and comes from a transcript supplied by the committee.

66. Quoted in Ferguson, *Texas Observer*, August 7, 1992, p. 6.

67. On the strange history of the manuscript, compare carefully what Monika Jensen-Stevenson writes in her letter to Senator John Kerry of October 6, 1991, with the discussion as recorded in the relevant parts of the hearings. Her letter appears on pp. 2–4 of part 2 of *Hearings Before the Select Committee on POW/MIA Affairs*, United States Senate, 102nd Congress, First Session (1991).

68. See the United Press International story on Perot dated May 21, 1981 (available through various computerized retrieval systems).

69. "Deposition of H. Ross Perot," pp. 122–135.

70. Ibid., pp. 144–55.

71. See the almost unbelievable story recounted by Perot about his efforts to squeeze out information on possible CIA involvement in one case in ibid., p. 171 ff.; for another involving the Defense Intelligence Agency, pp. 178 ff.

72. Jensen-Stevenson and Stevenson, *Goodbye*, p. 245; their p. 237 puts at least some of Perot's alleged fears for his safety in quite a different light than that suggested by the media during the campaign.

73. See Alfred McCoy, *The Politics of Heroin: CIA Complicity in the Global Drug Trade*, New York: Lawrence Hill, 1991.

74. Jensen-Stevenson and Stevenson, *Goodbye*, p. 337.

75. "Deposition of H. Ross Perot," p. 197. Perot continues, saying that he told Bush this during one of a series of personal visits to report on the progress of his investigation. On the next page, saying that the CIA has "a lot of fine, dedicated people," Perot says: "No, that's not fair, to say CIA agents. It's not that crisp in who they are. I said specifically—her quote is not accurate. To say I bump into drug and gun trafficking, then that would be accurate." Here one must note, however, that the actual quote is never used

by the investigators, so that exactly what is being affirmed or denied is obscure. Perot appears to be reacting to the words the interrogator is using.

76. See *Barron's*, February 23, 1987, pp. 34–35.

77. The deposition, Jensen-Stevenson and Stevenson, and many additional sources may be consulted about the Perot-Armitage controversy. Note that some observers, including Jonathan Kwitney, strongly defend Armitage. From this distance, it is simply impossible to judge. Not the least of the puzzles surrounding this controversy is the startlingly different tone in Jack Anderson's columns before and after the campaign started. Compare, for example, his column in the *Dallas Morning News* of February 2, 1987, with those he coauthored in the *Washington Post* for July 5, 1992 and July 7, 1992.

78. For Gargan, see, e.g., *Christian Science Monitor*, October 12, 1990. In Vermont, the core of Perot's volunteer efforts came from the the the failed campaign for the Democratic presidential nomination by Tom Laughlin (of *Billy Jack* fame). See Gail Russell Chaddock, "Perot's Volunteers," *Christian Science Monitor*, May 12, 1992. Perot opposed a balanced budget amendment during the campaign, only to endorse it afterward.

Perot's suggestions for changing the system of campaign financing amount to little in the way of serious reform proposals. According to Common Cause, in 1974 he was the largest single individual contributor to congressional campaigns. See the illuminating review of Perot's history of political investment by Ross Ramsey in the *Houston Chronicle*, May 10, 1992.

79. Among the first to urge Perot to run for president, for example, was John J. Hooker, a wealthy business figure from Tennessee. An aide to Jackson in the 1988 campaign, Hooker had also run twice for governor and remained very active in Southern politics. See the *Washington Times*, May 8, 1992. Another important figure behind the scenes was a well-known Southern banker, one Bert Lance. See the column on this notable "undeclared supporter" of Perot and his discussions with Jackson, Hamilton Jordan and others, by Rowland Evans and Robert Novak in the *Chicago Sun-Times*, June 28, 1992.

80. Some suggestive evidence exists about Perot's influence on the perception of Bush. The CBS/*New York Times* poll, for example, occasionally asked whether respondents thought "George Bush has strong qualities of leadership." Between March and April of 1992, the number saying "yes" dropped 14 points. See the press release for the poll of April 20–23, 1992. While other things were happening besides Perot's attacks on the president, it is difficult to believe that his influence was not felt. Unfortunately, this question was only rarely repeated.

Most survey indicators of interest in the race ran well above 1988's level: More people said they were interested, more people reported talking about the race, etc. Some of this new interest probably derived from the economic crisis, and thus should not be entirely attributed to Perot. Still, overall turnout in both the Democratic and Republican primaries was down as a percentage of the voting-age population, suggesting that much of this new interest was not coming from enthusiasts for Bush or Clinton (or anyone else in the major parties). In addition, the move upward in many of these indicators appears broadly to coincide with Perot's rise.

One wants to be careful about the frequently repeated assertion that Perot voters would have split down the middle between Clinton and Bush if Perot had not been on the ballot. It is a fair guess that a good percentage of such voters would not in fact have voted at all had Perot been absent from the ticket (more, that is, than those who claimed to pollsters that they would not have). Gallup's experience in its final polls also suggests that most undecided voters cast their vote for Perot at the end, instead of going to Clinton as they otherwise would have.

Though it is harder to show, I believe that in the spring, Perot also protected Clinton by drawing Bush's fire at a time when Clinton was vulnerable indeed.

81. The reference is to the now well-attested apparent effort by GOP operatives to disrupt the Massachusetts State Democratic Convention in 1990.

Perot's celebrated comments during the campaign about Citicorp (in whose stock he reportedly held a short position) and the banking system, while reflecting a real trend, suggest that he did not completely grasp Fed Chair Greenspan's strategy for dealing with the weakness in the banking sector. The Fed was clearly using a variety of tools, including the federal funds rate, to help the banks recapitalize. It was, in other words, virtually guaranteeing the profitability of the banking sector. This extraordinary development merits more attention than it has received; particularly as the United States recommends "free enterprise" to other countries.

82. See Perot to H. R. Haldeman of Feb. 24, 1970, quoted in Ferguson, *Texas Observer,* August 7, 1992, p. 8.

83. See my discussion in ibid., pp. 8–9.

84. For Tsongas on Perot, see the *Boston Globe,* June 27, 1992.

85. For the Toshiba warning, see "Perot cautions careful use of trade sanctions," United Press International, April 21, 1987.

86. Perot's substantial rise in the polls following the first debate leaves little doubt about his relative success in that first round. See the *New York Times,* October 15, 1992. The roundup of polls following the second debate reported in the *Boston Globe* of October 16, 1992, suggests that Clinton might qualify as the likely winner of the second debate. Polls split following the third debate over whether Clinton or Perot had won. See the *Boston Globe,* October 20, 1992. But perhaps the most important detail to watch is the difference between a candidate's support and the percentage of viewers suggesting he had won. Because these surely are normally highly correlated, a substantial number of people conceding that the less popular candidate won indicates a strong performance indeed.

87. For sharply contrasting versions of the CBS end-of-campaign interview with Perot, see the *Boston Globe,* October 28, 1992. Selective leaking to the press also complicates evaluation of other stories in the campaign, for example, those in which Perot was suggested to have engaged in practices, such as employing detectives, that are unfortunately widespread in American business.

88. See the *Boston Globe,* January 27, 1993.

89. E.g., Rubin, formerly of Goldman, Sachs, chairs the National Economic Council; Rubin formerly served as personal financial adviser to Bentsen, the former Texas senator who now serves as secretary of the treasury. (See the *New York Times,* March 7, 1993.) Bentsen's first deputy, Altman, formerly of Blackstone, worked with Rubin for many years in both state and national Democratic Party fund-raising. (See, e.g., note 31 above.)

90. Walter Dean Burnham, private communication.

91. For the poll results on the population's (brief) optimism, see the *New York Times,* January 31, 1993.

92. A preliminary analysis of the final budget legislation by H&R Block, dated Au-

gust 12, 1993 (distributed to me by the Office of Management and Budget), suggests that poor Americans are net beneficiaries of the bill's tax provisions, middle-income and most elderly taxpayers acquire no new burdens at all, and only the wealthiest Americans are likely to pay more. I think it is fair to say that the impression conveyed by most critics of the bill was quite different and that this misinformation affected the polls. The Congressional Budget Office and the Office of Management and Budget disagree somewhat on the exact numbers by which the deficit will be reduced. See, e.g., the unsympathetic analysis in *Investor's Business Daily*, September 9, 1993. But all the various tax, deficit, and GNP estimates imply reductions in federal spending as a percentage of GNP. Over time, these reductions add up to substantial sums. See, e.g., DRI/McGraw-Hill, *Review of the U.S. Economy*, September, 1993, pp. 73–79.

93. On the likely contractionary effects of cutting the deficit, see particularly Eisner, *Misunderstood Economy*. Another excellent discussion is Robert Blecker, "Low Savings Rates and the 'Twin Deficits': Confusing the Symptoms and Causes of Economic Decline," in Paul Davidson and J. A. Kregel, eds., *Economic Problems of the 1990s*, Brookfield, Vt.: Edward Elgar, 1991, pp. 161–93. See also his *Beyond the Twin Deficits*, Armonk, N.Y.: M. E. Sharpe, 1992.

94. See James Galbraith, "A Two-Track Growth Program," pp. 5, 11.

95. For the Kennedy administration's efforts to work with and on the Fed. see, e.g., E. Ray Canterbury, *Economics on A New Frontier*, Belmont, Cal: Wadsworth, 1968; Walter Heller's papers, now at the John F. Kennedy Library in Boston, contain much material on this question. A view of this sort implies a rejection of the fashionable view that the U.S. economy is now so open that the government cannot reasonably expect to do anything but please "the market," or, in some versions of the argument, only the capital markets. Such claims grossly overgeneralize from some celebrated cases of the seventies and eighties. It *is* obvious that governments cannot introduce socialism into open economies, but that was clear in the thirties. Current orthodoxy on this question resembles the debate over the "capitalist" state of a decade or so ago, which suffered sadly from neglect of the variety of historical forms capitalist societies can take. International economic forces are indeed powerful and need to be dealt with, but recent experiences with the European Monetary System show that countries like Britain and Italy can break with conventional wisdom and increase their rate of growth without the roof falling in. But more of this another time.

96. Lewis B. Kaden and Lee O. Smith, "Just Leave Laura Tyson Alone," the *New York Times*, January 17, 1993, draw a clear connection between efforts to address "structural" problems of competitiveness and the avoidance of devaluation. The authors were the chair and the executive director of a commission whose best-known report was signed by, among others, Robert Rubin. While I lack the space for a full discussion, it seems clear that no Japanese government is likely to find it very easy further to open its markets to foreign goods and investment. And it seems no less evident that many American analysts overestimate the strength of the very real forces in Japan that would like to bring about such a transformation.

97. A number of foreign analysts have raised pointed questions about the unwillingness of the American media to discuss potential balance-of-payments problems with the Clinton economic plan. See, in particular, the *Frankfurter Allgemeine Zeitung*, February 21, 1994. This also raises the possibility of an eventual flight from the dollar depending upon whom the president nominates to the Fed board of governors.

98. Because I broke the industry down into comparatively small subsegments to search for patterns, the results are not always statistically significant. Thus I do not report them in a table.

But the pattern is very striking. In most parts of the industry, rates of contribution to the Democrats approach zero. But in certain other segments, the rates of contribution to the Democrats are much higher.

Nursing homes, for example, are very highly mobilized. A great many firms on my list contributed—about half of them to Clinton or the Democratic soft money funds. (On the boards of such concerns, one also encounters rather a lot of political figures, including Mondale and top Bush campaign operative Frederic Malek.) Even more strikingly, *every single* contribution that I have been able to identify from the part of the industry concerned with long-term health care went to the Democrats. Upon examination, a single factor may explain most of this: these industry segments have been hurt badly by or fear further cuts in Medicaid or Medicare.

Another big bloc of Democrats comes from staff and administrators of many top research and teaching hospitals—where many of the Clinton campaign's health policy advisers appear to come from. Though some health policy analysts suggest that factors like the Clinton's campaign's emphasis on "choice" attracts such people, I am very skeptical that this explains anything. (The private sector as a whole does not appear to differ much on this dimension, for example.) The research hospitals, are, first of all, nonprofit. They fought a running battle with the Bush administration over the allocation of basic research support between them and the for-profit sector. Second, they are hugely dependent on subsidies for their teaching and research functions, and often in close touch with many foundations that are concerned that the present health-care system is collapsing. Because the status quo is a situation that figures every year to squeeze their high-cost research and training activities more and more, they must change the system before the system changes them.

Some Democratic contributors also turn up among the health maintenance organizations (HMOs). My sample of these, however, is very small, and I am checking further to see if this result is perhaps a statistical mirage or represents a clear subsector, such as nonprofits.

It may also be worth noting that many "nonphysician" providers—including nurses, psychiatrists (who, of course, do hold medical degrees), psychologists, and chiropractors show up as Democratic contributors. (Other studies indicate that their trade associations have historically been very heavily oriented to congressional Democrats.) One can conjecture that insurance coverage figures as an issue in several of these cases, as well as the ubiquitous question of relations with the heavily Republican physicians.

Finally, there are the special cases of pharmaceuticals and insurance. Overall, of course, these industries were highly mobilized in favor of Bush. Both industries were subsequently attacked in public by the Clinton campaign. In mid-summer, however, came reports of meetings between the insurers and the Clinton campaign. In the late stages of the campaign, Clinton gave a major campaign speech at the headquarters of a large drug company.

The administration is now reported to be eyeing a bill regulating pharmaceuticals recently introduced by Senator David Pryor of Arkansas, a close Clinton ally and friend. That bill relies on tying research-and-development tax credits to prices. As a consequence, large drug firms with big flows of new products generating rapid unit volume growth—such as the one which played host to Clinton during the campaign—would gain relative to smaller firms that rely more on price increases for revenue growth.

Note that for some years, Perot Systems has been striving to employ technology that could create the possibility of a "paperless hospital." See *Dallas Observer*, April 30, 1992, p. 9.

99. Vicente Navarro, "Swaying the Health Care Task Force," The *Nation*, September 6–13, 1993, pp. 1 ff.

100. Mishel and Bernstein, *State of Working America 1992–93*, chapters 3, 4, and 6, present a wide variety of data on the squeeze on ordinary Americans. Particularly striking is their table 3.1, which shows how hours of work have risen sharply as Americans have tried to cope with the pay squeeze. This stratagem can maintain annual incomes, particularly as women with families enter the labor force, but the process obviously also has inherent limits.

101. Both major parties, and indeed virtually the whole of the American establishment, now appear to consider unemployment of between 5½ and 6½ percent as "full employment." To the extent this view represents anything more than pure cynicism, it expresses a now fashionable conservative claim about an alleged "natural" rate of unemployment. But the underpinnings of this claim are flimsy indeed. Almost never is it treated as, for example, an empirical hypothesis subject to evidence. But as Eisner emphasizes, the view does have testable implications—and the evidence tells heavily against it. See his discussion in *Misunderstood Economy*, especially chapter 8.

CONCLUSION

Money and Destiny in Advanced Capitalism:
Paying the Piper, Calling the Tune

ON JANUARY 29, 1848, Alexis de Tocqueville rose to issue an urgent warning to his colleagues in the French Chamber of Deputies. "I am told," he said, "that there is no danger because there are no riots." But, he continued, "I believe that we are at this moment sleeping on a volcano. . . ."

"Think, gentlemen, of the old monarchy: it was stronger than you are, stronger in its origin; it was able to lean more than you upon ancient customs, ancient habits, ancient beliefs; it was stronger than you are, and yet it has fallen into dust. And why did it fall? Do you think it was by some particular mischance? Do you think it was by the act of some man, by the [budget] deficit . . . No, gentlemen; there was another reason: the class that was then the governing class had become, through its indifference, its selfishness and its vices, incapable and unworthy of governing the country."

"Do you not feel," finally asked the famous author of *Democracy in America*, "by some intuitive instinct which is not capable of analysis, but which is undeniable, that the earth is quaking once again?"[1]

De Tocqueville's fellow deputies listened, but few heard him. Virtually to a man (all, of course, were males), they were astounded when, a few weeks later, a tide of revolution engulfed Paris and the rest of Europe.

In the mid-1990s, the ominous sounds of the earth "quaking once again" are suddenly becoming audible to many Americans who never expected to hear them. Under pressure in the swiftly moving global economy, one corporate giant after another is "downsizing," announcing massive layoffs, wage cuts, plant closings, and reductions in benefits, including health insurance. In some parts of the country, real estate values appear likely to remain low for years. Almost everywhere, cash-starved governments are cutting back on social programs long viewed as untouchable, while many "not-for-profit" institutions such as universities, museums, and schools waste away.

Although the press still covers elections as though they were so many Kentucky Derbies and increasingly appears to believe that strange bedfellows are all there are to American politics, even the mainstream media sometimes betray doubts about the future of the "American dream." Alongside its now well-stereotyped stories illustrating the indifference, the selfishness, and the vices of official Washington (the congressional pay raise and bank overdrafts scandals, savings and loans, Whitewater, the Capitol Post Office and Congressman Rostenkowski, or the Packwood debacle) appear occasional memorable vignettes of giddily leveraged buyouts and mergers, flagrant abuses of the tax code and employee pension funds, breathtaking statistics about the increase in the wealth of the top 1 percent of the American rich in the eighties, and the fabulous rise in executive compensation—running, in many cases, far ahead of corporate performance. Former Secretary of State George Shultz, now a professor at Stanford University and director of many concerns, including Boeing, Bechtel, and Weyerhauser, has even wondered out loud if the feeble state of American labor unions is really healthy for the system as a whole.[2]

But America in the nineties is a long way from Paris in 1848. When the earth began to rumble then, the City of Light had a revolution. By contrast, the United States sports perhaps the most smoothly efficient money-driven electoral system in the world.

This ensures a strikingly different outcome. The essays in this book have shown how, in the midst of the greatest depression in world history, capital-intensive, multinationally oriented financiers and industrialists and their allies in export-oriented industry coalesced in support of Franklin D. Roosevelt's Second New Deal. This multinational bloc can be demonstrated to have contributed in hugely disproportionate numbers to the financing of FDR's critical 1936 reelection campaign. Many of its leaders, in addition, played key roles in the administration or the policy-making process that produced the New Deal's epoch-making legislative achievements.

Depending on the strength of labor and the changing balance of power within the Republican Party between these liberal internationalists and their more protectionist and nationalist opponents, the multinational bloc's attachment to the Democrats waxed and waned. But the political formula of this System of 1936—free trade and social welfare—dominated the American political landscape and inspired much of the rest of the world until the 1970s.

Then the world economy turned decisively against it. In a complex process summarized in chapters 5 and 6, virtually the entire business community abandoned the Democrats. Facing intense pressure from foreign competitors, more and more enterprises sought to shift or lower costs by intensifying the globalization of production, lowering wages, reducing government regulation, and reducing taxes. Though the general public's views on most issues of public policy either remained basically the same or actually shifted a bit in a liberal direction, a consensus formed within the business community in favor of rearmament, macroeconomic austerity, and domestic budgetary retrenchment.[3]

Responding to these sentiments, the Carter administration tilted further and further to the right—most memorably by appointing Paul Volcker to chair the Federal Reserve and by chopping the budget on its own mass constituencies just ahead of the 1980 election, as it ratcheted up military spending. Not surprisingly, the party's efforts to simulate the GOP availed it nothing. Its policies of economic austerity turned voters massively against it, bringing the Republicans to power.[4]

Unlike the Democrats, the GOP had never strongly championed the ideas that governmental power not only could but should help ordinary Americans as well as business, and that it was imperative to temper the often ferocious workings of the "invisible hand."

The new dominance of the Republicans, however, did not last. Very soon, extreme laissez faire proved unacceptable not only to the poor and vulnerable, but also to important parts of the business community. Led and, of course, financed by prominent business figures, the Democrats regrouped. In the early 1980s, many investment bankers, real estate magnates, and high-tech firms promoted a more activist course for government, as well as stricter budget discipline. Because of the budget crisis, this stance automatically implied limits to Pentagon spending, though neither the investment bankers nor the high-tech firms disputed the importance of maintaining a high level of military spending. In 1992, after four years of virtually no growth under the Bush administration, the coalition of businesses committed to the basic multinational project, but in favor of carefully limited state intervention, widened appreciably. Often citing the need for a break with (relatively) strict laissez faire orthodoxy, an important minority of business leaders defected to the Democrats. With major assistance from a superrich Texan who could afford to chart his own unique course of conservative national renewal, this coalition triumphed with much less than a majority of votes.

Now, however, average Americans who can hear the earth quaking—who are anxious about their jobs, education, health costs, pensions, and personal security—confront a severe problem. While there is no reason to doubt that many members of President Bill Clinton's team devoutly hope some day to be able to promote bolder domestic policy initiatives, the business groups that dominate the new administration's financing and many of its top policy-making slots differ only modestly from their Republican predecessors. The slight rise in upper bracket tax rates so narrowly—and noisily—wrought by the Clinton budget program in 1993 marks the pillars of Hercules of their tolerance for "sacrifice." Almost neurotically sensitive to the risk of even tiny amounts of inflation, these groups are as committed as any Republicans to macroeconomic austerity and free trade (with everyone save perhaps parts of Asia). And in the end, quite like the Republican elites which dominated the Reagan and Bush administrations, they are likely to spend a plenary share of their time and attention pondering foreign, rather than domestic, policy conundrums—how to preserve peace and economic progress in Hong Kong or Western Europe, for example, rather than in Los Angeles.

Not surprisingly, in recent years substantial numbers of Americans have come to feel that something is desperately wrong with their political system. Many polls indicate a growing demand for reforms, and the grass roots are stirring in all directions—on the left, on the right, and even in the center. Not one but several budding new parties have sprouted, while Ross Perot's following continues to hold itself aloof from both the Democrats and the Republicans. Though it is perhaps an unlikely outcome, it is possible that 1996 will see not three, but four candidates with a plausible claim to national followings in the final leg of the race for the White House.[5]

As the fluctuations in Perot's popularity since the election suggest, these signs of discontent will surely vary not only over the course of the business cycle, but with every twist and turn of national politics.[6] Still, all around the United States, campaigns on behalf of all sorts of "reforms" are kicking into gear: constitutional amendments to require a balanced budget; term limitations; various secession movements; any number of referenda. But one idea which stands out, though it certainly does not preempt all others, is the notion that the time has come for serious campaign finance reform.

Obviously this is a sentiment that I completely share. I have no objection to term limits—if, as I suspect, they would slightly enhance the significance of party identification, they might do a little good. But they will do nothing to end the dependence of candidates and parties on big money. Anyone who wants to run will still have to pay to play, even if the number of lucrative go-rounds is limited by statute. By contrast, the balanced budget amendment is pre-Keynesian nonsense. It would virtually guarantee a major depression if seriously adhered to. And all forms of secession run up against the hard truth that motivated Trotsky's famous old gibe that while you may not be interested in history, history is interested in you. Balkanization, I fear, is a poor answer, even in the Balkans.

In the end, the only political change that will guarantee real reform is a wholesale restructuring of campaign financing. But as one contemplates the range of proposals that are crowding the agenda, it is impossible to escape a certain all-too-familiar sinking feeling.

Precisely because the subject really is crucial all sorts of sham proposals now crowd the docket. Because these change with every legislative session, it is pointless to linger over the details of any one in particular. Suffice it to say that while reasonable people might disagree over whether the various bills supported at different times by the Clinton administration add up to a baby step in the right direction, neither the president's proposals, nor those of the congressional leaders, nor—*a fortiori*—of the Republicans, nor of Perot come close to dealing seriously with the problem.[7]

Like Common Cause, most of these blow hard about a peripheral problem—the notorious political action committees. PACs, however, are simply not that important in the grand scheme of political money. They account for slightly more than a third of all receipts in House races and about a quarter of receipts in Senate races. Their role in presidential races is insignificant; many candidates now routinely make the grand gesture of refusing money from them, as they open for business.[8]

Because what really matters is individual contributions and soft money, PACs could be completely banned without changing anything fundamental. The major consequence would be that groups such as unions or eyeglass vendors, whose members are scattered over wide areas and not particularly rich individually, would have a much harder time coordinating. Large firms, which can organize themselves comparatively easily, would be little affected in the long run. The value of endorsements by the media would almost certainly be enhanced considerably—indeed, I am not alone in regarding this, along with the obstacle presented to unions, as one of the principal reasons this proposed "reform" is so popular.

Most of the widely touted campaign finance reform proposals, including President Clinton's, leave the door open for colossal amounts of the soft money that, as we saw in the previous chapters, now fuels both major parties. The president's latest proposal, for example, suggests a limit on the size of such donations that must surely be very close to the median soft money contribution.

Equally ineffective are the limits usually proposed on individual contributions (current federal law mandates a limit of $1,000, with primaries and general elections counting as two separate races), or, *a fortiori*, the much higher limits on total donations in a year. These simply codify candidates' dependence on one set of very special interests—the comparative handful of Americans who can routinely afford to make donations of this size. (Indeed, the current system of presidential matching funds, which doubles the first $250 of suitably qualifying presidential primary contributions, amounts to a roundabout device for leveraging the contributions of major investors with public money.)

The reforms proposed by the usual suspects also hurry past most of the other problems identified in essays in this book as sources of politically significant money. Long before Ed Rollins drew spectacular attention to such practices, parties and candidates had figured out that charities, foundations, and think tanks were all potential vehicles for money that in fact, if not in law, was campaign money. Nor do any amount of limits on spending and reports on funds help much to control the many other ways money is funneled to politicians all the time (see Figure 1). Nor do they address the more ramified ways, discussed earlier, that money deforms the political system, such as the question of media access, or the way big money links up with professional hierarchies at the bar, in the universities, and even in the pulpit.

Does this mean that nothing can be done? That no specific reform, short of a transformation of the political system on at least the scale of the New Deal, can accomplish anything substantial?

In an age in which the corrupting influence of political money has recently helped topple regimes in no less than three of the G7 countries (Italy, Japan, France); is a major issue in at least two others (the United States and Germany); and has become the object of significant public concern in a sixth (Great Britain, where a special parliamentary commission is investigating), it would be idle to pretend that the millennium lies around the corner.

But from an investment theory perspective, the problem is by no means hopeless. The usual regulatory formulations, however, are not the most helpful.

Consider instead how the problem might be transformed. Let us agree that bribery and most other forms of funnelling cash to politicians should be sharply penalized. Let us also agree that campaign expenditures require some limitation, if only to prevent more and more of society's resources from going down a black hole. Yet, no matter how diligent the regulators, it is likely that de Tocqueville's "governing class," with its "selfishness and its vices," will contrive to find ways to corrupt the system. It is also likely that the favored candidates and parties of this class will from time to time attempt to circumvent spending limits.

Therefore, turn the problem around. The first essay in this book (like the appendix, where the point emerges with particular starkness) argued that the classical approaches to democratic control of the state fatally underestimate the costs facing citizens who seriously try to exert

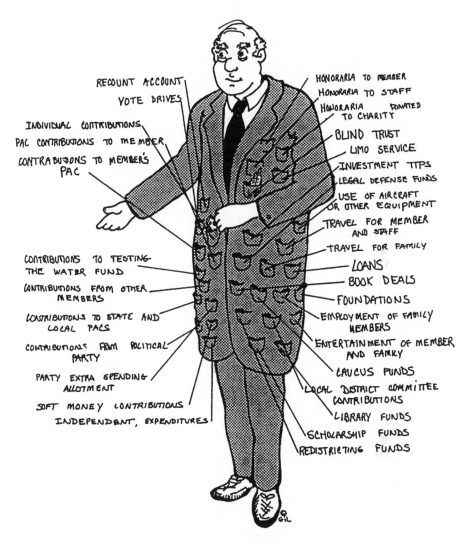

FIGURE 1. The Many Pockets of a Politician's Coat

that control. Not one but a host of barriers must be surmounted, including the often high costs of acquiring and verifying information,
and the costs of finding allies, negotiating agreements, building a party,
choosing candidates, campaigning, and so forth. Unless some way can
be devised to share these costs, control of the state remains literally
beyond the means of average citizens.

It is extraordinarily inefficient, and sometimes quite impossible, for individual citizens or even groups of citizens to cope with this problem on an individual basis. At best, everyone ends up duplicating work that could have been shared at a far lower unit cost if overhead costs had been spread out over the whole group and economies of scale tapped. At worst, an endless series of "let George do it" collective-action problems stymies all progress.

A sensible public policy, accordingly, would build on the practices that virtually all modern democratic states have evolved to cope with these dilemmas. Whether or not they trumpet the facts, all modern states extensively subsidize many of these costs. The political parties of the United States and many other countries receive subsidies of various sorts. They qualify for matching funds; representatives frank mail; the state stages elections and counts the ballots, etc. They also teach civics, and require courses in government for a diploma from college or high school. As recent German discussions, in particular, have emphasized, even the practice of paying for legislative staff is a valuable form of subsidy.[9]

What these nations, and particularly the United States, with its private domination of the airwaves, do *not* do is subsidize enough of these costs to do average citizens much good. Instead, most modern states pick up much of the tab for parties that only the rich can afford to control, because the "threshold" costs of entry are so high.[10]

This is the aspect of the system that needs to be changed. And the remedy is straightforward: Apply the "Golden Rule" for the benefit of the public as a whole: Provide sufficient public financing to allow ordinary people to run for office with a reasonable chance of getting their message out and getting elected. This could be done in any number of ways. One could simply extend some of the proposals now before Congress that would establish various voluntary schemes, probably with a variety of qualifying hurdles. Or one could take over the proposals advanced by some private groups with no particular axes to grind— those of the Center for Responsible Politics and the Working Group on Electoral Democracy are quite sensible and fair.[11]

One can also envision other possible formulas: Congress could simply establish a system of modest tax credits for political contributions conferred by individuals on candidates or parties of their choice. A system like this would, for the first time, give candidates an incentive to appeal to the poor. If it was coupled with the requirement that radio and TV stations make available a certain amount of time to candidates as a condition for holding broadcasting licenses, its cost would be comparatively low.[12]

However it was done, almost any system of public financing would have an extra benefit that is only rarely appreciated. It would seriously limit the harm that can be done by all the other ways wealth corrupts the system. Financing elections, after all, somewhat resembles a nuclear arms race. There is a limit to the advantages to be derived from blowing up the entire world twenty-seven or forty-four times. For virtually any practical situation, destroying everything ten times over should suffice.

Analogously, if citizens with grievances or (what appear to be) heterodox points of view are able to get their messages out, respond to critics, and have a chance to counterattack (a stage of campaigning that is particularly expensive, as the appendix notes), the logic of the situation alters dramatically. Though last-minutes charges could sow confusion in particular races, it would be much more difficult to distort or suppress policy alternatives that would benefit the bulk of the citizenry in the long run. Other illicit uses of wealth in politics would also recede in importance, since no matter how corrupt any set of politicians were, they could not escape public criticism and competition from outsiders. Voters would have a real chance to hear alternative points of view. They could reflect upon these points of view, even if the press and the leaders of the academy were hostile or indifferent. If the electorate wanted, it could vote the critics in—whether or not any investor bloc at all was willing to finance the campaign.

In the mid-1990s, hard-pressed taxpayers who are already irate about paying more for less from their government may not instantly see the logic of such a scheme. But there are ways to frame the issue to get the point across. Perhaps the most telling is simply to restate the "Golden Rule" as it applies to popular democracy: In politics, you get what you pay for. Or someone else does.

NOTES

1. *The Recollections of Alexis de Tocqueville,* ed. by the Comte de Tocqueville and translated by Alexander Teixeira de Mattos, New York: Macmillan, 1896, pp. 14–15.

2. For Shultz's views, see the discussion in the *New York Times,* December 13, 1991. Surveys of the relation between chief executive officers' pay and corporate performance are becoming numerous. See, e.g., *Executive Compensation in Corporate America '91,* United Shareholders Association, 1991, for a very striking analysis. (The data are for 1990; Graef S. Crystal, perhaps the leading authority in the field, presents the analysis.)

3. It is presumably unnecessary to remind readers that this discussion is a summary of a much longer analysis that included discussions of the roles of think tanks, shifts within the media, and even religious movements. See the discussion and notes to references in the chapters concerned, particularly those to Ferguson and Rogers, *Right Turn: The Decline of the Democrats and the Future of American Politics,* New York: Hill & Wang, 1986.

4. See the careful review of interpretations of the 1980 election in Stanley Kelley Jr., *Interpreting Elections,* Princeton: Princeton University Press, 1983, chapter 9; and the

statistical evidence in Kelley, "Democracy And The New Deal Party System," in Amy Guttman, ed., *Democracy and the Welfare State,* Princeton: Princeton University Press, 1988; John Geer, "The Electorate's Partisan Evaluations: Evidence of A Continuing Democratic Edge," *Public Opinion Quarterly* 55, no. 2, summer 1991, pp. 218–31, and Geer's "New Deal Issues and the American Electorate, 1952–88," *Political Behavior* 14, no. 1, 1992, pp. 45–65; as well as the discussion in Ferguson and Rogers, *Right Turn,* pp. 33–36. These sources document the observation that despite many claims, foreign policy was plainly not the chief catalyst of voter switches in this election, or in later ones.

5. The best-known poll evidence on the public's demand for reforms is probably Gordon Black's "The Politics of American Discontent: A Study of Voter Discontent," prepared for a press conference at the National Press Club, June 3, 1992, which is quite comprehensive; organizers of one of the new parties were associated with this poll. It would be possible to compare this poll with others, but this level of detail is not necessary for the points made here. Perot's entry into Republican primaries also should not be ruled out.

6. I should like to emphasize that this discontent should not be identified solely with any single movement, including Perot's, though I also believe that the wish is father to the thought in the claims, repeated by many in the media, that the NAFTA debate discredited the Texan. This is the second time Perot has been pronounced dead based on declines in polls. By comparison with the first decline, the latest is quite small. In Michigan and elsewhere, I think, his stance in due course may well be differently perceived.

7. Useful overviews of recent proposals for campaign finance reform are "Constitutional Doubts Bedevil Hasty Campaign Finance Bill," *Congressional Quarterly,* August 14, 1993, pp. 2215–18 and the "Provisions" on pp. 2239–43. Ellen Miller, "The Senate's Sham Reform Plan," the *Washington Post,* June 28, 1993, is an excellent criticism of one widely touted reform plan. Miller's statement "On Campaign Finance Reform," at the hearings before the Connecticut House of Representatives Government Administration and Elections Committee, March 15, 1993, available from the Center for Responsive Politics in Washington, D.C., is a useful outline of a number of practical issues in public financing, of which the United States has more experience than usually recognized. See also the discussion in the last chapter of Frank Sorauf, *Money in American Elections,* Glenview, Il: Scott, Foresman, 1988.

8. The percentages are for the years 1987–88 (1988 elections) and come from table 3 of Thomas Ferguson, "Money and Politics," in Godfrey Hodgson, ed., *Handbooks to the Modern World—The United States,* vol. 2, New York: Facts On File, 1992, p. 1066. It will be understood that the percentages vary over time.

9. See Hans Herbert von Arnim, "Die Politischen Parteien und Das Geld," Vortrag bei den 26. Bitburger Gespraeche zum Thema 'Parteienrecht—Parteienfinanzierung'," am 14–16 April 1993 in Bischofsgruen. Arnim is probably the leading German student of campaign finance. Note that an important consequence of the German system is that because the parties are associated with recognized think tanks, far more of the politically relevant money comes to public attention. As is several times discussed in this book, many U.S. foundations and think tanks which are quite obviously involved in politics, in an extended sense, escape scrutiny by claiming to be "nonpolitical."

10. Chapter 1 and the appendix discuss at length the "public goods" ("collective action") aspects of political action. These have an important consequence: they cannot in principle be remedied by any laissez faire policy. This point will be obvious to anyone

familiar with this now large literature, but I mention it here for the benefit of readers from other fields. Any textbook on public finance will have a thorough treatment of the problem.

11. See, for the center's proposals, Ellen Miller, "Money, Politics, and Democracy," *Boston Review*, March/April 1993, p. 5 ff.; the Washington, D.C.–based center has a wide variety of shorter and longer literature available describing its proposals. The Working Group on Electoral Democracy has also produced detailed proposals. See, e.g., Marty Jezer, Randy Kehler, Ben Senuria, "A Proposal for Democratically Financed Congressional Elections," *Yale Law and Policy Review* 11, no. 2, 1993, pp. 333–360; the group's convenient "Summary of Model Proposal for Democratically Financed Elections" summarizes its longer proposed measure. See also Randy Kehler, "Is Change on the Horizon?" *Sojourners*, November 1992, pp. 21–23; particularly interesting, considering the silence of much of organized labor on this question, is the working group's "Labor Needs Democratically Financed Elections," n.d. One of the working group's excellent ideas is to require candidates to use a specific "credit card" for all campaign expenditures, making it much easier to track spending.

12. The stations, of course, oppose requirements for free time. They would rather sell the time. In a world marked by the ascent of giant, vertically integrated world-wide communications companies, such a scheme is certain to have powerful opponents.

Note also that a system of tax credits would miss the relatively small number of low-income Americans who do not pay significant taxes.

The 1994 Explosion

"Our issues are basically safe now, the health mandates, the employer mandates, the minimum wage. . . . I don't think those will be high priorities in a Republican Congress."
GOPAC Contributor Thomas Kershaw
Described by the Boston *Globe* as "a $10,000-a-year charter member" of
Newt Gingrich's "grand effort to engineer a Republican takeover of Congress"

DOWN THROUGH THE AGES, survivors of truly epic catastrophes have often recounted how their first, chilling presentiment of impending doom arose from a dramatic reversal in some feature of ordinary life they had always taken for granted. Pliny the Younger's memorable account of the destruction of Pompeii and Herculaneum by an eruption of Mt. Vesuvius in A.D. 79, for example, remarks how, in the hours before the volcano's final explosion, the sea was suddenly "sucked away and apparently forced back . . . so that quantities of sea creatures were left stranded on dry sand."[1]

Sudden, violent changes in an ocean of money around election time are less visually dramatic than shifts in the Bay of Naples. But long before the Federal Election Commission unveils its final report on the financing of the 1994 midterm elections, it is already clear that in the final weeks before the explosion that buried alive the Democratic Party, changes in financial flows occurred that were as remarkable as anything Pliny and his terrified cohorts witnessed two thousand years ago: A sea of money that had for years been flowing reliably to Congressional Democrats and the party that controlled the White House abruptly reversed direction and began gushing in torrents to Republican challengers.

Throughout most of the 1993–94 "election cycle" a reversal of these proportions seemed about as likely as the sudden extinction of two important Roman towns did to Pliny's contemporaries. The Republican Party, virtually everyone agreed, normally enjoyed a lopsided overall national advantage in campaign fundraising. But in the Congress, incumbency was decisive. Because big business, the Democratic Party's putative opponent, ultimately preferred "access" over "ideology," Democratic Congressional barons could reliably take toll—enough to make them all but invulnerable for the indefinite future.[2]

In addition, the Democrats now also controlled the White House. By comparison with its recent past, the party was thus exquisitely positioned to raise funds for the 1994 campaign. It could extract vast sums of "soft money" (funds allegedly raised for state and local party-building purposes, but in fact closely coordinated with national campaigns) from clients (i.e., patrons) in the business community. It could also exploit the unrivalled advantages occupants of the Oval Office enjoy in hitting up big ticket individual contributors.

The glib contrast between "access" and "ideology" was always at best a half-truth. Particularly if one reckons over several election cycles, the differences in total contributions flowing to a Democratic leader who literally opened for business, such as former House Ways and Means chair Dan Rostenkowski, and a populist maverick like outgoing House Banking Committee chair Henry Gonzalez, are quite fabulous. Between 1982 and 1992, for example, FEC figures indicate that Rostenkowski succeeded in raising more than four million dollars in campaign funds. Over the same period, Gonzalez's campaigns took in less than $700,000. Among Democratic Congressional leaders, Rostenkowski's was far from a record-setting pace. Not including funds formally raised for his forays into presidential politics, Richard Gephardt, formerly House majority leader and now minority leader, raised over seven million dollars in the same stretch.[3]

Differences of this order demonstrate that, in the long run, "access" eventually leads to favorable policy outcomes—or the money goes elsewhere. Airy talk about mere "access" also subtly diverted attention from the historically specific stages of the accommodation between the Democrats and big business as the New Deal System died its painful, lingering death of 1,000 contributions.[4]

Early reports by the FEC for the 1993–94 election cycle appeared to confirm the conventional wisdom. In August, the FEC released a survey of national party fundraising efforts (a much narrower category than the name suggests, since it takes no account of, for example, the separately tabulated efforts of individual campaigns for Congress, where the consolidated totals run far higher). This indicated that the Republicans were continuing to cling to their overall lead. Fundraising by the national Democratic party, however, was up by 34 percent compared to the same period in 1991–92, when George Bush was president.[5]

In the bellwether category of soft money, one of the best available indicators of sentiment among America's largest investors, the contrast in regard to the same period was even sharper: Democratic receipts had doubled, to $33 million, while GOP receipts were down 28 percent, to a mere $25 million.[6]

Early statistics on Congressional races indicated much the same trend. One FEC report released during the summer showed the early flow of contributions to Democratic candidates in all types of races—incumbencies, challenges, and, especially, open seats—running well above the levels of 1991–92. By contrast, House Republican candidates in every category trailed well behind their Democratic counterparts in average (median) total receipts. Other FEC statistics indicated that in House races, corporate PACs were tilting strongly in favor of Democratic candidates.[7]

As late as October, reports continued to circulate in the media of persisting large Democratic advantages in fundraising in regard to both Congressional races and soft money.[8] By then, however, little puffs of smoke were appearing over Mt. Vesuvius. Leaks in the press began to appear, suggesting that the Republicans, led by the redoubtable Newt Gingrich, were staging virtual revivals with enthusiastic corporate donors, lobbyists, and, especially, PACs.[9]

On November 2 came what could have become the first public premonition of the coming sea change: New figures for soft money published by the FEC indicated that between June 30 and October 19, the Democrats had managed to raise the almost laughable sum of $10 million dollars, while the Republicans had pulled down almost twice that much. Alas, the media and most analysts concentrated on each party's now closely similar take over the full two-year cycle. No one asked what had happened to dry up money to the Democrats in a period in which most observers still took for granted continued Democratic control of at least the House. Neither did anyone think to project the new trend, which was undoubtedly gathering additional fierce momentum in the final, delirious weeks of fundraising as the GOP scented victory.[10]

Two days later, the Commission published data on Congressional races throughout October 19. Though almost no one noticed, the new data pointed to a startling turnabout: funds to House Republican challengers and candidates for open seats were now pouring in at approximately twice the rate of 1992. Democratic totals were up only slightly, save for a somewhat larger rise among candidates in races for open seats (that, unlike 1992, left their median receipts well behind those of their GOP counterparts).[11] The ceaseless drumbeating by Newt Gingrich and other Republicans was beginning to pay off. Only a few months before, corporate PACs investing in House races had been sending 60 percent of their funds to Democrats. By October, the PACs, along with other donors, were swinging back toward the GOP.

The trend was strongest where it probably mattered most: in races waged by challengers and candidates for open seats. A study by Richard Keil of the Associated Press indicates that in 1992 PACs as a group favored Democratic challengers and open-seat aspirants by a 2 to 1 margin. By October 1994, however, the AP found that PACs had switched dramatically: More than half of their donations to challengers and open-seat aspirants were going to GOP candidates. The Associated Press figures are for PACs as a group, and thus include contributions from Labor PACs, which give lopsidedly to Democrats. The real size of the shift within the business community and related ideological PACs is, accordingly, significantly understated.[12]

Pressed by Gingrich, who wrote what the AP described as a "forceful memo" on the subject to would-be Republican leaders of the new House, the GOP also made efficient use of another emergency fundraising vehicle: the shifting of excess campaign funds from Republican incumbents with a high probability of reelection. Additional last minute spending against Democratic candidates also appears to have come from organizations "independent" of the parties, but favoring issues firmly associated with Gingrich and the Republicans, such as the recently founded Americans for Limited Terms.[13]

With so many races hanging in the balance (the Republicans, in the end, garnered only 50.5 percent of the total vote, according to a study by Stanley Greenberg for the Democratic Leadership Council), the tidal wave of late-arriving money surely mattered a great deal. But the AP's striking analysis of the effects of this blitz underscores just how wide of the mark were the establishment pundits who rushed to claim that "money can't buy everything" in the wake of razor-thin defeats suffered by high-visibility, high-spending Republican Senate candidates in California and Virginia.[14]

The AP examined sixteen House contests decided by four percentage points or less. Campaign funds from Republican incumbents to other Republican candidates came in at three times the rate of donations from Democratic incumbents to their brethren. The Republicans won all sixteen. Even more impressive, of the 146 Republicans estimated by the AP to have received $100,000 or more in PAC donations, 96 percent were victorious—a truly stunning result when one reflects that much of the late money was clearly funnelled into close races.[15]

Most election analysts in the United States habitually confuse the sound of money talking with the voice of the people. Thus it was only to be expected that as they surveyed the rubble on the morning after the election, many commentators gleefully broadjumped to the conclusion that the electorate had not merely voted to put the Democratic Party in Chapter 11, but had also embraced Newt Gingrich's curious

"Contract with America." But the evidence is very strong that it's still "the economy, stupid," and that the 1994 election was essentially the kind of massive no-confidence vote that would have brought down the government in a European-style parliamentary system.

Let us start with some obvious, if once again relatively neglected, facts. As an anointed representative of massive blocs of money, Newt Gingrich may indeed be on his way to becoming a figure of towering significance in American politics. But until the sunburst of publicity that followed the election, he was just another face in the crowd to most Americans. In a Yankelovich poll of 800 adult Americans taken for *Time*/CNN immediately following the vote, 68 percent of respondents said they were not familiar with him. (Another 3 percent were unsure of their response; of those who were, slightly more people— 16 percent vs. 13 percent—viewed him unfavorably rather than favorably.)[16]

It is true that a few late Democratic ads targeted the Contract and that the White House briefly attacked it. But the Contract itself was essentially an inside-the-beltway gimmick, publicized in the closing weeks of the campaign to answer the charge—coming mostly from desperate rival elites who saw all too clearly what was happening— that the GOP stood for nothing in its own right, and was simply trying to win by opposing Clinton and the Democrats. Based on what we know about the way ideas play off personalities in American politics, it is hard to believe that in such a short, distracted time stretch the Contract could have become much more visible or attractive than Gingrich himself.[17]

Neither does survey evidence about the public's attitudes support sweeping claims about a sharp new "right turn" by the mass public. Virtually all polls released so far rely on various forms of so-called forced-choice questions. Because these squeeze the respondent to make choices between alternatives selected by the survey designer, they are not always a happy tool for sorting out views and opinions that were actually important to voters as they made up their minds from the welter of other convictions that they have, but which were irrelevant to their voting decisions. For example, it does not automatically follow that, because voters do not care for a president's foreign policies, their distaste will actually carry over to their voting decisions. Many may simply vote their pocketbooks. Their truthful answer to a foreign policy question might be irrelevant.[18]

Forced-choice questions also lend themselves to misinterpretation, by posing choices that the electorate (or pollsters) may not realize are in fact incompatible, or by omitting alternatives that voters consider important. Depending on which responses receive emphasis, the electorate can appear to be moving in almost any direction. Thus, 85 percent of those interviewed in the Yankelovich poll, attached "high priority" to reducing the federal budget deficit; 75 percent attached a similar priority to a Constitutional amendment to balance the budget; 54 percent agreed that legislation to limit the terms of members of Congress to twelve years was also a "high priority" item; 82 percent thought tougher crime enforcement legislation was also. The same poll showed large majorities favor placing a "high priority" on actions to limit welfare payments (66%) and a line-item veto for the president (59%).[19] But this particular survey (which is quite well crafted by the standards of the trade) did not ask voters a number of other questions. For example, respondents were not asked whether they ranked economic growth above deficit reduction. In all polls known to me, whenever that question is asked, growth is the landslide winner.[20]

Nor was the public asked its views about cutting Social Security or the wisdom of making many specific budget cuts (e.g., in Medicare and Medicaid) that the affluent sponsors of the balanced budget are seeking to impose by what is, in reality, stealth. In a post-election poll by Greenberg for the DLC of people who said they had voted, 62 percent of those interviewed indicated that protecting Social Security and Medicare should be either the "single highest" or one of the "top few" priorities of the president and the next Congress. Sixteen percent placed increasing defense spending within those two categories. Gingrich and the GOP's stalwart opposition to raising the minimum wage is also unlikely to resonate strongly with most Americans.[21]

One also needs to remember that many Americans have been ideologically conservative and programmatically liberal for decades. At no time before, during, or after the New Deal were new taxes, more bureaucracy, or "big government" ever anyone's idea of shrewd political appeals. This is one of several reasons for skepticism about the meaning of the discovery, by Greenberg working for the DLC, that if respondents are forced to choose between "traditional Democrats who believe government can solve problems and protect people from adversity" and "New Democrats who believe government should help people equip themselves to solve their own problems," 66 percent say they identify with the latter.[22]

To the extent the answer does not reflect unalloyed familiarity with beltway buzzwords, I suspect strongly that one would find roughly the same pattern of responses at any point in the high New Deal. Who now remembers, for example, that in the very first Gallup Poll published in 1935, 60 percent of respondents said that too much money was being spent on "relief and recovery"? On the other hand, Greenberg's survey does show clearly enough that whatever the popular mood about government action (which, as indicated below, has hardened), a majority of respondents flatly reject what certainly qualifies as the guiding idea of the Contract that "government should leave people alone to solve their own problems."[23]

Nor is this all. Fifty-four percent of respondents in the Yankelovich poll also came out for tougher legislation to regulate lobbying, which Gingrich staunchly opposed as he solicited corporate cash. (This news was reported in a preelection leak to the *Washington Post;* a Democratic Party less hopelessly mortgaged to pecuniary interests could have trumpeted it until the heavens resounded.) Forty-five percent also indicated campaign finance reform as another "high priority." In the great tradition of predictive social science, one can venture to suppose that Mt. Vesuvius will freeze over before House Republicans offer anything except cosmetics on this decisive issue.[24]

Surveys also suggest that the Clinton administration's own Rube Goldberg scheme for health-care reform did finally become unpopular with many voters. In the later stages of the mammoth onslaught against health-care reform by industry groups, opinion also wavered on related health issues. Still, 72 percent of those polled by Yankelovich wanted health-care "reform" to be a "high priority" in the next Congress. Health-care reform also topped all other responses in the poll when respondents were asked to pick one issue as the top priority of the new Congress. Whatever senses of "reform" respondents read into those questions, most surely intend something quite different from anything Gingrich and the new GOP majority in Congress have in mind.[25]

More abstract—and hence, perhaps, less clearcut—benchmarks also show no sudden new turn to starboard. While election day surveys do not exhaust the complicated question of how the public labels itself, the party identification figures in the (very large) *New York Times* election-day exit poll actually moved the wrong way for a new "right turn" hypothesis: this year the percentage of self-described Democrats was 41 percent, compared to 38 percent in 1992. (The percentage of self-described Republicans did not change; while the percentage of Independents dropped one percent.)[26]

Based on the percentages of the mass population who—in contrast to Democratic presidential candidates—remain willing to identify themselves with a specific political ideology, even the dreaded "L-word" does not yet seem quite ready to join the spotted owl on the list of politically endangered species. In 1994, 18 percent of respondents in the *New York Times* election-day survey described themselves as—or perhaps, confessed to being—"Liberal." A drop of 3 percent from 1992, this looks provocative, until one realizes that the figure in, for example, 1988, was again 18 percent. The trend in the percentage of self-described "Conservatives" was essentially a mirror image of these small zigs and zags: 34 percent in 1994, 29 percent in 1992, but 33 percent in 1988; the only other choice given in all three years was "moderate."[27] It may also be suggestive that some Democrats—including Massachusetts senator Edward Kennedy—who were sagging dangerously in the polls, but who still commanded sufficient financial resources to make effective counterarguments rallied to victory as they attacked the Contract.

Polls by the *Los Angeles Times Mirror* Center suggest that opinions about race have fallen back somewhat since 1992, when the publicity and protests surrounding the Rodney King case led to sharp increases in the percentages of respondents reacting sympathetically to African-American concerns. Yet, despite the noise about Republican gains in the South (which have a solid basis in that region's changing industrial structure and institutional obstacles to unionization and community organizations that the press and most scholars virtually ignore), one cannot plausibly blame the staggering Democratic losses nationwide on some inchoate perception that the administration was "excessively" partial to minorities, or even to cities. The Clinton administration too obviously turned its back on all such concerns, and people associated with them.[28]

A number of Republicans, of course, made a major issue out of illegal immigration. But this scarcely explains the across-the-board GOP victory. First, the issue in fact cuts across party lines, both in Congress and in the states (e.g., Florida). During the campaign, Republican elites divided sharply on the question, not least because so many see it as intimately bound up with "economic growth" (translated into plain "English only": low wages).[29]

Most fatefully, however, immigration's emergence as an object of mass political concern in American politics very much resembles the gathering trend toward greater hostility to government activity or the various other (mostly far smaller) rightward shifts in public opinion mentioned above or documented in other recent polls.[30] It is essentially a reactive phenomenon, an emergent, constructed reality that grows out of the persisting failure by (money-driven) governments to do much more than talk about problems like high unemployment, which, along with the federal reluctance to share revenues with states receiving large numbers of immigrants, surely is the key to the upsurge in anxiety about immigration.

Senator Feinstein's narrow victory in the California Senate race that will, at least until 1996, go down in the *Guinness Book of World Records* as the most expensive nonpresidential campaign in world history is one more proof that, where there are resources and a will to counterargument, issues of this sort can be effectively engaged.

What destroyed Bill Clinton and the Democrats in 1994, however, was precisely what derailed his Republican predecessor only two years earlier: in the midst of a steadily deepening economic crisis, it is impossible to beat something—even a fatuous, heavily subsidized something—with *nothing*.

But this was the hopeless task Clinton set for himself and his party after he (precisely as some of us predicted on the basis of the outpouring of Wall Street support for his "New Democrat" candidacy in 1992) betrayed his campaign promise to "grow out" of the deficit by "investing in America" as he assumed office in 1993. By deciding to make the bond market the supreme arbiter of economic policy, by ostentatiously refraining from jawboning the Federal Reserve to restrain rises in interest rates, by abandoning his much touted plan for an economic stimulus and instead bringing in a budget that was contractionary over the medium term, the president embraced precisely the program of continuing austerity that the electorate elected him to break with.[31]

Once he had embarked on this course, most, if not quite everything else he tried to do was doomed. No amount of PC posturing, homilies about values, or pathetically funded demonstration schemes for worker training or education could long disguise the fact that 5.5 or 6 percent unemployment is not really full employment, and a fortiori, not a "boom." Note that, as usual, no one in the administration spoke up in public to support Alan Blinder, the President's own nominee to the Federal Reserve Board, during the firestorm of criticism that followed his few brief remarks in a nonpublic speech about the weakness of the case for the much touted [high] "natural rate of unemployment" hypothesis. Because of this incident's chilling effect on future discussions of Fed policy, it may well be every bit as significant as the 1994 election itself.[32]

By some estimates, based on census data, the economic situation of as much as 80 percent of the population has not substantially improved since 1989. Such statistics may slightly underestimate the true level of economic welfare, particularly as this is affected by the thorny problem of valuing new products and changing quality.[33]

But this is arguing about decimal points. What matters is the real "chain reaction" that now threatens to blow apart the political system. This chain reaction begins with the desperate economic squeeze a largely unregulated world economy now places on ordinary Americans. It leads next to the decay of public services and nonprofit institutions that sustain families and communities, including schools, court systems, and law enforcement. In the end, it makes the daily life of more and more Americans increasingly unbearable.

Given that the Democrats controlled both the White House and Congress, it is scarcely surprising that so many Americans are fed up with them. Or that substantial numbers of citizens should be increasingly attracted to the only public criticisms of the system that they are consistently allowed to hear (particularly on talk radio or the generally right wing "new media")—that their real problem is the bell curve, immigrants, welfare, or indeed, the very notion of government action itself, which does inevitably cost money.[34] That the system is so obviously money-driven and frequently corrupt only enrages people, while the administration's all out efforts for NAFTA and GATT underscored the fact that Clinton's priorities and his real constituency were somewhere else.

Sixty percent of those in the Yankelovich poll expressed the belief that the outcome of the 1994 election was more a "rejection" of Democratic policies than a "mandate" for Republican policies. Fifty-six percent of the voters in the Greenberg survey claimed that they were "trying to send a message about how dissatisfied [they] were with things in Washington." Invited to be more specific, 15 percent said the message referred to "Bill Clinton," 15 percent pointed to "Congress," 5 percent each indicated "Republicans" and "Democrats"; while *45 percent* said the problem was "politics as usual."[35]

But the most striking evidence about what is now happening in the American political system comes from the *New York Times* election-day exit poll. This broke down the vote in terms of whether the respondent reported that his or her standard of living was becoming better or worse. The results are astonishing in the light of the publicity garnered after the election by the eight-point spread in the overall party vote by men and women, as well as conventional views that the Democrats mobilize less-well-off voters. In both the overall national vote and major state campaigns that were separately reported (including the New York gubernatorial and Massachusetts Senate race), those whose standard of living was improving voted roughly *2 to 1 (66%/34% in the national sample) for the Democrats*. By contrast, those whose standard of living was getting worse went roughly *2 to 1 (63%/37% in the national sample) for the Republicans*, while the group in the middle split 50/50.[36]

The contrast with 1992 is glaring: at that time, according to the *New York Times* exit poll, Clinton lost the former camp by 62 percent to 24 percent (with 14% going to Perot). He split the group in the middle, 41 percent to 41 percent (with 18% voting for Perot). But he swept the group whose standard of living had declined by an overwhelming 61 percent to 14 percent (with, suggestively, 25% going to Perot).[37]

The 1994 surveys still show a sizeable pocket of people with low incomes and relatively little schooling who, when they vote, remain stalwart Democrats. But these numbers show just how upside down patterns of mobilization are now becoming in America. The 1994 elections essentially suggest that the party that commands by far the most money is now succeeding by mobilizing increasing numbers of disenchanted poor- and middle-class voters against their traditional champions.[38] This is a voting pattern more reminiscent of some European elections in the 1930s than most American elections. It ought to ring some alarm bells. Asked whether the Republicans would do a better job of running Congress than did the Democrats, 61 percent of respondents in the Yankelovich poll declared that they would either do a worse job (16%) or make no difference (45%). Sixty-one percent, in other words, expect no major improvement.[39]

A full analysis of Newt Gingrich's Contract with America is not possible here. There is space only to observe that the voters may well be right. Nothing in the Contract really addresses the problems of a world economy in which many of the biggest American businesses increasingly do not need most of the American workforce or even the infrastructure—apart from the defense and foreign relations establishments—for anything. Nor will the suggestion by Gingrich and other Republican leaders after the election that price stability should perhaps be legally enshrined as the sole target for Federal Reserve policy.[40]

What will happen as the economic crisis deepens, and voters discover that their suspicions were right? Perhaps for a while, the merry-go-round in Washington will spin with the speed of light.[41] But in the long run? In all probability, I suspect, Mt. Vesuvius's greatest blowouts are still to come. As in the thirties, those who scorn Keynes will be astonished at the outcomes for which they will have to accept responsibility.

ACKNOWLEDGMENTS

I am grateful to Richard Keil, Benjamin Page, Robert Shapiro, and seminar audiences at Columbia University and the New School for Social Research for comments on early versions of this postscript.

NOTES

The Kershaw quotation, which along with the paper's description forms the epigraph, appeared in the *Boston Globe*, November 20, 1994. The article noted that Kershaw's holdings include the Bull and Finch Pub of Boston, which inspired the "setting of the 'Cheers' television show." GOPAC is a vehicle for various organizing efforts of Gingrich's.

Some advice proffered by Gingrich on a GOPAC "training tape" for other would-be

GOP candidates is of considerable interest from the standpoint of the discussion in the appendix on "rational expectations" and conditions of public debate in the United States. "'A shield issue is just, you know, your opponent is going to attack you as lacking compassion,' Gingrich says on the tape [provided to the newspaper]. 'You better find a good compassion issue where, you know, you show up in the local paper holding a baby in the neonatal center, and all you're trying to do is shield yourself from the inevitable attack.'"

As observed earlier, this strategy absolutely requires the cooperation of the press to be effective.

1. Pliny's description appears in his letter to Cornelius Tacitus, in *Pliny: Letters and Panegyricus,* trans. Betty Radice (Loeb Classical Library; Cambridge: Harvard University Press, 1969), vol. 1, p. 443.

2. Because the introduction to this book references so many discussions of campaign finance, there is no point in detailed citations to the campaign; but on the expected primacy of incumbents, see, e.g., the *Washington Post,* November 3, 1994. Note also that, of course, the advantages entrenched incumbents enjoyed were considered to be stronger in the House; many recognized that the Senate could easily go Republican.

3. The campaign finance totals come from the Federal Election Commission; they are arrived at by summing the appropriate figures for total receipts in the Commission's various final reports on financial activity for the years indicated. Note that fees received from speaking, stamp sales, and other activities are not included in these figures. These would almost certainly considerably increase the disparities.

4. See the discussion above in chapters 5 and 6.

5. See the statistics presented in the FEC press release of August 8, 1994.

6. Ibid.

7. For the Congressional races, see the FEC press release of August 12, 1994, especially the comparative figures on median receipts for House candidates on p. 4; for the party balance among (House) corporate PAC contributions, see the FEC release of September 19, 1994 (the data reflect contributions through June 30; the exact percentage varies slightly depending on whether one calculates figures for only 1994 or through the whole cycle to that point), especially p. 4. Note that donations to GOP Senate candidates, where many observers saw a chance of a GOP turnaround, unsurprisingly held up very well.

8. In a spirit of collegial goodwill, let us dispense with specific references. See, instead, the surprise various commentators registered after the election in, e.g., Richard Keil's story of November 17, 1994 for the Associated Press. My reference is to the full text supplied to me by the AP; AP stories are often edited severely before running in local papers.

9. E.g., *Washington Post,* October 14, 1994.

10. See the FEC press release of November 2, 1994, which focused on the two-year totals. The real news comes only when one goes back and compares its statistics to those in the earlier FEC press release of August 8, 1994. It then becomes fairly clear that the real "break" in the trend of soft money probably came in the late spring or early summer. This is well before any widespread anticipation of the GOP takeover of the House, and is thus of considerable interest. What happened?

In the absence of the FEC's final report on the 1994 election, it is difficult to be sure. Because the available evidence defies brief summary, all that is possible here is to record my belief that two developments that were closely related to the great bond crash that roiled world markets in the spring of 1994 played important roles in this shift of funds. First, the administration's policy of talking down the dollar against the yen drove a wedge between it and many of its supporters on Wall Street as chapter 6, n. 47 suggested could happen. Second, Congressional inquiries into hedge funds led other Wall Street supporters of the president either to switch to the GOP, or simply withdraw from previously made commitments to help finance the Democrats.

11. See the FEC press release of November 4, 1994, especially pp. 3 and 8. This constitutes, in my opinion, the truly clinching evidence for the late turn in funding House races, since it can be compared cautiously, but directly, with the earlier FEC release of August 12, 1994. Note that over the campaign as a whole, Democratic incumbents succeeded in raising very substantial sums.

12. See the AP story of November 15, 1994 by Richard Keil. I rely here on the full text the AP supplied me. I took considerable pains to resolve various ambiguities in statistics the story reported. I am grateful to Keil for the patience and good humor he displayed in dealing with my queries.

13. On the excess campaign funds, see Keil's story for the AP of November 17, 1994, which also alludes to the Gingrich memo. Again, I rely on the uncut text supplied me by the AP. On the independent organizations, see, e.g., *Wall Street Journal*, November 4, 1994.

14. See page 1 of the draft dated November 17, 1994 of Greenberg's "The Revolt Against Politics," which accompanies his survey for the DLC discussed here.

15. See (the uncut text to) Richard Keil's stories for the AP of November 9, 15, and 17, 1994.

16. See the "Memorandum" to "Data Users" from Hal Quinley of Yankelovich Partners, November 11, 1994, which reports the poll in detail. See p. 5 for the question on Gingrich.

17. In a press release of November 29, 1994 released over a computer network, Kathy Frankovic of CBS News reported that 28 percent of those polled by CBS in late November had heard of the Contract With America.

18. See the discussion of the work of Stanley Kelley, Jr. and John Geer in chapters 5 and 6. Some recent work using panel data that is critical of Kelley or Geer's reliance on open-ended questions relies on statistical assumptions that simply cannot be accepted. But this controversy exceeds the scope of this discussion.

19. See pp. 14–17 of the Quinley memorandum cited above, n. 16.

20. See the discussion in chapter 6, n. 5.

21. For the Greenberg poll, see "Survey of Voters, with Figures and Tables," by Greenberg Research Inc. for the Democratic Leadership Council, November 8–9, 1994, p. 32. The Yankelovich survey, reported in the Quinley memo, p. 15, found slightly more support for increasing defense spending—31 percent thought it should be a "high priority." But compare that to the other numbers quoted earlier. I think we can safely conclude that the rush by both Democrats and Republicans to raise defense spending after the election has nothing to do with satisfying public opinion.

22. See the Greenberg "Survey of Voters," pp. 12–13.

23. See George Gallup, *The Gallup Poll: Public Opinion 1935–71* (New York: Random House, 1972), p. 1. For the Greenberg data, see his "Survey of Voters," p. 13.

24. For the Yankelovich data, see the Quinley memo, pp. 14–18; for the *Washington Post*, see its October 14, 1994 issue.

25. The "single highest" Yankelovich result is on p. 18 of the Quinley memo; for the "high priority" statistic, see pp. 14 and 16. In addition to supporting data in the Greenberg survey already cited, see among many other analyses, Lawrence R. Jacobs and Robert Shapiro, "Public Opinion's Tilt Against Private Enterprise," *Health Affairs*, Spring (I) 1994, pp. 285–98; Jacobs, Shapiro, and Eli Schulman, "Medical Care in the United States—An Update," *Public Opinion Quarterly* 57 (1993), pp. 394–427.

26. For the *New York Times* exit polls, see the paper for November 13, 1994 and November 5, 1992.

27. See the poll results reported in ibid; for 1988, see the press release to the *Times/* CBS exit poll dated November 8, 1988. The latter year, of course, saw the question emerge as a campaign issue.

28. Along with the discussion in chapter 6, see also the critical discussion of claims that reapportionment explains the GOP gains in the South by Allan J. Lichtman, "Quotas Aren't the Issue," *New York Times*, December 7, 1994. This is an effective critique of suggestions advanced by other analysts quoted in news sections of the *Times* for November 13. On recent trends in opinion on racial issues, see, e.g., Larry Hugick and Andrew Kohut, "Taking The Nation's Pulse," in *The Public Perspective* 6, no. 2 (November/December 1994), p. 4.

29. For GOP differences on immigration, see the *Boston Globe*, November 22, 1994; cf. Thomas Ferguson, "From Boiling Pot to Melting Pot: The Real Lessons of the American Experience of Immigration and 'Assimilation,'" in Roger Benjamin, C. R. Neu, and Denise Quigley, *Between States and Markets: The Limits of the Transatlantic Alliance* (New York: St. Martin's Press, in press).

30. In light of this study's earlier critical remarks on public opinion trends since the sixties, I should like to add that I agree with Robert Shapiro's suggestion (offered in conversation) that, in broad terms, opinion drifted somewhat to the right around the time Clinton entered office, after mostly moving the other way for a long time. A number of obvious exceptions to this generalization exist on both sides of the time line, and the nineties shifts are usually, but not always, minor, but this topic simply cannot be developed any further here. Note, however, the time trends of the data discussed in Hugick and Kohut, "Pulse," pp. 3–6; their material omits discussion of health care, where "self reliance" usually looks rather hollow. Compare also the shifts in the *Los Angeles Times Mirror* Center for the "People and the Press" press release of September 21, 1994, "The People, The Press and Politics: The New Political Landscape," e.g., the small shift on environmentalism (p. 41) between 1992 and 1994.

31. See the discussion in my introduction and chapter 6.

32. See chapter 6, especially the reference to Robert Eisner's evidence against the "natural rate" hypothesis.

33. Compare the data presented in Lawrence Mishel and Jared Bernstein, *The State of Working America, 1994–95* (Washington, D.C.: Economic Policy Institute, in press), especially chapters 1, 3, and 4. For one explicit 1989–94 comparison from census data, see their table 1.6. Note that the downturn of the early 90s influences the trend of virtually all such data. The widespread switch to variable rate mortgages in the United States may also be a factor in the '94 outcome, as an earlier move to them appears to have influenced British politics in the previous decade.

Hugick and Kohut ("Pulse," p. 5), report that in a mid-October 1994 *Times Mirror* survey, 50 percent of respondents could not name a single achievement of the Clinton administration.

Robert Samuelson ("False Economic Report Card?" *Boston Globe,* November 1, 1994) offers several criticisms of the pessimistic critique of the American economy's recent trend. Mishel and Bernstein, I believe, provide a convincing (implicit) rejoinder, along with the fact that, as suggested, many of the proposed corrections don't add up to a major difference. I would also emphasize the negative effects on individual lives of the decay of the nonprofit sector, which is not really reflected in any of the usual statistics.

A *New York Times* report of October 17, 1994 that recent jobs data did not support the pessimists' position(s) appears to have rested on a statistical confusion. See the letters by Lawrence Chimerine and Edward S. Herman in the *Times* of October 24, 1994 and Robert Kuttner's "Inequality Sours Economic Recovery," *Boston Globe,* October 24, 1994.

34. An election day Gallup Poll indicated that voters who listened frequently to talk radio disproportionately favored Republican candidates. See *USA Today,* November 10, 1994. Without access to the original poll, it is impossible to pin down the factors that could be contributing to this result. Other published research, however, suggests that it might be fruitfully approached along the lines of the discussion in the appendix on the sources of error in mass populations.

First, it now seems clear that lower-income, less-educated males have been particularly hard hit by the cumulative changes in the U.S. world economic position and that many respond to long term sub- or unemployment by withdrawing from the labor market (see the *New York Times,* December 1, 1994). It is a fair guess—one that is consistent with other research into the audience for talk radio—that these out-of-work Americans with time on their hands tune into talk radio at disproportionately high rates (see, e.g., the brief discussion in Benjamin Page, "Populist Deliberation: The Zoe Baird Uprising" [manuscript], or the *Los Angeles Times Mirror* Center for the People and the Press, "The Vocal Minority in American Politics," press release, July 16, 1993, both of which comment on the position of males within the talk-show audience, without, however, making the link to the economy that the recently reported Census data appear to support).

Second, it is obvious that talk radio and most cable TV shows, despite a few clear exceptions, have taken advantage of the new, less regulated climate (and the shift rightward by most of the owners of the media since the sixties) to move much further to the right than the major television networks. (As the discussion of the media in chapters 5 and 6 implies, the major networks remain nested in the older political and economic establishment structures of the high Cold War, and are far more multinationally oriented.) Even if one had never heard of Rush Limbaugh & Co., it does not require profound insight to see how a disproportionately out-of-work, male audience dreaming fondly of the good old days is likely to respond to certain very obvious conservative messages. Or how describing the effects of all this simply in terms of, say, a "gender gap" misses an important part of the truth.

Attempts to characterize the differences between the mainline networks and other media outlets in terms of a contrast between "mediated" vs. "unmediated" politics are, in my opinion, similarly unhelpful. (See, e.g., the otherwise very interesting and thoughtful "The Rise and Fall of Candidate Perot" [Part I: "Unmediated vs. Mediated Politics," and Part II: "The Outsider vs. the Political System"] of John Zaller with the assistance of Mark Hunt, forthcoming in *Political Communication.*) Real progress in analyzing how the media relates to politics requires a plain acknowledgment that watching Larry King cheer on Ross Perot as he decides to become a candidate cannot possibly be described as "unmediated." One also needs to understand the institutional reasons why the much more progressive New Party does not receive similar invitations.

Studies of the media that do not test for the effects of specific investor coalitions, however subtle, are likely to produce only statistical misspecifications. It is also essential to consider how money affects candidate "viability" and poll success. (From an investment theory perspective, Zaller's "prior political experience" is rather obviously related to previous investor choices). For different quantitative approaches to dealing with such questions, see chapter 6, n. 49 and the analysis of the 1976 election in Thomas Ferguson & Joel Rogers, *Right Turn: The Decline of the Democrats and the Future of American Politics* (New York: Hill & Wang, 1986), p. 259, n. 7.

35. See Greenberg, "Survey of Voters," pp. 6–7; for Yankelovich, see the Quinley memo, p. 7.

36. See the *New York Times* exit poll reported in the paper on November 13, 1994. Michael Kagay kindly made the exact form of the question available to me. For results in particular state elections, see the polls printed in ibid., November 10, 1994.

37. See the *New York Times*, November 5, 1992.

38. One should note the possibility that a form of "rationalization" perhaps influenced some pro- or anti-Clinton voters in making up their minds about the economy. But the numbers in the exit poll are far too large for that to be the main explanation.

39. For the Yankelovich results, see pp. 9–13 of the Quinley memo.

40. For Gingrich, the GOP, and the Fed, see *Wall Street Journal*, November 18, 1994.

41. It is clear that the midterm election results considerably complicate any hopes the Clinton administration entertains for a political business cycle in 1996, since it has lost control of Congress and does not firmly control the Fed. On the other hand, post-election polls also suggest that much of the population credits the president with good intentions, if not with any results. See, e.g., the Greenberg "Survey of Voters," pp. 10–11, where 73 percent of voters say "It is too early too tell" if Clinton will become a failed President; 68 percent assert that they are still hopeful Clinton "can succeed"; and 64 percent agree that Clinton "has tried to move the country in the right direction."

Former Massachusetts senator Paul Tsongas has also begun circulating a memo suggesting that General Colin Powell would be a good candidate for president. Tsongas, currently a leader of the Concord Coalition discussed in chapter 6, explicitly invokes both fiscal and foreign policy motives for the choice of Powell (see *Boston Globe*, December 13, 1994). A candidacy of this sort is likely to be of considerable interest to more investors than one might first suppose. Whatever Tsongas's own intentions, cutting entitlements could permit a rise in the military budget without threatening the progress Clinton has made in reducing the deficit. A Powell candidacy also cannot fail to have an interesting relation to Ross Perot. Among Powell's close associates is Richard Armitage (cf. *Newsweek*, October 10, 1994, pp. 22, 26 and chapter six).

In the absence of the FEC's final report on the midterm elections, it is impossible to characterize the investor coalition that is lining up behind Newt Gingrich and his wing of the GOP. It is obvious that most of the health industry and many opponents of Clinton enlisted early. So, also, has a part of finance and many service sector firms. But more of this another time. I think, however, that, as the quotation that opens this "Postscript" suggests, one fundamental result of the 1994 election will be a powerful reenforcement of existing trends for a "low wage" strategy of international competition.

Along with Eisner's work discussed in chapter six, perhaps the most interesting recent discussion of alternative economic policies are John Cornwall, *Economic Breakdown and Recovery* (Armonk, N.Y.: M. E. Sharpe, 1994), and Alain Parguez, "Full Employment and Inflation," Department of Economics, University of Ottawa, Working Paper # 9424E, December 1994.

Deduced and Abandoned:
Rational Expectations, the Investment Theory of Political Parties, and the Myth of the Median Voter

> We are here plunged in politics funnier than words can express
> . . . The public is angry and abusive. Everyone takes part. We are
> all doing our best and swearing like demons. But the amusing
> thing is that no one talks about real interests. By common consent
> they agree to let these alone. We are afraid to discuss them. Instead
> of this, the press is engaged in a most amusing dispute whether
> Mr. Cleveland had an illegitimate child.
> Henry Adams

> If you truly had a democracy and did what the people wanted,
> you'd go wrong every time.
> Dean Acheson

IN THE TURBULENT spring of 1919, Bronson Cutting, a wealthy Progressive who controlled one of New Mexico's leading newspapers, decided to throw in with the enthusiasts who were pushing General Leonard Wood for the 1920 Republican presidential nomination. For a few months Cutting and like-minded local acquaintances worked by themselves, in virtual isolation, for the general, who was widely perceived as the heir to the mantle of the recently deceased Theodore Roosevelt.

Late in the summer, however, Wood's own powerful, Eastern-centered national campaign organization reached out to them. John T. King, the former Republican national committeeman from Connecticut who was one of the general's key national organizers, wrote to Cutting. Inviting cooperation, King requested an assessment of the local political scene.

The publisher responded at once. In a lengthy letter, Cutting reported:

> The Republican party in New Mexico has for a long time been split
> up into two bitterly antagonistic factions, one of which has controlled
> the northern and the other the southern counties of the state. Each

group has been to a large extent controlled by rival corporate interests.

The northern group represents the Maxwell Land Grant Company, the northern coal mines and the St. Louis and Rocky Mountain railroad. In the background is the powerful but unobtrusive influence of the A[tchison] T[opeka] & S[anta] F[e] Railway. The chief figures in this group are:

Charles Springer, of Cimarron, manager of the Maxwell Land Grant Company and president of the State Council of Defense [a privately funded, but state-sanctioned "voluntary" organization that was then crusading against labor unions and "radical" agitation].

Jan Van Houten, of Raton, vice president of the St. Louis & Rocky Mountain Railway.

John S. Clark, of Las Vegas, president pro tem of the state senate.

Secundino Romero, of Las Vegas, sheriff and boss of San Miguel County.

Judge Clarence J. Roberts, of the supreme court, residing in Santa Fe.

Governor O. A. Larrazolo, who, however, has kept free of factional alliances since he has been governor.

The controlling interest in the southern group is the Phelps Dodge Company (El Paso & Southwestern Railroad) with such allied corporations as the Chino Copper Company, etc. Its principal figures are:

H. O. Bursum, of Socorro, national committeeman.

Senator A. B. Fall.

W. A. Hawkins, of El Paso, counsel for the E. P. & S. W.

Eduardo M. Otero, Los Lunas, sheep man and boss of Valencia County.[1]

In a sparsely populated, semi-peripheral state where human life was often cheap, Bronson Cutting stood out. He was a genuine Progressive, frequently at odds with the rest of the state's political establishment, someone who, years later, would end up switching parties and supporting Franklin D. Roosevelt. In sharp contrast to King, whose corrupt relations with a powerful bloc of business leaders exploded into a scandal that eventually brought down the Wood campaign, he was on no one's payroll except his own.

If in 1919, accordingly, he initially disregarded warnings from his friends that "there is no sincerity in the advocacy of the Republican ring here for the General, and that their intention is to trade him for [Illinois Governor Frank] Lowden or [Ohio Senator Warren G.] Harding at the convention," it was only because—for a time—he still reposed too much starry-eyed trust in the publicly professed principles of Progressive Republicanism.[2]

This appendix, however, is not concerned with Cutting's political biography or the 1920 campaign. Its focus is broader, and concerns whether the account of party competition implicitly put forward in the New Mexico publisher's letter to King—according to which rivalries and competition between major investor blocs provide the mainspring (but not the *only* spring) of partisan competition—might provide a better guide to politics in countries like the United States than the usual "median voter" model.[3]

In a series of recent essays (some of which are reprinted in revised form in this book) I argue in effect that the answer is yes—that classical theories of democracy greatly underestimate the costs facing ordinary voters as they attempt to control the state. As a consequence, political parties in countries such as the United States

> are not what . . . most American election analyses . . . treat them as, viz . . . the political analogues of "entrepreneurs in a profit-seeking economy" who "act to maximize votes" . . . Instead, the fundamental market for political parties usually is not voters. . . . Most of these possess desperately limited resources and—especially in the United States—exiguous information and interest in politics. The real market for political parties is defined by major investors, who generally have good and clear reasons for investing to control the state. . . . Blocs of major investors define the core of political parties and are responsible for most of the signals the party sends to the electorate. (chapter 1, p. 22)[4]

In such investor-driven systems, the dynamics of political competition are very different from what traditional democratic theory imagines:

> [P]olitical parties dominated by large investors try to assemble the votes they need by making very limited appeals to particular segments of the potential electorate. If it pays some other bloc of major investors to advertise and mobilize, these appeals can be vigorously contested, but . . . on all issues affecting the vital interests that major investors have in common, no party competition will take place. Instead, all that will occur will be a proliferation of marginal appeals to voters—and if all major investors happen to share an interest in ignoring issues vital to the electorate, such as social welfare, hours of work, or collective bargaining, so much the worse for the electorate. Unless significant portions of it are prepared to try to become major investors in their own right, through a substantial expenditure of time and (limited) income, there is nothing any group of voters can do to offset this collective investor dominance. (chapter 1, p. 28)

As publicly recorded campaign expenditures have skyrocketed in the United States and other countries, this argument has won some favorable notice. Several analysts have recently concluded that their case studies support an investment theory approach. Among these are the author of an imaginative quantitative assessment of press coverage of the 1964 presidential election (Devereux, 1993), a historian of the 1920s Democratic Party (Craig, 1992, pp. 7, 155) and, *mirabile dictu,* the *Wall Street Journal,* which recently informed readers that "the 1992 election proves that the investment theory of political parties is correct" (*Wall Street Journal,* 1992).

But not everyone, to put it mildly, is equally enthusiastic. Ever since 1983, when my first essay appeared, some analysts have complained that the investment approach implies that elections should go automatically to the highest bidder—an outcome which, they insist, simply cannot be true, however superficially attractive it may appear to casual consumers of FEC statistics. Other critics allege that the investment approach implies a passive role for voters, or even ignores them all together.

Two very prominent rival schools of thought, in addition, have claimed to refute the investment approach. Champions of the well-known "retrospective voting" approach assert that by simply "voting the rascals out," the electorate can bypass all the problems my original essay raised about the tendency to investor dominance of parties and policymaking. Two celebrated "rational choice" analysts, Richard McKelvey and Peter Ordeshook, reach essentially the same conclusion by a somewhat different route. They claim that a consistent "rational expectations" approach to questions about the use of information by voters invalidates my earlier essay. By relying on easily available "cues," they argue, voters can learn all they need to know to enforce majority (median) control (McKelvey and Ordeshook, 1986).[5]

This appendix responds to these critics by restating in a compact and, I hope, pointedly accessible, fashion the fundamental propositions of my investment approach to party competition. It begins by setting out a simple example to make the key point crystal clear: the general failure of the median position in elections "in which money matters." This same case is then analyzed more closely, to point up the fallacy in suggestions that an investment approach makes electoral outcomes a linear function of total spending. A last glance at the example reveals an important implication of the investment approach that many critics have missed—that even voters who were virtually perfectly informed might easily be unable to control policy.

The striking implications of this point are developed in the course of an effort to pin down more precisely the role voters play in money-driven political systems. By broadening the original single-issue model to incorporate the role of (subsidized) political ideas and rhetoric, it is easy to show how choices voters make affect elections and parties—

without any tendency for the parties to converge on the median position.

The essay then tackles head-on the important, and much neglected, question of how "systematic error" by voters can be reconciled with the abundant empirical evidence that most of them are *not* passive, or foolish, and that they clearly attempt to make sense of campaigns. This exercise, which is essentially a critique of McKelvey and Ordeshook, yields a clear statement—at last—of just what is required, both objectively and subjectively, for voters to be systematically mistaken over long periods of time about candidates and parties.

The essay's theoretical argument is supported throughout by references to empirical analyses, by Stanley Kelley, John Geer, and other analysts, of actual voting decisions. By contrasting the role information plays in the functioning of politics and the stock market, this discussion exposes the hollowness of claims that free markets guarantee voters all the information they need to vote in their own best interests—whether the "markets" in question are served by political parties or the media.

The final section of the appendix considers Fiorina's retrospective voting model (Fiorina, 1981). This "just say no" approach to popular democracy, I suggest, solves no fundamental problem of democratic control of elections.

THE MYTH OF THE MEDIAN VOTER

Let us begin, however, with the investment theory's bedrock claim: what might be termed the general failure of control by the so-called median voter (the voter whose strategic position exactly in the middle of a distribution of voters guarantees a candidate one more vote than he or she needs to defeat all comers).

The argument can be developed with any degree of detail and formal rigor. But it is perhaps most easily and convincingly outlined in terms of a single concrete example designed to demonstrate with the clarity of a laboratory experiment just how money-driven political systems can thwart the will of even overwhelming majorities of voters.

Imagine a world in which labor-intensive textile producers command virtually all pecuniary resources beyond those necessary for ordinary wage earners to live (a world, that is, in which the so-called "classical savings function" popularized by Kalecki, Kaldor, and Robinson applies). Such a situation is perhaps most conveniently pictured along the lines of some company town of the early Industrial Revolution, but as will shortly be evident, conditions long ago and far away are not the essence of the problem. A fortiori, neither is the classical savings function.

Suppose, further, that an election is being staged, in which everyone votes for one of two political parties. There is only one issue, and everyone agrees on what it is: passage of legislation that is likely to lead to 100 percent unionization of the labor force. All wage earners agree that the law is desirable. All textile magnates (3 percent of the total voting population) vehemently disagree.

What stance do the political parties take?

Analysts impressed by the familiar spatial models of party competition will of course reply that the parties must head immediately to the median position at the far right of figure A.1, where virtually all voters are located.[6]

The investment theory, however, spotlights a detail that leads to a dramatically different expectation: *When money matters importantly to mounting campaigns,* no party can afford to take up the median position that represents the views of the vast majority, if investors disagree. The mere fact that votes are out there does not imply that any party can afford to campaign for them, even if its message is what they would want to hear.

In this instance, all parties depend on textiles for funding. The textile industry, of course, will not pay to undermine itself. It thus subsidizes only candidates opposed to passage of the law. (Readers who have been exposed only to the median voter model are often inclined to object: But wouldn't the textile party improve its chances of winning

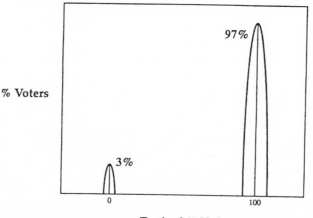

FIGURE A.1. Voters, Investors, and Unionization: An Idealized Example

by embracing unionization? The all-but-irresistible tendency to this mistaken inference illustrates perfectly how a bad model can blind social scientists—and many ordinary people, who intuitively know better—to the harsh realities of money-driven political systems. The short answer is that if the cost of winning the election really were sponsoring unionization, textiles would, paradoxically, lose by adopting the "winning" strategy.)

Given that the textile industry is the only source of campaign funds, all parties must comply with the industry's demand for a union-free environment, or else they cannot afford to compete at all. Without collusion or "conspiracy" of any kind, accordingly, each party *independently* discovers that available funds constrain it to champion the very same rate of unionization as all others: 0 percent, ironically, on the far left in figure A.1.[7]

The conclusion is sweeping, but while the example is carefully constructed, it is not contrived. In particular, it does *not* represent a "special case" dependent on the improbably stark contrast between the very rich and the very poor, assumed here for simplicity's sake, or on features unique to unionization as a political issue. (Or, of course, on the lopsided 97 percent to 3 percent opinion distribution, which simply defines a case that, on the face of it, should be a knockdown for the median voter model since an overwhelming majority consensus has actually crystallized.)

Instead, what is critical are the brute implications of a very pedestrian fact: that entry into politics (and, for that matter, subsequent campaigning) is normally very expensive in terms of the time and incomes of ordinary voters. As a consequence of this "campaign cost condition," whenever the generic policy interests of all large investors diverge from those of ordinary people (and there is certainly no presumption that they should always do so), voters are checkmated. As long as money matters importantly, and efforts to offset the costs of political activity by pooling resources confront high transaction costs or other obstacles, including overt repression, the electorate can shake, rattle, and roll. But it cannot float an alternative of its own to force the issue onto the agenda—even if, as in this case, the majority comprises an overwhelming 97 percent of the electorate. By virtue of what my earlier essay summarized as the "principle of noncompetition across all investor blocs," only investors can compel (at least one of the) parties to take up an issue—because only investors can afford to pay the high "replacement cost" of nonresponsive parties (candidates, etc.).[8]

Does the campaign cost condition imply then that elections go automatically to the highest bidder, or render electoral outcomes a linear function of total spending? Hardly. As will become even clearer below, in the analysis of elections with more than one issue, what is pivotal is ready access to the comparatively large sums of money necessary to mount a real campaign, not necessarily *the most* money. (In light of recent developments in American politics, it may be worth raising a yellow caution flag about a related misconception: Multiplying the sheer number of parties in the system does nothing by itself to solve the conundrum facing the voters. Their situation would not improve if there were three, four, five or *n* parties on the ballot. To refer back to my example, only if one or the other of these new parties were financed independently of the textile industry, by some group that wanted unionization, would the electorate shake loose from its golden fetters.)

One final point about this example merits notice, since it brings us to the heart of some of the most important differences between median voter models and the investment approach. Note that while democracy is failing miserably, no one is being fooled about anything. Neither misinformation nor voters' lack of time nor ability to process campaign appeals is relevant here. There is no money, hence no campaign appeal. *The electorate is not too stupid or too tired to control the political system. It is merely too poor.*

Though some rational choice analysts profess exasperation, it is convenient to summarize this state of affairs as one in which the electorate is "virtually perfectly" informed—while still being quite unable to control the money-driven political system.[9]

VOTER CHOICE IN A WORLD RULED BY MONEY

In the example just discussed, ordinary voters desperately want something else from their party system, but cannot achieve it. I suspect that some complaints that the investment approach assumes a passive electorate are really disguised refusals to recognize that real-life electorates may often be trapped in such "no (cheap) exit" situations. On the other hand, for simple reasons of space, my earlier essays said relatively little directly about voters. It may, therefore, be helpful to discuss in more detail the roles voters play in money-driven political systems.

To make the basic point as clear as possible, let us consider once more a very simple example—an extension of the case just discussed, in which a handful of textile magnates controlled all the political money. Now, however, in place of the single dominant sector, let us picture how the situation might look 50 or so years later, when the economy has diversified a bit. We can imagine that a second, capital-intensive industry—the oil industry, perhaps—has firmly established itself alongside textiles in the local economy.

Let us further assume that at some point, the handful of oil magnates decide to acquire control of the state. One morning, accordingly, a new political party, which they finance, emerges. Since the oil industry is far more capital-intensive than textiles, its labor costs as a percentage of total value added are much lower. The investors who control the new party conclude, accordingly, that they can afford to support a scheme for, say, company unions, or even, perhaps, the organization of 20 percent of the workforce into independent (i.e., real) unions. As a consequence, funding suddenly becomes available for a party prepared to offer the electorate another deal—a "New Deal," one might say.

Now consider the situation of the electorate, for whom the long-deferred dream of unionization remains, by hypothesis, as attractive as ever. As long as the costs of mounting serious campaigns exceed sums that the voting majority can readily raise, its only alternative (other than abstention or collective self-organization, both here ruled out by assumption) is to calculate, along the lines of Kelley's (1983, pp. 11–12) linear model (according to which voters tally up the pluses and minuses of each candidate/party and then vote for the one with the highest net score), that the proposed "New Deal" is a better deal for them. They, accordingly, vote to put the new, oil-financed party in power. Here, indubitably, is real voter choice exercised by a superbly informed electorate—yet the median is never approached. The system goes from 0 percent to 20 percent unionization, and that is all.

Now let us consider how this "New Deal" example can be adapted to shed light on problems now widely discussed in the literature on real-life political campaigns. In the case just described, as long as nothing changes, the capital-intensive party will obviously win election after election in a manner reminiscent of the "dominant party" scenarios of some "realignment" theories. (Indeed, from an investment-theory standpoint, the rise to power of new, dominant blocs of industries, or firms, is historically the most common cause of realignment, which explains why Burnham and the other realignment theorists who have never developed a consistent approach to investor blocs have such difficulty pinning down the precise role of the electorate in their otherwise very illuminating discussions.)[10]

How might the textile party try to reply to break its rival's hold? From the perspective of comparative political history, the number of likely strategies does not seem enormous. First of all, in the spirit of the maxim that the best defense is a good offense, conservative parties facing this kind of pressure almost invariably begin a relentless campaign of vilification directed against their opponents. In the intellectual equivalent of radio jamming, they hammer away at the principles and the leaders (in some cases, even the dogs of the leaders: witness FDR's dog Falla) of the opposition with virtually any argument that seems likely to fly. Sometimes their campaigns focus on rival values ("freedom" or rather, "Freedom," is said to be in danger, or the Constitution is declared to be at risk); in other cases, the goal is lauded, but the means are scorned, while charges of corruption resound everywhere. Almost invariably, however, as the social temperature begins to rise, previously accepted rules of social intercourse fray. In a word gravid with implications, we can summarize all this by saying that all sorts of cues—not only the good, but the bad, and the ugly—quickly fill the air.

Such campaigns usually succeed in instilling enough doubt in some portion of the electorate's mind to at least slow down a developing mass movement (and they certainly raise the level of investment required to stay in the game). In particularly backward regions and specially circumstanced voting groups (including, many times in the past, at least upper-class women and the conventionally religious at every level of society), they sometimes stop agitation altogether. On the other hand, the historical evidence also shows that purely negative campaigns often are not enough. At some point, another strategy often comes into play: Try to change not minds, but the subject.

Historically, this step leads to a "Heinz 57 varieties" of concrete proposals. Sorting them into rough, but illuminating, categories is not too difficult. One class of options involves a deliberate decision to counter by emphasizing another economic issue (or, obviously, issues). From a comparative historical standpoint, perhaps the most common contraposition to unionization and similar broad "populist" issues has been the attempt to celebrate economic "growth." Depending on time, circumstance, and the business cycle—for the historical association of free enterprise with economic growth is far more problematic than most contemporary discussions are willing to recognize—the textile party could, for example, froth on about the liberating possibilities of, say, "supply-side" economics à la Ronald Reagan or Jack Kemp.

More concrete alternatives are also sometimes posed. If an incumbent regime dominated by textile magnates is not easily imagined as a plausible champion of advanced technology, still, for completeness, it is worth observing that, on occasion, investor-dominated political parties have emphasized not only state-assisted "modernization" or "great leaps forward" in technology (as did, for instance, many Fascist groups, Roosevelt's own New Deal, or Ernest Mercier's Redressement Français, in the interwar period; or François Mitterrand's "Socialists" in the 1980s), but also the introduction of modern financial systems (e.g.,

Napoleon III, who famously availed himself of many other appeals as well) as ways of projecting an economic appeal.[11] In other cases, for example, the case of the American Populists of the 1890s, or the recent European controversies over currency integration, concerns about monetary standards have incited major blocs of investors to organize politically.

Other historically important political formulas of a broadly "economic" type include the campaigns for sweeping deregulation, lower taxes, and reduced governmental fiscal "extravagance" waged in the nineteenth century by liberal parties in Europe and Andrew Jackson, Martin Van Buren, and company in the United States; and in the twentieth century by Reagan, Margaret Thatcher, and many other right-wing leaders. In other circumstances, however, investors have also coalesced behind programs of spending on various tangible "public goods" such as canals, bridges, roads, or "a navy second to none." How to pay for these programs has sometimes, of course, become a troublesome issue. But a historically very popular combination appears to be apparently progressive spending programs financed, without fanfare, by regressive taxes on their putative beneficiaries in the mass electorate.[12] (Later in this essay, we will see how this pattern derives in part from characteristic defects of the systems of public deliberation normally evolved by market societies.)

Though comparatively few electoral analysts pay much attention, often such tactics lead to party systems divided at least partially over "horizontal" economic cleavages, in which the major national parties represent coalitions of investor blocs dominant in different regions, sections, or other spatially defined groups.[13] In France, Japan, the United States, and many other countries, a variant of this strategy has led investor-dominated, predominantly urban-based conservative parties to coddle agriculture to secure an electoral base (a fact which, because the link to urban investor blocs is rarely acknowledged, leads many electoral analysts to tie themselves into knots trying to explain the apparently magical ability of comparatively small numbers of farmers to succeed where millions of workers have failed). The case of "free trade" or "protection" in Germany, the United States, Great Britain, and other countries in the last two centuries is analogous, and too well known to require any comment.

On the other hand, while many American readers may be skeptical, it is a fact that such economic appeals rarely suffice for long. As party systems decay with, in many cases, the economy remaining stuck for long periods far below full employment, economic appeals by themselves often become dangerously unreliable. Any investor-dominated party that relied solely on them would be swiftly over-whelmed by a tide of triumphant unionization or populist farm organi-zations.

The anthropologist Marvin Harris (1979, p. xi) has observed that groups dominated by the wealthy are usually the most conspicuous champions of the importance of ideals and values in political practice.[14] Though I know of no clear-cut statistical inquiries into the question, I suspect strongly that he is right, and that what accounts for this is the overwhelming incentive conservative parties frequently have to change the subject from economic questions to the flag, eternal values, or patriotism; or even to foreigners, blacks, or Jews.

Moves of this sort, which centrally involve "discourse" or "rheto-ric" (in plain, nonmystifying English: sustained political arguments and appeals), have sweeping implications for the level of investment re-quired to become a player in the political system.[15] First, as new issues surface, complex, ramified arguments proliferate. The threshold of fi-nance required for credible entry and subsequent argument into the political system, accordingly, rises markedly. As the 1992 campaign il-lustrates, even nationally known political figures, with clearly articu-lated initial positions on major issues, some free TV time, and an 800 number, require really vast sums of money once the campaign heats up. (Rarely, however, will the relation between money and political success become linear, as many critics of the investment approach seem to think.)

Second, money's influence on the election now becomes more subtle. In part mediated by campaign rhetoric and language, it is not only direct in the senses discussed earlier, but indirect as well: not only are issues vital to the electorate not being discussed, but other issues apparently quite unrelated to pecuniary interests are being deployed or emphasized instead. As simpleminded contrasts between a pristine "politics of ideas" and a grubby "politics of money" dissolve, analysts who try to estimate money's influence on politics (*or on voters,* who are struggling to make up their minds) by attending to, say, direct discus-sions of economic issues will be almost comically mistaken—though only investors will be laughing. And statistical studies of the correlation of policy with opinion are very likely to be systematically misinter-preted, since the whole point of hyping these other issues (which will work if and only if some constituency can be persuaded that they are "real") is precisely to raise the apparent correlation, while guarantee-ing investor dominance.[16]

Much more could be said about the role political ideas play in money-driven political systems. But the above suffices to explain Hobsbawm's observation, in his masterly survey of comparative politics, that everywhere in the nineteenth century the generalization of suffrage vastly denatured the political rhetoric of the (non-socialist) parties (Hobsbawm, 1989, pp. 87–88). It should also be apparent why an established church is so often connected with conservative parties; why, in money-driven political systems like that of the contemporary United States, both major parties show strong preferences for highly stylized discussions of the economy (e.g., abstract talk about "growth" or, when someone wishes to look daring, very guarded, highly stereotyped New Deal tub thumping); and why so much American political rhetoric concentrates on "social" or "cultural" issues that are peripheral to most investors, even though most voters indicate in responses to open-ended questions that economic issues stand high on their list of concerns. Not to mention why, in 1992, all three major candidates flatly declined an invitation in the debates to discuss even modest changes in the Federal Reserve System.[17]

More broadly, it should be equally easy to understand why investor blocs in the United States (and, mutatis mutandis, many other countries) so often pursue two apparently contradictory grand strategies in regard to public opinion. On the one hand, inspired sometimes by elaborate normative theories articulated within the establishment by opinion leaders such as A. Lawrence Lowell or Walter Lippman, and in other instances by much cruder pressures, they are quite prepared to force through public policies opposed by majorities (or, if "don't knows" are included, pluralities) of the electorate. (Choice recent examples include the North American Free Trade Agreement, which free-traders in both George Bush's and Bill Clinton's administrations pushed forward in the face of polls showing strong public opposition; most policy switches that defined the Reagan-Bush "right turn" of the 1980s; or the all but incredible spectacle of insistent congressional pressure to scale back President Clinton's already anemic proposals for an economic stimulus, in the face of polls showing truly gigantic majorities of voters ranking job creation above deficit reduction as a priority.)[18]

Some of these efforts involve organized (and subsidized) campaigns to "marginalize" adverse opinion by blandly redescribing the facts of either policy or opinion until the inconsistency disappears in a cloud of verbiage. (One example: most of the discussion of America's "right turn" in the 1980s, discussion which also featured that reliable staple of the attempted "marginalization" strategy, vituperative attacks on the heterodox.) In other cases, investor blocs and the media simply ignore or fudge the inconsistency (as in the discussion of the North American Free Trade Agreement or the efforts to cut back the Clinton administration's economic stimulus). Frequently, when majority opinion is obviously hostile, no one prints or analyzes any polls at all in public. (It is certainly not accidental that major polls virtually never report the public's views about, say, Federal Reserve high interest-rate policies; while, in a careful study of *New York Times* polls on aid to the Contras, Lance Bennett has demonstrated that the paper simply stopped printing the polls—which ran strongly against the U.S. government's position—as major congressional votes approached.[19]

On the other hand, American political history is also filled with wave after wave of clever publicists who became rich teaching big business and politicians the latest refinements of "the engineering of consent." Among these have been, appropriately, the inventor of the three-ring circus (and father of the adage that "there's a sucker born every minute"), P. T. Barnum himself, who served as a Republican state legislator and mayor of Bridgeport, Connecticut; any number of journalists and publishers, from Thurlow Weed to Warren G. Harding (the genial newspaper publisher from Marion, Ohio, who at least once recommended the use of Gatling guns to quell labor unrest); and some fabulously successful retailers (including John Wanamaker, chair of the Republican National Finance Committee in the late nineteenth century). More recently, an army of handsomely remunerated "public relations consultants" has taken the field, from Edward L. Bernays (an American nephew of Sigmund Freud) and Ivy Lee (the man who told John D. Rockefeller to hand out dimes to children) at the turn of the century, to more gemütlich bamboozlers in the last decades than can be conveniently enumerated.[20]

The message of virtually all of these eminently respectable gentlemen (all, so far, have been men, though women are now becoming increasingly prominent in the "profession") consists of variations on a single theme: that often it is easier and, in the long run, cheaper, to change mass opinion than to brush it aside (Bernays, 1928).

Such public relations activities, and the simple fact that, as Ginsberg recently emphasized, even dictatorial regimes will sometimes find it in their interests to appear to court public opinion, almost guarantee that some positive correlations will exist between public policies and mass opinion in most historical periods (Ginsberg, 1982, pp. 8–9). Given that politicians still have to talk about something, even if debarred by their dependence on investor blocs from addressing many issues most important to voters, we can be quite certain that elections, and scholars of elections, will inevitably celebrate the idea of such correlations.

But How Is Systematic Error by Voters Possible?

We thus arrive at a first, preliminary statement from a practical research perspective on how to tackle questions of mass voting behavior and actual campaigns in political systems like that of the United States, where most of the population is very weakly organized and a minority is almost hyperorganized. Clearly the initial, and most critical, task is to form a coherent picture of bloc formation within big business ("major investors") as an election approaches. Once this is achieved, the next problem is to relate these blocs (and their associated policies) to candidates and parties (if reasonably comprehensive campaign finance records are available, an application of the "Golden Rule"—to see who rules, follow the gold—can help greatly to resolve these problems, though I would caution against excessively mechanical applications of this dictum).[21]

By paying careful attention to the slogans, buzzwords, and oratory that constitute the collective deliberative process—such as it is—of political campaigns, one then tries as best as one can to sort out the signals that are being sent to the electorate. (This step is a rough, linguistic equivalent of tracing campaign financing. It is an area in which current measurement practices leave much to be desired.) If the problem is finally to explain voting behavior, then the last stage of the inquiry involves analyzing how voters draw on their own particular interpretative resources, which are very closely related to their particular forms of social activity (and thus, as discussed below, differ radically from the cognitive activities assumed in neoclassical economies in general and "rational expectations" in particular) to reach a decision.

In practice, these last steps can be accomplished in a number of ways. But empirical studies of voting behavior, I think, would gain a lot from closer acquaintance with the practice of writing "history from below," as George Rudé, E. P. Thompson, or a few members of the (overrated) *Annales* school have attempted to do. In sharp contrast to most conventional "public opinion" analysts, these historians take pains to disentangle elite from mass opinion and to analyze the latter in its own right. They pay great attention to subtle differences in the flow of information within and between social classes, racial and ethnic groups, political institutions, and gender hierarchies, and to how various groups experience the same events. Precisely who reads which newspapers or books (or watches which TV programs), along with the interpretative theories historical actors bring to bear on these experiences, not to mention who subsidizes what, and how all of this changes over time, all figures in their explanations.[22]

One strand of contemporary voting research deliberately bends over backward to avoid the great pitfall of all such inquiries: the likelihood of inadvertently putting words into people's mouths and, without meaning to, mistranslating popular culture into familiar (elite) viewpoints. Relying exclusively on open-ended questions, Stanley Kelley has shown that voters' decisions in two-party races can be predicted with remarkable accuracy (more than 80 percent in most elections, within at least respectable hailing distance of eclipse studies, the stock social science example of a good theory) by attending to what voters volunteer they like and dislike about candidates and parties (Kelley, 1983). Though he does not refer to it, Kelley's "linear model" approach to voters' decisions is supported by a substantial psychological literature on decision making. His findings, in addition, have been extended by John Geer (1988, 1991a, 1991b, 1992), who has also shown empirically that a number of plausible objections to the method—for example, that it might disproportionately favor articulate or educated respondents—are invalid. Additional buttressing comes from two sociologists who independently developed what amounts to virtually the same praxis (Ajzen and Fishbein, 1980).[23]

Both Kelley and Geer stress their conviction that voters' decisions on the smallish list of considerations that actually appear to move them are importantly affected by campaigns, the media and other influences. From an investment theory standpoint, this sounds exactly right, and while one would like to explore the point in detail, there is no reason to quarrel with their empirical results. Indeed, I regard their analyses of recent elections as entirely consistent with my own studies of the behavior of investor blocs in those elections, particularly of the way the austerity policies sponsored by Democratic investor blocs have crippled the party's mass appeal.[24]

But this view of voters, political campaigns, and public discussion raises a fundamental question. Kelley's and Geer's research with open-ended questions shows that most ordinary voters are definitely not passive spectators of electoral contests. At least during presidential elections, most are certainly not voting randomly, or on the basis of "off-the-top-of-the-head" whims, as other analysts have sometimes suggested. Many try rather hard to make sense of campaigns. Despite the publicity about alleged "single-issue voters," almost all cast their ballots on the basis of more than one issue.[25]

On the other hand, this research, along with other studies, suggests quite a mixed picture about the overall consistency and coherence of the electorate's views. For example, in sharp contrast to political scientists, a large majority of the population apparently finds it very plausible that the rich and powerful dominate the political system. At the same time, however, they "rally 'round the flag" and give many responses to other questions that are often jarringly inconsistent with this viewpoint. While one could perhaps redescribe this behavior to reduce the impression of incoherence, it is obvious that the American electorate is light years from the case discussed at the outset of this essay, in which only the sheer existence of the campaign cost constraint prevents aroused voters from controlling the state.[26]

But how is it possible to square the evidence of intelligent, goal-directed behavior on the electorate's part with the persistence of so much ambiguous and contradictory thought about politics? Or, to make the question as pointed as possible by raising the level of generalization, how is persistent, "systematic error" reproduced in social systems that is consistent with the historical and contemporary evidence regarding both investor bloc strategies and voters' behavior?

This is the real question raised by McKelvey and Ordeshook's critique of my earlier essay. Their use of rational expectations to analyze "whether incomplete information precludes effective competition among groups, as Ferguson suggests" is really an argument that systematic error of this sort should not occur on what are, essentially, theoretical grounds (McKelvey and Ordeshook, 1986, p. 912). Because their case is the polar opposite of mine, it is very helpful to consider their argument in detail:

> Our definition of an equilibrium here is inspired by recent attempts at incorporating considerations of imperfect information into economics. Just as voters are unlikely to be informed about the details of candidate platforms, consumer-investors are not likely to satisfy, even approximately, the information assumptions of neoclassical microeconomics. The rational expectations hypothesis assumes that consumers and investors condition their decisions on a belief about how true states are related to observed signals (e.g., prices). In equilibrium, they must be acting optimally, conditional on their beliefs, and these beliefs must be consistent with what they observe; otherwise, there is additional information available that might change their decisions. (McKelvey and Ordeshook, 1986, p. 914)

McKelvey and Ordeshook therefore attempt to analyze a process of expectation formation and verification that teaches citizens "to vote correctly in terms of their self-interests by using relatively costless sources of information" (McKelvey and Ordeshook, 1986, p. 934).

They proffer two models which they suggest lead to plausible reconstructions of actual voter practices. The first, which they admit assumes rather a lot, postulates that uninformed voters know exactly where they usually sit in relation to the entire distribution of voter opinions (while possessing an internalized sense of self-discipline worthy of Saint Ignatius of Loyola and a strong, intuitive sense of stochastic processes).[27] By tracking a series of polls showing how various candidates fare over time, voters initially ignorant of where candidates stand on an issue spectrum running from left to right learn to recognize which candidate is nearest to them. By eventually matching up with the right candidates, voters force the candidates to move to the median.

McKelvey and Ordeshook's second model, by contrast, appears to assume much less about the voters. Accordingly, it seems on the surface much more plausible. Essentially, they suggest that by paying careful attention not only to polls, but to endorsements from reference groups and similar campaign announcements, voters can find out which candidate is nearest them. This, McKelvey and Ordeshook argue, will again force candidates to the median after a while, even though all that voters know about the candidates is who is closest to them, not what they stand for, or even what the precise issues in question are (McKelvey and Ordeshook, 1986, p. 933–4).

As in many parts of economics where rational expectations has been tried, the argument is ingenious and stimulating, at least up to a point. But also like many parts of economics, including those concerned with stock prices (once considered the area of the theory's greatest success, but now marked by many negative appraisals and even recantations of onetime champions); foreign exchange markets; many macroeconomic adjustment questions; and asset market bubbles in the United States and Japan, their ultimate conclusions have a distinct air of *Through The Looking Glass.*[28]

To anyone sensitive to the Niagaras of on-the-record cash that now swirl indubitably around Washington and state capitals, for example, McKelvey and Ordeshook's argument appears more than a little quixotic. While rational expectations does not (as sometimes supposed) imply perfect foresight on everyone's part, the claim certainly does entail what might be termed perfect foresight on average; i.e., a random distribution of hits and misses nestling around the theoretically true mean value of whatever one is trying to predict. This is why the argument implies an absence of systematic error (Begg, 1982, pp. 29 ff).

Thus, if the Cal Tech analysts were correct in arguing that voters' rational expectations normally ensure the triumph of the median, it would be pointless for the average (self-interested) investor to contribute to political campaigns at all. The expected value of contributions, on average, would be zero, because democracy would be working, and the investment theory would be wrong. Investors, who must perforce also be assumed to be acting with rational expectations, would know it, and would not contribute. (Note that since McKelvey and Ordeshook's principal models work because voters use cues to cut through the fog of political campaigns and inform themselves, investors do not need to contribute to protect themselves against contributions by rivals—when the median decides, the median decides.)[29]

But the gravest problems with their argument emerge when it is examined in the light of the textile magnates/pro-union majority case already discussed above. Though their argument is, in effect, designed to dispute it, McKelvey and Ordeshook completely fail to confront the campaign cost condition. Their model *simply assumes away* the problem that the textile example highlights: that, somehow, the candidates are able to get on the ballot and continue finding the resources to stay in the race to the finish.

In effect, their argument presupposes that money grows on trees or, perhaps, that the leftmost candidate is running some as-yet-unknown form of green campaign that burns something other than money for fuel. If there is no campaign at all, their case falls completely apart, since informed voters would have nothing to respond to and the candidate would not appear in the polls. (It may be instructive to recall that even Jerry Brown kicked off his now legendary 1992 campaign with widespread national name recognition worth, in effect, millions of dollars. He also spent an additional $8 million before he was emulsified by the Clinton campaign's lavishly financed TV blitz—and his own mistakes, but mostly the TV blitz—in the New York primary.)[30]

The critical realignment case discussed earlier also qualifies as a disastrous counterexample of why, in the real world, the ability of the voters to recognize which candidate is nearest to them *does not* lead to an iterative process in which all, or indeed, any candidates have to converge on the median. (Recall that the "New Deal" example led only to 20 percent unionization, and no more.) To get to the median, candidates have to be able to go to the median. But unless they can float not only freely, but free, over the political spectrum, they can't afford to do much travelling. Indeed, in a world where money matters, they can't even pack their bags without seeing their receipts fall off literally with the speed of light, in the case of wired funds.

THE ORIGINS OF SYSTEMATIC VOTER ERROR I— THE "OBJECTIVE" SIDE

McKelvey and Ordeshook's disregard of the campaign cost condition is aided by an important equivocation. Their exposition equates voters' reliance on rational expectations with the use of "all available" information. While this formulation is common in the literature, the best accounts carefully note a major qualification: that the "available" information is free or obtainable at negligible cost. As an exceptionally lucid statement of the view concedes:

> Improving the quality of information about the structure of the economy will generally be a costly activity which will be pursued only up to the point at which marginal benefits from better information equal

the marginal costs of obtaining it. Thus it is unlikely that it will ever be profitable or rational to obtain complete information. Without a more detailed examination of these costs and benefits, it is hard to decide how much information will be collected. While the assumption of any particular information is therefore arbitrary, many models implicitly assume that the relevant information set is precisely the widely available public information used by economists in empirical specification of the model itself. (Begg, 1982, p. 67)

That is, what makes expectations "rational" is not that they incorporate all potentially available information, but that they incorporate all *affordable* information. As Begg goes on to underline:

By a Rational Expectations equilibrium we then mean a path along which individuals cannot improve their forecasting by using the information which they cheaply acquire. (Begg, 1982, p. 69.)

By eliding this point, McKelvey and Ordeshook brush aside all the differences in the real-life political economy of information that are created by social class and education, or one's slot within the industrial structure, and the rather obvious "public good" character of much political information (to be discussed shortly). By assumption, in other words, and not by any compelling evidence or reasoning, voters are put on the same footing as investment banks.

Since McKelvey and Ordeshook's exposition relies heavily on the notion of a "poll," and then quite deliberately elongates that concept into the still broader idea of "cues," it is important to observe that their case depends absolutely on the existence of a neutral source that freely supplies voters with unbiased polls and other "cues" throughout the campaign. Along with the neglect of the campaign cost condition, and the implicit confusion of "affordable" with "available," this last point gives the game away. It is not simply that the use voters would have to make of the polls is, practically speaking, computationally impossible and conflicts with virtually everything that is known about the logic of everyday inference.[31] Nor is it that rational expectations as a general theory of cognition is incompatible with the results of contemporary empirical research on human judgment and reasoning—though, as we shall see, the implications of this fact are indeed striking.[32]

From the standpoint of the investment theory, the most profound problem with their argument is that no such neutral, "Archimedean" point exists in the real world's political economy of information.

This fact comprises at least half of the answer to the question about how "systematic error" arises and persists, so the argument is worth tracing in detail. We are all aware that ever since that *annus mirabilis* of American party politics, 1896, the *New York Times* has promised readers "all the news that's fit to print." Unfortunately, it is a fact that on all too many occasions—e.g., the Bay of Pigs, the notorious transfer of Raymond Bonner for his politically incorrect reporting on Latin America, or the articles on local politics that appear to have occasioned the departure of Pulitzer Prize–winning columnist Sydney Schanberg—the paper deemed unfit to print information that would have been of great interest to many voters. (It is also a fact, and a very interesting fact, that no other major media outlet picked up the torch when the *Times* let it fall.) Independent analysts have also raised important questions about the paper's coverage of two very important recent national controversies: the North American Free Trade Agreement and national health care.[33]

Considering McKelvey and Ordeshook's uncomplicated confidence in polls, it is worth recalling Bennett's penetrating demonstration of the *Times'* manipulative coverage of public opinion about Nicaragua. One might also note the many years the same preeminent journal spent touting Ronald Reagan as one of the most popular presidents in American history—a claim which it abandoned only long after evidence to the contrary had been widely publicized. Then there is the matter of its improbable, but nonetheless reiterated, claims that higher participation by nonvoters would not have affected the outcome of 1988 and other presidential elections, which I believe played a role in various prenomination struggles within the Democratic Party in 1992.[34]

Even more telling against McKelvey and Ordeshook's case, however, is the simple fact that the *Times* and the rest of the U.S. prestige press rarely cover endorsements, or other politically significant activities of most major investors. (They do devote some space to political endorsements by movie stars and pop singers.) Unless major party campaigns choose to publicize (a select few of) their business supporters for special reasons, as for example, the Clinton campaign did in 1992, at best the major media provide very general, "no fault" campaign finance analysis. Neither do they cover the Business Council, the Trilateral Commission, the Council on Foreign Relations and other influential investor-dominated organizations in any detail, though the latter two, at least, must be well known to many leading media figures, since so many have been members. This pattern of benign neglect also extends to most research institutes, think tanks, foundations, and other places where investors, scholars, and journalists, if rarely median voters, converge to formulate policy proposals. Save when they are financed by groups that are pariahs even to major blocs of investors in the media (e.g., some, though far from all, foreign interests), journalists will cover the scholars, but not the donors who may or may not be gratefully acknowledged in the annual reports and publications of the institutions concerned. Other "special interests" such as unions occasionally receive coverage, but little of it is likely to be helpful to voters, particularly if they are suspicious of the official union leadership.

But this unhappy catalogue does not even hint at the true dimensions of the problem with reliance on the media for "polls" (and other cues). Consider just the relatively clear-cut case of real polls. For all the questions that cluster about the *Times'* use of opinion polls in its news coverage—and there are many more than there is space here to mention—it is important to remember that the actual CBS/*Times* polling operation is a model of care and professionalism. Real care is taken not to cook the questions; the staff is sensitive to question wording, interviewer, and order effects; and requests for fuller information are readily and courteously filled.

Apart from Gallup and a few other leading surveys, the same cannot be said about most other polls published in the media. Questions are frequently slanted in any number of ways both in primaries (where, it often seems, almost anything goes) and general elections. Candidates who should be included in surveys are not. Potential candidates and noncandidates who shouldn't be included are. (We pause here in memory of frustrated 1992 Democratic presidential hopeful Larry Agran, and note that in the early stages of the New Hampshire primary, his poll numbers, but not his press notices or fund-raising totals, were little different from those of, say, Bill Clinton. We also underline the fact—calamitous for McKelvey and Ordeshook—that in this instance, as in many others, newspaper editors were sometimes willing to admit in public that both their coverage and their polls were affected by candidates' success in raising money.)[35]

Outrageously loaded questions about issues and referenda are common even in very respectable newspapers (and are not unknown in even the "name brand" polls). Results are frequently published with no indication of sample size, the exact wording of the question, or hints about what other questions preceded it. While one would like to believe that these horrors are a consequence of simple incompetence, often they are not. Studies of journalism content confirm what is suggested to me by my own archival work and firsthand acquaintance with many "analysts" in the "business": that newspapers' coverage and use of polls is usually correlated with their support for particular candidates.[36]

In general, what is true of polls holds for all the rest of the "cues" voters often rely on. In terms of a critical approach to rational expectations, what is problematic is not merely the empirical fact that voters have often paid demonstrably inordinate attention to the ethnic origins of candidates, or their religion, or whether they can claim the title "Dr.", or are listed first on the ballot, or irrelevant traits of personality, character, facial features, or even their names. (I recall an Ohio Senate candidate named John Kennedy who received over a million votes, as well as the legendary deal Nelson Rockefeller struck with the Hatters Union to install one Frank D. Roosevelt, Jr. on the Liberal line to siphon votes from Frank O'Connor [Kramer and Roberts, 1976, pp. 317–19].)

The truly mortifying circumstance is that all through American history, voters have received all kinds of institutional encouragement to rely on such cues. Even the prima facie absurd ballot position and same-name cues can be and have been systematically manipulated by parties, newspapers, and investor blocs, in many instances for years. The same holds for the generous tolerance these same groups—parties, media, and investor blocs—have so long extended to the venerable practice of religious and ethnic "balancing" of tickets by political parties whose top leadership indubitably and literally is or was "in the money"; to the way the contemporary Democratic Party, which should probably take out formal membership in the Investment Bankers Association of America, disguises itself as a congeries of more politically correct and far less affluent "special interest" groups; and to the widening practice among Republicans of grabbing for a "moderate" label by talking up "choice" or, occasionally, gay rights. In some of these cases (e.g., ballot position and same-name candidacies), the promotion of the cue may be explicable, but plainly amounts to encouraging irrationality, if that protean term is to have any meaning at all. In other cases, the cue arguably (the rubber quality of this qualifying term points to a major part of the problem) made sense once, or made sense in special, limited circumstances, but has long since deteriorated into a complex fraud that, however, still retains (some) effectiveness, particularly as long as the media wink at the practice.[37]

McKelvey and Ordeshook's claim that endorsements are an avenue for voters to obtain cheap information is equally flimsy. We have already noticed most endorsements fail to make the papers, but there are a variety of other problems with this suggestion. In money-driven systems, endorsements are frequently sold and bartered by both businesses and unions, as a variety of striking cases from recent Democratic primaries can illustrate. Endorsements can also be affected by a host of considerations that are clearly irrelevant to voters' interests in the best possible "signal" value. For example, strategic silences by interest groups are very common, but virtually impossible for voters to "read." Neither would it be a very good idea for average voters to try to "go to school" on their more affluent compatriots' voting preferences, as

McKelvey and Ordeshook suggest at one point, unless they enjoy, for example, regressive taxes.[38]

The cumulative effect of all these influences defies straightforward quantitative summary. But, in general, there is no reason either empirically or theoretically to believe that the media do anything but exacerbate voters' problems in obtaining and evaluating reliable information.

We can, for example, dismiss the still-fashionable notion that the media have "few political effects." Particularly if one gives up silly *1984* notions of Big Brother controlling everyone at election time, and thinks in terms of marginal influences on various percentages of the electorate (Robinson, 1974), a wave of new studies suggests that this old chestnut is absurd. (Some studies suggest that the voters most susceptible to media influence are usually those who know the least, which, interestingly for money-driven political systems, turns out to be precisely those who watch the most TV. These are mostly middle-class and lower-middle-class voters, whose opinions as a result resemble not those of their similarly circumstanced compatriots, but of upper-class voters who do not watch nearly as much television.)[39]

As Erik Devereux has observed, for all the rodomontade about journalistic independence, what might be termed the "practical party identification" of newspapers and other media (indicated, for example, by which party's presidential candidates are normally endorsed; though these are often important less in their own right than because they have been shown to be correlated with other aspects of coverage [Wilhoit and Auh, 1974]) is at least as stable and predictable as analysts of electoral behavior used to believe individual party identifications were.[40]

From an investment theory standpoint, none of this is surprising. In the United States and most other advanced postindustrial societies, most major media are privately controlled and a wave of pressure for deregulation is leading to the erosion of the few state-supported systems that still exist. As a consequence, one can generalize the investment theory's "principle of non-competition" across all investor blocs within the party system into a "black hole" maxim applicable to the public sphere as a whole under "free enterprise": Just as large profit-maximizing investors in parties do not pay to undermine themselves, major media (i.e., those big enough to have potentially significant effects on public opinion) controlled by large profit-maximizing investors do not encourage the dissemination of news and analyses that are likely to lead to popular indignation and, perhaps, government action hostile to the interests of all large investors, themselves included.

This does not imply that such media will not print some "bad" news—a newspaper that reports none at all is likely to lose credibility.

Nor, as emphasized by a variety of recent empirical studies of politically significant differences within the media, does the claim imply that the press cannot be critical. It can, and it will be critical, to the point of destroying presidencies, when major differences within investor blocs are involved, or, of course, when mobilizing against anti-investor groups. (As the recent upsurge of corporate-backed lawsuits and subsidized studies of "bias" in press coverage of oil spills, Vietnam, and other hot topics attests, however, rival investor blocs can hit back hard.)[41]

But all this "diversity" is diversity among large investor blocs. While greatly underestimated in contemporary social science, it will not necessarily do much for the average voter. Unions, the poor, and other groups who are not major investors cannot count on the press to present their cases. Indeed, since so many political arguments turn ultimately on (mostly implicit) judgments by voters of the net effects of various complicated policy options, a profit-maximizing media often can readily help transform an unorganized electorate into a disorganized one by a variety of very simple techniques: By hyping estimates of the magnitude of the benefits of particular policies; by eliding questions of costs (a factor, probably, in the frequent association of "progressive"-sounding policies with regressive taxation mentioned earlier, and an all-but-universal practice within the U.S. press, in regard to Reaganomics during most of the 1980s [Hertsgaard, 1988]); by practicing a version of "confirmation bias," that is, the tendency to dwell disproportionately on cases favorable to one's pet theory (e.g., cases in which "free markets" produce economic growth or "democracy" [cf. Therborn, 1977, for a devastating empirical critique]); or by framing a wide variety of spurious "contrast effects" (for example, by a simple failure to cover interest groups lined up behind a preferred policy option, creating the impression that protectionism, but not free trade, is an issue promoted by peculiarly narrow "special interests.)"[42]

As a consequence, all sorts of subsidized misinformation will be circulating in the press, even in regard to major public issues that appear to be "well covered." In the political equivalent of Gresham's law, bad information repeated by most of the major media may even drive out good information, and—via "Asch effects," "spirals of silence," or simple fear of ridicule—sow additional public confusion.[43]

But, it may be urged in response, would it not, accordingly, be profitable for some individuals to attempt to organize new enterprises to improve the quality of the information and analysis available to them? Here, I fear, the answer is obvious, if rarely incorporated into empirical democratic theory.

Of course it will (or, as will momentarily become evident, might). That is why my original essay on the investment theory included the passages that McKelvey and Ordeshook take special exception to (p. 934) on the importance of government policy toward the secondary organization of the citizenry—toward unions, cooperatives, etc. Precisely because these organizations have such revolutionary (in many senses) potential, governments controlled by large investors have always been extremely sensitive to their political activities. That is why the history of labor or agrarian protest cannot be reduced to a chronicle of attempts to raise wages or farm prices. It is also part of the reason why in so many parts of the world, including the United States, the specter of honest, free trade unions arouses so much passion—and brings forth such strenuous efforts from major investors and governments to raise the costs of starting or maintaining such movements. And the success of this repression in so many parts of the world is probably the major reason for the comparative failure of voter control in most existing states.[44]

In the case of new newspapers, additional considerations are relevant. Ginsberg's historically sensitive discussion of the role of advertising (paid for, or course, by other investors) in reducing the newsstand and subscription prices of newspapers and magazines helps greatly to explain why almost all new publications that focus on politics are subsidized (Ginsberg, 1986, pp. 135–37). As Curran documents, really aggressive papers have historically faced all sorts of other transaction costs, including (often groundless) libel suits and police harassment (Curran, 1982). And if, as has not been likely since the mid-nineteenth century, the owners successfully thread their way around all these hazards, at some point they begin to think like major investors themselves. As with the once "populist" Scripps-Howard chain, interest withers in the original mission (Lundberg, 1946, pp. 279–82).

From a purely theoretical standpoint, in addition, the public's prospects in a free market for information peopled only by profit-maximizing producers and totally self-interested consumers are even bleaker than indicated by existing discussions of "imperfect markets" for information.[45] In strict, neoclassical logic, for political information such as we are considering, a market is unlikely to exist at all.

Perhaps the most convenient way to demonstrate the point is to contrast two cases: First, that of a newsletter that accurately predicts the stock market; second, that of a magazine that attempts to inform voters about the political activities of the very same businesses, and perhaps, their relations with high government officials. The first has an obvious market and may expand rapidly. People will buy it, read it, invest on the basis of its reports, and make money, at least until word leaks out. In the other case, however, people buy it, read it, and then face massive collective-action problems (Olson, 1971) plus, commonly, direct repression and formidable transaction costs. While the social value of the information may be enormous, there is, from a purely self-interested individual economic standpoint, no reason to purchase the magazine at all. All one gets is a headache, accompanied perhaps by long-term demoralization.[46]

THE ORIGINS OF SYSTEMATIC VOTER ERROR II—
THE "SUBJECTIVE" SIDE

All these influences collectively constitute what might be termed the "objective" side of the genesis of systematic error—the part that is ecologically external to individual voters. But as was hinted earlier, this comprises but half the story. No less important is the "subjective" side of this process—what individual voters add as they deliberate and attempt to act.

The literature in experimental social psychology is now quite clear that rational expectations, with its reliance on a single, unanimously accepted, unambiguous (and quantitatively formulated) true model, caricatures the way human perception and judgment actually work. Real-life human perception proceeds not only from "the bottom up" (by inducing from particulars), but also from the "top down," (from preconceived ideas). Frequently stereotypical, full of "false consensus," "anchoring," and "halo" effects, and relying extensively on "heuristics" of "representativeness," or "availability," human judgment can be shown to be highly fallible and not self-correcting in many clear-cut cases in ordinary life (Hogarth, 1980; Tversky and Kahneman, 1974; Nisbet and Ross, 1980). When group pressures and values figure importantly, the likelihood of major persistent error rises even further, not least because of a raft of perceptual anomalies that can seriously distort even simple physical comparisons of the relative sizes of everyday material objects (Tajfel, 1981, chapters 5 and 6). A variety of other "cognitive illusions" also exist, including some that may cause special problems for voters.[47]

This does not mean that humans cannot respond sensibly to new situations. They can, and they do—particularly if they already have a clue as to the real nature of the situation they are up against, or if somebody takes the trouble to teach them how to respond appropriately. But even at an individual level, such efforts are often very expensive, in terms of not only money but time, since human learning often has a motor aspect requiring some repetition, and always involves an appropriate level of emotional commitment. At a mass level the real cost of developing and disseminating reasonably accurate accounts of how political systems really work is enormous (Goodwyn, 1976). Not surprisingly, therefore, empirical studies of mass public opinion in history and political science powerfully suggest that controversies among elites and older elite theories usually have major influence on popular culture (Cf. e.g., Rudé [1980] or Zaller [1992]; though the latter, perhaps because it draws its evidence almost exclusively from the mass communications–dominated recent past, is less sensitive to the way these older views are sometimes assimilated into independently derived conceptual schemas and to developments such as those discussed by Goodwyn, 1976).

The implications of all this for the discussion here can be summarized by observing that for all but the very simplest levels of human performance, successful human activity is a function of culture (Wygotski, 1985; Luria, 1982). But "human activity in general" is an empty abstraction. What is real are humans acting in particular contexts (including the very abstract contexts of mathematics and formal reasoning) with particular tools (including the great tool of language itself). As a consequence, without deliberate organized effort (which is very costly, since it involves a kind of formal instruction), knowledge tends to be "local" and domain specific. The so-called "transfer problem" (recognition of A should entail recognition of B, by voters and everyone else) is ubiquitous—and, normally, solvable only in culturally sanctioned contexts (Tulviste, 1991; Laboratory of Comparative Human Cognition, 1983).

Considering that in most real-life systems of public deliberation the parts most easily controlled by ordinary voters—their own discussions at home or work, for example—are precisely the most informally organized, while the rest of the system is normally owned and operated by investor blocs of one sort or another, there is nothing contradictory in the claim that voters in an ordinary language sense usually do the "best they can" even if they only intermittently succeed in grasping the essence of a political system that few political scientists can describe correctly. As Granberg and Holmberg demonstrate, in the United States the quality of political information conveyed by the media, parties, and other institutions is wretched, even by the standards of other countries—which are usually nothing to be proud of (Granberg and Holmberg, 1988). Moreover, as many recent studies of political "rhetoric" remind us, political commentary is far from a "random" stream of impressions. In most cases, it has been skillfully crafted to appeal to its audiences's prejudices and stereotypes—making it precisely the sort of material that the literature in experimental psychology suggests is difficult for most humans to see through under normal conditions (Bennett, 1992).

Not surprisingly, in such an environment the everyday "theories" most voters hold about the political system rarely provide much help. Thanks to generations of hard work by investor blocs, most voters are usually saddled (this term is carefully chosen) with some high school civics textbook version of the median voter model, supplemented perhaps by almost endlessly manipulable personality-based accounts of high-level decision making gleaned from popular novels, television, and, sometimes, the educational system—including higher education and, alas, political science textbooks. Ignorant of alternative ways of thinking about either the polity or the economy, many citizens sometimes appear to possess few general notions about politics at all.[48]

But however inadequate these everyday theories are, they are usually well entrenched. In part, this is because voters, like the rest of the human race, approach reality with particular hopes, fears, and interests, and with a definite, historically circumscribed knowledge base, rather than behaving as statistically unbiased detectors that impartially pick up and decode every signal in the environment. In part, it is also because many mistakes voters make are luxuriantly encouraged by the very processes of social deliberation they are attempting to master.

Not surprisingly, therefore, voters share the general human tendency toward "overconfidence" in judgments. They stick with bad interpretative theories far longer than they rationally should (Hogarth, 1980). Even when everyday life is breaking up, nothing resembling impartial hypothesis testing usually results. With the set of alternatives all too easily restricted to proposals that grow naturally out of the previous era's elite discourse, good new ideas frequently have a difficult time getting a hearing, even from the people they could benefit. The problem of building political support is compounded by the high costs of inventing serious, credible new hypotheses that are worth sticking one's neck out for, since, as Thomas Kuhn noted, even scientists rarely break with existing theories without a well-developed alternative to sharpen their perception and given them confidence (Kuhn, 1970). And, of course, the sheer massive fact of political repression often overrides everything else.

WHEN "JUST SAYING NO" IS NOT ENOUGH

There remains only the argument in the literature on retrospective voting as a challenge to the investment approach. At first hearing, this view sounds very plausible: Voters may not know or care very much about the particulars of governing. But they still should be able to decide whether they like what the governing party has brought about. Members of the electorate, accordingly, have a perfectly sensible basis

for casting their ballots. If they like the effects of the incumbent's policies, they vote for him or her. If they don't, they throw the rascal out.
As Fiorina has argued: "What policies politicians follow is their business; what they accomplish is the voter's" (Fiorina, 1981, p. 12).

This innocent-sounding proposal, however, suffers from two grave
drawbacks. The most fundamental is apparent from the aforementioned case of the textile magnates confronting a 97 percent majority
in favor of unionization. I noted then that merely multiplying parties
did nothing to solve the electorate's problem. The situation with regard
to expelling a series of incumbents is similar.

By installing a swivel chair in the Oval Office, voters can "just say
no" and ensure a circulation of the elite's representatives. But in a
world in which money matters, they do not thereby achieve circulation of the elite: If, for example, voters want unions, they still need a
pro-union party. Otherwise, all they get is a fresh (and affluently rewarded) face and timeworn (protextile) policies. Nor is this a purely
theoretical deduction from airy first principles: As more than one electorate in American history has discovered, to ensure a break with persistently deflationary macroeconomic policies it is essential to find
someone willing to try out a genuinely new policy. Otherwise, all voters can do is substitute Grover Cleveland (one of whose closest advisers
happened to be J. P. Morgan's principal attorney, and who himself
spent the four years between his first and second presidential terms
in Morgan's law firm) for Benjamin Harrison (backed actively by J. P.
Morgan, Wanamaker, and Company), and then dump him for William
McKinley (backed by—J. P. Morgan, Wanamaker and an almost wall-
to-wall coalition of finance and industry). Or, as almost happened in
1932, the populace will be asked to hail as the alternative to Herbert
Hoover the honorable Newton D. Baker, Cleveland bank attorney and
counsel to the Federal Reserve System that was strangling the
economy.[49]

There is another problem with the notion of retrospective voting.
Like McKelvey and Ordeshook's rational expectations argument, the
notion is remarkably innocent in its approach to the real-life political
economy of information. For at bottom, the view takes voters' judgments of a regime's policy success to be essentially incorrigible. It thus
succumbs to what might be termed the "fallacy of immaculate perception."

Considering the amount of political commentary that is concerned
with managing perceptions of past policy, this is difficult to abide. It
was Friedrich Nietzsche who observed, in his celebrated essay "On the
Use and Abuse of History," that a culture's ability to function was essentially bound up with the view of the past it maintained (Nietzsche,

1957). In the twentieth century, Nietzsche's point has been seized upon by any number of regimes, think tanks, and foundations. They have grasped keenly the logic of making massive investments in the rewriting of history—with results visible to all, not least in the fluctuating answers recorded by pollsters to questions about the reputations of former presidents and candidates, and policy questions such as exactly how successful people believe the War on Poverty really was, or how the rich responded to the Reagan tax cuts.[50]

Such facts are a warning that eternal vigilance is likely to be the least of the costs of democratic control of the state. In politics, as in the economy, voters get what they pay for—or else investors do, exactly as my original essays argued.

ACKNOWLEDGEMENTS

I am grateful to Erik Devereux and Benjamin Page for helpful comments on earlier drafts; to Edward Reed for many discussions of the experimental literature on human perception and judgment; and to Edward Herman for drawing my attention to several valuable studies on the press. The Henry Adams quotation that opens this paper comes from Adams, 1930, p. 360; the Acheson quotation is in Cumings, 1993, p. 557, n. 53.

Some arguments in this appendix date back to my "Deduced and Abandoned: McKelvey and Ordeshook's Rational Expectations-Augmented-Myth of the Median Voter," paper for the Conference on Politics, Information, and Political Theory, February 13–15, 1986; Thompson Conference Center, University of Texas at Austin. An earlier version of the discussion also appeared under the same title as this essay in a special issue, edited by William Crotty and sponsored by the Political Organizations and Parties Section of the American Political Science Association, of The *American Review of Politics*, vol. 14, winter 1993, pp. 497–532. My discussion of the "black hole" thesis in regard to profit-maximizing media is quite different from, but inevitably brings to mind, Stephen Magee, William Brock, and Leslie Young's (1989); we have all, of course, borrowed this attractive usage from astronomy.

NOTES

1. Bronson Cutting to John T. King, September 4, 1919, Bronson Cutting Papers, Library of Congress, Box 4. This letter also briefly discusses how ethnic politics fitted into this pattern—as if that were not clear enough already between the lines. H. J. Hageman to Cutting, Feb. 9, 1920, in Box 5, suggests that Cutting's was the only sizable paper in the state not clearly affiliated with the mining companies and their allies.

Note that, strictly speaking, Cutting's missive deals with intraparty competition. But the Democrats were no different—indeed, the New York-based chair of Phelps Dodge, Cleveland Dodge, was one of the most prominent Democrats in the United States and a close friend of President Woodrow Wilson.

For reasons of space, this paper attempts to provide the minimum of documentation consistent with precision of argument; references are therefore collected, whenever possible, and inserted into a single note.

2. The warning is in the Hageman letter cited above.

3. The classic account of the median voter is that put forward in Downs (1957); there have been many restatements and refinements since. See also the lucid discussion in Barry (1970, chap. 5); and, for a later treatment, McLean (1987, pp. 49–50).

4. This essay was originally quite long, and had to be divided for publication. Its first part appeared as Ferguson (1986); a revised version of Ferguson (1983) appears in this book as chapter 1; the quotations are found there.

5. McKelvey and Ordeshook (1986) reference several other essays they wrote on the question of democratic control of the state. The "retrospective voting" objection has not appeared in print, but ever since the 1986 panel at the Texas conference referred to above, at which McKelvey, Ordeshook, and I all appeared, it has been advanced informally by various commentators, as have the other objections mentioned in the text. Perhaps the best-known general statement of the retrospective voting view is Fiorina (1981).

It may also be worth mentioning that after McKelvey and Ordeshook performed some experiments with a median voter model of elections, Gavan Duffy designed and carried out several from an investment perspective. Though all these are interesting, it is difficult not to be skeptical of their ecological validity.

6. This discussion draws very slightly from Ferguson (1991; in this volume chapter 4). It should not be necessary to caution that the discussion below is informal. But the critical points should nevertheless be clear; I certainly see no point to attempt to specify a minimum dollar amount for when "money matters." Note, however, that Ross Perot, the walking incarnation of the investment theory of political parties, appears to have spent rather more than $60 million in his two very brief campaigns in 1992; and that every single major losing candidate in the 1992 Democratic presidential race was forced to quit the race for lack of funds before being finished off electorally in the primaries. Serious campaigns for the White House, accordingly, now seem to require at least $100 million or so to go all the way—and that is a low estimate that takes no account of the "free" publicity that true insurgent candidacies are rarely afforded.

One other point about the example may need to be emphasized—the language about voters choosing a general rate of unionization is chosen carefully to avoid a variety of technical complications that would waste considerable time and distract from the essence of the argument. For the average semi-skilled or unskilled worker, in any case, the treatment is probably quite realistic.

7. So far, the discussion is about one issue. But if no one could speak affirmatively to it, voters would end up flipping coins to decide who to vote for, or the candidates would start competing on who has the best smile, or whatever. Many such moves would amount to adding "issues." Filling in these details would clutter the exposition, so I omit them.

8. This notion of "replacement cost," in my opinion, is basic to discussions of competition. It clearly varies with the overall state of the political system; an unpopular incumbent, for example, might have a lower replacement cost.

9. The truly significant assumption here is that information which is immediately recognized as reliable does not flow instantaneously and costlessly from candidates to

voters, who are otherwise clear about what they want. Of course, this broad condition, which certainly fits our world, is precisely what brings parties into existence in the first place. Parties, in this respect, resemble banks, which depend for their existence on the fact that funds do not flow effortlessly from savers to investors as they would in a "perfect" credit market. Note also that, depending on how one defines terms, even in such a "frictionless" world, information costs may not exhaust the obstacles facing voters; there might exist various transaction costs, for example.

10. Ferguson (1986) discusses various contradictions reflected in different versions of realignment theory. The reference here to the New Deal is not casual, though in that case class conflict squeezed the capital-intensive party to change its initial offer. See Ferguson (1984; chapter 2 in this volume); Ferguson (1991; chapter 4 in this volume) presents detailed quantitative tests of the earlier paper's central hypotheses.

11. Here a caution is in order. In outlining how adding issues can help investor blocs, I am *not* suggesting that these additional issues are necessarily "pseudo" issues. While each concrete case is different, as discussed below, the general case is likely to be one that is in accord with the evidence from experimental psychology that people are often poor judges of everyday events, and consistent with the "black hole" maxim, also analyzed below, that applies to the public sphere in market societies. Typically, in other words, plausible arguments are overstated, and alternatives are underplayed or suppressed. This "cultural-historical" emphasis on social factors in cognition itself sharply differentiates the investment approach from rational choice theory.

12. The heavy reliance on various regressive taxes to finance many modern benefits that used to be thought part of the "welfare state" is a staple in the literature; see e.g., Page (1983). Nineteenth-century outlays that were often financed by tariffs fall right into this general pattern, since most tariffs were surely regressive overall.

13. The sectional interpretation of American history was long a mainstay of political history, but until recently it cut little ice with political scientists. In many respects, however, the revival of interest in regionalism is a giant step backward theoretically, for in treating regions as homogeneous, all the important questions of class, race, ethnicity and gender are dodged. Save perhaps in a few cases of peripheral nationalism (largely outside the United States), in which virtually the whole of some large social group has been mired for generations in relative poverty, it can be taken as a rule that where regionalism dominates a political system, other basic cleavages are usually being suppressed.

14. Perhaps I should note that while I think very highly of the work of Harris and his students, the "cultural-historical" approach to language and cognition discussed below is quite different from "cultural materialism."

15. "Discourse" is a term that means many things to many people. But it is now used widely to signal a commitment to a view that meaning is an attribute of texts, with no necessary (or, sometimes, possible) relation to a larger world. In my view, this is entirely wrong even as an empirical theory of reading, which is a practice that always requires the reader to draw on his or her knowledge of the world even to get started. See, e.g., Cole (1990).

16. Thus a classic study by Warren Miller and Donald Stokes (1966) of constituency influence in Congress found a fairly strong correlation between a district's views and its congressional representative's record on racial issues, but only a weak fit between the district's economic views and the representative's record. This result is exactly what an investment approach would predict, but, somehow, the paradox has never been per-

ceived by the discipline. We may also note that in many instances where new issues are being invented, the target group is likely to be very far from median voters. Thus, for example, in the 1980s, the basic GOP strategy for the White House was rather clearly to appeal broadly to wealthy Americans, while trying to splinter blue-collar Democrats around race, gun control, pornography, etc. For this to work, the economy had to be reasonably strong and the Democrats had to eschew strong cross-cutting appeals to social class or New Deal issues and avoid efforts to raise turnout. Ferguson (1993) and Ferguson and Rogers (1986) analyze in detail how Democratic investor blocs blocked such appeals, thereby "winning" even as they "lost."

One other point, for clarity: note that adding issues never amounts to a step back toward the median voter, in the sense that no money-driven party can afford to add an issue that all investors abominate. I repeat this point, which is implicit in the main text, because some readers have suggested "synthesizing" the investor approach with the median voter view, or trying to assess "how much" each is true in a concrete case. Alas, this catholicity is inconsistent: for voters to control the state, either they organize and pay the costs, or money grows on trees.

17. Readers dubious about the "invention" of other issues should consult Hobsbawm's "Mass Producing Traditions: Europe, 1870–1914," (in Hobsbawm and Ranger, 1983), and Hobsbawm's devastating (1990) book. For evidence on voter's desires, see Kelley (1983). A very stimulating analysis of rhetoric and the investment approach is in Bennett (1992).

18. Lippman's writings and viewpoint are well known, but my own examination of Lowell's papers at Pusey Library, Harvard University, makes it clear that Lippman, who had been a student at Harvard, wrote up ideas that Lowell had already put in the air. (The conservative Lowell was president of Harvard and heir to a large textile fortune.) Based on the empirical evidence at the time the essay went to press, Ferguson (1993) described public sentiment as opposed to NAFTA by an "overwhelming" margin. It is clear that the split between opponents and proponents closed up as the decisive congressional vote approached. But this scarcely touches my point—that elites persisted with their policy in the face of very strong popular resistance. Note that, according to the *New York Times*/CBS poll published the week of the vote, the treaty was still a loser by 41 percent to 37 percent (the poll, which appeared in the Nov. 16, 1993, *Times* had a 3 percent margin of sampling error). I do not believe it can plausibly be contended that NAFTA proponents were going ahead in the conviction that public opinion would necessarily come round to their point of view. My own observations of an exceptionally wide range of East Coast business groups at the time of the Perot-Gore debate indicate quite the opposite. In addition, the public discussion betrayed many characteristic signs of elite anxiety, including, in some polls, subtle changes in question wording that bordered on the manipulative (notably a shift to the full, formal usage of "North American Free Trade Agreement"). Though I lack the space for a detailed analysis, I believe this inflated the number of apparent undecideds and perhaps nudged some respondents in a more favorable direction.

For the Reagan-Bush right turn, see Ferguson and Rogers (1986, chap. 1); for jobs vs. the deficit under Clinton, see Schneider (1993); other sources report even bigger majorities. There are no doubt ways to frame the questions about Clinton's budget to show lower numbers, but no poll suggests that the population would rather have a higher rate of unemployment and a lower deficit, even if some polls suggest many voters might choose more budget cuts over higher taxes. (The latter question, in my judgment, is highly manipulative when asked in isolation.) It should also perhaps be added that polls taken in the weeks just before the final passage of the Clinton deficit reduction program were undoubtedly muddied by the charge, widely believed but quite untrue, that most of the population would see its taxes rise markedly as a consequence of the plan. Such was the case only for the most affluent Americans.

19. On marginalization, see especially Bennett (1989). On the controversy over public opinion and the right turn, cf. Page and Shapiro (1992, pp. 169–70), whose well-nigh exhaustive review of polls over time concludes that "Ferguson and Rogers are correct, therefore, in arguing that the policy right turn of the Reagan years cannot be accounted for as a response to public demands." On the *Times* and Nicaragua, see Bennett (1989) for an excellent discussion. Note that his "institutional voice" really amounts to "investor voice."

20. Most of these cases are well known, but for the little-known Harding quote, see Downes (1970, p. 86).

21. For the necessary cautions, see Ferguson, (1991 [this volume, chapter 4], 1992). Note that this paragraph's suggestions presuppose a prior assessment of the level of popular organization—that yields a rough estimate of how much control ordinary citizens can afford to exert over the system. This point requires strong emphasis: there is nothing metaphysical about voter control of the state. Given the proper institutional support, it really can happen.

22. See, e.g., Rudé (1959); E. P. Thompson (1968); the *Annales* group has produced more work than can possibly be referenced here.

23. On linear models in psychology, see especially Dawes (1988, pp. 202–27). Ajzen and Fishbein (1980, p. 192) claim that campaigns normally give voters highly accurate information on candidates by election time. But this is easy to refute. See the works discussed below, or Center for the Study of Communication (1993); this shows, for example, that large numbers of voters greatly overestimate the number of children welfare mothers have and, in general, that they possessed little true information about any candidate in 1992. They did, however, know the name of George Bush's dog. This imaginative piece of research should embarrass a large number of far better-funded political scientists.

One should also note that Kelley himself observed that his model was virtually equivalent to one developed by Brody and Page (1973).

24. In particular, their findings suggest strongly that the turnaround in voters' ratings of the Democrats in regard to economic issues is probably the largest single cause of the party's decline—not race, or crime, or any other issue, including religious fundamentalism. This is why the dominance of the investment houses and other forces in the party committed to austerity since the late seventies is so significant for the party's electoral chances: they block more attractive economic appeals.

25. This is implied in Kelley's and Geer's tables, though there is perhaps minor ambiguity about how to correlate issues with responses. But more of this another time; the population clearly has multiple reasons for its votes.

26. Almost every poll now finds very large numbers of Americans suspicious of the role money plays in the system. Kelley, Ajzen and Fishbein, and Geer all present data that raise questions about consistency, though all consider the question only briefly. Perhaps the best overall treatment of this question is Granberg and Holmberg (1988) e.g, pp. 27–37, who present a number of devastating survey results.

27. The latter is particularly vulnerable, to judge from the literature on decision making cited below. People, in general, are poor judges of probabilities, and often don't think stochastically at all.

28. On the increasing difficulties of rational expectations in economics, see Sheffrin (1989, pp. 133 ff.), Shiller (1989), and Thaler (1992), among a large and rapidly growing literature that only incompletely assimilates the various failed European efforts to introduce "credible" macroeconomic policies in the 1980s. (The American failure at the start of the 1980s has been taken to heart, in many quarters.) My own coauthored work on stock markets turned up clear evidence that adjustments to unexpected developments were far from instantaneous (Epstein and Ferguson, 1991, p. 195, n. 16).

Within political science, the discussion of such questions would be much easier if works like Carvalho (1992) or Lavoie (1993) were better known.

29. In section 3 of their paper, McKelvey and Ordeshook do present a model of campaign contributions that is specifically aimed at the investment theory for which this is not true. But that model is outlandish, in that only turnout is affected by contributions and politicians cannot keep any of the money. Both of their really interesting models work by giving the electorate full information equivalents.

30. For Brown, see Ferguson (1993). The $8 million figure is an estimate that assumes that many bills that were paid in June were run up in May, as was surely the case.

31. See, e.g., Lave (1988). Her discussion of shopping is highly relevant to McKelvey and Ordeshook's suggestions, particularly the observations about how individuals frequently give up and go do something else if a particular problem resists solution. As can be seen from her discussion, this does not imply that any satisfactory solution to the original conundrum ever appears; the people in question may be in equilibrium, but it is not of a rational expectations variety. This point should also be considered below, in connection with the observation that the parts of the system of public deliberation that are most in the control of ordinary citizens are usually the most informally organized. The literature in Hogarth (1980) on the role errors in memory play in systematic mistakes is also highly relevant to any example in which people are expected to compare polls over time. In all probability, many people would end up reconstructing their memories of precisely the polls McKelvey and Ordeshook imagine them relying on. Those who doubt this should consider the evidence on retrospective reports of voting: surely the well-known phenomenon of overreporting voting for the winner is not entirely derived from dishonesty.

32. This literature is enormous, but see the references below.

33. The Bay of Pigs case is now well known; for Bonner, see Wypijewski (1990, p. 14), and Parry (1992, pp. 208–09); for Schanberg, see Lee and Solomon (1991, pp. 21–22). For other cases, see Herman (1992) and Herman and Chomsky (1988). On NAFTA and the *Times*, see the quantitative survey of the paper's coverage reported in Fairness and Accuracy in Reporting's *Extra* (1993) and its account of the newspaper's refusal to sell space in its special "advertorials" to NAFTA opponents.

34. For the participation claim, cf. the discussion of unpublished data supplied by the Gallup poll in Ferguson (1989) [this volume, chapter 5, n. 3]; see also Ginsberg (1986, pp. 198–99). For an even more striking case involving the *Washington Post* and the number of voters Jesse Jackson helped register, see note 35 of Ferguson, "By Invitation Only" (this volume, chapter 5).

35. I owe this point to Dr. Erik Devereux, who pointed out to me various media

interviews during the 1992 campaign in which news editors themselves drew connections to decisions on coverage, polls, and large amounts of early money. See also the discussion in note 49 of Ferguson, "Real Change?" (this volume, chapter 6). This essay also contains a discussion with detailed references to a critical incident in the 1992 Clinton campaign when fund-raisers deliberately aimed to signal the media and other elite groups, and helped save the campaign (p. 303).

36. Most studies of newspaper reporting of polls end up concluding that newspaper coverage of polls is at least moderately biased in favor of candidates that the paper endorses. See, e.g., Wilhoit and Auh (1974).

37. On the Democrats, investment houses and alleged "special interests," cf. Ferguson (1993). Public promotion of dubious cues is certainly no nineteenth-century phenomenon. As I finished a draft of this paper, the Boston papers were touting a possible set of ethnic-based mayoral candidates with an élan that recalls Henry Adams's famous characterization of Massachusetts politics as the systematic organization of hatreds. Indeed, it appears many urban newspapers treat local politics almost entirely in terms of clashes between racial and ethnic groups. Such influences indubitably exist, but it is difficult not to suspect that here one has a particularly clear-cut case of elite rhetoric influencing mass politics. (Economic conflicts, for example, receive much less newspaper discussion.)

38. The vast literature on the diffusion of innovations identifies one pattern as characteristic: that lower-status individuals often copy higher-status people. See Rogers (1983, p. 153, 206, 215 ff). For voters concerned about political economy, relying on such cues is often clearly irrational, unless one is prepared to swallow "supply-side" economics whole. The example, however, illustrates how the group process of self-informing touted by McKelvey and Ordeshook (1986, p. 926) easily goes off the rails.

39. For TV, voters, and knowledge, see Ginsberg (1986, pp. 146–48); for the limits of the "limited effects" literature, see e.g., Page, Shapiro, and Dempsey (1987). Chapter 9 of Page and Shapiro (1992) has a good empirical survey of some of the biases in the media, though its claim that the world of think tanks and research institutes is highly decentralized is mistaken from an investment theory standpoint. Virtually all such institutions are highly subsidized by a very small percentage of the population—the very wealthy. See their discussion, pp. 365–66.

40. The point, suggested to me by Devereux, is obvious, if one notices it in such older accounts of the press as Lundberg (1946).

41. See, e.g., the discussion and references in Ferguson and Rogers (1986, pp. 104, 248, n. 50). See also Devereux (1993).

42. On contrast effects, see Eiser (1990) and the work by Tajfel (1981). Recent elections have been full of carefully engineered "contrast effects" as "New Democrats" and other sorts of Democrats competed for public attention. Most such manipulations require considerable aid from the press—which can, whenever its various parts choose, spotlight facts inconsistent with these labels. Note that one famous study of the Smoot-Hawley Tariff, E. E. Schattschneider's (1935), never even bothered to analyze the array of interests opposed to the bill. It is perhaps of interest to note that an important segment of the American press has long made an excellent business publishing so-called "tombstone" ads announcing the completion of major deals by leading financial houses.

43. The "Asch effect" refers to Solomon Asch's famous experiments in which individual dissenters or small minorities were induced to change their views to conform to

a larger group's opinions, even on matters that were obviously dead wrong. The "spiral of silence" refers to the discussion started by Elizabeth Noelle-Neumann (1984). (It is an effect, I believe, that does exist but is normally fairly small in voting democracies.)

44. At the 1986 Texas conference, where I first presented this analysis, Peter Aronson responded that unions would be able to borrow all the finance they required in (perfect) credit markets. But this is not only empirically false, it is theoretically mistaken. For exactly the same reasons that major investors do not promote political parties favoring a dangerous degree of unionization (the reference is to the limited "New Deal" case discussed above), they would not rationally make direct loans to unions either.

45. E.g., Page and Shapiro (1992, p. 397), who recognize that the market is less than perfect.

46. This conclusion, I think, should lead one to investigate changes in the "non-profit" sector over time and their relation to the diffusion of political information. One striking example is the study of campaign finance itself: many tax-exempt research centers fear to name names during political campaigns lest they lose their "nonpolitical" tax-exempt status. None, however, admit this in public, though it can be surprising indeed to see what the more conscientious do with true hot potatoes.

Were there space enough, it would also be desirable to look a bit more closely at the notion of self-interest, though only subsidized academics would dream of arguing that self-interest in a very crass sense is not a basic feature of the existing world economy.

A recent argument that is fated—because of the growing worldwide strength of vertically integrated media companies—to have a great future should also receive a moment's notice, so that it may be dismissed with the contempt it deserves. This is the claim, advanced by any number of spokespersons (see, e.g., a recent *New York Times* essay by Mario Cuomo [Cuomo, 1993]) that recent advances in cable technology imply that a scarcity of publicly licensed airwaves no longer exists, so that "diversity of viewpoints is virtually assured by the explosion in outlets for informational programming." From both theoretical and empirical perspectives, however, this is sheer confusion. First, stations and networks certainly are scarce goods—they have hugely positive prices. Far from being given away, they are among the hottest stocks in the market, and the object of takeover efforts by some of the world's largest (and most ruthless) corporations. For someone—particularly someone often thought to harbor ambitions for the Supreme Court—to pretend otherwise is sheer sophistry. Second, there is no reason to believe that we now live in a new era of unlimited "free speech." As Fairness and Accuracy in Reporting (FAIR)'s *Extra* has recently documented, even the so-called "public" network, PBS, is massively biased by subsidies from arch-conservative foundations. (See FAIR [1992a]; in regard to the for-profit sector, see FAIR's survey of coverage of the 1992 election by the commercial networks, FAIR [1992b].) This is scarcely surprising—from the standpoint of the investment theory's "black hole" approach, arguments like those made by Cuomo reflect at best a deep-seated confusion of variance with the mean. On average, profit-making stations give their audience U.S.-average programming. That some tiny, low-power station in New York or Los Angeles is sometimes more adventuresome does not meet the argument. Freedom of the press remains guaranteed to those who can buy it—and the vast majority of the population still has no chance of purchasing a cable station.

47. Compare, for example, Langer (1975) on the "illusion of control" with Ginsberg's argument and data (1982, pp. 165 ff.) that the act of voting by itself tends to

produce the feeling in citizens that they control the state. The work of James Gibson on perception and context suggests a variety of quite specific illusions which may be important in electoral contests, but I lack the space here to develop the point. See Reed (1988).

These sorts of considerations make it quite impossible to accept the notion that voters simply maximize perceived "income." Rather, as Kelley's work suggests, income or related economic considerations are likely to be (at least) one consideration in the voting decision. This means, of course, that a shift in national income will still move large numbers of voters on the margin, and it is the explanation for what appears to be a paradoxical set of contentions: one, that most voters are not simple income maximizers, and two, that shifts in economic conditions nevertheless often have massive effects on elections.

A closely related misconception attends many studies of the influence of money on congressional votes. Simple correlations between money and votes are usually quite useless. One first has to control for votes that are clearly going to be in one camp or another for obvious constituency considerations and such. It is on the marginal congressional votes not obviously committed that such tests should be performed. Judging from work recently discussed with me by other scholars but mostly as yet unpublished, pursuing this point is likely to lead to real progress in studies of Congress. A useful study using a similar methodology is Ginsberg and Green (1986).

48. Some critics of my earlier essay have objected that poorer citizens can always contribute time instead of money. But if one imagines costing out all the time contributed by the people described in Goodwyn, the amounts are still enormous. The point emerges with even greater clarity if one also tries to value that time at the wage rate prevailing for unskilled labor, which would be the appropriate price for most campaign work.

49. For Morgan and his associates in these quite complicated elections, cf. Josephson (1963, p. 423 ff.), and Burch (1981, p. 97); for FDR's narrow convention win, e.g., Rosen (1977, chapter 10).

50. One other point may be relevant on the logic of retrospective evaluations. In refusing to look forward at all, retrospective theories end up throwing out too much valuable information, even if it is difficult to assess. Anyone who tried to buy stocks purely off past records would suffer far more losses than necessary if he or she never glanced ahead to, say, the condition of the macroeconomy.

REFERENCES

Adams, Henry. 1930. *Letters of Henry Adams, 1858–91.* Boston: Houghton Mifflin.

Ajzen, Icek and Martin Fishbein. 1980. *Understanding Attitudes and Predicting Social Behavior.* Englewood Cliffs, NJ: Prentice Hall.

Barry, Brian. 1970. *Sociologists, Economists, and Democracy.* New York: Collier-Macmillan.

Begg, David. 1982. *The Rational Expectations Revolution in Macroeconomics.* Baltimore: Johns Hopkins University Press.

Bennett, Lance. 1989. "Marginalizing the Majority: Conditioning Public Opinion to Accept Managerial Democracy." Pp. 321–361 in *Manipulating Public Opinion,* edited by Michael Margolis and Gary Mauser. Pacific Grove: Brooks/Cole.

———. 1992. *The Governing Crisis: Media, Money, and Marketing in American Elections.* New York: St. Martin's.

Bernays, Edward L. 1928. "Manipulating Public Opinion." *American Journal of Sociology* 33:958–971.

Brody, Richard and Benjamin Page. 1973. "Indifference, Alienation, and Rational Decisions: The Effects of Candidate Evaluations on Turnout and the Vote." *Public Choice* 15:1–17.

Burch, Philip. 1981. *Elites in American History, Vol. II.* New York: Holmes & Meier.

Carvalho, Fernando J. Cardim de. 1992. *Mr. Keynes and the Post-Keynesians.* Brookfield, VT: Edward Elgar.

Center for the Study of Communication, University of Massachusetts, Amherst. 1993. "Images/Issues/Impact: The Media and Campaign 92."

Cole, Michael. 1990. "Cultural Psychology: A Once and Future Discipline." Pp. 279–335 in *Nebraska Symposium on Motivation, 1989*, edited by John Berman. Lincoln: University of Nebraska.

Craig, Douglas. 1992. *After Wilson: The Struggle for the Democratic Party, 1920–34.* Chapel Hill: University of North Carolina Press.

Cumings, Bruce. 1993. "Revising Postrevisionism, or the Poverty of Theory." *Diplomatic History*, vol. 17, no. 4.

Cuomo, Mario. 1993. *New York Times* September 20.

Curran, James. 1982. "Communications, Power, and Social Order." Pp. 202–235 in *Culture, Society, and The Media*, edited by Michael Gurevitch, Tony Bennett, James Curran and Janet Woollacott. London: Methuen.

Cutting, Bronson. 1919. Papers. The Library of Congress.

Dawes, Robyn. 1988. *Rational Choice in an Uncertain World.* New York: Harcourt.

Devereux, Eric. 1993. "Media Coalitions in the 1964 Campaign: A Political Investment Analysis." Working paper 92–38. H.J. Heinz School of Public Policy and Management, Carnegie-Mellon University.

Downes, Randolph. 1970. *The Rise of Warren Gamaliel Harding.* Columbus: Ohio State University Press.

Downs, Anthony. 1957. *An Economic Theory of Democracy.* New York: Harper.

Eiser, J. Richard. 1990. *Social Judgment.* Milton Keynes: Open University Press.

Epstein, Gerald and Thomas Ferguson. 1991. "Answers to Stock Questions: Fed Targets, Stock Prices, and the Gold Standard in the Great Depression." *Journal of Economic History* 51:190–200.

Fairness and Accuracy in Reporting. 1992a. "Special Section on PBS." *Extra* 5, no. 4 (June).

———. 1992b. "Campaign '92 Wrap-up." *Extra* 5, no. 8 (December).

———. 1993. "Update" and "Action Alert." *Extra* (October).

Ferguson, Thomas. 1983. "Party Realignment and American Industrial Structure: The Investment Theory of Political Parties in Historical Perspective." Pp. 1–82 of *Research in Political Economy, Volume VI.* Greenwich, Conn.: JAI Press.

———. 1984. "From 'Normalcy' to New Deal: Industrial Structure, Party Competition, and American Public Policy in the Great Depression." *International Organization* 38:41–92.

———. 1986. "Elites and Elections, or: What Have They Done to You Lately?" Toward an Investment Theory of Political Parties and Critical Realignment." Pp. 164–88 in *Do Elections Matter?* edited by Benjamin Ginsberg and Alan Stone. First Edition. Armonk, NY: Sharpe.

———. 1989. "By Invitation Only: Party Competition and Industrial Structure in the 1988 Election." *Socialist Review* 19:73–103.

———. 1991. "Industrial Structure and Party Competition in the New Deal." *Sociological Perspectives* 34:493–526.

———. 1992. "Money and Politics." Pp. 1060–1084 in *Handbooks to the Modern World— The United States*, vol. 2, edited by Godfrey Hodgson. New York: Facts On File.

———. 1995. "'Real Change'? 'Organized Capitalism,' Fiscal Policy, and the 1992 Election." Chapter 6, this volume.

Ferguson, Thomas and Joel Rogers. 1986. *Right Turn: The Decline of the Democrats and the Future of American Politics*. New York: Hill & Wang.

Fiorina, Morris. 1981. *Retrospective Voting in American National Elections*. New Haven: Yale University Press.

Geer, John. 1988. "What Do Open-Ended Questions Measure?" *Public Opinion Quarterly* 52:365–371.

———. 1991a. "Do Open-Ended Questions Measure 'Salient' Issues?" *Public Opinion Quarterly* 55:360–370.

———. 1991b. "The Electorate's Partisan Evaluations: Evidence of a Continuing Democratic Edge." *Public Opinion Quarterly* 55:218–231.

———. 1992. "New Deal Issues and the American Electorate, 1952–88." *Political Behavior* 14:45–65.

Ginsberg, Benjamin. 1982. *The Consequences of Consent: Elections, Citizen Control, and Popular Acquiescence*. Reading, MA: Addison Wesley.

———. 1986. *The Captive Public*. New York: Basic Books.

Ginsberg, Benjamin and John Green. 1986. "The Best Congress Money Can Buy." Pp. 75–89 of *Do Elections Matter?* edited by Benjamin Ginsberg and Alan Stone. First ed.; Armonk, NY: Sharpe.

Goodwyn, Lawrence. 1976. *Democratic Promise*. New York: Oxford University Press.

Granberg, Donald and Soren Holmberg. 1988. *The Political System Matters*. New York: Cambridge University Press.

Harris, Marvin. 1979. *Cultural Materialism*. New York: Random House.

Herman, Edward. 1992. *Beyond Hypocrisy*. Boston: South End Press.

Herman, Edward and Noam Chomsky. 1988. *Manufacturing Consent*. New York: Pantheon.

Hertsgaard, Mark. 1988. *On Bended Knee*. New York: Farrar, Straus & Giroux.

Hobsbawm, Eric. 1989. *The Age of Empire*. New York: Vintage.

———. 1990. *Nations and Nationalism Since 1780*. New York: Cambridge University Press.

Hobsbawm, Eric and Terence Ranger. 1983. *The Invention of Tradition*. New York: Cambridge University Press.

Hogarth, Robin. 1980. *Judgment & Choice*. New York: Wiley.

Josephson, Matthew. [1963]. *The Politicos*. New York: Harcourt, Brace & World.

Kelley, Stanley, Jr. 1983. *Interpreting Elections*. Princeton: Princeton University Press, 1983.

Kramer, Michael and Samuel Roberts. 1976. *"I Never Wanted to Be Vice President of Anything."* New York: Basic Books.

Kuhn, Thomas. 1970. *The Structure of Scientific Revolutions*. Second ed. Chicago: University of Chicago Press.

Laboratory of Comparative Human Cognition. 1983. Pp. 295–356 in *Handbook of Child Psychology, Vol. I*, edited by Paul H. Mussen. Fourth edition. New York: Wiley.

Langer, Ellen J. 1975. "The Illusion of Control." *Journal of Personality and Social Psychology* 32:311–328.

Lave, Jean. 1988. *Cognition in Practice.* New York: Cambridge University Press.

Lavoie, Marc. 1993. *Foundations of Post-Keynesian Economic Analysis.* Brookfield, VT: Edward Elgar.

Lee, Martin and Norman Solomon. 1991. *Unreliable Sources.* New York: Carol Publishing Group.

Lundberg, Ferdinand. [1938] 1946. *America's 60 Families.* New York: Citadel.

Luria, A.R. 1982. *Language and Cognition.* New York: Wiley.

Magee, Stephen, William Brock, and Leslie Young. 1989. *Black Hole Tariffs and Endogenous Policy Theory.* New York: Cambridge University Press.

McKelvey, Richard and Peter Ordeshook. 1986. "Information, Electoral Equilibria, and the Democratic Ideal." *Journal of Politics* 48:909–937.

McLean, Iain. 1987. *Public Choice.* Oxford: Blackwell.

Miller, Warren and Donald Stokes. 1966. "Constituency Influence in Congress." Pp. 351–372 of *Elections and the Political Order,* edited by Angus Campbell, Philip Converse, Warren Miller, and Donald Stokes. New York: Wiley.

Nietzsche, F.W. 1957. *The Use and Abuse of History,* translated by Adrian Collins. Second edition. Indianapolis: Bobbs-Merrill.

Nisbet, R. and L. Ross. 1980. *Human Inference: Strategies and Shortcomings of Human Judgment.* Englewood Cliffs, NJ: Prentice Hall.

Noelle-Neumann, Elizabeth. 1984. *The Spiral of Silence.* Chicago: University of Chicago Press.

Olson, Mancur. 1971. *The Logic of Collective Action.* Second edition. Cambridge: Harvard University Press.

Page, Benjamin. 1983. *Who Gets What from Government.* Berkeley: University of California Press.

Page, Benjamin and Robert Shapiro. 1992. *The Rational Public.* Chicago: University of Chicago Press.

Page, Benjamin, Robert Shapiro, and Glenn Dempsey. 1987. "What Moves Public Opinion." *American Political Science Review* 81:23–43.

Parry, Robert. 1992. *Fooling America.* New York: Morrow.

Reed, Edward. 1988. *James J. Gibson and the Psychology of Perception.* New Haven: Yale University Press.

Robinson, John P. 1974. "The Press As King-Maker: What Surveys From [the] Last Five Campaigns Show." *Journalism Quarterly* 51:587–594.

Rogers, Everett M. 1983. *The Diffusion of Innovations.* Third edition. New York: Free Press.

Rosen, Elliot. 1977. *Hoover, Roosevelt and the Brains Trust.* New York: Columbia University Press.

Rudé, George. 1959. *The Crowd in the French Revolution.* New York: Oxford University Press.

———. 1980. *Ideology and Popular Protest.* New York: Pantheon.

Schattschneider, E.E. 1935. *Politics, Pressures, and the Tariff.* New York: Prentice Hall.

Schneider, William. 1993. "The President's Call To Arms." Boston *Herald,* February 19.

Sheffrin, Steven. 1989. *The Making of Economic Policy.* Oxford: Blackwell.

Shiller, Robert. 1989. *Market Volatility.* Cambridge: MIT Press.

Tajfel, Henri. 1981. *Human Groups and Social Categories*. New York: Cambridge University Press.

Thaler, Richard. 1992. *The Winner's Curse: Paradoxes and Anomalies of Economic Life*. Princeton: Princeton University Press.

Therborn, Goran. 1977. "The Rule of Capital and the Rise of Democracy." *New Left Review*, no. 103 (May-June):3–41.

Thompson, E.P. 1968. *The Making of the English Working Class*. London: Penguin.

Tulviste, Peeter. 1991. *The Cultural-Historical Development of Verbal Thinking*. Commack, N.Y.: Nova Science Publishers.

Tversky, Amos and Daniel Kahneman. 1974. "Judgment Under Uncertainty: Heuristics and Biases." *Science* 184:1124–1131.

Wall Street Journal. 1992. November 19, p. A16.

Wilhoit, G.C. and Auh, T.S. 1974. "Newspaper Endorsement and Coverage of Public Opinion Polls in 1970" *Journalism Quarterly* 51:654–658.

Wygotski, Lew. [Vygotsky, Lev]. 1985. *Ausgewaehlte Schriften, Bd. I*. Koeln: Pahl-Rugenstein Verlag.

Wypijewski, JoAnn. 1990. "Shirley Christian and the *Times* on Chile." *Lies of Our Times* 1, no. 1:14.

Zaller, John. 1992. *The Nature and Origins of Mass Opinion*. New York: Cambridge University Press.

Index

Made in the USA
San Bernardino, CA
27 August 2018